278

D0871953

08|89   Purchase

INDIANS
of North and South America:

*A Bibliography based on the collection at
the Willard E. Yager Library-Museum
Hartwick College, Oneonta, N.Y.*

Supplement

by

CAROLYN E. WOLF

and

NANCY S. CHIANG

The Scarecrow Press, Inc.
Metuchen, N.J., & London
1988

Library of Congress Cataloging-in-Publication Data

Wolf, Carolyn E., 1941-
    Indians of North and South America : a biblio-
graphy based on the collection at the Willard E.
Yager Library-Museum, Hartwick College, Oneonta,
N.Y. Supplement / by Carolyn E. Wolf and Nancy
S. Chiang.
    p.   cm.
    Includes indexes.
    ISBN 0-8108-2127-3
    1. Indians--Bibliography--Catalogs.   2.
Willard E. Yager Library-Museum--Catalogs.   I.
Chiang, Nancy S.   II. Willard E. Yager Library-
Museum.   III. Title.
Z1209.W82 Suppl.   88-6055
[E58]

to

Irving

TABLE OF CONTENTS

PREFACE

All items in this bibliography have been added
to the Yager Library-Museum collection, Hartwick
College since the late spring of 1976 when the main
bibliography was prepared and subsequently published in 1977 by Scarecrow Press. Entry numbers which
are decimals indicate books added to the collection
in the process of typing this list and all items
included were on the shelves and available for use
before May 1987.

All materials circulate and are available
through interlibrary loans except rare books, items
in the Yager collection and papers donated by Con-
gressman James Hanley (retired, D, Syracuse, N. Y.
area) Mr. Hanley's papers deal primarily with the
Oneida land claim case which at this date is not
yet settled.

The following types of materials have been included: (1) Books primarily on Indians; (2) individual periodical articles or issues of periodicals
which have been added to the Yager collection; (3)
collections of essays in which some or all of the
essays discuss Indians (each essay is listed individually in the main bibliography and in the
title index); (4) books on archaeology and anthropology that deal primarily with Indians; (5) doctoral dissertations purchased from University
Microfilms International and (6) major collections
of documents on microfilm such as the Iroquois
Treaty Documents.

The bibliography is arranged alphabetically by
main entries. The alphabetical subarrangement of
the author's works is without regard to coauthors.
Wherever possible OCLC authority files have been
used to establish a main entry, series entry, or
subject entry. No attempt has been made to class-
ify this bibliography by broad subjects.

Notes concerning reprints have been included.
The following spellings have been interfiled: "Mac"

vii

and "Mc"; "Navaho" and "Navajo"; and "Archaeology" and "Archeology".

The Library has continued to purchase the microfiche edition of the Human Relations Area Files and the file is current.

The college is committed to developing and enhancing its collection of materials on Native Americans and providing scholars with a major research collection.

This manuscript was prepared using Wordperfect, version 4.1 and printed on a NEC Pinwriter P2, using font 7.

We would like to thank the Hartwick College administration for their support in preparation of this supplement.

Carolyn Wolf
Nancy Chiang

BIBLIOGRAPHY

0001 Abbott, Charles C. Primitive Industry: or
Illustrations of the Handiwork in Stone,
Bone and Clay of the Native Races of the
Northern Atlantic Seaboard of America.
Salem, MA., G. A. Bates, 1881.
The Antiquities and Origin of the Trenton
Gravel by Prof. Henry Carville Lewis, pp.
521-551.
OCLC # 1820289

0002 _____. Stone Age in New Jersey. In the
Annual Report of the Board of Regents of
the Smithsonian Institution, Washington,
Govt. Print. Off. 1876, pp. 246-422.
OCLC # 781945

0003 Abel, Annie Heloise, 1873- . The American
Indian Under Reconstruction. by... (Mrs.
George Cockburn Henderson) Cleveland, A.
H. Clark Co., 1925, New York, Johnson
Reprint, 1970.
Original ed. issued as v. 3 of the
author's The Slaveholding Indians.
OCLC # 488341

Abel-Vidor, Suzanne see 0256

0004 Aberle, David Friend, 1918- . Navaho and
Ute Peyotism; a Chronological and Dis-
tributional Study. by ... and Omer C.
Stewart. Boulder, University of Colorado
Press, 1957.
University of Colorado Studies. Series in
Anthropology, no. 6.
OCLC # 3387667

0005 Aberle, Sophie Bledsoe de, 1899- . The
Pueblo Indians of New Mexico, Their Land,
Economy and Civil Organization. New York,

Kraus Reprint, 1969.
American Anthropological Association Memoir
no. 70. Supplement to American Anthropologist, v. 50, no. 4, pt. 2, 1948.
OCLC # 558765

0006   Abler, Thomas S. The Kansas Connection: The
       Seneca Nation and the Iroquois Confederacy
       Council. In 0979, pp. 81-93.

0007   Ablon, Joan. American Indian Relocation:
       Problems of Dependency and Management in
       the City. In 2304, pp. 269-280.
       Reprinted from Phylon v. 24, no. 4, Win-
       ter 1965, pp. 362-371.

0008   Aboriginal Sign Languages of the Americas and
       Australia. Edited by D. Jean Umiker-Sebeok
       and Thomas Sekeok. New York, Plenum
       Press, 1978.
       V. 1 North America: Classic Comparative
       Perspectives. V. 2 The Americas and
       Australia. Essays in this collection are
       also listed individually and refer to this
       citation.
       OCLC # 3650174

       Aborigines Protection Society. London see
       3153

0009   Abramova, Z. A. Concerning the Cultural
       Contacts Between Asia and America in the
       Late Paleolithic. In 0905 pp. 133-139.

0010   Abrams, H. Leon. The Mixtec People: A
       Glance at Their Background, Their Condi-
       tion a Quarter of a Century Ago, and Their
       Position Today. Greeley, Co. University
       of Northern Colorado, Museum of Anthropol-
       ogy, 1984.
       University of Northern Colorado. Museum of
       Anthropology, Misc. Series v. 57.
       OCLC # 11216273

0011   Ackerman, Lillian A. Sexual Equality in the
       Plateau Culture Area. Ann Arbor, MI.,
       University Microfilms International, 1982.
       Microfilm - PhD Thesis - Washington State
       University.
       OCLC # 11979702

0012   Ackerman, Robert E. <u>Microblades and Prehis-
        tory: Technological and Cultural Consider-
        ations for the North Pacific Coast</u>. In
        0905, pp. 189-197.

0013   Acosta, Jorge R. <u>Excavations at Palenque,
        1967-1973</u>. In 2920, pp. 265-285.

0014   <u>Across the Chichimec Sea: Papers in Honor of
        J. Charles Kelley</u>. Edited by Carroll L.
        Riley and Basil C. Hedrick. Carbondale.
        Southern Illinois University Press. 1978.
        Essays in this collection are also listed
        individually and refer to this citation.
        OCLC # 3627497

0015   Adair, James. ca. 1709- ca. 1783. <u>Adair's
        History of the American Indians</u>. Edited un-
        der the auspices of the National Society of
        the Colonial Dames of American in Ten-
        nessee. Promontory Press. 1974?
        Reprint of 1930 ed. published by Watauge
        Press, Johnson City, TN. Originally pub-
        lished in 1775.
        OCLC # 1172155

0016   Adam, Paul. <u>Future of Fisheries as a Basic
        Resource for Arctic Communities: With Ac-
        cent on the Greenland Case</u>. In 1875. pp.
        519-531.

0017   Adams, Alexander B. <u>The Disputed Lands</u>. New
        York. Putnam. 1981.
        OCLC # 6378699

0018   Adams, Andy. <u>He Looked Every Inch a Chief</u>.
        In 1566. pp. 141-162.
        Reprinted from Adams. A. <u>The Log of a
        Cowboy: A Narrative of the Old Trail Days</u>.
        Boston. Houghton Mifflin and Co.. 1903.
        pp. 136-143.

        Adams, Charles L. <u>see</u> 0965

        Adams, George R. <u>see</u> 2304

0019   Adams, Karen R. 1946- . <u>Pollen, Parched
        Seeds and Prehistory: A Pilot Investiga-
        tion of Prehistoric Plant Remains from
        Salmon Ruin. A Chacoan Pueblo in North-</u>

western New Mexico.   Portales.   NM.   Llano
Estacado Center for Advanced Professional
Studies and Research.   1980.
Contributions in Anthropology.   v. 9.   San
Juan Valley Archaeological Project.
OCLC # 5893303

0020   Adams.   Richard E.   W.   Comments on the
       Glyphic Texts of the "Alter Vase".   In
       2920.   pp.   409-420.

0021   _____ and Culbert T. Patrick.   The Origins
       of Civilization in the Maya Lowlands.   In
       2378.   pp.   3-21.

0022   _____.   Rio Bec Archaeology and the Rise of
       Maya Civilization.   In   2378.   pp.   77-99.

       _____.   see also 2378.

       Adams.   Richard Newbold   see   0111.

0023   Adaptive Responses of Native Amazonians.
       Edited by Raymond B.   Hames.   William T.
       Vickers.   New York.   Academic Press.   1983.
       Studies in Anthropology.   Essays in this
       collection are also listed individually and
       refer to this citation.
       OCLC # 8827760

0024   Adovasio.   J.   M.   et. al.   Evidence from
       Meadowcroft Rock Shelter.   In   0903.   pp.
       163-189.

0025   _____.   et. al.   Meadowcroft Rock Shelter.
       In 0902.   pp.   140-180.

0026   _____.   et.   al.   The Meadowcroft Rockshel-
       ter/   Cross Creek Archaeological Project:
       Retrospect.   1982.   In   2111.   pp.   257-
       270.

0027   _____.   Prehistoric Basketry of Western
       North America and Mexico.   In   0905.   pp.
       341-362.

       _____.   see also   2111.

Advanced Seminar on Lower Central American
Archaeology (1980: School of American Re-

search) see 0123.

0028 Adventure of a Young English Officer. New
      York, Garland Pub., 1977.
      The Garland Library of Narratives of North
      American Indian Captivities, v. 10. Re-
      print of an anonymous article in the 1768
      ed. of Bickerstaff's Boston Almanac,
      printed by Mein and Fleeming. Boston.

0029 Afansiev, V. The Literary Heritage of
      Bartolomé de las Casas. In 0193, pp.
      539-578.

0030 The Affecting History of Mrs. Howe. New
      York. Garland Pub.. 1977.
      The Garland Library of Narratives of North
      American Indian Captivities, v. 19. Re-
      print of the 1815 ed. published by J.
      Bailey, London.
      OCLC # 3104352

0032 Agenbroad, Larry D. Cultural Implications
      from the Distributional Analysis of a Lith-
      ic Site, San Pedro Valley, Arizona. In
      0822. pp. 55-71.

0033 _____. Geology and Lithic resources of the
      Grasshopper Region. In 2239, pp. 42-45.

      _____. see also 2239

0034 Aggressions of Civilization: Federal Indian
      Policy Since the 1880's. Edited by Sandra
      L. Cadwalder and Vine Deloria. Philadel-
      phia. Temple University Press. 1984.
      Essays in this collection are also listed
      individually and refer to this citation.
      OCLC # 10432467

0035 Aginsky, Bernard W. The Socio-psychological
      Significance of Death Among the Pomo Indi-
      ans. In 2276. pp. 319-330.

0036 Agnew, Brad. 1939- . Fort Gibson: Termi-
      nal on the Trail of Tears. Norman. Uni-
      versity of Oklahoma Press. 1980.
      OCLC # 5147493

0037 Ahler, Janet Goldstein. The Formal Education

of Plains Indians. In 0113. pp. 245-
254.

0038   Aikens, C. Melvin. Archaeology of the Great
        Basin. In the Annual Review of Anthro-
        pology. 1978. v. 7. pp. 71-87.

0039   _____. The Far West. In 0097. pp. 149-
        201.

0040   Akweks. Aren. Collection of Mohawk Legends.
        Hogansburg, NY., Akwesasne Counselor Organ-
        ization. St. Regis Mohawk Reservation.
        1948.

0041   _____. Conservation as the Indian Saw It.
        Hogansburg, NY., Akwesasne Counselor Organ-
        ization. St. Regis Mohawk Reservation.
        1948.

0042   _____. Costume of Iroquois. Hogansburg.
        NY., Akwesasne Counselor Organization. St.
        Regis Mohawk Reservation. 194?

0043   _____. Costume of the Six Nation Man.
        Hogansburg. NY., Akwesasne Counselor Organ-
        ization. St. Regis Mohawk Reservation.
        1948.

0044   _____. Cultural Areas of the North Amer-
        ican Indians. Hogansburg. NY., Akwesasne
        Counselor Organization. St. Regis Mohawk
        Reservation. 1948.

0045   _____. The Formation of the Ho-de-no-sau-
        ne or the League of the Five Nations.
        Hogansburg. NY., Akwesasne Counselor Organ-
        ization. St. Regis Mohawk Reservation.
        194?

0046   _____. Four Happenings in Indian History.
        Hogansburg, NY., Akwesasne Counselor Organ-
        ization, St. Regis Mohawk Reservation.
        1948.

0047   _____. The Gift of the Great Spirit.
        Hogansburg. NY., Akwesasne Counselor Organ-
        ization. St. Regis Mohawk Reservation.
        1948?

0048 _____. The Great Gift, Tobacco. Hogans-
       burg,   NY., Akwesasne Counselor Organiza-
       tion,   St. Regis Mohawk Reservation,   1947.

0049 _____. History of the St.   Regis Akwesasne
       Mohawks. Hogansburg, NY.,   Akwesasne Coun-
       selor Organization,   St.   Regis Mohawk Res-
       ervation,   1947.

0050 _____. Honayawas, Fish Carrier, Logan and
       Cornplanter. Hogansburg, NY.,   Akwesasne
       Counselor Organization,   St.   Regis Mohawk
       Reservation,   194?

0051 _____. Key to Indian Pictographs. Hogans-
       burg,   NY.,   Akwesasne Counselor Organiza-
       tion,   St.   Regis Mohawk Reservation,   194?

0052 _____. Migration of the Iroquois. Hogans-
       burg,   NY.,   Akwesasne Counselor Organiza-
       tion,   St.   Regis Mohawk Reservation,
       1948.

0053 _____. Migration of the Tuscaroras.
       Hogansburg,   NY.,   Akwesasne Counselor Or-
       ganization,   St.   Regis Mohawk Reservation,
       194?

0054 _____. Monuments to Six Nation Indians.
       Hogansburg,   NY.,   Akwesasne Counselor   Or-
       ganization,   St.   Regis Mohawk Reservation,
       1947?

0055 _____. Sa-ko-ri-on-nie-ni,   Our Great
       Teacher. Hogansburg, NY.,   Akwesasne Coun-
       selor Organization,   St.   Regis Mohawk Res-
       ervation,   1947?

0056 _____. Seven Dances. Hogansburg,   NY.,
       Akwesasne Counselor Organization,   St.
       Regis Mohawk Reservation,   1947.

0057 _____. Wampum Belts. Hogansburg,   NY.,
       Akwesasne Counselor Organization,   St.
       Regis Mohawk Reservation,   194?

0058 _____. Why We Have Mosquitoes. Hogans-
       burg,   NY.,   Akwesasne Counselor Organiza-
       tion,   St.   Regis Mohawk Reservation,
       1947.

_____. see also 982-985

0059   Albers, Patricia. New Perspectives on Plains
       Indian Women. In 1438, pp. 1-26.

0060   _____ and Beatrice Medicine. The Role of
       Sioux Women in the Production of Ceremonial
       Objects: The Case of the Star Quilt. In
       1438, pp. 123-140.

0061   _____. Sioux Women in Transition: A Study
       of Their Changing Status in a Domestic and
       Capitalist Sector of Production. In 1438,
       pp. 175-234.

       _____. see also 1438

       Albert, James William, 1820-1897 see 3187

0062   Alcina Franch, Josbe. Pre-Columbian Art.
       Translated from the French by I.   Mark
       Paris. New York, H. N.   Abrams, 1983,
       c. 1978.
       Translation of L`art Precolombien.
       OCLC # 8929943

0063   Alden, Dauril. Black Robes Versus White Set-
       tlers: The Struggle for "Freedom of the
       Indians" in Colonial Brazil. In 0114,
       pp. 19-45.

0064   Alexander, Eveline Martin, 1843-1922. The
       Diary of Eveline M. Alexander, 1866-1867,
       Being a Record of Her Journey from New York
       to Fort Smith to Join Her Calvary-officer
       Husband, Andrew J. Alexander, and Her
       Experiences with Him on Active Duty Among
       the Indian Nations and in Texas, New Mex-
       ico, and Colorado. College Station, Tex-
       as A & M University Press, 1977.
       OCLC # 2655408

0065   Alexander, Hartley Burr, 1873-1939. The
       Worlds Rim: Great Mysteries of the North
       American Indians. With a foreword by Clyde
       Kluckhorn, Lincoln, University of
       Nebraska Press, 1967, 1953.
       A Bison Book
       OCLC # 4144092

0066   Alexseev, Valeri.   Anthropology of Siberian
        Peoples.   In 1052.   pp.   57-90.

0067   Alford, Dan.   Linguistic Speculation on the
        Pre-history of the Cheyenne People.   In
        0068.   pp.   10-29.

0068   Algonquian Conference, 6th Ottawa, 1974.
        Papers of the Sixth Algonquian Conference,
        1974.   William Cowan, editor.   Ottawa, Na-
        tional Museum of Canada, 1975.
        Mercury Series,   Canadian Ethnology Series,
        no. 23.   Essays in this collection are
        also listed individually and refer to this
        citation.
        OCLC # 1913249

0069   Allaire, Louis.   A Native Mental Map of Coast
        Tsimshian Villages.   In 3162,   pp.   82-98.

        _____.   see also 2711

        Allan, Peter, 1898- , see 0234

0070   Allen, Jamey D.   The Manufacture of Intricate
        Glass Canes and a New Perspective on the
        Relationship Between Chevron-Star Beads and
        Mosaic-Millefiori Beads.   In 1204,   pp.
        173-191.

        Allen, Paula Gunn see 3033

0071   Allen, Robert S.   A Witness to Murder: The
        Cypress Hills Massacre and the Conflict at-
        titudes Towards the Native Peoples of the
        Canadian-American West During the 1870's.
        In 0137,   pp.   229-246.

        Allen, T. D. (Pseud.) see 2174

0072   Allison, Marvin J., et. al.   Tuberculosis
        in Pre-Columbian Andean Population.   In
        2526,   pp.   49-61.

0073   Ambler, Marjane.   The Three Affiliated Tribes
        at Fort Berthold--Mandan, Hidatsa,
        Arikara--Seek to Control Their Energy Re-
        Sources.   In 2274,   pp.   194-199.

0074   _____.   Uncertainity in CERT.   In 2274.

pp.   71-78.

0075   American Anthropologist.   Selected Papers
       from the American Anthropologist, 1888-
       1920.   Evanston, IL., Row, Peterson,
       1960.
       OCLC # 421581

0076   American Association for the Advancement of
       Science.   Section on Anthropology.   Asia
       and North America, Transpacific Contacts.
       Assembled by Marion W.   Smith.   Salt Lake
       City, UT..   Utah Society for American An-
       thropology.   1953.   Millwood, NY..   Kraus
       Reprints.   1974.
       Society for American Archaeology.   Memoirs.
       no.   9.   Supplement to American Antiquity.
       v.   18.   no.   3,   pt.   2,   Jan.   1953.
       OCLC # 1183477

0077   American Bottom Archaeology: A Summary of
       the FAI-270 Project Contribution to the
       Culture History of the Mississippi River
       Valley.   Edited by Charles J.   Bareis and
       James W.   Porter.   Urbana.   Published for
       the Illinois Department of Transportation
       by the University of Illinois Press.   1984.
       American Bottom Archaeology
       OCLC # 9827894

0078   American Ethnological Society.   Cultural Sta-
       bility and Cultural Change.   American Eth-
       nological Society.   edited by Verne F.
       Ray.   Seattle.   University of Washington.
       Press, 1969.   1957.
       Essays in this collection are also listed
       individually and refer to this citation.
       OCLC # 1744556

       American Federation of Arts see 391.   2248

0079   American Indian Environments: Ecological is-
       sues in Native American History.   With Con-
       tributions from Kai T.   Erikson.   et.   al.
       edited by Christopher T.   Vecoey and Robert
       W.   Venables.   Syracuse.   Syracuse Univer-
       sity Press,   1980.
       Essays in this collection are also listed
       individually and refer to this citation.
       OCLC # 6941713

American Indian Historical Society see 1418

0080 **American Indian Intellectuals.** Edited by
Margot Liberty, St. Paul, West Pub. Co.,
1978.
Essays in this collection are also listed
individually and refer to this citation.
Proceedings of the American Ethnological
Society, 1976.
OCLC # 4119714

0081 **American Indian Leaders: Studies in Diversity.** Edited by R. David Edmunds. Lincoln, University of Nebraska Press, 1980.
Essays in this collection are also listed
individually and refer to this citation.
OCLC # 5946604

0082 **American Indian Literature: An Anthology.**
Edited with an introd. by Alan R. Velie;
illus. by Danny Timmons. Norman, University of Oklahoma Press, 1979.
OCLC # 4835339

0083 **American Indian Myths and Legends.** Selected
and edited by Richard Erdoes and Alfonso
Ortiz. New York, Pantheon Books, 1984.
Pantheon Fairy Tale and Folklore Library
OCLC # 10799274

0084 American Indian Policy Review Commission.
Task Force Five. **Report on Indian Educa-
tion:** Final report of the American Indian
Policy Review Commission/ Task Force Five;
Indian Education. Washington, Govt. Print.
Off., 1976.
OCLC # 2993726

0085 American Indian Policy Review Commission.
**Final Report Submitted to Congress May 17,
1977.** Washington, Govt. Print. Off.,
1977.
Printed for the use of the American Indian
Policy Review Commission
OCLC # 4241886

0086 **American Indian Reference Book.** Portage,
MI., Earth, 1976.
OCLC # 3170763

0087 **American Indians and the Law**. Edited by
      Lawrence Rosen. New Brunswick, NJ.,
      Transaction Books, 1976.
      Reprint of the 1976 ed. published by
      School of Law, Duke University, Durham,
      NC. which was issued as v. 40, no. 1 of
      Law and Contemporary Problems. Essays in
      this collection are also listed individual-
      ly and refer to this citation.
      OCLC # 4005558

0088 American Land Title Association. **Indian Land**
      Claims Under the Nonintercourse Act: The
      Constitutional Basis and a Need for a Leg-
      islative Solution. Washington, American
      Land Title Association, 1978.
      OCLC # 4727245

      American Museum of Natural History **see** 2248

0089 American Philosophical Society. Library. **A**
      Supplement to a Guide to Manuscripts Relat-
      ing to the American Indian in the Library
      of the American Philosophical Society.
      Compiled by Daythal Kendall. Philadelphia,
      American Philosophical Society, 1982.
      Memoirs of the American Philosophical Soc-
      iety, v. 65.

      American Society for Ethnohistory **see** 1099

0090 **America's Fascinating Indian Heritage**. Edit-
      ed by James A. Maxwell. Pleasantville,
      NY., Reader's Digest Association, 1978.
      OCLC # 4612484

0091 **America's First Big Parade**, by the unknown
      author. Little Rock, AR., Central Print-
      ing Co., 1932.
      OCLC # 4269264

0092 Amon Carter Museum of Western Art. **Institute**
      of American Indian Arts' Alumni Exhibition.
      Fort Worth, TX., 1973?
      Catalogue of an exhibition to be held at
      the Museum of American Indian Arts, Dec.
      17, 1973- Jan. 28, 1974; Amon Carter
      Museum, Feb. 14- Mar. 31; New Orleans
      Museum of Art, Ap. 27- June 10; and
      Oklahoma Art Center, July 21- Sept. 5.

OCLC # 867708

0093   Amoss, Pamela T. The Power of Secrecy Among
        the Coast Salish. In 0111,   pp.   131-140.

0094   Amsden, Charles Avery, 1899-1941.   Prehistor-
        ic Southwesterners from Basketmaker to
        Pueblo. With an introd. by Alfred V.
        Kidder. New York, AMS Press, 1980.
        Reprint of the 1949 ed. published by
        Southwest Museum, Los Angelos.
        OCLC # 5941036

0095   Anawalt, Patricia Rieff, 1924- . Indian
        Clothing before Cortez: Mesoamerican Cos-
        tume from the Codices. Foreword by H. B.
        Nicholson; charts prepared by Jean Cuker
        Sells. Norman, University of Oklahoma
        Press, 1981.
        Civilization of the American Indian Series,
        no. 156.
        OCLC # 7272788

0096   Ancient Man: A Handbook of Puzzling Arti-
        facts. Illus. by John C. Holden. Glen
        Arm, MD., Sourcebook Project, 1978.
        OCLC # 3905412

0097   Ancient North Americans. Edited by Jesse D.
        Jennings. San Francisco, W. H. Freeman,
        1983.
        Includes some chapters from Ancient Native
        Americans pub. in 1978. Essays in this
        collection are also listed individually and
        refer to this citation.
        OCLC # 8708839

0098   Ancient South Americans. Edited by Jesse D.
        Jennings. San Francisco, W. H. Freeman,
        1983.
        Includes some chapters from Ancient Native
        Americans pub. in 1978. Essays in this
        collection are also listed individually and
        refer to this citation.
        OCLC # 8708835

        Anderson, Arthur J. O. see 0260, 2729

0099   Anderson, Douglas D. Western Arctic and Sub-
        arctic. In 0577, pp. 29-50.

0100	Anderson, Edward F., 1932- . *Peyote, the
	Divine Cactus*. Tucson, University of
	Arizona Press, 1980.
	OCLC # 5336861

	Anderson, Elaine *see* 0893

0101	Anderson, Gary Clayton. *Kinsmen of Another
	Kind: Dakota-White Relations in the Upper
	Mississippi Valley, 1650-1682*. Lincoln,
	University of Nebraska Press, 1984.
	OCLC # 10162792

	Anderson, Melville Best, 1851-1933 *see*
	1677

	Anderson, Ned *see* 0198

0102	Andrefsky, William. *Late Archaic Prehistory
	in the Upper Delaware Valley: A Study of
	Classification, Chronology, and Interac-
	tion*. Ann Arbor, MI., University Micro-
	films International, 1984.
	Microfilm - PhD Thesis - SUNY at Binghamton

0103	Andrews, Anthony P. *Maya Salt Production and
	Trade*. Tucson, University of Arizona
	Press, 1983.
	OCLC # 9827682

0104	Andrews, David H. *Ridged Fields in the Andes
	of Peru*. In 0120, pp. 147-153.

0105	Andrews, E. Wyllys. *Chronology and Astrono-
	my in the Maya Area*. In 2105, pp. 150-
	161.

0106	_____. *Dzibilchaltun*. In 0122, pp. 313-
	341.

0107	_____. *The Southeastern Periphery of Meso-
	America: A View from Eastern El Salvador*.
	In 2920, pp. 113-134.

	Andrews, Patricia A. *see* 0122, 1903

	The Anonymous Conqueror *see* 2259

0108	Antevs, Ernst. *Geological Dating*. In 2768,

pp.   26-43.

0109 Anthropology and History in Yucatan.   Edited
      by Grant D.   Jones.   Austin,   University of
      Texas Press,   1977.
      Texas Pan American Series.   Essays in this
      collection are also listed individually and
      refer to this citation.
      OCLC # 2202479

0110 Anthropology in North America.   New York,   G.
      E.   Stechert,   1915.
      Essays in this collection are also listed
      individually and refer to this citation.
      OCLC # 822786

0111 The Anthropology of Power: Ethnographic
      Studies from Asia, Oceania and the New
      World.   Edited by Raymond D. Fogelson,
      Richard N.   Adams.   New York,   Academic
      Press, 1977.
      Studies in Anthropology.   Essays in this
      collection are also listed individually and
      refer to this citation.
      OCLC # 2633478

0112 The Anthropology of St.   Katherines Island.
      David Hurst Thomas,   et.   al.   New York,
      American Museum of Natural History, 1978.
      Anthropological Papers of the American
      Museum of Natural History v.   55,   pt.   2.
      OCLC # 4441944

0113 Anthropology on the Great Plains.   Edited by
      W.   Raymond Wod and Margot Liberty.   Lin-
      coln, University of Nebraska Press, 1980.
      Essays in this collection are also listed
      individually and refer to this citation.
      OCLC # 5831790

0114 Anyon, Roger, 1952- .   The Galaz Ruin: A
      Prehistoric Mimbres Village in Southwestern
      New Mexico.   By ...   and Steven A.   LeBlanc
      with contributions by Paul E. Minnis,   Mar-
      garet C.   Nelson,   James Lancaster;   edited
      by Paul L.   W.   Sabloff;   foreword by J.
      J.   Brody.   Albuquerque,   Maxwell Museum of
      Anthropology,   University of New Mexico
      Press,   1984.

Maxwell Museum of Anthropology Publication
Series.
OCLC # 10324965

0015   Applebee, Alan C. The Relationship of Val-
ues, Attitudes, and Interests to Participa-
tion in Interscholastic Athletics Among
Selected American Indian Youth. Ann Arbor,
MI., University Microfilms International,
1983.
Microfilm - PhD Thesis - Temple University.
OCLC # 11608558

0116   Applegarth, J. D. Excavations at Cross
Creek Village (36WH293) and the Avella
Mound (36WH415), Washington County,
Southwestern Pennsylvania. In 2111, pp.
241-256.

0117   Aquila, Richard, 1946- . The Iroquois
Restoration: Iroquois Diplomacy on the
Colonial Frontier, 1701-1754. Detroit,
Wayne State University Press, 1983.
OCLC # 8666973

0118   _____. The Iroquois Restoration: A Study
of Iroquois Power, Politics, and Relations
with Indians and Whites, 1700-1744. Ann
Arbor, MI., University Microfilms International, 1977.
Microfilm - PhD Thesis - Ohio State University.

0119   Archaeoastronomy in Pre-Columbian America.
Austin, University of Texas Press, 1975.
OCLC # 1654706

0120   Archaeological Investigations in Columbia,
Venezuela, and the Amazon. Thomas P.
Meyers, et. al., Greeley, Museum of An-
thropology, University of Northern Color-
ado, 1984.
Occasional Publications in Anthropology:
Archaeological Series, Museum of Anthro-
pology, University of Northern Colorado,
no. 15.
OCLC # 10647240.

0121   Archaeological Investigations in Peru. Selected Papers by John R. Cole ... et.

al., Greeley, Museum of Anthropology,
University of Northern Colorado, 1983.
Occasional Papers in Anthropology. Archae-
ological Series, Museum of Anthropology,
University of Northern Colorado, no. 17.
Essays in this collection are also listed
individually and refer to this citation.
OCLC # 11291361

0122 Archaeology. Jeremy A. Sabloff, volume editor with the assistance of Patricia A.
Andrews. Austin, University of Texas
Press, 1981.
Supplement to the Handbook of Middle American Indians, v. 1. Essays in this collection are also listed individually and
refer to this citation.
OCLC # 7306936

0123 The Archaeology of Lower Central America.
Edited by Frederick W. Lange and Doris Z.
Stone. Albuquerque, University of New
Mexico Press, 1984.
School of American Research Advanced Semin-
ar Series. Papers presented at the advanc-
ed seminar on lower Central American Ar-
chaeology held April 8-14, 1980 at the
School of American Research, Santa Fe, NM.
OCLC # 10045443

0124 Archaic Hunters and Gathers in the American
Midwest. Edited by James L. Phillips,
James A. Brown, New York, Academic
Press, 1983.
New World Archaeological Record. Based on
a symposium held at Midwest Archaeological
Conference, University of Illinois at
Chicago, October, 1980. Essays in this
collection are also listed individually and
refer to this citation.
OCLC # 9133123

Archivo General de Indias see 0697

Arctic Institute of North America see 0700

0125 Arese, Francesco, conte 1805-1881. A Trip
to the Prairies and in the Interior of
North America, 1837-1838. Travel notes,

now first translated from the original
French by Andrew Evans. New York, Cooper
Square Publishers, 1975.
Reprint of the 1934 ed. published by Harbor
Press, New York.
OCLC # 1008051

Arima, E. Y. see 0126

0126 Arima, P. Q. and Arima, E. Y. Notes on
      the Kayak and its Equipment at Ivuyivik.
      In the National Museum of Canada Bulletin,
      no. 194, Anthropological Series, no.
      62. Contributions to Anthropology, 1961-
      1962, pt. II. Ottawa, Department of the
      Secretary of State, 1964, pp. 221-261.

0127 Armour, David. The Merchants of Albany, N.
      Y. 1686-1760. Evanston, IL., Ann Arbor,
      MI.,   University Microfilms International,
      1965.
      Microfilm - PhD Thesis - Northwestern Uni-
      versity
      OCLC # 4141864

0128 Armstrong, Perry A., 1823- . The Sauks
      and the Black Hawk War: With Biographical
      Sketches, etc. New York, AMS Press,
      1979, c1886.
      Reprint of the 1887 ed. published by H.
      W. Rokker, Springfield, IL.
      OCLC # 4933769

0129 Armstrong, William Howard, 1932- . Warri-
      or in Two Camps: Ely S. Parker, Union
      General and Seneca Chief. Syracuse,
      Syracuse University Press, 1978.
      An Iroquois Book
      OCLC # 3844302

0130 Arnold, Bingham. Surface Evidence of Early
      Man in Arid Lands. In 0902, pp. 181-182.

0131 Arnold, Dean E. Ethnography of Pottery mak-
      ing in the Valley of Guatemala. In 0531,
      pp. 327-400.

0132 _____, et. al. Neutron Activation Analy-
      sis of Contemporary Pottery and Pottery
      from the Valley of Guatemala. In 0531,

pp.   543-586.

0133   Arnold,   James MacKeever and James Robert
       Moriarty,   III.   A Survey of Maya State,
       Religious and Secular Architecture.
       Greeley,   University of Northern Colorado,
       Museum of Anthropology,   1971.
       University of Northern Colorado,   Museum of
       Anthropology,   Misc.   Series,   no.   27.
       OCLC # 261012

0134   Arnold,   Mary Ellicott.   In the Land of the
       Grasshopper Song: Two Women in the Klamath
       River Indian Country in 1908-09.   By ..
       and Mabel Reed.   Lincoln,   University of
       Nebraska Press,   1980,   c1957.
       Reprint of the ed.   published by Vantage
       Press,   New York.
       OCLC # 6143499

       Art Institute of Chicago see 2101

0135   Art of the Huichol Indians,   with contribu-
       tions by Lowell John Bean,   et.   al.;
       introd.   and edited by Kathleen Berrin;
       preface by Thomas K.   Seligman.   San
       Francisco,   Fine Arts Museum of San
       Francisco,   1978.
       OCLC # 3845461

       Arthur C.   Parker Fund for Iroquois Research
       see 1204,   1583

0136   Artigas-Padilla,   Maria Del Carmen.   Fruitful
       Encounter: The Meeting of the Spanish-
       MesoAmerican Civilizations in the Sixteenth
       Century.   Ann Arbor, MI.,   University
       Microfilms International,   1984.
       Microfilm - PhD Thesis - Bowling Green
       State University.
       OCLC # 12257397

       Arts Council of Great Britain see 0608

0137   As Long as the Sun Shines and the Water
       Flows: A Reader in Canadian Native Studies.
       Edited by Ian A.   L.   Getty and Antoine S.
       Lussier.   Vancouver,   University of British
       Columbia Press,   1983.

Nakoda Institute Occasional Paper,   no. 1.
Essays in this collection are also listed
individually and refer to this citation.
OCLC # 10134484

0138   Asch, David. The Middle Woodland Population
        of the Lower Illinois Valley: A Study in
        Paleodemographic Methods.   Evanston, IL.,
        Northwestern Archaeological Program,   1976.
        Northwestern University Archaeological Pro
        gram, Scientific Papers,   no. 1.
        OCLC # 3551355

        _____. see also 2635

0139   Ascher, Marcia,   1935- . Code of the Quipu:
        A Study in Media, Mathematics, and Culture.
        By ... and Robert Ascher.   Ann Arbor, Uni-
        versity of Michigan Press,   1981.
        OCLC # 7169684

        Ascher, Robert, 1931- . see 0139

        Ashton, Robert H. see 3030

0140   Ashton, Roger. The Oatman Site: A Single
        Component of the Late Archaic in Washington
        County, NY.   New York State Archeological
        Association,   Bulletin 48,   pp. 15-19,
        March 1970.   Millwood, NY.,   Kraus Reprint,
        1976.

        Association for the Advancement of Native
        North American Arts and Crafts see 1582

        Association on American Indian Affairs see
        3499

0141   Aten, Lawrence E. Indians of the Upper
        Texas Coast. New York, Academic Press,
        1983.
        New World Archaeological Record
        OCLC # 8688554

0142   Atlas of the Lewis and Clark Expedition.
        Gary E. Moulton, editor.   Lincoln, Uni-
        versity of Nebraska Press,   1983.
        Sponsored by the Center for Great Plains

Studies,   University of Nebraska - Lincoln,
and the American Philosophical Society,
Philadelphia.
OCLC # 8629853

0143   Attenborough,   David.   The Tribal Eye.   New
       York,   Norton,   1976.
       OCLC # 2745067

0144   Attitudes of Colonial Powers Toward the Amer-
       ican Indian.   Howard Peckham and Charles
       Gibson,   editors.   Salt Lake City,   Univer-
       sity of Utah Press,   1969.
       University of Utah Publications in the
       American West, v. 2. Essays in this col-
       lection are also listed individually and
       refer to this citation.
       OCLC # 137356

       Attneave, Carolyn L. see 1731

0145   Aubin,   George F.   The Edison Insight and the
       Williams Materials.   In 0068,   pp.   180-
       195.

0146   Authentic Indian Designs: 2500 Illustrations
       from Reports of the Bureau of Indian Af-
       fairs.   Edited by Maria Naylor.   New York,
       Dover Pubs.,   1975.
       Dover Pictorial Archive Series
       OCLC # 1848847

0147   Aventi, Anthony F.   Concepts of Positional
       Astronomy Employed in Ancient Mesoamerican
       Architecture.   In 2270,   pp.   3-19.

0148   _____.   Skywatchers of Ancient Mexico.
       Foreword by Owen Gingerich,   Aus-
       tin,   University of Texas Press,   1980.
       Texas Pan American Series
       OCLC # 5893613

       _____.   see also 2270

0149   Axtell,   James.   Dr.   Wheelock and the
       Iroquois.   In 0979,   pp.   51-64.

0150   _____.   The European and the Indian: Es-
       says in the Ethnohistory of Colonial North

America. New York, Oxford University
Press, 1981.
OCLC # 6864212

0151 _____. The European Failure to Convert the
Indians: An Autopsy. In 0069, pp. 274-
290.

0152 _____. The Invasion Within: The Contest
of Cultures in Colonial North America. New
York, Oxford University Press, 1985.
OCLC # 11971236

_____. see also 1567, 2695

0153 Axtell, Juliet L. The Indian Sign Language
in Indian Education. In 0008, pp. 27-35.
Reprinted from The Indian Sign Language and
the Invention of Lewis F. Hadley, as Applied to the Speedy Christian Civilization
and Education of the Wild Adult Indian.
Chicago, Western Label Co., 1891, pp.
3-11.

0154 The Aztecs of Mexico. Selected papers by
James R. Moriarty, et. al. Greeley, Uni-
versity of Northern Colorado, Museum of
Anthropology, 1982.
University of Northern Colorado, Museum of
Anthropology Occasional Publications in
Anthropology, Ethnology Series no. 42.
Essays in this collection are also listed
individually and refer to this citation.
OCLC # 9603823

Babcock, Molly see 3123

0155 Bad Heart Bull, Amos. Letter from Pine
Ridge. In 3335, pp. 130-131.
Source - New York Times, Nov. 19, 1967,
Letters to the Editor.

0156 Bailey, Garrick. John Joseph Mathews,
Osage, 1894- . In 0080, pp. 205-214.

0157 Bailer, Garrick. Social Control on the
Plains. In 0113, pp. 153-163.

0158 Bailey, John W. 1934- . Pacifying the
Plains: General Alfred Terry and the De-

cline of the Sioux, 1866-1890. Westport,
CT., Greenwood Press, 1979.
Contributions to Military History, v. 17.
OCLC # 4495751

0159 Bailey, Kenneth P. 1912- . Christopher
Gist: Colonial Frontiersman, Explorer and
Indian Agent. Hamden, CT., Archon Books,
1976.
OCLC # 1733479

0160 Baird, W. David. The Quest for a Red Faced
White Man: Reservation Whites View Their
Indian Wards. In 2602, pp. 113-131.

0161 Baker, Nancy Roux-Teepen. American Indian
Women in an Urban Setting. Ann Arbor, MI.,
University Microfilms International, 1982.
Microfilm - PhD Thesis - Ohio State Univer-
sity
OCLC # 10366735

0162 Baker, Robert Charles, 1949- . North
American Tribal Arts and Crafts; Towards a
New Interpretation. Ann Arbor, MI., Uni-
versity Microfilms International, 1983.
Microfilm - PhD Thesis - American Univer-
sity.
OCLC # 11120705

      Bakker, Dirk see 0256

0163 Ball, Eve. Indeh, an Apache Odyssey. ...
with Nora Henn and Lynda Sanchez. Provo,
Utah, Brigham Young University Press,
1980.
OCLC # 6195018

      _____. see also 1702

0164 Ball Joseph W. An Hypothetical Outline of
Coastal Maya Prehistory: 300 B. C. to
A. D. 1200. In 2920, pp. 167-196.

0165 _____. The Rise of the Northern Maya
Chiefdoms: A Socioprocessual Analysis. In
2378, pp. 101-132.

0166 Ballard, George Alexander, 1862- . Amer-

ia and the Atlantic. New York,   Dutton,
1923.
OCLC # 1542415

0167 Bancroft-Hunt, Norman. The Indians of the
Great Plains. Photos by Werner Forman.
New York,   Morrow,   1982, c1981.
OCLC # 8660047

0168 _____. People of the Totem: The Indians
of the Pacific Northwest. Photos by Werner
Forman. New York,   Putman,   1979.
Echoes of the Ancient World
OCLC # 4990225

0169 Bandelier,   Adolph Francis Alphonse,   1840-
1914.   and Edgar L.   Hewett. Indians of
the Rio Grande Valley. New York,   AMS
Press,   1978.
Reprint of the 1937 pub. by the University
of New Mexico Press,   Albuquerque.   Hand-
books of Archaeological History Series.
CONTENTS: Hewett, E. L. The Rio Grande
Pueblos Today. Bandelier, A. F. A. Documentary History of the Rio Grande Pueblos.
OCLC # 3872511

0170 _____. On the Social Organization and Mode
of Government of the Ancient Mexicans. New
York,   Cooper Square Publishers,   1975.
From the 12th Annual Report of the Peabody
Museum of Archaeology and Ethnology,   Cambridge,   1879.   Reprint of the 1879 ed.
printed at the Salem Press, Salem.   Library
of Latin American History and Culture.
OCLC # 1031464

0171 _____. Pioneers in American Anthropology:
The Bandelier-Morgan Letters,   1873-1883.
Edited by Leslie A.   White.   New York,   AMS
Press,   1978,   c1940.
Reprint of the ed. published by University
of New Mexico Press,   Albuquerque,   issued
in series: Coronado Cuarto Centennial Pub-
lications, 1540-1940: Bandelier Series.
OCLC # 3934699

0172 Bankes,   George. Peru before Pizarro.   Oxford,   England,   Phaidon,   1977.
OCLC # 3321375

0173 Barbeau,   Charles Marius,   1883- . Huron-
      Wyandot Traditional Narratives in Transla-
      tion and Native Texts. Ottawa,   Queen's
      Printer,   1960.
      National Museum of Canada.   Bulletin 165,
      Anthropological Series no.   47.
      OCLC # 1990439

0174 _____.   The Indian Days on the Western
      Prairies. Portraits by W. Langdon Price.
      Ottawa,   Department of Northern Affairs and
      National Resources.   National Museum of
      Canada,   1960.
      National Museum of Canada.   Bulletin 163.
      Anthropological Series no.   46.
      OCLC # 2569896

0175 _____.   Totem Poles of the Gitksan, Upper
      Skeena River,   British Columbia. Facsimile
      ed. Ottawa,   National Museum of Canada,
      1973.
      National Museum of Canada.   Bulletin 61.
      Anthropological Series no.   12.
      OCLC # 4688596

0176 Barbeau,   Marius. The Language of Canada in
      the Voyages of Jacques Cartier (1534-1538).
      In   National Museum of Canada.   Bulletin
      173.   Anthropological Series no.   50. Con-
      tributions to Anthropology,   1959.   1961,
      pp.   108-229.

0177 Barbour,   Phillip L. Notes on Anglo-Algon-
      kian Contacts, 1605-1624. In 0068,   pp.
      112-127.

0178 Barber,   Russell J. Post-Pleistocene Anadro-
      mous Fish Exploration at the Buswell Site,
      Northeastern Massachusetts. In 0901,   pp.
      97-113.

      Bareis,   Charles J. see 0077

0197 Barker,   A.   J. Redcoats. London,   Gordon
      and Cremonesi,   1976.
      OCLC # 2230011

0180 Barnes,   Will C.   (Will Croft).   1858-1936.
      Apaches and Longhorns: The Reminiscences
      of Will C.   Barnes. Edited by Frank C.

Lockwood; with a decoration by Cas Duchow.
Tucson, University of Arizona Press, 1982.
Originally published in Los Angelos by Ward
Ritchie, 1941.
OCLC # 8430344

0181   Barney, Ralph A. Legal Problems Peculiar to
        Indian Claims Litigation. In 2304, pp.
        255-262.
        Reprinted from Ethnohistory vol. 2, no.
        4, Fall 1955, pp. 315-24.

0182   Barnitz, Albert. Life in Custer's Cavalry:
        Diaries and Letters of ALbert and Jenny
        Barnitz. Edited by Robert M. Utley. New
        Haven, Yale University Press, 1977.
        Yale Western Americana Series v. 31
        OCLC # 2694967

0183   Barnouw, Victor. Acculturation and Person-
        ality Among the Wisconsin Chippewa. Mill-
        wood, NY., Kraus Reprint, 1974.
        American Anthropological Association Mem-
        oirs no. 72. Supplement to American An-
        thropologist v. 52, no. 4, pt. 2,
        1950.
        OCLC # 1409842

0184   _____. Wisconsin Chippewa Myths and Tales
        and Their Relation to Chippewa Life. Based
        on folktales collected by Victor Barnouw,
        Joseph B. Casagrande, Ernestine Friedl
        and Robert E. Ritzenthaler. Madison,
        University of Wisconsin Press, 1977.
        OCLC # 2968389

0185   Barron, F. Laurie. Alcoholism, Indians
        and the Anti-drink Cause in the Protestant
        Indian Missions of Upper Canada, 1822-
        1850. In 0137, p. 191-202.

0186   Barrows, David Prescott, 1873- . The
        Ethnobotany of the Coahuilla Indians of
        Southern California. New York, AMS Press,
        1978.
        Reprint of the 1900 ed. published by Uni-
        versity of Chicago Press, Originally
        presented as the author's thesis, Univer-
        sity of Chicago, 1897.
        OCLC # 4137432

27   BARRY

0187   Barry, John Willard, 1934- . American In-
       dian Pottery: An Identification and Value
       Guide. Florence, AL., Books Americana,
       1981.
       OCLC # 7384410

0188   Barsh, Russell Lawrence. The Road: Indian
       Tribes and Political Liberty. By ... and
       James Youngblood Henderson. Berkeley,
       University of California Press, 1980.
       OCLC # 6076803

0189   _____, and J. Youngblood Henderson.
       Tribal Courts, the Model Code and the
       Police Idea in American Indian Policy. In
       0087, pp. 26-60.

0190   Barta, Richard Lee. An Evaluation of an In-
       dian Health Management Training Program and
       its Counseling Component as Perceived by
       the Program's Participants. Ann Arbor,
       MI., University Microfilms International,
       1984.
       Microfilm - PhD Thesis - University of
       South Dakota
       OCLC # 11323838

0191   Bartlett, Charles E. Jesse J. Cornplanter.
       New York State Archaeological Association
       Bulletin 10, July 1957, pp. 1-3. Mill-
       wood, NY., Kraus Reprint, 1976.

0192   _____. Some Seneca Songs from Tonawanda
       Reservation. New York State Archaeological
       Association Bulletin 5, Nov. 1955, pp.
       8-16. Kraus Reprint, 1976.
       Abstract of paper presented at annual meet-
       ing, April 16, 1955.

0193   Bartolome de la Casas in History: Toward an
       Understanding of the Man and His Work. Ed-
       ited by Benjamin Keen. Dekalb, Northern
       Illinois University Press, 1971.
       Essays in this collection are also listed
       individually and refer to this citation.

0194   Barton, Charles. The Wadsworth Fort Site
       (CDA 11-4). New York State Archaeological
       Association Bulletin 32, Nov. 1964, pp.
       2-5. Millwood, NY., Kraus Reprint, 1976.

0195   Baskets of the Dawnland People. Under the
       direction of Joseph A. Nichols. Calais,
       ME., Project Indian Pride, 1980?
       OCLC # 6530117

0196   Basso, Keith H. 1940- . Portraits of "The
       Whiteman": Linguistic Play and Cultural
       Symbols Among the Western Apache. Illus.
       by Vincent Craig. Cambridge, England. New
       York, Cambridge University Press, 1979.
       OCLC # 4592954

0197   _____. Southwestern Ethnology: A Critical
       Review. In the Annual Review of Anthro-
       pology vol. 2, 1973, pp. 221-252.

0198   _____. A Western Apache Writing System.
       By ... and Ned Anderson. Lisse, Nether-
       lands, P. de Ridder Press, 1975.
       P. de Ridder Press Publications on writing
       systems. Reprinted from Linguistics and
       Anthropology: In Honor of C. F. Vogelin
       edited by M. Dale Kinkade, Kenneth Hale
       and Oswald Werner.
       OCLC # 3530767

0199   Bataille, Gretchen M., 1944- . American
       Indian Women, Telling Their Lives. By ...
       and Kathleen Mullen Sands. Lincoln, Univ-
       ersity of Nebraska Press, 1984.
       OCLC # 9621968

       _____. see also 2533

0200   Bataillon, Marcel. The Clerigo Casas, Col-
       onists and Colonial Reform. In 0193, pp.
       353-440.

0201   Battey, Thomas C. The Life and Adventures
       of a Quaker Among the Indians. With an
       introd. by Alice Marriott. Norman, Univ-
       ersity of Oklahoma Press, 1968.
       Western Frontier Library no. 36.
       OCLC # 165802

0202   Battiste, Marie Ann. An Historical Inves-
       tigation of the Social and Cultural Conse-
       quences of Micmac Literacy. Ann Arbor,
       MI., University Microfilms International,
       1984.

Microfilm - EdD Thesis - Stanford University.

0203 Bauer, Mark Carl. Navaho Conflict Management. Ann Arbor, MI., University Microfilms International, 1983.
Microfilm - PhD Thesis - Northwestern University
OCLC # 11612809

0204 Baumbach, Otto Schondube. Deidades Prehispanicas en el Area de Tamazula-Tuxpan-Zapotlan en el Estado de Jalisco. In 0231, pp. 168-181.

0205 _____. Introduccion: Algunas Consideraciones Sobre la Arqueologia del Occidente de Mexico. In 0231, pp. 1-5.

0206 Baurley, Marion E. American Indian Law, Relationship to Child Abuse and Neglect. By ... and Matthew H. Street. Washington, U. S. Department of Health and Human Services, Office of Human Development Services, Administration for Children, Youth and Families, Children's Bureau, National Center on Child Abuse and Neglect. Govt. Print. Off. 1981.
A Special report from the National Center on Child Abuse and Neglect.
OCLC # 7507002

0207 Beads - Their Use by Upper Great Lake Indians: An Exhibition. Produced by the Grand Rapids Public Museum and the Cranbrook Academy of Art Museum. Grand Rapids, The Public Museum, 1977.
Grand Rapids Public Museum Publication no. 3.
OCLC # 3446969

0208 Beaglehole, Ernest. Hopi of the Second Mesa. By ... and Pearl Beaglehole. New York, Kraus Reprint, 1964.
American Anthropological Association Memoirs no. 44, 1935. Supplement to American Anthropologist v. 37, no. 3, pt. 2.
OCLC # 558757

Beaglehole, Pearl see 00208

0209   Bean, Lowell John.   California Indian
        Shamanism and Folk Curing.   In   3180,   pp.
        109-123.

0210   _____.   California Indians: Primary Re-
        sources: A Guide to Manuscripts,   Arti-
        facts,   Documents,   Serials,   Music and Il-
        lustrations.   By ... and Sylvia Brakke
        Vane.   Ramona, CA.,   Ballena Press,   1977.
        Ballena Press Anthropological Papers no.   7
        OCLC # 3206224

0211   _____.   Power and Its Application in Native
        Californians.   In   0111,   pp.   117-129.

0212   _____.   Power and Its Application in Native
        Californians.   In   2276,   pp.   407-420.

0213   _____.   Social Organization in Native Cali-
        fornia.   In   2276,   pp.   99-124.

0214   _____.   Some Explanations for the Rise of
        Cultural Complexity in Native California
        with Comments on Proto-agriculture and
        Agriculture.   In   2276,   pp.   19-48.

        _____.   see also   0135,   2276

0215   Beatty,   John.   Kiowa-Apache Music and Dance.
        Greeley,   University of Northern Colorado,
        Museum of Anthropology,   1974.
        University of Northern Colorado,   Museum of
        Anthropology,   Occasional Publications in
        Anthropology,   Ethnology Series no.   31.
        OCLC # 1448593

0216   Beauchamp,   William Martin,   1830-1925.
        Civil, Religious and Mourning Councils and
        Ceremonies of Adoption of the New York
        Indians.   University of the State of New
        York,   State Education Department,   1975.
        New York State Museum Bulletin 113.   Re-
        print of the 1907 ed.   which was issued as
        Bulletin 113,   Archaeology 13 of the New
        York State Museum.
        OCLC # 4036379

0217   _____.   History of the New York Iroquois,
        Now Commonly Called the Six Nations.   New
        York,   AMS Press,   1976.

Reprint of the 1905 ed. published by New
York State Education Department, ALbany,
which was issued as Bulletin no. 329 of
the University of the State of New York,
Bulletin 788 of the New York State Museum,
and as no. 9 in the subseries Archaeology
of the Museum's Bulletin,
OCLC # 1693797

0218 _____. Horn and Bone Implements of New
York Indians. Albany, University of the
State of New York, 1902.
New York State Museum Bulletin no. 50.
Reprinted by AMS in 1978.
OCLC # 1574733

0219 _____. Indian Names in New York, with a
Selection from Other States, and Some
Onondaga Names of Plants, etc. Fayette-
ville, NY., Printed by H. C. Beauchamp,
1893.
OCLC # 635605

0220 _____. Metallic Implements of the New York
Indians. Albany, University of the State
of New York, 1902.
New York State Museum Bulletin no. 55,
Archaeology no. 7.
OCLC # 4714893

0221 _____. Papers on Iroquois Personal Names.
Onondaga Historical Association, Originals
in Syracuse (NY) Public Library. Microfilm
supplied by American Philosophical Society,
Philadelphia. Material collected by W. M.
Beauchamp, 1909.
Film #643, Freeman reference #203

0222 _____. Wampum and Shell Articles Used by
the New York Indians. Albany, University
of the State of New York, 1901.
New York State Museum Bulletin no. 41, v.
8.
OCLC # 3892075

0223 Beaver, Robert Pierce, 1906- . The Native
American Christian Community: A Directory
of Indian, Aleut and Eskimo Churches.
Monrovia, CA., MARC, 1979.
OCLC # 5103055

0224   Becker,   Marshall Joseph.   Theories of An-
       cient Maya Social Structure: Priests,
       Peasants and Ceremonial Centers in Histor-
       ical Perspective. Greeley, Museum of An-
       thropology,   University of Northern Colo-
       rado Press,   1984.
       University of Northern Colorado,   Museum of
       Anthropology,   Occasional Papers in An-
       thropology,   Ethnology Series no.   53.
       OCLC # 1541447

0225   _____.   Priests,   Peasants and Ceremonial
       Centers: The Intellectual History of a
       Model.   In 0472,   pp.   3-20.

0226   Beckerman,   Stephen.   Carpe Diem: An Opti-
       mal Foraging Approach to Bari Fishing.   In
       0023,   pp.   269-299.

0227   Beckwith, H. W. (Hiram Williams) 1833-1903.
       The Illinois and Indiana Indians.   New
       York,   Arno Press,   1975, c1884.
       Mid-American Frontier.   Reprint of the ed.
       published by Fergus Printing Co.,   Chicago,
       which was issued as no.   27 of Fergus'
       Historical Series, 1884.
       OCLC # 1218311

0228   Bedwell,   Stephen Ferguson,   1930-1972.   Fort
       Rock Basin: Prehistory and Environment.
       Foreword by L. S. Cressman,   Eugene,
       University of Oregon Books,   1973.
       OCLC # 960762

       Begay,   Gishin see 3226

0229   Beidler,   Peter G.   The American Indian in
       Short Fiction: An Annotated Bibliography.
       By ... and Marion F. Egge.   Metuchen, NJ.,
       Scarecrow Press,   1979.
       OCLC # 5336873

0230   Belize,   David A.   Maritime Adaptation and
       the Rise of Maya Civilization: The View
       from Cerros, Belize.   In 2524,   pp.   239-
       265.

       Bell,   Amelia see 1079

0231   Bell,   Betty.   Archaeology of West Mexico.
       Ajijic,   Jalisco,   Mexico,   West Mexican
       Society for Advance Study,   1974.
       Essays in this collection are also listed
       individually and refer to this citation.
       OCLC # 1042439

0232   _____.   Excavations at El Cerro Encantado,
       Jalisco.   In   0231,   pp.   147-167.

       _____ see also 2342

       Bell,   Robert E.   see   0410

0233   Bellamy,   Gail Rochelle,   1950-   .   Policy
       Implications for Adolescent Deviance: The
       Case of Indian Alcohol Prohibition.   Ann
       Arbor,   University Microfilms Internation-
       al,   1984.
       Microfilm - PhD Thesis - Johns Hopkins
       University
       OCLC # 12994563

0234   Bellamy,   Hans Schindler,   1901-   .   The Cal-
       endar of Tiahuanaco;   A Disquisition on the
       Time Measuring System of the Oldest Civili-
       zation in the World.   By ... and P.   Allan.
       London,   Farber and Farber,   1956.
       OCLC # 1983190

0235   Bemister,   Margaret,   1877-   .   Thirty Indian
       Legends of Canada.   Illus.   by Douglas
       Tait.   Vancouver,   Douglas and McIntyre,
       1973.
       OCLC # 875179

0236   Bennett,   Ben.   Death,   Too,   for the-Heavy-
       Runner.   Illus.   by Tom Saubert.   Missoula,
       MT.,   Mountain Press Pub.   Co.,   1982.
       OCLC # 6356620

0237   Bennett,   Kenneth A.   Skeletal Remains from
       Mesa Verde National Park,   Colorado.
       Washington,   Govt.   Print.   Off.,   1975.
       OCLC # 1056783

0238   Bennett,   Monte.   Glass Trade Beads from Cen-
       tral New York.   In 1204,   pp.   51-58.

0239   Bennett, Wendell Clark, 1905- . A Reap-
        praisal of Peruvian Archaeology. Menasha.
        WI., Published jointly by the Society for
        American Archaeology and the Institute of
        Andean Research, 1948. Millwood, NY.,
        Kraus Reprint, 1974.
        Memoirs of the Society for American Archae-
        ology no. 4. Supplement to American Anti-
        quity v. 13, no. 4, pt. 2, April 1948.
        Includes papers and comments submitted to
        a conference entitled A Reappraisal of
        Peruvian Archaeology held in New York,
        July 17-19, 1947, under the auspices of
        the Viking Fund and the Institute of Andean
        Research.
        OCLC # 1185158

        Bennyhoff, James Allen, 1926- . see
        2150

0240   Benson, Charles L. Explaining Organization-
        al Change: Anasazi Community Patterns.
        Ann Arbor, MI., University Microfilms
        International, 1984.
        Microfilm - PhD Thesis - University of
        Washington
        OCLC # 12578952

        Benson, Elizabeth P. see 2519

0241   Berdan, Frances. The Aztecs of Central Mex-
        ico: An Imperial Society. New York.
        Holt, Rinehart, and Winston, 1982.
        Case Studies in Cultural Anthropology
        OCLC # 7795704

        _____. see also 0260

0242   Berger, Rainer. New Dating Techniques. In
        0903, pp. 159-161.
        This is publication no. 2267 of the Insti-
        tute of Geophysics and Planetary Physics,
        UCLA.

        Bergs, Lilita see 1391

0243   Berkhofer, Robert F. Protestants, Pagans,
        and Sequences Among the North American In-
        dians, 1760-1860. In 2304, pp. 120-

131.
Abridged and reprinted from Ethnohistory v.
10, no. 3, Summer 1963, pp. 201-16.

0244   _____.   The White Man's Indian: Images of
the American Indian from Columbus to the
Present. New York,   Knopf,   1978.
OCLC # 3345457

0245 Berlant,   Anthony.   Walk In Beauty: The
Navajo and Their Blankets. By ... and Mary
Hunt Kahlenberg.   Boston,   New York Graphic
Society, 1977.
OCLC # 2645462

0246 Berlant, Tony. Mimbres Painting: An Art-
ist's Perspective.   In 0391, pp.   13-22.

0247 Berlin,   Brent and Elois Ann Berlin.   Adaptation and Ethnozoological Classification:
Theoretical Implications of Animal Resources and Diet of the Aguaruan and
Huambisa.   In 0023, pp.   301-325.

0248   _____.   Principles of Tzeltal Plant Classi-
fication: An Introduction to the Botanical
Ethnography of a Mayan-speaking People of
Highland Chiapas. By ... and Dennis E.
Breedlove and Peter H.   Raven.   New York,
Academic Press,   1974.
Language Thought and Culture
OCLC # 1055254

Berlin,   Elois Ann see 0248

0249 Bernal, Ignacio. A History of Mexican Ar-
chaeology: The Vanishing Civilizations of
Middle America. New York,   Thames and
Hudson,   1980.
OCLC # 6371199

0250   _____.   Maya Antiquities.   In 2920, pp.
19-43.

0251 Berreman, Joel Van Meter, 1900- . Tribal
Distribution in Oregon. New York,   Kraus
Reprint,   1969.
American Anthropological Association Mem-
oirs no.   47,   1937. Supplement to Ameri-
can Anthropologist v.   39,   no.   3,   pt.

2.
OCLC # 561433

Berrin,   Kathleen <u>see</u>   0135

0252   Berry,   David Richard,   1941-   . <u>Disease and</u>
       <u>Climatological Relationships Among Pueblo</u>
       <u>III - Pueblo IV Anasazi of the Colorado</u>
       <u>Plateau</u>.   Ann Arbor,   MI.,   University
       Microfilms International,   1983.
       Microfilm - PhD Thesis -   University of
       California - Los Angelos.
       OCLC # 12626337

0253   Berthrong,   Donald John.   <u>Changing Concepts:</u>
       <u>The Indian Learns About the "Long Knives"</u>
       <u>and Settlers (1847-1890s)</u>.   In   2602,   pp.
       47-61.

0254   _____.   <u>The Cheyenne and Arapaho Ordeal:</u>
       <u>Reservation and Agency Life in the Indian</u>
       <u>Territory,   1875-1907</u>. Norman,   University
       of Oklahoma Press,   1976.
       Civilization of the American Indian Series
       v.   136.
       OCLC # 1504813

0255   Bettinger,   Robert L.   <u>Aboriginal Sociopolit-</u>
       <u>ical Organization in Owens Valley: Beyond</u>
       <u>the Family Band</u>.   In 0796,   pp.   45-58.

       _____.   <u>see also</u>   3106

0256   <u>Between Continents/ Between Seas: Precolum-</u>
       <u>bian Art of Costa Rica</u>.   Text by Suzanne
       Abel-Vidor,   photographs by Dirk Bakker.
       New York, H. N. Abrams,   Detroit,
       Detroit Institute of Arts,   1981.
       OCLC # 7596893

0257   Beuf,   Ann H.   1938-   .   <u>Red Children in</u>
       <u>White America</u>.   Philadelphia,   University
       of Pennsylvania Press,   1977.
       OCLC # 2645824

0258   Bevier,   Abraham Garret.   <u>The Indian: or</u>
       <u>Naratives of Massacres and Depredations on</u>
       <u>the Frontier,   in Wawasinic and it's Vicin-</u>
       <u>ity</u>.   Wawarsink, NY.,   American Bicentenni-
       al Commission;   Monroe,   NY.,   distributed

by Library Research Associates, 1975.
Reprint of the 1846 ed. published in
Rondout, NY.
OCLC # 1500168

0259 Beynon, D. and J. Donahue. The Geology and
Geomorphology of Meadowcroft Rockshelter
and the Cross Creek Drainage. In 2111,
pp. 31-52.

0260 Beyond the Codices: The Nahua View of Colo-
nial Mexico. Translated and edited by
Arthur J. O. Anderson, Frances Berdan,
James Lockhart; with a linguistic essay by
Ronald W. Langacker. Berkeley, Univer-
sity of California Press, 1976.
UCLA Latin American Studies Series. Texts
of documents in Nahuatl and English.
OCLC # 2557755

0261 Bia, Johnson. Agricultural-Related Issues
on the Navaho Nation. Ann Arbor, University Microfilms International, 1984.
Microfilm - MS Thesis - University of Arizona
OCLC # 12114672

Biblioteca Nazionale Centrale di Firenze.
Manuscript. Codex Magliabecchi, XIII, 11,
3. English. 1983. see 0330

0262 Bierhorst, John. American Indian Verbal Art
and the Role of the Literary Critic. In
2904, pp. 78-86.
Reprinted from Journal of American Folklore
v. 88, no. 350, 1975, pp. 401-8.

0263 _____. Mythology of North America. New
York, Morrow, 1985.
OCLC # 11754474

0264 Biermann, Benno M. Bartolome de las Casas
and Verapaz. In 0193, pp. 443-484.

0265 Bill, Willard. Curriculum Research for
American Indian Education: Alcohol and the
American Indian. In 2962, pp. 143-157.

0266 Bindel, Rosalie A. American Indian Education: An Overview of a Case Study. In

2962,   pp.   83-99.

0267 Binford,   Lewis R.   and Mark L.   Papworth.
      The Eastport Site,   Antrim County,   Michi-
      gan.   In   2189,   pp.   71-123.

0268 _____.   The Hodges Site;   A Late Archaic
      Burial Station.   In   2189,   pp.   149-192.

0269 _____.   A Proposed Attribute List for the
      Description and Classification of Project-
      ile Points.   In   2189,   pp.   193-221.

0270 Biocultural Adaptation in Prehistoric Ameri-
      ca.   Robert L.   Blakely,   editor.   Athens,
      University of Georgia Press,   1977.
      Papers presented at a symposium held during
      the 11th Annual Meeting of the Southern
      Anthropological Society in Atlanta.   Essays
      in this collection are also listed indi-
      vidually and refer to this citation.
      OCLC # 2646110

0271 Biographical Dictionary of Indians of the
      Americas.   Newport Beach, CA.,   American
      Indian Publishers,   1983.
      OCLC # 11060536

0272 Bird,   Junius and Richard Cooke.   The Occur-
      rence in Panama of Two Types of Paleo-In-
      dian Projectile Points.   In   0902,   pp.
      263-272.

0273 Bird,   Robert McK.   South American Maize in
      Central America.   In   2521,   pp.   39-65.

      _____.   see also   2521

0274 Birkby,   Walter H.   Biosocial Interpretations
      from Cranial Nonmetric Traits of Grasshop-
      per Pueblo Skeletal Remains.   In   2239,
      pp.   36-41.

0275 Birket-Smith,   Kaj,   1893- .   The Caribou
      Eskimos.   Translated by W.   E.   Calvert.
      AMS Press,   1976.
      Reprint of the 1929 ed. published by
      Glydenal,   Copenhagen which was issued as
      v.   5 of report of the 5th Thule Expedition
      1921-24.

OCLC # 3969421

0276 _____. Contributions to Chipewyan Ethnolo-
gy. Translated by W. E. Calvert. New
York, AMS Press, 1976.
Reprint of the 1930 ed. published by
Gyldendal, Copenhagen which was issued as
v. 6, no. 3 of report of the 5th Thule
Expedition 1921-24.
OCLC # 2332086

0277 _____. Studies in Circumpacific Culture
Relations. Kobenhavn Munksgaard, 1967.
Danske videnskabernes selskab, Copenhagen.
Historisk filosofiske meddelelser, bd.
42, nr. 3.
CONTENTS 1. Potlatch and feasts of merit.
3. Sundry Customs and notions.
OCLC # 1142251

0278 Bishop, Charles A. The First Century:
Adaptive Changes Among the Western James
Bay Cree Between the Early Seventeenth and
Early Eighteenth Centuries. In 3047, pp.
21-53.

0279 _____. Limiting Access to Limited Goods:
The Origins of Stratification in Interior
British Columbia. In 0796, pp. 148-161.

0280 _____. Northeastern Indian Concepts of
Conservation and Fur Trade: A Critique of
Calvin Martin's Thesis. In 1574, pp.
39-58.

0280.5 _____. The Origin of the Speakers of the
Severn Dialect. In 0068, pp. 196-208.

0281 Bittman, Bente. Arqueologia de Cobija,
Fechas Radiocarbonicas: Un Comentario. In
0873, pp. 97-115.
Article in Spanish

0282 _____. Fisherman, Mummies and Balsa Rafts
of the Coast of Northern Chile. In 0873,
pp. 53-96.

0283 _____. Historical Archaeology in Abandoned
Nitrate "Oficinas" in Northern Chile. In
0873, pp. 31-52.

0284   Bizarro, Ujpan Ignacio.   Campesino: The
       Diary of a Guatemalan Indian.   Trans. and
       edited by James D.   Sexton.   Tucson,   Uni-
       versity of Arizona Press.   1985.
       Sequel to Son of Tecun Uman
       OCLC # 11815692

0285   _____.   Son of Tecún Umán: A Maya Indian
       Tells His Life Story.   James D.   Saxton,
       editor.   Tucson,   University of Arizona
       Press,   1981.
       OCLC # 7671903

0286   Black, Lydia T.   The Nature of Evil: Of
       Whales and Sea Otters.   In   1574,   pp.
       109-153.

0287   Black,   Mary B.   Ojibwa Power Belief System.
       In 0111,   pp.   141-151.

       Black,   Nancy B.   see   3413

0288   Black Elk,   Oglala Indian,   1863-1950.   Black
       Elk Speaks: Being the Life Story of a Holy
       Man of the Oglala Sioux,   as Told Through
       John G.   Neihardt (Flaming Rainbow).
       Illus. by Standing Bear.   Lincoln,   Univer-
       sity of Nebraska Press,   1961.
       A Bison Book,   119.
       OCLC # 338775

0289   _____.   The Gift of the Sacred Pipe: Based
       on   Black Elk's Account of the Seven Rites
       of the Oglala Sioux as Originally Recorded
       and Edited by Joseph Epes Brown.   Edited
       and illus. by Vera Louise Drysdale.   Nor-
       man,   University of Oklahoma Press,   1982.
       Revised ed. of The Sacred Pipe, 1st ed.
       1953.
       OCLC # 7875676

       _____.   see also   2283

0290   Blackman,   Margaret B.   During My Time:
       Florence Edenshaw Davidson,   A Haida Woman.
       Seattle,   University of Washington Press,
       Vancouver,   Douglas and McIntyre,   1982.
       OCLC # 8476185

0291   Blackburn,   Thomas C.   Ceremonial Integra-
        tion and Social Interaction in Aboriginal
        California.   In 2276, pp.   225-244.

        _____.   see also 2276

        Blackman,   Margaret B.   see 1314

0292   Blackstone.   Sarah J.,   1954-   Buffalo Bill's
        Wild West: A Study of the History,   Struc-
        ture, Personal Imagery and Effect.   Ann
        Arbor, MI.,   University Microfilms   Inter-
        national,   1983.
        Microfilm - PhD Thesis - Northwestern Uni-
        versity
        OCLC # 11768753

0293   Blaine, Martha Royce,   1923- .The Ioway
        Indians.   Norman,   University of Oklahoma
        Press,   1979.
        Civilization of the American Indian Series,
        v.   151.
        OCLC # 4835340

0294   _____.   The Pawnees: A Critical Bibliog-
        raphy.   Bloomington.   Published for the
        Newberry Library by Indiana University
        Press,   1980.
        OCLC # 6891161

0295   Blakely,   Robert L.   Changing Strategies for
        the Biological Anthropologist.   In 0270,
        pp.   1-9.

0296   _____.   Sociocultural Implications of Demo-
        graphic Data From Ethowah,   Georgia.   In
        0270,   pp.   45-66.

        _____,   see also 0270

0297   Blanchard,   Kendall,   1942- .   The Missis-
        sippi Choctaws at Play: The Serious Side
        of Leisure.   Urbana,   University of Illi-
        nois Press,   1981.
        OCLC # 6982439

0298   Blanton, Richard E.   and Stephen A.   Kowalew-
        ski.   Monte Alban and After in the Valley
        of Oaxaca.   In 0122,   pp.   94-116.

0299   _____.   Monte Alban: Settlement Patterns
        at the Ancient Zapotec Capital.   with con-
        tributions by William O.   Autry,   et.   el.
        New York,   Academic Press,   1978.
        Studies in Archaeology
        OCLC # 3223848

0300   _____.   The Origins of Monte Alban.   In
        0710,   pp.   223-232.

0301   _____.   The Rise of Cities.   In   0122.   pp.
        392-400.

0302   _____.   The Role of Symbiosis in Adapta-
        tion and Sociocultural Change in the Valley
        of Mexico.   In   3237.   pp.   181-201.

0303   Bleecker,   Ann Eliza.   1752-1783.   The
        History of Maria Kittle.   New York,
        Garland Pub.,   1978.
        Garland Library of Narratives of North
        American Indian Captivities,   v.   20.   Re-
        print of the 1797 ed.   printed by E.   Bab-
        cock,   Hartford.
        OCLC # 3293322

0304   Bleeker,   Sonia.   The Navajo: Herders,
        Weavers,   and Silversmiths.   Illus. by
        Patricia Boodel.   New York,   Morrow,   1958.
        Fiction

0305   Blodgett,   Harold William,   1900-   .   Samson
        Occom.   Hanover, NH.,   Dartmouth College
        Publications,   1935.
        Dartmouth College Manuscript Series. no.   3
        OCLC # 2273255

0306   Blue Cloud,   Peter.   Elderberry Flute Song:
        Contemporary Coyote Tales.   Illus.   by Bill
        Crosby.   Trumansburg, NY.,   Crossing Press.
        1982.
        OCLC # 8346776

        Blumberg,   Baruch S.   see   1816

0307   Blumhagen,   Richard Hugo.   Dropout and Gradu-
        ates Among Native American Adults Schooled
        on a Reservation.   Ann Arbor,   University
        Microfilms International.   1984.
        Microfilm - EdD Thesis - Northern Arizona

University
OCLC # 10792314

0308   Boas, Franz, 1858-1942.   Decorative Art of
       the Indians of the North Pacific Coast.
       New York, AMS Press, 1976.
       Reprint of the 1897 ed. published by order
       of the Trustees of the American Museum of
       Natural History, NY., which was issued as
       v. 9 of its Bulletin.
       OCLC # 1945123

0309   _____.   The Eskimo of Bafflin Land and Hud-
       son Bay.   New York, AMS Press, 1975.
       Reprint of American Museum of Natural
       History Bulletin, v. 15, pt. 1, 1901
       and v. 15, pt. 2, 1907.
       OCLC # 3935189

0310   _____.   Gestures.   In 0008, pp. 21-25.
       Reprinted from Codere, Helen, Kwakiutl
       Ethnography.   Chicago,   University of
       Chicago Press, 1966, pp. 372-376.

0311   _____.   Kwakiutl Texts - Second Series.
       New York, AMS Press, 1975.
       English and Kwakiutl.   Reprint of the 1906
       ed. published by E. J. Brill, Leiden
       and G. E. Stechert, New York, which was
       issued as v. 14, pt. 1 of the Memoirs of
       the American Museum of Natural History,
       and as v. 10, pt. 1 of the Publications
       of the Jesup North Pacific Expedition.
       OCLC # 2668042

0312   _____.   Mythology and Folktales of the
       North American Indians.   In 0110. pp.
       306-349.

0313   _____.   Sign Language.   In 0008, pp. 19-
       20.
       Second general report on the Indians of
       British Columbia, 6th report of the Com-
       mittee...appointed to investigate the ...
       Northwestern Tribes of the Dominion of Can-
       ada.   Reprinted from Report of the Sixtieth
       Meeting of the British Association for the
       Advancement of Science. 1890, London,
       John Murray, 1891, pp. 638-641.

Boehm, Randolph. see 1277, 2599

0314 Boeri, David. People of the Ice Whale:
Eskimos, White Men, and the Whale. New
York, Dutton, 1983.
OCLC # 9759943

0315 Boggs, James P. The Challenge of Reservation Resource Development: A Northern
Cheyenne Instances. In 2274, pp. 205-
236.

0316 Bohrer, Vorsila L. Ethnobotanical Tech-
niques and Approaches at Salmon Ruin, New
Mexico. By ... and Karen R. Adams.
Portales, Eastern New Mexico University
Press. 1977.
Technical series San Juan Valley Archaeo-
logical Project. no. 2. Contributions in
Anthropology (Portales. NM.) v. 8. no.
1.
OCLC # 3168404

0317 _____. Plant Remains from Rooms at Grasshopper Pueblo. In 2239. pp. 97-105.

Boldt. Menno see 2429

0318 Bolian, Charles E. The Early and Middle
Archaic of the Lakes Region, New Hampshire. In 0901, pp. 115-137.

_____. see also 0901

0319 Bolland, O. Nigel. The Maya and the Colonization of Belize in the Nineteenth Century. In 0109, pp. 69-99.

0320 Bolles, John S. Las Monjas: A Major Pre-
Mexican Architectural Complex at Chichen
Itza, with New Contributions by Sir J.
Eric S. Thompson and Ian Graham. Introd.
by John H. Jennings. Norman, University
of Oklahoma Press. 1977.
Civilization of the American Indian Series.
no. 139.
OCLC # 1418933

Bolton. Ralph see 3068

0321   Bolton,   Reginald Pelham.   The Indians of
        Washington Heights.   In 3469,   pp.   75-109.

0322   Bombin,   Alan L.   and Maria C.   de M.   C.
        Beltrao.   An Early Stratified Sequence Near
        Rio Claro,   East Central Sao Paulo State.
        Brazil.   In 0902,   pp.   303-305.

0323   Bond,   Richmond Pugh,   1899-   .   Queen Ann's
        American Kings.   New York.   Octagon Books.
        1974.
        Reprint of the 1952 ed.   pub. by Clarendon
        Press, Oxford.
        OCLC # 494189

0324   Bones from Awatovi,   Northeastern Arizona:
        The Faunal Analysis.   Stanley J.   Olsen.
        Bone and Antler Artifacts,   Richard Page
        Wheeler.   Cambridge,   MA.,   Peabody Museum
        of Archaeology and Ethnology,   Harvard Uni-
        versity,   1978.
        Report of the Awatovi Expedition,   no.   11.
        Peabody Museum of Archaeology and Ethnology
        Papers,   v.   70,   no.   1-2.
        OCLC # 4933627

0325   Bonnichsen,   Robson.   Critical Arguments for
        Pleistocene Artifacts from the Old Crow
        Basin,   Yukon: A Preliminary Statement.
        In 0902,   pp.   102-118.

0326   Bonvillain,   Nancy.   A Grammar of Akwesasne
        Mohawk.   Ottawa,   National Museum of Can-
        ada,   1973.
        Ethnology Division Paper,   no.   8.   Mercury
        Series.   Abstract in French.
        OCLC # 1097877

0327   _____.   Iroquoian Women.   In   3035.   pp.
        47-58.

0328   _____.   Mohawk Dialects: Akwesasne,   Caugh-
        nawaga,   Oka.   In 0979,   pp.   313-323.

        _____.   see also 1823,   3033

0329   Book of the Life of the Ancient Mexicans:
        Containing an Account of Their Rites and
        Superstitions.   An anonymous Hispano-Mex-

ican manuscript preserved at the Biblioteca
Nazionale Centrale, Florence, Italy. Re
produced in facsimile, with introd.,
translation and commentary by Zelia Nuttall. Part I, Introduction and Facsimile. Berkeley, University of California
Press, 1983.
The manuscript formed part of the collection of Antonio Magliabechi, and is
classified in the Biblioteca as Cod. Magl.
XIII, 11, 3. Introd. in English; Facsimile text in Spanish. Facsimile of
Berkeley, University of California. 1903.
OCLC # 10719260

0330   Boone, Elizabeth Hill. Codex Magliabechiano
       and the Lost Prototype of the Magliabech-
       iano Group. Berkeley, University of Cal-
       ifornia Press, 1983.
       OCLC # 8113016

0331   Borah, Woodrow. The Historical Demography
       of Aboriginal and Colonial America: An At-
       tempt at Perspective. In 0779, pp. 13-
       34.

0332   _____. Some Problems of Sources. In 0978,
       pp. 23-39.

0333   Borchers, Perry E. Terrestrial Photogram-
       metry of Cliff Dwellings in the Canyons of
       Arizona. In 0711, pp. 347-370.

0334   Borden, Charles E. Prehistoric Art of the
       Lower Fraser Region. In 1562, pp. 131-
       165.

0335   Bornemann, Claus. Economic Development and
       the Specific Aspects of the Society in
       Greenland. In 1875, pp. 391-429.

0336   Boserup, Mogens. The Economic Future of
       the Greenland Society as a Problem of
       Regional Policy. In 1875, pp. 461-476.

0337   Boudinot, Elias, d. 1839. Cherokee Edi-
       tor, the Writings of Elias Boudinot. Edi-
       ted with an introd. by Theda Perdue.
       Knoxville, University of Tennessee Press,
       1983.

OCLC # 8865497

0338 Bowden, Henry Warner. American Indians and
      Christian Missions: Studies in Cultural
      Conflict. Chicago, University of Chicago
      Press, 1981.
      Chicago History of American Religion
      OCLC # 7170480

      _____. see also 0937

      Bowen, Abel, 1790-1850 see 3509

0339 Bowen, Thomas G. Seri Prehistory: The Ar-
      chaeology of the Central Coast of Sonora,
      Mexico. Tucson, University of Arizona
      Press, 1976.
      Anthropological Papers of the University of
      Arizona, no. 27.
      OCLC # 2377162

0340 Boyce, Douglas W. Did a Tuscarora Confeder-
      acy Exist? In 1099, pp. 28-45.

0341 Boyd, Maurice, 1921- . Kiowa Voices. By
      ... and Linn Pauahty, Kiowa consultant;
      the Kiowa Historical and Research Society,
      consultants. Fort Worth, TX., Texas
      Christian University Press, 1981, 1983.
      CONTENTS - v. 1 Ceremonial dance, ritual,
      and song. v. 2 Myths, legends, and
      folktales.
      OCLC # 7593978

0342 Boyer, W. Kent. Bipod Photogrammetry. In
      0711, pp. 327-345

0343 Brackenridge, H. H. (Hugh Henry), 1748-
      1816. Indian Atrocities: Captivities of
      Knight ans Slover. New York, Garland
      Pub., 1978.
      The Garland library of narratives of North
      American Indian captivities, v. 12.
      OCLC # 3871841

      _____. see also 1563.5

0344 Braddell, D., C. Minty and M. J.
      Tamplin. A Prehistoric Burial Site Near
      Reston, Manitoba. In 1467, pp. 191-

208.

Bradley.   Bruce A.   <u>see</u>   1129

0345   Bradley.   James W.   <u>Blue Crystals and Other</u>
       <u>Trinkets: Glass Beads from Sixteenth and</u>
       <u>Early Seventeenth Century   New England</u>.   In
       1204.   pp.   29-39.

0346   _____.   <u>Ironwork in Onondaga,   1550-1650</u>.
       In 3035.   pp.   109-117.

0347   _____.   <u>The Onondaga Iroquois,   1500-1655,</u>
       <u>A Study in Acculturative Change and its</u>
       <u>Consequences</u>.   Syracuse.   NY..   Syracuse
       University Press.   1979.
       Microfilm - Thesis - Syracuse University
       OCLC # 6183174

0348   Brady.   Cyrus Townsend,   1861-1920.   <u>Indian</u>
       <u>Fights and Fighters</u>.   Introd.   by James T.
       King.   Lincoln.   University of Nebraska
       Press.   1971.
       A Bison Book.   Reprint of the 1904 ed.
       with a new introd.   by James T. King.
       OCLC # 226795

0349   Brain.   Jeffrey P.   <u>Late Prehistoric Settle-</u>
       <u>ment Patterning in the Yazoo Basin and Nat-</u>
       <u>chez Bluffs Regions of the Lower Mississip-</u>
       <u>pi Valley</u>.   In   2172,   pp.   331-368.

0350   _____.   <u>Tunica Treasure</u>.   With Contribu-
       tions by T.   M.   Hamilton,   et.   al.   Cam-
       bridge.   MA..   Peabody Museum of Archaeol-
       ogy and Ethnology,   Salem,   MA..   Peabody
       Museum of Salem.   1979.
       Papers of the Peabody Museum of Archaeology
       and Ethnology.   Harvard University.   v.
       71.
       OCLC # 7384066

       _____.   <u>see also</u>   3446

       Brainerd.   George W.   (George Walton) 1909-
       1956 <u>see</u>   2215

0351   Brakel.   Samuel J.   <u>American Indian Tribal</u>
       <u>Courts: The Cost of Separate Justice</u>.
       Chicago,   American Bar Foundation.   1978.

OCLC # 4358421

0352 Brand, Donald D. Erroneous Locations of Two
      Sixteenth-century Spanish Settlements in
      Western Nueva Espana. In 0014, pp. 193-
      201.

0353 Brandon, William. American Indians and
      American History. In 2304, pp. 16-28.
      Reprinted and abridged from The American
      West, v. 2, no. 2, Spring 1965, pp. 14-
      25, 91-92.

0354 Brandt, John C. and Ray A. Williamson.
      Rock Art Representations of the A. D.
      1054 Super Nova: A Progressive Report. In
      2270, pp. 171-177.

0355 Braniff, Beatriz. Oscilación de la
      Frontera Septentrional Mesoamericana. In
      0231, pp. 40-50.

0356 _____. Preliminary Interpretations Regard-
      ing the Role of the San Miguel River, Son-
      ora, Mexico. In 0014, pp. 67-82.

0357 Brasch, Beatty. The "Y" Indian Guide and
      "Y" Indian Princess Program. In 1456,
      pp. 182-210.
      Reprinted from The Indian Historian v. 10,
      no. 3, 19__, pp. 49-61. "Y" refers to
      YMCA.

0358 Brasser, Ted J. The Coastal New York In-
      dians in the Early Contact Period. In
      2282, pp. 150-157.
      Paper presented at 3rd Eastern Regional
      Conference on the Native American at the
      State University College, New Paltz, NY.,
      May 4, 1974.

0359 _____. Riding on the Frontier's Crest:
      Mahican Indian Culture and Cultural Change.
      Ottawa, National Museums of Canada, 1974.
      National Museums of Canada, Ethnology
      Division, Paper no. 13. Mercury Series.
      OCLC # 1583169

      Braun, Molly see 3297

Brawer, Catherine Coleman see 2059

0360 Bray, Warwick. Maya Metalwork and its External Connections. In 2920. pp. 365-
403.

0361 Brennan, Louis A. Artifacts of Prehistoric
America. Photos and illus. by Harold
Simmons. Harrisburg, PA., Stackpole
Brooks. 1975.
OCLC # 1529399

0362 _____. Projectile Point Varieties Present
in a Pre-ceramic, Non-shell-midden Site in
the Lower Hudson Valley. New York State
Archaeological Association, Bulletin 30.
March 1964, pp. 2-10. Millwood. NY.,
Kraus Reprint, 1976.

0363 _____. The Q Tradition and the GO Horizon
in the Vicinity of the Mouth of the Croton
River. New York State Archaeological Association, Bulletin 24, March 1962, pp.
11-16. Millwood, NY., Kraus Reprint,
1976.
Paper presented at the annual meeting.
April 8, 1961.

0364 _____. Remarks on the Timeliness of a
Projectile Point Typology. New York State
Archaeological Association. Bulletin 18.
March 1960, pp. 12-16. Millwood, NY..
Kraus Reprint, 1976.

0365 _____. A Short Evaluation of the Current
State of Knowledge of New York Prehistory
Stated in Terms of the Problems Raised by
it. New York State Archaeological Asso-
ciation. Bulletin 28, July 1963, pp. 6-
15. Millwood. NY.. Kraus Reprint. 1976.
Paper presented at the annual meeting.
April 6, 1963.

0366 _____. A 6000 Year Old Midden of Virginia
Oyster Shell at Croton Point, Lower Mid-
Hudson. New York State Archaeological Association. Bulletin 29, Nov. 1963, pp.
14-18. Millwood, NY., Kraus Reprint,
1976.
Paper presented at the annual meeting of

the Eastern States Archaeological Federation, Philadelphia, Nov. 9, 1963.

0367 _____. **The Taconic Tradition and the Coe
Axion**. New York State Archaeological Association, Bulletin 39, March 1967, pp.
1-14. Millwood, NY., Kraus Reprint,
1976.

0368 _____. **Two possible Coeval Lamokoid Sites
Near Ossining**. New York State Archaeological Association. Bulletin 8: 11-15,
Nov. 1956. Millwood, NY., Kraus Reprint,
1976.

0369 _____. **The Twombly Landing Site**. New York
State Archaeological Association. Bulle-
tin 42: 11-28, Mar. 1968. Millwood.
NY., Kraus Reprint. 1976.

0370 _____. **The Twombly Landing Site II**. New
York State Archaeological Association.
Bulletin 49: 13-29, July 1970. Millwood.
NY., Kraus Reprint. 1976.

0371 _____. **Vinette I Pottery in the Croton
River Mouth Area**. New York State Archaeological Association. Bulletin 26: 12-15,
Nov. 1962. Millwood, NY., Kraus Reprint, 1976.

0372 Brenner, Elise Melanie, 1955- . **Strate-
gies for Autonomy: An Analysis of the Eth-
nic Mobilization in Seventeenth Century
Southern New England**. Ann Arbor, MI.,
University Microfilms International, 1984.
Microfilm - PhD Thesis - University of Mas-
sachusetts at Amherst
OCLC # 11208180

0373 Brew, J. O. **Mexican Influence Upon the Indian Cultures of the Southwestern United
States in the 16th and 17th Centuries**. In
2105. pp. 341-348.

0374 Bricker, Victoria Reifler. 1940- . **The
Caste War of Yucatán: The History of a
Myth and the Myth of History**. In 0109.
pp. 251-258.

0375 _____. The Indian Christ, The Indian King:
     The Historical Substrate of Maya Myth and
     Ritual. Austin, University of Texas
     Press, 1981.
     OCLC # 7554390

0376 _____. The Meaning of Masking in San Pedro
     Chenaldo. In 2502. pp. 110-115.

0377 Bridenbaugh, Carl. Jamestown, 1544-1699.
     New York, Oxford University Press, 1980.
     OCLC # 5007249

     Bridges, Sarah T. see 2738

0378 Briggs, Jean L. Aspects of Inuit Value So-
     cialization. Ottawa, National Museum of
     Canada, 1979.
     OCLC # 5817497

0379 Brill, Charles J. Conquest of the Southern
     Plains: Uncensored Narrative of the Battle
     of the Washita and Custer's Southern Cam-
     paign. Millwood, NY., Kraus Reprint,
     1975.
     Reprint of the 1938 ed. published by Golden
     Saga Publishers, Oklahoma City, which was
     issued in Golden Saga Series.
     OCLC # 1055619

0380 Brinkman. L. M. A Woodland Site in Wash-
     ington County. New York State Archaeologi-
     cal Association. Bulletin 9: 10-14. Mar.
     1957, Millwood, NY., Kraus Reprint,
     1976.

0381 Brintnall, Douglas E. 1946- . Revolt A-
     gainst the Dead: The Modernization of a
     Mayan Community in the Highlands of Guate-
     mala. With a foreword by Charles Wagley.
     New York, Gordon and Breach, 1979.
     Library of Anthropology
     OCLC # 4638179

0382 Brinton, Daniel Garrison, 1837-1899. The
     Floridian Peninsula. New York, Paladin
     Press, 1969.
     Reprint of the 1859 ed. published under
     the title Notes on the Floridian Peninsula,
     OCLC # 13212

British American Associates see 0608

British Museum   see 3400

British Museum.   Department of Ethnography
    see 0525

0383   Broch,   Harold Beyer.   The Blue Fish River
       Incident.   In 2484,   pp. 137-196.

0384   Broder, Patrick Janis.   American Indian
       Painting and Sculpture.   New York,
       Abbeville Press, 1981.
       Works are mainly from the collection of the
       Philbrook Art Center,   Tulsa,   Oklahoma.
       OCLC # 7652406

0385   Broder,   Patricia Janis.   Hopi Painting:
       The World of the Hopis.   New York.   Dutton.
       1978.
       OCLC # 4404392

0385.5 Brodeur,   Paul.   Restitution,   The Land
        Claims of the Mashpee,   Passamaquoddy and
        Penobscot Indians of New England.
        Afterword by Thomas N. Tureen.   Boston.
        Northeastern University Press.   1985.
        OCLC # 11621769

       Brodoff,   Maureen see 2430

0386   Brody, Hugh.   Maps and Dreams.   1st American
       Edition.   New York,   Pantheon Books,   1982.
       OCLC # 8032629

0387   Brody, J. J.   Chocoan Art and the Chaco
       Phenomenon.   In 2289,   pp.   13-18.

0388   _____.   Mimbres Painted Pottery.   Santa Fe,
       New Mexico,   School of American Research,
       1977.
       Southwest Indian Art Series
       OCLC # 2984415

0389   _____.   Mimbres Painting.   In 0391.   pp.
       69-125.

0390   _____.   Mimbres Painting and the Northern
       Frontier.   In 0014.   pp.   11-21.

0391 _____. Mimbres Pottery: Ancient Art of the
American Southwest. Essays by ..., Catherine J. Scott, Stephen A. LeBlanc;
introd. by Tony Berlant. New York, Published by Hudson Hills Press in association
with The American Federation of Arts:
Distributed in the United States by Viking
Penguin, 1983.
Published in conjunction with the exhibition ... organized by the American Federation of Arts... AFA exhibition #81-1 circu-
lated Jan. 1984 - Oct. 1985.
OCLC # 9647079

0392 Broendsted, Henning. Ruling in Greenland
and Forms of Integration into Denmark: The
Established Legal Components. In 1875,
pp. 553-570.

0393 Broennimann, Peter, 1924- . Auca on the
Cononaco: Indians of the Ecuadorian Rain
Forest. Text and Photographs, Peter
Broennimann. Basel, Boston, Birkhauser
Verlag, 1981.
OCLC # 7577963

0394 Broker, Ignatia. Night Flying Women: An
Ojibway Narrative. Illustrated by Steven
Premo; with a foreword by Paulette Fairbanks Molin. St. Paul, Minnesota Historical Society Press, 1983.
In the accounts of the lives of several
generations of Ojibway people in Minnesota
is much information about their history and
culture.
OCLC # 9783311

0395 Bronitsky, Gordon. Jemez and Tiguex: A
Test of an Ethological Inference. IN 0622,
pp. 22-46.

       _____. see also 0622

0396 Bronson, Bennet. Angkor, Anuradhapura,
Prambanan Tikal: Maya Subsistence in an
Asian Perspective. IN 2522, pp. 255-
300.

0397 Brooks, Edward. The Rivers Site, Addison
County, Vermont. New York State Archaeol-

ogical Association. Bulletin 3:   5-8.
Mar. 1955. Millwood. NY., Kraus Reprint. 1976.
Abstract of paper presented at annual
meeting, 1954.

Brooks, Edwin II see 3153

0398 Brooks, Richard H. A Loma San Gabriel /
      Chalchihuites Cultural Manifestation in the
      Rio Ramos Region, Durango, Mexico. In
      0014, pp. 83-95.

      _____, see also 0399

0399 Brooks, Sheilagh T. and Richard H. Brooks.
      Palaeoepidemology as a Possible Interpreta-
      tion of Multiple Child Burials Near Zape
      Chico, Durango, Mexico. IN 0014. pp.
      96-101.

0400 Brose, David S. and George W. Percy. Fort
      Walton Settlement Patterns. IN 2172. pp.
      81-114.

0401 _____. Locational Analysis in the Prehisto-
      ry of Northeast Ohio. In 0710, pp.   3-
      18.

0402 Brotherston, Gordon. Continuity in the Book
      of Chilam Balam of Chumayel. In 0472. pp.
      241-258.

0403 _____. Image of the New World: The Ameri-
      can Continent Portrayed in Native Texts.
      Translations prepared in collaboration with
      Ed Dorn. London, Thames and Hudson,
      1979.
      OCLC # 5158620

0404 Browman, David L. External Relationships of
      the Early Horizon Ceramic Style for the
      Jauja-Huancayo Basin. In 0120, pp.   26-
      48.

0405 Brown, Anthony D. Adjustment Programs for
      the American Indian College Student. In
      2962, pp. 117-131.

0406 Brown, Dee Alexander. The Ghost Dance and

the Battle of Wounded Knee. In 2304. pp.
221-229.
Reprinted from American History Illustrated
v. 1, no. 8, Dec. 1966, pp. 5-16.

0407   .   The Fetterman Massacre: Formerly
Fort Phil Kearny, an American Saga. Lin-
coln, University of Nebraska Press. 1984.
1962.
Originally published: Fort Phil Kearny,
an American Saga. New York, Putnam. 1962.
A Bison Book
OCLC # 9971279

0408 Brown, Donald N. Dance as Experience: The
Deer Dance of Picurus Pueblo. In 2931.
pp. 71-92.

0409 Brown, Galen N. Correlations between cover
type and Lithology in the Teshekpuk Lake
Area, Alaska: A Remote Sensing Analysis.
In 0711, pp. 55-78.

0410 Brown, James A. Caddoan Settlement Patterns
in the Arkansas River Drainage. In 2172.
pp. 169-200.

0411   .   Current Directions in Midwestern Archaeology. In the Annual Review of Anthropology, 1977, 6; 161-79.

0412   .   What Happened in the Middle Archaic?
Introduction to an Ecological Approach to
Koster Site Archaeology. In 0124. pp.
166-195.

0413 Brown, Jennifer, 1948- . Fur Traders,
Racial Categories and Kinship Networks. In
0068. pp. 209-222.

0414 Brown, Jennifer S. H.. 1940- . Strangers
in Blood: Fur Trade Company Families in
Indian Country. Vancouver. University of
British Columbia Press, 1980.
OCLC # 6675286

Brown, John Arthur see 2716

0415 Brown, Joseph Epes. The Roots of Renewal.
In 2818, pp. 25-34.

57   BROWN

0416   _____.   The Spiritual Legacy of the American
         Indian.   New York.   Crossroads.   1982.
         OCLC # 8708193

         _____.   see also   0289

0417 Brown,   Kenneth L.   The Ceramics of the
      Southern Half of the Valley of Guatemala.
      In 0531,   pp.   151-171.

0418   _____.   Towards a Systematic Explanation of
         Culture Change Within the Middle Classic
         Period of the Valley of Guatemala.   In
         3096,   pp.   410-440.

0419   _____.   The Valley of Guatemala: A Highland
         Port of Trade.   In 3096,   pp.   205-395.

0420 Brown,   Mark Herbert,   1900- .The Flight of
      the Nez Perce.   Lincoln.   University of
      Nebraska Press,   1982,   c1967.
      A Bison Book.   Reprint originally published
      New York,   Capricorn Books.   1971.   c1967.
      OCLC 8282205

0421 Brown,   Meredith Lynn.   Old Age and Childhood
      in a Sub-Arctic Community: A History of
      Age Relations in an Underdeveloped Economy.
      (Ontario).   Ann Arbor.   MI..   University
      Microfilms International.   1983.
      Microfilm - PhD Thesis - SUNY at Buffalo
      OCLC # 10658117

0422 Brown,   Thomas,   b.   1740.   A Plain Narra-
      tive.   New York.   Garland Pub..   1978.
      OCLC # 3843098
      Garland Library of Narratives of North
      American Indian Captivities,   v.   8

0423 Bruce,   Louis R.   The Bureau of Indian Af-
      fairs,   1972.   In 2265,   pp.   242-250.

0424 Bruchac,   Joseph,   1942- .   The Good Message
      of Handsome Lake.   Greensboro, NC..   Uni-
      corn Press,   Inc.,   1979.
      Unicorn Keepsake Series,   v.   9.
      OCLC # 5135306

         _____.   see also   2923

0425   Brugge,   David M.   The Chaco Navajos.   In
       2289,   pp.   73-90.

0426   _____.   History of the Chaco Navajos.   Albu-
       querque,   NM.,   U. S.   Department of the
       Interior,   National Park Service.   Division
       of Chaco Research,   1980.
       Reports of the Chaco Center,   no.   4.
       OCLC # 7089102

       _____.   see also   1386

       Brumbach,   Hetty Jo   see   1613

0427   Brumble,   H.   David.   An Annotated Bibliog-
       raphy of American and Eskimo Autobiog-
       raphies.   Lincoln,   University of Nebraska
       Press.   1981.
       OCLC # 6734304

0428   _____.   Indian Sacred Materials: Kroeber,
       Waters and Kroeber.   In 2904,   pp.   283-
       300.
       Reprinted from The Canadian Review of Amer-
       ican Studies vol. 1,   no. 1,   1980;   32-
       48.

0429   Brundage,   Burr Cartwright,   1912- .   Empire
       of the Inca,   With a foreword by Arnold J.
       Toynbee.   Norman,   University of Oklahoma
       Press,   1974, c1963.
       Civilization of the American Indian Series
       OCLC # 4233361

0430   _____.   The Fifth Sun: Aztec Gods,   Aztec
       World.   Illustrated by Roy E.   Anderson.
       Austin,   University of Texas Press.   1979.
       Texas Pan American Series
       OCLC # 4494945

0431   _____.   Two Earths, Two Heavens: An Essay
       Contrasting the Aztecs and the Incas.   Al-
       buquerque.   University of New Mexico Press.
       1975.
       OCLC 1924632

0432   Brush.   Edward Hale.   Iroquois Past and Pre-
       sent,   Including Brief Sketches of Red
       Jacket,   Cornplanter,   and Mary Jemison by
       Edward Dinwoodie Strickland.   New York.

AMS Press, 1975.
Reprint of the 1901 ed. pub. by Baker,
Jones, Buffalo.
OCLC # 1601809

0433 Brush, Stephen B., 1943- . Mountain Field
      and Family: The Economy and Human Ecology
      of an Andean Valley. Philadelphia, Uni-
      versity of Pennsylvania Press, 1977.
      OCLC 3120950

0434 Bryan, Alan Lyle. An Overview of Paleo-
      American Prehistory from a Circum-Pacific
      Perspective. In 0902, pp. 306-327.

0435 _____. South America. In 0903, pp. 137-
      146.

      _____. see also 0902

0436 Bryant, Charles S., 1808-1885. A History
      of the Great Massacre by the Sioux Indians,
      in Minnesota: including the Personal Nar-
      ratives of Many Who Escaped. By ... and
      Abel B. Murch. 2nd ed., Millwood, NY.,
      Kraus Reprint, 1977.
      Reprint of the 1864 ed. pub. NY., Rickey &
      Carroll, Cincinnati.
      OCLC # 3779913

      Buchanan, Robert W. see 3335

      Buchner, A. P. see 3393

0437 Budy, Elizabeth. The Politics of American
      Indian Identity: A Comparison of the Three
      Rural Mountain Communities in Northeastern
      California. Ann Arbor, MI., University
      Microfilms International, 1983.
      Microfilm - PhD Thesis - University of
      Oregon
      OCLC # 10094594

      Buffalo Bill Historical Center see 3109

0438 Buffalo Historical Society. Red Jacket.
      Buffalo, by order of the Society, 1885.
      Transactions of the Buffalo Historical
      Society, v. 3.
      OCLC # 1185130

0439   Buikstra,   Jane E.   Biocultural Dimensions of
        Archaeological Study: A Regional Perspec-
        tive.   In 0270.   pp.   67-84.

0440   _____.   Epigenetic Distance: A Study of
        Biological Variability in the Lower Illi-
        nois River Region.   In 0905.   pp.   271-299.

0441   ._____.   Hopewell in the Lower Illinois Val-
        ley: A Regional Approach to the Study of
        Human Biological Variability and Prehistor-
        ic Behavior.   Evanston.   IL.,   Northwestern
        Archaeological Program,   1976.
        Northwestern University Archaeological
        Program: Scientific Papers.   no. 2.
        OCLC # 3551375

0442   _____ and Della C.   Cook.   Pre-Columbian
        Tuberculosis in West-Central Illinois:
        Prehistoric Disease in Biocultural Perspec-
        tive.   In 2526.   pp.   115-139.

        Bullard,   William Rotch.   1926-1972 see
        0687

0443   Bullen.   Ripley P.   Fiber-tempered Pottery in
        Southeastern United States and Northern
        Columbia: Its Origins,   Context,   and
        Significance.   Ed. by ... and James B.
        Stoltman.   Fort Lauderdale.   FL..   Florida
        Anthropological Society, 1972.
        Florida Anthropological Society,   Publica-
        tion no.   6.   Reprinted from The Florida
        Anthropologist,   v.   25,   no.   2,   part 2.
        OCLC # 1861075

0444   Bullen,   Ripley P.   Tocobagan Indians and the
        Safety Harbor Culture.   In 3071,   pp.   50-
        58.

0445   Buller,   Galen.   Comanche and Coyote,   the
        Culture Maker.   In 2904,   pp.   245-258.

0446   Burch.   Ernest S.   1938- .   Eskimo Kinsmen;
        Changing Family Relationships in North
        West Alaska.   St. Paul.   West Publishing
        Co..   1975.
        American Ethnological Society.   Monograph
        no.   59.
        OCLC # 1218550

Co., 1975.
Monographs of the American Ethnological
Society, no. 59.
OCLC # 1218550

0447 _____ and C. G. Turner. The Outward
Appearance of the Average Maleface at Gran
Quivira. In 1387, pp. 141-143.

0448 Burckhalter, David L. The Seris. Tucson,
University of Arizona Press, 1976.
OCLC # 2610329

0449 Burgess, Larry E. Lake Mohonk Conference of
Friends of the Indian: A Guide to the An-
nual Reports. New York, Clearwater Press,
1975.
Library of the American Indian. With L.
M. Hauptman, The Lake Mohonk Conference on
the Negro Question.
OCLC # 1835627

0450 Burns, Allan F. The Caste Wars in the
1970's: Present Day Accounts from Village
Quintana Roo. In 0109, pp. 259-271.

0451 Burns, Allan F. (Allan Frank), 1945- .
An Epoch of Miracles: Oral Literature of
the Yucatec Maya. Translated with commen-
taries by Allan F. Burns; foreword by
Dennis Tedlock. Austin, University of New
Mexico Press, 1983.
Texas Pan American Series
OCLC # 8495025

0452 Burns, Barney T. Simulated Anasazi Storage
Behavior Using Crop Yield Reconstruction
from Tree Rings, A. D. 652-1968. Ann
Arbor, MI., University Microfilms Inter-
national, 1983.
Microfilm - PhD Thesis - University of
Arizona
OCLC # 11527536

0453 Burridge, K. O. L. Lévi-Strauss and Myth.
In 3547 of main bibliography, pp. 91-115.

0454 Burt, Larry W., 1950- . Tribalism in
Crisis: Federal Indian Policy, 1953-1961.

Albuqueque,   University of New Mexico
Press,   1982.
OCLC # 8552506

0455   Burton,   Bruce A.   Hail! Nene Karenna, the
       Hymn: A Novel on the Founding of the Five
       Nations, 1550-1590. Afterward (sic) by
       Stephen Butterfield. 1st ed.,   Rochester,
       NY.,   Security-Dupont Press,   1981.
       OCLC # 8794744

0456   Burton,   Charline Ladd.   Native American and
       Anglo Use of Compliance Gaining Strategies.
       Ann Arbor,   MI.,   University Microfilms
       International,   1984.
       Microfilm - PhD Thesis - University of
       Oklahoma

0457   Burton,   Henrietta Kolshorn, 1893- . Re-
       establishment of the Indians in their
       Pueblo Life Through the Revival of Their
       Traditional Crafts: A STudy in Home Ex-
       tension Education. Millwood,   NY.,   Kraus
       Reprint,   1975,   c1963.
       Reprint of the ed. published by Bureau of
       Publications, Teachers College, Columbia
       University, which was issued as no. 673
       of Contributions to Education, Teacher's
       College, Columbia University.
       OCLC # 1531824

0458   Burton,   Jimalee.   Indian Heritage, Indian
       Pride. Stories that Touched My Life.   by
       (Ho-chee-nee,   Cherokee). Foreword by W.
       W. Keeler. Paintings and sketches by the
       author. Norman,   University of Oklahoma
       Press,   1974.
       OCLC # 762387

0459   Burton,   Lloyd.   American Indian Water Rights
       in the Western United States: Litigation,
       Negotiation, and the Regional Planning
       Process. Ann Arbor,   MI.,   University
       Microfilms International,   1984.
       Microfilm - Phd Thesis - University of Cal-
       ifornia - Berkeley
       OCLC # 12635094

0460   Bush,   W. Stephen.   Moving Picture Absurd-
       ities. In 2533,   pp. 60.

Reprinted from Moving Picture World v. 9,
Sept. 16, 1911, pp. 773.

0461   Butler, Barbara H. Bones are as Important
       as Sherds and Stones. New York State
       Archaeological Association Bulletin 31,
       July 1964, pp. 8-12. Millwood, NY.,
       Kraus Reprint, 1976.
       Paper presented at the Annual Meeting,
       April 6,1964.

0462   Butler, Mary. A Pottery Sequence from the
       Alta Verapaz, Guatemala. In 2105, pp.
       250-267.

0463   Byler, Mary Gloyne. Introduction to Amer-
       ican Indian Authors for Young Readers. In
       1456, pp. 34-45.
       Reprinted from "Introduction", American In-
       dian Authors for Young Readers: A Selected
       Bibliography. Association of American In-
       dian Affairs, 1973, pp. 5-11.

       Cadwalader, Sandra L. see 0034

0464   Cadillac, Antoine de la Mothe, 1656(ca.)-
       1730. The Western Country in the 17th
       Century: The Memoir of Lamothe Cadillac
       and Pierre Liette. Edited by Milo Milton
       Quaife, Chicago, R. R. Donnelley,
       1947.
       The Lakeside Classics. The memoir of
       Cadillac was translated by Edith Moodie,
       the memoir of Liette by William Giese
       OCLC # 349005

0465   Cadzow, Donald A. Archaeological Studies of
       the Susquehannock Indians of Pennsylvania.
       Harrisburg, 1936.
       Publications of Pennsylvania Historical
       Commission, v. 3, no. 2. Safe Harbor Re-
       port, no. 2.
       OCLC # 1629481

       Cahill, Holger, 1893-1960. see 2250

0466   Cain, Barbara T. Guide to Private Manu-
       scripts in the North Carolina Archives.
       3rd rev. ed. Compiled and edited by Barba-
       ra T. Cain, with Ellen Z. McGrew and

CAIN   64

         Charles E. Morris. Raleigh, North Carol-
         ina Dept. of Cultural Resources, Division
         of Archives and History, 1981.
         OCLC # 8004476

0467 Cain, William C. Materials, Techniques,
         and Styles. In 2677, pp. 82-111.

0468 Caldwell, Joseph Ralston, 1916- . Trend
         and Tradition in the Prehistory of the
         Eastern United States. Millwood, NY.,
         Kraus Reprint, 1974.
         Memoirs of the American Anthropological As-
         sociation no. 88. Supplement to American
         Anthropologist v. 60, no. 6, pt. 2,
         1958. Scientific Papers, Illinois State
         Museum, v. 10.
         OCLC 1617994

0469 Caldwell, Warren W. (Warren Wendell) and
         Dale R. Henning, 1931- . North American
         Plains. In 0577, pp. 113-145.

         California. Department of Parks and
         Recreation see 0470

0470 California. University. Riverside. Archae-
         ological Research Unit. Perris Reservoir
         Archeology: Late Prehistoric Demographic
         Change in Southeastern California. Pre-
         pared by the Archaeological Research Unit,
         Dept. of Anthropology, University of Cal-
         ifornia, Riverside, CA., Submitted to
         the State of California, Dept. of Parks
         and Recreation; edited by James F.
         O'Connell, et. al. Sacramento, State of
         California, Resources Agency, Dept. of
         Parks and Recreation, 1973, 1974.
         OCLC # 2583614

         California Academy of Science, San Fran-
         cisco see 0938, 2520

0471 Calnek, Edward E. The Internal Structure of
         Tenochtitlan. In 3237, pp. 287-302.

0472 Cambridge Symposium on Recent Research in
         Mesoamerican Archaeology, 2nd, 1976.
         Maya Archaeology and Ethnohistory. Edited
         by Norman Hammond and Gordon R. Wiley.

Austin, University of Texas Press, 1979.
Texas Pan American Series. Papers present-
ed at the second Cambridge Symposium on
Recent Research in Mesoamerican Archae-
ology, Aug. 29-31, 1976 which was held
under the auspices of the Centre of Latin
American Studies, Cambridge University.
Essays in this collection are also listed
individually and refer to this citation.
OCLC # 4004520

0473 Camera, Spade and Pen: An Inside View of
Southwestern Archaeology. Marc Gaede,
photographer; Marnie Gaede, editor; Con-
tributing authors, J. Richard Ambler,
et. al. Tucson, University of Arizona
Press, 1980.
OCLC # 6533363

0474 Campbell, Ken. Hartley Bay, British Columbia: A History. In 3162, pp. 3-26.

Campbell, Lyle see 1824

0475 Campbell, Maria, 1940- . Halfbreed. Lin-
coln, University of Nebraska Press, 1982,
c1973.
Reprint, originally pub. New York,
Saturday Review Press, 1973.
OCLC 8452270

0476 Campisi, Jack. Fur Trade and Factionalism
of the 18th Century Oneida Indians. In
3035, pp. 37-46.

0477 _____. The Hudson Valley Indians Through
Dutch Eyes. In 2282, pp. 158-180.

0478 _____. National Policy, States' Rights,
and Indian Sovereignty: The Case of the
New York Iroquois. In 0979, pp. 95-108.

_____. see also 0979

Canada. Public Archives see 1568

Canadian Association of Geographers see
1398

0497 Canadian Ethnology Society. Papers from the

4th Annual Congress, 1977. Canadian Ethnology Society, editor, Richard J. Preston. Ottawa, National Musuems of Canada,
1978.
Papers of the Canadian Ethnology Society,
no. 40. This volume of papers is a com-
panion to the separately published Applied
Anthropology in Canada. Congress held in
Halifax, Feb. 23-27, 1977. Abstracts in
English and French.
Essays in this collection are also listed
individually and refer to this citation
OCLC 5262557

0480 _____. Proceedings of the First Congress.
Canadian Ethnology Service. Editor,
Jerome H. Barkow. Ottawa, National Muse-
ums of Canada, 1974.
Papers of the Canadian Ethnology Society,
no. 17. Mercury Series. Held Feb. 1974
at Levis, Quebec.
OCLC # 1525018

0481 _____. Proceedings of the Second Congress.
Canadian Ethnology Service. Editors Jim
Freedman and Jerome H. Barkow. Ottawa,
National Museums of Canada, 1975.
Papers of the Canadian Ethnology Society,
no. 28. Mercury Series. Held Feb. 1975
at Winnipeg, Manitoba.
OCLC # 2110510

Canadian Studies Foundation see 1398

0482 Caperton, Thomas J. An Archaeological Re-
connaissance of the Gran Quivira Area. In
1387, pp. 3-11.

Capps, Walter H. see 2818

0483 Caraman, Philip, 1911- . The Lost Para-
dise: The Jesuit Republic in South
America. New York, Seabury Press, 1976,
c1975.
A Continum Book
OCLC # 2532608

0484 Cardich, Augusto. Recent Excavations at
Lauricocha (Central Andes) and Los Toldos
(Patogonia). In 0902, pp. 296-300.

0485 Carleton,   James Henry,   1814-1873.   The
      Prairie Logbooks: Dragoon Campaigns to the
      Pawnee Villages in 1844,   and to the Rocky
      Mountains in 1845.   Edited with an introd.
      by Louis Pelzer.   Lincoln,   University of
      Nebraska Press,   1983.
      Reprint.   Originally pub.   Chicago,   Caxton
      Club,   1943.   A Bison Book.
      OCLC # 9154281

0486 Carley,   Kenneth.   The Sioux Uprising of
      1862.   2nd ed.   St. Paul, Minnesota Histor-
      ical Society,   1976.
      Publications of the Minnesota Historical
      Society.
      OCLC # 2225048

0487 Carlisle, J. M.   An Introduction to the
      Meadowcroft/Cross Creek Archaeological Pro-
      ject: 1973-1982.   In 2111,   pp.   1-30.

      Carlisle,   Ronald C.   see   2111

0488 Carlson,   John B.   (John Bertil).   The Case
      for Geomagnetic Alignments of Precolumbian
      Mesoamerican Sites - The Maya.   In   2208,
      pp.   87-99.

0489 _____.   Copan Altar Q: The Maya Astronom-
      ical Congress of A. D.   763?   In 2270,
      pp.   100-109.

0490 Carlson,   Leonard,   1947- .   Indians, Bu-
      reaucrats and Land: The Dawes Act and the
      Decline of Indian Farming.   Westport,   CT.,
      Greenwood Press,   1981.
      Contributions in Economics and Economic
      History,   no.   36.
      OCLC # 6555812

0491 Carlson,   Roy L.,   1930- .   Basket Maker
      III Sites Near Durango, Colo.   Introd. to
      the Earl Morris papers,   by Joe Ben Wheat.
      New York,   Kraus Reprint,   1974.
      The Earl Morris papers,   v. 1.   University
      of Colorado Studies In Anthropology,   no.
      8.   Reprint of the 1963 ed.   pub. by Uni-
      versity of Colorado Press,   Boulder.
      Carlson's work is based on field work and
      records of Earl H.   Morris.

OCLC # 2068613

0492 _____. Change and Continuity in Northwest Coast Art. In 1562, pp. 199-205.

0493 _____. The Far West. In 0903, pp. 73-96.

0494 _____. Prehistoric Art of the Central Coast of British Columbia. In 1562, pp. 122-129.

0495 _____. Prehistory of the Northwest Coast. IN 1562, pp. 13-32.

_____. see also 1562

0496 Carmack, Robert M., 1934- . The Quiche Mayas of Utatlan: The Evolution of a High-Land Guatemala Kingdom. Norman, University of Oklahoma Press, 1981.
Civilization of the American Indian Series
OCLC # 6555814

0497 _____. Quichean Art: A Mixteca Puebla Variant. By ... and Lynn Larmer. Greeley, University of Northern Colorado, Museum of Anthropology, 1971.
University of Northern Colorado, Museum of Anthropology, Misc. Series no. 23.
Feb., 1971.
OCLC # 1164854

0498 Carmack, Robert M., 1934- . Quichean Civilization: The Ethnohistoric, Ethno-graphic, and Archaeological Sources. Berkeley, University of California Press, 1973.
OCLC # 649816

0499 Carneiro, Robert L. (Robert Leonard), 1927- . The Civilization of Manioc Among the Kuikuru of the Upper Xingu. In 0023, pp. 65-111.

0500 _____. Leslie A. White. In 3139, pp. 209-252.

0501 Carpenter, Edmund Snow, 1922- . Eskimo Realities. Designed by Arnold Skolnick.

Photos by Eberhard Otto, Fritz Spiess and
Jorgen Meldgaard. New York, Holt, Rine-
hart and Winston, 1973.
OCLC 697672

0502   Carr, Pat and Willard Gingerick. The Vagina
Dentata Motif in Nahuatl and Pueblo Mythic
Narratives: A Comparative Study. In 2904,
pp. 187-203.

0503   Carrasco, David. Quetzalcoatl and the Irony
of Empire: Myths and Prophecies in the
Aztec Tradition. Chicago, University of
Chicago Press, 1982.
OCLC # 8626972

0504   Carrasco Pizana, Pedro, 1921- . The Joint
Family in Ancient Mexico: The Case of
Molotla. In 0958, pp. 45-63.

0505   _____. Royal Marriages in Ancient Mexico.
In 0978, pp. 41-81.

_____. see also 0958

0505.5   Carriker, Robert C. Joseph M. Cataldo,
S. J.: Courier of Catholicism to the Nez
Perces. In 0578.5, pp. 109-139.

0506   Carrington, Margaret Irvin, 1831-1870.
Absaraka, Home of the Crows: Being the
Experience of an Officer's Wife on the
Plains. Lincoln, University of Nebraska
Press, 1983.
Reprint. Originally pub. Philadelphia, J.
B. Lippincott, 1868.
OCLC # 9442380

0507   Carro, Venacio D. The Spanish Theological-
Juridical Renaissance and Ideology of
Bartolome de las Casas. In 0193, pp.
237-277.

0508   Carroll, Gail Julia. Cultural Values and
Survival: A Comparative Study of the
Oglala Sioux and the Hopi Indian Tribes
with Special Focus on the Maintenance of
Cultural Heritage. Ann Arbor, MI., Uni-
versity Microfilms International, 1984.
Microfilm - PhD Thesis - United States Int-

national University

Carroll,   John M.   (John Melvin)   1928-   .
see 1176,   2375,   3252

0509 Carter, George Francis, 1912-   .   The American Paleolithic. In 0902, pp.   10-19.

0510 _____.   Earlier Than You Think: A Personal
View of Man in America. 1st ed.,   College
Station,   Texas A & M University Press,
1980.
OCLC # 6304142

0511 _____.   The Metate: An Early Grain-grinding
Implement in the New World. In 0905, pp.
21-39.

Carter,   Harvey Lewis,   1904- . see   2234.5

Carterette,   Teresa see   1408

Casagrande,   Louis B. see   3018

Casas,   Bartolome de las,   Bp.   of Chiapa,
1474-1566 see 1334

0512 Cash,   Joseph H. The Reservation Indian
Meets The White Man (1860-1914).   In 2602,
pp.   93-111.

0513 Cashman,   Marc.   Bibliography of American
Ethnology. Barry Klein,   research editor.
Bicentennial. Rye,   NY.,   Todd Publica-
tions,   1976.
OCLC # 2283283

0514 Cass,   Elizabeth.   The Effects of Civilization on the Visual Acuity of the Eskimo.
In 1875, pp.   243-257.

0515 Castaneda,   Carlos.   The Second Ring of
Power. New York,   Simon and Schuster,
1977.
OCLC # 3168389

0516 _____.   A Separate Reality; Further Conver-
sations with Don Juan. New York,   Simon
and Schuster,   1971.
OCLC # 137692

0517 _____. _Tales of Power_. New York, Simon
     and Schuster, 1974.
     OCLC # 940633

0518 _____. _Teachings of Don Juan: A Yaqui Way_
     of Knowledge. New York, Simon and Schus-
     ter, 1973, c1968.
     OCLC # 268560

0519 Casteel, Richard W. _A Sample of Northern_
     North American Hunter-Gathers and the Mal-
     thusian Thesis: An Explicitly Qualified
     Approach. In 0905, pp. 301-319.

0520 Castetter, Edward Franklin, 1896- . _The_
     Ethnobiology of the Papago Indians. By ...
     and Ruth M. Underhill. New York, AMS
     Press, 1978.
     Reprint of the 1935 ed. pub. by Univer-
     sity of New Mexico Press, which was issued
     as University of New Mexico Bulletin no.
     275, Biological Series, v. 4, no. 3,
     and as the Ethnobiological Studies in the
     American Southwest, no. 2.
     OCLC # 4006018

0521 Castile, George Pierre. _North American In-_
     dians: An Introduction to the Chichimeca.
     New York, McGraw Hill, 1979.
     OCLC # 3869496

0522 Castro, Michael, 1945- . _Interpreting the_
     Indian: Twentieth - Century Poets and the
     Native American. Albuquerque, University
     of New Mexico Press, 1983.
     OCLC # 9762164

     Catal a Roca, Francesc _see_ 0956

0523 Catlin, George, 1796-1872. _Drawings of the_
     North American Indians. With an introd. by
     Peter H. Hassrick. Garden City, NY.,
     Doubleday, 1984.
     OCLC # 10606257

0524 _____. _The George Catlin Book of American_
     Indians. Royal Hassrick, NY., Watson-
     Guptill, 1977.
     OCLC # 2984175

0525 _____. Indian Art in Pipestone: George
Catlin's Portfolio in the British Museum.
John C. Ewers, editor. London, British
Museum Publications, Washington, Smith-
sonian Institution Press, 1978.
Includes the new publication of an original
Catlin manuscript found in the collections
of the Dept. of Ethnography at the British
Museum.
OCLC # 3771086

0526 _____. Letters and Notes on the North American Indians. Edited and with an introd.
by Michael Macdonald Mooney. New York, C.
N. Potter, distributed by Crown Publishers, 1975.
Original work published in 1841 under title
Letters and Notes on the Manners, Customs,
and Conditions of the North American Indians, has been condensed and rearranged
by the editor.
OCLC # 1738208

_____. see also 1134

0527 Cattanach, George S. Long House, Mesa
Verde National Park, Colorado. With con-
tributions by Richard P. Wheeler (et
al.). Washington, National Park Service,
U. S. Dept. of the Interior, U. S.
Govt. Print. Off., 1980.
Publications in Archeology, v. 7H,
Wetherill Mesa Studies
OCLC # 4775387

0528 Caverly, Robert Boodey, 1806-1887. Heroism
of Hannah Duston, Together with the Indian
Wars of New England. Boston, Russell,
1874.
OCLC # 891440

0529 Cawelti, John G. Reflections on the New
Western Films: The Jewish Cowboy, the
Black Avenger, and the Return of the Van-
ishing America. In 2533, pp. 112-114.
Reprinted from The University of Chicago
Magazine, v. 65, Jan.-Feb. 1973, pp.
25-32.

Cayuga County Historical Society, Auburn,
NY., see 1381

0530   Cazeau,   Charles J.   Heavy Minerals in Guate-
        malan Pottery.   In 0531,   pp.   587-590.

        Center for Inter-American Relations   see
        2248

0531   The Ceramics of Kaminaljuyu, Guatemala.
        Edited by Ronald K.   Wetherington.   Univer-
        sity Park,   Pennsylvania State University
        Press,   1978.
        Pennsylvania State University Press mono-
        graphic series on Kaminaljuyu.   Essays in
        this collection are also listed individual-
        ly and refer to this citation.
        OCLC # 4195798

0532   Chafe,   Wallace L.   How to Say They Drank in
        Iroquois.   In 0979,   pp.   301-311.

        Chafe,   William L.   see   1902

0533   Chalmers,   Harvey.   Tales of the Mohawk;
        Stories of Old New York State from Colonial
        Times to the Age of Homespun.   Illus.   by
        Nell Perret.   Port Washington,   NY.,   I.
        J.   Friedman,   1968.
        Empire State Historical Publication,   no.
        57-58.
        OCLC # 410579

0534   _____.   West to the Setting Sun.   Toronto,
        The Macmillan Company of Canada,   Ltd.,
        1947,   c1944.
        OCLC # 4960510

0535   Chamberlin,   J.   Edward,   1943- .   The Har-
        rowing Eden: White Attitudes Toward Native
        Americans.   New York,   Seabury Press,
        1975.
        OCLC # 1322859

0536   Chamberlin,   Ralph Vary,   1879- .   The
        Ethno-botany of the Gosiute Indians of
        Utah.   New York,   Kraus Reprint,   1964.
        Reprint of the 1911 ed.,   The New Era
        Printing Co.   American Anthropological As-
        sociation Memoirs v. 2   pt.   5.
        OCLC # 594298

        Chapman,   Abraham see   1919

0537   Chapman, Ann MacKaye, 1922- . Drama and
       Power in a Hunting Society: The Selknam of
       Tierra del Fuego. Cambridge, New York,
       Cambridge University Press, 1982.
       OCLC # 8346167

0538   Chapman, Carl Haley, 1915- . The Archae-
       ology of Missouri... Illus. by Eleanor F.
       Chapman. Columbia, University of Missouri
       Press, 1975-1980.
       2 volumes. Vol. 1 University of Missouri
       Studies, v. 62
       OCLC # 1632796

0539   _____. Internal Settlement Designs of Two
       Mississippian Tradition Ceremonial Centers
       in Southeastern Missouri. In 0710, pp.
       121-146.

       Chapman, Frederick T. see 2621

0540   Chapple, Eliot Dismore. Biocultural Adapta-
       tion in Prehistoric America: An Anthropol-
       ogical Biologist's Perspective. In 0270,
       pp. 131-141.

0541   Charles, Douglas K. and Jane E. Buikstra.
       Archaic Mortuary Sites in the Central Mis-
       sissippi Drainage: Distribution, Struc-
       ture, and Behavioral Implications. In
       0124, pp. 117-145.

0542   Chartkoff, Joseph L. The Archaeology of
       California. ... and Kerry Kona Chart-
       koff. Stanford, CA., Stanford University
       Press, 1984.
       OCLC # 11351549

       Chartkoff, Kerry Kona see 0542

0543   Chase, Thomas Christopher. Christian Fred-
       erick Post, 1715-1785: Missionary and
       Diplomat to the Indians of America. Ann
       Arbor, MI., University Microfilms Inter-
       national, 1982.
       Microfilm - PhD Thesis - Pennsylvania State
       University
       OCLC # 10050474

0544   Cheek,   Charles D.   Excavations at the Palan-
       gana and the Acropolis, Kaminaljuyu. In
       3096, pp. 1-24.

0545   _____. Teotihuacan Influence at Kaminal-
       juyu. In 3096, pp. 441-452.

0546   Chepesiuk,   Ronald. American Indian Archival
       Material: A Guide to Holdings in the
       Southeast. Compiled by ... and Arnold
       Shankman. Westport, CT., Greenwood
       Press, 1982.
       OCLC # 8728402

0547   The Cherokee Indian Nation. Edited by Duane
       H. King. Knoxville, University of Ten-
       nessee Press, 1979.
       Essays in this collection are also listed
       individually and refer to this citation.
       OCLC # 4194151

0548   Cherokee Nation. The Act of Union Between
       the Eastern and the Western Cherokees, the
       Constitution and Amendments, and the Laws
       of the Cherokee Nation. Passed During the
       Session of 1868 and Subsequent Sessions.
       Wilmington, DE., Scholarly Resources,
       1975.
       Constitutions and laws of the American In-
       dian tribes, series 2, v. 3. Reprint of
       the 1870 ed.
       OCLC # 1441982

0549   _____.   The Constitution and Laws of the
       Cherokee Nation, Passed at Tah-le-quah,
       Cherokee Nation, 1839. Wilmington, DE.,
       Scholarly Resources, 1975.
       Constitution and laws of the American In-
       dian tribes, series 2, v. 1. Reprint of
       the 1839 ed. printed by Gales and Seaton,
       Washington
       OCLC # 3104184

0550   _____.   Constitution and Laws of the
       Cherokee Nation, Published by an Act of
       the National Council, 1892. Wilmington,
       DE., Scholarly Resources, 1973.
       Constitution and laws of the American In-
       dian tribes, v. 10. Reprint of the 1893
       ed.

OCLC # 3142919

0551   _____.   Laws and Joint Resolutions of the
         Cherokee Nation,   Enacted by the National
         Council During the Regular and Extra Ses-
         sions of 1884,   1885,   1886.   Published by
         authority of the National Council.   Wilm-
         ington,   DE.,   Scholarly Resources,   1975.
         Constitutions and laws of the American In-
         dian tribes,   series 2,   v. 7.   Reprint of
         the 1887 ed.   Cherokee and English
         OCLC # 1435980

0552   _____.   Laws and Joint Resolutions of the
         Cherokee Nation,   Enacted During the Regu-
         lar and Special Sessions of the Years 1881-
         1883.   Published by authority of an act of
         the National Council,   1975.
         Constitutions and laws of the American In-
         dian tribes,   series 2,   v. 6.   Reprint of
         the 1884 ed.   Cherokee and English
         OCLC # 1427524

0553   _____.   Laws and Joint Resolutions of the
         National Council,   Passed and Adopted at
         the Regular and Extra Sessions of 1870,
         1871 and 1872.   Wilmington,   DE.,   Scholar-
         ly Resources,   1975.
         Constitutions and laws of the American In-
         dian tribes,   series 2,   v. 4.   Reprint of
         the 1871 ed.
         OCLC # 1435984

0554   _____.   Laws and Joint Resolutions of the
         National Council,   Passes and Adopted at
         the Regular Session of 1876.   Wilmington,
         DE.,   Scholarly Resources,   1975.
         Constitutions and laws of the American In-
         dian tribes,   series 2,   v. 5.   Reprint of
         the 1877 ed.
         OCLC # 1636789

0555   _____.   Laws of the Cherokee Nation Passed
         at Tahlequah,   Cherokee Nation,   1844-1845.
         Wilmington,   DE.,   Scholarly Resources,
         1975.
         Constitutions and laws of the American In-
         dian tribes,   series 2,   v. 2.   Reprint of
         the 1845 ed.
         OCLC # 3206062

Chicago Natural History Museum <u>see</u> 2075

0556 Chickasaw Nation. <u>Constitution, Laws and</u>
      <u>Treaties of the Chickasaws</u>. Wilmington,
      DE., Scholarly Resources, 1975.
      Constitutions and laws of the American In-
      dian tribes, series 2, v. 9. Reprint of
      the 1867 ed. printed by J. F. Wheeler,
      Fort Smith, AR.,
      OCLC # 3149791

0557 _____. <u>Constitution, Laws and Treaties of</u>
      <u>the Chickasaws</u>. by authority. Wilmington,
      DE., Scholarly Resources, 1975.
      Constitutions and laws of the American In-
      dian tribes, series 2, v. 8. Reprint of
      the 1860 ed. printed by E. J. Foster,
      Tishomingo City, MS.,
      OCLC # 1517587

0558 _____. <u>Laws of the Chickasaw Nation, I.</u>
      <u>T., Relating to Intermarried and Adopted</u>
      <u>Citizens and the Rights of Freedmen</u>. Com-
      piled by the Chickasaw Commission, Overton
      Love, Chairman. Wilmington, DE., Schol-
      arly Resources, 1975.
      Constitutions and laws of the American In-
      dian tribes, series 2, v. 12. Reprint
      of the 1860 ed. printed by E. J. Foster,
      Tishomingo City, MS.
      OCLC # 1517599

Chief Eagle, D. 1925- . <u>see</u> 1082

0559 Chisholm, James S. <u>Navajo Infancy: An Eth-</u>
      <u>nological Study of Child Development</u>. Haw-
      thorn, NY., Aldine Pub. Co., 1983.
      Biological Foundations of Human Behavior
      OCLC # 9762325

0560 Choctaw Nation. <u>Acts and Resolutions of the</u>
      <u>General Council of the Choctaw Nation, At</u>
      <u>the Called Sessions Thereof Held in April</u>
      <u>and June 1858, and the Regular Session</u>
      <u>Held in October, 1858</u>. Published by the
      authority of the General Council. Wilming-
      ton, DE., Scholarly Resources, 1975.
      Constitutions and laws of the American In-
      dian Tribes, series 2, v. 16. Reprint
      of the 1859 ed. published by J. Dotson,

Fort Smith, AK.,
OCLC # 1517679

0561   _____.   Acts and Resolutions of the General
          Council of the Choctaw Nation, Passed at
          its Regular Session, 1899. Wilmington,
          DE., Scholarly Resources, 1975.
          Constitutions and laws of the American In-
          dian Tribes, series 2, v. 24. Reprint
          of the 1900 ed. published by News Press,
          South M'Alester.
          OCLC # 1517682

0562   _____.   Acts and Resolutions of the General
          Council of the Choctaw Nation, Passed at
          its Regular session, 1901. Wilmington,
          DE., Scholarly Resources, 1975.
          Constitutions and laws of the American In-
          dian Tribes, series 2, v. 25. Reprint
          of the 1902 ed. published by Herald Press,
          Caddo.
          OCLC # 1517699

0563   _____.   Acts and Resolutions of the General
          Council of the Choctaw Nation, Passed at
          its Regular Session 1904: Acts and Resolu-
          tions of the General Council of the Choctaw
          Nation, Passed at its Extraordinary and
          Regular Session 1905. Wilmington, DE.,
          Scholarly Resources, 1975.
          Constitutions and laws of the American In-
          dian Tribes, Series 2, v. 26. Reprint
          of the 1904 and 1905 ed.
          OCLC # 4291830

0564   _____.   The Choctaw Laws, Passed at the
          Special Sessions in January, 1894 and
          April 1894, and the Regular Sessions,
          October 1894. Wilmington, DE., Scholarly
          Resources, 1975.
          Constitutions and laws of the American In-
          dian Tribes, series 2, v. 23. Reprint
          of the 1894 ed. National Advocate Print.,
          Antlers, I. T.
          OCLC # 1517675

0565   _____.   The Constitution and Laws of the
          Choctaw Nation. WIlmington, DE., Schol-
          arly Resources, 1975.
          Constitutions and laws of the American In-

dian Tribes, series 2, v. 14. Reprint
of the 1847 ed. printed by E. Archer,
Mission Press, Park Hill, Cherokee
Nation.
OCLC # 2858769

0566   _____. The Constitutions and Laws of the
Choctaw Nation. Wilmington, DE., Scholarly Resources, 1975.
Constitutions and laws of the American Indian Tribes, series 2, v. 15. Reprint
of the 1852 ed. printed at Doaksville.
OCLC # 1517648

0567   _____. The Constitution and Laws of the
Choctaw Nation: = Chahta Yakni, Nan
Ulhpisa Nishkoboka, Micha Anumpa Ulhpisa
Aiena. Wilmington, DE., Scholarly Re-
sources, 1975.
Constitutions and laws of the American In-
dian Tribes, series 2, v. 13. Reprint
of the 1840 ed., J. Candy, Printer,
Park Hill, Cherokee Nation. English and
Choctaw.
OCLC # 1517695

0568   _____. Constitution, Treaties and Laws of
the Choctaw Nation. Made and Enacted by
the Choctaw Legislature. Wilmington, DE.,
Scholarly Resources, 1975.
Constitutions and law of the American Indian Tribes, series 2, v. 19. Reprint
of the 1887 ed. published by Democrat
Steam Print., Sedalia, MO.
OCLC # 1509116

0569   _____. The Freedman and Registration Bills,
Passed at the Special Session of the
Choctaw Council, Indian Territory, May
1883: Laws of the Choctaw Nation Passed at
the Choctaw Council...1883: = Chanta Okla I
Nan Vhlpesa. Wilmington, DE., Scholarly
Resources, 1975.
Constitutions and laws of the American In-
dian Tribes, series 2, v. 18. Reprint
of the 1883 ed. printed at Murray's Steam
Print. House, Denison, TX. English and
Choctaw.
OCLC # 3104183

0570   _____.   General and Special Laws of the
Choctaw Nation Passed at the Regular Session of the General Council...October 3,
and Adjourned Nov. 12th, 1881. Wilmington, DE., Scholarly Resources, 1975.
Constitutions and law of the American Indian Tribes, series 2, v. 17. Reprint
of the 1881 ed. published by Murray and
Dearing, Denison, TX.
OCLC # 1517627

0571   _____.   Laws of the Choctaw Nation; Made
and Enacted by the General Council, from
1886 to 1890 Inclusive. Atoka, I. T.,
Indian Citizen Print. 1890. Wilmington,
De., Scholarly Resources, 1975.
Constitutions and laws of the American In-
dian Tribes, series 2, v. 21. Text in
English and Choctaw. Issued with Laws of
the Choctaw Nation...convened...Oct. 6,
1890, adjourned Nov. 14, 1890. Atoka,
I. T., 1890.
OCLC # 1950732

0572   _____.   Laws of the Choctaw Nation, Passed
at the Regular Session of the General Council...Oct. 7, 1889, Adjourned Nov. 15,
1889. Wilmington, DE., Scholarly Resources, 1975.
Constitutions and laws of the American Indian Tribes, series 2, v. 20. Reprint
of the 1890 ed. Indian Citizen Pub. Co.,
Atoka, I. T.
OCLC # 1517658

0573   _____.   Laws of the Choctaw Nation, Passed
at the Regular Session of the General Council... Oct. 3rd, 1892, and Adjourned
Nov. 4th, 1892; Laws of the Choctaw Nation Passed at the Regular Session of the
General Council ... Oct. 2, 1893 and Adjourned Oct., 27, 1893 and the Special
Sessions ...Feb. 1892...June 1893. Wilmington, DE., Scholarly Resources, 1975.
Constitutions and laws of the American Indian Tribes, series 2, v. 22. Reprint
of the 1893 and 1894 ed. published by the
Indian Citizen Pub. Co., Atoka, I. T.
OCLC # 1517740

0574   Chown,   Bruce and Marion Lewis.   Blood Groups
       in Anthropology: With Special Reference to
       Canadian Indians and Eskimos.   In   National
       Museum of Canada.   Bulletin no.   167.   Con-
       tributions to Anthropology,   1958.   Ottawa,
       Dept. of Northern Affairs and Natural Re-
       sources,   1960.   pp.   66-79.

0575   Christensen,   Erleen J.   Loren Eiseley: Mod-
       ern Shaman.   Ann Arbor,   MI.,   University
       Microfilms International,,   1984.
       Microfilm - PhD Thesis - University of
       Kansas
       OCLC # 11542273

0576   Christman, Edward B.   Steubenville Type
       Points in the Mid Husdon Valley.   New York
       State Archaeological Association Bulletin
       no. 20,   pp.   12-14,   Nov.   1960.   Mill-
       wood, NY.,   Kraus Reprint,   1976.
       Paper presented at the annual meeting,
       April 2,   1960.

0577   Chronologies in New Worls Archaeology.   Edit-
       ed by R.   E.   Taylor,   Clement W.   Meighan.
       New York,   Academic Press,   1978.
       Studies in Archaeology.   Essays in this
       collectiion are also listed individually
       and refer to this citation.
       OCLC # 3706928

0578   Chuinard,   Eldon.   Only One Man Dies: The
       Medical Aspects of the Lewis and Clark Ex-
       pedition.   Glendale,   CA.,   A.   H.   Clark
       Co.,   1979.
       Western Frontiersman Series,   no.   19
       OCLC # 5109672

0578.5   Churchmen and the Western Indians,   1820-
       1920.   Edited, and with an introd.   by
       Clyde A.   Milner II and Floyd A.   O'Neil.
       Norman,   University of Oklahoma Press,
       1985.
       Papers from a conference held at Utah State
       University,   Aug.   6-7,   1982,   which was
       sponsored by the Natiional Endowment for
       the Humanities.
       OCLC # 12189143

0579   Churchill,   Ward;   Mary Ann Hill and Norbet
       S. Hill,   Jr.,   Examination of Sterotyping:
       An Analytical Survey of the Twentieth Cent-
       ury Indian Entertainers.   In   2533,   pp.
       35-48.

0580   _____.   White Studies or Isolation: An Al-
       ternative Model for Native American Studies
       Programs.   In   2962,   pp.   19-33.

0581   Claiborne,   Robert.   The First Americans.
       New York,   Time Life Books,   1973.
       OCLC # 662250

0582   Clark,   Donald W.   and A.   McFadyen Clark.
       Fluted Points at the Batza Tena Obsidian
       Source, Northwestern Interior Alaska.   In
       0905,   pp.   141-159.

       Clarf,   Edward W.   1943- .   see   2562

0583   Clark,   Ella Elizabeth,   1896- .   Sacagawea
       of the Lewis and Clark Expedition.   By ...
       and Margot Edmonds.   Berkeley,   CA.,   Uni-
       versity of California Press,   1979.
       OCLC # 6301851

0584   Clark,   Walter,   1846-1924.   Indian Massacre
       and Tuscarora War, 1711-13.   North Carol-
       ina Booklet v.   2,   no.   3,   July 10,
       1902.   Raleigh,   Capital Printing Co.,
       1902.
       OCLC # 7519142

       Clark,   William,   1770-1838 see   0142

0585   Clarke,   John M.   1857- .   The Micmac Ter-
       centenary.   New York State Museum Bulletin
       no.   158,   1912,   pp.   189-197.

0586   Clements,   William M.,   1945- .   Native
       American Folklore, 1879-1979; An Annota-
       ted Bibliography.   Compiled by ... and
       Frances M.   Malpezzi.   Athens, OH.,   Swal-
       low Press,   1984.
       OCLC # 9556664

0587   Clemmer,   Richard O.   Black Mesa and the
       Hopi.   In   2273,   pp.   17-34.

0588   _____.   Effects of the Energy Economy on
        Pueblo Peoples. In 2274, pp. 79-115.

0589   Clifton,   James A.   A Place of Refuge for All
        Time: Migration of the American Potawatomi
        into Upper Canada 1830 to 1850.   Ottawa,
        National Museum of Canada,   1975.
        National Museum of Canada, Canadian Ethno-
        logy Service,   Paper no. 26.   Mercury
        Series.
        OCLC # 2967710

0590   _____.   Potowatomi Leadership Roles: On
        Okama and Other Influential Personages.   In
        0068,   pp. 42-99.

0591   _____.   The Prairie People: A Continuity
        and Change in Potawatomi Indian Culture,
        1665-1965.   Lawrence,   Regents Press of
        Kansas,   1977.
        OCLC # 2644469

0592   Cline,   S. L.,   1948- .   Land Tenure and
        Land Inheritance in Late Sixteenth Century
        Culhuacan. In 0978,   pp.   277-309.

0593   Closs,   Michael P.   The Date-Reaching Mecha-
        nism in the Venus Table of the Dresden
        Codex.   In   2270,   pp.   89-99.

0594   The Cloud People: Divergent Evolution of the
        Zapotec and Mixtec Civilizations.   Edited
        by Kent V.   Flannery,   Joyce Marcus.   New
        York,   Academic Press,   1983.
        A School of American Research Book
        OCLC # 8805988

0595   Clum,   Woodworth.   Apache Agent: The Story
        of John P.   Clum.   Lincoln,   University of
        Nebraska Press,   1976,   c1936.
        Reprint of the ed.   published by Houghton
        Mifflin,   New York.
        OCLC # 3274554

0596   The Coastal Archaeology Reader: selections
        from the New York State Archaeological As-
        sociation Bulletin,   1954-1977.   Stony
        Brook,   NY.,   Suffolk County Archaeological
        Association,   1978.
        Readings in Long Island Archaeology and

COBO   84

Ethnology v. 2.
OCLC # 6055237

0597 Cobo, Bernabe, 1582-1657. **History of the
      Inca Empire: An Account of the Indians'
      Customs and their Origin, Together with a
      Treatise on Inca Legends, History, and
      Social Institutions**. Translated and edited
      by Roland Hamilton from the holograph manu-
      script in the Biblioteca Capitular y Colom-
      bina de Sevilla, foreword by John Howland
      Rowe. Austin, University of Texas Press,
      1979.
      Texas Pan American Series. Sections trans-
      lated from Historia del Neuvo Mundo
      OCLC # 4933087

0598 Codex Nuttall. **The Codex Nuttall: A Picture
      Manuscript from Ancient Mexico: The Pea-
      body Museum Facsimile**. Edited by Zelia
      Nuttall; with new introductory text by
      Arthur G. Miller. New York, Dover Pub-
      lications, 1975.
      OCLC # 3242453

0599 Codex Pérez. English. **The Codex Pérez and
      the Book of Chilam Balam of Mani**. Trans-
      lated and edited by Eugene R. Craine and
      Reginald C. Reindorp. Norman, University
      Of Oklahoma Press, 1979.
      Civilization of the American Indian Series
      The Codes of Perez contains the Book of
      Chilam Balam of Mani within it; also,
      parts of the Chilam Balam of Kaua, of
      Ixil, and some think Oxkutzcab.
      OCLC # 4641849

0600 Coe, Joffre Lanning. **Formative Cultures of
      Carolina Piedmont**. Philadelphia, American
      Philosophical Society, 1964.
      Transactiona of the American Philosophical
      Society, new series, v. 54, pt. 5.
      OCLC # 501121

0601 Coe, Michael D. **In the Land of the Olmec**.
      By ... and Richard A. Diehl. Austin,
      University of Texas Press, 1980.
      2 volume set includes folder containing 4
      folded color maps. v. 1 **The Archaeology
      of San Lorenzo Tenochtitlan** v. 2 **The**

People of the River.
OCLC # 5170710

0602   _____. Lords of the Underworld, Masterpieces of Classic Maya Ceramics. Photographs by Justin Kerr. Princeton, Art
Museum, Princeton University; distributed
by Princeton University, 1978.
Exhibition Dates, March 4 - June 18,
1978.
OCLC # 3928095

0603   _____. The Maya Scribe and His World. New
York, Grolier Club, 1973.
Includes items from the Grolier Club Exhib-
it held April 20 - June 5, 1971 in New
York.
OCLC # 804680

0604   _____. Old Gods and Young Heros: The
Pearlman Collection of Maya Ceramics.
Photographs by Justin Kerr. Jerusalem,
Israel Museum, Maremont Pavilion of Ethnic
Arts, 1982.
Catalog of an exhibition
OCLC # 8824570

0605   _____. Olmec and Maya: A Study in Relationships. In 2378, pp. 183-195.

0606   _____. San Lorenzo Tenochtitlan. In 0122,
pp. 117-146.

0607   _____. Supernatural Patrons of Maya Scribes
and Artists. In 2920, pp. 327-347.

0608   Coe, Ralph T. Sacred Circles: Two Thousand
Years of North American Indian Art: Exhib-
ition organized by the Arts Council of
Great Britain with the support of the Brit-
ish-American Associates, (held at the) Hay-
wood Gallery, London, 7 Oct. 1976 - 16
Jan. 1977. Catalogue. London, Arts
Council of Great britain, 1976.
OCLC # 3274717

Coe, WIlliam R. see 1658

0609   Coel, Margaret, 1937- . Chief Left Hand,
Southern Arapaho. Norman, University of

Oklahoma Press,   1981.
Civilization of the American Indian Series,
v.   159.
OCLC # 7196759

0610   Coffer,   William E.   Phoenix: The Decline
       and Rebirth of the Indian People.   New
       York,   Van Nostrand Reinhold Co. ,   1979.
       OCLC # 4776592

0611   _____.   Spirits of the Sacred Mountains:
       Creation Stories of the American Indian.
       New York,   Van Nostrand Reinhold Co. ,
       1978.
       OCLC # 3730186

       Coffin,   James L.   see   0862

0612   Coggins,   Clemency.   A New Order and the Role
       of the Calendar: Some Characteristics of
       the Middle Classic Period at Tikal.   In
       0472,   pp.   38-50.

0613   Cogwill,   George L.   Teotihuacan,   Internal
       Militaristic Competition,   and the Fall of
       the Classis Maya.   In 0472,   pp.   51-62.

0614   Cohen,   Felix S. ,   1907-1953.   Americanizing
       the White Man.   In 2304,   pp.   29-41.
       Reprinted from The Legal Conscience: Se-
       lected Papers of Felix S.   Cohen,   ed.
       Lucy Kramer Cohen.   New Haven,   Yale Uni-
       versity Press,   1960,   pp.   315-32.

0615   _____.   Handbook of the Federal Indian Law.
       Felix S.   Cohen's Handbook of Federal In-
       dian Law,   1982 ed.,   board of authors and
       editors,   Rennard Strickland,   editor-in-
       chief ... et al.   Contributing writers
       Denis Binder ... et al.   Charlottesville,
       VA.,   Michie,   Bobbs-Merrill,   1982.
       OriginallyPublished,   1942.
       OCLC # 8341687

0616   Cohen,   Ronald and James W.   Van Stone.   De-
       pendency and Self-sufficiency in Chipewyan
       Stories.   In   National Museum of Canada
       Bulletin no.   194,   Anthropological Series
       no.   62.   Contributions to Anthropology,
       1961-62,   Part II,   Ottawa,   Dept.   of the

Secretary of State, 1964, pp. 29-55.

0616.5 Coker, William S. Indian Traders of the
        Southeastern Spanish Borderlands: Panton,
        Leslie & Company and John Forbes & Company,
        1783-1847. Foreword by J. Leitch Wright.
        Gainesville, FL. , University Presses of
        Florida, Pensacola, University of West
        Florida, 1986.
        OCLC # 11469679

0617   Colbert, Thomas Burnell, 1947- . Prophet
        of Progress: The Life and Times of Elias
        Cornelius Boudinot. Ann Arbor, MI. , Uni-
        versity Microfilms International, 1982.
        Microfilm - PhD Thesis - Oklahoma State
        University
        OCLC # 9769307

0618   Colby, Benjamin N. , 1931- . The Day-
        keeper, the Life and Discourse of an Ixil
        Diviner. ... and Lore M. Colby. Cam-
        bridge, MA. , Harvard University Press,
        1981.
        OCLC # 7197630

        Colby, Lore M. 1930- . see 0618

0619   Colden, Cadwallader, 1688-1776. History of
        the Five Indian Nations of Canada, Which
        are the Barrier Between the English and the
        French in that Part of the World. 2nd ed. ,
        London, Printed for J. Whiston (etc)
        c1750.
        OCLC 3326008

0620   Cole, John R. Lithic Evidence for Trans-
        Andean Contact in Preceramic South America.
        In 0121, pp. 1-10.

        _____. see also 0121, 3519

0621   Coleman, Michael C. Presbyterian Missionary
        Attitudes Towards American Indians, 1837-
        1893. Jackson, University Press of Mis-
        sissippi, 1985.
        OCLC # 11972268

0622   Collected Papers in Honor of Florence Hawley
        Ellis. Theodore R. Frisbie, editor;

Contributors,   Gordon Bronitsky... et al.
Norman,   OK.,   Published for the Archaeo-
logical Society of New Mexico by Hooper
Pub. Co., 1975.
Papers of the Archaeological Society of New
Mexico,   v. 2.   Essays in this collection
are also listed individually and refer to
this citation.
OCLC # 2382321

0623 Collier, George Allen, 1942- . Fields of
      the Tzotzil: The Ecological Bases of Tra-
      dition in Highland Chiapas. Austin, Uni-
      versity of Texas Press,   1975.
      Texas Pan American Series
      OCLC # 1341418

      _____. see also 1557

0624 Collier, John. A Lift for the Forgotten Red
      Man, too. In 3335, pp. 40-48.
      Reprinted from New York Times Magazine May
      6, 1934.

0625 Collins, Anne Cox. The Maestros Cantores in
      Yucatan. In 0109, pp. 233-247.

0626 Collins, Henry Bascom, 1899- . Recent
      Developments in the Dorset Culture Ares.
      In 0076, pp. 32-39.

      _____. see also 1063

      Colorado Historical Society see 3303

      Colorado State University,   Fort Collins see
      2602

0627 Colson, Elizabeth, 1917- . The Makah In-
      dians: A Study of an Indian Tribe in Mod-
      ern American Society. Westport, CT.,
      Greenwood Press, 1974.
      Reprint of the 1953 ed. pub. by the Uni-
      versity of Minnesota Press, Minneapolis
      OCLC # 737044

0628 Colton, Mary Russell Ferrell, 1889- . The
      Little Known Small House Ruins in Coconino
      Forest. By ... and Harold Sellers, New
      York, Kraus Reprint, 1964.

Memoirs of the American Anthropological Association, v. 5, no. 4, 1918.
OCLC # 3405008

0629 Comas, Juan, 1900- . Historical Reality
and the Detractors of Father Las Casas. In
0193, pp. 487-537.

0630 Combs, Richard. Ulzana's Rain. In 2533,
pp. 169-170.
Reprinted from Sight and Sound v. 42,
Spring 1973, pp. 115-116.

Comer, George see 0309

0631 The Commissioners of Indian Affairs 1924-
1977. Edited by Robert M. Kvasnicka and
Herman J. Vivlas, foreword by Phillio
Nash. Lincoln, University of Nebraska
Press, 1979.
OCLC # 4857939

0632 Comstock, W. Richard. On Seeing With the
Eye of the Native European. In 2818, pp.
58-78.

0633 Comunale, Anthony R. Art on Stone by the
American Indian of New Jersey. New York,
Vantage Press, 1963.
OCLC # 4991382

0634 Conard, Howard Louis. Uncle Dick Wootton:
The Pioneer Frontiersman of the Rocky
Mountain Region. Edited by Milo Milton
Quaife, Chicago, R. R. Donnelley,
1957.
Reprint of the 1890 ed., with a new
introd.
OCLC # 3704553

0635 Conaway, Mary Ellen. Still Guahibo, Still
Moving. A Study in Circular Migration and
Marginality in Venezuela. Greeley, CO.,
Museum of Anthropology, University of
Northern Colorado, 1984.
Occasional Papers in Anthropology, Ethno-
logy Series, v. 51.
OCLC # 11866048

0636 Condon, Richard G. (Richard Guy). Inuit

Behavior and Seasonal Change in the Canadian Arctic. Ann Arbor, MI., University
Microfilms International Research Press,
1983.

Studies in Cultural Anthropology, v. 2
OCLC # 9828479

0637 Conference on Iroquoian Research (1972:
Rensselaerville, NY.,) Papers in Linguis
tics from the 1972 Conference on Iroquoian
Research. Editor Michael K. Foster.
Ottawa, National Museum of Canada, 1974.
Mercury Series, National Museum of Canada,
Ethnology Division Paper no. 10. Summar-
ies in French.   Held Nov. 4, 1972.
OCLC # 1429124

0638 Conference on the History of Western America
(1st: 1961: Santa Fe, NM.,) Probing the
American West; Papers edited by K. Ross
Toole (and others). With an introd. by
Ray A. Billington. Santa Fe, Museum of
New Mexico Press, 1962.
OCLC # 4655278

0639 Conn, Richard. Circles of the World: Traditional Arts of the Plains Indians. Photographer Lloyd Rule. Denver, CO., Denver
Art Museum, 1982.
Catalog of the exhibition held at the Denver Art Museum and seven other museums,
1982-1984.
OCLC # 8618332

_____. see also 0788

0640 Conn, Stephen. The Extralegal Forum and
Legal Power: The Dynamics of the Relationship - Other Pipelines. In 0111, pp.
217-224.

0641 Connell, Evan S., 1924- . Son of the
Morning Star: Custer and the Little Big
Horn. San Francisco, CA., North Point
Press, 1984.
OCLC # 11266256

Conser, Walter H. see 2026

0642   Converse, Harriet Maxwell, 1836-1903. The
       Iroquois Silver Brooches. Albany, State
       University of New York, 1902.
       Reprinted from the 54th report of the New
       York State Museum, 1900.

0643   _____. Myths and Legends of the New York
       Iroquois. Albany, University of the State
       of New York, State Education Dept., 1974.
       In New York State Museum Bulletin no. 125,
       Reprint of the 1908 ed.
       OCLC # 1196357

0644   Cook, Angel Garcia. The Historical Import-
       ance of Tlaxcala in the Cultural Develop-
       ment of the Central Highlands. In 0122,
       pp. 244-276.

0645   Cooks, Charles. Iroquois Personal Names (ca.
       1900-1950). one reel microfilm provided by
       American Philosophical Society, Philadel-
       phia. Reel 1374 of Freeman Guide #1823 and
       Freeman Guide #43.
       Note from Freeman Guide - Alphabetical list
       of ca 6200 Iroquoian names...each entry in-
       cluding phonetic spelling, gender, tribe,
       location, date, clan...

       Cook, Della Collins see 0442

0646   Cook, Sherburne Friend, 1896-1974. The In-
       dian Population of New England in the Sev-
       enteenth Century. Berkeley, University of
       California Press, 1976.
       University of California Publications in
       Anthropology, v. 12.
       OCLC # 2633437

0647   _____. The Population of the California In-
       dians 1769-1970. With a foreword by Wood-
       row Borah and Robert F. Heizer. Berkeley,
       University of California Press, 1976.
       OCLC # 2466560

0648   Cook, Thomas Genn. Koster: An Artifact
       Analysis of Two Archaic Phases in Westcen-
       tral Illinois. Evanston, IL., Northwest-
       ern University Archeological Program,
       1976.
       Koster Research Reports no. 3. Prehistor-

ic Records - Northwestern University Archeological Program no. 1.
OCLC # 4168860

0469 Cooke,   Alan.   The Eskimos and the Hudson's
      Bay Company.   In 1875,   pp.   209-223.

      Cooke,   Richard see 0272

      Cooley, M. E. (Maurice E.) see 0921

0650 Coombs,   Elizabeth Lockwood.   Memorial to
      Cyrus Standing Bull.   The Lenape Archives,
      Sections 1,   2,   3.
      Photocopy of typescript copy.

0651 Cooper,   John Montgomery,   1881-1949.
      Snares,   Deadfalls and Other Traps of the
      Northern Algonquians and Northern Athapas-
      kans.   New York,   AMS Press,   1978.
      Reprint of 1938 ed.   pub.   by Catholic Uni-
      versity of America,   Washington,   as its
      no.   5 in its Anthropological Series.
      OCLC # 4137427

0651.5 Cooper,   Margaret Baba.   Task Force Eleven
      of the American Indian Policy Review Com-
      mission: A Developmental Overview.   In
      02961.5,   pp.   53-55.

0652 Copway,   George,   Chippewa Chief,   1818-1863?
      Indian Life and Indian History by an Indian
      Author: Embracing the Traditions of the
      North American Indians Regarding Them-
      selves,   Particularly of That Most Import-
      ant of all Tribes,   the Ojibways.   By Kah-
      ge-ga-gah-bowh,   known also by the English
      name of George Copway.   New York,   AMS
      Press,   1978.
      Reprint of the 1860 ed.   pub.   by A.
      Colby,   Boston.   Original title: The
      Traditional History and Characteristic
      Sketches of the Ojibway Nation.
      OCLC # 4137426

0653 Copy of a Journal Kept During the Siege of
      Fort William Henry,   Aug.   2 - 10,   1757.
      Microfilm supplied by American Philosophi-
      cal Society,   Philadelphia.   See Freeman
      Guide #44 for description

0654   Corbett, William Paul, 1948- . Oklahoma's
       Highway's: Indian Trails to Urban Express-
       ways. Ann Arbor, MI., University Micro-
       films International, 1982.
       Microfilm - PhD Thesis - Oklahoma State
       University
       OCLC # 9517806

0655   Cordry, Donald Bush. Mexican Masks. Aus-
       tin, University of Texas Press, 1980.
       OCLC # 5493859

0656   Cordy-Collins, Alana. The Dual Divinity
       Concept in Chavin Art. In 0121, pp. 90-
       120.

       _____. see also 2520

       Corey, Peter L. see 1486

0657   Corkran, David Husdon, 1902- . Iroquois
       Frontier. 1979. University Microfilms
       International, 1984.
       OCLC # 6992598

0658   Corley, Nora Teresa. Resources for Native
       Peoples Studies. Ottawa, Resources Survey
       Division, Collections Development Branch,
       National Library of Canada, 1984.
       Research Collections in Canadian Libraries,
       Special Studies, 9. Text in English and
       French on inverted pages.
       OCLC # 11390338

       Corliss, William R. see 0096

0659   Cornell, George Leslie. Native American
       Contributions to the Formation of the Mod-
       ern Conservation Ethic. Ann Arbor, MI.,
       University Microfilms International, 1982.
       Microfilm - PhD Thesis - Michigan State
       University
       OCLC # 10979168

0660   Cornplanter, Jesse J. Deswadeyon: Seneca
       Songs. 1952. 1 reel cassette tape, 89
       songs in cycle sung by Jesse Cornplanter.
       Tape provided by American Philosophical
       Society, Philadelphia.

0661 _____. Iroquois Indian Games and Dances.
Drawn by ..., Seneca Indian boy, n. p.,
1903? Drawings copyrighted by Frederick
Starr in 1903.
OCLC # 4454120

0662 Cornwell, W. S. An Artificially Deformed
Skull from the Dann Site. New York State
Archeological Association Bulletin 17,
Dec. 1959, pp. 10-12. Millwood, NY.,
Kraus Reprint, 1976.
Paper presented at annual meeting, April
18, 1959.

0663 Corry, John Pitts, 1900- . Indian Affairs
in Georgia, 1732-1756. New York, AMS
Press, 1980.
Originally presented as the author's
thesis, University of Pennsylvania, 1936.
Reprint of the 1936 ed. pub. by G. S.
Ferguson, Philadelphia.
OCLC # 6737147

0664 Corson, Christopher. Maya Anthropomorphic
Figurines from Jaina Island, Campeche.
Ramona, CA., Ballena Press, 1976.
Ballena Press Studies in Mesoamerican Art,
Archaeology and Ethnohistory, no. 1.
OCLC # 2231854

0665 Cortes, Hernan, 1485-1547. The Conquest of
Mexico. Greeley, CO., Museum of Anthro-
pology, University of Northern Colorado,
1984, c1760.
Occasional publications in anthropology.
Archaeology series v. 24. Translation of
Conquista de Mexico, reprint, originally
pub.: The World Displayed, v. 2. Lon-
don, printed for J. Newberry, 1760.
OCLC # 10854832

0666 _____. Fernando Cortes: His Five Letters
of Relation to the Emperor Charles V (1519-
1526). Trans. and edited, with a biographical introd. and notes compiled from
original sources, by Francis Augustus
MacNutt. Glorieta, NM., Rio Grande
Press, 1977, c1908.
A Rio Grande Classic. Reprint of the ed.
pub. by A. H. Clark co., Cleveland.

OCLC # 2798144

0667   Costo, Rupert. <u>Alcatraz</u>. In 2304, pp.
       281-291.
       Abridged and Reprinted from <u>The Indian His-</u>
       <u>torian</u> 3(1) winter, 1970, pp. 4-12,
       64.

0668   _____. <u>Indian Treaties: Two centuries of</u>
       <u>Dishonor</u>. By ... and Jeannette Henry. San
       Francisco, CA., Indian Historian Press,
       1977.
       American Indian Reader, v. 5.
       OCLC # 3904450

0669   Coulter, Robert T. and Steven M. Tullberg.
       <u>Indian Land Rights</u>. In 0034, pp. 185-
       213.

0670   Council on Inter-racial Books for Children.
       <u>Textbooks and Native Americans</u>. In 1456,
       pp. 81-110.
       Reprinted from "Native Americans" in <u>Stero-</u>
       <u>types, Distortions and Omissions in U. S.</u>
       <u>History Textbooks</u>. New York, Council on
       Inter-racial Books for Children, 1977.

0671   Couture, A. and J. O. Edwards. <u>Origin of</u>
       <u>Copper Used by Canadian West Coast Indians</u>
       <u>in The Manufacture of Ornamental Plaques</u>.
       In National Museum of Canada Bulletin no.
       194, Anthropological series, no. 62.
       Contributions to Anthropology, 1961-62,
       part II. Ottawa, Dept. of the Secretary
       of State, 1964. pp. 199-220.

0672   Covich, Alan P. <u>A Reassessment of Ecologi-</u>
       <u>cal Stability in the Maya Area: Evidence</u>
       <u>From Lake Studies of Early Agricultural Im-</u>
       <u>pacts on Biotic Communities</u>. In 2522,
       pp. 145-155.

0673   Covington, James W. <u>Relations Between the</u>
       <u>Eastern Timucuan Indians and the French and</u>
       <u>Spanish, 1564-1567</u>. In 1099, pp. 11-27.

       Cowan, William <u>see</u> 0068

0674   Coyne, Sheila. <u>Mandibular First Premolars</u>
       <u>of Gran Quivira</u>. In 1387, pp. 139-140.

0675 _____. Variations and Pathologies in the
Vertebral Columns of Gran Quivira Indians.
In 1387,   pp.   151-155.

0676 Coyote,   Fred and C.   Gregory Crampton.   An
Anecdote: In Search of Gold.   In 1556,
pp.   76-78.

0677 _____. The Indian Way of Teaching.   In
1556,   pp.   54-57.

0678 _____. Land Holds Families Together.   In
1556,   pp.   15-17.

0679 _____. Not Another Drop.   In 1556,   pp.
37-39.

0680 _____. Southwest Indians: Citizens Without
Lands.   In 1556,   pp.   67.

_____. see also 1556

0681 Coyote Was Going There,   Indian Literature of
the Oregon Country.   Complied and edited by
Jarold Ramsey.   Seattle,   University of
Washington Press,   1977.
OCLC # 2985280

0682 Craik,   Brian.   Fur Trapping and Food Sharing
in Fort George,   Quebec.   In 0068,   pp.
223-236.

0683 Crampton,   C.   Gregory (Charles Gregory),
1911- .   The Archives of the Duke Projects
in American Indian Oral History.   In 2265,
pp.   119-128.

0684 _____. Cultures in Perspective.   In 1556,
pp.   82-83.

0685 _____. The Zunis of Cibola.   Salt Lake
City,   University of Utah Press,   1977.
OCLC # 3727549

_____. see also 0676

Cranbrook Academy of Art.   Museum see 0207

0686 Crary,   Margaret.   Susette LaFlesche: Voice
of the Omaha Indians..   New York,   Hawthorn

Books,   1973.
OCLC # 677023

0687 Craven,   Roy C.   Ceremonial Centers of the
      Maya. Photography by Roy C.   Craven,   Jr.
      Introd. by William R.   Bullard,   Jr.   Site
      descriptions by Michael E.   Kampen.   Gain-
      esville,   University Presses of Florida,
      1974.
      OCLC # 821368

0688 Creek Nation. Laws of the Creek Nation.
      Edited by Antonio J.   Waring.   Athens,
      GA.,   University of Georgia Press,   1960.
      University of Georgia Libraries.   Miscella-
      nea publications no.   1.
      OCLC # 1616265

0689 _____. Acts and Resolutions of the National
      Council of the Muskogee Nation of 1893.
      Compiled by W.   A.   Rentie. Wilmington,
      DE.,   Scholarly Resources,   1975.
      Constitutions and laws of the American In-
      dian Tribes,   series 2,   v.   29.   English
      and Creek. Reprint of the 1894 ed.   print-
      ed by Phoenix Printing Co.,   Muskogee.
      OCLC # 3149786

0690 _____. Acts and Resolutions of the National
      Council of the Muskogee Nation of 1893 and
      1899, Inclusive. Compiled by A.   P.   Mc-
      Kellop,   Wilmington,   DE.,   Scholarly Re-
      sources,   1975.
      Constitutions and laws of the American In-
      dian Tribes,   series 2,   v.   30.   Reprint
      of the 1900 ed.   printed by Phoenix Print-
      ing Co.,   Muskogee.
      OCLC # 1517593

0691 _____. Constitution and Laws of the
      Muskogee Nation. Compiled by L.   C.
      Perryman,   March 1st,   1890. Wilmington,
      DE.,   Scholarly Resources,   1975.
      Constitutions and laws of the American In-
      dian Tribes,   series 2,   v.   28.   Reprint
      of the 1890 ed.   printed by Phoenix Print-
      ing Co.,   Muskogee.
      OCLC # 1535842

0692 _____. Constitution and Laws of the

Muskogee **Nation**. Published by authority of
the National Council. Wilmington, DE.,
Scholarly Resources, 1975.
Constitutions and laws of the American In-
dian Tribes, series 2, v. 27. Reprint
of the 1880 ed. published by Levison and
Blythe Stationary Co., St. Louis.
OCLC # 3104182

0693 Cressey, Pamela J. Post-conquest Develop-
ments in the Teotihuacan Valley, Mexico.
Early Colonial Obsidian Industry. Greeley,
CO., Museum of Anthropology, University
of Northern Colorado, 1984.
Occasional publications in anthropology.
Archaeological series, no. 22.
Originally presented as the author's MA
thesis under title The Early Colonial Ob-
sidian Industry: Teotihuacan Valley.
OCLC # 10646727

0694 Cressman, Luther Sheeleigh, 1897- . Pre-
history of the Far West: Homes of Vanished
Peoples. Salt Lake City, University of
Utah Press, 1977.
OCLC # 3004934

0695 Cridlebaugh, Patricia A. American Indian
and European Impact Upon Holocene Vegetation in the Lower Little Tennessee River
Valley, East Tennessee. Ann Arbor, MI.,
University Microfilms International,
1984.
Microfilm - PhD Thesis - University of Tennessee
OCLC # 11488282

0696 Crocker, Jon Christopher, 1938- . Being
an Essence: Totemic Representation Among
the Eastern Bororo. In 2502, pp. 157-
176.

0697 Croix, Teodoro de, 1730-1791. Teodordo de
Croix and the Northern Frontier of New
Spain, 1776-1783, From the Original Docu-
ment in the Archives of the Indies, Se-
ville. Translated and edited by Alfred
Barnaby Thomas. Norman, University of
Oklahoma Press, 1941.
American Exploration and Travel

OCLC # 2564159

0698   Croom, Edward M., 1948- . Medical Plants
       of the Lumbee Indians. Ann Arbor, Univer-
       sity Microfilms International, 1982.
       Microfilm - PhD Thesis - North Carolina
       State University
       OCLC # 10267459

0699   Crowe, Charles. Indians and Blacks in White
       America. In 1099, pp. 148-169.

0700   Crowe, Keith J. A History of the Original
       Peoples of Northern Canada. Montreal,
       McGill-Queen's University Press (for the)
       Arctic Institute of North America, 1974.
       A Technical report from the Man in the
       North project.
       OCLC # 1065922

0701   Crumrine, N. Ross. Mask Use and Meaning in
       Easter Ceremonialism: The Mayo Parisero.
       In 2502, pp. 93-101.

0702   _____. Masks, Participants and Audience.
       In 2502, pp. 1-11.

0703   _____. Mayo Social Organization, Ceremon-
       ial and Ideological Systems, Sonora,
       Northwestern Mexico. Greeley, CO., Uni-
       versity of Northern Colorado, Museum of
       Anthropology, 1982.
       Occasional Papers in Anthropology, Ethnol-
       ogy series no. 41.
       OCLC # 8934809

       _____. see also 2502

0704   Culbert, T. Patrick. Early Maya Develop-
       ment at Tikal, Guatemala. In 2378, pp.
       27-43.

0705   _____. Maya Development and Collapse: An
       Economic Perspective. In 2920, pp. 509-
       530.

0706   _____. Mesoamerica. In 0097, pp. 495-
       555.
       Also printed in 0098

0707   _____. *Mesoamerica*. In 0098, pp.   25-85.
          Also printed in 0097

0708   _____. *Regional Variability in Maya Lowland
          Agriculture*. In 2522, pp.   157-161.

          _____. see also 0021

0709 Culin,   Stewart,   1858-1929. *Games of the
      North American Indians*. New York,   Dover,
      1975.
      Reprinted from U. S.   Bureau of American
      Ethnology,   24th Annual Report,   1902-1903.
      OCLC # 5471058

          _____. see also 0880

0710 *Cultural Change and Continuity: Essays in
      Honor of James Bennett Griffin*. Edited by
      Charles E.   Cleland. New York,   Academic
      Press,   1976.
      Studies in Archaeology.   Essays in this
      collection are also listed individually and
      refer to this citation.
      OCLC # 2034758

0711 *Cultural Resources Remote Sensing*. Edited by
      Thomas R.   Lyons and Frances Joan Mathien.
      Washington, D. C.   Cultural Resources
      Management Division,   National Park Serv-
      ice,   Govt.   Print.   Off.,   1980.
      Essays in this collection are also listed
      individually and refer to this citation.
      OCLC # 7093142

0712 *Current Perspectives in Northeastern Archae-
      ology: Essays in Honor of William A.   Rit-
      chie*. Edited by Robert E.   Funk and
      Charles F.   Hayes III.   Rochester,   New
      York State Archaeological Association,
      1977.
      Researches and Transactions of the New York
      State Archaeological Association,   v.   17,
      no.   1.
      OCLC # 3080639

0713 Curtis,   Edward S.,   1868-1952. *In the Land
      of the Head-Hunters*. Illus.   with photos
      by the author.   Tamarack Press,   1975.
      Reprint of the 1915 ed.   pub.   by World

Book Co., Yonkers, NY., in the series
Indian Life and Indian Lore.
OCLC # 2165137

0714 _____. Indian Days of the Long Ago. Illus.
with plants by the author and drawings by
F. N. Wilson. Tamarack Press, 1975.
Reprint of the 1915 ed. pub. by World
Book Co., Yonkers, NY., in the series
Indian Life and Indian Lore.
OCLC # 2967530

0715 Cushing, Frank Hamilton, 1857-1900. Zuñi:
Selected Writings of Frank Hamilton Cush-
ing. Edited with an introd. by Jesse
Green; foreword by Fred Eggan. Lincoln,
University of Nebraska Press, 1979.
OCLC # 4135872

0716 Cushman, K. A. Floral Remains from Meadowcroft Rockshelter, Washington County,
Southwestern Pennsylvania. In 2111, pp.
207-220.

0717 Custer, Jay F., 1955- . Delaware Prehis-
toric Archaeology: An Ecological Approach.
Newark, University of Delaware Press.
London, Associated University Presses,
1984.
OCLC # 10161565

0718 Cutcliffe, Stephen Hosmer, 1947- . In-
dians, Furs, and Empires: The Changing
Policies of New York and Pennsylvania,
1674-1768. Ann Arbor, MI., University
Microfilms International, 1976.
Microfilm - PhD Thesis - Lehigh University
OCLC # 4541359

0719 Cvpvkke, Holatte (Clark, C. B.) "Drove
Off Like Dogs" - Creek Removal. In 1282,
pp. 118-124.

0720 Dahlin, Bruce H. Cropping Cask in the
Protoclassic: A Cultural Impact Statement.
In 0472, pp. 21-37.

0720.1 Dailey, Charles. Major Influences in the
Development of 20th Century Native American
Art. In 2831.5, pp. 39-47.

0721 Dall, WIlliam Healey, 1845-1927. On Masks,
      Labrets, and Certain Aboriginal Customs:
      With an Inquiry into the Bearing of their
      Geographical Distribution. Washington,
      Govt. Print. Off., 1884.
      OCLC # 9312410

      Davidson, Florence Edenshaw, 1896- . see
      0290

0722 Daniel, Thomas M. An Immunochemist's View
      of the Epidemiology of Tuberculosis. In
      2526, pp. 35-48.

0723 Danky, James Philip, 1947- . Native Amer-
      ican Periodicals and Newspapers, 1828-
      1982, Bibliography, Publishing Record,
      and Holdings. Compiled by Maureen E.
      Hady, Ann Bowles, Research Assistant,
      foreword by Vine Deloria. Westport, CT.,
      Greenwood Press, 1984.
      In Association with the State Historical
      Society of Wisconsin
      OCLC # 10071283

0724 Danziger, Edmund Jefferson, 1938- . The
      Chippewas of Lake Superior. Norman, Uni-
      versity of Oklahoma Press, 1978.
      Civilization of the American Indian series
      v. 148.
      OCLC # 4003642

0725 Daugherty, Richard and Janet Friedman. An
      Introduction to Ozette Art. In 1562, pp.
      183-195.

      Davis, Andrew McFarland, 1833-1920 see
      2017

0726 Davis, Emma Lou. Associations of People and
      a Rancholabrean Fauna at China Lake, Cal-
      ifornia. In 0902, pp. 183-217.
      China Lake Program, Publication no. 3

0727 _____ and James Winkler. Ceremonial Rooms
      as Kiva Alternatives SOC-45 and SDV-3. In
      0622, pp. 47-79.

0728 Davis, Kenneth Penn. Chaos in the Indian

Country: The Cherokee Nation, 1825-35.
In 0547, pp. 129-147.

0729 Davies, Nigel, 1920- . The Aztecs, a
History. Norman, University of Oklahoma
Press, 1980, c1973.
Reprint of the ed. pub. by Macmillan,
London,
OCLC # 6087363

0730 _____. The Toltec Heritage: from the Fall
of Tula to the Rise of Tenochtitlan. Norman, University of Oklahoma Press, 1980.
Civilization of the American Indian series,
v. 153.
OCLC # 5103377

0731 _____. The Toltecs, Until the Fall of
Tula. Norman, University of Oklahoma
Press, 1977.
Civilization of the American Indian series,
v. 144.
OCLC # 2646410

0732 Davis, Ogilvie H. Ceramic Horizons Northeast. Clinton, IN., Clinton Color Craft-
ers, 1970.
OCLC # 720785

0733 _____. Winney Island Synopsis. Salem,
NY., Davis, 1974.
OCLC # 2129077

0734 Davis, Richard Harding, 1864-1916. There
are a Great Many Indians and a Great Many
Reservations. In 1566, pp. 111-140.
Reprinted from Davis, Richard Harding,
The West From a Car Window, NY., Harper &
Bro., 1892, pp. 151-81.

0735 Davis, Shelton H. Victims of the Miracle:
Development and the Indians of Brazil.
Cambridge, New York, Cambridge University
Press, 1977.
OCLC # 2896320

0736 Dawdy, Doris Ostrander. Annotated Biblio-
graphy of American Indian Painting. New
York, Museum of the American Indian, Heye
Foundation, 1968.

Contributions from the Museum of the American Indian,   Heye Foundation,   v. 21,   pt.
2.
OCLC # 50619

0737   Dawson,   K.   A.   C.   The Western Area Algon-
kians.   In 0068,   pp.   30-41.

0738   Day,   Gordon M.   Early Merrimack Toponymy.
In 0068,   pp.   372-389.

0739   _____.   The "Mots Loup" of Father Mathevet.
Ottawa,   National Museum of Canada,   1975.
National Museum of Canada,   Publications in
Ethnology,   v.   8.   Summary in French.
OCLC # 2871849

0740   _____.   The Ouragie War: A Case History in
Iroquois - New England Indian Relations.
In 0979,   pp.   35-50.

0741   _____.   The Tree Nomenclature of the St.
Francis Indians.   In the National Museum of
Canada Bulletin no.   10.   Contributions to
Anthropology,   1960,   pt.   2.   Ottawa,
Dept.   of Northern Affairs and National Re-
sources,   1963,   pp.   37-48.

Dbavalos,   G.   Felipe see 2138

0742   Deagan,   Kathleen A.   Cultures in Transition:
Fusion and Assimilation Among the Eastern
Timucua.   In 3071,   pp.   89-119.

0743   Dean,   Jeffrey S.,   1939- and William J.
Robinson.   Dendrochronology of Grasshopper
Pueblo.   In 2239,   pp.   46-60.

0744   Dearborn,   H.   A.   S.   (Henry Alexander Scam-
mell)   1783-1851.   Journals of Henry A.   S.
Dearborn: A Record of Councils with the
Seneca and Tuscarora Indians at Buffalo and
Cattaraugus in the Years 1838 and 1839.
Publications of the Buffalo Historical Soc-
iety,   v.   7.
OCLC # 11005483

0745   Death Dances: Two Novellas on North American
Indians.   Cambridge,   Applewood Press,
1979.

CONTENTS v. 1. Marvin, John. *Wink of Eternity.* v. 2. Abbott, Raymond, *The Axing of Leo White Hat.*
OCLC # 5507377

0746 Debo, Angie, 1890- . *Apaches as Southeastern Indians.* In 1282, pp. 143-158.

0747 _____. *Geronimo: The Man, His Time, His Place.* Norman, University of Oklahoma Press, 1976.
Civilization of the American Indian series, v. 142,
OCLC # 2189189

0748 _____. *Major Indian Record Collections in Oklahoma.* In 2265, pp. 112-118.

0749 Decalves, Alonso. *New Travels to the Westward, 1788.* New York, Garland Pubs., 1978.
Garland Library of narratives of North American Indian captivities, v. 18. Reprint of the 1788 ed., printed and sold by John W. Folsom, Boston.
OCLC # 3543372

0750 _____. *New Travels to the Westward, 1797.* New York, Garland Pubs., 1978.
Garland Library of narratives of North American Indian captivities, v. 18. Reprint of the 1797 ed. issued with the reprint of the 1787 ed. of the *Returned Captive,* New York, 1978.
OCLC # 3542685

0751 Defour, Darna L. *Nutrition in the Northwest Amazon: Household Dietary Intake and Time-Energy Expenditure.* In 0023, pp. 329-355.

0752 deGonzalez, Dora and Ronald K. Wetherington. *Incensarios and Other Ceremonial Forms at Kaminaljuyu.* In 0531, pp. 279-298.

0753 DeGroot, Alfred Thomas, 1903- . *Churches and the North American Indians: A Chronology and a sample denominational bib-*

liography. Peoria, AZ., DeGroot, 1977.
OCLC # 3941653

0754   Dekin,   Albert A.   Arctic Archaeology: A
       Bibliography and History. New York, Gar-
       land Pubs., 1978.
       Garland Reference Library of Science and
       Technology, v. 1.
       OCLC # 3610009

0755   De Laguna, Frederica, 1906- . The Prehis-
       tory of Northern North America as Seen
       from the Yukon. Menasha, WI., Society
       for American Anthropology, 1947. Mill-
       wood, NY., Kraus Reprint, 1974.
       Society for American Archeology, Memoir
       no. 3. Supplement to American Antiquity,
       v. 12, no. 3, pt. 2, 1947.
       OCLC # 1185949

0756   _____. Some Problems in the Relationship
       Between Tlingit Archaeology and Ethnology.
       In 0076, pp. 53-57.

0757   _____. Voyage to Greenland: A Personal In-
       itiation into Anthropology. New York,
       Norton, 1977.
       OCLC # 2646088

0758   Delaware Indian Symposium, Seton Hall Uni-
       versity, 1972. A Delaware Indian Sympo-
       sium: Proceedings. Edited by Herbert C.
       Kraft. Harrisburg, Pennsylvania Historic-
       al and Museum Commission, 1974.
       Anthropological Series no. 4.
       OCLC # 2072666

0759   Delfeld, Paula The Indian Priest Philip B.
       Gordon, 1885-1948. Chicago, Franciscan
       Herald Press, 1977.
       OCLC # 2493555

0760   Delgado-P, Guillermo. The Devil Mask: A
       Contemporary Variant of Andean Iconography
       in Oruro. In 2502, pp. 128-148.

0761   De Ling, Eleanor Louise. Mending the Cir-
       cle: Processes in the Loss and Preserva-
       tion of and American Indian Language. Ann
       Arbor, MI., University Microfilms Inter-

national, 1982.
Microfilm - PhD Thesis - University of
Michigan
OCLC # 10790633

0762 Deloria, Vine. The American Indian Image in
North America. In 2533, pp. 49-54.
Reprinted from Encyclopedia of Indians of
the Americas, v. 1, St. Clair Shores,
MI., Scholarly Press, 1974, pp. 40-44.

0763 _____. "Congress in its Wisdom:" The
Course of Indian Legislation. In 0034,
pp. 105-130.

0764 _____. Grandfathers of Our Country. In
3335, pp. 211-213.
Source - New York Times, February 22,
1972.

0765 _____. The Indian Rights Association: An
Appraisal. In 0034, pp. 3-18.

0766 _____. The Nations Within: The Past and
Future of American Indian Sovereignty. ...
and Clifford M. Lytle. New York, Pantheon Books, 1984.
OCLC # 10799271

0767 _____. Of Utmost Good Faith. San Francisco, Straight Arrow Books, 1971.
OCLC # 126600

0678 _____. The Twentieth Century. In 2602,
pp. 155-166.

_____, see also 0034, 1577

0769 Delorme, Teresa. An Assessment of the Attitudes and Perceptions of Selected Elementary School Teachers Who Serve Native American Children Toward Instructional Supervision and Evaluation. Ann Arbor, MI.,
University Microfilms International, 1984.
Microfilm - EdD Thesis - University of
North Dakota
OCLC # 12388544

0770 DeMallie, Raymond J. 1946- . George Bush-
otter; The First Lakota Ethnographer:

Teton Sioux, 1864-1892. In 0080, pp.
91-102.

0771 _____. Male and Female in Traditional
Lakota Culture. In 1438, pp. 237-265.

0772 _____ and Robert H. Lavenda. Wakan:
Plains Siouan Concepts of Power. In 0111,
pp. 153-165.

_____. see also 2283, 3302, 3304, 3348

0773 Dempsey, Hugh Aylmer, 1929- . Big Bear:
The End of Freedom. Lincoln, University
of Nebraska Press; Vancouver, British
Columbia, Douglas & McIntyre, 1984.
OCLC # 10912723

0774 _____. History in their Blood: The Indian
Portraits of Nicholas de Grandmaison.
Introd. by J. Russell Harper; foreword
by Frederick J. Dockstader. New York,
Hudson Hills Press. Distributed by Viking
Penguin, 1982.
OCLC # 8388465

0775 _____. Sylvester Long, Buffalo Child Long
Lance, Catawba - Cherokee and Adopted
Blackfoot, 1891-1932. In 0080, pp. 197-
203.

0776 Dench, Ernest Alfred. The Dangers of Em-
ploying Redskins as Movie Actors. In 2533,
pp. 61-62.
Reprinted from Making the Movies, New
York, Macmillan, 1915, pp. 92-94.

0777 Dene Nation, The Colony Within. Edited by
Mel Watkins for the University League for
Social Reform. Toronto; Buffalo. Univer-
sity of Toronto Press, 1977.
A revision and abridgement of material
presented at the Mackenzie Valley Pipeline
Inquiry (Berger Inquiry) by the Dene
themselves and by others on their behalf.
OCLC # 2614384

0778 Denevan, William M. The Aboriginal Population of Amazonia. In 0779, pp. 205-234.
Reprinted, with corrections and revisions

from <u>The Aboriginal Population of Western
Amazonia in Relation to Habitat and Sub-
sistence</u>. Revista Geografica (Rio de
Janeiro, no. 72, 1970, pp. 61-86.

0779 Denevan, William M. <u>The Native Population
      of the Americas in 1492</u>. Madison, Univer-
      sity of Wisconsin Press, 1976.
      Essays in this collection are also listed
      individually and refer to this citation.
      OCLC # 3103540

0780 Denig, Edwin Thompson, 1812-1862? <u>Of the
      Crow Nation</u>. Edited with a biographical
      sketch and footnotes by John C. Ewers.
      New York, AMS Press, 1980.
      Reprint of the 1953 ed. pub. by the
      Smithsonian Institution, Washington, D.
      C., as no. 33 of the Bureau of American
      Ethnology's Anthropological papers and as
      no. 151 of the Bureau's Bulletin.
      OCLC # 5749988

0781 Denkin, Albert A. <u>The Arctic Small Tool
      Horizon: A Behavioral Model of the Dis-
      persal of Human Population into an Unoccu-
      pied Niche</u>. In 0908, pp. 156-163.

0782 _____. <u>Elliptical analysis: An Heuristic
      Technique for the Analysis of Artifact
      Clusters</u>. In 0908, pp. 79-88.

0783 Denny, J. Peter. <u>Semantic Organization in
      Relation to the Traditional Algonquian
      Economy</u>. In 0068, pp. 336-343.

0784 Denonville, Jacques Rene-de Brisay, Marquis
      de, d. 1710. <u>Narrative of the Expedition
      of the Marquis de Nonville, Against the
      Senecas, in 1687</u>. Trans. from the French
      with an introductory note by Orsamus H.
      Marshall. In New York Historical Society.
      Collections, 1848, 2nd series, v. 2,
      pp. 149-192.

0875 Densmore, Frances, 1867-1957. <u>Chippewa
      Customs</u>. Reprint ed. with an introd. by
      Nina Marchatti Archabal. St. Paul, Min-
      nesota Historical Press, 1979.
      Publications of the Minnesota Historical

Society. Reprint of the 1929 ed. pub. by
Govt. Print. Off. as Bulletin no. 86 of
the Bureau of American Ethnology
OCLC # 5101612

0786 _____. How Indians Use Wild Plants for
Food, Medicine and Crafts. New York,
Dover, 1974.
Reprint of Uses of Plants by the Chippewa
Indians from the 44th annual report (1926-
1927) of the Bureau of American Ethnology.
OCLC # 940463

0787 Denton, James F., 1928- . The Red Man
Plays Indian. In 2533, pp. 68-70.

0788 Denver Art Museum. Native American Art in
the Denver Art Museum. by Richard Conn.
Denver Art Museum, Seattle, Distributed
by the University of Washington Press,
1979.
OCLC # 5172446

_____ see also 0639, 3109

0789 DeOrio, Robert N. Perspectives on the Prehistoric Cayuga, Post Owasco Tradition,
Through the Correlation of Ceramic Types
with Area Development. In 1585, pp. 65-
85.

0790 Depratter, Chester Burton, 1947- . Late
Prehistoric and Early Historic Chiefdoms in
the Southeastern U. S. Ann Arbor, MI.,
University Microfilms International, 1983.
Microfilm - PhD Thesis - University of
Georgia
OCLC # 10242987

0791 DeRosier, Arthur H. Myths and Realities in
Indian Westward Removal: The Choctaw Example. In 1099, pp. 83-100.

0792 Deserontyon, John, Mohawk Chief, d. 1811.
A Mohawk Form of Ritual Condolence, 1782.
Translated with an introd. by J. N. B.
Hewitt. New York, Museum of the American
Indian, Heye Foundation, 1928.
Indian Notes and Monographs v. 10, no. 8.
OCLC # 3433717

0793 **Designs from the Ancient Mimbrenos with a
Hopi Interpretation** by Fred Kabotie.
Flagstaff, AZ., Northland Press, 1982.
OCLC # 9323375

Detroit Institute of Art see 0256

0794 Detwiler, Frederick Emrey, 1947- . **The
Sun Dance of the Oglala: A Case Study in
Religion, Ritual and Ethics**. Ann Arbor,
MI., University Microfilms International,
1983.
Microfilm - PhD Thesis - University of New
Mexico
OCLC # 11617670

0795 Deutsch, Herman J. **Indian and White in the
Inland Empire, The Contest for the Land,
1880-1912**. In 2304, pp. 209-220.
Reprinted from **Pacific Northwest Quarterly**
v. 47, no. 2, April 1956, pp. 44-51.

Deutsch, Warren N. see 0132

0796 **Development of Political Organizations in
Native North America**. Elizabeth Tooker,
editor, Morton H. Fried, symposium
organizer. Philadelphia, American Ethnol-
ogy Society, 1983.
Essays in this collection are also listed
individually and refer to this citation.
Proceedings of the American Ethnological
Society, 1979.
OCLC # 9112137

0797 Devereux, George, 1908- . **Mohave Soul
Concepts**. In 2276, pp. 331-336.

DeVos, G. A. see 1408

0798 Dewall, Barbara Jean. **Leisure Satisfaction
Profiles of Selected American Indian,
Anglo Americans and Hispanic Americans**.
Ann Arbor, MI., University Microfilms
International, 1983.
Microfilm - PhD Thesis - University of New
Mexico
OCLC # 10775275

0799   Dial,   Adolph.   Lumbee Indians.   In 1282,
        pp.   77-92.

0800   Diamond,   Stanley,   1922-   .   Paul Radin.   In
        3139,   pp.   67-99.

        Dibble,   Charles E.   see   2729

0801   Dickason,   Olive Patricia,   1920-   .   The
        Myth of the Savage: And the Beginnings of
        French Colonialism in the Americas.   Edmon-
        ton,   Alberta,   Canada,   University of Al-
        berta Press,   1984.
        OCLC # 10896411

0802   Dickens,   Roy S.,   1938-   .   Cherokee Pre-
        history: The Pisgah Phase in the Appalach-
        ian Summit Region.   Knoxville,   University
        of Tennessee Press,   1976.
        OCLC # 2006040

0803   _____.   Mississippian Settlement Patterns in
        the Appalachian Summit Area: The Pisgah
        and Qualla Phases.   In 2172,   pp.   115-139.

0804   _____.   The Origins and Development of Cher-
        okee Culture.   In 0547,   pp.   3-32.

0805   Dickinson,   Jonathan,   1663-1722.   God's Pro-
        tecting Providence.   New York,   Garland
        Pub.,   1977.
        Garland Library of narratives of North
        American Indian captivities,   v.   4.   Re-
        print of the 1699 ed.   printed by R.   Jan-
        sen,   Philadelphia.
        OCLC # 3104354

0806   Dickson,   Lovat,   1902-   .   Wilderness Man:
        The Strange Story of Grey Owl.   New York,
        Atheneum,   1973.
        OCLC # 853039

0807   Dictionary of Daily Life of Indians of the
        Americas.   Newport Beach,   CA.,   American
        Indian Publishers,   1982.
        OCLC # 8195064

0808   Dictionary of Indian Tribes of the Americas.
        Newport Beach,   CA.,   American Indian

Publishers, 1980.
OCLC # 7886382

0809 Dictionary of Indians of North America.
      Frank H. Gille, publisher; Harry Walde-
      man editor. St. Clair Shores, MI.,
      Scholarly Press, 1978.
      OCLC # 4992022

0810 Diehl, Richard A. Pre-Hispanic Relation-
      ships Between the Basin of Mexico and North
      and West Mexico. In 3237, pp. 249-286.

0811 _____. Tula. In 0122, pp. 277-295.

0812 _____. Tula: The Toltec Capitol of Ancient
      Mexico. London, Thames and Hudson, Ltd.,
      1983.
      OCLC # 11112955

      _____. see also 0601, 3034

0813 Diereville. Relation of the Voyage to Port
      Royal in Acadia or New France. A Facsimile
      edition. New York, Greenwood Press,
      1968.
      Champlain Society Publication, no. 20.
      Reprint of the 1933 ed., English and
      French.
      OCLC # 21652

      Dilke, Christopher Wentworth, 1913- . see
      2491

0814 Dillon, Richard H. North American Indian
      Wars. New York, Facts on File, Inc.,
      1983.
      A Bison Book
      OCLC # 8475379

0815 Din, Gilbert C. The Imperial Osages: Span-
      ish-Indian Diplomacy in the Mississippi
      Valley. ... and A. P. Nasatir. Norman,
      University of Oklahoma Press, 1983.
      Civilization of the American Indian Series,
      v. 161.
      OCLC # 9392905

0816 Dincauze, Dena Ferran. The Neville Site:
      8000 Years at Amoskeag, Manchester, New

Hampshire. Cambridge, MA., Peabody Muse-
um of Archaeology and Ethnology, Harvard
University, 1976.
Peabody Museum Monographs, no. 4.
OCLC # 2331054

0817 Diné bahane. English. Diné bahane: The
      Navajo Creation Story. Trans. by Paul G.
      Zolbrod. Albuquerque, University of New
      Mexico Press, 1984.
      OCLC # 11677806

0818 Dingle Steven Franklin. Factors Which Affect
      Traditionalism of Navajo High School Stu-
      dents. Ann Arbor, MI., University Micro-
      films International, 1984.
      Microfilm - MA Thesis - University of
      Arizona
      OCLC # 12260073

0819 Di Peso, Charles Corradeno, 1920- . The
      Babocomari Village Site on the Babocomari
      River, Southeastern Arizona. Dragoon,
      AZ., Amerind Foundation, 1951. Millwood,
      NY., Kraus Reprint Co., 1974.
      The Amerind Foundation Publications v. 5
      OCLC # 1283130

0820 Dippie, Brian W. Custer's Last Stand: The
      Anatomy of an American Myth. Missoula,
      University of Montana, 1976.
      University of Montana Publications in His-
      tory.
      OCLC # 2796289

0821 _____. The Vanishing American: White Atti-
      tudes and the U. S. Indian Policy. Mid-
      dletown, CT., Wesleyan University Press,
      1982.
      OCLC # 8193939

0822 Discovering Past Behavior: Experiments in
      the Archaeology of the American Southwest.
      Edited by Paul Grebinger. New York, Gor-
      don & Breach, 1978.
      Essays in this collection are also listed
      individually and refer to this citation.
      Library of Anthropology
      OCLC # 4500057

0823   Disselhoff, Hans Dietrich. The Art of An-
       cient America; Civilizations of Central
       and South America. ... and Sigvald Linne.
       Trans. by Ann E. Keep. Rev. ed., New
       York, Greystone Press, 1966.
       OCLC # 676542

0824   Dixon, Joseph Kossuth. They Have Moved Ma-
       jestically Down the Pathway of the Ages.
       In 1566, pp. 267-286.
       Reprinted from The Vanishing Race; The
       Last Great Indian Council, Garden City,
       NY., Doubleday, Page & Co., 1914, pp.
       3-36.

0825   Dixon, Roland Burrage, 1875-1934. The
       Northern Maidu. New York, AMS Press,
       1983.
       Reprint, originally pub. New York, Amer-
       ican Museum of Natural History, 1905.
       Bulletin of the American Museum of Natural
       History, v. 17, pt. 3.
       OCLC # 8627327

0826   _____. The Shasta. New York, AMS Press,
       1983.
       Reprint. Originally pub. New York, Amer-
       ican Museum of Natural History, 1907.
       Bulletin of the American Museum of Natural
       History, v. 17, pt. 5.
       OCLC # 8627315

       _____. see also 3064

0827   Dobyns, Henry F. Indians of the Southwest:
       A Critical Bibliography. ... and Robert C.
       Euler. Pub. for the Newberry Library.
       Bloomington, Indiana University Press,
       1980.
       Bibliography Series
       OCLC # 7177081

0828   _____. Native American Historical Demo-
       graphy: A Critical Bibliography. Pub.
       for the Newberry Library. Bloomington,
       Indiana University Press, 1976.
       Bibliographical Series
       OCLC # 2331652

0829   _____.   Native American Population Collapse
        and Recovery.   In 2789,   pp.   17-35.

0830   _____.   Peru: A Cultural History.   ... and
        Paul L.   Doughty.   New York,   Oxford Uni-
        versity Press,   1976.
        Latin American Histories
        OCLC # 2562565

0831   _____.   Their Numbers Become Thinned:
        Native American Population Dynamics in
        Eastern North America.   Including an essay
        with William R.   Swagerty as co-author.
        Knoxville,   TN.,   Pub.   by the University
        Press in cooperation with the Newberry
        Library Center for the History of the
        American Indian,   1983.
        Native American Historic Demography Series
        OCLC # 9392931

0832   Dobyns,   Henry F.   Thematic Changes in Yuman
        Warfare.   In 0078,   pp.   46-71.

0833   Dockstader,   Frederick J.   Great North Amer-
        ican Indians: Profiles in Life and Leader-
        ship.   New York,   Van Nostrand Reinhold,
        1977.
        A Norbach Book
        OCLC # 3167970

0834   _____.   Weaving Arts of the North American
        Indian.   New York,   Crowell,   1978.
        OCLC # 4192428

0835   Documents Relative to Indian Affairs.   Clay-
        ton and Kingsland,   1794?

0836   Dodge,   John,   1751-1800.   Narrative of the
        Capture and Treatment of John Dodge,   1779.
        New York,   Garland Pub.,   1978.
        Garland Library of narratives of North
        American Indian captivities,   v.   12.   Re-
        print of the 1779 ed.   printed by T.   Brad-
        ford,   Philadelphia,   under the title A Nar-
        rative of the Capture and Treatment of John
        Dodge,   by the English at Detroit.
        OCLC # 3843467

0837   Dodge,   Richard Irving,   1827-1895.   He
        Remains a Savage Simply from Lack   of a

Code of Morals. In 1566, pp. 17-
46.
Reprinted from Dodge, Richard Irving Our
Wild Indians: Thirty Three Years' Personal
Experience Among the Red Men of the Great
West, Hartford, A. D. Worthington &
Co., 1882, pp. 53-67, 204-18, 220-23.

0837.5 _____. Our Wild Indians: Thirty-Three
Years Personal Experience Among the Red Men
of the Great West: A Popular Account of
their Social Life, Religion, Habits,
Traits, Customs, Exploits, etc.: With
Thrilling Adventures and experiences on the
Great Plains and in the Mountains of Our
Wild Frontier. With an introd. by General
Sherman. Hartford, CT., A. D. Worth-
ington, 1883.
OCLC # 10440197

0838 _____. Sign Language Wonderful Expertness
of Indian Sign Talkers. In 0008, pp. 3-
18.
Reprinted from Our Wild Indians, Thirty-
Three Years Personal Experience Among the
Red Men of the Great West, Hartford,
Hartford Pub. Co., 1882, pp. 379-394.

Dodgen, Dulce N. see 3276

0839 Doelle, William Harper. Hohokam Use of Non-
riverine Resources. In 0822, pp. 245-
274.

Donahue, J. see 0025, 3263

Donald, Collier, 1911- . see 2075

0840 Donald, Leland. Was Nuu-chah-nulth-aht
(Nootka) Society Based on Slave Labor? In
0796, pp. 108-119.

0841 Donnan, Christopher B. Ancient Burial
Patterns of the Moche Valley, Peru. ...
and Carol J. Mackey. Austin, University
of Texas Press, 1978.
OCLC # 3204251

0842 Donnelly, Joseph P. Jacques Marquette, S.
J., 1637-1675. Chicago, Loyola Univer-

sity Press, 1968.
OCLC # 435714

0843 Dorsey, Ella Loraine, 1853-1935. Poca-
      hontas. Washington, D. C., G. E. How-
      ard, 1906.
      OCLC # 1833626

0844 Dorsey, George Amos, 1868-1931. Indians of
      the Southwest. Designs by A. S. Covey,
      New York, AMS Press, 1976.
      Reprint of the 1903 ed. pub. by Passenger
      Dept., Atchison Topeka & Santa Fe Railway
      System, Chicago.
      OCLC # 1959256

0845 Dorson, Richard Mercer, 1916- . Blood-
      Stoppers and Bearwalkers; Folk Traditions
      of the Upper Peninsula. Cambridge, Har-
      vard University Press, 1952.
      Reprinted 1972.
      OCLC # 295659

      Dort, Wakefield, 1923- . see 2147

0846 Douglas, Diane Miriam. A Semeiotic Approach
      to Meaning in Historical Archaeology:
      Examining the Ceramics from a Wilmington,
      Delaware Site. Ann Arbor, MI., Univer-
      sity Microfilms International, 1982.
      Microfilm - PhD Thesis - University of Del-
      aware.
      OCLC # 9467787

0847 Douglas, Mary Tew The Meaning of Myth,
      With Special Reference to LaGeste
      d'Asdiwal'. In 3547 of original volume.
      pp. 49-69.

0848 Dow, James. The Otomi of the Northern
      Sierra de Puebla, Mexico: An Ethnographic
      Outline. East Lansing, Latin American
      Studies Center, Michigan State University,
      1975.
      Monographic series - Latin American Studies
      Center, Michigan State University, no.
      12.
      OCLC # 1990773

      Dowanandenyo, Sgaoyadih see 3509

0849   Downes, Randolph C. A Crusade for Indian
       Reform, 1922-1934. In 2304, pp. 230-
       242.
       Abridged and reprinted from Mississippi
       Valley Historical Review v. 32, no. 3,
       Dec. 1945, pp. 331-354.

0850   Downey, Fairfax Davis, 1893- . The
       Red/Blue Coats; The Indian Scouts U. S.
       Army. ... and Jacques Noel Jacobson Jr.,
       Fort Collins, Colorado. The Old Army
       Press, 1973.
       OCLC # 848922

0851   Downs, Ernest C. The Struggle of the Louis-
       iana Tunica Indians for Recognition. In
       2931, pp. 72-89.

0852   Downs, James F. The Navajo. New York,
       Holt, Rinehart and Winston, 1972.
       Case Studies in Cultural Anthropology.
       OCLC # 281127

0853   Drager, Dwight L. Vegetative Stratifica-
       tions from Aerial Imagery. In 0711, pp.
       79-86.

0854   Dragoo, Don W. Prehistoric Iroquoian Occup-
       ation in the Upper Ohio Valley. In 0712,
       pp. 41-47.

0855   _____. The Trimmed-Core Tradition in Asiat-
       ic-American Contacts. In 0905, pp. 69-
       81.

0856   Drake, Percy W. The Fish Creek Site. New
       York State Archeological Association Bulle-
       tin no. 13, July 1958, pp. 7-8. Mill-
       wood, NY., Kraus Reprint, 1976.
       Paper presented at annual meeting, April
       2, 1958.

0857   Drake, Samuel Gardner, 1798-1875. The Old
       Indian Chronicle: Being a Collection of
       Exceeding Rare Tracts/written and Published
       in the Time of King Philip's War by Persons
       Residing in the Country; to which are add-
       ed an introd. and notes. New York, AMS
       Press, 1976.
       Reprint of the 1867 ed. pub. by S. A.

Drake,   Boston
OCLC # 2136316

0858   Drapeau,   Lynn,   Alan Ford and Micheline
       Noreau-Hebert.   Sur la Dialectologie Phono-
       logique de Montagnais.   In 0068,   pp.   344-
       361.

0858.5   Draper,   David Elliott,   1943- .   Sensi-
         tivity vs.   Objectivity: An Indian Re-
         searcher's Dilemma.   In 2831.5,   pp.   131-
         133.

       Drewitt,   Bruce see 2150

0859   Driben,   Paul,   1946- .   When Freedom is
       Lost: The Dark Side of the Relationship
       Between Government and the Fort Hope Band.
       ... and Robert S.   Trudeau.   Toronto,   Buf-
       falo,   University of Toronto Press,   1983.
       OCLC # 10384294

0860   Drimmer,   Frederick.   Scalps and Tomahawks:
       Narratives of Indian Captivity.   New York,
       Coward-McCann,   1961.
       OCLC # 1193793

0861   Drinnon,   Richard.   Facing West: The Meta-
       physics of Indian-Hating and Empire Build-
       ing.   Minneapolis,   University of Minnesota
       Press,   1980.
       OCLC # 5992449

0862   Driver,   Harold Edson,   1907- .   Classifica-
       tion and Development of North American In-
       dian Cultures: A Statistical Analysis of
       the Driver-Massey Sample.   ... and James
       L.   Coffin.   Philadelphia,   American Philo-
       sophical Society,   1975.
       Transactions of the American Philosophical
       Society,   new series v.   65,   pt.   3.
       OCLC # 1405324

0863   Droessler,   Judith,   1947- .   Craniometry
       and Biological Distance: Biocultural Con-
       tinuity and Change at the Late-Woodland-
       Mississippian Interface.   Evanston,   IL.,
       Center for American Archaeology at North-
       western University,   1981.
       Research Series/Center for American Ar-

chaeology, v. 1.
OCLC # 7574249

0864 Drucker, Philip, 1911- . Ecology and Po-
      litical Organization on the Northwest Coast
      of North America. In 0796, pp. 86-96.

0865 Druke, Mary A., 1951- . Calendar of Iro-
      quois Treaty Documents in the Collection at
      the State Historical Society of Wisconsin.
      Prepared 10-11 May, 1979.
      Unpublished

0866 _____. The Concept of Personhood in 17th
      and 18th Century Iroquois Ethnopersonality.
      In 3035, pp. 59-70.

0867 _____. Iroquois Treaties: Common Forms,
      Varying Interpretations. In 1463, pp.
      85-98.

0868 _____. List of Iroquois Documents in the
      Public Archives of Canada, and Wampum
      Belts in the National Museum of Man,
      Ottawa. Prepared 23-30 March, 1979.
      Unpublished

0869 _____. Structures and Meanings of Leader-
      ship Among the Mohawk and Oneida During the
      Mid 18th Century. Ann Arbor, MI., Univer-
      sity Microfilms International, 1981.
      Microfilm - PhD Thesis - University of
      Chicago

0870 Drumm, Judith. Iroquois Culture. Albany,
      University of the State of New York, State
      Education Dept., State Museum and Science
      Service, 1961?
      Educational Leaflet - State Museum and
      Science Service, no. 5.
      OCLC # 3647164

0871 Drury, Clifford Merrill, 1897- . Chief
      Lawyer of the Nez Perce Indians, 1796-
      1876. Glendale, CA., A. H. Clark Co.,
      1979.
      Northwest Historical Series v. 14.
      OCLC # 5654205

0872 _____. Nine Years With the Spokane Indians:

The Diary, 1838-1848, of Elkanah Walker.
Glendale, CA., A. H. Clark Co., 1976.
Northwest Historical Series, v. 13.
OCLC # 2200095

0873 Druss, Mark. Archaeological Investigations
      in Chile. Greeley, Museum of Anthropolo-
      gy, University of Northern Colorado Press,
      1984.
      University of Northern Colorado, Museum of
      Anthropology, Occasional Publications in
      Anthropology, Archaeological Series, no.
      19.
      OCLC # 1541399

0874 _____. Computer Analysis of Chiuchiu Com-
      plex Settlement Pattern. In 0873, pp. 8-
      30.

0875 _____. Environment, Subsistence Economy,
      and Settlement Patterns of the Chiuchiu
      Complex, Northern Chile. In 0873, pp.
      1-7.

      DuBois, David see 1134

0876 Du Bray, Wynne. Cultural Values: An As-
      sessment and Comparison of Value Orienta-
      tions of Anglo-American and American Indian
      Social Workers. Ann Arbor, MI., Univer-
      sity Microfilms International, 1983.
      Microfilm - PhD Thesis - University of San
      Francisco
      OCLC # 9845544

0877 Duchene, Marlys. The Relevancy of Indian
      Studies in Higher Education. In 2962, pp.
      13-18.

0878 Duff, Wilson, 1925- . Images, Stone, B.
      C.: Thirty Centuries of Northwest Coast
      Indian Sculpture: An Exhibition Originat-
      ing at the Art Gallery of Greater Victoria.
      Photos and drawings by Hilary Stewart.
      Seattle, University of Washington Press,
      1975.
      OCLC # 2225252

0879 _____. The World is as Sharp as a Knife:

Meaning in Northern Northwest Coast Art.
In 1562, pp. 47-66.

0880 Dumarest, Noel, 1868-1903. Notes on
Cochiti, New Mexico. Pref. by Stewart
Culin. Trans. and edited by Elsie Clews
Parsons. New York, Kraus Reprint, 1964.
Memoirs of the American Anthropological
Association, v. 5, no. 3, 1919.
OCLC # 1838885

0881 DuMars, Charles T. Pueblo Indian Water
Rights: Struggle for a Precious Resource.
... and Marilyn O'Leary, Albert E. Utton.
Tucson, University of Arizona Press,
1984.
OCLC # 10605135

0882 Dumond, Don E., 1929- . Alaska and the
Northwest Coast. In 0097, pp. 69-113.

0883 _____. The Eskimos and Aleuts. London,
Thames and Hudson, 1977.
Ancient peoples and places, v. 87.
OCLC # 3346937

0884 _____. Independent Maya of the Late Nineteenth Century: Chiefdoms and Power
Politics. In 0109, pp. 103-138.

0885 Dumont, Jean Paul, 1940- . The Headman
and I: Ambiguity and Ambivalence in the
Fieldworking Experience. Austin, Univer-
sity of Texas Press, 1978.
Texas Pan American Series
OCLC # 3869539

0886 _____. Under the Rainbow: Nature and
Supernature Among the Panare Indians. Aus-
tin, University of Texas Press, 1976.
Texas Pan American Series
OCLC # 1530729

0887 Dunbar Ortiz, Roxanne, 1938- . The Great
Sioux Nation: Sitting in Judgement on
America. San Francisco, American Indian
Treaty Council Information Center,
Berkeley, CA., Moon Books, 1977.
Based on and containing testimony heard at
the Sioux Treaty Hearings held December

1974,   in Federal District Court,   Lincoln,
Nebraska.
OCLC # 3439795

0888 Dunlay, Thomas W., 1944- . Wolves for the
Blue Soldiers: Indian Scouts and Auxiliar-
ies with the United States Army, 1860-90.
Lincoln,   University of Nebraska Press,
1982.
OCLC # 7947300

Dunn, Dorothy see 2479

0889 Dunn, Jacob Piatt, 1855-1924. Jack, I
Haven't Had an Indian to Eat for a Long
Time. In 1566, pp. 47-90.
Reprinted from Dunn, J. P. Massacres of
the Mountains: A History of the Indian
Wars of the Far West, New York, Harper &
Brothers, 1886, pp. 396-446.

0890 Dunn, John Asher. International Matri-
moieties: The North Maritime Province of
the North Pacific Coast. In 3162, pp.
99-109.

0891 Dunnell, Robert C., 1942- . The Prehis-
tory of Fishtrap, Kentucky. New Haven,
Dept., of Anthropology, Yale University
Press, 1972.
Yale University Publications in Anthropol-
gy, no. 75. Revised version of author's
thesis.
OCLC # 508511

0892 Dunning, Robert W. (Robert William), 1938-
. Social and Economic Change Among the
Northern Ojibwa. Toronto, Buffalo, Uni-
versity of Toronto Press, 1959.
OCLC # 418202

0892.5 Dupris, Joseph C. The National Impact of
Multicultural Education: A Renaissance of
Native American Culture Through Tribal
Self-determination and Indian Control of
Education. In 2238.5, pp. 43-54.

0893 Durango South Project: Archaeological Salvage of Two Late Basketmaker III Sites in
the Durango District. John D. Gooding,

editor,   with contributions by Elaine An-
derson.   Tucson,   University of Arizona
Press,   1980.
University of Arizona Anthropological Paper
v. 34.
OCLC # 6305069

0894 Durant, David N. Ralegh's Lost Colony.
New York, Atheneum, 1981.
OCLC # 6649884

Dustin, Fred, 1866- . see 1242

Duston, Hannah (Emerson), b. 1657 see
528

0894.4 Dyal, David E. Preserving Traditional
Arts in Times of Scarcity. In 2831.5, pp.
119-129.

0894.5 Dyal, Susan. Preserving Traditional Arts:
A Toolkit for Native American Communities.
Los Angeles, Presented by the American In-
dian Studies Center, University of Calif-
ornia, Los Angeles, 1985.
OCLC # 13979174

0895 Dyck, Noel. Representation and Leadership
of a Provincial Indian Association. In
2485, pp. 197-305.

0896 _____. Strangers in Our Midst: An Examination of Anthropological Thought About
Brokerage. In 0479, pp. 239-251.

0897 Dycherhoff, Ursula. Mexican Toponyms as a
Source in Regional Ethnohistory. In 0978,
pp. 229-252.

Dyk, Ruth see 1864

Dyk, Walter see 1864, 1865

0898 Earl, Guy Chaffee. Indian Legends and
Songs. Glendale, CA., A. H. Clark Co.,
1980.
Edition of 500 copies.
OCLC # 6943371

0899   The Earliest Recorded Description: The Mo-
       hawk Treaty with New France at Three
       Rivers, 1645. In 1463,   pp.   127-153.

0900   Early American Indian Documents: Treaties
       and Laws, 1607-1789. General editor Alden
       T.   Vaughan.   Washington,   D.   C.:   Univer-
       sity Publications of America,   1979.
       v.   1   Pennsylvania and Delaware Treaties,
       1629-1737,   edited by Donald H.   Kent.
       OCLC # 5435281
0901   Early and Middle Archaic Cultures in the
       Northeast.   Edited by David R.   Starbuck
       and Charles E.   Bolian.   Rindge,   NH.,
       Dept. of Anthropology,   Franklin Pierce
       College,   1980.
       Occasional Publications in Northeastern An-
       thropology,   v.   7.
       OCLC # 7011860

0902   Early Man in America From a Circum Pacific
       Perspective.   Edited by Alan Lyle Bryan.
       Edmonton,   Archaeological Researches In-
       ternational,   1978.
       Occasional papers of the Dept.   of Anthro-
       pology,   University of Alberta,   no.   1.
       Essays in this collection are also listed
       individually and refer to this citation.
       OCLC # 4315579

0903   Early Man in the New World.   Edited by Rich-
       ard Shutler.   Beverly Hills,   CA.,   Sage
       Publications,   1983.
       Essays in this collection are also listed
       individually and refer to this citation.
       OCLC # 9111264

0904   Early Mesoamerican Village.   Edited by Kent
       V.   Flannery.   New York,   Academic Press,
       1976.
       Studies in Archaeology.
       OCLC # 1602067

0905   Early Native Americans: Prehistoric Demo-
       graphy, Economy, and Technology.   Edited
       by David L.   Browman.   The Hague,   New
       York,   Mouton,   1980.
       Papers prepared for the 9th International
       Congress of Anthropological and Ethnologi-

cal Sciences.
OCLC # 6522152

0906 Early Papers in Long Island Archaeology.
Stony Brook, NY., Suffolk County Archae-
ological Association, 1977.
Readings in Long Island Archaeology and
Ethnohistory, v. 1. Articles originally
published in American Museum of Natural
History Anthropological papers and Museum
of the American Indian, Heye Foundation,
Indian Notes.
OCLC # 6054769

0907 Eastburn, Robert, 1710-1778. Faithful Nar-
rative. New York, Garland Pub., 1978.
Garland Library of narratives of North
American Indian captivities, v. 8.
OCLC # 3842894

0908 Eastern Arctic Prehistory: Paleoeskimo Problems: A Monograph Resulting from a Joint
Project Sponsored by the National Museums
of Canada and the School of American Research. Edited by Moreau S. Maxwell.
Washington, Society for American Archaeology, 1976.
Essays in this collection are also listed
individually and refer to this citation.
Memoirs of the Society for American Archaeology, no. 31.
OCLC # 3160849

0909 Eastman, Charles Alexander, 1858-1939. Indian Scout Craft and Lore. By ...
("Ohiyesa"). New York, Dover, 1974.
A full blooded Sioux trained as a warrior
to age sixteen discusses the crafts, lore,
and customs that were the essence of that
training. Reprint of the 1914 ed. pub.,
by Little, Brown, Boston, under the
title Indian Scout Talks.
OCLC # 979058

0910 Ebeit, James I. The Detection, Migration
and Analysis of Remotely-sensed, "Epherm-
eral" Archeological Evidence. In 0711,
pp. 119-122.

0911 _____. Locational Modeling in the Analysis

of the Prehistoric Roadway System at and
Around Chaco Canyon, New Mexico. In
0711, pp. 169-207.

0912 _____. Prehistoric Irrigation Canals Iden-
tified from Skylab III and Landsat Imagery
in Phoenix, Arizona. In 0711, pp. 209-
228.

0913 _____. Remote Sensing in Large-Scale Cultural Resources Survey: A Case Study from
the Arctic. In 0711, pp. 7-54.

_____. see also 0409

0914 Eccles, William John. Frontenac, The
Courtier Governor. Toronto, McClelland
and Stewart, 1968, c1959.
OCLC # 2941539

0915 Echohawk, John E. The Poorest of the Poor.
In 1556, pp. 48-51.

0916 _____. Postscript: 1979. In 1556, pp.
19-25.

0917 _____. A Trust Responsibility Issue. In
1556, pp. 6-9.

0918 _____. Who Owns the Rain? In 1556, pp.
26-30.

0919 Eckert, Allan W. The Conquerors; A Narrat-
ive. Boston, Little Brown, 1970.
His Winning of America.
OCLC # 104206

0920 _____. The Wilderness War: A Narrative.
1st ed., Boston, Little Brown, 1978.
His Winning of America Series
OCLC # 4114821

0921 Eddy, Frank W. Cultural and Environmental
History of Cienega Valley, Southwestern
Arizona. ... and Maurice E. Cooley; with
sections by Paul S. Martin, Bruce B.
Huckell. Tucson, University of Arizona
Press, 1983.
Anthropological Papers of the University of

Arizona no. 43.
OCLC # 9918379

0922 Eddy, John. Medicine Wheels and Plains
      Indian Astronomy. In 2270, pp. 147-169.

0923 Eder, Jeanne M. Oyawin. The History,
      Structure and Organization of the Indian
      Studies Departments at the University of
      North Dakota. In 2962, pp. 51-55.

      Edmonds, Margot. see 0583

      Edmonson, Munro S. see 1903

0924 Edmunds, R. David (Russell David, 1939-
      .) Indian Humor: Can the Red Man Laugh?
      In 2602, pp. 141-153.

0925 _____. Old Briton. In 0081, pp. 1-20.

0926 _____. The Potawatomis: Keepers of the
      Fire. Norman, University of Oklahoma
      Press, 1978.
      Civilization of the American Indian Series,
      no. 145.
      OCLC # 3844497

0927 _____. The Shawnee Prophet. Lincoln, Uni-
      versity of Nebraska Press, 1983.
      OCLC # 9112321

0928 _____. Tecumseh, and the Quest for Indian
      Leadership. Boston, Little Brown, 1984.
      OCLC # 9946361

      _____. see also 0081

      Edwards, J. O. see 0671

0929 Eggan, Fred, 1906- . Ojibwa Ecology and
      Social Organization. In 1318, pp. 313-
      350.

      Egge, Marion F. see 0229

0930 Ehrenhard, Ellen B. Ninety Six National
      Historic Sites in South Carolina. In 0711,
      pp. 229-291.

0931   Ehrenhard,   John E.   Cultural Resource Inven-
       tory of the Big Cypress Swamp: An Exper-
       iment in Remote Sensing.   In 0711,   pp.
       105-117.

0932   Eisenberg,   Leonard.   Paleo-Indian Settlement
       Pattern in the Hudson and Delaware River
       Drainages.   Rindge, NH.,   Dept.   of An-
       thropology,   Franklin Pierce College,
       1978.
       Occasional Papers in Northeastern Anthro-
       pology,   no.   4.
       OCLC # 4786440

0933   Ekholm,   Gordon.   The Archaeology of Northern
       and Western Mexico.   In 2105,   pp.   320-
       330.

0934   _____.   A Possible Focus of Asiatic Influ-
       ence in the Late Classic Cultures of Meso-
       america.   In 0076,   pp.   72-89.

0935   Ekholm-Miller,   Susanna.   The Lagartero Fig-
       urines.   In 0472,   pp.   172-186.

0936   El Guindi,   Fadwa .   The Structural Corre-
       lates of Power in Zapotec Ritual.   In 0111,
       pp.   299-307.

0937   Eliot,   John,   1604-1690.   John Eliot's Dia-
       loques: A Study in Cultural Interaction.
       Edited by Henry W.   Bowden and James P.
       Ronda.   Westport,   CT.,   Greenwood Press,
       1980.
       Contributions in American History,   no.
       88.   Originally published in Cambridge,
       MA.,   by M.   Johnson,   1671.
       OCLC # 7523574

       Elkus,   Charles de Young,   1881-1963   see
       0938

0938   The Elkus Collection: Southwestern Indian
       Art.   Edited by Dorothy K.   Washburn,   with
       a final editing by Robert Sayers.   San
       Francisco,   California Academy of Sciences.
       Seattle,   distributed by University of
       Washington Press,   1984.
       OCLC # 12861634

0939 Elliott, Dobres. Otsiningo, an Example of
      an Eighteenth Century Settlement Pattern.
      In 0712, pp. 93-105.

0940 _____. An Ethnohistorical Approach to Set-
      tlement Pattern Studies: Otsiningo, a
      Case Study. In 3519, pp. 100-114.

      Ellis, Florence. see 0622

0941 Elmendorf, Mary L. (Mary Lindsay). Nine
      Mayan Women: A Village Faces Change. NEW
      YORK, Schenkman Pub. Co., 1976.
      Pub. in 1972 under the title The Mayan
      Women and Change.
      OCLC # 2888062

0942 El-Najjar, Mahmoud Y. A Comparative Study
      of Facial Dimensions at Gran Quivira. In
      1387, pp. 157-159.

0943 _____. Skeletal Changes in Tuberculosis:
      The Hamann-Todd Collection. In 2526,
      pp. 85-97.

      Elasser, Albert B. see 1402

0944 Emboden, William A. Plant Hypnotics Among
      the North American Indians. In 3747 (of
      main bibliography) pp. 159-167.

0944.5 Emerson, Thomas E., 1945- . The BBB
      Motor Site (11-MS-595). by ... and Douglas
      K. Jackson with contributions by Sissel
      Johannessen, Lucy A. Whalley and George
      R. Milner. Urbana; Chicago, published
      for the Illinois Dept. of Transportation
      by the University of Illinois Press, 1984.
      American Bottom Archaeology: FAI-270 Site
      reports, v. 6.
      OCLC # 10207105

0945 _____. The Florence Street Site (11-S-458).
      by ... and George R. Milner and Douglas K.
      Jackson; with contributions by Paula
      Cross, Sissel Johannessen and William P.
      White. Urbana, published for the Illinois
      Dept. of Transportation by the University
      of Illinois Press, 1983.

American Bottom Archaeology,   v.   2.
OCLC # 9392768

0946   _____. A Settlement-subsistence Model of
        the Terminal Late Archaic Adaptation in the
        American Bottom,   Illinois. In 0124,   pp.
        219-242.

0947 Emmerich,   Andre. Sweat of the Sun and Tears
        of the Moon; Gold and Silver in Pre-Colum-
        bian Art. Seattle,   University of Washing-
        ton Press,   1965.
        OCLC # 280524

0948 Engel,   Frederic Andre,   1908- . An Ancient
        World Preserved;   Relics and Records of
        Prehistory in the Andes. Trans. by Rachel
        Kendall Gordon. Rev. and updated. New
        York,   Crown Publishers,   1976.
        Trans. of Le Monde Precolombien des Andes
        OCLC # 2331811

0949   _____. A Preceramic Settlement on the Cen-
        tral Coast of Peru. Asia,   Unit I. Phila-
        delphia,   American Philosophical Society,
        1963.
        Transactions of the American Philosophical
        Society,   n. s.,   v. 53,   pt. 3.
        OCLC # 500514

0950 Engelbrecht,   William E.,   The Kleis Site
        Ceramics: An Interpretive Approach. In
        0979,   pp. 325-339.

0951   _____. Methods and aims of Ceramic De-
        scription. In 1585,   pp. 27-29.

0952 Englebert,   Omer,   1893- . The Last of the
        Conquistadors,   Junipero Serra,   1713-
        1784. Trans. from the French by Katherine
        Woods. New York,   Harcourt,   Brace,   1956.
        OCLC # 1726842

0953 Ericksen,   Mary F. Patterns of Microscopic
        Bone Remodeling in Three Aboriginal Ameri-
        can Populations. In 0905,   pp. 239-270.

0954 Erickson,   Vincent O. Some Recent Micmac
        Witchcraft Beliefs. In 0479,   pp. 189-
        200.

0955 Erikson, Kai T. and Christopher Vecsey. A
     Report to the People of Grassy Narrows. In
     0079, pp. 152-161.

     _____. see also 0079

     Ermatinger, Edward, 1797-1876. see 2004

     Ermatinger, Francis, 1798-1858. see 2004

0956 Espejel, Carlos. Mexican Folk Ceramics.
     Photographer F. Catala Roca. Trans.
     from the Spanish by Diorki. Barcelona:
     Blume, 1975.
     Nueva imagen series
     OCLC # 2966979

0957 Esposito, Frank John, 1941- . Indian-
     White Relations in New Jersey, 1609-1802.
     Ann Arbor, MI., University Microfilms
     International, 1976.
     Microfilm - PhD Thesis - Rutgers University

0958 Essays on Mexican Kinship. University of
     Pittsburgh Press, 1976.
     Essays in this collection are also listed
     individually and refer to this citation.
     Pitt Latin American Series.
     OCLC # 1622050

0959 Essenpreis, Patricia Sue. Fort Ancient Set-
     tlement: Differential Response at a
     Mississippian-Late Woodland Interface. In
     2172, pp. 141-167.

0960 Esser, Janet Brody. Tarascan Masks of Women
     as Agents of Social Control. In 2502, pp.
     114-127.

     Estes, George. see 3538

0961 Estin, Ann Laquer. Lone Wolf v. Hitchcock:
     The Long Shadow. In 0034, pp. 215-245.

     Eubanks, William. see 0550

0962 Euler, Robert C. The Pai: Cultural Conser-
     vatives in Environmental Diversity. In
     0622, pp. 80-87.

Evans, Clifford. see 2116

0963 Evans, Nancy H. California: The Native
American Heritage Commission and Energy-re-
lated Issues. In 2274, pp. 200-204.

0964 Evans, W. McKee. The North Carolina Lum-
bees: From Assimilation to Revitalization.
In 2930, pp. 49-71.

0965 Evans-Wentz, W. Y. (Walter Yelling),
1878-1965. Cuchama and Sacred Mountains.
Edited by Frank Waters and Charles L.
Adams. Chicago, Swallow Press, Athens,
Ohio University Press, 1981.
OCLC # 7556001

0966 Evarts, Jeremiah, 1781-1831. Cherokee Re-
moval, The "William Penn" Essays and Other
Writings. Edited and with an introd. by
Francis Paul Prucha. Knoxville, Univer-
sity of Tennessee Press, 1981.
OCLC # 7206416

Everson Museum of Art. see 3483.5

0967 Ewers, John Canfield. Artifacts and Pictures as Documents in the History of Indian-White Relations. In 2265, pp. 101-
111.

0968 _____. A Century of American Indian Exhib-
its in the Smithsonian Institution. From
Annual Report of the Board of the Regents
of the Smithsonian Institution, 1958, pp.
513-525.

0969 _____. The Emergence of the Plains Indian
as the Symbol of the North American Indian.
In 1456, pp. 16-32.
Reprinted from Smithsonian Annual Report,
1964, pp. 531-544.

0970 _____. The George Catlin Paintings in the
U. S. National Museum. A Checklist taken
from "George Catlin, Painter of Indians
and the West" in the Annual Report of the
Smithsonian Institution, 1955. 1956, pp.
507-528.

0971 _____. Indian Views of the White Man Prior
to 1850: An Interpretation. In 2602, pp.
7-23.

0972 _____. Mothers of the Mixed-Bloods: The
Marginal Women in the History of the Upper
Missouri. In 0638, pp. 62-70.

0973 _____. Murals in the Round: Painted Tipis
of the Kiowa and Kiowa Apache Indians: An
Exhibition of Tipi Models Made for James
Mooney of the Smithsonian Institution Dur-
ing his Field Studies of Indian History and
Art in Southwestern Oklahoma, 1891- 1904.
Washington, Published for Renwick Gallery
of the National Collection of the Fine
Arts by the Smithsonian Press, 1978.
OCLC # 3966225

0974 _____. Richard Sanderville, Blackfoot Indian Interpreter, Blackfoot, ca1873-1951.
In 0080, pp. 117-126.

0975 _____. The Static Images. In 2533, pp.
16-21.
From Look to the Mountaintop edited by
Robert Iocopi, San Jose, Gousha Publications, 1972, pp. 107-109.

_____. see also 0525, 0780

0976 Ewert, Theodore, 1847-1906. Private Theodore Ewert's Diary of the Black Hills Expedition of 1874. Edited by John M. Carroll, Lawrence A. Frost. Piscataway,
NJ., CRI Books, 1976.
OCLC # 2754212

0977 Ewing, Douglas C. Pleasing the Spirits: A
Catalogue of a Collection of American In-
dian Art, with essays by Craig Bates and
Ted J. Brasser. New York, Ghylen Press,
1982.
OCLC # 9000747

0978 Explorations in Ethnohistory: Indians of
Central Mexico in the 16th Century.
Edited by H. R. Harvey, Hanns J. Prem.
Albuquerque, University of New Mexico

Press, 1984.
OCLC # 9895002

0979 Extending the Rafters: Interdisciplinary Ap-
      proaches to Iroquoian Studies. Edited by
      Michael K. Foster, Jack Campisi, Mari-
      anne Mithun. Albany, State University of
      New York Press, 1984.
      A Publication of the Center for the History
      of the American Indian of the Newberry
      Library.
      OCLC # 9646457

0980 Ezell, Paul Howard, 1913- . The Hispanic
      Acculturation of the Gila River Pimas.
      Millwood, NY., Kraus Reprint, 1974.
      Memoirs of the American Anthropological As-
      sociation, no. 90. Supplement to Ameri-
      can Anthropologist, v. 63, no. 5, pt.
      2, 1961.
      OCLC # 2192685

0981 Fadden, Ray. The Creation. by Aren Akweks.
      Illus. by the author. Hogansburg, NY.,
      Akwesasne Counselor Organization, St.
      Regis Mohawk Reservation, 1947.
      OCLC # 5117367

0982 _____. The Hermit Thrush. by Aren Akweks.
      Hogansburg, NY., Akwesasne Counselor
      Organization, St. Regis Mohawk Reserva-
      tion, 1948.
      OCLC # 5114147

0983 _____. History of the Oneida Nation. by
      Aren Akweks. Hogansburg, NY.,
      Akwesasne Counselor Organization, St.
      Regis Mohawk Reservation, nd.

0984 _____. The Story of the Monster Bear, The
      Great Dipper. by Aren Akweks. Hogansburg,
      NY., Akwesasne Counselor Organization,
      St. Regis Mohawk Reservation, 1948.
      OCLC # 5114179

0985 _____. The Thunder Boy. by Aren Akweks,
      illus. by the author. Malone, NY., Roy
      Smalley, 1948.
      OCLC # 5114203

_____, see also 0040-0058

0986 Fagan, Brian M. The Aztecs. New York, W.
      H. Freeman, 1984.

0987 Fairbanks, Charles Herron, 1913- . The
      Ethno-Archaeology of the Florida Seminole.
      In 3071, pp. 163-193.

0988 Farb, Peter. Man's Rise to Civilization:
      The Cultural Ascent of the Indians of North
      America. New York, Dutton, 1978.
      OCLC # 3167419

0989 Farber, Stephen. A Man Called Horse and
      Flap. In 2533, pp. 166-168.
      Reprint from Film Quarterly, v. 24, Fall
      1970, pp. 60-61.

0990 Farr, William E., 1938- . The Reservation
      Blackfeet, 1882-1945: A Photographic His-
      tory of Cultural Survival. with a foreword
      by James Welch, Seattle, University of
      Washington Press, 1984.
      OCLC # 10122441

0991 Farrer, Claire. Singing for Life: The
      Mescalero Apache Girls' Puberty Ceremony.
      In 2931, pp. 125-159.

0992 Farriss, Lorene Sanders. A Study of Factors
      Associated with Success of American Indians
      in Nursing and a Proposed Model for Cultur-
      al Content. Ann Arbor, MI., University
      Microfilms International, 1984.
      Microfilm - PhD Thesis - University of
      Miami
      OCLC # 11854113

0993 Farriss, Nancy M. (Nancy Marguerite),
      1938- . Maya Society under Colonial Rule:
      The Collective Enterprise of Survival.
      Princeton, NJ., Princeton University
      Press, 1984.
      OCLC # 9970717

      _____. see also 2139

0994 Fausz, John Frederick, 1947- . Anglo-In-

dian Relations in Colonial North America.
In, 2789, pp. 79-105.

0995 _____. The Powhatan Uprising of 1622: A
Historical Study of Ethnocentrism and Cultural Conflict. Ann Arbor, MI., University Microfilms International, 1977.
Microfilm - PhD Thesis - College of William
and Mary
OCLC # 6077951

0996 Fay, George Emory, 1927- . Charters,
Constitutions and By-laws of the Indian
Tribes of North America. Part I: The
Sioux Tribes of South Dakota. Greeley,
Colorado State College, Museum of Anthro-
pology, 1967.
University of Northern Colorado, Museum of
Anthropology, Occasional Publications in
Anthropology, Ethnology Series no. 1.
OCLC # 65921

0997 _____. Charters, Constitutions and By-laws
of the Indian Tribes of North America.
Part II. The Indian Tribes of Wisconsin
(Great Lakes Agency). Greeley, Colorado
State College, Museum of Anthropology,
1967.
University of Northern Colorado, Museum of
Anthropology, Occasional Publications in
Anthropology, Ethnology Series no. 2.
OCLC # 65921

0998 _____. Charters, Constitutions and By-laws
of the Indian Tribes of North America.
Part III. The Southwest (Apache-Mohave).
Greeley, Colorado State College, Museum
of Anthropology, 1967.
University of Northern Colorado, Museum of
Anthropology, Occasional Publications in
Anthropology, Ethnology Series no. 4.
OCLC # 65921

0999 _____. Charters, Constitutions and By-laws
of the Indian Tribes of North America.
Part IV. The Southwest (Navajo-Zuni).
Greeley, Colorado State College, Museum
of Anthropology, 1967.
University of Northern Colorado, Museum of
Anthropology, Occasional Publications in

Anthropology, Ethnology Series no. 5.
OCLC # 65921

1000   _____. Charters, Constitutions and By-laws
of the Indian Tribes of North America.
Part V. The Indian Tribes of Oklahoma.
Greeley, Colorado State College, Museum
of Anthropology, 1968.
University of Northern Colorado, Museum of
Anthropology, Occasional Publications in
Anthropology, Ethnology Series no. 6.
OCLC # 65921

1001   _____. Charters, Constitutions and By-laws
of the Indian Tribes North America. Part
VII. The Indian Tribes of California.
Greeley, University of Northern Colorado,
Museum of Anthropology, 1970.
University of Northern Colorado, Museum of
Anthropology, Occasional Publications in
Anthropology, Ethnology Series no. 8.
OCLC # 65921

1002   _____. Charters, Constitutions and By-laws
of the Indian Tribes of North America.
Part VIII. The Indian Tribes of California
(cont.). Greeley, University of Northern
Colorado, Museum of Anthropology, 1970.
University of Northern Colorado, Museum of
Anthropology, Occasional Publications in
Anthropology, Ethnology Series no. 9.
OCLC # 65921

1003   _____. Charters, Constitutions and By-laws
of the Indian Tribes of North America.
Part IX. The Northwest and Alaska.
Greeley, University of Northern Colorado,
Museum of Anthropology, 1970.
University of Northern Colorado, Museum of
Anthropology, Occasional Publications in
Anthropology, Ethnology Series no. 10.
OCLC # 65921

1004   _____. Charters, Constitutions and By-laws
of the Indian Tribes of North America.
Part X. The Northwest and Alaska (cont).
Greeley, University of Northern Colorado,
Museum of Anthropology, 1970.
University of Northern Colorado, Museum of
Anthropology, Occasional Publications in

Anthropology,   Ethnology Series no. 11.
OCLC # 65921

1005 _____.   Charters, Constitutions and By-laws
of the Indian Tribes of North America.
Part XI.   The Basin-Plateau Tribes.
Greeley,   University of Northern Colorado,
Museum of Anthropology,   1971.
University of Northern Colorado,   Museum of
Anthropology,   Occasional Publications in
Anthropology. Ethnology Series no. 12.
OCLC # 65921

1006 _____.   Charters, Constitutions and By-laws
of the Indian Tribes of North America.
Part XII.   The Basin-Plateau Tribes (cont).
Greeley,   University of Northern Colorado,
Museum of Anthropology,   1971.
University of Northern Colorado,   Museum of
Anthropology,   Occasional Publications in
Anthropology. Ethnology Series no.   13.
OCLC # 65921

1007 _____.   Charters, Constitutions and By-laws
of the Indian Tribes of North America.
Part XIII.   The Midwestern Tribes.
Greeley,   University of Northern Colorado,
Museum of Anthropology,   1972.
University of Northern Colorado,   Museum of
Anthropology,   Occasional Publications in
Anthropology.   Ethnology Series no. 14.
OCLC # 65921

1008 _____.   Charters, Constitutions and By-laws
of the Indian Tribes of North America.
Part XIV.   Great Lakes Agency: Minnesota-
Michigan.   Greeley,   University of Northern
Colorado,   Museum of Anthropology,   1972.
University of Northern Colorado,   Museum of
Anthropology,   Occasional Publications in
Anthropology.   Ethnology Series no.   15.
OCLC # 65921

1009 _____.   Charters, Constitutions and By-Laws
of the Indian Tribes of North America.
Part XV.   The Northwest and Alaska (cont).
Greeley,   University of Northern Colorado,
Museum of Anthropology,   1972.
University of Northern Colorado,   Museum of
Anthropology,   Occasional Publications in

Anthropology. Ethnology Series no. 16.
OCLC # 65921

1010 _____. A Guide to Archaeological Sites in
Mexico. Greeley, University of Northern
Colorado, Museum of Anthropology, 1970.
University of Northern Colorado, Museum of
Anthropology, Misc. Series no. 20.
OCLC # 3800362

1011 _____. Indian House Types of Sonora, Mex-
ico. I. Yaqui, II. Mayo and an Indian
House Type of Sinaloa. Greeley, Colorado
State College, Museum of Anthropology,
1970.
University of Northern Colorado, Museum of
Anthropology, Misc. Series no. 14.
OCLC # 261473

1012 _____. An Indian Mexican House Type in
Sonora, Mexico. Greeley, Colorado State
College, Museum of Anthropology, 1969.
University of Northern Colorado, Museum of
Anthropology, Misc. Series no. 5.
OCLC # 134521

1013 _____. Land Cessions in Utah and Colorado
by the Ute Indians, 1861-1899. Greeley,
University of Northern Colorado, Museum of
Anthropology, 1970.
University of Northern Colorado, Museum of
Anthropology, Misc. Series no. 13.
OCLC # 2634007

1014 _____. Military Engagements Between United
States Troops and Plains Indians. Documen-
tary Inquiry by the U. S. Congress, Part
Ia; 1854-1867. Part Ib; 1854-1867 (cont).
Assembled/edited by George E. Fay.
Greeley, University of Northern Colorado,
Museum of Anthropology, 1972.
University of Northern Colorado, Museum of
Anthropology, Occasional Publications in
Anthropology. Ethnology Series no. 26.
OCLC # 815435

1015 _____. Military Engagements Between Unites
States Troops and Plains Indians. Part
III; Report of the Secretary of the Inte-
rior Regarding the Origin and Process of

Indian Hostilities on the Frontier. As-
sembled/edited by George E. Fay. Greeley,
University of Northern Colorado, Museum of
Anthropology, 1973.
University of Northern Colorado, Museum of
Anthropology, Occasional Publications in
Anthropology. Ethnology Series no. 28.
OCLC # 815435

1016   _____. Military Engagements Between United
States Troops and Plains Indians. Part II.
Report of the Secretary of War on the In-
quiry into the Sand Creek Massacre. Assem-
bled/edited by George E. Fay. Greeley,
University of Northern Colorado, Museum of
Anthropology, 1973.
University of Northern Colorado, Museum of
Anthropology, Occasional Publications in
Anthropology. Ethnology Series no. 27.
OCLC # 815435

1017   _____. Military Engagements Between United
States Troops and Plains Indians. Part IV;
1872-1890. Assembled/edited by George E.
Fay. Greeley, University of Northern
Colorado, Museum of Anthropology, 1973.
University of Northern Colorado, Museum of
Anthropology, Occasional Publications in
Anthropology. Ethnology Series no. 29.
OCLC # 815435

1018   _____. Military Engagements Between United
States Troops and Plains Indians. Part 6;
1878-1902. Greeley, University of North-
ern Colorado, Museum of Anthropology,
1980.
University of Northern Colorado, Museum of
Anthropology, Occasional Publications in
Anthropology. Ethnology Series no. 35.
OCLC # 8381575

1019   _____. Salvage Archaeology of an Indian
Mound in Ouachita County, Arkansas.
Greeley, Colorado State College, Museum
of Anthropology, 1968.
University of Northern Colorado, Museum of
Anthropology, Misc. Series no. 3.
OCLC # 3583

1020   _____. Treaties and Land Cessions Between

Bands of the Sioux and the United States of
America, 1805-1906. Assembled/edited by
George E. Fay. Greeley, University of
Northern Colorado, Museum of Anthropology,
1972.
University of Northern Colorado, Museum of
Anthropology, Occasional Publications in
Anthropology. Ethnology Series no. 24.
OCLC # 1735572

1021 _____. Treaties, Land Cessions and Other
U. S. Congressional Documents Relative to
American Indian Tribes. Treaties between
the Tribes of the Great Plains and the
United States of America: Cheyenne and
Arapaho, 1825-1900, etc. Greeley, Uni-
versity of Northern Colorado, Museum of
Anthropology, 1971.
University of Northern Colorado, Museum of
Anthropology, Occasional Publications in
Anthropology. Ethnology Series no. 22.
OCLC # 3263869

1022 _____. Zuni Indian Pueblo, New Mexico.
Part I: U. S. Congressional Documents,
1877-1967. Greeley, University of North-
ern Colorado, Museum of Anthropology,
1971.
University of Northern Colorado, Museum of
Anthropology, Occasional Publications in
Anthropology. Ethnology Series no. 20.
OCLC # 1676598

1023 _____. Zuni Indian Pueblo, New Mexico.
Part II. Pueblo Indian Agents' Reports,
and Related Historical Documents, 1849-
1914. Greeley, University of Northern
Colorado, Museum of Anthropology, 1971.
University of Northern Colorado, Museum of
Anthropology, Occasional Publications in
Anthropology no. 21. Ethnology Series.
OCLC # 1052401

_____. see also 3148, 3216-3219

1024 Featherstonhaugh, George William, 1780-
1866. Canoe Voyage up the Minnay Sotor;
with an Account of the Lead and Copper De-
posits in Wisconsin; of the Gold Region in
the Cherokee Country; and Sketches of Pop-

ular Manners. St. Paul, Minnesota
Historical Society, 1970.
Reprint of the 1847 ed., with an introd.
by William E. Lass.
OCLC # 140742.

1025 Federal Training Seminar for American Indian
      Women (1978: Dept. of Labor). Native
      American Women and Equal Opportunity: How
      to Get Ahead in the Federal Government.
      Washington, Dept. of Labor, Women's
      Bureau, Govt. Print. Off., 1979.
      OCLC # 5468334

1026 Feest, Christian. Native Arts of North
      America. New York, Oxford University
      Press, 1980.
      OCLC # 6251178

1027 Feister, Lois M. Linguistic Communications
      Between the Dutch and Indians in New
      Netherlands. In 2282, pp. 181-196.

1028 Fejes, Claire. Villagers, Athabaskan
      Indian Life Along the Yukon River. New
      York, Random House, 1981.
      OCLC # 7247720

1029 Feldman, Lawrence H. Archaeometric Species
      of Northwest Mesoamerica: Patterns of Nat-
      ural and Cultural Distribution. In 0231,
      pp. 225-239.

1030 _____. "Riverine Maya" The Torquegua and
      Other Chols of the Lower Montagua Valley.
      Columbia, Museum of Anthropology, Univer-
      sity of Missouri, 1975.
      Museum Briefs, v. 15
      OCLC # 1735138

      _____. see also 1607

1031 Feldman, Robert A. and Michael Edward
      Moseley. The Northern Andes. In 0098,
      pp. 139-177.

1032 Felstiner, John. Translating Neruda: The
      Way to Macchu Picchu. Stanford, CA.,
      Stanford University Press, 1980.
      Includes Alturas de Macchu Picchu in

English and Spanish.
OCLC # 7152250

1033 Fenton, William Nelson, 1908- . "Aborig-
      inally Yours" Jesse Cornplanter, Hah-
      Yonh-Wonh-Ish, The Snipe, Seneca, 1889-
      1957. In 0080, pp. 177-195.

1034 _____. The "Great Good Medicine". New York
      State Journal of Medicine, v. 79, Sept.
      1979, pp. 1603-1609.
      Reprint Copy

1035 _____. Long-Term Trends of Change Among the
      Iroquois. In 0078, pp. 30-35.

1036 _____. Problems in the Authentication of
      the League of the Iroquois. In 2282, pp.
      261-276.
      Paper presented at the 3rd Eastern Region-
      al Conference on the Native American at the
      State University College, New Paltz, NY.,
      1974.

1037 _____. The Science of Anthropology and the
      Iroquois Indians. New York State Archae-
      ological Association Bulletin no. 6,
      March 1956, pp. 10-14. Millwood, NY.,
      Kraus Reprint, 1976.
      Paper read to the WGY Science Forum, March
      2, 1955.

1038 _____. Structure, Continuity, and Change
      in the Process of Iroquois Treaty Making.
      In 1463, pp. 3-36.

1039 _____. Tonawanda Reservation, 1935: The
      Way it Was. In 1583, pp. 37-45.

      Ferenci, Andrea see 2417

1040 Ferguson, Brian. Warfare and Redistributive
      Exchange on the Northwest Coast. In 0796,
      pp. 133-147.

1041 Ferguson, Henry L. Archeological Explora-
      tion of Fishers Island, N. Y. New York,
      Museum of the American Indian, Heye Found-
      ation, 1935.
      Indian Notes and Monographs, v. 11, no.

1.
OCLC # 1823509

Ferguson, John P., *see* 1582

1042 Ferguson, Robert. An Overview of Southwestern Indian Culture. In 1282, pp. 37-41.

1043 Ferguson, William M. Maya Ruins of Mexico
in Color. Palenque, Uxmal, Kabah,
Sayil, Xlapak, Labna, Chichen Itza,
Coba Tulum. By ... and collaboration with
John Q. Royce; Color photos by William M.
Ferguson and John Q. Royce. 1st ed. Nor-
man, University of Oklahoma Press, 1977.
OCLC # 3241008

1045 Feurer, Hanny, The Acquisition of Mohawk:
Observations of First Language Development.
In 3050, pp. 119-130.

1046 Fiedler, Leslie A., The Demon of the Continent. In 2533, pp. 9-15.

1047 Finch, James K., Aboriginal Remains on Manhattan Island. In 3469, pp. 63-73.

1048 Findlow, Frank J. and Neil J. Goldberg.
Some Simple Measures for the Study of Prehistoric Political Organization. In 0796,
pp. 214-226.

Fine Arts Museum of San Francisco *see* 0135

1049 Finerty, John F. Their Music is Fitter for
Hell Than for Earth. In 1566, pp. 91-98.
Reprinted from Finerty, John F. War-Path
and Bivouac, or, the Conquest of the
Sioux, Chicago, M. A. Donahue & Co.,
1890, pp. 99-109.

1050 Finger, John R., 1939- . The Eastern Band
of Cherokees, 1819-1900. Knoxville, University of Tennessee Press, 1984.
OCLC # 9644210

1051 Finlayson, William David and Robert H.
Pihl. Some Implications for the Attribute
Analysis of Rim Shards from the Draper

Site, Pickering, Ontario. In 1585, pp.
113-131.

Finney, Fred A., 1954- . see 1091

1052 The First Americans: Origins, Affinities
and Adaptations. Edited by William S.
Laughlin and Albert B. Harper. New York,
G. Fischer, 1979.
Proceedings of a conference held at the
European Conference Center of the Wenner-
Gren Foundation for Anthropological Re-
search, Burg-Wartenstein, Austria, Au-
gust 21-30, 1976.
OCLC # 5310329

1053 First People, First Voices. Edited by Penny
Petrone. Toronto, Buffalo, University of
Toronto Press, 1983.
OCLC # 10119863

1054 Firth, Raymond William, 1901- . Bronislaw
Malenowski. In 3139, pp. 101-139.

1055 Fish, Joseph, 1706-1781. Old Light on Separate Ways: The Narragansett Diary of Joseph Fish, 1765-1776. William S. Simmons
and Cheryl L. Simmons, editors. Hanover,
NH., University of New England Press,
1982.
OCLC # 8451958

1056 Fish, Louise. Figurines with Up-tilted
Noses from Colima, Mexico. In 0331, pp.
212-214.

Fisher, Howard J. see 3453

1057 Fisher, Robin, 1946- . Contact and
Conflict: Indian-European Relations in
British Columbia, 1774-1890. Vancouver,
University of British Columbia Press,
1977.
OCLC # 2925629

1058 Fitting, James Edward. The Kaminaljuyu Test
Trenches: Description and Artifact Yield.
In 2825, pp. 309-589.

1059 _____. Patterns of Acculturation at the

Straits of Mackinac. In 0710, pp. 321-334.

1060 Fitzgibbons, P. T. Lithic Artifacts from Meadowcroft Rockshelter and the Cross Creek Drainage. In 2111, pp. 91-111.

1061 Fitzhugh, William W., 1934- . Environmental Factors in the Evolution of Dorset Culture: A Marginal Proposal for Hudson Bay. In 0908, pp. 139-149.

1062 _____. Paleoeskimo Occupations of the Labrador Coast. In 0908, pp. 103-118.

1063 _____. Inua; Spirit World of the Bering Sea Eskimo. ... and Susan A, Kaplan with contributions by Henry B. Collins. Washington, Published for National Museum of Natural History by the Smithsonian Institution Press, 1982.
Prepared in conjunction with an exhibit of the Edward William Nelson Bering Sea Eskimo ethnology collection of the National Museum of Natural History.
OCLC # 8387734

Five Civilized Tribes see 3192

1063.5 Fixico, Donald Lee, 1951- . Modernization and the Native American Middle Class, 1945-1970. In 2831.5, pp. 75-87.

1064 _____. Twentieth Century Federal Indian Policy. In 2789, pp. 123-161.

1065 Fladmark, Knut, R. The Feasibility of the Northwest Coast as a Migration Route for Early Man. In 0902, pp. 119-128.

1066 _____. Times and Places: Environmental Correlates of Mid-to-Late Wisconsinan Human Population Expansion in North America. In 0903, pp. 13-41.

1067 Flanagan, Thomas, 1944- . Louis Riel and Aboriginal Rights. In 0137, pp. 247-262.

1068 Flannery, Kent V. and Joyce Marcus. Evolu-

149   FLANNERY

tion of the Public Building in Formative
Oaxaca. In 0710, pp. 205-221.

1069 _____. The Preceramic and Formative of the
Valley of Oaxaca. In 0122, pp. 48-93.

_____. see also 0594

1070 Flannery, Regina. An Analysis of Coastal
Algonquian Culture. New York, AMS Press,
1983.
Reprint . Originally pub. Washington,
D. C., Catholic University of America,
1939. Anthropological Series, Catholic
University of America, no. 7.
OCLC # 9853743

1071 Flasete, Richard. American Indians: Still
a Stereotype to Many Children. In 1456,
pp. 3-6.
Reprinted from The New York Times, Sept.
27, 1974.

1072 Fleisher, P. Jay (Penrod Jay(, 1937- .
Deglacial Chronology of the Oneonta, New
York Area. In 3519, pp. 41-50.

Fleming, Elizabeth, d. 1756. see 1073

1073 Fleming, William. A Narrative of Suffering
and Deliverance. Fleming, NY., Garland
Pub., 1978.
Garland Library of narratives of North
American Indian captivities, v. 8. Re-
print of the 1756 ed. printed and sold by
Green and Russell, Boston, under title A
Narrative of the Sufferings and Surprizing
Deliverances of William and Elizabeth Flem-
ing. Issued with the reprint of the 1758
ed. of Maylem, J. Gallic Perfidy. The
Reprint of the 1758 ed. of Eastburn, R. A
Faithful Narrative. The reprints of the
1759 ed. of LeRoy, M. Die Erzehlungen von
Maria LeRoy und Barbara Leininger. 1760
ed. of Brown, T. A Plain Narrative.
1760 ed. of Hammon, B. A Narrative of the
sufferings and deliverance of Briton
Hammon. 1760 ed. of Lowry, J. A.
Journal of the captivity of Jean Lowry.
1762 ed. of Urssenbacher, A. Erzehlung

FLETCHER   150

        eines unter den Indianern gewesener
        Gefangenen..
        OCLC # 3842906

1074   Fletcher, John Gould, 1886-1950. John
       Smith - also Pocahontas. New York,
       Brentano's; New York, Kraus Reprint Co.,
       1972.
       OCLC # 526973

       Flint, Timothy, 1780-1840. see 2431

1075   Flores Ochoa, Jorge A., Pastoralists of the
       Andes: The Alpaca Herders of Paratia.
       Ralph Bolton, Trans., Philadelphia,
       Institute for the Study of Human Issues,
       1979.
       Translation of Los Pastores de Paratia.
       OCLC # 4549421

1076   Flowers, Nancy M. Seasonable Factors in
       Subsistence, Nutrition, and Child Growth
       in a Central Brazilian Indian Community.
       In 0023, pp. 357-390.

       Fodor, Eugere see 1440

1077   Fogelson, Raymond D. An Analysis of Chero-
       kee Sorcery and Witchcraft. In 1099, pp.
       113-131.

1078   _____. The Cherokee, a Critical Biblio-
       graphy. Bloomington: Published for the
       Newberry Library by Indiana University
       Press, 1978.
       Bibliographical Series
       OCLC # 4004973

1079   _____, and Amelia R. Bell. Cherokee Booger
       Mask Tradition. In 2502, pp. 48-69.

1080   _____. Cherokee Notions of Power. In
       0111, pp. 185-194.

       _____. see also 0111

       Folk, Karen R. see 3484

       Folsom, James K., 1942- . see 2919

1081   Fontana, Bernard L. *Tarahumara Where Night
       is the Day of the Moon*. with photos by
       John P. Schaefer. 1st ed., Flagstaff,
       AZ., Northland Press, 1979.
       OCLC # 4902559

1082   Fools Crow, Frank, 1890 or 1891- . *Fools
       Crow, Recorded by Thomas E. Mails,
       Assisted by Dallas Chief Eagle*. Garden
       City, NY., Doubleday, 1979.
       OCLC # 4884828

1082.5 Forbes, Bruce David. *John Jasper Methvin:
       Methodist "Missionary to the Western
       Tribes*. In 0785.5, pp. 41-73.

1082.7 Forbes, Jack, 1941- . *Traditional Nat-
       ive American Philosophy and Multicultural
       Education*. In 2238.5, pp. 3-13.

1083   Forbes, Jack D. *The Indians in America's
       Past*. Englewood Cliffs, NJ., Prentice
       Hall, 1964.
       A Spectrum Book
       OCLC # 419760

1084   _____. *Native Americans and Nixon: Presi-
       dential Politics and Minority Self-deter-
       mination, 1969-1972*. Los Angeles, Amer-
       ican Indian Studies Center, UCLA, 1981.
       OCLC # 8262716

       Ford, Alan *see* 0858

1085   Ford, James Alfred, 1911-1968. *Crooks
       Site, a Marksville Period Burial Mound in
       La Salle Parish, Louisiana*. ... and Gor-
       don Willey; partially based on field re-
       ports by William T. Mulloy and Arden King.
       Millwood, NY., Kraus Reprint, 1975,
       c1940.
       Reprint of the ed. published by Dept. of
       Conservation, Louisiana Geological Survey,
       New Orleans, which was issued as no. 3 of
       the Department's Anthropological study.
       OCLC # 1273528

1086   Ford, Richard I. *Communication networks and
       Information Hierarchies in Native American*

Folk Medicine: Tewa Pueblos, New Mexico.
In 3180, pp. 143-157.

1087 _____. Prehistoric Phytogeography of Economic Plants in Latin America. In 2521,
pp. 175-183.

1088 Foreman, Carolyn Thomas. Lewis Francis
Hadley: "The Long-Haired Sign Talker". In
0008, pp. 157-174.
Reprinted from Chronicles of Oklahoma v.
27, no. 1, 1949, pp. 41-55.

Forman, W. (Werner) see 2910

1089 Forsino, Falken C. R. B., 1941- . Cos-
mography at the Caracol, Chichen Itza,
Yucatan, Mexico. Ann Arbor, MI.,
University Microfilms International, 1984.
Microfilm - PhD Thesis - University of
Oregon
OCLC # 11558873

1090 Forsium, Henrick The Effects of Civilization on the Eyes of the Eskimos. In 1875,
pp. 259-264.

1091 Fortier, Andrew C., 1947- . The Mund Site
(11-S-435). ... and Fred A. Finney and
Richard B. Lacampagne; with contributions
by Sissel Johannessen and Paula G. Cross.
Urbana, Published for the Illinois Dept.
of Transportation by the University of
Illinois Press, 1983.
American Bottom Archaeology v. 5.
OCLC # 9853479

1092 _____. Settlement and Subsistence at the
Go-Kart North Site: A Late Archaic Titter-
ington Occupation in the American Bottom,
Illinois. In 0124, pp. 243-260.

_____. see also 2007

1093 Foster, Laurence, 1903-1969. Negro-Indian
Relationships in the Southeast. New York,
AMS Press, 1978.
Originally presented as the author's
thesis, University of Pennsylvania, 1931,
reprint of the 1935 ed. published by the

author, Philadelphia.
OCLC # 4137423

1094 Foster, Michael K.   Another Look at the
      Function of Wampum in Iroquois-White
      Councils.   In 1463,   pp.   99-114.

1095 _____. From the Earth to Beyond the Sky:
      An Ethnographic Approach to Four Longhouse
      Speech Events.   Ottawa,   National Museum of
      Canada,   1974.
      Canadian Ethnology Service paper no.   20.
      Mercury Series.
      OCLC # 1584535

1096 _____. One Who Spoke First at Iroquois-
      White Councils: An Exercise in the Methods
      of Upstreaming.   In 0979,   pp.   183-207.

      _____. see also 0979

1097 Foulks, Edward F.   The Arctic Hysterias of
      the North Alaskian Eskimo.   Washington, D.
      C.,   American Anthropological Association,
      1972.
      Anthropological Studies no.   10.
      OCLC # 1374949

1098 Foundations of Northeast Archaeology.   Edited
      by Dean R.   Snow.   New York,   Academic
      Press,   1981.
      Studies in Archaeology.   Based on papers
      delivered at a conference held Feb.   29-
      Mar.   1,   1980,   at the State University of
      New York at Albany.
      OCLC # 7947823

1099 Four Centuries of Southern Indians.   Charles
      M.   Hudson,   editor.   Athens,   University
      of Georgia Press,   1975.
      All the papers in this volume were origin-
      ally presented at the 19th annual meeting
      of the American Society for Ethnohis-tory
      held in Athens,   GA.,   Oct.   13-16,   1971.
      Essays in this collection are also listed
      individually and refer to this citation.
      OCLC # 1365856

1100 Fowler, Catherine S.   Sarah Winnemucca,

Northern Paiute, 1884-1891. In 0080, pp. 33-42.

1101 Fowler, Loretta, 1944- . Arapaho Politics, 1851-1978: Symbols in Crisis of Authority. Foreword by Fred Eggan. Lincoln, University of Nebraska Press, 1982.
OCLC # 7554180

1102 _____. Oral Historian or Ethnologist?: The Career of Bill Shakespeare, Northern Arapaho, 1901-1975. In 0080, pp. 227-240.

1103 Fowler, Melvin L. Cahokia and the American Bottom: Settlement Archaeology. In 2172, pp. 455-478.

1104 _____. The Temple Town Community: Cahokia and Amalucan Compared. In 0905, pp. 391-400.

1105 Fox, Nancy. Potsui'i Incised Cylindrical Vessels. In 0622, pp. 88-97.

1106 Fox, Robin. Totem and Taboo Reconsidered. In 3547 of 1977 volume, pp. 161-177.

1107 Francis, Convers, 1795-1863. Life of John Eliot, the Apostle to the Indians. Garrett, 1969.
Library of American Biography, v. 5. Reprint of the 1854 ed. pub. by Harper, New York.
OCLC # 1012162

1108 Francis, Peter. Some Thoughts on Glass Beadmaking. In 1204, pp. 193-202.

1109 Francisco, Alice Enderton, 1933- . An Archeological Sequence from Carchi, Ecuador. Ann Arbor, MI., University Microfilms International, 1976.
Microfilm - PhD Thesis - University of California; Berkeley
OCLC # 4100810

1110 Franks, Kenny Arthur, 1945- . Stand Watie and the Among of the Cherokee Nation. Memphis, Memphis State University Press,

1979.
OCLC # 5243586

1111 Franz Boas, 1858-1942. By A. L. Kroeber
and Ruth Benedict, Murray B. Emaneau,
Melville J. Herskovits, Gladys A. Reich-
ard and J. Alden Mason. New York, Kraus
Reprint, 1969.
Memoirs of the American Anthropological
Association no. 10. Supplement to Ameri-
can Anthropologist, v. 45, no. 3, pt.
2, 1943.
OCLC # 1728219

1112 Frazier, Gregory W., 1947- . The American
Indian Index: A Directory of Indian Coun-
try, USA. Edited by Randolph J. Punley.
Denver, CO., Arrowstar Pub., 1985.
OCLC # 12669318

       Frederickson, David A. (David Allen) see
       2201

       Freeman, Donald B. see 2593

1113 French, Mansfield Joseph, 1872- . Samuel
de Champlain's Incursion Against the Onondaga Nation. Ann Arbor, Edwards Bros.,
1949.
OCLC # 3572654

1114 French, Philip. The Indian in the Western
Movie. In 2533, pp. 98-105.

       French, Thomas see 3449

1115 French Vikki. Subjective Judgement Analysis
of Maya Pottery. University of Northern
Colorado, Museum of Anthropology, Occa-
sional Publications in Anthropology.
Archaeological Series no. 23.
OCLC # 1541399

       Friar, Natashe A. see 1116

1116 Friar, Ralph E. and Natasha A. Friar.
White Man Speaks With Split Tongue, Forked
Tongue, Tongue of Snake. In 2533, pp.
92-97.

1117   Fried,   Jacob.   Two Orders of Authority and
       Power in Tarahumara Society.   In 0111,   pp.
       263-269.

       Fried,   Morton Herbert,   1923- .   see
       0796

1118   Friede,   Juan.   Las Casas and Indigenism in
       the Sixteenth Century.   In 0193,   pp.   127-
       234.

       Friedman,   Janet   see   0725

1119   Friends Society of (Hicksite).   Joint Commit-
       tee on Indian Affairs.   Case of the Seneca
       Indians of the State of New York.   Printed
       for the information of the Society of
       Friends (Hicksite),   1840;   also including,
       a further illustration of the case of the
       Seneca Indians in the State of New York,
       1841, and a brief statement of the rights
       of the Seneca Indians in the State of New
       York to their lands in that State,   1872.
       Stanfordville,   NY.,   E.   M.   Coleman,
       1979.
       American Indian at Law Series.   Reprint of
       the 3 works,   the first 2 printed by Mer-
       rihew and Thompson,   Philadelphia and the
       third printed by W.   H.   Pile.
       OCLC # 5564787

1120   Friesen,   Gerald.   The Canadian Prairies: A
       History.   Lincoln,   University of Nebraska
       Press,   1984.
       OCLC # 11403877

1121   Frisbie,   Charlotte J.   Fieldwork as a "Sin-
       gle Parent":   To Be or Not to Be Accompa-
       nied by a Child.   In 0622,   pp.   98-119.

1122   _____.   Music and Dance Research of South-
       Western United States Indians: Past
       Trends,   Present Activities,   and
       Suggestions for Future Research.   Detroit,
       Information Coordinators,   1977.
       Detroit Studies in Music Bibliography,   no.
       36.
       OCLC # 2995340

1123 _____. Ritual Drama in the Navaho House
        Blessing Ceremony. In 2931, pp. 161-198.

        _____. see also 2931

1124 Frisbie, Theodore R. High Status Burials in
        the Greater Southwest: An Interpretative
        Synthesis. In 0014, pp. 202-227.

1125 _____. Hishi as Money in the Puebloan
        Southwest. In 0622, pp. 120-142.

        _____. see also 0622

1126 Frison, George C. The Agate Basin Site: A
        Record of the Paleoindian Occupation of the
        Northwest High Plains. ... and Dennis J.
        Stanford, New York, Academic Press,
        1982.
        OCLC # 8346187

1127 _____. The Casper Site: A Hell Gap Bison
        Kill on the High Plains. New York, Aca-
        demic Press, 1974.
        Studies in Archaeology
        OCLC # 1235666

1128 _____. The Chronology of Paleo-Indian and
        Althermal Cultures in the Big Horn Basin,
        Wyoming. In 0710, pp. 147-173.

1129 _____. Folsom Tools and Technology at the
        Hanson Site, Wyoming. ... Bruce A. Brad-
        ley, Albuquerque, University of New Mex-
        ico Press, 1980.
        OCLC # 5939984

1130 _____. Prehistoric Hunters of the High
        Plains. New York, Academic Press, 1978.
        New World Archaeological Record
        OCLC # 3396613

1131 _____. The Western Plains and Mountain
        Region. In 0901, pp. 109-124.

1132 Fritz, Henry Eugene. The Board of Indian
        Commissioners and Ethnocentric Reform,
        1878-1893. In 2265, pp. 57-78.

        Fritz, John M see 3540

Fritz, Margaret C. <u>see</u> 3540

Frohlich, Bruno <u>see</u> 1842

1133 <u>Frontier Adaptations in Lower Central Amer-
      ica.</u> Essays originally presented at the
      9th annual meeting of the Southern Anthro-
      pological Society in April 1974. Philadel-
      phia, Institute for the Study of Human
      Issues, inc., 1976.
      Essays in this collection are also listed
      individually and refer to this citation.
      OCLC # 2346164

1134 Fronval, George. <u>Indian Signs and Signals</u>.
      New York, Sterling Pub. Co., 1978.
      Translation of <u>Les Signes Mysterieux des
      Peaux-Rouhes</u>, Paris, 1976.
      OCLC # 4597328

1135 Frost, Lawrence A. <u>Custer Legends</u>. Bowling
      Green, Ohio, Bowling Green University
      Popular Press, 1981.
      OCLC # 7674095

      _____. <u>see also</u> 0976

1136 Fry, G. F. <u>Prehistoric Diet and Parasites
      in the Desert West of North America</u>. In
      0905, pp. 325-339.

1137 Fryman, R. F. <u>Prehistoric Settlement Pat-
      terns the Cross Creek Drainage</u>. In 2111,
      pp. 53-68.

1138 Funk, Robert E. <u>Adaptation Continuity and
      Change in Upper Susquehanna Prehistory</u>.
      ... and Bruce E. Rippeteau. George's
      Mills, NH., Man in the Northeast, 1977.
      Occasional Publications in Northeastern
      Anthropology, no. 3
      OCLC # 3483745

1139 _____. <u>Archeological Investigations at the
      Dennis Site Albany County, N. Y.</u> New
      York State Archaeological Association Bul-
      letin no. 32, Nov. 1964, pp. 18-21.
      Millwood, NY., Kraus Reprint, 1976.

1140 _____. The Burnt Hills Phase: Regional
      Middle Woodland at Lake George, N. Y.
      New York State Archaeological Association
      Bulletin no. 37, July 1966, pp. 1-20.
      Millwood, NY., Kraus Reprint, 1976.

1141 _____. Earliest Aboriginal Occupations of
      New York State. In 2519, pp. 32-40.

1142 _____. Early to Middle Archaic Occupations
      in Upstate New York. In 0712, pp. 21-29.

1143 _____. Excavations of Fish Club Cave
      (COX6), Albany, Co., N. Y. New York
      State Archaeological Association Bulletin
      no. 30, March 1964, pp. 23-25. Mill-
      wood, NY., Kraus Reprint, 1976.

1144 _____. Fluted Point Discovery in Orange
      County Cave. New York State Archaeological
      Association Bulletin no. 34, July 1965,
      pp. 2-6. Millwood, NY., Kraus Reprint,
      1976.

1145 _____. Hudson Valley Prehistory: Current
      Status, Problems, Prospects. In 2282,
      pp. 1-87.
      This article has an extensive bibliography

1146 _____. The Kings Road Site: A Recently
      Discovered Paleo-Indian Manifestation in
      Green County, N. Y. New York State
      Archaeological Association Bulletin no.
      45, March 1969, pp. 1-23. Millwood,
      NY., Kraus Reprint, 1976.

1147 _____. The Knapp Site: A Small Multicom-
      ponent Camp on Lake George, N. Y. New
      York State Archeological Association Bul-
      letin no. 41, Nov., 1967, pp. 1-10.
      Millwood, NY., Kraus Reprint, 1976.

1148 _____. A New Middle Woodland Complex in
      Eastern New York. New York State Ar-
      chaeological Association Bulletin no. 44,
      Nov. 1968, pp. 1-7. Millwood, NY.,
      Kraus Reprint, 1976.
      Paper presented at the annual meeting,
      April 20, 1968.

1149 _____. The Northeastern United States. In
       0097, pp. 303-371.

1150 _____. Preliminary Report of Excavations at
       Taghkanick Rock Shelter. New York State
       Archaeological Association Bulletin no.
       25, July 1962, pp. 9-12. Millwood,
       NY., Kraus Reprint, 1976.
       Paper presented at the annual meeting,
       April 7, 1962.

1151 _____. The Sylvan Lake Rock Shelter (CLO2)
       and its Contributions to Knowledge of the
       Archaic Stage in Eastern New York: A Brief
       Report. New York State Archaeological As-
       sociation Bulletin no. 33, March 1965,
       pp. 2-12. Millwood, NY., Kraus Reprint,
       1976.

       _____. see also 0712

1152 Furst, Peter T. North American Indian Art.
       ... and Jill L. Furst. New York, Riz-
       zoli, 1982.
       An Artpress Book
       OCLC # 8627614

1153 _____. Some Problems in the Interpretation
       of West Mexican Tomb Art. In 0231, pp.
       32-146.

1154 Fynn, Arthur John. The American Indian as a
       Product of Environment, With Special Ref-
       erence to the Pueblos. Boston, Little,
       Brown, 1908.
       OCLC # 1019841

1154.5 Gabriel, Ralph Henry, 1890- . Elias
       Boudinot: Cherokee and his America.
       Norman, University of Oklahoma Press,
       1941.
       Civilization of the American Indian Series,
       no. 20.
       OCLC # 607468

1155 Gale, George, 1816-1868. Upper Mississip-
       pi: Or, Historical Sketches of the Mound
       Builders, The Indian Tribes and the Pro-
       gress of Civilization in the North-west
       from A. D. 1600 to the Present Time. New

York,   Kraus Reprint Co.,   1975,   c1867.
Reprint of the ed.   published by Clarke,
Chicago.
OCLC # 1230737

Gallagher,   Marsha V.   see   1676

1156   Gallagher,   Patrick Francis,   1930- .   La
Pit'ia: An Archaeological Series in the
Northwestern Venezuela.   New Haven,   Yale
University Press,   1976.
Yale University Pubs.   in Anthropology no.
76.
OCLC # 2884378

1157   Gallatin,   Albert,   1761-1849.   A Synopsis of
the Indian Tribes Within the United States
East of the Rocky Mountains,   and in the
British and Russian Possessions in North
America.   New York,   AMS Press,   1973.
Originally published in Archaeological
Americana,   Transactions and Collections of
the American Antiquarian Society,   v.   2,
1836
OCLC # 489504

1157.2   Gallerito,   Cecelia.   Indian Health,   Fed-
erally or Tribally Determined?   Health Recommendations of the American Indian Policy Review Commission.   In 2961.5,   pp.
29-43.

1157.5   Galli,   Marcia J.   A Transportable Model
for Cultural Awareness In-Service Training:
Rationale and Overview.   In 2238.5,   pp.
145-150.

Galloway,   Patricia Kay   see   1830

Galvan,   L.   Javier   see   2791

Galvin,   John,   1963-   see   3187

1158   Gannett,   William B.,   1952- .   The American
Invasion of Texas,   1820-1845:   Patterns of
Conflict Between Settlers and Indians.   Ann
Arbor,   MI.,   University Microfilms Inter-
national,   1984.
Microfilm - PhD Thesis - Cornell University
OCLC # 12169648

Ganong,   William Francis,   1864-1941.   <u>see</u>
1858

1159   Garber,   Clark M.   (Clark McKinley),   1891- .
       <u>Stories and Legends of the Bering Strait</u>
       <u>Eskimos</u>.   New York,   AMS Press,   1975.
       Reprint of 1940 ed.,   Christopher Pub.
       House,   Boston.
       OCLC # 1501901

1160   Garcia,   Martha W.   <u>Greater Voice,   Greater</u>
       <u>Share: A Study of Role Changes of Cheyenne</u>
       <u>and Navajo Women</u>.   Ann Arbor,   MI.,   Univer-
       sity Microfilms International,   1984.
       Microfilm - MA Thesis - University of
       Louisville

1161   Garfield,   Viola Edmundson,   1899- .   <u>Possi-</u>
       <u>bilities of Genetic Relationships in North-</u>
       <u>ern Pacific Moiety Structures</u>.   In 0076,
       pp.   58-61.

1162   Garland,   Hamlin,   1860-1940.   <u>Hamlin Gar-</u>
       <u>land's Observations on the American Indian,</u>
       <u>1895-1905</u>.   Compiled and edited by Lonnie
       E.   Underhill and Daniel F.   Littlefield.
       Tucson,   University of Arizona Press,
       1976.
       OCLC # 2609502

1163   Garmhausen,   Winona M.   <u>The Institute of</u>
       <u>American Indian Arts 1962-1978:   With His-</u>
       <u>torical Background 1890-1962</u>.   Ann Arbor,
       MI.,   University Microfilms International,
       1982.
       Microfilm - PhD Thesis - University of New
       Mexico
       OCLC # 11963307

1164   Garrad,   Charles.   <u>Petun Pottery</u>.   In 1585,
       pp.   105-111.

1165   Garth,   Thomas R.   <u>Emphasis on Industrious-</u>
       <u>ness Among the Atsugewi</u>.   In 2276,   pp.
       337-354.

1166   Gasaway,   Laura.   <u>American Indian Legal Mat-</u>
       <u>erials: A Union List</u>.   Compiled by ...
       James L.   Hoover,   Dorothy M.   Warden;

foreword by Rennard Strickland.   Stanford-
ville, ¯NY., E. M. Coleman, 1980.
American Indian at Law Series
OCLC # 5492598

1167   Gasparini, Graziano. Inca Architecture and
Luise Margolies. Trans. by Patricia J.
Lynn.   Bloomington, Indiana University
Press, 1980.
Translation of Arquitectura Inka
OCLC # 5670419

1168   Gatschet, Albert Samuel, 1832-1907. Klamath Indians of Southwestern Oregon. Washington, Govt. Print. Off., 1890.
Contributions to North American Ethnology,
v. 2, part I -II. Dept. of the Interior
U.S. Geographical and Geological Survey of
the Rocky Mountain Region. Part I. Letter
of transmittal, ethnographic sketch,
texts, grammar. Part II. Dictionary:
Klamath-English; English-Klamath
OCLC # 1738984

————. see also 1432

Gay, Bunker, 1735-1815 see 1513

1169   Gay, Carlo T. E. Chalcacingo. Drawings by
Frances Pratt. Portland, OR., Interna-
tional Scholarly Book Service Inc., 1972.
American rock paintings and petroglyphs.
Monographs and documentations
OCLC # 333856

1170   Gay, E. Jane, 1830-1919. With the Nez
Perces: Alice Fletcher in the Field,
1889-92. Edited, with an introd. by
Frederick E. Hoxie and Joan T. Mark.
Lincoln, University of Nebraska Press,
1981.
OCLC # 6789956

1171   Gayton, Anna H. Culture-Environment Integration: External References in Yokuts
Life. In 2276, pp. 79-98.

1172   Gearing, Fred O., 1922- . Priests and
Warriors: Social Structure for Cherokee
Politics in the 18th Century. Millwood,

NY., Kraus Reprint, 1974.
Memoirs of the American Anthropological
Association no. 93. Supplement to _Amer-
ican Anthropologist_ v. 64, no. 5, pt.
2, 1962.
OCLC # 1303687

1173 Gedicks, Al. _Resource Wars in Chippewa
      Country_. In 2274, pp. 175-193.

1174 Geier, Philip Otto. _A Peculiar Status-
      Microform: A History of Oneida Indian
      Treaties and Claims: Jurisdictional Con-
      flict Within the American Government,
      1775-1920_. Microfilm of transcript. Ann
      Arbor, MI., University Microfilms Inter-
      national, 1980.
      OCLC # 8117405

1175 Geiogamak, Hanay, 1945- . _New Native
      American Drama: Three Plays_. Introd. by
      Jeffrey Huntsman. Norman, University of
      Oklahoma Press, 1980.
      OCLC # 5892185

1176 _General Custer and the Battle of the Washita:
      The Federal View_. Edited by John M. Car-
      roll; introd. by Georg W. Schneider-
      Wettengel. Bryan, TX., Guidon Press,
      1978.
      Custeriana Series
      OCLC # 4762209

1177 Geogakas, Dan. _They Have Not Spoken: Amer-
      ican Indians in Film_. In 2533, pp. 134-
      142.

      Geological Survey (U. S.) _see_ 1953

      George, Dan _see_ 2226

      Getches, David H. _see_ 2263

      Gibbins, Roger, 1947- . _see_ 2492

1178 Gibbs, Sharon L. _Mesoamerican Calendrics as
      Evidence of Astronomical Activity_. In
      2270, pp. 21-35.

1179 Gibson, Arrell Morgan. _The American Indian:_

Prehistory to the Present. Lexington,
MA., D. C. Health, 1980.
OCLC # 5940087.

Gibson, Charles, 1920- . see 0144

1180   Gidley, M. (Mick). Kopet, a Documentary
Narrative of Chief Joseph's Last Years.
Seattle, University of Washington Press,
1981.
OCLC # 7551711

1181   _____. With One Sky Above Us: Life on an
Indian Reservation at the Turn of the Cen-
tury. Photos by Edward H. Latham, New
York, Putman, 1979.
OCLC # 5589018

Giese, William Frederick, 1864- . see
0464

1182   Giffin, James B. Eastern United States. In
0577, pp. 51-70.

Gifford, Carol A. see 1185

1183   Gifford, James C. Ancient Maya Pottery - 2:
A Second Folio of Maya Pottery from the
Site of Barton Ramie in British Honduras
(Belize). ... and Muriel Kirkpatrick;
color illus. by Muriel Kirkpatrick.
Philadelphia: Order from Kirkpatrick,
Laboratory of Anthropology, Temple Univer-
sity, 1975.
OCLC # 1912983

1184   _____. Archaeological Exploration in Caves
of the Point of Pines Region. Tucson,
University of Arizona Press, 1980.
Anthropological Papers of the University of
Arizona, no. 36. Contributions to Point
of Pines Archaeology, no. 27.
OCLC # 5101901

1185   _____. Gray Corrugated Pottery from Awatovi
and Other Jeddito Sites in Northeastern
Arizona. ... and Watson Smith, with the
assistance of Carol A. Gifford, Muriel
Kirkpatrick and Robert O'Haire, Compiled
by Carol A. Grifford. Cambridge, MA.,

Peabody Museum of Archaeology and Ethnology, Harvard University, 1978.
Papers of the Peabody Museum of Archaeology
and Ethnology, Harvard University, v.
69. Reports of the Awatovi Expedition,
no. 10.
OCLC # 4172848

1186 _____. Prehistoric Pottery Analysis and
the Ceramics of Barton Ramie in the Belize
Valley; with special sections or assist-
ance by Robert J. Sharer. Compiled by
Carol A. Gifford, illus. by Muriel Kirk-
patrick and Michael Nicolazoo. Cambridge,
MA., Peabody Museum of Archaeology and
Ethnology, Harvard University, 1976.
Memoirs of the Peabody Museum of Archae-
ology and Ethnology, v. 18.
OCLC # 2512901

1187 Gilbert, B. Miles. The Plains Setting. In
0113, pp. 8-15.

1188 Gilbert, Robert I. Applications of Trace
Element Research to Problems in Archaeology. In 0270, pp. 85-100.

1189 Gilbert, William Harlen, 1904- . The
Eastern Cherokee. New York, AMS Press,
1978.
Originally presented as the author's
thesis, University of Chicago, 1934.
Reprint of the 1943 ed. pub. by Smithsonian Institution, Washington, which was
issued as no. 23 of Smithsonian Institution, Bureau of American Ethnology, Anthropological Papers in 133 of its Bulletin.
OCLC # 4196110

1190 Gill, George W. Toltec-period Burial Customs Within the Marismas Nacionales of
Western Mexico. In 0231, pp. 83-105.

1191 Gill, Sam D., 1943- . Native American
Religions: An Introduction. Belmont,
CA., Wadsworth Pub. Co., 1982.
Religious Life of Man Series
OCLC # 7203563

1192   _____. Native American Traditions: Sources
        and Interpretations. Belmont,   CA.,   Wads-
        worth Pub. Co., 1983.
        The Religious Life of Man Series
        OCLC # 8931505

1193   _____. Sacred Words: A Study of Navaho
        Religion and Prayer. Westport, CT.,
        Greenwood Press, 1981.
        Contributions in Intercultural and
        Comparative Studies, v. 4.
        OCLC # 6142467

1194   _____. The Shadow of a Vision Yonder. In
        2818, pp. 44-57.

1195   Gillespie, Susan Dale, 1952- . Aztec Pre-
        history as Postconquest Dialogue: A Struc-
        tural Analysis of the Royal Dynasty of
        Tenochtitlan. Ann Arbor, MI., University
        Microfilms International, 1983.
        Microfilm - PhD Thesis - University of
        Illinois at Urbana-Champaign
        OCLC # 10287605

1196   Gillespie, William B. The Environment of
        the Chaco Anasazis. In 2289, pp. 37-44.

        _____. see also 2504

1197   Gillman, Henry, 1833-1915. Certain Char-
        acteristics Pertaining to Ancient Man in
        Michigan. In Annual Report to the Board of
        Regents of the Smithsonian Institution,
        Govt. Print. Off., 1876, pp. 234-245.

1198   Gillmor, Frances, 1903- . Symbolic Re-
        presentation in Mexican Combat Plays. In
        2502, pp. 101-110.

1199   Gilmore, Melvin Randolph, 1868-1940. Uses
        of Plants by the Indians of the Missouri
        River Region. Foreword by Hugh Cutler.
        Lincoln, University of Nebraska Press,
        1977.
        A Bison Book. Reprint of the 1919 ed.
        which was reprinted from the 33rd annual
        report of the Bureau of American Ethnology
        OCLC # 3168014

1200   Gilstrap,   Roger.   Algonquin Dialect Rela-
       tionships in Northwestern Quebec.   Ottawa,
       National Museum of Canada,   1978.
       Canadian Ethnology Service,   Paper 44.
       Mercury Series
       OCLC # 5291174

1200.5 Gimenez Fernandez,   Manuel.   Fray Bartolomé
       de las Casas: A Biographical Sketch.   In
       0193,   pp.   67-125.
       This essay has an extensive bibliography

1201   Gingerich,   Willard.   Critical Models for the
       Study of Indigenous Literature: The Case
       of Nahuatl.   In 2904,   pp.   112-125.

1202   Glamm,   A.   C.   The Cain Mound (CTG 5-2),
       Erie County, N. Y.   New York State Archae-
       ological Association Bulletin 9,   March
       1957,   pp.   8-10.   Millwood,   NY.,   Kraus
       Reprint,   1976.

1203   Glasbrenner,   Kimberly.   American Indian Med-
       icine Aims to Add Physicians,   Improve
       Health.   JAMA,   v.   254,   no.   14,   Oct.
       11,   1985,   pp.   1871-1878.

1203.5 Glass,   Anthony,   ca.1773-1819?   Journal of
       an Indian Trader: Anthony Glass and the
       Texas Trading Frontier,   1790-1810.   Edited
       by Dan L.   Flores.   College Station,   Texas
       A & M University Press,   1985.
       Texas A & M Southwestern Studie4s,   v.   4
       OCLC # 12108082

1204   Glass Trade Bead Conference (1982 Rochester,
       N. Y.)   Proceedings of the 1982 Glass
       Trade Bead Conference Sponsored by the
       Arthur C.   Parker Fund for Iroquois Re-
       search.   General editor Charles F.   Hayes
       III;   Associate editors Nancy Bolger,
       Karlis   Karklins,   Charles F.   Wray.   Roch-
       ester,   NY.,   Rochester Museum and Science
       Center,   1983.
       Rochester Museum and Science Center,   Re-
       search Division,   Research Records no.   16.
       Essays in this collection are also listed
       individually and refer to this citation.
       OCLC # 11202271

1205 Glenn,   James Lafayette. My Work Among the
      Florida Seminoles. Edited and with an
      introd. by Harry A. Kersey, Jr., Or-
      land, University Presses of Florida,
      1982.
      A University of Central Florida Book
      OCLC # 8451517

1206 Glossary of Figures of Speech in Iroquois
      Political Rhetoric. In 1463, pp. 115-
      124.

1207 Goddard, Ives, 1941- . Agreskwe, a
      Northern Iroquoian Deity. In 0979, pp.
      229-235.

1208 Goddard, Ives. The Ethnohistorical Im-
      plications of early Delaware Linguistic
      Materials. In 2282, pp. 88-102.
      Reprint from Man in the North East, v. 1,
      Mar. 1971, pp. 14-26.

1209 _____. Fox Social Organization 1650-1859.
      In 0068, pp. 128-140.

1210 Goddard, Pliny Earle, 1869-1928. Dancing
      Societies of the Sarsi Indians. In 3473,
      pp. 461-473.
      Anthropological Papers of the American
      Museum of Natural History v. 11, pt. 5.

1211 _____. The Present Condition of our
      knowledge of the North American Languages.
      In 0110, pp. 182-228.

      Godfrey, Laurie R. see 3519

      Goetz, Thomas H. see 2220

1212 Goetzmann, William H. The West as Romantic
      Horizon: Selection from the Collection of
      the InterNorth Art Foundation. ... and
      Joseph C. Porter; with artist's biograph-
      ies by David C. Hunt. Omaha, NB., Center
      for the Western Studies, Joslyn Art Mus-
      eum, InterNorth Art Foundation: Dis-
      tributed by University of Nebraska Press,
      1981.
      OCLC # 7733734

1213   Goldberg,   Carole E.   A Dynamic View of
       Tribal Jurisdiction to Tax Non-Indians.   In
       0087,   pp.   166-189.

       Goldberg,   Neil J.   see   1048

1214   Goldenweiser,   A.   A.   Social Organization of
       the North American Indians.   In 0110,   pp.
       350-378.

1215   Goldfrank,   Esther Schiff.   Changing Config-
       urations in the Social Organization of a
       Blackfoot Tribe During the Reserve Period.
       Observations on Northern Blackfoot kinship
       by L.   M.   Hanks,   Jr.   and Jane Richard-
       son.   Seattle,   University of Washington
       Press,   1966,   c1945.
       American Ethnological Society Monographs
       no.   8,   9.
       OCLC # 958086 and 230593

1216   _____.   The Social and Ceremonial Organiza-
       tion of Cochiti.   New York,   Kraus Reprint,
       1964.
       Memoirs of the American Anthropological
       Association no.   33,   1927.
       OCLC # 559476

1217   Goldschmidt,   Walter Rochs,   1913-   .   The
       Anthropology of Franz Boas;   Essays on the
       Centennial of his Birth.   Millwood,   NY.,
       Kraus Reprint,   1974.
       Memoirs of the American Anthropological
       Association no.   89.   Supplement to the
       American Anthropologist v.   61,   no.   5,
       pt.   2,   1959.
       OCLC # 2192708

1218   _____.   Social Organization and Status Dif-
       ferentiation Among the Nomlaki.   In 2276,
       pp.   125-174.

1219   Goldstein,   Lynne.   Mississippian Mortuary
       Practices: A Case Study of Two Cemeteries
       in the Lower Illinois Valley.   Evanston,
       IL.,   Northwestern University Archae-
       ological Program,   1980.
       Scientific Papers/ Northwestern Univer-
       sity Archaeological Program,   v.   4.
       OCLC # 7472102

1220   Gomara, Francisco Lopez de, 1510-1560?
        Conquest of the Weast Indian. Readex
        Microprint, 1966.
        Original t. p. reads The pleasant his-
        torie of the conquest of the Weast India,
        now called New Spayne, atchieued by the
        worthy prince Hernando Cortes, Marques of
        the valley of Huaxacac, most delectable
        to reach. Trans. out of the Spanish ton-
        gue by T. N., anno 1578. Imprinted at
        London by Henry Bynneman. Some pages in-
        correctly numbered. Trans. by Thomas Nic-
        holas, of the second part of the author's
        Historia General de las Indias.
        OCLC # 2127441

1221   Gomberg, S. Northwest Indians: "I Found
        the Future. In 1556, pp. 73-74.

        Gonyea, Ray see 3483.5

1222   Good, Mary Elizabeth. A Comparison of
        Glass Beads from Upper Creek Indian Towns
        in the Southeast and in Oklahoma. In 1204,
        pp. 159-166.

1223   Good, Mary Elizabeth. Guebert Site: An
        18th Century Historic Kashashia, Indian
        Village in Randolph County, Illinois.
        Wood River?, IL., Central States Ar-
        chaeological Societies, 1972.
        Central States Archaeological Societies
        Memoir no. 2.
        OCLC # 483044

        _____. see also 2895

        Gooding, John D. see 0893

1224   Goodman, James Marion. The Navaho Atlas;
        Environments, Resources, People, and
        History of the Dine' Bikeyah. Drawings and
        Cartographic assistance by Mary E,
        Goodman. Norman, University of Oklahoma
        Press, 1982.
        Civilization of the American Indian Series
        v. 157.
        OCLC # 8386632

1125   Goodman,   Jeffrey.   American Genesis: The
       American Indian and the Origins of Modern
       Man.   New York,   Summit Books,   1981.
       OCLC # 6532267

1126   Goodwin,   Gary C.,   1940-   .   Cherokees in
       Transition: A Study of Changing Culture
       and Environment Prior to 1775.   Chicago,
       University of Chicago,   Dept. of Geography,
       1977.
       Research Paper - University of Chicago,
       Dept. of Geography no.   181.
       OCLC # 3072738

1127   Goodwin,   Grenville.   Myths and Tales of the
       White Mountain Apache.   New York,   The
       American Folklore Society,   J.   J.   Augus-
       tin,   Agent.   New York,   Kraus Reprint,
       1969.
       Memoirs of the American Folk-lore Society,
       v.   33.   Reprint of the 1939 ed.
       OCLC # 606359

       Goodwin,   Mary E.   see   1224

1228   Gookin,   Daniel.   1612-1687.   Historical Ac-
       count of the Doings and Sufferings of the
       Christian Indians in New England,   in the
       Years 1675,   1676,   1677.   New York,   Arno
       Press,   1972.
       Research Library of Colonial America.
       Reprint of th1 1836 ed.   pub.   in v.   2 of
       Archaeological Americana: Transactions and
       Collections of the American Antiquarian
       Society.
       OCLC # 384224

       Goossen,   Irvy W.   see   3326

1229   Gorenstein,   Shirley.   Tepexi el Viejo: A
       Postclassic Fortified Site in the Mixteca-
       Puebla Regions of Mexico.   Philadelphia,
       American Philosophical society,   1973.
       Transactions of the American Philosophical
       Society,   New Series v.   63,   pt.   1.
       OCLC # 618509

1230   Gorman,   Frederick J.   E.   Inventory Oper-
       ations Research in Southwestern Prehistory:

An Example From East Central Arizona. In
0822, pp. 165-194.

1231 Gorospe, Larry Darwin. A Comparison of
Graduates of the Native American Program
and Non-Indian Graduates in Educational Ad-
ministration. Ann Arbor, MI., University
Microfilms International, 1983.
Microfilm - PhD Thesis - Pennsylvania State
University

1232 Gosner, Kevin Marlin. Soldiers of the Vir-
gin: An Ethnohistorical Analysis of the
Tzeltal Revolt of 1712 in Highland Chiapas
(Mexico). Ann Arbor, MI., University
Microfilms International,
Microfilm - PhD Thesis - University of
Pennsylvania
OCLC # 13476907

1233 Goss, Charles Wayne, 1943- . The French
and the Choctaw Indians, 1700-1763. Ann
Arbor, MI., University Microfilms Inter-
national, 1977.
Microfilm - PhD Thesis - Texas Tech
University
OCLC # 4669542

1234 Gossen, Gary H. Chamulas in the World of
the Sun; Time and Space in a Maya Oral
Tradition. Cambridge, Harvard University
Press, 1974.
OCLC # 1040313

1235 Gough, Barry M. Gunboat Frontier: British
Maritime Authority and Northwest Coast In-
dians, 1846-1890. Vancouver, University
of British Columbia Press, 1984.
University of British Columbia Press
Pacific Maritime Studies, v. 4.
OCLC # 10787267

1236 Gould, Richard A. Ecology and Adaptive Response Among the Tolowa Indians of Northwestern California. In 2276, pp. 49-78.

1237 Gourd, Charles Allen. No Contest: A de-
pendent Sovereignty from Tribe to Nation.
Ann Arbor, MI., University Microfilms
International, 1984.

Microfilm - PhD Thesis - University of
Kansas
OCLC # 12574937

1237.5   Gove, Chris Moyers Leddy. The Conflict
Between Cultural Persistance and Accultura-
tion as it Affects Individual Behavior of
Northwestern Alaskan Eskimos. Ann Arbor,
MI., University Microfilms International,
1982.
Microfilm - PhD Thesis - United States
International University
OCLC # 11980478

1238   Grace, Henry, b. 1730? History of the Life
and Suffering of Henry Grace. New York
Garland Pub., 1977.
Garland Library of narratives of North
American Indian captivities, v. 10. Re-
print of the 1764 ed. printed for the
author in Reading, Eng.
OCLC # 2798776

1239   Gradwohl, David M., 1934- . Prehistoric
Village Sites in Eastern Nebraska.
Lincoln, NB., Nebraska State Historical
Society, 1969.
Nebraska State Historical Society Pubs. in
Anthropology no. 4.
OCLC # 259606

1240   Graham, Elizabeth. Medicine Man to
Missionary: Missionaries as Agents of
Change Among the Indians of Southern
Ontario, 1784-1867. Toronto, P. Martin
Associates, 1975.
Canadian Experience Series
OCLC # 2930738

1241   Graham, John, b. 1740. John Graham's
Address to the Master and Worthy Family of
this House. New York, Garland Pub.,
1978.
Garland Library of narratives of North
American Indian captivities, v. 18.
Reprint of the 1787 ed. pub. by W. Ap-
pleton. Issues with the reprint of the
1737 ed. of the Returned Captive.
OCLC # 3558743

1242 Graham, W. A. (William Alexander), 1875-
      1954. _The Custer Myth, a Source Book of_
      Custeriana. To which is added important
      items of Custeriana and a Complete and
      Comprehensive Bibliography by Fred Dus-
      tin. New York, Bonanza, 1953.
      OCLC # 351131

      Grand Rapids Public Museum _see_ 0207

1243 Grange, Roger T. _Pawnee and Lower Loup_
      Pottery. Lincoln, NB., Nebraska State
      Historical Society, 1968.
      Nebraska State Historical society
      Publications in Anthropology no. 3.
      OCLC # 616247

      Granger, Erastus _see_ 2915

1244 Grant, Campbell, 1909- . _Canyon de_
      Chelly; Its People and Rock Art. Tucson,
      University of Arizona Press, 1978.
      OCLC # 3732735

1245 _____. _Rock Art of the North American_
      Indian. New York, Cambridge University
      Press, 1983.
      Imprint of Man Series
      OCLC # 9153452

1246 Grant, John Webster. _Moon of Wintertime:_
      Missionaries and the Indians of Canada in
      Encounter Since 1534. Buffalo, University
      of Toronto Press, 1984.
      OCLC # 11025390

1247 _Graphic Sketches from old and Authentic_
      Works, Illustrating the Costume, Habits,
      and Character of the Aborigines of America;
      Together with Rare and Curious Fragments
      Relating to the Discovery and Settlement
      of the Country. (pt. 1), New York, J.
      and H. G. Langley, 1841.
      Plates accompanied by leaves with
      descriptive letterpress, Halftitle _Graphic_
      Sketches. Part 1. The Natives of Virginia
      by John Wyth, 1585-1588. Added t. p.
      Portraits to the life and manner of the in-
      habitants of that province in America,

called Virginia... No more published.
OCLC # 5301734

Grasmick, Harold G. , 1947- . see 3120

Grasmick, Mary K. , 1953- . see 3119

1248 Graves, Michael W. <u>Aggregation and Abando-
ment at Grasshopper Pueblo: Evolutionary
Trends in the Late Prehistory</u> of East-
Central Arizona. In 2239, pp. 110-121.

_____. see also 1479, 2239

1248.5 Graves, William Hilton, 1950- . <u>The
Evolution of American Indian Policy: From
Colonial Times to the Florida Treaty
(1819)</u>. Ann Arbor, MI. , University
Microfilms International, 1982
Microfilm - PhD Thesis - Florida State
University
OCLC # 10320385

1249 Gray, John Stephen, 1910- . <u>Centennial
Campaign: The Sioux War of 1876</u>. Maps by
John A. Popovich. Ft. Collins, CO. ,
Old Army Press, 1976.
Source Custeriana Series v. 8
OCLC # 2693348

1250 Graymont, Barbara. <u>American Indian History
of the Hudson Valley: Needs and Opportu-
nities</u>. In 2282, pp. 269-276.

1251 _____. <u>The Six Nations Indians in the Revolutionary War</u>. In 1583, pp. 25-36.

Great Britain. Board of Trade <u>see</u> 2599

Great Britain. Colonial Office <u>see</u> 2599

Great Britain. Commission of Indian Affairs,
Albany, Minutes <u>see</u> 1568

1252 Grebinger, Paul. <u>Prehistoric Social Organization in Chaco Canyon, New Mexico: An
Evolutionary Perspective</u>. In 0822, pp.
73-100.

1253 _____ and David P. Adam. <u>Santa Cruz Valley</u>

Hohokam: Cultural Development in the Clas-
sical Period. In 0822, pp. 215-244.

_____. see also 0822

Green, Jesse, 1928- . see 0715

1254 Green, Michael D., 1941- . Alexander Mc-
      Gillivary. In 0081, pp. 41-63.

1255 _____. The Creeks: A Critical Biblio-
      graphy. Bloomington, Published for the
      Newberry Library by Indiana University
      Press, 1979.
      Bibliographical Series
      OCLC # 5499018

1256 _____. The Politics of Indian Removal:
      Creek Government and Society in Crisis.
      Lincoln, University of Nebraska Press,
      1982.
      OCLC # 7773031

1257 Green, Rayna. Native American Women: A
      Contextual Bibliography. Bloomington,
      Indiana University Press, 1983.
      Newberry Library Center for the History of
      the American Indian Bibliographical Series
      OCLC # 9019547

1258 Green, Thomas J., 1946- , and Cheryl A.
      Munson. Mississippian Settlement Pattern
      in Southwestern Indiana. In 2172, pp.
      293-300.

Greenberg, Georgia, 1919- . see 1259

1259 Greenberg, Henry, 1921- . Carl Gorman's
      World. ... and Georgia Greenberg.
      Albuquerque, University of New Mexico
      Press, 1984.
      OCLC # 10277418

1259.5 Greene, A. C., 1923- . The Last Cap-
      tive. Austin, Encino Press, 1972.
      OCLC # 354470

1260 Greene, Jerome A. Slim Buttes, 1876: An
      Episode of the Great Sioux War. Norman,

University of Oklahoma Press, 1982.
OCLC # 7737239

1261   Greenleaf, J. Cameron.   Excavations at
       Punta de Agua in the Santa Cruz River Bas-
       in, Southeastern Arizona.   Tucson,   Uni-
       versity of Arizona Press,   1975.
       Contributions to highway salvage archae-
       ology in Arizona,   no. 40.   Anthropolog-
       ical papers of the University of Arizona,
       no. 26.
       OCLC # 1852892

1261.2 Gregonia, Linda M.   Hohokam Indians of the
        Tucson Basin.   ... and Karl J. Reinhard.
        Tucson,   University of Arizona Press,
        1979.
        OCLC # 5336916

1261.3 Grey, Herman.   Tales from the Mohaves.
        With a foreword by Alice Marriott.   Norman,
        University of Oklahoma Press,   1970.
        Civilization of the American Indian Series,
        v. 107.
        OCLC # 107911

1261.5 Grieder, Terence.   The Art and Archaeology
        of Pashash.   Austin,   University of Texas
        Press,   1978.
        OCLC # 3003030

1261.7 Griffin, James Bennett, 1905- . Fort
        Ancient Aspect: its Cultural and Chrono-
        logical Position in Mississippi Valley
        Archaeology.   Ann Arbor, MI.,   University
        of Michigan,   Museum of Anthropology,
        1966,   c1943.
        University of Michigan Museum of Anthropol-
        ogy.   Anthropological Papers no.   28.
        OCLC # 214699

1261.8 _____.   The Origin and Dispersion of Amer-
        ican Indians in North America.   In 1052,
        pp.   43-55.

1261.9 _____.   Lake Superior Copper and the In-
        dians: Miscellaneous Studies of Great
        Lakes Prehistory.   Ann Arbor,   University
        of Michigan,   1961.
        University of Michigan Museum of Anthropol-

ogy. Anthropological Papers no. 17.
OCLC # 627592

_____. see also 0710

1262 Griffith, A. Kinney. Mickey Free, Manhun-
ter. Caldwell, IO. , Caxton Printers,
1969.
OCLC # 34401

1263 Griffith, Roberta Jean. Ramey Incised Pot-
tery. Urbana, Illinois Archaeological
Survey, 1981.
Circular, Illinois Archaeological Survey
no. 5.
OCLC # 8328569

1264 Griffith, Winthrop. The Taos Indians Have a
Small Generation Gap. In 3335, pp. 147-
161.
Source - New York Times - Feb. 21, 1971.

1265 Grim, John. The Shaman: Patterns of Siberian and Ojibway Healing. Norman, University of Oklahoma Press, 1983.
Civilization of the American Indian Series
v. 165.
OCLC # 9758677

1266 Grinde, Donald A. , 1946- . The Iroquois
in the Founding of the American Nation.
Illus. by Peter Jemison, San Francisco;
Indian Historian Press, 1977.
OCLC # 3462392

1266.5 _____. Politics and the American Indian
Policy Review Commission. In 2961.5, pp.
19-28.

1267 Grinnell, George Bird, 1849-1938. The Pun-
ishment of the Stingy and Other Indian
Stories. Introd. by Jarold Ramsey, Lin-
coln, University of Nebraska Press, 1982.
Reprint of the 1901 ed. pub. in New York,
Harper
OCLC # 8031564

_____. see also 2800

1268 Grobsmith, Elizabeth S. Lakota of the Rose-

bud: A Contemporary Ethnography.   New
York,   Holt,   Rinehart,   and Winston,
1981.
Case studies in cultural anthropology
OCLC # 7171821

Grolier Club,   NY.,   see   0603

1269   Gross,   Daniel R.   Village Movement in Relation to Resources in Amazonia.   In 0023,
pp.   429-449.

1271   Grove,   David C.   Chalcatingo,   Excavations
on the Olmec Frontier.   New York,   Thames
and Hudson,   1984.
New aspects of antiquity
OCLC # 11786472

1272   _____.   The Formative Period and the Evolution of Complex Culture.   In 0122,   pp.
373-391.

1273   Grumet,   Robert Steven.   Native Americans of
the Northwest Coast.   Bloomington,   Pub-
lished for the Newberry Library by Indiana
University Press,   1979.
The Newberry Library Center for the History
of the American Indian Bibliographical
Series
OCLC # 5563433

1275   Guedon,   Marie Francoise.   An Introduction to
Tsimshian World View and its Practitioners.
In 3162,   pp.   137-159.

1276   _____.   Tsimshian Shamanic Images.   In
3162,   pp.   174-211.

1277   A Guide to British Public Record Office,
Colonial Office,   Class 5 Files.   Edited by
Randolph Boehm,   guide compiled by Linda
Womaski and Randolph Boehm.   Frederick,
MD.,   University Publications of America,
1983.
Contents.   Pt.   1,   Westward Expansion.
Pt.   2.   Board of Trade.   Pt.   3.   French
and Indian War.
OCLC # 9471047

Guilday,   J.   see   0025

1278   Guilday, John E. <u>A Possible Caribou-Paleo-</u>
       <u>Indian Association from Dutchess Quarry</u>
       <u>Cave, Orange County, New York</u>. New York
       State Archaeological Association Bulletin
       45, Mar. 1969, pp. 24-29. Millwood,
       NY., Kraus Reprint, 1976.

1279   _____. <u>Vertebrate Faunal Remains from Mead-</u>
       <u>owcroft Rock Shelter, Washington County,</u>
       <u>Pennsylvania: Summary and Interpretation</u>.
       In 2111, pp. 163-174.

1280   Guillemin, George F. <u>Urbanism and Hierarchy</u>
       <u>at Iximche</u>. In 2920, pp. 227-264.

1281   Guinn, Marcia Ann Fitzgerald. <u>Gender Toy</u>
       <u>Preference of Native American, Non-Native</u>
       <u>American Preschool Children in Day Care,</u>
       <u>Non-day Care Settings</u>. Ann Arbor, MI.,
       University Microfilms International, 1984.
       Microfilm - EdD Thesis - University of
       Oklahoma

1282   Gulf Coast History and Humanities Conference,
       5th, 1974: Pensacola. <u>Indians of the</u>
       <u>Lower South: Past and Present</u>. Gulf Coast
       History and Humanities Conference: John
       K. Mahon, ed. Pensacola. The Confer-
       ence, 1975. Proceedings - Gulf Coast
       History and Humanities Conference, v. 5.
       Essays in this collection are also listed
       individually and refer to this citation.
       OCLC # 1748201

1283   Gumerman, George J. <u>Regional Variation in</u>
       <u>the Southwest and the Question of Mesoamer-</u>
       <u>ican Relationships</u>. In 0014, pp. 22-33.

       Gunn, J. D. <u>see</u> 0025

1283.5 Gunsky, Frederick R. <u>Multicultural Educa-</u>
       <u>tion: Implications for American Indian</u>
       <u>People</u>. In 2238.5, pp. 69-75.

1284   Gusinde, Martin, 1886-1969. <u>Folk Litera-</u>
       <u>ture of the Yamana Indians: Martin</u>
       <u>Gusinde's Collection of Yamana Narratives</u>.
       Johannes Wilbert, editor. Berkeley, Uni-
       versity of California Press, 1977.

UCLA Latin American Studies series v. 40.
Translation of the 2d vol. of the author's
Die Feuerland Indianer
OCLC # 2958741

1285 Gustafson, Paula. Salish Weaving. With
photos by Robert Warick; sketches by the
author. Vancouver, B. C., Douglas &
McIntyre; Seattle, University of Washington Press, 1980.
OCLC # 6357613

1286 Guthe, Alfred K. (Alfred Kidder), 1920-
1983. Current Trends in American Prehistory. New York State Archaeological Association Bulletin 12, Mar. 1958, pp.
7-10. Millwood, NY., Kraus Reprint,
1976.
Revised paper, presented to Morgan
Chapter, March 8, 1957.

1287 _____. The Frog Mound - A Hopewellian Mani-
festation. New York State Archeological
Association Bulletin 13, July 1958, pp.
9-10. Millwood, NY., Kraus Reprint,
1976.
Paper presented at the annual meeting April
12, 1958.

1288 Guthe, Carl E. Sequence of Culture in the
Eastern United States. In 2105, pp. 368-
374.

1289 Gutierrez, Helen. Salvage Archaeology: A
Status Report. In 3519, pp. 87-90.

1290 Guy, Camil. The Weymontaching Birchbark
Canoe. Ottawa, National Museums of
Canada, 1974.
Anthropological papers no. 20. Trans-
lation of Le canot d'ecorce a Weymontaching
OCLC # 1993602

1290.5 Guyette, Susan. Suggestions for Priority
Alcohol and Drug Abuse Research: A Comment
on the Recommendations of Task Force Eleven
of the American Indian Policy Review Commission. In 2961.5, pp. 45-52.

1291 Gryles, John, 1678?-1755. Memoirs of Odd

Adventures, Strange Deliverances, etc.
Garland Library of narratives of North
American Indian captivities,   v.   6
Garland Pub.,   1977.
OCLC # 2896232

1291.5   Gyles,   John,   1678?-1755.   Memoirs of Odd
Adventures, Strange Deliverances, etc.   In
2562,   pp.   91-131.

Gendrop,   Paul.   see   1434

1292   HRAF (Human Relations Area Files) on
microfiche.   As of 1/17/87 the library has
the following.   NA6 Aleut,   NA10 South
Alaska Eskimo,   NA12 Tlingit,   ND8 Cooper
Eskimo,   ND9 Hare,   ND12 Nahane,   NE6 Bel-
lacoola,   NE11 Nootka,   NF6 Blackfoot,   NG6
Ojibwa,   NH6 Montagnis,   NJ5 Micmac,   NM7
Delaware,   NM9 Iroquois,   NN11 Creek,   NO6
Comanche,   NP5 Fox,   NP12 Winnebago,   NQ6
Arapaho,   NQ10 Crow,   NQ12 Dhegiha,   NQ13
Gros Ventie,   NQ17 Mandan,   NQ18 Pawnee,
NR4 Plateau Indians,   NR10 Klamath,   NR13
Northern Paiute,   NR19 Southeast Salish,
NS18 Pomo,   NS22 Tubatulabal,   NS29 Yokuts,
NS31 Yurok,   NT8 Eastern Apache,   NT9
Hopi,   NT13 Navaho,   NT14 Plateau Yumans,
NT15 River Yumans,   NT16 Southern Paiute,
NT18 Tewa,   NT19 Utes,   NT20 Washo,   NT21
Western Apache,   NT23 Zuni,   NT24 Mormons,
NT25 Mescalero,   NU7 Aztec,   NU28 Papago,
NU31 Seri,   NU33 Tarahumara,   NU34 Tarasco,
NU37 Tepoztlan,   NU44 Zapotec,   NU54 Mexico
City,   NV9 Tzeltal,   NV10 Yucatec Maya,
NW8 Mam,   SA15 Mosquito,   SA19 Talamanca,
SB5 Cuna,   SC7 Cagaba,   SC13 Goajiro,   SC15
Paez,   SD6 Cayapa,   SD9 Jivaro,   SE13 Inca,
SF5 Aymara,   SF10 Chiriguano,   SF21
Siriono,   SF24 Uru,   SG4 Araucanians,   SH4
Ona,   SH5 Tehuelche,   SH6 Yahgan,   SI4
Abipon,   SI7 Mataco,   SI12 Toba,   SK6
Choroti,   SK7 Guana,   SM3 Caingang,   SM4
Guarani,   SO8 Timbira,   SO9 Tupinamba,
SO11 Bahia,   SP7 Bacairi,   SP8 Bororo,   SP9
Caraja,   SP17 Nambicuara,   SP22 Tapirape,
SP23 Trumai,   SQ13 Munduruco,   SQ18 Yah-
oama,   SQ19 Tucano,   SQ20 Tucuna,   SR8 Bush
Negroes,   SR9 Carib,   SS16 Pemon,   SS18

Warao,   SS19 Yaruro,   ST13 Callinago,   SU1
Puerto Rico,   SV3 Haiti,   SY1 Jamaica.

1293 Haas, Marilyn L. Indians of North America:
      Methods and Sources for Library Research.
      Hamden, CT. , Library Professional Public-
      ations, 1983.
      OCLC # 9682796

1294 Haas, Mary. Boas, Sapir and Bloomfield.
      In 1902, pp. 59-74.

1295 Haan, Richard L., 1946- . The Covenant
      Chain: Iroquois Diplomacy on the Niagara
      Frontier, 1697-1730. Ann Arbor, MI.,
      University Microfilms International, 1976.
      Microfilm - PhD Thesis - University of
California, Santa Barbara
      OCLC # 4161973

1296 Haberland, Wolfgang. Lower Central America.
      In 0577, pp. 395-430.

1297 Haboo: Native American Stories from Puget
      Sound. Trans. and edited by Vi Hilbert;
      with a foreword and introd. by Thom Hess;
      illus. by Ron Hilbert. Seattle, Univer-
      sity of Washington Press, 1985.
      OCLC # 12313955

      Hady, Maureen E., 1952- . see 0723

1298 Haefer, J. Richard. Oodham Celkona: The
      Papago Skipping Dance. In 2931, pp. 239-
      273.

      Hafen, LeReuben, 1893- . see 2234.5

1299 Haffenreffer Museum of Anthropology. Hau
      Kola! The Plains Indian Collection of the
      Haffenreffer Museum of Anthropology. Bar-
      bara A. Hail. Providence, RI., Haffen-
      reffer Museum of Anthropology, 1980.
      Studies in anthropology and material cul-
      ture, v. 3
      OCLC # 7811464

1300 Hagan, William Thomas. The Indian Rights
      Association: The Herbert Welsh Years,
      1882-1904. Tucson, University of Arizona

Press, 1985.
OCLC # 12133782

1301   _____. Justifying Dispossession of the Indian: The Land Utilization Argument. In
0079, pp. 65-80.

1302   _____. Longhouse Diplomacy and Frontier
Warfare: The Iroquois Confederacy in the
American Revolution. Albany(?) New York
State American Revolution Bicentennial Com-
mission, 1976(?)
OCLC # 2799980

1303   _____. Private Property, the Indian's Door
to Civilization. In 2304, pp. 200-208.
Reprinted from Ethnohistory v. 3, no. 2,
Spring 1956, pp. 126-137.

1304   _____. Quanah Parker. In 0081, pp. 175-
191.

1305   _____. Quanah Parker, Indian Judge. In
0638, pp. 71-78.

1306   _____. The Reservation Policy: Too Little
and Too Late. In 2265, pp. 157-169.

1307   _____. United States-Comanche Relations:
The Reservation Years. New Haven, Yale
University Press, 1976.
Yale Western Americana Series, v. 28.
OCLC # 2435187

1308   Hagerty, Gilbert W., 1908-1984. The Iron
Trade Knife in Oneida Territory. Phila-
delphia? 1963?
Cover title: reprint from Pennsylvania
Archaeologist, Bulletin of the Society for
Pennsylvania Archaeology, v. 22, July
1963, nos. 1-2.
OCLC # 958090

Hail, Barbara A. see 1299

Haile, Berard, 1874-1961 see 3226

1309   Hale, Kenneth L. (Kenneth Locke), 1934-
Theoretical Linguistics in Relation to

American Indian Communities. In 1902, pp. 35-58.

Hales, Donald M. see 2669

1310 Haley, James L. Apaches: A History and Culture Portrait. Garden City, NY., Doubleday, 1981.
OCLC # 6764029

1311 Haley, James L. The Buffalo War: The History of the Red River Indian Uprising of 1874. Garden City, NY., Doubleday, 1976.
OCLC # 1733203

1312 Hall, David J. Clifford Sifton and Canadian Indian Administration 1896-1905. In 0137, pp. 120-144.
Reprinte4d from Prairie Forum v. 2, no. 2, 1977.

1313 Hall, Edwin S., 1939- . The Eskimo Storyteller: Folktales from Noatak Alaska. Knoxville, University of Tennessee Press, 1976, c1975.
OCLC # 1009773

1314 _____. Northwest Coast Indian Graphics: An Introduction to Silk Screen Prints. ... and Margaret B. Blackman, Vincent Rickard. Seattle, University of Washington Press, 1981.
OCLC # 7459954

1315 Hall, Gilbert L. Federal-Indian Trust Relationship: Duty of Protection: Legal Curriculum and Training Program of the Institute for the Development of Indian Law. Washington, The Institute, 1979.
OCLC # 5100430

1316 Hall, Robert L. An Interpretation of the Two-Climax Model of Illinois Prehistory. In 0905, pp. 401-462.

1317 Halliburton, R. Red Over Black: Black Slavery Among the Cherokee Indians. Westport, CT., Greenwood Press, 1977.
Contributions in Afro-American and African

Studies,   no.   27.
OCLC # 2644717

1318   Hallowell,   A.   Irving (Alfred Irving),
       1892-1974.   Contributions to Anthropology:
       Selected Papers of A.   Irving Hallowell.
       With introd.   by Raymond D.   Fogelson.
       Chicago,   University of Chicago Press,
       1976.
       Some essays in this collection are also
       listed individually and refer to this
       citation.
       OCLC # 1958125

1319   Halpin,   Marjorie.   Feast Names at Hartley
       Bay.   In 3162,   pp.   57-64.

1320   _____.   The Mask of Tradition.   In 2502,
       pp.   219-226.

1321   _____.   "Seeing" in Stone: Tsimshian Mask-
       ing and the Twin Stone Masks.   In 3162,
       pp.   281-307.

1321.5   _____.   Totem Poles: An Illustrated
       Guide.   Foreword by Michael M.   Ames,
       Vancouver,   University of British Columbia
       Press,   Seattle,   University of Washington
       Press,   1981.
       Museum Note no.   3
       OCLC # 11852544

1322   _____.   William Beynon,   Ethnographer,
       Tsimshian,   1888-1958.   In 3162,   pp.   141-
       156.

       _____.   see also   2502

1323   Hamell,   George R.   Gannagaro State Historic
       Site: A Current Perspective.   In 3035,
       pp.   91-108.

1324   _____.   Trading in Metaphors: The Magic of
       Beads.   In 1204,   pp.   5-28.

1325   Hames,   Raymond B.   The Settlement Pattern of
       a Yanomamo Population Bloc: A Behavioral
       Ecological Interpretation.   In 0023,   pp.
       393-427.

_____. see also 0023

Hamilton, Roland, 1936- . see 0597

Hamilton, Thomas D. see 2510

1326 Hammon, Briton. A Narrative of the Uncommon
     Sufferings and Deliverance of Briton Ham-
     mon, a Negro Man. New York, Garland
     Pub., 1978.
     Garland Library of narratives of North
     American Indian captivities, v. 8. Re-
     print of the 1760 ed. printed and sold by
     Green & Russell, Boston, under title A
     Narrative of the Uncommon Sufferings, and
     Surprizing Deliverance of Briton Hammon, a
     Negro Man. Issued with the reprint of the
     1756 ed. of Fleming, W. A Narrative of
     Sufferings and Deliverance.
     OCLC # 3842907

1327 Hammond, Norman. The Early Formative in the
     Maya Lowlands. In 2920, pp. 78-101.

1328 _____. Ex Oriente Lux: A View from Belize.
     In 2378, pp. 45-76.

1329 _____. The Myth of the Milpa: Agricultural
     Expansion in the Maya Lowlands. In 2522,
     pp. 23-34.

     _____. see also 0472, 2920

Hand, Wayland Debs, 1907- . see 3180

1330 Handbook of North American Indians. William
     C. Sturtevant general editor. Washington,
     Smithsonian Institution, Govt. print.
     Off., 1978.
     Library has vols. 6 Subarctic, v. 8
     California, v. 9 Southwest, v. 15
     Northeast.
     OCLC # 3414504

1331 Handelman, Don. The Development of a Washo
     Shaman. In 2276, pp. 379-406.

1332 Handsome Lake, 1735-1815. The Code of Hand-
     some Lake, the Seneca Prophet. by Arthur
     C. Parker. Albany, University of the

State of New York, 1913. New York State
Museum, Museum Bulletin no. 163.
Part 2, Field notes on the rites and
ceremonies of the Ganio dal'lo religion:
pp. 81-138.
OCLC # 4312091

1333   Hanihara, Kazuro. Dental traits in Ainu,
Australian Aborigines and New World Populations. In 1052, pp. 125-134.

1334   Hanke, Lewis. All Mankind is One; A Study
of the Disputation Between Bartolome de las
Casas and Juan Gines de Sepulveda in 1550
on the Intellectual and Religious Capacity
of the American Indians. DeKald, Northern
Illinois University Press, 1974.
OCLC # 841323

1335   _____. Indians and Spaniards in the New
World: A Personal View. In 0144, pp.
1-18.

Hanks, Jane (Richardson), 1908- . see
1336

1226   Hanks, L. M. (Lucien Mason), 1910- .
Observations on Northern Blackfoot Kinship.
Seattle, University of Washington Press,
1966, c1945.
Monographs of the American Ethnological
Society, v. 9.
OCLC # 675029

_____. see also 1215

Hansell, Pat see 2584

1337   Hanson, Elizabeth. God's Mercy Surmounting
Man's Cruelty. In 2563, pp. 227-244.

1338   Hanson, Jeffery R. (Jeffery Raymond),
1949- . Hidatsa Culture Change, 1780-
1845: A Cultural Ecological Approach. Ann
Arbor, MI., University Microfilms Inter-
national, 1983.
Microfilm - PhD Thesis - University of
Missouri-Columbia
OCLC # 11146332

1339   Harby,   Lee (Cohen),   1849- . The Tejas,
       Their Habits,   Government,   and Supersti-
       tions.   In American Historical Association.
       Annual Report for the year 1894.
       Washington,   1895,   pp.   63-82.
       One reel microfilm,   from the Library of
       Congress Class E - Miscellaneous Monographs
       and pamphlets,   shelf #44140-44175,
       #44141.
       OCLC # 12232463

1340   Harn,   Alan D.   Mississippian Settlement Pat-
       terns in the Central Illinois River Valley.
       In 2172,   pp.   233-268.

1341   Harner,   Michael J.   The Way of the Shaman:
       A Guide to Power and Healing.   San Fran-
       cisco,   Harper and Row,   1980.
       OCLC # 6485731

       Harney,   Michael see 2063

1342   Harp,   Elmer.   Dorset Settlement Patterns in
       Newfoundland and Southeastern Hudson Bay.
       In 0908,   pp.   119-138.

1343   _____.   Pioneer Cultures of the Sub-Arctic
       and the Arctic.   In 0097,   pp.   115-147.

1344   Harper,   Albert B.,   1950- . Life Expect-
       ancy and Population Adaptation: The Aleut
       Centenarian Approach.   In 1052,   pp.   309-
       330.

       _____.   see also 1052

1345   Harrington,   John Peabody.   The American In-
       dian Sign Language.   In 0008,   pp.   109-
       142.
       Reprinted from Indians at Work,   v. 5,   no.
       7,   pp.   8-15;   v.   5,   no.   11,   pp.   28-
       32;   v.   5,   no.   12,   p.   25039;   v.   6,
       no.   1,   pp.   24-32;   v.   6,   no.   3,   pp.
       24-29,   1938.

1346   _____.   Tomol: Chumash Watercraft as De-
       scribed in the Ethnographic Notes of John
       P.   Harrington.   Edited and annotated by
       Travis Hudson,   Janice Timbrook and Melissa
       Rempe;   art work by Jane Jolley Howorth.

Socorro, NM., Ballena Press, 1987.
Ballena Press Anthropological Papers, no.
9.
OCLC # 4003253

1347 Harrington, M. R. (Mark Raymond), 1882-
      1971. Sacred Bundles of the Sac and Fox
      Indians. New York, AMS Press, 1983.
      Reprint, originally published, Philadel-
      phia, University Museum, 1914. Anthro-
      pological Publications, University of
      Pennsylvania, The University Musuem, v.
      4, no. 2.
      OCLC # 9732377

1348 _____. Ancient Shell Heaps new New York
      City. In 3469, pp. 167-179.

1349 _____. Indians of New Jersey. Dickon Among
      the Lenapes. Illus. by Clarence Ells-
      worth. New Brunswick, NJ., Rutgers Uni-
      versity Press, 1966.
      First publisheder under the title Dickson
      Among the Lenape Indians.
      OCLC # 1841844

1350 _____. The Rock-shelters of Armonk, New
      York . In 3469, pp. 123-138.

1351 Harris, David R. The Agricultural Founda-
      tions of Lowland Maya Civilization: A
      Critique. In 2522, pp. 301-323.

      Harris, Stuart Kimball, 1906-1969 see
      3517

1352 Harrison, Peter D., 1937- . Bajos Re-
      visited: Visual Evidence for one System of
      Agriculture. In 2522, pp. 247-253.

1353 _____. The Lobil Postclassic Phase in the
      Southern Interior of the Yucatan Peninsula.
      In 0472, pp. 189-207.

1354 _____. The Rise of the Bajos and the Fall
      of the Maya. In 2920, pp. 469-508.

1355 _____. So the Seeds Shall Grow: Some In-
      troductory Comments. In 2522, pp. 1-11.

_____. see also 2522

Hartmann,   Gayle Harrison see 1724,   3276

1356   Hartney,   Patrick C. Tuberculosis Lesions in
       a Prehistoric Population Sample from South-
       ern Ontario. In 2526,   pp.   141-160.

1357   Hartung,   Horst. Ancient Maya Architecture
       and Planning: Possibilities and Limita-
       tions for Astronomical Studies. In 2270,
       pp.   111-129.

1358   _____. Astronomical Signs in the Codices
       Bodley and Selden. In 2270,   pp.   37-41.

Harvey,   Frank see 2476

1359   Harvey,   H. R. Aspects of Land Tenure in
       Ancient Mexico. In 0978,   pp.   83-102.

_____. see also 0978

Hassrick,   Peter H. see 3109

1360   Hassrick,   Royal B. Cowboys and Indians: An
       Illustrated History. London,   Octopus
       Books,   1976.
       OCLC # 3186333

_____. see also 0524

1361   Hatcher,   Evelyn Payne. Visual Metaphors:
       A Formal Analysis of Navaho Art. With an
       introd. by Anthony F. C. Wallace. St.
       Paul,   West Publishing Co.,   1974.
       Monograph - The American Ethnological
       Society,   58.
       OCLC # 1056779

Hatoff,   Brian W. see 3106

1362   Haupt,   Carol Magdalene. The Image of the
       American Indian Female in the Biographical
       Literature and Social Studies Textbooks of
       the Elementary Schools. Ann Arbor,   MI.,
       University Microfilms   International,
       1984.
       Microfilm - PhD Thesis - Rutgers,   The
       State University of New Jersey

1363   Hauptman, Laurence M. Between a Rock and a
       Hard Place: William N. Fenton in the In-
       dian Service, 1935-1937. In 0978, pp.
       359-369.

1364   _____. The Dispersal of the River Indians:
       Frontier Expansion and Indian Dispossession
       in the Husdon Valley. In 2282, pp. 242-
       260.

1365   _____. The Indian Reorganization Act. In
       0034, pp. 131-148.

1366   _____. The Iroquois and the New Deal.
       Syracuse, NY., Syracuse University Press,
       1981.
       An Iroquois Book
       OCLC # 7978087

1367   _____. Raw Deal: The Iroquois View the In-
       dian Reorganization Act of 1934. In 3035,
       pp. 15-25.

1368   _____. Refugee Havens: The Iroquois Vil-
       lages of the Eighteenth Century. In 0079,
       pp. 128-139.

1369   _____. Smallpox and American Indian. New
       York State Journal of Medicine, v. 79,
       Nov. 1979, pp. 1945-1949.
       A Reprint copy

1370   Haury, Emil W. (Emil Walter), 1904- .
       Concluding Remarks. In 2768, pp. 158-
       166.

1371   _____. The Hohokam, Desert Farmers and
       Craftsmen: Excavations at Snaketown,
       1964-1965. Tucson, University of Arizona
       Press, 1976.
       OCLC # 2283003

1372   _____. The Stratigraphy and Archaeology of
       Ventana Cave. Collaborators Kirk Bryan ...
       Tucson, University of Arizona Press,
       1950, 1975 printing.
       1975 printing preface by Emil W. Haury and
       Julian D. Hayden.
       OCLC # 1965699

_____. see also 1725

Hausfater, Glenn see 3527

1373 Haviland, John Beard. Gossip, Reputation
      and Knowledge in Zinacantan. Chicago,
      University of Chicago Press, 1977.
      OCLC # 2464509

1374 Haviland, William A. The Ancient Maya and
      the Evolution of Urban Society. Greeley,
      University of Northern Colorado, Museum of
      Anthropology, 1975.
      University of Northern Colorado, Museum of
      Anthropology, Misc. Series no. 37
      OCLC # 2484751

1375 _____. The original Vermonters: Native In-
      habitants, Past and Present. ... Marjory
      W. Power. Hanover, NH., Published for
      University of Vermont by University Press
      of New England, 1981.
      OCLC # 7277340

      _____, see also 1658

1376 Hawk, William. The Revitalization of the
      Matinnecock Indian Tribe of New York. Ann
      Arbor, MI., University Microfilms Inter-
      national, 1984.
      Microfilm - PhD Thesis - University of
      Wisconsin, Madison
      OCLC # 11602977

      Hawkes, Kristen see 1448

1377 Hawkins, Benjamin, 1754-1816. Letters of
      Benjamin Hawkins, 1796-1806. Savannah,
      GA., Georgia Historical Society, 1916.
      Collections of the Georgia Historical Soc-
      iety v. 9. Hawkins was U. S. agent for
      Indian Affairs south of the Ohio River dur-
      ing the period covered by the letters.
      OCLC # 3428708

1378 _____. A Sketch of the Creek Country, in
      1798 and 1799. New York, Kraus Reprint,
      1971.
      Collection of the Georgia Historical Soc-
      iety v. 3, pt. 1. Reprint of the 1848

ed.   published by the Society.   Introd.
and historic sketch of the Creek Confederacy by W.   B.   Hodgson.
OCLC # 1141267

1379 _____. Sketch of the Creek Country,   in the
Years 1789 and 1799. A combinaztion of a
sketch of the Creek Country,   in the years
1798 and 1799;   and letters of Benjamin
Hawkins,   1796-1806.
Reprint of 2 works,   1st originally published in 1848 by Georgia Historical Society,   Savannah,   which was issued as part
1, v. 3 of Georgia Historical Society
Collections,   2nd originally published in
1916 by Georgia Historical Society,   Savannah,   which was issued as v. 9 of Georgia
Historical Collections
OCLC # 8964419

Hawkins,   Gerald S.   see   2224

1380 Hawley,   Charles,   1819-1885.   Early Chapters
of Cayuga History: Jesuit Missions in Goi-
o-gotten,   1656-1684.   Also an Account of
the Sulpitian Mission Among the Emigrant
Cayugas About Quint Bay,   in 1668.   With an
introd.   by John Gilmary Shea.   Auburn,
NY.,   Knapp & Peck Printers,   1879.

1381 _____. Early Chapters of Seneca History:
Jesuit Missions in Sonnontouan 1656-1684.
Auburn,   NY.,   Knapp,   Peck & Thomson,
Book & Job Printers,   1884.
Reprinted from Collections of Cayuga County
Historical Society no. 3.

1382 Hawthorn,   Audrey.   Kwakiutl Art.   Seattle,
University of Washington Press,   1979.
Includes much of what appeared in Art of
the Kwakiutl Indians an Other Northwest
Coast Tribes
OCLC # 5102078

1383 Hayden,   Brian D.   Material Culture in the
Mayan Highlands: Preliminary Study.   In
2825,   pp. 183-222.

1384 Hayden,   Robert.   The Patrilineal Determina-

tion of Band Membership at the Six-Nation
Reserve. In 3035, pp. 27-36.

1385 Hayes, Alden C. and Thomas C. Winders. An
Anasazi Shrine in Chaco Canyon. In 0622,
pp. 143-156.

1386 _____. Archeological Surveys of Chaco Can-
yon, New Mexico. ... David M. Brugge,
W. James Judge. Washington, National
Park Service, U. S. Dept. of the In-
terior, 1981.
OCLC # 5750491

1387 _____. Contributions to Gran Quivira
Archaeology: Gran Quivira National Mon-
ument, New Mexico. With contributions by
Thomas J. Caperton, et al. Washington,
National Park Service, U. S. Dept. of
the Interior, Govt. Print. Off.,
Distributors, 1981.
Essays in this collection are also listed
individually and refer to this citation.
Publications in Archaeology v. 17
OCLC # 5008222

1388 _____. Excavations of Mound 7, Gran
Quivira National Monument, New Mexico.
... Jon Nathan Young and A. H. Warren.
Washington, National Park Service, U. S.
Dept. of the Interior, Govt. Print.
Off., 1981.
Publications in Archaeology v. 16
OCLC # 5008223

1389 Hayes, Charles F. An Approach to Iroquois-
White Acculturation Through Archeology.
New York State Archeological Association
Bulletin 22, July 1961, pp. 15-18.
Paper presented at the annual meeting,
April 8, 1961.

1390 _____. An Overview of the Current Status of
Seneca Ceramics. In 1585, pp. 87-93.

1391 _____. A Progress Report on an Archaic Site
on the Farrell Farm: The Cole Gravel Pit
1966-1968. New York State Archeological
Association Bulletin 47, Nov. 1969, pp.

1-12. Millwood, NY., Kraus Reprint, 1976.

1392 _____. <u>Projectile Point Classification</u>. New York State Archeological Association Bulletin 32, Nov. 1964, pp. 17-18. Millwood, NY., Kraus Reprint, 1976.

_____. see also 0712, 1204

Haywood Gallery see 0608

1393 Heckewelder, John Gottlieb Ernestus, 1743-1823. <u>An Account of the History, Manners, Customs of the Indian Nations</u>. Philadelphia, A. Small, 1819.
Detached from Transactions of the Historical and Literary Committee of the American Philosophical Society, held at Philadelphia for promoting useful knowledge, v. 1.
OCLC # 2430700

1394 _____. <u>Indian Tradition of the First Arrival of the Dutch at Manhattan Island, Now New York</u>. In Collections of the New York State Historical Society, second series, v. 1, pp. 69-74.

1395 Hedlund, Ann Lane. <u>Contemporary Navajo Weaving: An Ethnography of a Native Craft</u>. Ann Arbor, MI., University Microfilms International, 1983.
Microfilm - PhD Thesis - University of Colorado
OCLC # 11368491

1396 Hedren, Paul L. <u>First Scalp for Custer: The Skirmish at Warbonnett Creek, Nebraska, July 17, 1876: With a Short History of the Warbonnett Battlefield</u>. Introd. by Don Russell, Glendale, CA., A. H. Clark Co., 1980.
Hidden Springs of Custeriana, v. 5. "of this book 350 copies have been printed" verso of t. p.
OCLC # 7344955

1397 Hedrick, Basil Calvin, 1932- . <u>The Loca-</u>

tion of Corazones.   In 0014,   pp.   228-
232.

_____. see also 0014

1398 Heidenreich,   Conrad,   1936- . The Early
Fur Trades: A Study in Cultural Inter-
action.   ... Arthur J.   Ray.   Toronto,   Mc-
Cleeland and Steward,   1976.
A Canada Studies Foundation/ Canadian
Assoiation of Geographers Project
OCLC # 3792379

1399 Heizer,   Robert Fleming,   1915- . Califor-
nia Indian History: A Classified and An-
notated Guide to Source Materials.   ...
Karen M.   Nissen and Edward D.   Castillo.
Ramona,   CA.,   Ballena Press,   1975.
Ballena Press Publications in Archaeology,
Ethnology and History,   no.   4.
OCLC # 1647606

1400 _____.   and Thomas R.   Hester.   Great Basin.
In 0577,   pp.   147-199.

1401 _____.   The Indians of California: A Criti-
cal Bibliography.   Bloomington,   Indiana
University Press,   1976.
Bibliographical Series,   Newberry Library
Center for the History of the American In-
dian
OCLC # 2331653

1402 _____.   The Natural World of the California
In-dians.   ... Albert B.   Elsasser.   Berk-
eley,   University of California Press,
1980.
California Natural History Guides,   v.   46
OCLC # 5336725

_____. see also 1589

1403 Hellmuth,   Nicholas M.   Cholti-Lacandon
(Chiapas) and Petén-Ytza-Agriculture,   Settlement Pattern and Population.   In 2920,
pp.   421-448.

1404 _____.   The Escuintla Hoards: Teotihuacan
Art in Guatemala.   Guatemala City,   Foundation for Latin American Anthropological Re-

search, 1975.
F. L. A. A..R. Progress Reports, v.
1, no. 2.
OCLC # 2069667

1405 _____. Maya Archaeology, Tikal, Copan:
Travel Guide, 1978; A Complete Guide to
all the Maya Ruins of Central America. St.
Louis, MO., Foundation for Latin American
Anthropological Research, 1978, c.1976.
OCLC # 4619199

1406 Hellson, John C. Ethnobotany of the Black-
foot Indians. Ottawa, Natiional Museum of
Canada, 1974.
OCLC # Paper - Canadian Ethnology Service,
no. 19, Mercury Series. Abstracts in
French
OCLC # 3053606

1407 Helm, June, (formerly June Helm MacNeish),
1924- . The Indians of the Subarctic.
Bloomington, Indiana University Press,
1976.
Bibliographical Series, Newberry Library
Center for the History of the American In-
dian
OCLC # 2868610

1408 _____. and G. A. De Vos and Teresa Carterette. Variations in Personality and Ego
Identification Within a Slave Indian Kin-
community. In National Musuem of Cananda
Bulletin no. 10. Contributions to Anthropology, 1960, pt. 2. Ottawa, Dept. of
Northern Affairs and National Resources,
1963, pp. 94-138.

1409 Helms, Mary W. Coastal Adaptating as Contact Phenomena Among the Miskito and Cuna
Indians of Lower Central America. In 2524,
pp. 121-149.

_____. see also 1133

1410 Hemmerdinger, Catherine C. Design. In
2677, pp. 112-161.

1411 Hemming, John, 1935- . Monuments of the
Incas. Photographs by Edward Ranney. Bos-

ton. Little, Brown, 1982.
A New York Graphic Society Book
OCLC # 8589532

1412 _____. Red Gold: The Conquest of the Bra-
zilian Indians, 1500-1760. Cambridge,
MA., Harvard University Press, 1978.
OCLC # 3121140

Henderson, James Youngblood see 0189

1413 Henderson, John S. Atopula Guerrero and
Almec Horizons in Mesoamerica. New Haven,
Dept. of Anthropology, Yale University
Press, 1979.
Yale University Publications in Anthro-
pology, no. 77.
OCLC # 5630577

1414 _____. The World of the Ancient Maya.
Ithaca, NY., Cornell University Press,
1981.
OCLC # 7464206

1415 Henley, Paul. The Panare Tradition and
Change on the Amazonian Frontier. New
Haven, Yale University Press, 1982.
OCLC # 7575001

Henn, Nora see 0163

1416 Hennessy, Alistair. The Frontier in Latin
American History. Albuquerque, University
of New Mexico Press, 1978.
History of the American Frontier
OCLC # 4118190

Henning, Dale R. see 0469

1417 Henfrey, Colin. Through Indian Eyes: A
Journey Among the Indian Tribes of Guiana.
New York, Holt, Rinehart and Winston,
1965.
First published in London in 1964 under
title The Gentle People
OCLC # 410666

1418 Henry, Jeannette. Textbooks and the
American Indian. by The American Indian
Historical Society. Rupert Costo, editor.

San Francisco, Indina Historian Press,
1970.
OCLC # 106388

_____. see also 0668

1419 Henry, Jules, 1904-1969. Doll Play of Pil-
aga Indian Children; An Experimental and
Field Analysis of the Behavior of the Pil-
agá Children. ... and Zunia Henry. With a
new introd. by Stanley Diamond. New York,
Vintage Books, 1974.
Reprint of the 1944 ed. by American Ortho-
psychiatric Assoc. which was issued as
Research Monograph no. 4. American Ortho-
psychiatric Association
OCLC # 754455

1420 Henry, William, fl 1768. Account of the
Captivity of William Henry. New York,
Garland Pub., 1977.
Garland Library of narratives of North
American Indian captivities, v. 10. Re-
print of an article which appeared in the
London Chronicle v. 23, no. 1798, June
23, 1768 and no. 1799, June 25, 1768.
Issued with the reprint of the 1764 ed. of
Saunders, C. The Horrid Cruelty of the In-
dians.
OCLC # 2798668

Henry, Zunica see 1419

1421 Hensley, William. Arctic Development and
the Future of the Eskimo Societies. In
1875, pp. 111-121.

1422 Herbert, Belle. Shandaa in my Lifetime;
Recorded and edited by Bill Pfisterer with
the assistance of Alice Moses; transcribed
and translated by Katherine Peter; edited
by Jane McGary, drawings by Sandy
Jamieson; photographs by Rob Stapleton.
Alaska Native Language Center, University
of Alaska, 1982.
OCLC # 9112401

Herbstritt, J. see 3263

1423 Herskovitz, Robert M. Fort Bowie Material

Culture. Tucson, University of Arizona
Press, 1978.
University of Arizona Anthropological
Papers no. 31.
OCLC # 3844278

1424 Hertzberg, Hazel W. _Arthur C. Parker,
Seneca, 1881-1955_. In 0080, pp. 129-
138.

1425 Hess, Milton Jerome. _The Origin and
Implementation of the Dawes Act in the
Dakotas, 1865-1914_. Ann Arbor, MI.,
University Microfilms International, 1982.
Microfilm - PhD Thesis - Columbia Univer-
sity
OCLC # 12618331

1426 Hesse, Franklin J. _The Egli and Lord Sites:
The Historic Component - "Unadilla" 1753-
1778_. In 3519, pp. 92-99.

1427 _____. _The Fredenburg Site: A Single Component Site of the Fox Creek Complex_. New
York State Archeological Association Bulletin 44, Nov. 1968, pp. 27-32. Millwood, NY., Kraus Reprint, 1976.
Paper presented at the annual meeting,
April 20, 1968.

Hester, Thomas R. _see_ 1400

1428 _The Héta Indians: Fish in a Dry Pond_.
Vladimir Kozak. New York, American Museum
of Natural History, 1979.
Anthropological Papers of the American
Museum of Natural History v. 55, pt. 6.
OCLC # 5616027

1428.5 Heth, Charlotte. _Update on Indian Music:
Contemporary Trends_. In 2831.5, pp. 89-
100.

_____. _see also_ 2831.5

1429 Hewatt, Alexander. _An Historical Account of
the Rise and Progress of the Colonies of
South Carolina and Georgia_. London, A.
Donaldson, 1779. (Spartanburg, SC.,
Reprint Co., 1971.)

South Carolina heritage series no.   7-8.
The first set of the fundamental
constitutions of South Carolina as compiled
by Mr. John Locke.
OCLC # 264203

1430   Hewes,   Gordon Winaut,   1917-   .   A Conspec-
       tus of the World's Cultures in 1500 A. D.
       Millwood,   NY.,   Kraus Reprint,   1974.
       Essays in this collection are also listed
       individually and refer to this citation.
       University of Colorado Studies series in
       anthropology no. 4. Orig. pub. Univer-
       sity of Colorado Press,   1954.
       OCLC # 1302088

1431   Hewett,   Edgar L.   (Edgar Lee),   1865-1946.
       The Proposed "National Park of the Cliff
       Cities".   Washington?,   1916.
       Archaeological Institute of America.   Pa-
       pers of the School of American Archaeology
       no.   34.   1 reel microfilm from Library of
       Congress Class E - Miscellaneous Monographs
       and pamphlets,   shelf #44140-44175,
       #44140.
       OCLC # 2286569

       _____.   see also   0169

1432   Hewitt,   John Napoleon Brinton.   Myths, Leg-
       ends,   Ethnological Notes,   Historical In-
       formation in re Tuscaroras of New York
       State (1883-1890).   1 reel microfilm pro-
       vided by American Philosophical Society,
       Philadelphia.   For description see Freeman
       Guide #88.
       Transcripts of originals in Bureau of
       American Ethnology

       _____.   see also   0792

1433   Hewson,   John.   New Resources for Comparative
       Work in Algonkian Languages.   In 0068,
       pp.   3-9.

1434   Heyden,   Doris.   Pre-Columbian Architecture
       of Mesoamerica.   ... Paul Gendrop;   trans.
       by Judith Stanton,   New York,   H. N.
       Adams,   1975.
       History of World Architecture.   Translation

of Architettura Mesoamericana
OCLC # 1365109

1435 Hibben, Frank C. (Frank Cummings), 1910- .
Kiva Art on the Anasazi at Pottery Mound,
New Mexico. Las Vegas, KC Publications,
1975.
OCLC # 1902936

1436 Hickerson, Harold, 1923- . The Southwest-
ern Chippewa: An Ethnohistorical Study.
Millwood, NY., Kraus Reprint, 1974.
Memoirs of the American Anthropological As-
sociation, no. 92. Suppl. to American
Anthropologist v. 64, no. 3, pt. 2,
1962.
OCLC # 1187706

1437 Hicks, Frederic. Rotational Labor and Urban
Development in Prehistoric Tetzcoco. In
0978, pp. 147-174.

1438 The Hidden Half: Studies on Plains Indian
Women. Patricia Albers, Beatrice Medi-
cine. Lanham, MD., University Press of
America, 1983.
Essays in this collection are also listed
individually and refer to this citation.
Consists chiefly of papers presented at a
symposium entitled The Role and Status of
Women in Plains Indian Cultures, held in
1977 at the Plains Conference, Lincoln,
Nebraska.
OCLC # 9110693

1439 Highwater, Jamake. Arts of the Indian
Americas: Leaves from the Sacred Tree.
New York, Harper & Row, 1983.
OCLC # 9325268

1440 _____. Fodor's Indian America. illus. by
Asa Battles; Eugene Fodor, editor. New
York, McKay, 1975.
OCLC # 1529087

1441 _____. The Primal Mind: Vision and Reality
in Indian America. New York, Harper &
Row, 1981.
OCLC # 7177774

1442   _____.   Ritual of the Wind: North American
           Indian Ceremonies,   Music,   and Dance.
           Drawings by Asa Battle.   New York,   Viking
           Press,   1977.
           OCLC # 3072355

1443   _____.   Song from the Earth: American In-
           dian Painting.   Boston,   New York Graphic
           Society,   pub.   by Little,   Brown,   1976.
           OCLC # 2372147

           Hilbert,   Vi.   see   1297

1444   Hill,   Beth,   1924- .   Indian Petroglyphs of
        the Pacific Northwest.   ...   Ray Hill.
        Saanichton,   B.   C.,   Hancock House Pub-
        lishers,   1974.
        OCLC # 1450019

1445   Hill,   Edward E.   Guide to Records in the Na-
        tional Archives of the United States Relat-
        ing to American Indians.   Washington,   D.
        C.,   National Archives and Records Service,
        General Services Administration,   1981.
        OCLC # 8052651

1446   Hill,   Frank Ernest.   A New Pattern of Life
        for the Indian.   In 3335,   pp.   48-56.

1447   Hill,   Jonathan and Emilio F.   Moran.   Adapt-
        ive Strategies of Wakunai Peoples to the
        Oligotrophic Rain Forest of the Rio Negro
        Basin.   In 0023,   pp.   113-135.

1448   Hill,   Kim and Kristen Hawkes.   Neotropical
        Hunting Among the Ache of Eastern Paraguay.
        In 0023,   pp.   139-188.

        Hill,   Mary Ann   see   0579

        Hill,   Norbet S.,   see   0579

        Hill,   Ray   see   1444

1448.5 Hill,   Richard.   The Impact of a Museum on
        the Native Community.   In 2831.5,   pp.
        147-154.

        Hill,   Robert M.   see   2616

1449 Hill,   W.   W.   (Willard Williams),   1902-
      1974. An Ethnology of Santa Clara Pueblo,
      New Mexico. Edited and annotated by
      Charles H. Lange. Albuquerque, Univer-
      sity of New Mexico Press, 1982.
      Constitutions and Bylaws of the Pueblo of
      Santa Clara
      OCLC # 7306003

1450 _____. The Agricultural and Hunting Methods
      of the Navaho Indians. New York, AMS
      Press, 1978.
      Reprint of the 1938 ed. pub. for Dept.
      of Anthropology, Yale University by Yale
      University Press, which was issued as no.
      18 of Yale University Publications in
      Anthropology
      OCLC # 4500149

1451 Hind, Henry Youle, 1823-1908. Explorations
      in the Interior of the Labrador Peninsula,
      the Country of the Montagnais and Nasquapee
      Indians. London, Longman, Green, Long-
      man, Roberts, and Green, 1863. Millwood,
      NY., Kraus Reprint Co., 1973.
      OCLC # 677631

1452 Hinsdale, W. B. (Wilbert B.), 1851-1944.
      ...Perforated Indian Crania in Michigan.
      ... Emerson F. Greenman. Ann Arbor, MI.,
      University of Michigan Press, 1936.
      Michigan. University. Museum of Anthro-
      pology. Occasional Contributions, no. 5.
      OCLC # 627450

1453 Hinshaw, Robert E., 1933- . Panajachel:
      A Guatemalan Town in Thirty-Year Perspect-
      ive. Foreword by Sol Tax. Pittsburgh,
      University of Pittsburgh Press, 1975.
      Pitt Latin American Series
      OCLC # 1195044

1454 Hinton, Leanne. Vocables in Havasupai Song.
      In 2931, pp. 275-305.

1455 Hippler, Arthur E. Patterns of Migration,
      Urbanization and Acculturation of the
      Alaskan Natives. In 1875, pp. 171-177.

1456 Hirschfelder, Arlene B. American Indian

Stereotypes in the World of Children: A
Reader and Bibliography. Metuchen, NJ.,
Scarecrow Press, 1982.
Essays in this collection are also listed
individually and refer to this citation.
This volume has an extensive bibliography
OCLC # 7948627

1457   _____. Annotated Bibliography of the Liter-
ature on American Indians Published in
State Historical Society Publications, New
England and Middle Atlantic States. Mill-
wood, NY., Kraus Reprint, 1982.
OCLC # 8763655

1458   _____. Toys with Indian Imagery. In 1456,
pp. 145-180.

1459   _____. The Treatment of the Iroquois in
Selected History Textbooks. In 1456, pp.
121-137.
Reprinted from The Indian Historian v. 8,
no. 2, Fall 1975, pp. 32-39.

1460   Historic Clay Tobacco Pipe Studies. v. 1-
Ponca City, OK., B. Sudbury, 1980.
OCLC # 10618601

1461   Historical Indian - Colonial Relations of New
Hampshire; Treaties, Letters of Agree-
ment, Land Sales, Leases and Other Perti-
nent Information, 17th - 18th Centuries.
Manchester, NH., Pennacook/ Sokoki Inter-
Tribal Nation, NH., Indian Council,
1977.
OCLC # 4765216

Historical Society of Pennsylvania see 1569

1462   History and Archaeology of the Montauk In-
dians. Lexington, MA., Ginn Custom Pub.,
Stony Brook, NY., (Available from Suffolk
County Archaeological Association), 1979.
Readings in Long Island Archaeology and
Ethnohistory, v. 3.
OCLC # 6357913

1463   The History and Culture of Iroquois Diplomacy: An Interdisciplinary Guide to the
Treaties of the Six Nations and their Lea-

gue. Francis Jennings, editor, for the
D'Arcy McNickle Center for the History of
the American Indian, The Newberry Library.
Syracuse, NY., Syracuse University Press,
1985.
OCLC # 11187575

Hitchcock, Robert K. see 0911

1464 Hlady, Walter M. The Harris Bison Run Near
Brandon. In 1467, pp. 175-179.

1465 _____. Manitoba - The Northern Woodlands.
In 1467, pp. 93-121.

1466 _____. Southeastern Manitoba Resurveyed.
In 1467, pp. 269-281.

1467 _____. Ten Thousand Years: Archaeology in
Manitoba. Commorating Manitoba's Centen-
nial, 1870-1970. Winnipeg, Manitoba
Archaeological Society, 1970.
Essays in this collection are also listed
individually and refer to this citation.
OCLC # 2656426

1468 Hodges, B. Frank. The Arthur Harris Site.
New York State Archeological Association
Bulletin 3, March 1955, pp. 10-11.
Millwood, NY., Kraus Reprint, 1976.
Abstract of paper presented at the annual
meeting 1954.

Hodgson, William Brown, 1800- . see 1378

1469 Hoebel, E. Adamson (Edward Adamson), 1906-
The Influence of Plains Ethnography on the
Development of Anthropological Theory. In
0112, pp. 16-22.

1470 _____. Plains Indians: A Critical Biblio-
graphy. Bloomington, Published for the
Newberry Library by Indiana University
Press, 1977.
Bibliographical Series
OCLC # 3275660

1471 _____. The Political Organization and Law-
ways of the Comanche Indians. New York,
Kraus Reprint, 1969.

Memoirs of the American Anthropological Association, no. 54, Contributions from
the Laboratory of Anthropology 4, Suppl.
to American Anthropologist v. 42, no. 3,
pt. 2.

_____. see also 3311

1472 Hoegh, Erling. The Historical Development
of Political Institutions in Greenland. In
1875, pp. 371-390.

1473 Hoffman, Albert J. Additional Data on Historic Burials at the Boughton Hill Site
(Can 2-2), Victor Township, Ontario County, N. Y. New York State Archeological
Association Bulletin 40, July 1967, pp.
4-17. Millwood, NY., Kraus Reprint,
1976.
For additional information see New York
State Archeological Association Bulletin
32, Nov. 1964, pp. 6-16.

1474 _____. The McClintock Burial Site. New
York State Archeological Association Bul-
letin 7, Aug. 1956, pp. 3-5. Millwood,
NY., Kraus Reprint, 1976.

1475 Hofling, Charles K. Custer and the Little
Big Horn: A Psychobiological Inquiry.
Detroit, MI., Wayne State University
Press, 1981.
OCLC # 6734115

1476 Hofsinde, Robert (Gray Wolf). Talk-Without-
Talk. In 0008, pp. 143-155.
Reprinted from Natural History v. 47,
Jan. 1941, pp. 32-39.

1477 Hoig, Stan The Battle of the Washita: The
Sheridan-Custer Indian Campaign of 1867-69.
Garden City, NY., Doubleday, 1976.
OCLC # 2020143

1477 _____. The Peace Chiefs of the Cheyennes.
Foreword by Boyce D. Timmons. Norman,
University of Oklahoma Press, 1980.
OCLC # 5197005

1479 Holbrook, Sally J. and Michael W. Graves.

Modern Environment of the Grasshopper Region. In 2239, pp. 5-11.

1480   _____. Prehistoric Environmental Reconstruction by Mammalian Microfaunal Analysis, Grasshopper Pueblo. In 2239, pp.
73-86.

        _____. see also 2239

1481   Hole, Frank. Changing Directions in Archeological Thought. In 0097, pp. 1-23.
Also printed in 0098

1482   _____. Changing Directions in Archeological
Thought. In 0098, pp. 1-23.
Also printed in 0097.

1482.5   _____. Prehistoric Archaeology: A Brief
Introduction. ... Robert F. Heizer. New
York, Holt, Rinehart and Winston, 1977.
OCLC # 2646231

1483   Holien, Thomas. Pseudo-Cloisonne in the
Southwest and Mesoamerica. In 0622, pp.
157-177.

1484   Hollister, Isaac, b. 1750? A Brief Nar-
ration of the Captivity of Isaac Hollister.
New York, Garland Pub., 1977.
Garland Library of narratives of North
American Indian captivities, v. 10. Re-
print of the 1767 ed. printed and sold at
the printing office, New London, CT.
OCLC # 2798772

        Hollow, Kitty see 1575

1485   Hollow, Robert C. and Douglas R. Parks.
Studies in Plains Linguistics: A Review.
In 0112, pp. 68-97.
This paper has an extensive bibliography

1486   Holm, Bill, 1925- . The Box of Daylight:
Northwest Coast Indian Art. With contribu-
tions by Peter L. Corey ... Seattle, WA.,
Seattle Art Museum; University of Washing-
ton Press, 1983.
Catalog of an exhibition held at Seattle
Art Museum, Sept. 15, 1983- Jan. 8,

1984
OCLC # 9758809

1487 _____. Form in Northwest Coast Art. In
1562, pp. 33-45.

1487.5 Holm, Thomas. The Discovery of Indian
Art: Awareness or Choices? In 2831.5,
pp. 67-74.

1488 Holm, Thomas Mark. Indians and Progres-
sives: From Vanishing Policy to the Indian
New Deal. Ann Arbor, MI., University Mi-
crofilms International, 1978.
Microfilm - PhD Thesis - University of
Oklahoma
OCLC # 4979833

1489 Holm, Thomas Campanius, 1670(ca)-1702.
Description of the Province of New Sweden,
Now Called by the English, Pennsylvania in
America: Compiled From the Relations and
Writings of Persons Worthy of Credit, and
Adorned with Maps and Plates. Translated
from the Swedish, for the Historical Soc-
iety of Pennsylvania, with notes by Peter
S. DuPonceau. Millwood, NY., Kraus Re-
print Co., 1975.
Reprint of the 1834 ed. published by
M'Carty & Davis, Philadelphia. Transla-
tion of Kort Beskrifning om Provincien Nya
Swerige uti America.
OCLC # 1530787

1490 Holm, Tom. Methodology in Cherokee Tribal
History. In 2962, pp. 167-174.

1490.5 _____. Racial stereotypes and Government
Policies Regarding the Education of Native
Americans, 1879-1920. In 2238.5 pp. 15-
24.

1491 Holmes, Jack D. L. Spanish Policy Toward
the Southern Indians in the 1790's. In
1099, pp. 65-82.

1492 Holmes, Oliver W. Indian-related Records in
the National Archives and their Use:
Observations over a Third of a Century. In
2265, pp. 13-32.

1493 Holmes, W. H. Areas of American Culture
      Characterization Tentatively Outlined as an
      Aid in the Study of the Antiquities. In
      0110, pp. 42-75.

1494 Hooton, Earnest A. Skeletons from the
      Cenote of Sacrifice at Chichen Itza. In
      2105, pp. 272-280.

1495 Hoover, Dwight W. , 1926- . The Red and the
      Black. Chicago, Rand McNally College Pub.
      Co. , 1976.
      Rand McNally series on the history of Amer-
      ican thought and culture
      OCLC # 2401323

1496 Hoover, Herbert T. The Sioux: A Critical
      Bibliography. Bloomington, Published for
      the Newberry Library by Indian University
      Press, 1979.
      Bibliographical Series
      OCLC # 4983586

1497 _____. Sitting Bull. In 0081, pp. 152-
      174.

      Hoover, James L. see 1166

1498 Hopi Kachina: Spirit of Life: Dedicated to
      the Hopi Tricentennial, 1680-1980. Edit-
      ed by Dorothy K. Washburn. San Francisco,
      California Academy of Sciences, Seattle,
      distributed by University of Washington
      Press, 1980.
      Published in conjunction with the
      exhibition of Hopi Kachina: Spirit of Life
      OCLC # 6707575

1499 Hopi Photographers, Hopi Images. Compiled
      by Victor Masayesva and Erin Younger.
      Tucson, AZ. , Sun Tracks and University of
      Arizona Press, 1983.
      Sun Tracks v. 8. Published in conjunction
      with a touring exhibition of Hopi photo-
      graphy , 7 views of Hopi, Organized by
      Northlight Gallery, Arizona State Univer-
      sity.
      OCLC # 9593047

1500 Hopkins, David M. Landscape and Climate of

Beringia During Late Pleistocene and Holocene Time. In 1052, pp. 15-41.

1501 Horowitz, David. The First frontier: The
      Indian Wars and America's Origins. New
      York, Simon and Schuster, 1978.
      OCLC # 4194194

1502 Horsfield, Timothy. Papers, Chiefly on
      Indian Affairs of Pennsylvania (1733-1771).
      One reel microfilm provided by American
      Philosophical Society, Philadelphia. For
      further information consult the Freeman
      Guide #90.

1503 Horsmanden, Daniel. Papers Pertaining to
      Six Nations, 1714-1747. Originals in New
      York Historical Society. One reel of
      microfilm provided by American Philosophi-
      cal Society, Philadelphia. Reel also
      contains some papers of Van Shack family

1504 Hosler, Dorothy, Jeremy A. Sabloff and
      Dale Runge. Situation Model Development:
      A Case Study of the Classic Maya Collapse.
      In 2920, pp. 553-590.

1505 Hothem, Lar, 1938- . North American In-
      dian Artifacts: A Collector's Identifica-
      tion and Value Guide. 3rd ed., Florence,
      AL., Books Americana, 1984.
      OCLC # 10954151

1505.5 Hough, Franklin Benjamin, 1822-1885.
      Notices of Peter Penet, and of His Opera-
      tions Among the Oneida Indians, Including
      a Plan Prepared by Him for the Government
      of that Tribe. Read before the Albany In-
      stitute, Jan. 23, 1866. Lowville, NY.,
      1866.
      Selected Americana from Sabin's Dictionary
      OCLC # 2637021

1506 How, Nehemiah, 1693-1747. A Narrative of
      the Captivity of Nehemiah How. New York,
      Garland Pub., 1977.
      Garland Library of narratives of North
      American Indian captivities, v. 6. Re-
      print of the 1748 ed. printed and sold by
      S. Kneeland, Boston. Issued with the re-

print of the 1728 ed. of E. Hanson God's
Mercy Surmounting Man's Cruelty.
OCLC # 2896265

1507 Howard, Helen Addison. American Frontier
Tales. Missoula, MT., Mountain
Publishing Co., 1982.
A Rendezvous Book
OCLC # 4775812

1508 _____. Saga of Chief Joseph. Maps and
illus. by George D. McGrath. Lincoln,
University of Nebraska Press, 1978,
c1965.
A Bison Book. Reprint of the 1971 ed.
published by Caxton Printers, Caldwell,
ID., first published in 1941 under title
War Chief Joseph.
OCLC # 4036996

1509 _____. War Chief Joseph. Assisted in the
Research by Dan L. McGrath; maps and
illus. by George D. McGrath. Caldwell,
ID., Caxton Printers, 1946.
OCLC # 1385500

1510 Howard James Henri, 1925- . Canadian
Sioux. Lincoln, University of Nebraska
Press, 1984.
Studies in the Anthropology of North
American Indians
OCLC # 10183997

1510.5 _____. Shawnee!: The Ceremonialism of a
Native Indian Tribe and its Cultural Background. Athens, Ohio University Press,
1981.
OCLC # 6533399

1511 Howrad, O. O. (Oliver Otis), 1830-1909.
Famous Indian Chiefs I Have Known. With
illus. by George Varian and by photographs. New York, Century, 1908.
OCLC # 854776

1512 Howard, Richard M. An Adobe-Lines Pit at
Gran Quivira. In 1387, pp. 13-14.

1513 Howe, Jemima Sartwell, 1713?-1805. A

Genuine and Correct Account of the Captiv-
ity, Sufferings & Deliverance of Mrs.
Jemima Howe. (Taken from her Own Mouth,
and Written by Bunker Gray, ie Gay). New
York, Garland Pub., 1977.
Garland Library of narratives of North
American Indian captivities, v. 19. Re-
print of the 1792 ed. published by Belknap
and Young, Boston. Issued with the re-
print of the 1788 ed. of D. Humphreys An
Essay on the Life of the Honorable Major
General Israel Putnam.
OCLC # 2929563

1514 Howells, H. H. The Origins of American
      Indian Race Types. In 2105, pp. 3-9.

1515 Howley, James Patrick, 1847-1918. The
      Beothucks or Red Indians: The Aboriginal
      Inhabitants of Newfoundland. New York,
      AMS Press, 1979.
      Reprint of the 1915 ed. pub. by Univer-
      sity Press, Cambridge, Eng.
      OCLC # 4500147

      Howling Wolf see 2479

1516 Hoxie, Frederick E., 1947- . A Final
      Promise: The Campaign to Assimilate the
      Indians, 1880-1920. Lincoln, University
      of Nebraska Press, 1984.
      OCLC # 9488717

1517 _____. Indian-White Relations: 1790-1900.
      In 2789, pp. 106-122.

      _____. see also 1170

1518 Hrdlicka, Ales, 1869-1943. The Anthropol-
      ogy of Florida. New York, AMS Press,
      1980.
      Reprint of the 1922 ed. published by
      Florida State Historical Society, Deland,
      as no. 1 of its publications.
      OCLC # 6737151

1519 _____. Physical Anthropology in America.
      In 0110, pp. 135-181.

1520 Hubbard, John Niles, 1815-1897. A Account

of Sa-go-ye-wat-ta,   or Red Jacket,   and
His People, 1750-1830.   Albany,   NY.,
Munsell,   1886.
Munsell's Historical Series no.   13.
OCLC # 1207756

1521 Hudanick,   Andrew.   The Pima Indians and Ari-
zona Water Policy,   1840-1907.   Ann Arbor,
MI.,   University Microfilms International,
1983.
Microfilm - PhD Thesis - Northern Arizona
University
OCLC # 10453836

1522 Hu-DeHart,   Evelyn.   Missionaries,   Miners
and Indians: Spanish Contact With the
Yaqui Nation of Northwestern New Spain,
1533-1820.   Tucson,   University of Arizona
Press,   1981.
OCLC # 7772749

1523 Hudson,   Charles M.   The Catawba Indians of
South Carolina: A Question of Ethnic Survival.   In 2930,   pp.   110-120.

1524 _____.   Southeastern Indians.   Knoxville,
University of Tennessee Press,   1976.
OCLC # 1818252

1525 _____.   Why the Southeastern Indians Slaugh-
tered Deer.   In 1574,   pp.   155-176.

_____,   see also 1099

Hudson,   Travis see 1346

1526 Huel,   Raymond.   A Parting of the Ways:
Louis Schmidt's Account of Louis Riel and
the Metis Rebellion.   In 0137,   pp.   263-
279.

1527 Huelsbeck,   David Richard.   Mammals and Fish
in the Subsistence Economy of Ozette.   Ann
Arbor,   MI.,   University Microfilms Inter-
national,   1983.
Microfilm - PhD Thesis - Washington State
University

1528 Huey,   Paul R.   Glass Trade Beads from Fort

Orange, Albany, New York c. A. D. 1624-
1676. In 1204, pp. 83-110.

1529 Hughes, Charles C. (Charles Campbell). Reference Group Concepts in the Study of a
Changing Eskimo Culture. In 0078, pp. 7-
14.

1530 Hughes, J. Donald (Johnson Donald), 1932-.
American Indian Ecology. Preface by Jamake
Highwater. El Paso, Texas Western Press,
1983.
OCLC # 9772596

1531 Hughes, Thomas. Treaty of Traverse des
Sioux in 1851, Under Governor Alexander
Ramsey, With Notes of the Former Treaty
There, in 1841, Under Governor James D.
Doty, of Wisconsin. St. Paul, Minnesota
Historical Society, 1905.
From the Minnesota Historical Society Col-
lection, v. 10, 1905.
OCLC # 6598317

1532 Hughey, David V. An Overview of Great
Plains Physical Anthropology. In 0112,
pp. 52-67.
This paper has an extensive bibliography

1533 Hugo, Richard. Indians of the Imagination.
In 1556, pp. 86

1534 _____. Northwest Indians: Taking Steps for
Themselves. In 1556, pp. 72-73.

1535 Hultkrantz, Ake. Belief and Worship in Native North America. Edited with an introd.
by Christopher Vecsey. Syracuse, NY.,
Syracuse University Press, 1981.
OCLC # 7948560

1536 _____. The Contribution of the Study of
North American Indian Religions to the
History of Religions. In 2818, pp. 86-
106.

1537 _____. The Religions of the American Indians. Translated by Monica Setterwall.
Berkeley, University of California Press,
1979.

Hermeneutics,   studies in the history of
religions, 7.
OCLC # 5509289

_____. see also 2818

Hulton, P. H. (Paul Hope) see 3400

1538   Humfreville,   J.   Lee.   The Sign Language,
       Its Mysterious Origin and Significance.   In
       0008, pp. 69-76.
       Reprinted from Twenty Years Among Our Hos-
       tile Indians, New York,   Hunter & Co.,
       1899, pp. 108-111.

1539   Humphreys,   David,   1752-1818.   An Essay on
       the Life of the Honorable Major General
       Israel Putnam. New York,   Garland Pub.,
       1977.
       Garland Library of narratives of North
       American Indian captivities, v. 19. Re-
       print of the 1788 ed. printed by Hudson
       and Goodwin, Hartford. Issued with the
       reprint of the 1792 ed. of J. S. Howe A
       Genuine and Correct Account of the Captiv-
       ity, Sufferings & Deliverances of Mrs.
       Jemima Howe & Others.
       OCLC # 2965642

1539.5 Humphreys,   Paul.   The Tradition of Song
       Renewal Among the Pueblo Indians,   Part II.
       In 2831.5, pp. 25-37.

1540   Hungry Wolf,   Adolf.   The Blood People: A
       Division of the Blackfoot Confederacy: An
       Illustrated Interpretation of the Old Ways.
       New York,   Harper and Row, 1977.
       OCLC # 2283793

1541   _____.   Shadows of the Buffalo: A Family
       Odyssey Among the Indians.   ... and Beverly
       Hungry Wolf. New York, W. Morrow, 1983.
       OCLC # 9693164

1542   Hungry Wolf,   Beverly.   The Ways of My Grand-
       mothers. New York,   William Morrow Co.,
       Inc., 1980.
       OCLC # 6014468

_____. see also 1541

1543 Hunn, Eugene S. Tzeltal Folk Zoology: The
      Classification of Discontinuities in Na-
      ture. New York, Academic Press, 1977.
      Language, thought, and culture
      OCLC # 2646105

      Hunt, David C. see 1212, 1676

1544 Hunt, Eva. Kinship and Territorial Fission
      in the Cuicatec Highlands. In 0958, pp.
      97-135.

1545 Hunter, C. Bruce. A Guide to Ancient Mex-
      ican Ruins. Norman, University of Oklaho-
      ma Press, 1974.
      OCLC # 922707

1546 Hunter, George. Journals. 1796-1809. One
      reel microfilm provided by American Philo-
      sophical Society. Reel 200, for detailed
      description see the Freeman Guide #93.

1547 Huntsman, Jeffrey F. Traditional Native
      American Literature: The Translation Di-
      lemma. In 2904, pp. 87-97.
      Reprinted from Shantik v. 4, no. 2,
      1979, pp. 5-9.

1548 Hurley, William M. An Analysis of Effigy
      Mound Complexes in Wisconsin. Ann Arbor,
      Museum of Anthropology, University of
      Michigan, 1975.
      University of Michigan, Museum of Anthro-
      pology, Anthropological Papers no. 59.
      OCLC # 3018287

1549 _____. Coding and Cluster Analysis of Wis-
      consin Ceramics. In 0905, pp. 373-390.

1550 Hutchins, Francis G. Mashpee, the Story of
      Cape Cod's Indian Town. West Franklin,
      NH., Amarta Press, 1979.
      OCLC # 5939233

1551 Hyde, Dayton O., 1925- . The Last Free
      Man; The True Story Behind the Massacre of
      Shoshone Mike and His Band of Indians in
      1911. New York, Dial Press, 1973.
      OCLC # 632376

1552   Hymes, Dell H. *The Americanist Tradition*.
       In 1902, pp. 11-33.

1553   _____. *"In Vain I Tried to Tell You": Es-
       says in Native American Ethnopoetics*.
       Philadelphia, University of Pennsylvania
       Press, 1981.
       Studies in Native American Literature v. 1.
       University of Pennsylvania Pubs. in
       Conduct and Communications
       OCLC # 7555043

1554   _____. *Victoria Howard's "Gitskux and his
       Older Brother": A Clackamas Chinook Myth*.
       In 2904, pp. 129-170.

1555   *I Am the Fire of Time: The Voice of Native
       American Women*. Edited by Jane B. Katz.
       New York, Dutton, 1977.
       OCLC # 3588149

1556   *I Will Die an Indian*. By Fred Coyote ... et
       al. Sun Valley, ID., Sun Valley Center
       for the Arts and Humanities, 1980.
       Essays in this collection are also listed
       individually and refer to this citation.
       This publication made possible through a
       grant from Levi Strauss & Co.
       OCLC # 7811015

       Illinois Dept. of Transportation *see*
       0944.5, 1091, 2007

1557   *Inca and Aztec States, 1400-1800: Anthro-
       pology and History*. Edited by George A.
       Collier, Renato I. Rosaldo, John D.
       Wirth. New York, Academic Press, 1982.
       Studies in Anthropology
       OCLC # 8389637

1558   Indergaard, Michael LeRoy. *Urban Renewal
       and the American Indian Movement in Minnea-
       polis: A Case Study in Political Economy
       and the Urban Indian*. Ann Arbor, MI.,
       University Microfilms International, 1983.
       Microfilm - PhD Thesis - Michigan State
       University
       OCLC # 10901437

1559   *Index to the Decisions of the Indian Claims*

Commission. Edited by Norman A. Ross.
New York, Clearwater Pub. Co., 1973.
The Library of American Indian Affairs.
Index to 221 sheets of microfiche, Decisions of the Indian Claims Commission:
findings, opinions, orders, and final
awards of the U. S. Indian Claims Commission, 1948 et seq.
OCLC # 982464

1560 Index to the Expert Testimony Before the
Indian Claims Commission: The Written
Reports. Compiled and edited by Norman A.
Ross. New York, Clearwater Pub. Co.,
1973.
The Library of American Indian Affairs.
Index to 1270 sheets of microfiche, expert
testimony before the Indian Claims Commis-
sion.
OCLC # 2741489

1561 Indian Affairs Papers, American Revolution.
Compiled by Maryly B. Penrose. Franklin
Park, NJ., Liberty Bell Association,
1981.
OCLC # 6580106

1562 Indian Art Traditions of the Northwest Coast.
Roy L. Carlson, editor. Burnaby, B. C.
Archaeology Press, Simon Fraser Univer-
sity, 1982.
Essays in this collection are also listed
individually and refer to this citation.
OCLC # 10949306

1563 Indian as a Soldier at Fort Custer, Montana,
1890-1895: Lieutenant Samuel C. Robert-
son's First Cavalry Crow Indian Contingent.
Compiled and edited by Richard Upton. El
Segundo, CA., R. Upton, 1983.
Montana and the West v. 1
OCLC # 10080405

1563.5 Indian Atrocities. Narratives of the Per-
ils and Sufferings of Dr. Knight and John
Slover, Among the Indians During the Rev-
olutionary War, ... Cincinnati, U. P.
James, 1867.
Reprinted from the Nashville ed. of 1843
OCLC # 1021229

1564 The Indian Awakening in Latin America. Edit-
      ed by Yves Materne; postscript by Michel
      de Certeau. New York, Friendship Press,
      1980.
      Translation of Le Reveil Indien en Amerique
      Latine.
      OCLC # 6092570

1565 Indian Legal Curriculum and Training Program.
      Indian Sovereignty. (Authors Kirke Kick-
      ingbird... et al.); Indian Legal Curricu-
      lum and Training Program of the Institute
      for the Development of Indian law, Wash-
      ington, The Institute, 1977.
      OCLC # 4468859

1566 Indian Life: Transforming an American Myth.
      Edited and with an introd. by William W.
      Savage. Norman, University of Oklahoma
      Press, 1977.
      Essays in this collection are also listed
      individually and refer to this citation.
      OCLC # 3119702

1567 Indian Peoples of Eastern America: A Docu-
      mentary History of the Sexes. Edited by
      James Axtell, New York, Oxford University
      Press, 1981.
      Collection of 67 short descriptions taken
      from many original sources
      OCLC # 5831792

1568 Indian Records; Record Group 10, Series 2,
      1722-1855. Manuscript Collection in the
      Public Archives of Canada. Includes Min-
      utes of the Commission of Indian Affairs at
      Albany, Minutes and Other Records of Sir
      William Johnson and Guy Johnson, Superin-
      tendents-General of Indian Affairs in North
      America. Microfilm of MSS. Ottawa, Pub-
      lic Archives of Canada, Photographic
      Branch, 1956.
      Photocopies of a few items are negative.
      Library has rolls 1-4, 1772-1842.
      OCLC # 3989233

1569 Indian Rights Association. Indian Rights As-
      sociation Papers, 1885-1901. Wilmington,
      DE., Scholarly Resources Inc., 1973.
      26 reels, microfilm of manuscript collec-

tion in the Historical Society of Pennsylvania
OCLC # 9006920

1570 Indian Slaves of King Philip's War. In Rhode
      Island Historical Society,   Publications.
      Providence,   1893.   v. 1,   no. 3,   pp.
      234-238.
      One reel microfilm from Library of
      Congress,   Class E - Miscellaneous Mono-
      graphs and pamphlets,   shelf # 44140-44175,
      #44142.

1571 Indian Territory. Grand Council. Journal of
      the General Council of the Indian Terri-
      tory: Composed of Delegates...Assembled in
      Council at Okmulgee, in the Indian Terri-
      tory. Wilmington, DE., Scholarly Re-
      sources, 1975.
      Constitutions and Laws of the American In-
      dian Tribes, series 2, v. 32. Reprint
      of the 1871 ed. pub. by Excelsior Book
      and Job Printing Office, Lawrence, KS.
      OCLC # 2343836

1572 Indian Territory. General Council. Journal
      of the Sixth Annual Session of the General
      Council of the Indian Territory: Composed
      of Delegates...Assembled in Council at Ok-
      mulgee, Indian Territory. Wilmington,
      DE., Scholarly Resources, 1975.
      Constitutions and Laws of the American In-
      dian Tribes, series 2, v. 33. Reprint
      of the 1875 ed. pub. by Republican
      Journal Steam Printing Establishment, Law-
      rence, KS.
      OCLC # 2343771

1573 The Indians and Their Captives. Edited and
      compiled by James Levernier and Hennig
      Cohen. Westport, CT., Greenwood Press,
      1977.
      Contributions in American Studies, 31
      OCLC # 3001998

1574 Indians, Animals, and the Fur Trade; A
      Critique of Keepers of the Game. Edited by
      Shepard Krech. Athens, University of
      Georgia Press, 1981.
      Essays in this collection are also listed

individually and refer to this citation.
Initial versions of these papers were
presented in the Symposium Ethnohistorical
Perspectives on Keepers of the Game,   at
the 27th annual meeting of the American
Society for Ethnohistory,   ALbany,   NY.,
Oct. 11-14,   1979.
OCLC # 7283836

1575 Indians in Careers: Interviews by Neal
      Starkman,   Kitty Hollow,   Bill Brescia.
      Edited by Kitty Hollow,   Jeanne Heuving;
      photography by Roger Fernandes,   Yasu
      Osawa.   Seattle,   WA.,   United Indians of
      All Tribes Foundation,   1979.
      OCLC # 9902367

1576 Indians of the United States and Canada: A
      Bibliography.   Dwight L.   Smith,   editor;
      John C.   Ewers,   introd.   Santa Barbara,
      ABC Clio,   1976.
      Clio Bibliography Series v. 3. A compila-
      tion of descriptive annotations of litera-
      ture of the years 1954-1972.
      OCLC # 1272447

      Institute for Andean Research see 0239

1577 Institute for the Development of Indian Law.
      A Chronological List of Treaties and Agree-
      ments made by Indian Tribes,   with the
      United States.   Introd.   by Vine Deloria,
      Washington,   1973.
      OCLC # 1099187

      Institute for the Development of Indian Law
      see 1880,   3185

      Institute of American Indian Arts see 0092

      Institute of Social and Economic Research
      see 2485

1578 Inter-American Conference on Indian Life.
      Final Act of the First Inter-American Con-
      ference on Indian Life.   Washington,   Of-
      fice of Indian Affairs,   1941.
      OCLC # 3904764

      InterNorth Art Foundation see 1212

1579 Iobst, Richard W. <u>William Holland Thomas</u>
      <u>and the Cherokee Claims</u>. In 0547, pp.
      181-201.

1580 <u>Iontenwennaweienstahkhwa': Mohawk Spelling</u>
      <u>Dictionary</u>. Compiled by Mary McDonald,
      et al., Marianne Mithun, editor. Albany,
      New York State Museum, 1977.
      New York State Museum Bulletin no. 429
      OCLC # 3590523

1581 Ireland, Arthur K. <u>Cost Effective Mapping</u>.
      In 0711, pp. 371-387

1582 <u>Iroquois Art: A Directory of a People and</u>
      <u>Their Work</u>. Edited by Christina B. Jo-
      hannsen and John P. Ferguson. Warner-
      ville, NY., Association for the Advance-
      ment of Native North American Arts and
      Crafts, 1983. (Peterborough, NH., Sim's
      Press)
      OCLC # 10927657

1583 <u>Iroquois in the American Revolution: 1976</u>
      <u>Conference Proceedings, Sponsored by the</u>
      <u>Arthur C. Parker Fund for iroquois Re-</u>
      <u>search</u>. Rochester, NY., Research Divi-
      sion, Rochester Museum and Science Center,
      1981.
      Research records, Research Division, Ro-
      chester Museum and Science Center, v. 14.
      OCLC # 8668338

1584 <u>Iroquois Indians (Microform): A Documentary</u>
      <u>History of the Diplomacy of the Six Nations</u>
      <u>and Their League</u>. Francis Jennings, edit-
      or ... et al., introd. written by Mary A.
      Druke. Woodbridge, CT., Research Public-
      ations, 1984.
      50 reels of microfilm. Filmed from the
      holdings of the Newberry Library. Publish-
      ed for the D'Arcy McNickle Center for the
      History of the American Indian at the New-
      berry Library.
      OCLC # 11247894

1585 Iroquois Pottery Conference (1979: Rochester
      Museum and Science Center). <u>Proceedings of</u>
      <u>the 1979 Iroquois Pottery Conference Spon-</u>
      <u>sored by the Arthur C. Parker Fund for</u>

Iroquois Research. General editor Charles
F. Hayes III. Associate editors George R.
Hamell, Barbara M. Koenig. Drawings by
Gene MacKay, Rochester, NY., Rochester
Museum and Science Center, Research Divi-
sion, 1980.
Essays in this collection are also listed
individually and refer to this citation.
OCLC # 7444202

1586 Irving, W. N. Pleistocene Archaeology in
Eastern Beringia. In 0902, pp. 96-101.

1587 Isaacs, Hope L. Orenda and the Concept of
Power Among the Tonawanda Seneca. In 0111,
pp. 167-184.

1588 Isbell, William Harris, 1943- . The Rural
Foundation for Urbanism: Economic and
Stylistic Interaction Between Rural and Ur-
ban Communities in Eighth-Century Peru.
Urbana, University of Illinois Press,
1977.
Illinois Studies in Anthropology, v. 10
OCLC # 2799113

1589 Ishi, the Last Yahi: A Documentary History.
Edited by Robert Heizer and Theodora
Kroeber. Berkeley, University of Calif-
ornia Press, 1979.
OCLC # 5077569

1590 Iverson, Peter. Carlos Montezuma. In 0081,
pp. 206-220.

1591 _____. Carlos Montezuma and the Changing
World of American Indians. Albuquerque,
University of New Mexico Press, 1982.
OCLC # 8708777

1592 _____. Indian Tribal Histories. In 2789,
pp. 205-222.

1593 _____. The Navajo Nation. Westport, CT.,
Greenwood Press, 1981.
Contributions in Ethnic Studies v. 3
OCLC # 6330613

1594 _____. The Navajos: A Critical Biblio-

graphy. Bloomington, University of Indiana Press, 1976.
Newberry Library Center for the History of
the American Indian Bibliographical Series
OCLC # 2331654

1595 _____. Peter MacDonald. In 0081, pp.
222-241.

_____. see also 2480

1596 Ives, Ralph S. The Davis Site at Margaret-
ville, N. Y. New York State Archeological Association Bulletin 3, March 1955,
pp. 11-14. Millwood, NY., Kraus Reprint, 1976.
Abstract of paper presented at annual
meeting, 1954.

1597 Jackson, Curtis Emanuel and Marcia J.
Galli. History of the Bureau of Indian Af-
fairs and its Activities Among Indians.
San Francisco, Research Associates, 1977.
OCLC # 3058348

Jackson, Douglas K., 1956- see 0944.5,
0945

1598 Jackson, Helen Hunt. Here is a Picture of a
Helpless People. In 1566, pp. 171-208.
Reprinted from A Century of Dishonor: A
Sketch of the United States Government's
Dealings With Some of the Indian Tribes.
New York, Harper & Bros., 1881, pp.
136-43, 147-85.

1599 Jackson, Jean E. (Jean Elizabeth), 1943-
Recent Ethnography of Indigenous Northern
Lowlands South America. In Annual Review
of Anthropology, 1975, v. 4, pp. 307-
340.

1600 _____. The Fish People: Linguistic Exogamy
and Tukanoan Identity in Northwest Amazonia. New York, Cambridge University Press,
1983.
Cambridge Studies in Social Anthropology v.
39
OCLC # 9112189

1601 Jackson, Laurie James. Late Wisconsin En-
      vironments and Paleo-Indian Occupations in
      the Northeastern U. S. and Southern
      Ontario.
      Ann Arbor, MI., University Microfilms
      International, 1979.
      Microfilm - MA Thesis - Trent University

1602 Jackson, William Henry, 1843-1942. De-
      scriptive Catalogue of Photographs of
      North American Indians. Columbus, OH.,
      R. M. Weatherford Books, 1978.
      Reprint of the 1877 ed. pub. by Govt.
      Print. Off., Dept. of the Interior, U.
      S. Geological Survey of the Territories
      Misc. pub. no. 9.
      OCLC # 4111910

1603 Jacobs, Wilbur R. British-Colonial Atti-
      tudes and Policies Toward the Indian in
      the American Colonies. In 0144, pp. 81-
      106.

1604 _____. Indians as Ecologists and Other En-
      vironmental Themes in American Frontier
      History. In 0079, pp. 46-64.

      Jacobsen, Jacques Noel see 0850

1605 Jacobson, Angeline, 1910- . Contemporary
      Native American Literature: A Selected and
      Partially Annotated Bibliography. Metuch-
      en, NJ., Scarecrow Press, Inc., 1977.
      OCLC # 2896058

1606 Jacobson, Jerome. Archeology at Totten-
      ville, Staten Island. New York Archeo-
      logical Association Bulletin 23, Nov.
      1961, pp. 5-10. Millwood, NY., Kraus
      Reprint, 1976.
      Paper presented at the annual meeting April
      8, 1961

1607 Jade Workers in the Montagua Valley: The
      Late Classic Terzuola Site. Lawrence H.
      Feldman, et al. Columbia, Museum of
      Anthropology, University of Missouri -
      Columbia, 1975.
      Museum Briefs no. 17
      OCLC # 1735726

1608 Jaenen, Cornelius J. Friend and Foe: As-
      pects of French-Amerindian Cultural Contact
      in the 16th and 17th Centuries. New York,
      Columbia University Press, 1976.
      OCLC # 1976120

1609 Jahner, Elaine A., 1942- . Stone Boy:
      Persistent Hero. In 2904, pp. 171-186.

      _____. see also 3302, 3303

1610 Jahoda, Gloria. The Trail of Tears: The
      Story of the American Indian Removals 1813-
      1855. New York, Holt, Rinehart and Wins-
      ton, 1975.
      OCLC # 1363928

1610.5 James, William C. A Fur Trader's Photo-
      graphs: A. A. Chesterfield in the Dis-
      trict of Ungava, 1901-4. Kingston, On-
      tario: Montreal, McGill-Queens's
      University Press, 1985.
      OCLC # 12780333

1611 Jamison, Susan Mary. Neutral Iroquois
      Lithics: Technological Process and Its Im-
      plications (Northeast Ontario). Ann Arbor,
      MI., University Microfilms International,
      1984.
      Microfilm - PhD Thesis - Washington State
      University

1612 Jaquith, James R. Alonso de Molina as
      Ethnosemanticist: The Case of Classical
      Aztec Numbers. In 0154, pp. 77-94.
      Article in Spanish and Nahuatl

1613 Jarvenpa, Robert and Hetty Jo Brumbach. The
      Microeconomics of Southern Chipewyan Fur-
      Trade History. In 3047, pp. 147-183.

1614 Jefferies, Richard W. Dimensions of Middle
      Archaic Cultural Adaptation at the Black
      Earth Site, Saline County, Illinois. In
      0124, pp. 299-322.

1615 Jelinek, Arthur J. Form, FUnction, and
      Style in Lithic Analysis. In 0710, pp.
      19-33.

1616 Jelks,   Edward B.   Diablo Range.   In 0577,
      pp.   71-111.

1617 Jenness, Diamond, 1886-1969. Canada's In-
      dians Yesterday. What of Today? In 0137,
      pp.   158-163.
      Reprinted from CJEPS,   v.   20,   no.   1,
      Feb. 1954.

1618 _____.   The Corn Goddess and Other Tales
      from Indian Canada.   Illus.   by Winnifred
      K.   Bentley,   2nd ed.,   Ottawa,   National
      Museum of Canada,   1975,   c1960.
      National Museum of Canada Bulletin 141,
      Anthropological Series no.   39.
      OCLC # 4880072

1619 _____.   Life of the Copper Eskimos.   New
      York,   Johnson Reprint Corp.,   1970.
      Landmarks in Anthropology.   Reprint of Part
      A of volume 12,   a report of the Canadian
      Arctic Expedition 1913-1918.
      OCLC # 108411

1620 _____.   Notes on the Beothuk Indians of New-
      foundland.
      pages 36-40 from a book,   no clues indicate
      the original source

1621 Jennings, Francis Paul, 1918- . The Am-
      biguous Iroquois Empire: The Covenant
      Chain Confederation of Indian Tribes with
      English Colonies from Its Beginnings to the
      Lancaster Treaty of 1744.   New York,   Nor-
      ton,   1983.
      Continues: The Invasion of America,   1976,
      c1975
      OCLC # 9066383

1622 _____.   The Invasion of America: Indians,
      Colonialism,   and the cant of Conquest.
      Chapel Hill,   Published for the Institute
      of Early American History and Culture by
      the University of North Carolina Press,
      1975.
      OCLC # 1176061

1623 _____.   Iroquois Alliances in American His-
      tory.   In 1463,   pp.   37-65.

1624 _____. Miquon's Passing. Indian-European
      Relations in Colonial Pennsylvania, 1674-
      1755. Ann Arbor, MI., University Micro-
      films International, 1965.
      Microfilm - PhD Thesis - University of
      Pennsylvania
      OCLC # 2093031

      _____. see also 1463

1625 Jennings, Jesse David, 1909- . Danger
      Cave. With a chapter on textiles by Sara
      Sue Rudy and 6 appendices by Charles B.
      Hunt (and others). Salt Lake City, Uni-
      versity Press, 1957. Millwood, NY.,
      Kraus Reprint, 1974.
      Memoirs of the Society for American
      Archaeology no. 14. Suppl. to American
      Antiquity v. 23, pt. 2, Oct. 1957.
      OCLC # 1428201

1626 _____. Origins. In 0097, pp. 25-67.

      _____. see also 0098, 2947

      Jensen, Richard E. see 1769, 1770

      Jensen, Vickie, 1946- . see 1938, 2499

1627 Jernigan, E. W. Jewelry of the Prehistoric
      Southwest. Santa Fe, NM., School of
      American Research, 1978.
      Southwest Indian Art Series
      OCLC # 3516179

      Jester, William A. see 0132

1628 Jett, Stephen C., 1938- . Navajo Archi-
      tecture: Forms, History, Distribution.
      ... Virginia E. Spencer. Tucson, Univer-
      sity of Arizona Press, 1981.
      OCLC # 7170131

1629 _____. Precolumbian Transoceanic Contacts.
      In 0097, pp. 557-613.
      Also printed in 0098

1630 _____. Precolumbian Transoceanic Contacts.
      In 0098, pp. 337-393.
      Also printed in 0097

1631   Jogues,   Isaac.   <u>The Jogues Papers</u>.   Trans.
       and arranged,   with a memoir by John Gil-
       mary Shea.
       New York State Historical Society.   Collec-
       tions,   1857,   2nd series,   v.   3,   pt.   1,
       pp.   161-229.

1632   Johannsen,   Christina B.   <u>Efflorescence and
       Identify in Iroquois Art</u>.   Ann Arbor,   MI.,
       University Microfilms International,   1984.
       Microfilm - PhD Thesis - Brown University
       OCLC # 13472216

       _____.   <u>see also</u> 1582

       Johannessen,   Sissel <u>see</u> 0944.5

1633 Johansen,   Bruce E.   (Bruce Elliott),   1950- .
       <u>Forgotten Founders: Benjamin Franklin,
       the Iroquois,   and the Rationale for the
       American Revolution</u>.   Ipswich,   MA.,   Gam-
       bit,   1982.
       OCLC # 8115189

1634   _____.   <u>Wasi'chu: The Continuing Indian
       Wars</u>.   New York,   Monthly Review Press,
       1979.
       OCLC # 4775896

1635   Johnson,   Alfred E.   and W.   Raymond Wood.
       <u>Prehistoric Studies on the Plains</u>.   In
       0112,   pp.   35-51.

       _____.   <u>see also</u> 3329

1636   Johnson,   Allen.   <u>Machiguena Gardens</u>.   In
       0023,   pp.   29-63.

1638   Johnson,   Donald L.   <u>The CAlifornia Coastal
       Region: Its Late Pleistocene and Holocene
       Climate and Functions as an Ice Age
       Refugium</u>.   In 0905,   pp.   99-116.

       Johnson,   Eastman,   1834-1906.   <u>see</u> 1654

1639   Johnson,   Edward C.   <u>Future Use</u>.   In 1556,
       pp.   34-36.

1640   _____.   <u>The Miner's Canary</u>.   In 1556,   pp.
       13-14.

1641 _____. Northwest Indians: The Rights Can-
       not Be Taken Away. In 1556, pp. 75.

1642 Johnson, Elias, Tuscarora Chief. Legends,
       Traditions and Laws of Iroquois, or Six
       Nations, and History of the Tuscarora In-
       dians. New York, AMS Press, 1978.
       Reprint of the 1881 ed. pub. by Union
       Print. & Pub. Co., Lockport, NY.'
       OCLC # 3892072

1643 Johnson, Frederick, 1904- . Grassy Is-
       land: Archaeological and Botanical Inves-
       tigations of an Indian Site in the Taunton
       River, Massachusetts. ... Hugh M. Raup.
       Andover, MA., Phillips Academy, the
       Foundation, 1947.
       Papers of the Phillips Academy, Andover,
       MA., Robert S. Peabody Foundation for
       Archaeology, v. 1, no. 2.
       OCLC # 2671690

1644 _____. The Linguistic Map of Mexico and
       Central America. In 2105, pp. 88-114.

1645 _____. Man in Northeastern North America.
       Andover, MA., Phillips Academy, the
       Foundation, 1946.
       Papers of the Robert S. Peabody Foundation
       for Archaeology, v. 3.
       OCLC # 2104450

1646 _____. Radiocarbon Dating: A report on the
       Program to Aid in the Development of the
       Method of Dating. Salt Lake City, Society
       for American Anthropology, 1951. Mill-
       wood, NY., Kraus Reprint, 1974.
       Memoirs of the Society for American Arche-
       ology, v. 8. Reprint of 1951 ed. Suppl.
       to American Antiquity v. 17, no. 1, Pt.
       2, July 1951.
       OCLC # 1118723

1647 Johnson, Hervey, 1839-1923. Tending the
       Talking Wire: A Buck Soldier's View of In-
       dian Country; 1863-1866. Edited by Will-
       iam E. Unrau. Salt Lake City, University
       of Utah Press, 1979.
       OCLC # 5633933

1648 Johnson, R. Arthur. <u>A Vosburg Site on Bar-</u>
<u>ren Island Excavated During the Summer of</u>
<u>1959</u>. New York State Archeological Assoc-
iation Bulletin 20, Nov. 1960, pp. 9-
12. Millwood, NY., Kraus Reprint, 1976.
Paper presented at the annual meeting April
2, 1960

1649 Johnson, Steven L., 1949- . <u>Guide to</u>
<u>American Indian Documents in the Congres-</u>
<u>sional Serial Set, 1817-1899</u>. New York,
Clearwater Publishing Co., 1977.
Library of American Indian Affairs
OCLC # 3103367

1650 Johnson, W. C. <u>Ceramics from Meadowcroft</u>
<u>Rockshelter: A Reevaluation and Interpre-</u>
<u>tation</u>. In 2111, pp. 142-162.

1651 Johnson, W. Fletcher. <u>He Was Lazy and Vi-</u>
<u>cious, and Men Never Told the Truth When a</u>
<u>Lie Would Serve Better</u>. In 1566, pp.
231-247.
Reprinted from <u>Life of Sitting Bull and</u>
<u>History of the Indian War of 1890-91</u>.
Edgewood Pub. Co., 1891, pp. 17-48.

1652 Johnston, Charles M. <u>To the Mohawk Station:</u>
<u>The Making of a New England Company Mis-</u>
<u>sionary - the Rev. Robert Lugger</u>. In
0979, pp. 65-80.

Johnston, Eastman, 1824-1906. <u>see</u> 1654

1653 Johnston, Francis E. and Lawrence M.
Schell. <u>Anthropometric Variation of Native</u>
<u>American Children and Adults</u>. In 1052,
pp. 275-291.

1654 Johnston, Patricia Condon. <u>Eastman John-</u>
<u>son's Lake Superior Indians</u>. Afton, MN.,
Johnston Pub., 1983.
OCLC # 9782306

1655 Johonnet, Jackson. <u>The Remarkable Adven-</u>
<u>tures of Jackson Johonnet 1816</u>. New York,
Garland Pub., 1978.
Garland Library of narratives of North
American Indian captivities, v. 18. Re-
print of the 1816 ed. printed by Ansel

Phelps, Greenfield, MA. Issued with reprint of the 1787 ed. of The Returned Captive, New York.
OCLC # 3543969

1655.5 Jonaitis, Aldona, 1948- . Art of the
Northern Tlingit. Seattle, University of
Washington Press, 1986.
OCLC # 12108177

1656 _____. Tlingit Halibut Hooks: An Analysis
of the Visual Symbols of a Rite of Passage.
New York, American Museum of Natural His-
tory, 1981.
Anthropological Papers of the American
Museum of Natural History v. 57, pt. 1.
OCLC # 7351004

1657 Jones, Charles Colcock, 1831-1893. Historical Sketch of Tomo-Chi-Chi, Mico of
the Yamacraws. Millwood, NY., Kraus Reprint, 1975.
Reprint of the 1868 ed. pub. by J.
Munsell, Albany, NY.

1658 Jones, Christopher, William R. Coe and
William A. Haviland. Tikal: An Outline
of its Field Study (1956-1970) and a Project Bibliography. In 0122, pp. 296-312.

1659 Jones, Dorothy Miriam, 1923- . A Century
of Servitude: Pribilof Aleuts Under U. S.
Rule. Lanham, MD., University Press of
America, 1980.
OCLC # 6942903

1660 _____. Aleuts in Transition: A Comparison
of Two Villages. Seattle, Published for
the Institute of Social, Economic and Government Research, University of Alaska,
University of Washington Press, 1976.
OCLC # 2345594

1661 Jones, Dorothy V. Licence for Empire:
Colonialism by Treaty in Early America.
Chicago, University of Chicago Press,
1982.
OCLC # 7978073

1662 Jones, Douglas C. The Court Martial of
George Armstrong Custer. New York, Scrib-

ners, 1976.
OCLC # 2188995

1663 Jones, Eugene H. Native Americans As Shown
      on the Stage, 1753-1916. Ann Arbor, MI.,
      University Microfilms International, 1984.
      Microfilm - PhD Thesis - City University of
      New York
      OCLC # 12499007

1664 Jones, Grant D., 1941- . Levels of Set-
      tlement Alliance Among the San Pedro Maya
      of Western Belize and Eastern Peten, 1857-
      1936. In 0109, pp. 139-189.

      _____. see also 0109, 3146

1665 Jones, Oakah L. Los Paisanos: Spanish Set-
      tlers on the Northern Frontier of New
      Spain. Norman, University of Oklahoma
      Press, 1979.
      OCLC # 4193224

1666 Jones, Richard S. Indians: Land Claims by
      Eastern Tribes. Issue brief number IB
      77040. Library of Congress, Congres-
      sional Research Service. 4/5/77, updated
      12/12/79.

      Jorgensen, Jorgen B. see 1842

1667 Jorgensen, Joseph G., 1934- . and Shelton
      H. Davis and Robert O. Mathews. Energy,
      Agriculture, and Social Science in the
      American West. In 2273, pp. 3-16.

1668 _____. The Political Economy of the Native
      American Energy Business. In 2274, pp.
      10-51.

1669 _____. Western Indians: Comparative Envi-
      ronments, Languages and Cultures of 172
      Western American Indian Tribes. Research
      Collaborators Harold E. Driver, et al.
      San Francisco, W. H. Freeman, 1980.
      OCLC # 6143513

      _____. see also 2273, 2274

1669.5 Jornada Mogollon Archaeology Conference

(2nd: 1981: Eastern New Mexico Univer-
sity). Views of the Jornada Mogollon:
Proceedings of the Second Jornada Mogollon
Archaeology Conference. Edited by Colleen
M. Beck. Portales, Eastern New Mexico
University Press, 1985.
Contributions in Anthropology v. 12.
OCLC # 11043310

1670 Josephy, Alvin M., 1915- . The Highest
      and Best Use. In 1556, pp. 32-33.

1671 _____. Now That the Buffalo's Gone: A
      Study of Today's American Indians. New
      York, Knopf, Distributed by Random House,
      1982.
      OCLC # 8493650

1672 _____. A Period of Sudden Emergency. In
      1556, pp. 2-5.

1673 _____. Plains Indians: Appearances and
      Environment. In 1556, pp. 58-59.

1674 _____. Sovereignty. In 1556, pp. 52-53.

1675 _____. Spreading the Canvas. In 1556, pp.
      84-85.

1676 Joslyn Art Museum. Legacy of the West. By
      David C. Hunt, with a contribution by
      Marsha V. Gallagher. Omaha, NB., Joslyn
      Art Museum, 1982.
      OCLC # 8533322

      _____. see also 1212

1677 Joutel, Henri, 1640?-1735. Joutel's Jour-
      nal of La Salle's Last Voyage: a reprint
      (page for page and line for line) of the
      first English translation, London, 1714.
      With the map of the original French edi-
      tion, Paris, 1713 in facsimile; and
      notes by Melville B. Anderson, New York,
      B. Franklin, 1968.
      Burt Franklin: Research source works
      series no. 187. American Classics in His-
      tory and Social Science no. 29. Reprint
      of 1896 ed.
      OCLC # 432574

1678 Joyce, Thomas Athol. 1878-1945. <u>South</u>
      <u>American Archaeology; An Introduction to</u>
      <u>the Archaeology of the South American Con-</u>
      <u>tinent with Special Reference to the Early</u>
      <u>History of Peru</u>. New York, Hacker Art
      Books, 1969.
      Reprint of the 1912 American Edition
      OCLC # 253846

1679 Joyes, Dennis C. <u>The Cultural Sequence at</u>
      <u>the Avery Site at Rock Lake</u>. In 1467, pp.
      209-222.

1680 Juan, Jorge, 1713-1773. <u>Noticias Secretas</u>
      <u>de America, Discourse and Political Re-</u>
      <u>flections on the Kingdoms of Peru, Their</u>
      <u>Government, Special Regimen of Their In-</u>
      <u>habitants, and Abuses Which Have Been In-</u>
      <u>troduced into one and Another, With Spe-</u>
      <u>cial Information on Why They Grew Up and</u>
      <u>Some Means to Avoid Them</u>. Written by Jorge
      Juan and Antonio de Ulloa; edited and with
      an introd. by John J. TePaske; trans.
      by John J. TePaske and Besse A. Clement.
      Norman, University of Oklahoma Press,
      1978.
      Translations of <u>Noticias Secretas de</u>
      <u>America</u>
      OCLC # 3870098

1681 Judd, Carol M. <u>Sakie, Esquawenoe, and the</u>
      <u>Foundation of a Dual-Native Tradition at</u>
      <u>Moose Factory</u>. In 3047, pp. 81-97.

1682 Judge, W. James (William James). <u>New</u>
      <u>Light on Chaco Canyon</u>. In 2289, pp. 1-
      12.

      _____. see also 1386

1683 Judson, Katharine Berry. <u>Myths and Legends</u>
      <u>of Alaska</u>. Slected and edited. Chicago,
      A. C. McClurg & Co., 1911.
      OCLC # 2159760

1684 Jussim, Estelle. <u>Frederic Remington, the</u>
      <u>Camera and the Old West</u>. Fort Worth, TX.,
      Amon Carter Museum, 1983.
      Ann Burnett Tandy Lectures in American

Civilization v.   3.
OCLC # 9579620

Kabotie,   Fred   see   0793

1685 Kadlecek,   Edward.   To Kill an Eagle;   Indian
      Views on the Death of Crazy Horse.   ...
      Mabell Kadlecek,   maps by Llyn French.
      Boulder,   Johnson Books,   1981.
      OCLC # 7913541

      Kadlecek,   Mabell   see   1685

1686 Kael,   Pauline.   Americana: Tell Them Why
      Willie Boy is Here.   In 2533,   pp.   163-
      165.
      Reprinted from The New Yorker and Deeper
      into the Movies

1687 Kaeser,   Edward J.   The Cherry Orchard Rock
      Site.   New York State Archeological As-
      sociation Bulletin 34,   July 1965,   pp.
      10-19.   Millwood,   NY.,   Kraus Reprint,
      1976.

1688 _____.   The Middle Woodland Placement of
      Steubenville-Like Projectile Points in
      Coastal New York's Abbott Complex.   New
      York State Archeological Association Bul-
      letin 44,   Nov.   1968,   pp.   8-26.   Mill-
      wood,   NY.,   Kraus Reprint,   1976.

1689 _____.   The Morris Estate Club Site.   New
      York State Archaeological Association Bul-
      letin 27,   March 1963,   pp.   13-22.   Mill-
      wood,   NY.,   Kraus Reprint,   1976.

1690 _____.   A Primer for Pottery Classification,
      Metropolitan Coastal New York.   New York
      Archeological Association Bulletin 31,
      July 1964,   pp.   2-8.   Millwood,   NY.,
      Kraus Reprint,   1976.

      Kahlenberg,   Mary Hunt   see   0245

1691 Kakumasu,   Jim.   Urubú Sign Language.   In
      0008,   pp.   247-253.
      Reprinted from International Journal of
      American Linguistics v.   34,   1968,   pp.
      275-281.

1692 Kalinoski, Lynda L. The Termination
      Crisis: The Menominee Indians Versus the
      Federal Government, 1943-1961. Ann Arbor,
      MI., University Microfilms International,
      1982.
      Microfilm - PhD Thesis - University of
      Toledo
      OCLC # 10673833

1693 Kammer, Jerry, 1949- . The Second Long
      Walk: The Navajo-Hopi Land Dispute. Albu-
      querque, University of New Mexico Press,
      1980.
      OCLC # 6734685

      Kampen, Michael Edwin see 0687

      Kaplan, Susan A., 1951- . see 1063

1694 Karamanski, Theodore J., 1953- . Fur
      Trade and Exploration: Opening the Far
      Northwest, 1821-1852. Norman, University
      of Oklahoma Press, 1983.
      OCLC # 9083899

1695 Karklins, Karlis. Dutch Trade Beads in
      North America. In 1204, pp. 111-126.

      Karl V, Emperor of Germany, 1500-1558. see
      0666

1696 Karok Myths. Compiled by A. L. Kroeber,
      E. W. Gifford; edited by Grace Buzaljko;
      foreword by Theodora Kroeber; folkloristic
      commentary by Alan Dunes; linguistic index
      by William Bright. Berkeley, University
      of California Press, 1980.
      OCLC # 5354663

1697 Karsten, Rafael, 1879-1956. The Head-
      hunters of Western Amazonas: The Life and
      Culture of the Jibaro Indians of Eastern
      Ecuador and Peru. New York, AMS Press,
      1979.
      Reprint of the 1935 ed. pub. in Helsing-
      fors, which was issued as VII of Commenta-
      tiones Humanarum Litterarum.
      OCLC # 4500123

1698 _____. Indian Tribes of the Argentine and

Bolivian Chaco: Ethnological Studies. New
York, AMS Press, 1979
Reprint of the 1935 ed. pub. in Helsing-
fors, which was issued as VII of Commenta-
tiones Humanarum Litterarum.
OCLC # 4500122

1698 _____. Indian Tribes of the Argentine and
Bolivian Chaco: Ethnological Studies. New
York, AMS Press, 1979.
Reprint of the 1932 ed. pub. by Societas
Scientiarum Fennica, Helsinki, which was
issued as v. 4, no. 1 of its series Com-
mentationes Humanarum Litterarum
OCLC # 4500122

Katich, Joseph see 3172

Katonah Gallery see 2059

1699 Kaufmann, Donald L. The Indian as Media
Hand-Me-Down. In 2533, pp. 22-34.
Reprint from The Colorado Quarterly v. 23,
Spring 1975, pp. 489-504.

Kautz, Robert see 3104, 3146

1700 Kavena, Juanita Tiger. Hopi Cookery. Tucson, University of Arizona Press, 1980.
OCLC # 5946589

1701 Kay, Marvin. Archaic Period Research in the
Western Ozark Highland, Missouri. In
0124, pp. 41-70.

1702 Kaywaykla, James, 1873-1963. In the Days
of Victorio; Recollections of a Warm
Springs Apache by Eve Ball... Narrator,
1970.
OCLC # 101473

1703 Kazimiroff, Theodore L. Last Algonquin.
New York, Walker, 1982.
OCLC # 7977016

1704 Kealunohomoku, Joann W. The Drama of the
Hopi Ogres. In 2931, pp. 37-69.

1705 Keehn, Pauline A. Effect of Epidemic Diseases on the Natives of North America: An

Annotated Bibliography. London,   Survival
International,   1978.
Survival International;   Document V
OCLC 4713495

1706 Keen, Benjamin. Approaches to Las Casas,
1535-1970. In 0193, pp. 3-63.

1707 _____. Latin American Civilization. 3rd
ed. Boston, Houghton, Mifflin, 1974.
Previous ed. pub. under title Readings in
Latin American Civilization: 1492 to
Present. CONTENTS. v. 1. The Colonial
Origins. v. 2. The National Era.
OCLC # 858248

1708 _____.   Short History of Latin America. ...
Mark Wasserman, cover and frontpiece by
David Alfaro Siqueiros. Boston, Houghton,
Mifflin, 1980.
OCLC # 6086728

1709 Keesing, Roger M., 1935- . Kin Groups and
Social Structure. New York, Holt, Rine-
hart, and Winston, 1975.
OCLC # 1009488

1710 Kegg, Maude, 1904- . Gabekanaansing/Art
at the End of the Trail: Memoirs of
Chippewa Childhood in Minnesota. With
texts in Ojibwe and English, told by Maude
Kegg; ed. and transcribed by John Nich-
ols. Greeley, Museum of Anthropology,
University of Northern Colorado, 1978.
University of Northern Colorado, Museum of
Anthropology, Occasional Publications in
Anthropology, Linguistic Series, no. 4
OCLC # 4520716

1711 Kehoe, Alice B., 1936- . North American
Indians: A Comprehensive Account. Engle-
wood Cliffs, NJ., Prentice Hall, 1981.
OCLC # 6761280

1712 _____.   The Shackles of Tradition. In 1438,
pp. 53-73.

1713 Kellaway, William. The New England Co.,
1649-1776: Missionary Society to the
American Indians. Westport, CT., Green-

wood Press, 1975.
Reprint of the ed.   pub.   by Longmans,
London, 1961.
OCLC # 1323852

1713.5 Keller, Betty. Black Wolf: The Life of
        Ernest Thompson Seton. Vancouver, Douglas
        & McIntyre, 1984.
        OCLC # 11871282

1714 Keller, Robert H. American Protestantism
      and U. S. Indian Policy, 1869-82. Lin-
      coln, University of Nebraska Press, 1983.
      OCLC 8495047

1715 Kelleran, Ann. Old Fort Niagara. Buffalo,
      Buffalo Historical Society, 1960.
      Adventures in Western New York History, v.
      1, no. 1.
      OCLC # 3434722

1716 Kellet, Alexander. A Pocket of Prose and
      Verse. New York, Garland Pub., 1975.
      The Garland Library of Narratives of North
      American Indian Captivities, v. 11. Re-
      print of the 1778 ed. printed by R.
      Cruttwell, Bath.
      OCLC 1531704

1717 Kelley, David H. A Possible Maya Eclipse
      Record. In 2920, pp. 405-408.

1718 _____. Maya Astronomical Tables and In-
      scriptions. In 2270, pp. 57-73.

1719 Kelley, Ellen Abbott. The Temple of the
      Skulls at Alta Vista, Chalckihuites. In
      0014, pp. 102-126.

      _____. see also 1720

1720 Kelley, J. Charles, 1913- and Ellen
      Abbott Kelley. An Alternative Hypothesis
      for the Explanation of Anasazi Culture His-
      tory. In 0622, pp. 178-223.

1721 _____. Speculations on the Culture History
      of Northwestern Mesoamerica. In 0231, pp.
      19-39.

_____. see also 0014

1722 Kelley, Jane Holden, 1928- . Yaqui Women:
      Contemporary Life Histories. Lincoln, Uni-
      versity of Nebraska Press, 1978
      OCLC # 3274628

1723 Kelley, John Edward, 1853- . Remarks of
      Hon. J. E. Kelley and Others in the
      House of Representatives...Jan. 26, 1898.
      Washington, Govt. Print. Off., 1898.
      On the Indian appropriation bill. One reel
      microfilm - Library of Congress Class E -
      Miscellaneous Monographs and Pamphlets -
      Shelf #44140-44175, #44151.

      Kelley, N. E. see 2498

      Kelley, Patricia M. see 3522

1723.5 Keeling, Richard. Tribal Music and Cult-
      ural Revival. In 2831.5. pp. 165-173.

1724 Kelly, Isabel Truesdell, 1906- . The
      Hodges Ruin: A Hohokam Community in the
      Tucson Basin. ...with collaboration of
      James E. Officer and Emil W. Haury:
      edited by Gayle Harrison Hartmann. Tucson,
      University of Arizona Press, 1978.
      Anthropological Papers of the University of
      Arizona, no. 30.
      OCLC # 3729690

1725 _____. Stirrup Pots from Colima: Some
      Implications. In 0231, pp. 206-211.

      _____. see also 2181

      Kelly, Jerry. see 1726

1726 Kelly, Joyce, 1933- . The Complete Visit-
      or's Guide to Mesoamerican Ruins. Photo-
      graphs by Jerry Kelly and by the author;
      drawings and maps by the author. Norman,
      University of Oklahoma Press, 1982.
      OCLC # 7246953

1727 Kelly, Lawrence C. The Assault on Assim-
      ilation: John Collier and the Origins of
      Indian Policy Reform. Foreword by John

Collier, Jr., Albuquerque, University of
New Mexico Press, 1983.
OCLC # 9280575

1728 _____. John Collier and the Indian New
Deal: An Assesment. In 2265, pp. 227-
214.

1729 Kelsay, Isabel Thompson. Joseph Brant,
1743-1807, Man of Two Worlds. Syracuse,
NY., Syracuse University Press, 1984.
OCLC # 9413344

1730 Kelsey, Morton T. Tales to Tell: Legends
of the Senecas. Compiled and edited by
Morton T. Kelsey. Pecos, NM., Dove
Publ., 1978.
OCLC # 4335672

1731 Kelso, Dianne R. Bibliography of North
American Indian Mental Health. Compiled by
... and Carolyn L. Attneave, prepared un-
der the auspices of the White Cloud Center.
Westport, CT., Greenwood Press, 1981.
OCLC # 7282096

1732 Kelso, Gerald K. Two Pollen Profiles from
Grasshopper Pueblo. In 2239, pp. 106-
109.

1733 Kemper, Robert V., 1945- . Migration and
Adaptation: Tzintzuntzan Peasants in Mex-
ico City. Beverly Hills, Sage Pubs.,
1977.
Sage Library of Social Research, v. 43.
OCLC # 2818738

1734 Kemnitzer, Luis S. Research in Health and
Healing in the Plains. In 0113, pp. 272-
283.
This article has an extensive bibliography

1735 Kemrer, Meade F. (Meade Francis), 1939- .
Maximizing the Interpretive Potential of
Archaeological Tree-Ring Dates. In 0822,
pp. 29-53.

1736 Kendall, Aubyn. Art and Archaeology of Pre-
Columbian Middle America - an Annotated
Bibliography of Works in English. Boston,

G. K. Hall, 1977.
Reference Pubs. in Latin American Studies
OCLC # 3274547

Kendall, Daythal _see_ 0089

1737 Kennan, William Ray, 1949- . An Explor-
      atory Study of Intercultural Communication
      Between Native American and Anglo-American
      College Students. Ann Arbor, University
      Microfilms International, 1981.
      Microfilm - PhD Thesis - University of
      Oklahoma
      OCLC # 10920050

1738 Kent, Barry C. The Susquehanna Bead Se-
      quence. In 1204, pp. 75-81.

1739 _____. An Update on Susquehanna Iroquois
      Pottery. In 1585, pp. 99-103.

1739.5 Kent, Kate Peck. Navajo Weaving: Three
      Centuries of Change. With a catalogue of
      the School of American Research Collection.
      Santa Fe, NM., School of American Re-
      search, Seattle, WA., distributed by
      University of Washington Press, 1985.
      Studies in American Indian Art
      OCLC # 12107341

1740 _____. Prehistoric Textiles of the South-
      west. Santa Fe, NM., School of American
      Research, 1983.
      Southwest Indian Art Series
      OCLC # 8866731

1741 _____. Pueblo Indian Textiles: A Living
      Tradition. Santa Fe, NM., School of
      American Research, 1983.
      Studies in American Indian Art. With a
      catalogue of the School of American Re-
      search collection
      OCLC # 9370870

1742 Kentfield, Calvin. Dispatch From Wounded
      Knee. In 3335, pp. 121-130.
      Source - New York Times, Oct. 15, 1967.

1743 Kenyon, Ian T. Comments on Seventeenth

Century Glass Trade Beads from Ontario. In
1204, pp. 59-74.

1744 Kenyon, Victoria Bunker. River Valleys and
Human Interaction: A Critical Evaluation
of Middle Woodland Ceramics in the Merrimack River Valley. Ann Arbor, MI., University Microfilms International, 1983.
Microfilm - PhD Thesis - Boston University
OCLC # 10967134

Kerr, Justin see 0604

1745 Kerri, James N. Unwilling Urbanites: The
Life and Experiences of Canadian Indians in
a Prairie City. Washington, University
Press of America, 1978.
OCLC # 5169246

1746 Kersey, Harry A., 1935- . The Cherokee,
Creek and Seminole Responses to Removal: A
Comparison. In 1282, pp. 112-117.

1747 _____. Pelts, Plumes, and Hides: White
Traders Among the Seminole Indians, 1870-
1930. Gainesville, University Presses of
Florida, 1975.
OCLC # 1418851

1748 _____. Those Left Behind: The Seminole
Indians of Florida. In 2931, pp. 174-
190.

_____. see also 1205

1749 Keshena, Rita. The Role of the American Indians in Motion Pictures. In 2533, pp.
106-111.
Reprinted from American Indian Culture and
Research Journal v. 1, 1974, pp. 25-28.

1750 Kessell, John L. Kiva, Cross and Crown:
The Pecos Indians and New Mexico, 1540-
1840. Washington, National Park Service,
U. S. Dept. of the Interior, 1979.
OCLC # 3516524

1751 Keur, Dorothy Louise, 1904- . Big Bead
Mesa: An Archaeological Study of Navaho
Acculturation. Menasha, WI., Society for

Ameican Archaeology, 1941. Millwood,
NY., Kraus Reprint, 1974.
Memoirs of the Society for American
Archaeology, no. 1. Suppl. to American
Antiquity, v. 7, no. 2pt. 2, 1941.
Bound with Ford, James Alfred, The Tche-
functe Culture, PhD Thesis, Columbia
University, 1941.
OCLC # 1181177

Kickingbird, Kirke see 1565, 1752

1752   Kickingbird, Lynn. Indians and the U. S.
Government. ... Kirke Kickingbird; Indian Legal Curriculum and Training Program
of the Institute for the Development of Indian Law. Washington, The Institute,
1977.
OCLC # 3799874

1753   Kidd, Kenneth E. A Prehistoric Site Near
Phelps. New York State Archeological Association Bulletin no. 5, Nov. 1955,
pp. 7-8. Millwood, NY., Kraus Reprint,
1976.
Abstract of paper presented at annual
meeting, April 16, 1955.

1754   _____. Problems in Glass Trade Bead Research. In 1204, pp. 1-4.

1755   Kidder, Alfred Vincent, 1885-1963. Archaeological Problems of the Highland Maya.
In 2105, pp. 117-125.

1756   _____. South American Penetrations in
Middle America. In 2105, pp. 441-459.

1757   Kidwell, Clara Sue. The Choctaws: A Critical Bibliography. ... and Charles Roberts. Bloomington, Published for the Newberry Library by Indiana University Press,
1980.
OCLC # 6891203

Kilpatrick, Anna Gritts se 1758

1758   Kilpatrick, Jack Frederick. Friends of
Thunder, Folktales of the Oklahoma
Cherokees. ... and Anna G. Kilpatrick.

Dallas,   Southern Methodist University
Press,   1964.
OCLC # 418620

1759 Kimber,   Edward, 1719-1769. History of the
Life and Adventures of Mr. Anderson. New
York,   Garland Pub.,   1975.
The Garland Library of Narratives of North
American Indian Captivities, v. 7. Re-
print of the 1754 ed.,   printed for W.
Owen,   London.
OCLC # 1582499

1760 King,   Arden Ross. Cattle Point: A Strat-
ified Site in the Southern Northwest Coast
Region. Millwood,   NY.,   Kraus Reprint,
1974.
Memoirs of the Society for American
Archaeology no. 7. Reprint of the 1950
ed. pub. by the Society,   Menasha, WI.,
Suppl. to American Antiquity v. 15, no.
4, pt. 2, April 1950.
OCLC # 2182401

_____. see also 1085

1761 King,   Charles, 1844-1933. Campaigning with
Crook and Stories of Army Life. New York,
Readex Microprint, 1974?, 1966.
Original title page has imprint, New York,
Harper, 1890.
OCLC # 2850033

1762 King,   Chester. Chumash Inter-village
Economic Exchange. In 2276, pp. 289-318.

1763 King,   Duane H. The Origin of the Eastern
Cherokees as a Social and Political Entity.
In 0547, pp. 164-180.

1764 King,   Seth S. Lo! The Rich Indian. In
3335, pp. 100-106.

Kinietz,   Vernon, 1907. see 3158

1765 Kinietz,   William Vernon, 1907- . The Indians of the Western Great Lakes, 1615-
1760. Ann Arbor, MI.,   University of
Michigan Press, 1965.
University of Michigan Museum of Anthro-

pology. Occasional Contributions,   no.
10.
OCLC # 3550863

1766 Kinsey, W. Fred, 1929- . Archeology in
      the Upper Delaware Valley: A Study of the
      Cultural Chronology of the Tocks Island
      Reservoir. Contributors: Herbert C.
      Kraft, Patricia Marchiando, and David
      Werner. Harrisburg, Pennsylvania
      Historical and Museum Commission, 1972.
      Anthropological Series no. 2
      OCLC # 521119

1767 Kirk, Robert L. Genetic Differentiation in
      Australian and the Western Pacific and its
      Bearing on the Origins of the First Amer-
      icans. In 1052, pp. 211-237.

1768 Kirkland, Samuel, 1741-1808. Journals of
      Samuel Kirkland, November 1764-February
      1765. Clinton, NY., Alexander Hamilton
      Private Press, 1966.
      Excerpt from the original mss in the
      Hamilton College Library. 150 copies
      printed
      OCLC # 207796

      Kirkpatrick, Muriel. see 1285

      Kirsch, Richard I. see 0132

      Kissick, Janice. see 1944

1769 Kivett, Marvin F. Archaeological Invest-
      igations at the Crow Creek Site (39BF11).
      ... and Richard E. Jensen. Lincoln,
      Nebraska State Historical Society, 1976.
      Pubs. in Anthropology, no. 7
      OCLC # 3187276

1770 _____. The Crow Creek Site (39BF11) ... and
      Richard E. Jensen. Lincoln, Nebraska
      State Historical Society, 1976.
      Pubs. in Anthropology, no. 7.
      OCLC # 3187276

1771 _____. Woodland Sites in Nebraska.
      Lincoln, Nebraska State Historical
      Society, 1952.

Nebraska State Historical Society Pubs. in
Anthropology, no. 1. Reprinted in 1970.
OCLC # 345717

Kirwin, W. J. see 2814

1772 Klausner, Stephanie. Bipod Photography:
Procedures for Photographic Mapping of
Archaeological Sites. In 0711, pp. 293-
325.

1773 Klein, Alan M. Plains Economic Analysis:
The Marxist Complement. In 0113, pp.
129-140.

1774 _____. The Political Economy of Gender: A
19th Century Plains Indian Case Study. In
1428, pp. 143-173.

Klein, Barry T. see 2608, 2608.5

1775 Kluckhorn, Clyde, 1905-1960. The
Conceptual Structure in Middle American
Studies. In 2105, pp. 41-51.

1776 Knab, Tim. Words Great and Small: Sierra
Nahuat Narrative Discourse in Everyday
Life. Ann Arbor, MI., University Micro-
films International, 1983.
Microfilm - PhD Thesis - State University
of New York at Albany
OCLC # 11181088

1777 Knack, Martha C. As Long As the River Shall
Run, an Ethnohistory of Pyramid Lake In-
dian Reservation. ... and Omer C. Stewart.
Berkeley, University of California Press,
1984.
OCLC # 9622519

1777.5 Kniffen, Fred Bowerman, 1900- . The
Indians of Louisiana. With illus. by Mil-
dred Compton. 2nd ed., Gretna, LA.,
Pelican, 1976.
OCLC # 10866211

_____. see 1789

Knight, Dr. (John) d. 1838 see 0343

Knight,   Vernon J.   see   2786

1778   Koch,   Ronald P.   Dress Clothing of the
       Plains Indians.   Norman,   University of
       Oklahoma Press,   1977.
       Civilization of the American Indian Series
       v.   140
       OCLC # 2525247

1779   Kochan,   Edward.   Riverhaven #1   (TWA 4-3)
       Site,   Grand Island,   N.   Y.   New York
       Archeological Association Bulletin 26,
       Nov. 1962, pp. 9-12. Millwood,   NY.,
       Kraus Reprint,   1976.

1780   _____.   Riverhaven Sites #1 and #2 Grand
       Island,   N.   Y.   New York State Archeolog-
       ical Association Bulletin 22,   July 1961,
       pp.   13-14. Millwood,   NY.,   Kraus Re-
       print,   1976.

       Kock,   Frederick H. see   2070

1780.5 Kolata,   Alan L.   The South Andes.   In
       0098,   pp.   241-285.

       Koonce,   Naurice see   2057

       Kowalewski,   Stephen A.   see   0298,   1069

       Kozák,   Vladimir see   1428

1781   Kraft,   Herbert C.   The Miller Field Site in
       New Jersey and its Influence Upon the Ter-
       minal Archaic and Transitional Stages in
       New York State and Long Island.   New York
       State Archeological Association Bulletin
       48,   March 1970,   pp.   1-13. Millwood,
       NY.,   Kraus Reprint,   1976.

1782   _____.   Paleo-Indian Sites at Port Mobil,
       Staten Island.   In 0712,   pp.   1-19.

       _____.   see also   2059

1783   Krech,   Shepard, III.   "Throwing Bad Med-
       icine":   Sorcery,   Disease and the Fur
       Trade Among the Kutchin and Other Northern
       Athapaskans.   In 1574,   pp.   73-108.

1784   _____.   The Trade of the Slavery and the
        Dogrib at Fort Simpson in the Early Nine-
        teenth Century, In 3047, pp. 99-146.

        _____. see also 1574, 3047

Krieger,   Alex D. see 2299

1785 Kroeber A. L. (Alfred Louis), 1876-1960.
      The Arapaho. Fairfield, WA., Ye Galleon
      Press, 1975.
      Reprinted from the American Museum of
      Natural History Bulletin v. 18, 1902.
      OCLC # 1945470

1786   _____.   Basket Designs of the Mission In-
        dians of California. Preface by Robert F.
        Heizer. Romona, CA., Ballena Press,
        1973.
        Pages 55-99 were originally pub. as v.
        20, pt. 2 of Anthropological papers of
        the American Museum of Natural History,
        1922
        OCLC # 1052375

1787   _____.   Conclusions: the Present Status of
        Americanistic Problems. In 2105, pp.
        460-489.

1788   _____.   Sign Language Inquiry. In 0008,
        pp. 185-203.
        Reprinted from International Journal of
        American Linguistics v. 24, 1958, pp.
        1-19.

1789   _____.   Walapai Ethnography. By Fred
        Kniffen, Gordon MacGregor, Robert McKen-
        nan, Scudder Mekeel and Maurice Mook.
        Edited by A. L. Kroeber. New York,
        Kraus Reprint, 1964.
        Memoirs of the American Anthropological As-
        sociation no. 42, 1935. Contributions
        from the Laboratory of Anthropology I.
        OCLC # 1926077

1790   _____.   Yurok Myths. Berkeley, University
        of California Press, 1976.
        OCLC # 2197814

        _____.   see also 1111

1791 Kroeber, Karl, 1926- . Poem, Dream, and
      the Consuming of Culture. In 2904, pp.
      323-333.
      Reprinted from The Georgia Review v. 32,
      no. 2, 1978, pp. 266-80.

1792 _____. The Wolf Comes: Indian Poetry and
      Linguistic Criticism. In 2904, pp. 98-
      111.

      _____. see also 3144

      Kroeber, Theodora see 1589

1793 Krug, Merton E. DuBay: Son-in-law of Osh-
      kosh. With an introduction by Marvin B.
      Rosenberry; decorations by Russell Fager-
      burg. Appleton, WI., C. C. Nelson,
      1946.
      His Americana Series, no. 1.
      OCLC # 3997855

1794 Krupat, Arnold. The Indian Autobiography:
      Origins, Types, and Function. In 2904,
      pp. 261-282.
      Reprinted from American Literature v. 53,
      no. 1, 1981, pp. 22-42.

1795 Kunitz, Stephen J. Disease Change and the
      Role of Medicine: The Navajo Experience.
      Berkeley, University of California Press,
      1983.
      Comparative Studies of Health Systems and
      Medical Care
      OCLC # 9393923

1796 Kunkel, Peter H. The Pomo Kin Group and the
      Political Unit in Aboriginal California.
      In 2276, p. 271-288.

1797 Kupperman, Karen Ordahl, 1939- . Settling
      With the Indians: The Meeting of English
      and Indian Cultures in America, 1580-1640.
      Totowa, NJ., Rowman and Littlefield,
      1980.
      OCLC # 5219644

1798 Kurath, Gertrude Prokosch. Motion Pictures
      of Tewa Ritual Dance. In 2931, pp. 93-
      102.

_____. **see also** 2032

1798.5 Kutsche, Paul, 1927- . A Guide to Cherokee Documents in the Northeastern United States. Metuchen, NJ., Scarecrow Press, 1986.
Native American Bibliography Series no. 7.
OCLC # 12133302

Kvasnicka, Robert M. **see** 0631, 2265

1799 Laba, Martin. Ethnography and the Description and Analysis of Folklore Behavior. In 0479, pp. 201-210.

1799.5 La Barre, Weston, 1911- . The Peyote Cult. 4th ed., enl. Hamden, CT., Archron Books, 1975.
OCLC # 2004888

1800 _____. The "Diabolic Root". In 3335, pp. 193-197.
Source - The New York Times, Nov. 1, 1964.

1801 LaBlanc, Steven A. The Mimbres Culture. In 0391, pp. 23-38.

_____. see also 0391

1802 Laccetti, Michael F. A Postulated Early Owasco Component: The Round Top Site. New York State Archeological Association Bulletin 33, March 1965, pp. 12-20. Millwood, NY., Kraus Reprint, 1976.

1803 Lacey, Laurie Npisun (My Medicine): Change Over Time in the Micmac Indian Approach to Health and the Maintenance of Well-being. In 0479, pp. 179-187.

1804 Lackey, Louana M. (Louana May), 1926- . The Pottery of Acatlan: A Changing Mexican Tradition. Norman, University of Oklahoma Press, 1982.
OCLC # 7459652

1805 LaDuke, Winona. The Council of Energy: Resource Tribes. In 2274, pp. 58-70.

1806 La Forge, Oliver. The Indians Want a New
      Frontier. In 3335, pp. 111-121.
      Source - The New York Times June 11, 1961

1807 _____. Maya Ethnology: The Sequence of
      Cultures. In 2105, pp. 281-291.

1808 _____. Myths That Hide the American Indian.
      In 2304, pp. 1-15.
      Reprinted from American Heritage Oct.
      1956, pp. 59-69, 103-107.

1809 _____. A Plea for a Square Deal for the
      Indians. In 3335, pp. 71-77.
      Source - The New York Times June 27, 1948.

1810 Lafaye, Jacques. Quetzalcoatl and Guada-
      lupe: The Formation of Mexican National
      Consciousness, 1531-1813. With a foreword
      by Octavio Paz; trans. by Benjamin Keen.
      Chicago, University of Chicago Press,
      1976.
      OCLC # 2034700

1811 Lafitau, Joseph-Francois, 1681-1746. Cus-
      toms of the American Indians Compared With
      the Customs of Primitive Times. Edited and
      trans. by William N. Fenton and Elizabeth
      L. Moore. Toronto, Champlain Society,
      1974-1977.
      Publications of the Champlain Society, no.
      48-49. Translation of Moeurs des Sauvages
      Ameriquains
      OCLC # 1903593

1812 Laforet, Andrea. Tsimshian Basketry. In
      3162, pp. 215-280.

1813 LaFrance, Albert D. Onondaga Chance Phase
      Ceramic Trends - an Attribute Approach. In
      1585, pp. 51-63.

1814 Laird, Carobeth, 1895- . The Chemehuevis.
      Banning, CA., Malki Museum Press, 1976.
      OCLC # 2831468

      Laird, George see 1814

1814.2 Lake Mohonk Conference. Address to the
        Public of the Lake Mohonk Conference: Half

at Lake Mohonk, N. Y., Oct. 1883, in
Behalf of the Civilization and Legal Pro-
tection of the Indians of the United
States. 1st, 1883. Philadelphia, PA.,
Executive Committee of the Indian Rights
Association, 1883.
OCLC # 9783209

1814.3   _____. Proceedings of the Lake Mohonk
Conference. 4th, 1886. Washington,
Govt. print. Off., 1887.
Continues Lake Mohonk Conference of Friends
of the Indians
OCLC #9783219

1814.4   Lake Mohonk Conference of Friends of the
Indian. Proceedings of the ...Annual Meeting of the Lake Mohonk Conference of
Friends of the Indian. 5th-21st, 1887-
1903. Lake Mohonk Conference, 1887-1904.
17 volumes
OCLC # 4863564

1814.5   _____. Proceedings of the Third Annual
Meeting of the Lake Mohonk Conference of
Friends of the Indian. 3rd, 1885. Phila-
delphia, PA., Sherman, 1886.
OCLC # 9783216

1814.6   Lake Mohonk Conference of Friends of the
Indian and Other Dependent Peoples. Proceedings of the...Annual Meeting of the
Lake Mohonk Conference of Friends of the
Indians and Other Dependent Peoples. 22nd-
25th, 1904-1907. Lake Mohonk COnference,
1904-1907.
4 volumes
OCLC # 7851473

1814.7   _____. Report of the...Annual Meeting of
the Lake Mohonk Conference of Friends of
the Indian and Other Dependent Peoples.
26th-28th, 1908-1910. Lake Mohonk Conference of Friends of the Indian and Other
Dependent Peoples, 1908-1910.
3 volumes
OCLC # 7851489

1814.8   _____. Report of the...Annual Lake Mohonk
Conference of Friends of the Indian and

Other Dependent Peoples. 29th-31st, 1911-
1913. Mohonk Lake, NY., The Conference,
1911-1913.
3 volumes
OCLC # 9563908

1814. 85 _____.   Report of the...Annual Lake
Mohonk Conference on the Indian and Other
Dependent Peoples. 32nd-34th, 1914-1916.
Mohonk Lake, NY., The Conference, 1914-
1916.
3 volumes
OCLC # 9563932

1814.9 Lake Mohonk Conference on the Indian.
Report of the...Lake Mohonk Conference on
the Indian. 35th, 1929- . Lake Mohonk,
NY., The Conference, 1930- .
Library has 1929 only
OCLC # 9783228

Lake Superior Indians see 1654

1815 Lallo, John, Jerome Carl Rose and George J.
Armelagos. An Ecological Interpretation of
Variation in Mortality Within Three Prehis-
toric American Indian Populations from
Dickson Mounds. In 0905, pp. 203-238.

11816 Lampl, Michelle and Baruch S. Blumberg.
Blood Polymorphisms and the Origins of New
World Populations. In 1052, pp. 107-123.

Land, Lewis K. see 2520

Landauer, Karyn. see 0370

1817 Landsman, Anne Cheek. Needlework Designs
from the American Indian: Traditional Patterns of the Southeastern Tribes. South
Brunswick, NJ., A. S. Barnes, 1977.
OCLC # 3017769

1818 Landsman, Gail H. The Ganienkeh: Symbol
and Politics in an Indian White Land Dis-
pute. Ann Arbor, MI., University Microfilms International, 1983.
Microfilm - PhD Thesis - Catholic
University of America
OCLC # 9881981

Langacker, Ronald W. see 0260

1820   Lange, Charles H. The Spanish American
        Presence in the Cochiti-Bandelier Area,
        New Mexico. In 0014, pp. 34-52.

1821   _____. A Time Capsule for the 1880's:
        Bandelier's "Memoranda of Investigations
        Required". In 0622, pp. 224-245.

1822   Lange, Frederick W., 1944- . Coastal Set-
        tlement in Northwestern Costa Rica. In
        2524, pp. 101-119.

        _____. see also 0123

1823   Languages and Lore of the Long Island In-
        dians. Edited by Gaynell Stone Levine and
        Nancy Bonvillain. Stony Brook, NY., Suf-
        folk County Archaeological Association,
        Lexington, MA., Ginn Custom Pub., 1980.
        OCLC # 8053096

1824   The Languages of Native America; Historical
        and Comparative Assessment. Edited by Lyle
        Campbell and Marianne Mithun. Austin,
        University of Texas Press, 1979.
        OCLC # 5840226

1825   Lapiner, Alan C. Pre-Columbian Art of South
        America. New York, H. N. Abrams, 1976.
        OCLC # 1177648

1826   LaPotin, Armand Shelby. The Minisink Pat-
        ent: A Study in the Consequences of In-
        dian Habitation on White Settlement in
        Eighteenth Century New York. In 2282, pp.
        210-223.

1827   Larrabee, E. (Edward McMillan). Recurrent
        Themes and Sequences in North American In-
        dian European Culture Contact. Philadel-
        phia, American Philosophical Society,
        1976.
        OCLC # 2747514

1828   Larsen, Tord. Negatiating Identity: The
        Micmac of Nova Scotia. In 2485, pp. 37-
        136.

1829   Larson, Lewis H. ,   1927- . Historic Guale
        Indians of the Georgia Coast and the Impact
        of the Spanish Mission Effort.   In 0307,
        pp. 120-140.

1830   La Salle and his Legacy: Frenchmen and In-
        dians in the Lower Mississippi Valley.   Pa-
        tricia K.   Galloway,   editor.   Jackson,
        University of Mississippi Press,   1982.
        Chiefly papers presented at the 1982 annual
        meeting of the Mississippi Historical Soc-
        iety
        OCLC # 8826902

        Latham,   Edward H.   see 1181

1831   Latham, Roy.   A Cache of Graphite Found on
        Long Island, N. Y.   New York State Archeo-
        logical Association Bulletin 6,   March
        1956, pp. 14-15.   Millwood, NY. ,   Kraus
        Reprint,   1976.
        Abstract of paper presented at the annual
        meeting April 16,   1955.

1832   _____.   A Cache of Split Quartz Pebbles in
        Orient, Long Island, N. Y.   New York
        State Archeological Association Bulletin
        34,   July 1965, pp.   19-20,   Millwood,
        NY. ,   Kraus Reprint,   1976.

1833   _____.   More Notes on the Stone Utensils in
        the Orient Burials.   New York State Archeo-
        logical Association Bulletin 30,   March
        1964, pp. 30-32.   Millwood, NY. ,   Kraus
        Reprint,   1976.

1834   _____.   A Preliminary Report of the Smith
        Site, Shelter Island.   New York State
        Archeological Association Bulletin 11,
        Nov.   1957, pp.   1-7.   Millwood, NY. ,
        Kraus reprint,   1976.
        Paper presented at the annual meeting April
        6,   1957

1835   _____.   A Quartz Flaking Station on Eastern
        Long Island, N. Y.   New York State Archeo-
        logical Association Bulletin 13,   July
        1958.   Millwood,   NY. ,   Kraus Reprint,
        1976.

Paper presented at the annual meeting April
12, 1958.

1836 Latham, Roy. The Sebonac-Niantic Fusion on
Eastern Long Island, N. Y. New York
State Archeological Association Bulletin
17, Dec. 1959, pp. 9-10. Millwood,
NY., Kraus Reprint, 1976.
Paper presented at the annual meeting April
18, 1959.

1837 _____. Seventeenth Century Graves at
Montauk, Long Island, N. Y. New York
State Archeological Association Bulletin 9,
March 1957, pp. 5-6. Millwood, NY.,
Kraus Reprint, 1976.
Paper presented at the annual meeting April
14, 1956.

1838 _____. Three Mile Harbor Sites, East
Hampton, Long Island, N. Y. New York
State Archeological Association Bulletin
23, Nov, 1961, pp. 16-17. Millwood,
NY., Kraus Reprint, 1976.
Paper presented at the annual meeting April
8, 1961.

1839 Latta, Martha A. A Decorative Paradigm:
The Late Ontario Iroquois Ceramic
Tradition. In 1585, pp. 159-177.

Laubin, Gladys see 1840

1840 Laubin, Reginald. Indian Dances of North
America: Their Importance to Indian Life.
... and Gladys Laubin; with paintings,
drawings, and photos by the authors;
foreword by Louis R. Bruce. Norman,
University of Oklahoma Press, 1977.
Civilization of the American Indian Series
no. 141
OCLC # 3002160

Laughlin, Charles see 3343

1841 Laughlin, Robert M. Of Wonders Wild and
New. Washington, Govt. Print. Off.,
1976.
Smithsonian Contributions to Anthropology

no. 22
OCLC # 1735114

1842 Laughlin, William S., Jorgen B. Jorgensen
      and Bruno Frohlich. Aleuts and Eskimos:
      Survivors of the Bering Land Bridge Coast.
      In 1052, pp. 91-104.

1843 _____. Aleuts, Survivors of the Bering
      Land Bridge. New York, Holt, Rinehart
      and Winston, 1980.
      Case studies in cultural anthropology
      OCLC # 6143680

1844 _____ and William E. Taylor. A Cape Dorset
      Culture Site on the West Coast of Ungava
      Bay. In National Museum of Canada Bulle-
      tin 167. Contributions to Anthropology,
      1958. Ottawa, Dept. of Northern Affairs
      and national resources, 1960, pp. 1-28.

      _____. see also 1052

      Lavenda, Robert H. see 0772

1845 Lavin, Lucianne, Marie. Patterns of Chert
      Acquisition Among Woodland Groups Within
      the Delaware Watershed: A Lithologic
      Approach. Ann Arbor, MI., University
      Microfilms International, 1983.
      Microfilm - PhD Thesis - New York
      University

1846 La Violette, Forrest Emmanuel, 1904- .
      Struggle for Survival: Indian Cultures and
      the Protestant Ethic in British Columbia.
      Reprinted with additions. Toronto, Uni-
      versity of Toronto Press, 1978, c1973.
      First published 1961
      OCLC # 418261

1847 Laws of the Colonial and State Governments
      Relating to Indians and Indian Affairs,
      From 1633 to 1831, Inclusive; With an
      Appendix Containing the Proceedings of the
      Congress of Confederation and the Laws of
      Congress From 1800-1830, on the same Sub-
      ject. Stanfordville, NY., E. M. Cole-
      man, 1979.
      American Indian at Law series. Reprint of

the 1832 ed.   pub.   by Thompson and Homans,
Washington
OCLC # 5608155

1848 Lawson, Michael L. Damned Indians: The
Pick-Sloan Plan and the Missouri River
Sioux, 1944-1980. Foreword by Vine
Deloria, Norman, University of Oklahoma
Press, 1982.
OCLC # 7947912

Lawton, Hartry see 0214

1849 Layng, Anthony. Carib Reserve: Identity
and Security in the West Indies. With a
foreword by Leo A. Despres. Washington,
D. C., University Press of America,
1983.
OCLC # 9017725

1850 Layton, Thomas N. Archaeology of Silent
Snake Springs, Humboldt County, Nevada.
... and David Hurst Thomas. New York,
American Museum of Natural History, 1979.
Anthropological papers of the American
Museum of Natural History v. 55, pt. 3.
OCLC # 4980422

1851 Lazarus, Arthur and W. Richard West. The
Alaska Native Claim Settlement Act: A
Flawed Victory. In 0087, pp. 132-165.

1582 Lazell, J. Arthur. Alaskan Apostle: The
Life Story of Sheldon Jackson. New York,
Harper, 1960.
OCLC # 1331757

1583 Leacock, Eleanor Burke, 1922- . Ethnohistorical Investigations of Egalitarian Politics in Eastern North America. In 0796,
pp. 17-31.

1854 _____. The Montagnais "Hunting Territory"
and the Fur Trade. Millwood, NY., Kraus
Reprint, 1974.
Memoirs of the American Anthropological As-
sociation, no. 78. Supple. to American
Anthropologist v. 56, no. 5, pt. 2,
1954
OCLC # 2045747

1855 League of Women Voters. <u>Childrens Impressions</u>
     <u>of American Indians</u>. In 1456, pp. 7-14.
     Reprinted from <u>Children's Impressions of</u>
     <u>American Indians</u>, League of Women Voters,
     New Brighton, MN. , 1975.

1856 LeBlanc, Steven A. <u>The Mimbres People:</u>
     <u>Ancient Pueblo Painters of the American</u>
     <u>Southwest</u>. New York, Thames and Hudson,
     1983.
     OCLC # 9681311

     _____. <u>see also</u> 0114

1857 Lebrasseur, Margot Marie. <u>A Content Analy-</u>
     <u>sis of Selected Print Instructional Mater-</u>
     <u>ials Developed by American Indian Authors</u>
     <u>Since 1970</u>. Ann Arbor, MI. , University
     Microfilms International, 1983.
     Microfilm - PhD Thesis - Pennsylvania State
     University

1858 Le Clercq, Chestien, ca.1630-ca.1695. <u>New</u>
     <u>Relation of Gaspesia with the Customs and</u>
     <u>Religion of The Gaspesian Indians</u>. Trans.
     and ed. by William F. Ganong. New York,
     Greenwood Press, 1968.
     Champlain Society Publications no. 5.
     Reprint of the 1910 ed, English and French
     OCLC # 21645

     Lee, Bong K. <u>see</u> 0132

1859 Lee, Dorothy Sara. <u>Native North American</u>
     <u>Music and Oral Data: A Catalogue of Sound</u>
     <u>Recordings, 1893-1976</u>. Bloomington, Uni-
     versity of Indiana Press, 1979.
     OCLC # 4495483

1860 Lee, Thomas E. <u>Coapa, Chiapas: A Six-</u>
     <u>teenth-century Coxoh Maya Village on the</u>
     <u>Camino Real</u>. In 0472, pp. 208-222.

1861 _____. <u>The Lucas Site, Inverhuron, Ont</u>.
     In National Museum of Canada Bulletin no.
     167. Contributions to Anthropology, 1958.
     Ottawa, Dept. of Northern Affairs and Na-
     tional Resources, 1960, pp. 29-65.
     OCLC # 14087290

1862 Leforge, Thomas H. 1850-1931. Memoirs of a
      White Crow Indian (Thomas H. Leforge) as
      Told by Thomas B. Marquis. With an In-
      trod. by Joseph Medicine Crow and Herman
      J. Viola. Lincoln, University of
      Nebraska Press, 1974, c. 1928.
      A Bison Book, Reprint of the ed. pub. by
      Century Co., New York
      OCLC # 874127

1863 LeFree, Betty. Santa Clara Pottery Today.
      Albuquerque, University of New Mexico
      Press, 1975.
      Monograph Series - School of Social
      Research no. 29.
      OCLC # 1620536

1864 Left Handed, Navaho Indian, 1868- . Left
      Handed: A Navajo Autobiography. Recorded
      and edited by Walter and Ruth Dyk. New
      York, Columbia University Press, 1980.
      Translated from Navaho, Continues Son of
      Old Man Hat
      OCLC # 6086616

1865 _____. Son of Old Man Hat, A Navajo Auto-
      biography. Recorded by Walter Dyk. With a
      foreword by Edward Sapir. Lincoln, Uni-
      versity of Nebraska Press, 1967.
      OCLC # 1070169

1866 Legalistic Approaches to Early Man Studies.
      IN 0902, pp. 20-22.

1867 Lehmann, Henri. Pre-columbian Ceramics.
      Translated by Galway Kinnell, New York,
      Viking Press, 1962, c. 1959.
      OCLC # 421793

1867 Lehmann, Henri. Pre-Columbian Ceramics.
      Trans. by Galway Kinnell, New York,
      Viking Press, 1962, c. 1959.
      OCLC # 421793

1868 Leighton, Douglas. A Victorial Civil Ser-
      vant at Work: Lawrence Vankoughnet and the
      Canadian Indian Department, 1874-1893. In
      0137, pp. 104-119.

      Leininger, Barbara see 1877

1869   Leitch,   Barbara A.   A Concise Dictionary of
        Indian Tribes of North America.   Algonac,
        MI.,   Reference Publications,   1979.
        OCLC # 5899500

        Lekson,   Stephen H.   see 2504

1870   Lenig,   Donald.   The Getman Quarry and Work-
        shop Site (CNK67-2).   New York State Arche-
        ological Association Bulletin 13, July
        1958,   pp.   4-7.   Millwood, NY.,   Kraus
        Reprint,   1976.
        Paper presented at annual meeting April 12,
        1958

1871   _____.   The Getman Site.   New York State
        Archeological Association Bulletin 3,
        March 1955,   pp.   8-10.   Millwood,   NY.,
        Kraus Reprint,   1976.
        Abstract of paper presented at the annual
        meeting 1954

1872   _____.   Of Dutchmen,   Beaver Hats and
        Iroquois.   In 0712,   pp.   71-84.

1873   Leon,   Jorge.   The Spread of Amazonian Crops
        Into Mesoamerica: The Botanical Evidence.
        In 2521,   pp.   165-173.

1874   Leons,   William,   1935- .   Anthropological
        Investigations in Bolivia.   ... and Allyn
        MacLean Spearman.   Greeley,   University of
        Northern Colorado,   Museum of Anthropology,
        1984.
        Museum of Anthropology Miscellaneous Series
        v.   58.
        OCLC # 11076369

1875   Le Peuple Esquimau Aujourd'hui et Demain.
        The Eskimo People Today and Tomorrow.
        Quatrieme congres international de la
        Fondation francaise d'etudes nordiques.
        Rapports scientifiques publies avec une
        pref.   et sous la direction de Jean
        Malaurie.   Paris,   Mouton,   1973.
        Bibliotheque arctique et antarctique 4.
        Essays in English or French.
        Essays in this collection are also listed
        individually and refer to this citation
        (English language essays only)
        OCLC # 814743

Le Poer, Barbara A. see 1869

Le Poer, Kendall T. see 1869

1876 Lerner, Shereen A. Modelling Spatial
Organization in the Hohokam Periphery. Ann
Arbor, MI., University Microfilms Inter-
national, 1984.
Microfilm - PhD Thesis - Arizona State
University
OCLC # 12575640

1877 LeRoy, Marie. Die Erzehlungen von Maria le
Roy und Barbara Leininger. New York, Garland Pub., 1978.
Garland Library of Narratives of North
American Indian Captivities, v. 8. Reprint of the 1759 ed. pub. in Philadelphia by Deutsche Buchdruckerei. Issues
with the reprint of the 1756 ed. of Fleming, W. A Narrative of Suffering and
Deliverance.
OCLC # 3842908

1878 Lescarbot, Marc. The Defeat of the
Armouchiquois Savages by Chief Membertou
and His Savage Allies, in New Franch, in
the Month of July, 1607. In   , pp.
159-179.
Trans. from the French by Thomas H. Goetz

1879 Leslie, Vernon. Faces in the Clay; The
Archaeology and Early History of the Red
Man in Upper Delaware Valley. Middletown,
NY., T. E. Henderson, 1973.
Limited to 1000 copies, copy 291 signed by
the author
OCLC # 666756

1879.5 Lesser, Alexander, 1902- . Franz Boas.
In 3139, pp. 1-33.

1880 Leubben, Thomas E. American Indian Natural
Resources: Oil and Gas. Washington, D.
C. Institute for the development of Indian
Law, 1980.
Legal curriculum and training program of
the Institute for the Development of Indian
Law
OCLC # 7364889

Leventhal, Richard M. see 3438

1881 Levesque, Carole. **La Culture Materielle des Indiens du Quebec: Une Étude de Raquettes, Mocassins et Toboggans**. Ottawa, Musées nationaux de Canada, 1976.
Mercury series. Paper - Canadian Ethnology Series no. 33. Summary in English and French
OCLC # 4230023

1882 Lévi-Strauss, Claude. **From Honey to Ashes**. Trans. from the French by John and Doreen Weightman. New York, Harper and Row, 1973.
His Introduction to a Science of Mythology 2. Trans. of **Du Miel Aux Cendres**.
OCLC # 655646

1883 _____. **The Naked Man**. Trans. from the French by John and Doreen Weightman. New York, Harper and Row, 1981.
Introduction to a Science of Mythology 4. Trans. of **L' homme Nu**.
OCLC # 7383653

1884 _____. **The Origin of Table Manners**. Trans. from the French by John and Doreen Weightman. New York, Harper and Row, 1978.
Introduction to a Science of Mythology 3. Trans. of **L' origine des Manieres de Table**
OCLC # 4478175

1885 _____. **The Story of Asdiwal**. See original vol. #3547, pp. 1-47.

1886 _____. **La Voie des Masques**. Geneve, A. Skira, 1975.
OCLC # 2133958

1887 _____. **The Way of the Masks**. Trans. from the French by Sylvia Modelski. Seattle, University of Washington Press, 1982.
Trans. of **La Voie des Masques**
OCLC # 8282215

Levi Strauss & Co. see 1556

1888 Lewis, Albert Buell. **Tribes of the Columbia**

Valley and the Coast of Washington and
Oregon. New York, Kraus Reprint, 1964.
Memoirs of the American Anthropological As-
sociation, v. 1, pt. 2, 1907.
OCLC # 561565

1889 Lewis, Clifford M. The Calusa. In 3071,
      pp. 19-49.

      Lewis, Henry Carville, 1853-1888. see
      0001

      Lewis, Marion. see 0574

      Lewis, Meriwether, 1774-1809. see 0142

1890 Lewis, R. Barry. Archaic Adaptations to
      the Ilinois Prairie: The Salt Creek
      Region. In 0124, pp. 99-116.

1891 Lewis and Clark's America: Seattle Art
      Museum, July 15 - September 26, 1976.
      Contributors to the catalogue, Willis F.
      Woods...et al., Seattle, Seattle Art
      Museum, 1976,
      V. 1 A Voyage of Discovery. v. 2. A
      Contemporary Photo Essay
      OCLC # 2331964

1892 Lex, Barbara and Hope L. Isaacs. Handling
      Fire: Treatment of Illness by The Iroquois
      False Face Medicine Society. In 3035,
      pp. 5-13.

1893 Liberty, Margot. American Indians and
      American Anthropology. In 0080, pp. 1-
      13.

1894 _____. Francis La Flesche: The Osage
      Odyssey, Omaha, 1857-1932. In 0080, pp.
      45-59.

1895 _____. and Robert Morais. Psychological
      Anthropology. In 0112, pp. 230-244.

1896 _____. The Sun Dance. In 0112, pp. 164-
      178.

      _____. see also 0080, 0113, 2417, 2969

1897   Lichenstein,   Grace.   Northeast Indian Land
       Claims: More Than Twenty Four Bucks.   In
       1556,   pp.   60-61.

       Liette,   Pierre de,   d.   1729.   see   0464

1897.5 Linares,   Olga F.   Cultural Chronology of
       the Gulf of Chirqubi,   Panama.   Washington,
       Smithsonian Press,   1968.
       OCLC # 3218

1898   Lincoln,   Kenneth.   Native American
       Literatures.   In 2904,   pp.   3-38.

1899   _____.   Native American Literatures.   In
       2962,   pp.   175-184.

1900   _____.   Native American Renaissance.
       Berkeley,   University of California Press,
       1983.
       OCLC # 8845493

1901   Linderman,   Frank Bird,   1869-1938.   Indian
       Why Stories: Sparks from War Eagle's
       Lodge-fire.   by...(Co-skee-see-co-cot);
       Illus.   by Charles M.   Russell (Cah-ne-ta-
       wah-see-na-e-ket),   the cowboy artist.
       Millwood,   NY.,   Kraus Reprint,   1975,
       1915.
       Reprint of the ed.   published by Scribner,
       New York.   Retells 22 "Why STories" of the
       Blackfoot,   Chippewa,   and Cree tribes,
       including tales of the creation and of the
       willful and wily doings of the creator,
       Old-man.
       OCLC # 1322800

1902   Linquistic Society of America.   American In-
       dian Languages and American Linguistics:
       Papers of the Second Golden Anniversary
       Symposium of the Linguistic Society of
       America,   helf at the University of Cali-
       fornia,   Berkeley,   on Nov. 8 and 9,   1974.
       Edited by Wallace L.   Chafe.   Lisse: Peter
       de Ridder Press,   1976.
       Essays in this collection are also listed
       individually and refer to this citation
       OCLC # 2614857

1903   Linguistics.   Munro S.   Edmonson,   volume

editor with the assistance of Patricia A.
Andrews. Austin, University of Texas
Press, 1984.
Supplement to the Handbook of Middle Ameri-
can Indians v. 2.
OCLC # 10207920

1904 Link, Martin A. Navajo, a Century of Progress 1868-1968. Window Rock, AZ., Published by the Navajo Tribe, 1968.
Limited edition of 500 copies
OCLC # 91312

1905 Linne, Sigvald, 1899- . Archaeological Researches at Teotihuacan, Mexico. Stock-
holm, V. Patterson, 1924.
The Ethnographical Museum of Sweden (Riks-
museets Etnografiska Avdelning) New
Series. Publication no. 1.
OCLC # 941929

_____. see also 0823

1906 Linskey, Patricia K. Cochise and Mogollon
Hunting Patterns in West-central New
Mexico. In 0622, pp. 246-271.

1907 Linton, Ralph, 1893-1953. Crops, Soils
and Cultures in America. In 2105, pp.
32-40.

1908 Lipe, William D. The Southwest. In 0097,
pp. 421-493.

1909 Lipsett, Brenda McGee. A Comparative Study
to Determine the Origin of Some Canadian
Shield Rock Paintings. In 1467, pp. 181-
189.

1910 Lischka, Joseph J. A Functional Analysis of
Middle Classic Ceramics at Kaminaljuyu. In
0531, pp. 223-278.

1911 Lish, Lawrence R. Big Laugh: A Maya Set-
tlement-Type. In 2208, pp. 60-67.

1912 _____. Distribution of Southern Lowland
Maya Ceremonial Centers. In 2208, pp.
68-86.

Lister, Florence see 1914, 1918

1913 Lister, Robert Hill, 1915- . Archaeologi-
      cal Excavations in the North Sierra Madre,
      Occidental, Chihuahua and Sonora, Mexico.
      With reports by Paul C. Mangelsdorf and
      Kate Peck Kent. Boulder, University of
      Colorado Press, 1958. Millwood, NY.,
      Kraus Reprint, 1974.
      University of Colorado Studies. Series in
      Anthropology no. 7
      OCLC # 2521627

1914 _____. Chaco Canyon: Archaeology and Ar-
      chaeologists. ... and Florence C. Lister.
      Albuquerque, University of New Mexico
      Press, 1981.
      OCLC # 7461325

1915 _____. Chaco Canyon Archaeology Through
      Time. In 2289, pp. 25-36.

1916 _____. Mesoamerican Influence at Chaco
      Canyon, New Mexico. In 0014, pp. 233-
      241.

1917 _____. The Present Status of the Archae-
      ology of Western Mexico; A Distributional
      Study. Millwood, NY., Kraus Reprint,
      1974.
      University of Colorado Studies. Series in
      Anthropology no. 5. Originally pub. Uni-
      versity of Colorado Press, 1955.
      OCLC # 1302071

1918 _____. Those Who Came Before: Southwestern
      Archaeology in the National Park System;
      Featuring Photographs from the George A.
      Grant Collection and a Portfolio by David
      Muench. ... and Florence Lister; foreword
      by Emil W. Haury. Globe, AZ., Southwest
      Parks and Monuments Association; Tucson,
      University of Arizona Press, 1983.
      OCLC # 10152853

1919 Literature of the American Indian: Views and
      Interpretations: A Gathering of Indian
      Memories, Symbolic Context, and Literary
      Criticism. Edited, with an introd. and
      notes by Abraham Chapman. New York, New

American Library,   1975.
A Meridian Book
OCLC # 1990989

1920   Little,   Bryce Pennoyer.   "People of the Red
       Path": An Ethnohistory of the Dakota Fur
       Trade. Ann Arbor, MI.,   University Micro-
       films International,   1984.
       Microfilm - PhD Thesis - University of
       Pennsylvania
       OCLC # 12528443

1921   Little,   Ronald L.   Energy Boom Towns;   Views
       from Within. In 2273,   pp. 63-85.

       Little Bear,   Leroy. see 2429

1922   Littlefield,   Daniel F.   Africans and Creeks:
       From the Colonial Period to the Civil War.
       Westport, CT.,   Greenwood Press,   1979.
       Contributions in Afro-American and African
       Studies no. 47.
       OCLC # 4883992

1923   _____.   Africans and Seminoles: From Re-
       moval to Emancipation. Westport,   CT.,
       Greenwood Press,   1977.
       Contributions in Afro-American and African
       Studies no. 32.
       OCLC # 3001103

1924   _____.   Bibliography of Native American
       Writers,   1772-1924. ... and James W.
       Parins. Metuchen, NJ.,   Scarecrow Press,
       1981.
       Native American Bibliography Series v. 2
       OCLC # 7596642

1924.5 _____.   A Bibliography of Native American
       Writers,   1772-1924:   A Supplement.   ...
       and James W. Parins. Metuchen, NJ.,
       Scarecrow Press, 1985.
       Native American Bibliography Series v. 5
       OCLC # 11756039

1925   _____.   The Cherokee Freedmen: From the
       Emancipation to American Citizenship.
       Westport, CT. Greenwood Press, 1978.
       Contributions in Afro-American and African

Studies no. 40
OCLC # 4036340

1926 _____. The Chickasaw Freedmen: A People
Without a Country. Westport, CT. Green-
wood Press, 1980.
Contributions in Afro-American and African
Studies no. 54.
OCLC # 5990277

Littmann, Edwin R. see 2138

Litto, Frank. see 1927

1927 Litto, Gertrude, 1929- . South American
Folk Pottery. Studio photography by Robert
Emerson Willis; illus. by Frank Litto.
New York, Watson-Guptill Publications,
1976.
OCLC # 2035218

1928 Litzau, Kenneth. Psychological and Environ-
mental Factors Related to the Survivability
of American Indian Students in Higher Edu-
cation. Ann Arbor, MI., University
Microfilms International, 1984.
Microfilm - PhD Thesis - University of
North Dakota
OCLC # 11717609

1929 Litzinger, William Joseph. The Ethnobiology
of Alcoholic Beverage Production by the
Lacandon, Tarahumara and other Aboriginal
Mesoamerican Peoples. Ann Arbor, MI.,
University Microfilms International, 1983.
Microfilm - PhD Thesis - University of
Colorado
OCLC # 11752611

1930 Ljung, Magnus. Principles of a Stratifica-
tional Analysis of the Plains Indian Sign
Language. In 0008, pp. 213-222.
Reprinted from International Journal of
American Linguistics v. 31, 1965, pp.
119-127.

Lloyd, Herbert Marshall, 1862- . see
2203

1931 Lloyd, Peter. Emergence of a Racial Pre-

judice Toward the Indians in 17th Century
New England: Some Notes on an Explanation.
Ann Arbor, MI., University Microfilms In-
ternational, 1975.
Microfilm - PhD Thesis - Ohio State
University
OCLC # 2040276

1932 Lloyd, Trevor. The Development of the North
American Arctic and the Future of the
Eskimo Society. In 1875, pp. 51-62.

Lockhart, James Marvin. see 0260

Lockwood, Frank C. 1864-1948. see 0180

1933 Lodgsdon, Guy. Indian Studies Resources at
the University of Tulsa. Reprinted from
the Chronicles of Oklahoma, v. 55, no.
1, Spring 1977, pp. 64-77.

1934 Loftfield, Thomas C. Archaeological and
Ethno-historical Data Bearing on the Southern Boundary of Algonkian Indian Occupation. In 0068, pp. 100-111.

1935 Loftin, John D. Emergence and Ecology: A
Religio-Ecological Interpretation of the
Hopi Way. Ann Arbor, MI., University
Microfilms International, 1982.
Microfilm - PhD Thesis - Duke University
OCLC # 10675154

1936 Logan, Michael H. and William T. Sanders.
The Model. In 3237, pp. 31-58.

Long, J. Anthony. see 2429

1937 Long, Jeffrey C. and Charles F. Merbs.
Coccidioidomycosis: A Primate Model. In
2526, pp. 69-83.

1938 Long, J. (John), Indian Trader. Voyages
and Travels of an Indian Interpreter and
Trader, Describing the Manners and Customs
of the North American Indians; With an Account of Posts Situated on the River Saint
Laurence, Lake Ontario, etc. To Which
is Added a Vocabulary of the Chippeway Language... a List of Words in the Iroquois,

Mohegan, Shawanee, and Esquimeaux Ton-
gues, and a Table, Shewing the Analogy
Between the Algonkin and Chippeway
Languages. New York, Johnson Reprint
Corp. 1968.
Series in American Studies. Reprint of the
1791 ed. printed for the author and sold
by Robson, London and others.
OCLC # 1729011

1939 Longacre, William A., 1937- and Michael W.
Graves. Multidisciplinary Studies at
Grasshopper Pueblo. In 2239, pp. 1-4.

_____. see also 2239

1940 Longie, Joel D. Alcohol and American Indian
Children: An Assessment of Attitudes and
Behavior. Ann Arbor, MI., University
Microfilms International, 1983.
Microfilm - PhD Thesis - Pennsylvania State
University

1941 Longyear, John M. The Ethnological Significance of Copan Pottery. In 2105, pp.
268-271.

1942 Lopez, Julius. The Ryders Pond Site, Kings
County, New York. New York State Archeological Association Bulletin 53, Nov.
1971, pp. 2-21. Millwood, NY., Kraus
Reprint, 1976.

Lopez, Raul Alberto, 1937- . see 2677

1943 Lord, K. Invertebrate Faunal Remains from
Meadowcroft Rockshelter, Washington
County, Southwestern Pennsylvania. In
2111, pp. 186-206.

_____. see also 0025

1944 Lord, Philip. Prehistoric Archeology and
the New York State Museum. Prepared by the
New York State Museum Staff; written and
compiled by Philip Lord ... designed by
Janice Kissick. Albany, The University of
the State of New York, State Education
Dept., New York State Museum, 1979.
OCLC # 5625466

1945 Lorenzo, Jose Luis. Early Man Research in
      the American Hemisphere. In 0902, pp. 1-

      Lorraine, Edward K. see 2294

1946 Lasada, Angel. The Controversy Between
      Sepulveda and Las Casas in the Junta of
      Valladolid. In 0193, pp. 279-307.

1947 Lothrop, Samuel Kirkland, 1804-1886. In-
      dians of the Parana Delta, Argentina. New
      York, AMS Press, 1980.
      Reprint of the 1923 ed. which was publish-
      ed by the New York Academy of Sciences in
      v. 33 of its annals.
      OCLC # 5941059

1948 _____. The Indians of Tierra del Fuego.
      New York, AMS Press, 1978.
      Reprint of the 1928 ed. pub. by Museum of
      the American Indian, Heye Foundation,
      which was issued as v. 10 of its contribu-
      tions
      OCLC # 3935045

1949 _____. Pre-Columbian Designs from Panama:
      591 illus. of Cocle Pottery. New York,
      Dover Publications, 1976.
      Dover Pictorial Archiv Series. Selected
      illus. from pt. 2 of the authors Cocle,
      An Archaeological Study of Central Panama.
      OCLC # 2150759

1950 _____. South America as Seen from Middle
      America. In 2105, pp. 417-429.

      Lottinville, Savoie, 1906- . see 2343

1951 Lounsbury, Floyd G. Iroquois Place Names in
      the Champlain Valley. In 2282, pp. 103-
      149.
      Report of the New York-Vermont Interstate
      Commission on the Lake Champlain Basin,
      1960 Legislative Document (1960) no. 9,
      pp. 23-68.

1952 Love, Marian F. A Survey of the Distribu-
      tion of T-Shaped Doorways in the Greater
      Southwest. In 0622, pp. 296-311.

1953 Love, William DeLoss, 1851-1918. <u>Samson Occom and the Christian Indians of New England</u>. Boston, Chicago, Pilgrim Press, 1899.
OCLC # 892582.

1954 <u>Love in the Armpit, Tzeltal Tales of Love, Murder and Cannibalism</u>. Compiled by Brian Stross. Columbia, Museum of Anthropology, University of Missouri-Columbia, 1977.
Museum Brief no. 23
OCLC # 3294120

1955 Lovelace, Martin. <u>The Life History as an Oral Narrative Genre</u>. In 0479, pp. 211-223.

Loveland, Franklin O. <u>see</u> 1133

Levine, Gaynell Stone. <u>see</u> 1823

1956 Lowe, Gareth W. <u>Eastern Mesoamerica</u>. In 0577, pp. 331-393.

1957 _____. <u>The Mixe-Zoque as Competing Neighbors on the Early Lowland Maya</u>. In 2378, pp. 197-248.

Lowe Art Museum. <u>see</u> 2519

1958 Lowie, Robert Harry, 1883-1957. <u>Ceremonialism in North America</u>. In 0110, pp. 229-258.

1959 _____. <u>Dance Associations of the Eastern Dakota</u>. In 3473, pp. 101-141.
American Museum of Natural History.
Anthropological Papers v. 11, pt. 2.

1960 _____. <u>Dances and Societies of the Plains Shoshone</u>. In 3473, pp. 803-835,
American Museum of Natural History.
Anthropological Papers, v. 11, pt. 10.

1961 _____. <u>Material Culture of the Crow Indians</u>. New York, AMS Press, 1975.
Reprint of the 1922 ed. published by the American Museum of Natural History, New York, which was issued as v. 21, pt. 3

of its Anthropological papers.
OCLC # 1551050

1962   _____. Military Societies of the Crow
Indians. In 3473, pp. 143-217.
American Museum of Natural History.
Anthropological Papers v. 11, pt. 3.

1963   _____. Notes on the Social Organization and
Customs of the Mandan, Hidatsa, and Crow
Indians. New York, AMS Press, 1976.
Reprint of the 1917 ed. which was issued
as v. 21, pt. 1 of Anthropological Papers
of the American Museum of Natural History
OCLC # 1693798

1964   _____. Plains Indian Age-Societies: Historical and Comparative Summary. In 3473,
pp. 877-985.
American Museum of Natural History.
Anthropological Papers v. 11, pt. 13.

1965   _____. Societies of the Arikara Indians.
In 3473, pp. 645-677.
American Museum of Natural History.
Anthropological Papers v. 11, pt. 8.

1966   _____. Societies of the Hidatsa and Mandan
Indians. In 3473, pp. 219-357.
American Museum of Natural History.
Anthropological Papers v. 11, pt. 3.

1967   _____. Societies of the Kiowa. In 3473,
pp. 837-851.
American Museum of Natural History.
Anthropological Papers v. 11, pt. 11.

1968   _____. Sun Dance of the Crow Indians. New
York, AMS Press, 1978.
Reprint of the 1915 ed. published by order
of the Trustees of the American Museum of
Natural History, New York, which was is-
sued as v. 16, pt. 1 of the Museums
Anthropological Papers.
OCLC # 4500145

1969   _____. Tobacco Society of the Crow Indians.
New York, AMS Press, 1975.
Reprint of the 1919 ed. published by the
American Museum of Natural History, New
York, which was issued as v. 21, pt. 2

of its Anthropological Papers.
OCLC # 1582328

1970 Lowry, Jean, fl. 1756. A Journal of the
      Captivity of Jean Lowry. New York, Gar-
      land Pub., 1978.
      The Garland Library of Narratives of North
      American Indian Captivities, v. 8. Re-
      print of the 1760 ed. printed by W.
      Bradford, Philadelphia, under title A
      Journal of the Captivity of Jean Lowry and
      Her Children. Issued with the reprint of
      the 1756 ed. of Fleming, W. A Narrative
      of Sufferings and Deliverances.
      OCLC # 3842893

1971 Luckert, Karl W., 1934- . Olmec Religion:
      A Key to Middle America and Beyond. Nor-
      man, University of Oklahoma Press, 1976.
      Civilization of the American Indian Series
      v. 137
      OCLC # 1341430

      _____. see also 3226

1972 de Luguna, Frederica. Aboriginal Tlingit
      Sociopolitical Organization. In 0796, pp.
      71-85.

1973 Lujan, Philip and L. Brooks Hill. Inter-
      cultural Communication as an Academic Haven
      for Native American Studies. In 2962, pp.
      193-206.

      Lukens-Wahrhaftig, Jane. see 2295

1974 Lummis, Charles Fletcher, 1859-1928. Date-
      line Fort Bowie, Charles Fletcher Lummis
      Reports on an Apache War. Ed. and Annot-
      ated, and with an introd. by Dan L.
      Thrapp. Norman, University of Oklahoma
      Press, 1979.
      Contains the entire collection of dispatch-
      es filed by the author from the Arizona
      front and published by the Los Angeles
      Times in 1886.
      OCLC # 4193225

1975 Lumpkins, William. Reflections of Chacoan
      Architecture. In 2289, pp. 19-24.

1976   Lundy, Doris. Styles of Coastal Rock Art.
       In 1562, pp. 89-97.

1977   Luomala, Katharine. Flexibility in Sin
       Affiliation Among the Diegueno. In 2276,
       pp. 245-270.

1978   Lurie, Nancy Oestreich. Indian Cultural
       Adjustment to European Civilization. In
       2304, pp. 42-60.
       Abridged and reprinted from Seventeenth
       Century America, ed. James M. Smith,
       Chapel Hill, University of North Carolina
       Press, 1959, pp. 33-60.

1978.5 _____. North American Indian Lives.
       Milwaukee, WI., Milwaukee Public Museum,
       1985.
       OCLC # 11187123

       _____. see also 2032

1979   Lurie, Rochelle, 1849- . Economic Models
       of Stone Tool Manufacture and Use: The
       Koster Site   Middle Archaic. Ann Arbor,
       MI., University Microfilms International,
       1982.
       Microfilm - PhD Thesis - Northwestern
       University
       OCLC # 11482020

1980   Lutes, Steven V. The Mask and Magic of the
       Yaqui Paskola Clowns. In 2502, pp. 80-
       92.

1981   Luther, Daniel Dana, 1840-1923. Nun-da-
       wa'-o, the Oldest Seneca Village. In New
       York State Archeological Association Bul-
       letin 140, 1910, pp. 213-222.

1982   Lyman, Christopher M. The Vanishing Race
       and Other Illusions: Photographs of In-
       dians by Edward S. Curtis. Introd. by
       Vine Deloria, Washington, D. C., Smith-
       sonian Institution Press, 1982.
       Published in conjunction with the exhib-
       ition...organized and circulated by the
       Smithsonian Institution Traveling Exhibi-
       tion Service.
       OCLC # 7998512

1983   Lynch,   Thomas F.,   1938-   . The Paleo-
       Indians.   In 0098,   pp.   87-137.

1984   Lynge,   Father Finn.   The Principles and Main
       Characteristics of Missionary Activity.   In
       1875,   pp.   570-584.

1985   Lyons,   Oren.   An Iroquois Perspective.   In
       0079,   pp.   171-174.

1986   Lyons,   Thomas R.   and Ronald R.   Switzer.
       Archaeological Excavations at Tillery
       Springs,   Estancia,   New Mexico.   In 0622,
       pp.   312-337.

       _____.   see also 0711,   0910,   0912

       Lytle,   Clifford M.   see   0766

1987   Lytle-Webb,   Jamie.   Pollen Analysis in
       Southwestern Archaeology.   In 0822,   pp.
       13-28.

1988   McAdam,   R.   W.   Chickasaws and Choctaws;   a
       Pamphlet of Information Concerning Their
       History,   Treaties,   Government,   Country,
       Laws,   Politics and Affairs.   Wilmington,
       DE.,   Scholarly Resources,   1975.
       Constitutions and laws of the American In-
       dian tribes series 2,   v.   11.   Reprint of
       the 1891 ed.   pub.   by Chieftain Print.,
       Ardmore,   I.   T.
       OCLC # 1509103

1898   McAllester,   David P.   Shootingway,   An Epic
       Drama of the Navajos.   In 2931,   199-2931.

1990   McAllister,   Bernice.   The Setting.   In 2677,
       p.   1-51.

       Macapia,   Mary E.   see   1891

       Macapia,   Paul.   see   1891

1991   McCartney,   Peter Howard.   An Archaeological
       Analaysis of Bison Remains From the Cody
       Paleo-Indian Site of Lamb Springs,   Colo-
       rado.   Ann Arbor,   MI.,   University Micro-
       films International,   1983.
       Microfilm - PhD Thesis - University of

Arizona
OCLC # 10983780

1992 McCarthy, Richard L. <u>A Stratified Site at
     Lewiston</u>. New York State Archeological As-
     sociation Bulletin 13, July 1958, pp.
     10-11. Millwood, NY., Kraus Reprint,
     1976.
     Paper presented at annual meeting April 12,
     1958

1993 McCaskill, Don. <u>Native Peoples and the
     Justice System</u>. In 0137, pp. 288-298.

1994 McClellan, Catherine. <u>The Inland Tlingit</u>.
     In 0076, pp. 47-52.

1995 McConnell, Michael N. <u>The Search for Secu-
     rity: Indian-English Relations in the
     Trans-Appalachian Region, 1758-1763</u>. Ann
     Arbor, MI., University Microfilms Inter-
     national, 1983.
     Microfilm - PhD Thesis - College of William
     and Mary
     OCLC # 12685377

1996 McCool, Daniel Craig. <u>Indian and Non-Indian
     Water Development</u>. Ann Arbor, MI., Uni-
     versity Microfilms International, 1983.
     Microfilm - PhD Thesis - University of
     Arizona
     OCLC # 11542699

1997 McCoy, Ronald. <u>Winter Count: The Teton
     Chronicles to 1799</u>. Ann Arbor, MI., Uni-
     versity Microfilms International, 1983.
     Microfilm - EdD Thesis - Northern Arizona
     University
     OCLC # 11748748

1998 McCulloh, James Haines, 1793?-1870. <u>Re-
     searches on America; Being an Attempt to
     Settle Some Points Relative to the Aborig-
     ines of America, 1817</u>. 2nd ed., Center
     Conway, NH., Walker's Pond Press, 1976.
     Reprint of the Archbald Memorial Library,
     Fryeberg, Maine
     OCLC # 6413283

     McDonald, David R. <u>see</u> 2042

1999 MacDonald,   George. The Epic of Nekt: The
     Archaeology of Metaphor.   In 3162,   pp.
     65-81.

2000 _____. Prehistoric Art of the Northern
     Northwest Coast.   In 1562,   pp. 99-120.

2001 MacDonald,   George F.   Eastern North America.
     In 0903,   pp. 97-108.

2002 _____. Haida Monumental Art: Villages of
     the Queen Charlotte Islands.   Foreword and
     graphics by Bill Reid;   commentary by Rich-
     ard J. Huyda.   Vancouver,   University of
     British Columbia Press,   1983.
     OCLC # 9611554

2003 McDonald,   James A.   Images of the Nine-
     teenth-Century Economy of the Tsimashian.
     In 3162,   pp. 40-54.

2004 McDonald,   Lois Halliday.   Fur Trade Letters
     of Francis Ermatinger: Written to His Bro-
     ther Edward During His Service with the
     Hudson's Bay Company,   1818-1853.   Glen-
     dale,   CA.,   A.   H.   Clark Co.,   1980.
     Northwest Historical Series,   v. 15.
     OCLC # 6534995

2005 MacDonald,   Peter.   Navajo Natural Resources.
     In 0079,   pp. 162-170.

2006 MacDonald,   Robert,   1930- .   The Uncharted
     Nations: A Reference History of the Canad-
     ian Tribes.   Calgary,   Alberta,   Canada.
     Ballantrae Foundation,   1978.
     The Romance of Canadian History.   Canada
     3.
     OCLC # 4442877

     McDowell,   William L.   see 2928,   2929

2007 McElrath,   Dale L.,   1949- .   The Missouri
     Pacific #2 Site (11-S-46).   ... Andrew C.
     Fortier;   with contributions by Sissel
     Johannessen,   Richard B.   Lacampagne and
     Marlene Moshage.   Urbana,   Published for
     the Illinois Dept.   of Transportation by
     the University of Illinois Press,   1983.

American Bottom Archaeology v. 3
OCLC # 9465019

McGary, Mary Jane. <u>see</u> 1422

2008   McGee, R. Jon. <u>Sacrifice and Cannibalism:</u>
        <u>An Analysis of Myth and Ritual Among the</u>
        <u>Lacandon Maya of Chiapas, Mexico</u>. Ann
        Arbor, MI., University Microfilms Inter-
        national, 1984.
        Microfilm - PhD Thesis - Rice University
        OCLC # 10951789

2009   McGhee, Robert. <u>Paleoeskimo Occupations of</u>
        <u>Central and High Arctic Canada</u>. In 0908,
        pp. 15-39.

2010   _____ and James Tuck. <u>Un-dating the</u>
        <u>Canadian Arctic</u>. In 0908, pp. 6-14.

2011   McGimsey, Charles Robert. <u>Mariana Mesa:</u>
        <u>Seven Prehistoric Settlemenmts in West-</u>
        <u>Central New Mexico: A Report of the Upper</u>
        <u>Gila Expedition</u>. Cambridge, MA., Peabody
        Museum of Archaeology and Ethnology,
        Harvard University, 1980.
        Papers of the Peabody Museum of Archaeology
        and Ethnology, Harvard University, v. 72.
        OCLC # 6524435

2012   McGowan, Charlotte. <u>The Identification and</u>
        <u>Interpretation of Name and Place Glyphs of</u>
        <u>the Xolotl Codex</u>. Greeley, Museum of
        Anthropology, University of Northern
        Colorado Press, 1984.
        University of Northern COlorado. Museum of
        Anthropology. Occasional Publications in
        Anthropology. Archaeological Series, no.
        21.
        OCLC # 10749706

2013   _____. <u>The Philosophical Dualism of the</u>
        <u>Aztecs</u>. In 0154, pp. 28-42.

2014   McGregor, John C. (John Charles). <u>The Pool</u>
        <u>and Irving Villages: A Study of Hopewell</u>
        <u>Occupation in the Illinois River Valley</u>.
        Urbana, University of Illinois Press,
        1958.
        OCLC # 420091

McGrew, Ellen Z. see 0466

2015 McInnes, Simon. The Inuit and the
     Constitutional Process, 1978-81. In 0137,
     pp. 317-336.
     Reprinted from Journal of Canadian Studies
     16, no. 2.

McIntosh, Isabel. see 2464

Mackay, Gene. see 2540

2016 McKee, Jesse O. The Choctaws: Cultural
     Evolution of a Native American Tribe.... Jon
     A. Schlenker, Jackson, University Press
     of Mississippi, 1980.
     OCLC # 5170921

2017 McKendry, William. Sullivan's Expedition
     Against the Indians of New York. A Letter
     from Andrew McFarland Davis to Justin Win-
     sor, Corresponding Secretary Massachusetts
     Historical Society. With the Journal of
     William McKendry. Cambridge, MA., J.
     Wilson and Son, 1886.
     One reel microfilm - Library of Congress -
     Class E - Miscellaneous monographs and pam-
     phlets, shelf #44140-44175, #44164. 100
     copies privately printed from the proceed-
     ings of the Massachusetts Historical
     Society, 186.
     OCLC # 13648858

2018 McKenney, Thomas Loraine, 1785-1859.
     Memoirs, Official and Personal. Introd.
     by Herman J. Viola. Lincoln, University
     of Nebraska Press, 1973.
     Reprint of v. 1 of the 1846 ed. pub. by
     Paine and Burgess, NY., A Bison Book
     OCLC # 796874

2019 McKeown, James S., 1945- . Return J.
     Meigs, United States Agent in the Cherokee
     Nation, 1801-1823. Ann Arbor, MI., Uni-
     versity Microfilms International, 1984.
     Microfilm - PhD Thesis - Pennsylvania State
     University
     OCLC # 12618594

2020 McKesson, Charles L. Papers Pertaining to

Indian Affairs 1714-1790. Originals in New
York Historical Society. 1 reel microfilm
provided by American Philosophical Society,
Philadelphia.
For complete description see the Freeman
Guide item # 228.

Mackey, Carol J., 1933- . see 0841

2021 McKinney, Whitney. History of the Shoshone-
Paiutes of the Duck Valley Indian Reserva-
tion. With contributions by E. Richard
Hart and Thomas Zeidler. Salt Lake City,
Institute of the American West and Howe
Bros., 1983.
OCLC # 9084661

2022 McKusick, Charmion R. Avifauna From Grasshopper Pueblo. In 2239, pp. 87-96.

2023 _____. The Faunal Remains of Las Humanas.
In 1387, pp. 39-65.

2024 MacLachlan, Colin M. The Forging of the
Cosmic Race: A Reinterpretation of
Colonial Mexico. ... and Jaime E. Rodri-
quez. Berkeley, University of California
Press, 1980.
OCLC # 5939323

2025 MacLean, John. The Sign Language. In 0008,
pp. 43-51.
Reprinted from Canadian Savage Folk, The
Native Tribes of Canada, Toronto, William
Briggs, 1896, pp. 486-495.

McLoughlin, Virginia Duffy. see 2026

2026 McLoughlin, William Gerald. The Cherokee
Ghost Dance: Essays on the Southeastern
Indians, 1789-1861. ... with Walter H.
Conser, and Virginia Duffy McLoughlin.
Macon, GA., Mercer, 1984.
OCLC # 10996661

2027 _____. Cherokees and Missionaries, 1789-
1839. New Haven, Yale University Press,
1984.
OCLC # 9682857

2028   McManamon, Francis Patrick. <u>Middle Archaic
        Chipped Stone Variations: Collections,
        Researches and Hypothesis Testing.</u> In
        0901,   pp.   39-57.

2029   _____. <u>Prehistoric Cultural Adaptations on
        Cape Cod: Ecological Niches, Adaptive
        States and Temporal Variation.</u> Ann Arbor,
        University Microfilms International, 1984.
        Microfilm - PhD Thesis - S. U. N. Y. at
        Binghamton

        McMillan,   Robert Bruce. <u>see</u> 2525

2030   McNab,   David T.   <u>The Administration of
        Treaty 3: The Location of the Boundaries
        of Treaty 3 Indian Reservations in Ontario,
        1873-1915.</u> In 0137,   pp.   145-157.

2031   _____. <u>Herman Merivale and Colonial Office
        Indian Policy in the Mid-Nineteenth Cen-
        tury.</u> In 0137,   pp.   85-103.
        Reprinted from <u>Canadian Journal of Native
        Studies</u> v. 1,   no. 2,   1981.

2032   MacNeish,   June Helm, 1924- . <u>The Dogrib
        Hand Game.</u> ...and Nancy Oestreich Lurie
        with Gertrude Kurath on Dogrib choreography
        and music. Ottawa, Queens Printer, 1966.
        National Museum of Canada Bulletin 205.
        Anthropological Series no. 71.
        OCLC # 3191295

2033   MacNeish,   Richard S. <u>Iroquois Types 32 Years
        Later.</u> In 1585, pp.   1-6.

2034   _____. <u>The "In Situ " Iroquois Revisited
        and Rethought.</u> In 0710,   pp.   79-98.

2035   _____. <u>Mesoamerica.</u> In 0903,   pp.   125-
        135.

2036   _____. <u>Tehuacan's Accomplishments.</u>   In
        0122,   pp.   31-47.

2037   McNutt,   Charles H. <u>Wing-walls and Weeping
        Eyes.</u> In 0622,   pp.   360-370.

        McNutt,   FRancis Auguatus,   1863-1927. <u>see</u>
        0666

2038   McQuown, Norman A. American Indian
       Linguistics in New Spain. In 1902, pp.
       105-133.

2039   McWilliams, Kenneth R. Non-Metric Oral
       Traits in Gran Quivira Skeletons. In 1387,
       pp. 147-149.

2040   Magnus, Richard Werner. The Prehistoric and
       Modern Subsistence Patterns of the Atlantic
       Coast of Nicaragua: A Comparison. In
       2524, pp. 61-80.

       Mahey, John. see 2426

2041   Mahon, John K. The White Man's Image of the
       Indian: A Rebuttal. In 1282, pp. 25-36.

       _____. see also 1282

2042   Mail, Patricia D. Tulapai to Tokay: A
       Bibliography of Alcohol Use and Abuse Among
       Native Americans of North America. Compil-
       ed by ... and David R. McDonald; with a
       foreword and literature review by Joy H.
       Leland and indexes by Sandra Norris. New
       Haven, HRAF Press, 1980.
       OCLC # 7244219

2043   Mailhot, Jose. La Geographie: Noyaude
       Savoir Montagnais sur l'Environnement
       Physique. In 0068, pp. 314-323.

2043.5 Mails, Thomas E. Plains Indians: Dog
       Soldiers, Bear Man and Buffalo Women. New
       York, Bonanza Books, Distributed by
       Crown Publishers, 1985, c1973.
       Reprint. previously pub. Galahad Books,
       1973.
       OCLC # 12746321

2044   Mails, Thomas E. The Pueblo Children of the
       Earth Mother. Garden City, NY., Double-
       day, 1983.

       _____. see also 1082

2045   Major Council Meetings of American Indian
       Tribes, Part I and II. 1914-1971. Fred-
       erick, MD., University Publications of

America, 1981-.
OCLC # 8695473

2046 Makarius, Laura. The Mask and the Violation
      of Taboo. In 2502, pp. 195-203.

2047 The "Make Believe" Indian. In 2533, pp.
      59.
      Reprinted from Moving Picture World v. 8,
      March 4, 1911, pp. 473.

2048 Malaurie, Jean. The Last Kings of Thule:
      With the Polar Eskimos, as They Face Their
      Destiny. Translated from the French by
      Adrienne Foulke. New York, Dutton, 1982.
      Translation of Les Derniers Rois de Thule
      OCLC # 7283150

      Malaurie, Jean. see also 1875

2049 Maler, Teobert, 1842-1919. Explorations in
      the Department of Peten, Guatemala,
      Tikal; Report of Explorations for the
      Museum. Cambridge, MA., The Museum,
      1911. New York, Kraus Reprints Co.,
      1976.
      Memoirs of the Peabody Musuem of American
      Archaeology and Ethnology v. 5, no. 1.
      OCLC # 4864023

2050 Malin, Edward. A World of Faces: Masks of
      the Northwest Coast Indians. With line
      illustrations in Chapter II and IV by the
      writer, Portland, Oregon, Timber Press;
      Forest Grove, Oregon; exclusive distribu-
      tion, ISBS, 1978.
      OCLC # 3516488

      Malki Museum see 2831.5

2051 Mallery, Garrick. Introduction to the
      Study of Sign Language Among the North
      American Indians as Illustrating the Ges-
      ture Speech of Mankind.
      V. 1 of 0008. Contents - Part 1.
      Inquiries and suggestions upon sign lan-
      guage among the North American Indians,
      p. 5-70. Part 2. A Collection of gesture-
      signs and signals of the North American In-
      dians with some comparisons, p. 71-406.
      Part 3. The gesture of speech of man, pp.

407-439. Reprinted from U. S. Bureau of American Ethnology, Introduction series no. 3, 1880, pt. 1. Pt. 3, reprinted from American Association Advances Science Proceedings, 30th meeting, August, 1881, pp. 283-311, 1882.

2052 Mallery, Garrick, 1831-1894. Picture-Writing of the American Indians. New York, Dover Publications, 1972.
OCLC # 410455

2053 Maloney, Thomas J. Human Adaptation in San Miguel County: Human Waves on a Sea of Grass. In 0622, pp. 338-359.

2054 Malotki, Ekkehart. The Story of the 'Tsimonmamant" or Jimson Weed Girls: A Hopi Narrative Featuring the Motif of the Vagina Dentata. In 2904, pp. 204-220.

2055 Mandelbaum, David Goodman, 1911- . The Plains Cree. AMS Press, 1979.
American Museum of National History, Anthropological Papers v. 37, pt. 2.
Reprint of the 1940 ed.
OCLC # 4500144

2056 Manfred, Frederick. The Devil's Tower Reservation. In 1556, pp. 80-81.

Manley, Alan. see 2057

2057 Manley, Ray J. Ray Manley's Portraits and Turquoise of Southwest Indians. Texts by Clara Lee Tanner, Joe Ben Wheat; photography by Naurice Koonce and Alan Manley. Tucson, AZ., Ray Manley Photography, 1975.
OCLC # 2055477

2058 _____. Ray Manley's Southwest Indian Arts and Crafts. Tucson, AZ., Ray Manley Photography, 1975.
Southwestern Indian Arts and Crafts
OCLC # 1729557

Manson, Speco M. see 2556

2059 Many Trails: Indians of the Lower Hudson

Valley. Catherine Coleman Brawer, general editor; C. A. Weslager, consultant; essays by Herbert C. Kraft, et al., Katonah, NY., Katonah Gallery, 1983. Catalogue of an exhibition held at the Katonah Gallery from March 13-May 22, 1983.
OCLC # 10340232

Marcellin, Jean _see_ 1134

2059.5   Marcus, Joyce. _The Origins of Meso-american Writing_. In Annual Review of Anthropology, v. 5, 1976, pp. 35-67.

_____. _see also_ 0594, 1068

2060   Marcus, Raymond. _Las Casas: A Selective Bibliography_. In 0193, pp. 603.

2061   _____. _Las Casas in Literature_. In 0193, pp. 581-600.

2062   Margolies, Luise. _Princes of the Earth: Subcultural Diversity in a Mexican Municipality_. Washington, American Anthropological Association, 1975.
A special publication of the American Anthropological Association v. 2.
OCLC # 1958592

_____. _see also_ 1167

2063   Margolin, Malcome. _The Ohlone Way: Indian Life in the San Francisco-Monterey Bay Area_. Illus. by Michael Harney. Berkeley, CA., Heyday Books, 1878.
OCLC # 4628382

Mark, Joan T. _see_ 1170

2064   Marken, Jack W. _Bibliography of the Sioux_. Metuchen, NJ., Scarecrow Press, 1980. Native American Bibliography Series no. 1.
OCLC # 6625996

2065   Markov, Gretchen Koch, 1936- . _The Legal Status of Indians Under Spanish Rule_. Ann Arbor, MI., University Microfilms International, 1983.

Microfilm - PhD Thesis - University of
Rochester
OCLC # 10571424

2066   Marquardt, William H. The Shell Mound Arch-
       aic of Western Kentucky. In 0124, pp.
       323-339.

2067   Marquis, Thomas Bailey, 1869-1935. Keep
       the Last Bullet for Yourself: The True
       Story of Custer's Last STand. New York,
       Two Continents Publishing Group, Ltd.,
       1976.
       OCLC # 1991100

       _____. see also 1862, 3412, 3493

2068   Marriott, Alice Lee, 1910- . Dance Around
       the Sun: The Life of Mary Little Bear
       Inkanish, Cheyenne. ... and Carol K.
       Rachlin. New York, Crowell, 1977.
       OCLC # 2797913

2069   _____. Plains Indian Mythology. ... and
       Carol K. Rachlin. New York, Crowell,
       1975.
       OCLC # 1584078

2070   Marshall, S. L. A. (Samuel Lyman Atwood),
       1900-1977. Crimsoned Prairie: The Indian
       Wars. Da Capo Press pbk. ed. New York,
       De Capo Press, 1984, c1972.
       OCLC # 10778344

       Masayeova, Victor. see 1499

2071   Marshe, Witham. Lancaster in 1744. Journal
       of the Treaty at Lancaster in 1744, with
       the Six Nations. By Witham Marshe, sec-
       retary of the Maryland Commissioners. An-
       notated by William H. Egle, M. D. Lan-
       caster, PA., The New Era Steam and Job
       Print., 1884.

2072   Martin, Calvin. Keepers of the Game: In-
       dians-Animal Relationships and the Fur
       Trade. Berkeley, University of California
       Press, 1978.
       OCLC # 4019088

2073 _____. Subarctic Indians as Wildlife. In
      0079, pp. 38-45.

2074 _____. The War Between Indians and Animals.
      In 1574, pp. 11-18.
      Reprinted from Natural History June/July
      1978.

2075 Martin, Paul Sidney, 1899- . Indians
      Before Columbus: Twenty Thousand Years of
      North American History Revealed by Archae-
      ology. Chicago, University of Chicago
      Press, 1947.
      A contribution of the Chicago Natural His-
      tory Museum
      OCLC # 261281

2076 Martinez, Manuel M. Las Casas on the Con-
      quest of America. In 0193, pp. 309-349.

2077 Mary-Rousseliere, Guy. The Paleoeskimo in
      Northern Baffinland. In 0908, pp. 40-57.

2078 Mason, Bernard Sterling, 1896-1953. The
      Book of Indian Crafts and Customs. Draw-
      ings by Frederick H. Kock. New York,
      Ronald Press, 1946.
      OCLC # 1358205

2079 _____. Dances and Stories of the American
      Indians. Photographs by Paul Boris and
      others; drawings by Frederic H. Kock.
      New York, Ronald Press, 1944.
      OCLC # 965828

2080 Mason, Carol I. Historic Identification and
      Lake Winnebago Focus Oneota. In 0710, pp.
      335-348.

2081 Mason, John Alden, 1885-1967. The Native
      Languages of Middle America. In 2105, pp.
      52-87.

2082 Mason, Ronald J. Ethnicity and Archaeology
      in the Upper Great Lakes. In 0710, pp.
      349-361.

2083 _____. Great Lakes Archaeology. New York,
      Academic Press, 1981.

New World Archaeological Record
OCLC # 7306239

2084 Masthay, Carl. Mahican-Language Hymns,
      Biblical Prose, and Vocabularies from Mor-
      avian Sources, with 11 Mohawk Hymns
      (Transcription and Translation). St.
      Louis, MO., Masthay, 1980.
      English, German, Mahican and Mohawk
      OCLC # 7114986

2085 Material Pertaining to Pennsylvania Indian
      Affairs, 1755-1758. One reel microfilm
      provided by American Philosophical Society,
      Philadelphia.
      For description see the Freeman Guide to
      American Philosophical Society collection,
      #118.

      Materne, Yves. see 1564

2086 Matheny, Ray T. Northern Maya Lowland
      Water-Control Systems. In 2522, pp. 185-
      210.

2087 Mather, Cotton, 1663-1728. Decennium
      Luctuosum. New York, Garland Pub., 1978.
      Garland Library of Narratives of North
      American Indian Captivities, v. 3.
      Reprint of the 1699 ed. printed by B.
      Green for S. Philips, Boston, under
      title Decennium Luctuosum: An History of
      Remarkable Occurrences in the Long War
      Which New England Hath Had With the Indian
      Salvages, from the Year 1688 to the Year
      1698.
      OCLC # 2694987

2088 _____. Good Fetch'd Out of Evil. New York,
      Garland Pub., 1977.
      Garland Library of narratives of North
      American Indian captivities, v. 4
      OCLC # 2818145

2089 _____. Humiliations Follow'd with
      Deliverances. New York, Garland Pub.,
      1977.
      Garland Library of narratives of North
      American Indian captivities, v. 1.
      Reprint of the 1697 ed. printed by B.

Green and F. Allen for S. Philips,
Boston. Issued with reprint of the 1682
London ed. by M. Rowlandson, originally
printed under title The Soveraignty and
Goodness of God.
OCLC # 3104356

2090   _____. A Memorial of the Present Deplorable
State of New England. New York, Garland
Pub., 1977.
Garland Library of narratives of North
American Indian captivities, v. 4.
OCLC # 2797983

2091   _____. A Narrative of Hannah Dustan's
Notable Deliverance from Captivity. In
2562, pp. 159-164.
First published in Humiliations Followed
with Deliverances, Boston, 1697.

2092   _____. A Narrative of Hannah Swarton Containing Wonderful Passages Relating to Her
Captivity and Deliverance. In 2562, pp.
145-157.
First published in Humiliations Followed
with Deliverance, Boston, 1697.

2093   _____. "New Assaults from the Indians" and
"The Condition of the Captives". In 2562,
pp. 133-144.

2094   Mather, Increase, 1639-1723. Quentin
Stockwell's Relation of His Captivity and
Redemption. In 2562, pp. 77-89.
First published in Increase Mather's An
Essay for the Recording of Illustrious
Providences, Boston, 1684.

2095   Mathews, Zena Pearlstone. The Relation of
Seneca False Face Masks to Seneca and On-
tario Archaeology. New York, Garland
Pub., 1978.
OCLC # 3710615

2096   _____. Seneca Figurines: A Case of
Misplaced Modesty. In 3035, pp. 71-90.

2097   Mathiassen, Therkel, 1892- . Archaeology
of the Central Eskimos. New York, AMS
Press, 1976.

Reprint of the 1927 ed. pub. by
Gyldendal, Copenhagen, which was issued
as v. 4 of Report of the Fifth Thule Expedition, 1921-24.
OCLC # 2331391

Mathien, Frances John. see 0711

2098 Matthiessen, Peter. In the Spirit of Crazy
Horse. New York, Viking Press, 1983.
OCLC # 8475580

2099 _____. Indian Country. New York, Viking
Press, 1984.
OCLC # 9894676

Mattina, Anthony. see 2828

2100 Maud, Ralph. A Guide to B.C. Indian Myth
and Legend: A Short History of Myth-Col-
lecting and a Survey of Published Texts.
Vancouver, Talonbooks, 1982.
OCLC # 9772768

2101 Maurer, Evan M., 1944- . The Native Amer-
ican Heritage: A Survey of North American
Indian Art: The Art Institute of Chicago,
July 16-October 30, 1977. (Exhibition
Catalogue). Chicago, The Institute,
1977.
Distributed by University of Nebraska
Press, Lincoln.
OCLC # 3383015

2102 Mauss, Marcel, 1872-1950. Seasonal Var-
iations of the Eskimo: A Study in Social
Morphology. In collaboration with Henri
Beuchat; trans. with a foreword by James
J. Fox. Boston, Routledge & Kegan Paul,
1979.
Trans. of Sociologie et Anthropologie, Pt.
7. Essai Sur les Variations Saisonnieres
des Societes Eskimos.
OCLC # 5620144

Maxwell, James A., 1912- . see 0090

2103 Maxwell, Jean A. Colvilles on the Verge of
Development. In 2274, pp. 146-174.

2104 Maxwell,   Moreau S.   Pre-Dorset and Dorset
      Artifacts: The View from Lake Harbour.   In
      0908,   pp.   58-78.

      _____.   see also 0908

      Maxwell Museum of Anthropology see 0114

2105 Maya and Their Neighbors: Essays on Middle
      American Anthropology and Archaeology.   Ed.
      by Clarence L.   Hay.   New York,   Dover Pub-
      lications,   1977.
      OCLC # 3239842

2106 Mayer,   Dorothy.   An Examination of Miller's
      Hypothesis.   In 2270,   pp.   179-201.

      Mayer,   Enrique,   1944- .   see 3068

2107 Mayer,   Joseph Ralph,   1897- .   Flintlocks
      of the Iroquois,   1620-1687.   Rochester,
      NY.,   Rochester Museum of Arts and Sci-
      ences,   1943.
      Research Records of the Rochester Museum of
      Arts and Sciences,   no.   6.   History I.
      OCLC # 3923951

2108 Maylem,   John,   1739-1762? Gallic Perfidy:
      A Poem.   New York,   Garland Pub.,   1978.
      Garland Library of narratives of North
      American Indian captivities,   v.   8.   Re-
      print of the 1758 ed.   printed and sold by
      B.   Mecom,   Boston.   Issued with the re-
      print of the 1756 ed.   of Fleming,   W.   A
      Narrative of Sufferings and Deliverance.
      OCLC # 3845414

2109 Mazzarelli,   Marcella.   Ancient Maya Food
      Producing Systems in the Upper Belize
      Valley: Suggestions for Strategies and
      Implications for Population.   In 2208,   pp.
      42-59.

2110 Mead,   George Richard,   1934- .   Ethnobotany
      of the California Indians.   A Compendium of
      the Plants,   Their Users,   and Their Uses.
      Greeley,   University of Northern Colorado,
      Museum of Anthropology,   1972.
      Greeley,   University of Northern Colorado,
      Museum of Anthropology,   Occasional pubs.

in anthropology, Ethnology Series, no.
30, 1972.
OCLC # 2339859

2111 Meadowcroft: Collected Papers on the
Archaeology of Meadowcroft Rockshelter and
the Cross Creek Drainage. Edited by R. C.
Carlisle and J. M. Adovasio. Pittsburgh,
PA., Dept. of Anthropology, University
of Pittsburgh, 1982?
Prepared for the Symposium The Meadowcroft
Rockshelter Rolling Thunder Review: Last
Act, 47th annual meeting of the Society
for American Archaeology, Minneapolis,
MN., April 14-17, 1982. Final present-
ation of data on Meadowcroft and Cross
Creek and supersedes all previous publica-
tions.
OCLC # 8525306

2112 Means, Philip Ainsworth. The Philosophic
Interrelationship Between Middle American
and Andean Religions. In 2105, pp. 430-
440.

2112.5 Medicine, Beatrice. An Ethnography of
Drinks and Sobriety Among the Lakota Sioux.
Ann Arbor, MI., University Microfilms
International, 1983.
Microfilm - PhD Thesis - University of
Wisconsin-Madison
OCLC # 11748798

2113 _____. "Warrior Women" - Sex Role Alter-
natives for Plains Indian Women. In 1438,
pp. 267-280.

_____. see also 1438

2114 Meeds, Lloyd. The Indian Policy Review
Commission. In 0087, pp. 9-11.

2115 Megapolensis, Johannes. A Short Sketch of
the Mohawk Indians in New Netherland,
Their Land, Stature, Dress, Manner, and
Magistrates, Written in the Year 1644.
Revised from the trans. in Hazard's
historical collections, with an introduc-
tion and notes by John Romeyn Brodhead. In
New York State Historical Society Collec-

tions, 1857 2nd series, v. 3, pt. 1,
pp. 137-160.

2116 Meggers, Betty Jane and Clifford Evans.
      Lowland South America and the Antilles. In
      0098, pp. 287-335.

2117 Meighan, Clement Woodward, 1925- .
      Application of Obsidian Dating to West
      Mexican Archaeological Problems. In 0014,
      pp. 127-133.

2118 _____. California. In 0577, pp. 223-240.

      _____. see also 0577

      Meldgaard, Jorgen. see 0501

2119 Melody, Michael Edward. The Apaches: A
      Critical Bibliography. Bloomington, Pub-
      lished for the Newberry Library by Indiana
      University Press, 1977.
      Bibliographical Series
      OCLC # 3505301

2120 Meltzer, David J., 1955- . Late Pleis-
      tocene Human Adaptation in Eastern North
      America. Ann Arbor, MI., University
      Microfilms International, 1984.
      Microfilm - PhD Thesis - University of
      Washington
      OCLC # 11215242

      Memorial University of Newfoundland see
      2485

2121 Mendelson, E. Michael. The "Uninvited
      Guest": Ancilla to Lévi-Strauss on To-
      temism and Primitive Thought. In main vol.
      3547, pp. 119-139.

2122 Mengarini, Gregory, 1811-1886. Recollec-
      tions of the Flathead Mission: Containing
      Brief Observations, Both Ancient and Con-
      temporary, Concerning This Particular Na-
      tion. Trans. and edited with a biographi-
      cal introd. by Gloria Ricci Lothrop.
      Glendale, CA., A. H. Clark Co., 1977.
      Northwest Historical Series 12. Trans. of

Memorie della Missioui della Teste Piatte.
OCLC # 3059811

2123 Mera, Harry Percival, 1875- . Reconnais-
      sance and Excavations in Southeastern New
      Mexico. New York, Kraus Reprint, 1969.
      Memoirs of the American Anthropological As-
      sociation, no. 51, 1938. Contributions
      from the Laboratory of Anthropology 3.
      Supplement to American Anthropologist v.
      40, no. 4, pt. 2.
      OCLC # 2743261

      Merbs, Charles F. see 1937

2124 Mercer, Henry Chapman, 1856-1930. The Hill
      Caves of Yucatan: A Search for Evidence of
      Man's Antiquity in the Caverns of Central
      America. With a new introd. by Sir J.
      Eric S. Thompson. Norman, University of
      Oklahoma Press, 1975.
      Civilization of the American Indian Series
      v. 135. Reprint of the 1896 ed. pub. by
      Lippincott, Philadelphia.
      OCLC # 1910730

2125 Merrell, James Hart, 1953- . Natives in a
      New World The Catawba Indians of Carolina,
      1650-1800. Ann Arbor, MI., University
      Microfilms International, 1984.
      PhD Thesis - Johns Hopkins University
      OCLC # 9232643

2126 Merrill, Elizabeth J. Bryant. Subsistence
      and Persistence: Adaptation in the Trans-
      mission of Artistic Skills Among the Sho-
      shone-Bannock Since Euroamerican Contact.
      Ann Arbor, MI., University Microfilms
      International, 1984.
      Microfilm - PhD Thesis - State University
      of New York at Buffalo
      OCLC # 12580643

      Merritt, Carolyn. see 0370

      Merritt, Charles W. see 0370

2127 Messiter, Charles Alston. Indians Never
      Spare Anyone Who is in Their Power. In
      1566, pp. 99-109.

Reprint from Messiter, Charles Alston,
Sports and Adventures Among the North
American Indians, London, R. H. Porter,
1890, pp. 211-227.

2128 Meyer, Roy Willard, 1925- . The Canadian
Sioux. In 2304, pp. 168-182.
Abridges and reprinted from Minnesota History v. 41, no. 1, Spring 1968, pp.
13-28.

2129 _____. The Village Indians of the Upper
Missouri: The Mandans, Hidatsas and
Arikaras. Lincoln, University of Nebraska
Press, 1977.
OCLC # 2875144

Meyers, J. Thomas. see 3527

2130 Michéa, Jean. Les Chritra-Gottinéke (Essai
de Monographie d'un Groupe Athapascan des
Montagres Rocheuses.) In National Museum
of Canada Bulletin no. 10. Contributions
to Anthropology, 1960, pt. 2. Ottawa,
Dept. of Northern Affairs and National
Resources, 1963, pp. 49-93.
Article in French only

2131 Michels, Joseph W. A History of Settlement
at Kaminaljuyu. In 2825, pp. 277-306.

2132 _____ and Ronald K. Wetherington. The
Kaminaljuyu Test Trench: Component Assemblage Definition and Phasing. In 2825,
pp. 619-740.

2133 _____. Political Organization at Kaminaljuyu: Its Implications for Interpretating
Teotihuacan Influence. In 3096, pp. 453-
467.

_____. see also 2825, 3096

2134 Milanich, Jerald T. The Western Timucua:
Patterns of Acculturation and Change. In
3071, pp. 59-88.

_____. see also 3071

2135 Miles, James S. Orthopedic Problems of the

Wetherhill Mesa Populations, Mesa Verde
National Park, Colorado. Washington, Na-
tional Park Service, U. S. Dept. of the
Interior, 1975.
Publications in Archeology 7G
OCLC # 1119621

2136 Milfort, Louis, 1750(ca.)-1817. Memoirs;
Or a Quick Glance at My Various Travels and
My Sojourn in the Creek Nation. Trans.
and edited by Ben C. McCary. Savannah,
GA., Beehive Press, 1972, c1959.
OCLC # 482883

2137 Miller, Arthur G., 1942- . "Captains of
the Itza": Unpublished Mural Evidence from
Chichen Itza. In 2920, pp. 197-225.

2138 _____. The Mural Painting of Teotihuacán.
With drawings by Felipe Davalos G. and an
appendix by Edwin R. Littlemann. Washington, Dumbarton Oaks, 1973.
OCLC # 816551

2139 _____ and Nancy M. Farriss. Religious
Syncretism in Colonial Yucatan: The Archaeological and Ethnohistorical Evidence
from Tancak, Quintana Roo. In 0472, pp.
223-240.

2140 Miller, David. The Fur Men and Explorers
Meet the Indian. In 2602, pp. 25-45.

2141 Miller, David Humphreys. Ghost Dance. Lin-
coln, University of Nebraska Press, 1985,
c1959.
Reprint - originally pub. New York, Duell,
Sloan and Pearce, 1959. A Bison Book
OCLC # 11972455

2141 Miller, David Reed. Charles Alexander
Eastman, the "Winner"; From Deep Woods to
Civilization, Santee Sioux, 1858-1939.
In 0080, pp. 61-73.

2143 Miller, Henry M. Beads from the Seventeenth
Century Chesapeake. In 1204, pp. 127-
144.

2144 Miller, Jay. _Feasting with the Southern Tsimshian_. In 3071, pp. 27-39.

2145 _____. _Kokopelli_. In 0622, pp. 371-380.

2146 Miller, Joaquin, 1837-1913. _(Life Amongst the Modocs). My Own Story_. Authorised ed. London, Saxon & Co. Pub., 1891, c1980. Revised from his _Life Amongst the Modocs: Unwritten History_. 1st ed. London, 1873. Later ed. pub. under titles _Unwritten History: Life Amongst the Modocs_. Hartford, 1874; _Paquita, The Indian Heroine_, Hartford, 1881; _My Life Among the Indians_, Chicago, 1892; _Joaquin Miller's Romantic Life Amongst the Red Indians_, London, 1898.
OCLC # 3772521

2147 Miller, Susanne J. and Wakefield Dort. _Early Man at Owl Cave: Current Investigations at the Wasden Site, Eastern Snake River Plain, Idaho_. In 0902, pp. 129-139.

2148 Miller, Virginia P. _Ukomno'm: The Yuki Indians of Northern California_. Socorro, MN., Ballena Press, 1979. Ballena Press Anthropological Papers no. 14.
OCLC # 5446020

2149 Millon, René Francis. _Chronological and Developmental Terminology: Why They Must be Divorced_. In 3237, pp. 23-27.

2150 _____. _Pyramid of the Sun at Teotihuacán: 1959 Investigations_. ... and Bruce Drewitt and James A. Bennyhoff. Philadelphia, American Philosophical Society, 1965. American Philosophical Society Transactions. New Series v. 55, pt. 6.
OCLC # 525851

2151 _____. _Social Relations in Ancient Teotihuacán_. In 3237, pp. 205-248.

2152 _____. _Teotihuacán: City, State and Civilization_. In 0122, pp. 198-243.

2153 Milloy, John S. The Early Indian Acts: De-
      velopmental Strategy and Constitutional
      Change. In 0137, pp. 56-64.

2154 Milne, Tom. Buffalo Bill and the Indians.
      In 2533, pp. 171-174.

2154.5 Milner, Clyde A., 1948- . Albert K.,
      Smiley: Friend to Friends of the Indians.
      In 0578.8, pp. 143-175.

2155 _____. With Good Intentions: Quaker Work
      Among the Pawnees, Otos, and Omahas in
      the 1870's. Lincoln, University of Ne-
      braska Press, 1982.
      OCLC # 7946891

      _____. see also 0578.5

2156 Milner, George R., 1953- . The East St.
      Louis Stone Quarry Site Cemetery: (11-S-
      468). Urbana, Published for the Illinois
      State Dept. of Transportation by the
      University of Illinois Press, 1983.
      American Bottom Archaeology v. 1
      OCLC # 9324431

2157 _____. The Turner and DeMange Sites (11-S-
      50) (11-S-477). Assisted by Joyce A.
      Williams; with contributions by Paula G.
      Cross and Lucy A. Whaley. Urbana, Pub-
      lished for the Illinois Dept. of Transpor-
      tation by University of Illinois Press,
      1983.
      American Bottom Archaeology v. 4
      OCLC # 9684549

      _____. see also 0945

2158 Milton, John R. Materialism and Mysticism
      in Great Plains Literature. In 3275, pp.
      31-43.

2159 Miner, H. Craig. The Corporation and the
      Indian: Tribal Sovereignty and Industrial
      Civilization in Indian Territory, 1865-
      1907. Columbia, University of Missouri
      Press, 1976.
      OCLC # 1991143

2160   _____. Dennis Bushyhead. In 0081, pp.
        192-205.

2161   _____. The End of Indian Kansas: A Study
        in Cultural Revolution, 1854-1871. ...
        and William E. Unrau. Lawrence, Regents
        Press of Kansas, 1978.
        OCLC # 2874695

        _____. see also 3222

2162   Minge, Ward Allen. Acoma, Pueblo in the
        Sky. Albuquerque, University of New
        Mexico Press, 1976.
        OCLC # 2371854

2163   Minnesota Historical Society. Chippewa and
        Dakota Indians: A Subject Catalog of Book,
        Pamphlets, Periodical Articles, and
        Manuscripts in the Minnesota Historical
        Society. St. Paul, 1969.
        OCLC # 44545

2164   Minshall, Herbert L. 1912- . The Broken
        Stones. Paintings and sketches by the
        author; commissioned by Helen K. Copley;
        edited by Richard F. Pourade. La Jolla,
        CA., Copley Books, 1976.
        OCLC # 2331589

2165   Mintz, Sidney Wilfred, 1922- . Ruth Bene-
        dict. In 3139, pp. 141-168.

2166   Minutes of Indian Affairs (Pennsylvania)
        (1758-1760). One reel microfilm provided
        by American Philosophical Society, Phila-
        delphia.
        For description see Freeman Guide item
        #121.

2167   Minutes of Indian Conference Held at Easton
        in July, 1756. One reel microfilm pro-
        vided by American Philosophical Society,
        Philadelphia.
        For description see Freeman Guide item
        #122.

2168   Minutes of the Third Indian Treaty Council
        Held at Easton, July 21-August 7, 1757.
        One reel microfilm provided by American

Philosophical Society, Philadelphia.
For description see Freeman Guide item #
124.

2169 Mirambell, Lorena. Tlapacoya; A Late
Pleistocene Site in Central Mexico. In
0902, pp. 221-230.

2170 Mishkin, Bernard, 1913- . Rank and Wel-
fare Among the Plains Indians. Seattle,
University of Washington Press, 1973.
Monographs of the American Ethnological
Society 3. Reprint of the 1940 ed.
OCLC # 3315390

2171 Missionaries, Outlaws and Indians: Taylor
F. Ealy at Lincoln and Zuni, 1878-1881.
Edited and annotated by Norman J. Bender.
Albuquerque, University of New Mexico
Press, 1984.
Published in cooperation with the Histori-
cal Society of New Mexico
OCLC # 10532445

Missions Advanced Research and Communications
Center see 0223

Mississippi Historical Society see 1830

2172 Mississippian Settlement Patterns. Edited by
Bruce D. Smith; with a foreword by James
B. Griffin. New York, Academic Press,
1978.
Essays in this collection are also listed
individually and refer to this citation.
Studies in Archeology.
OCLC # 4005009

2173 Mitchell, D. H. (Donald H.). Seasonal
Settlements, Village Aggregations and
Political Autonomy on the Central Northwest
Coast. In 0796, pp. 97-107.

2174 Mitchell, Emerson Blackhorse. Miracle Hill:
The Story of a Navaho Boy. ... and T. D.
Allen. Norman, University of Oklahoma
Press, 1967.
OCLC # 179917

2175 Mitchell, Frank, 1881-1967. Navajo

Blessingway Singer: The Autobiography of
Frank Mitchell,   1881-1967.   Edited by
Charlotte J.   Frisbie and David P.   McAl-
lester.   Tucson,   University of Arizona
Press,   1978.
OCLC # 3071473

2176   Mitchell,   John Hansom.   Ceremonial Time:
Fifteen Thousand Years on One Square Mile.
Drawings by Gordon Morrison.   Garden City,
NY.,   Anchor Press,   Doubleday,   1984.
OCLC #10163068

2177   Mithun,   Marianne.   A Northern Iroquoian
Dating Strategy.   In 3035,   pp. 131-148.

2178   _____.   The Proto-Iroquoians: Cultural Reconstruction From Lexical Materials.   In
0979,   pp.   259-281.

_____.   see also   0979,   1824,   2334

2179   Mixco,   Mauricio J.   Kiliwa Texts: 'When I
Have Donned My Crest of Stars'.   Salt Lake
City,   University of Utah Press,   1983.
Anthropological Papers.   University of
Utah,   no.   107.
OCLC # 9609965

2180   Mochanov,   Ju A.   Early Migrations to America
in the Light of a Study of the Dyuktai
Paleolithic Culture in Northeast Asia.   In
0905,   pp.   119-131.

2181   Moctezuma,   Eduardo Matos and Isabel Kelly.
Una Vasija Que Segiere Relaciones Entre
Teotihuacán y Colima.   In 0231,   pp.   202-
205.

2182   Moeller,   Roger W.   Archaeological Bibliography for Eastern North America.   Compiled
by ... and John Reid;   edited by Roger W.
Moeller.   Published jointly by Eastern
States Archeological Federation and American Indian Archaeological Institute,   1977.
Supplement to an anthropological bibliography of the eastern seaboard,   v. 2.   Edited by Alfred K.   Guthe and Patricia B.
Kelly.
OCLC # 3475106

2183 Moerman, Daniel E. Geraniums for the Iro-
      quois: A Field Guide to American Indian
      Medicinal Plants. Illus. by Marie Cole.
      Algonac, MI., Reference Publications,
      1982.
      OCLC # 7836357

2184 Molitor, Martha. The Hohokam-Toltec Con-
      nection: A Study in Culture Diffusion.
      Greeley, Musuem of Anthropology, Univer-
      sity of Northern Colorado, 1981.
      Katunob, Occasional Pubs. in Mesoamerican
      Anthropology no. 19.
      OCLC # 9016760

2185 Molly, John Patrick. Dynasts and Revolu-
      tionists: A Synthesis of Toltec Chronology
      and History. Ann Arbor, MI., University
      Microfilms International, 1983.
      Microfilm - PhD Thesis - University of
      Arizona
      OCLC # 12109927

2185.5 Momaday, N. Scott. American Indian
      Literature. In 2831.5, pp. 177-184.

2186 _____. Native American Attitudes to the
      Environment. In 2818, pp. 79-85.

2187 Montet-White, Anta, 1933- . Analytic
      Descriptions of the Chipped Stone Industry
      from Snyders Site, Calhoun County,
      Illinois. In 2189, pp. 1-70.

2188 _____. The Lithic Industries of the
      Illinois Valley in the Early and Middle
      Woodland Period. Ann Arbor, MI., Univer-
      sity of Michigan, 1968.
      Museum of Anthropology, University of
      Michigan, Anthropological Papers no. 35.
      OCLC # 28005

2189 _____. Miscellaneous Studies in Typology
      and Classification. ... Lewis R. Binford
      and Mark L. Papworth. Ann Arbor, MI.,
      University of Michigan, 1963.
      Museum of Anthropology, University of
      Michigan, Anthropological Papers no. 19.
      OCLC # 665463

2190 Montgomery, John L. (John Lawrence). An-
      asazi Household Economic Autonomy; A Lith-
      ic Analysis. Ann Arbor, MI., University
      Microfilms International, 1983.
      Microfilm - PhD Thesis - University of
      Colorado
      OCLC # 11617949

2191 Monkman, Leslie. Native Heritage; Images
      of the Indian in English-Canadian Litera-
      ture. Toronto, Buffalo, University of
      Toronto Press, 1981.
      OCLC # 7809035

      Moodie, Edith. see 0464

2192 Mooney, James, 1861-1921. The Cheyenne
      Indians. ... and Radolphe Petter, Sketch
      of the Cheyenne Grammar. New York, Kraus
      Reprint, 1964.
      Memoirs of the American Anthropological
      Association v. 1, pt. 6, 1907.
      OCLC # 681793

2193 _____. Historical Sketch of the Cherokee.
      Foreword by W. W. Keeler. Introd. by
      Richard Mack Bettis. Chicago, Aldine Pub.
      Co., 1975.
      A Smithsonian Institution Press Book.
      Native American Library. Reprint of a
      portion of the 1900 ed. of the author's
      Myths of the Cherokee which appeared in
      the 19th Annual Report of the U. S.
      Bureau of American Ethnology.
      OCLC # 2053238

      _____. see also 0973

2194 Moore, James T. Indian and Jesuit: A
      Seventeenth-century Encounter. Chicago,
      Loyola University Press, 1982.
      A Campion Book
      OCLC # 8660922

2195 Moore, John H. Morgan's Problem: The
      Influence of Plains Ethnography on the
      Ethnography of Kinship. In 0113, pp.
      141-152.

2196 Moore, Martin. Memoirs of the Life

Character of Rev. John Eliot, Apostle of the N. A. Indians. Boston, T. Bedlington, 1822.

2197 Moore, Richard B., 1953- . Distribution and Source of Barium in Ground Water at Cattaraugus Indian Reservation, Southwestern New York. ... and Ward W. Staubitz; prepared in co-operation with the Seneca Nation of Indians. Ithaca, NY., U. S. Dept. of the Interior, Geological Survey; Denver, CO., Open File Services Section, Western Distributional Branch, 1984. U. S. Geological Survey Water-Resources Investigations Report, v. 84-4129. OCLC # 11857588

2198 Moore, Robert B., and Alrene B. Hirschfelder. Feathers, Tomahawks and Tipis. In 1456, pp. 46-79. Reprinted from Unlearning "Indian" Stereotypes, the Council on Interracial Books for Children, 1841 Broadway, New York, 1977.

2199 Moorehead, Warren King, 1866-1939. The Hopewell Mound Group of Ohio. New York, AMS Press, 1980. Reprint of the 1922 ed. pub. in Chicago, which was issued as Publication 211 of Field Museum of Natural History and as v. 6, no. 5 of Anthropological Series. OCLC # 6764037

Morais, Robert. see 1895

Moran, Emilio F. see 1447

2201 Moratto, Michael J. California Archaeology. With contributions by David A. Frederickson, Christopher Raven, Claude N. Warren, with a foreword by Francis A. Riddle. Orlando, Academic Press, 1984. New World Archaeology Series OCLC # 9576098

2202 Morgan, John Sydney, 1923- . When the Morning Stars Sang Together. Artists Jackson Beardy and Ron Hamilton. Agincourt,

Ont.,   Book Society of Canada,   1974.
OCLC # 1255158

2203 Morgan, Lewis Henry, 1818-1881. League of
      the Ho-de-no-sau-nee or Iroquois. A New
      ed., with additional matter. Edited and
      annotated by Herbert M. Lloyd. New York,
      B. Franklin, 1266.
      Burt Franklin research source works series
      #185. American classics in history and
      social sciences #28. Reprint of the 1901
      ed.
      OCLC # 29144

      _____. see also 0171

2204 Morgan, William N. Prehistoric Architecture
      in the Eastern United States. Cambridge,
      MA., MIT Press, 1980.
      OCLC # 6421322

2200 Morantz, Toby Elaine, 1943- . Economic
      and Social Accommodations of the James Bay
      Inlanders to the Fur Trade. In 3047, pp.
      55-79.

2205 Moriarty, James R. (James Robert). Aztec
      Jade. In 0154, pp. 71-76.
      Reprinted from The Lapidary Journal v. 26,
      no. 10, Jan. 1973.

2206 _____. Floating Gardens (Chinampas) Agri-
      culture in the Old Lakes of Mexico. In
      0154, pp. 1-18.
      Reprinted from American Indigena v. 18,
      no. 2, April 1968.

2207 _____. The Influence of Recent Climate
      Change on the Development of Maya Civil-
      ization. In 2208, pp. 1-11.

2208 _____. Maya Civilization. I. Selected
      Papers. Greeley, Museum of Anthropology,
      University of Northern Colorado Press,
      1983.
      University of Northern Colorado. Museum of
      Anthropology. Occasional Publications in
      Anthropology. Archaeological series no.
      13. Essays in this collection are also
      listed individually and refer to this cita

tion.
OCLC # 1541399

2209 _____. The Preconquest Aztec State. A
Comparison Between Progressive Evolution
and Other Historical Interpretations. In
0154, pp. 18-27.
Reprinted from Sobretiro de Estudios de
Cultura Nahuatl, Mexico, v. 8, 1969.

2210 _____. A General Syllogy of Maya Medicine.
Greeley, University of Northern Colorado,
Museum of Anthropology, 1970.
University of Northern Colorado, Museum of
Anthropology, Misc. series no. 15, May
1970.
OCLC # 2324188

2211 _____. Ritual Combat, A Comparison of the
Aztec "War of Flowers" and the Medieval
"Melee" and the Origin and Development of
Maya Militarism. Greeley, Colorado State
College, Museum of Anthropology, 1969.
University of Northern Colorado, Museum of
Anthropology, Misc. Series no. 9, Nov.
1969.
OCLC # 213626

2212 Morisset, Jean. La Conquête du Nord-Ouest,
1885-1985, or the Imperial Quest of British North America. In 0137, pp. 280-287.

2213 Morlan, Richard E. Early Man in Northern
Yukon Territory: Perspectives as of 1977.
In 0902, pp. 78-95.
Paper is contribution no. 30 of the Yukon
Refugium Project

2214 _____. Pre-Clovis Occupation North of the
Ice Sheets. In 0903, pp. 47-63.
This is contribution no. 4 to the Yukon
Refugium Project

2215 Morley, Sylvanua Griswold, 1883-1948. The
Ancient Maya. ... and George W. Brainard.
4th ed. revised by Robert J. Sharer.
Stanford, CA., Stanford University Press,
1983.
OCLC # 9996662

2216 _____. _Maya Epigraph_. In 2105, pp. 139-
         149.

         Morris,   Charles E. (Charles Eugene), 1884-
         . see 0466

2216.5 Morris, Don P. _Archeological Investiga-_
         tions at Antelope House. Washington,   D.
         C.,   National Park Service, U. S. Dept.
         of the Interior, Govt. Print. Off.,
         1986.
         OCLC # 11519045

2217 Morris, Elizabeth Ann, 1932- . _Basket-_
         maker Caves in the Prayer Rock District,
         Northeastern Arizona. Tucson, University
         of Arizona Press, 1980.
         Anthropological papers of the University of
         Arizona, no. 35.
         OCLC # 5336876

2217.5 Morris, Joann S. _Indian Portrayal in_
         Teaching Materials. In 2238.5, pp. 83-
         92.

2218 Morris, Nancy Tucker. _The Occurrence of_
         Mandibular Torus at Gran Quivira. In 1387,
         pp. 123-127.

         Morris, Swadesh, 1909-1967. see 2757

2219 Morrison, Alvin Hamblen, 1935- . _Dawnland_
         Decisions: 17th Century Wabanaki Leaders
         and Their Responses to Differential Contact
         Stimuli in the Overlap Area of New France
         and New England. Ann Arbor, MI., Univer-
         sity Microfilms International, 1974.
         Microfilm - PhD Thesis - S. U. N. Y.
         Buffalo
         OCLC # 3643740

2220 _____ and Thomas H. Goetz. _Membertou's_
         Raid on the Chouacoet "Almouchiquois" -
         The Micmac Sack of Saco in 1607. English
         trans. of _Marc Lescarbot_. In 0068, pp.
         141-159.

2221 Morrison, Charles Randall. _A Historical_
         Multiple Burial at Fort Union, New Mexico:

An Exercise in Forensic Archaeology. In
0622, pp. 381-406.

2222 Morrison, Dane Anthony. "A Praying People":
The Transition from Remnant to Convert
Among the Indians of Massachusetts Bay
Colony. Ann Arbor, MI., University
Microfilms International, 1983.
Microfilm - PhD Thesis - Tufts University
OCLC # 12679411

2223 Morrison, Kenneth M. The Embattled North-
east: The Elusive Ideal of Alliance in
Abenaki-Euramerican Relations. Berkeley,
University of California Press, 1984.
OCLC # 10072696

2224 Morrison, Tony. The Pathways to the Gods:
The Mystery of the Andes Lines. Incorpora-
ting the works of Gerald S. Hawkins. New
York, Harper & Row, 1978.
OCLC # 4972700

2225 Morse, Dan F. Archaeology of the Central
Mississippi Valley. ... and Phyllis A.
Morse. New York, Academic Press, 1983.
New World Archaeology Record
OCLC # 9083557

Morse, Phyllis A. see 2225

2226 Mortimer, Hilda. You Call Me Chief: Im-
pressions of the Life of Chief Dan George.
With Chief Dan George. Toronto, Doubleday
Canada; Garden City, NY., Doubleday,
1981.
OCLC # 6861633

2227 Morton, Thomas. That the Savages Live a
Contented Life. In 3413, pp. 28-31.
From The New English Canaan by Thomas
Morton in Publications of the Prince
Society XIV, Boston, 1883, pp. 175-78.

2228 Mosely, Michael Edward. Central Andean
Civilization. In 0098, pp. 179-239.

_____. see also 1031

2229   Moser,   Christopher L.   The Basketmakers.   In
       2677,   pp.   208.

2230   _____.   Collecting and Collectors.   In 2677,
       pp.   162-207.

2231   Moses,   L.   G.   (Lester George),   1948-   .
       The Indian Man,   A Biography of James
       Mooney.   Urbana,   University of Illinois
       Press,   1984.
       OCLC # 9442241

2232   Motolinia,   Toribio,   d.   1568.   History of
       the Indians of New Spain.   Westport,   CT.,
       Greenwood Press,   1973.
       Translation of Historia de los Indios de la
       Neuva Espana.   Reprint of the ed.   pub.   by
       the Cortes Society,   Berkeley,   CA.,   which
       was issued as no.   4 of Documents and Nar-
       ratives Concerning the Discovery and
       Conquest of Latin America,   New Series #4,
       1950.
       OCLC # 789410

2233   Moulton,   Gary E.   John Ross,   Cherokee
       Chief.   Athens,   University of Georgia
       Press,   1977.
       OCLC # 3018203

2234   _____.   John Ross.   In 0081,   pp.   88-106.

       _____.   see also   0142,   2704

2234.5 Mountain Men and the Fur trade of the Far
       West.   Selections.   Trappers of the Far
       West: Sixteen Biographical Sketches.
       Edited by LeRoy R.   Hafen;   selected with
       an introd.   by Harvey L.   Carter.   Lincoln,
       University of Nebraska Press,   1983.
       A Bison Book.   Companion to Mountain Men
       Fur Traders of the Far West.   Reprinted
       from The Mountain Man and the Fur Trade of
       the Far West.   Glendale,   CA.,   A.   H.
       Clark,   1965-1972.
       OCLC # 9392775

2235   Mountjoy,   Joseph B.   San Blas Complex
       Ecology.   In 0231,   pp.   106-119.

2236   Mulholland,   Michell T.,   1944-   .   Patterns

of Change in Prehistoric Southern New Eng-
land: A Regional Approach. Ann Arbor,
MI., University Microfilms International,
1984.
Microfilm - PhD Thesis - University of
Massachusetts at Amherst
OCLC # 12192594

2237 Muller, Jon. The Kincaid System: Mississippian Settlement in the Environs of a
Large Site. In 2172, pp. 269-292.

2238 _____. The Southeast. In 0097, pp. 373-
419.

Mullog, William Thomas, 1917- . see 1085

2238.5 Multicultural Education and the American
Indian. Los Angeles, American Indian
Studies Center, University of California,
1979.
Contemporary American Indian Issues v. 2
Essays in this collection are also listed
individually and refer to this citation.
OCLC # 6469876

2239 Multidisciplinary Research at Grasshopper
Pueblo, Arizona. Edited by William A.
Longacre, Sally J. Holbrook, Michael W.
Graves; contributors, Larry D. Agen-
broad. Tucson, University of Arizona
Press, 1982.
Essays in this collection are also listed
individually and refer to this citation.
Anthropological papers of the University of
Arizona, no. 40.
OCLC # 8688408

2240 Munkres, Robert L. The Arrival of Emigrants
and Soldiers: Curiosity, Contempt, Con-
fusion and Conflict. In 2602, pp. 63-91.

Munson, Cheryl A. see 1258

Murch, Abel B. see 0436

2241 Murdock, George Peter, 1897- . Ethnographic Bibliography of North America. ...
and Timothy J. O'Leary, with the assistance of John Beierle. 4th ed. New Haven,

Human Relations Area Files Press, 1975.
Behavior Science Bibliographies. 5 vols.
CONTENTS: v. 1. General North America.
v. 2. Arctic and Subarctic. v. 3. Far
West and Pacific Coast. v. 4. Eastern
United States. v. 5. Plains and South-
west.
OCLC # 2067450

2242 Murie, James R. Ceremonies of the Pawnee.
Edited by Douglas R. Parks. Washington,
Smithsonian Institution Press, 1981.
Smithsonian Contributions to Anthropology
no. 27. CONTENTS: Pt. 1. The Skiri.
Pt. 2. The Southern Bands.
OCLC # 4881720

2243 _____. Pawnee Indian Societies. In 3473,
pp. 543-643.
Reprinted from Anthropological Papers of
the American Museum of Natural History, v.
11, pt. 7.

2244 Murphy, James Emmett, 1940- . Let My
People Know, American Indian Journalism,
1828-1978. ... and Sharon M. Murphy.
Foreword by Jeannette Henry. Norman,
University of Oklahoma Press, 1981.
OCLC # 7272785

2245 Murphy, Robert F. Julian Steward. In 3139,
pp. 171-206.

Murphy, Sharon. see 2244

2246 Murphy, Timothy D. Marriage and Family in a
Nahuat-Speaking Community. In 0958, pp.
187-205.

2247 Murra, John V. On Inca Political Structure.
In Systems of Political Control and Bureau-
cracy in Human Societies, Proceedings of
the 1958 Annual Spring Meeting of the
American Ethnological Society, pp. 30-41.

Muse, on Yibsra, el (jerusalem) see 0604

2248 Museo del Oro (Colombia). El Dorado, the
Gold of Ancient Colombia: From el Museo
del Oro, Banco de la Republica, Bogota,

Colombia: An Exhibition. Organized by the
Center for Inter-American Relations and the
American Federation of Arts. New York,
The Center for Inter-American Relations and
the American Federation of Arts, 1974.
Catalog of an exhibition which travelled to
major museums throughout the United States
and Canada including the American Museum of
Natural History.
OCLC # 7414165

2249 Muser, Curt. Facts and Artifacts of Ancient
Middle America: A Glossary of Terms and
Words Used in the Archaeology and Art His-
tory of Pre-Columbian Mexico and Central
America. New York, Dutton, 1978.
OCLC # 4178679

2250 Museum of Modern Art (New York, NY.).
American Sources of Modern Art, May 10-
June 30, 1933. The Museum of Modern Art,
New York, Published for the Museum of
Modern Art by Arno Press, 1969, c1933.
Reprint edition
OCLC # 88201

2251 Museum of the American Indian, Heye Found-
ation. The Ancestors: Native Artisans of
the Americas. Edited by Anna Curtenius
Roosevelt, James G. E. Smith, maps and
line drawings by Tom Martin. New York,
Museum of the American Indian, 1979.
Catalog of an exhibition presented at the
U. S. Custom House in New York City,
Aug. 1-Oct. 31, 1979.
OCLC # 5708072

2251.5 Muskrat, Jerry. Recommendations of the
American Indian Policy Review Commission
and the Supreme Court. In 2961.5, pp.
99-114.

2252 Musters, George Chaworth, 1841-1879. At
Home with the Patagonians: A Year's Wan-
derings Over Untrodden Ground from the
Straits of Magellan to the Rio Negro. New
York, Greenwood Press, 1969.
Reprint of the 1897 ed.
OCLC # 49394

Mutch,   James C.   see   0309

2253   Nabhan,   Gary Paul.   The Desert Smells Like
       Rain: A Naturalist in Papago Indian
       Country.   San Francisco,   North Point
       Press,   1982.
       OCLC # 8246569

2254   _____.   Papago Fields: Arid Lands Ethno-
       botany and Agricultural Ecology.   Ann
       Arbor,   MI.,   University Microfilms Inter-
       national,   1983.
       Microfilm - PhD Thesis - University of
       Arizona
       OCLC # 11539020

2255   Nabokov,   Peter.   Indian Running.   Santa
       Barbara,   Capra Press,   1981.
       OCLC # 6916184

2256   _____.   The Peyote Road.   In 3335,   pp.
       197-210.
       Source -   New York Times,   March 9,   1969.

       _____.   see also   2272

2257   Nader,   Laura.   Powerlessness in Zapotec and
       United States Societies.   In 0111,   pp.
       309-324.

2258   Nagle,   Christopher Lippincott.   Lithic Raw
       Materials Procurement and Exchange in Dor-
       set Culture Along the Labrador Coast.   Ann
       Arbor,   MI.,   University Microfilms Inter-
       national,   1984.
       Microfilm - PhD Thesis - Brandeis
       University
       OCLC # 11645484

2259   Narrative of Some Things of New Spain and of
       the Great City of Temestitan,   Mexico.
       Written by the anonymous conqueror,   a com-
       panion of Hernan Cortes;   trans.   into Eng-
       lish and annotated by Marshland H. Saville.
       Boston,   Longwood Press,   1978.
       Trans. of Relacion de Algunas Cosas de la
       Nueva Espana,   which was a trans. of Rela-
       tione di Alcune cose della Nueva Spagna.
       The original Spanish text has been lost.
       Reprint of the 1917 edition pub.   by Cortes

Society, New York.
OCLC # 3446976

Nash, Bary B. see 3028

2260 Nash, Ronald J. Cultural Systems and Culture
Change in the Central Arctic. In 0908,
pp. 150-155.

2261 _____. Prehistory and Cultural Ecology -
Cape Breton Island, Nova Scotia. In 0479,
pp. 131-156.

2262 _____. The Prehistory of Northern Manitoba.
In 1467, pp. 77-92.

2263 National American Indian Court Judges As-
sociation. Long Range Planning Project.
Indian Courts and the Future: Report of
the NAICJA Long Range Planning Project.
Judge Orville N. Olney, project director,
David H. Getches, project planner/co-
ordinator. Washington, National American
Indian Court Judges Association, 1978.
OCLC # 3803737

2264 National Anthropological Archives. North
American Indians, Photographs from the
National Anthropological Archives, Smith-
sonian Institution. Compiled by Herman
Viola. Chicago, University of Chicago
Press, 1974.
52 Microfiche
OCLC # 2829177

2265 National Archives Conference on Research in
the History of Indian White Relations,
Washington, D. C., 1972. Indian-White
Relations: A Persistent Paradox: Papers
and Proceedings of the National Archives
Conference on Research in the History of
Indian White Relations, June 15-16, 1972,
the National Archives Building, Washing-
ton, D. C. Edited by Jane F. Smith and
Robert M. Kvasnicka, sponsored by the Na-
tional Archives and Records Service, Wash-
ington, Howard University Press, 1976.
National Archives Conferences, v. 10.
Essays in this collection are also listed

individually and refer to this citation.
OCLC # 1530849

National Center on Child Abuse and Neglect
see 0206

National Endowment for the Humanities. see
0578.5

2266 National Geographic Society, Washington, D.
C. National Geographic on Indians of the
Americas; A Color Illustrated Record by
Matthew W. Stirling. With contributions
by Hiram Bingham and others. Illus. with
full color reproductions of 149 paintings
by W. Langdon Kihn and H. M. Herget.
Foreword by John Oliver La Gorce. Washing-
ton, 1957, c1955.
National Geographic Story of Man Library
OCLC # 2420725

_____. see also 3500

2267 National Museum of Man. The Athapaskans:
Strangers of the North: An International
Travelling Exhibition from the Collection
of the National Museum of Man, Canada and
the Royal Scottish Museum. Ottawa, National Museums of Canada, 1974.
OCLC # 2072931

2268 _____. The Inuit Print: A Travelling Ex-
hibition of the National Museum of Man,
National Museums of Canada, and the De-
partment of Indian and Northern Affairs.
Ottawa, National Museum of Man, 1977.
Text in English and French
OCLC # 5777050

National Museum of Natural History (United
States). see 1063

National Native American Co-operative. see
2271

2269 Nations Remembered: An Oral History of the
Five Civilized Tribes, 1865-1907. Select-
ed by Theda Perdue. Westport, CT.,
Greenwood Press, 1980.
Contributions in Ethnic Studies, no. 1.

Extracted from Indian-Pioneer History, a
112 vol. oral history collected by the
Works Progress Administration in conjunction with the University of Oklahoma and
the Oklahoma Historical Society.
OCLC # 5892392

2270   Native American Astronomy. Edited by Anthony
       F. Aveni. Austin, University of Texas
       Press, 1977.
       Edited versions of papers presented at a
       symposium held at Colgate University, 23-
       26, Sept. 1975.
       Essays in this collection are also listed
       individually and refer to this citation.
       OCLC # 2968473

2271   Native American Directory: Alaska, Canada,
       United States. San Carlos, AZ., National
       Native American Co-operative, 1982.
       OCLC # 8920173

2272   Native American testimony: An Anthology of
       Indian and White Relations: First Encount-
       ers to Dispossession. Edited by Peter
       Nabokov; pref. by Vine Deloria. New
       York, Crowell, 1978.
       Summary: A collection of documents in
       which Native American describe their re-
       sponses to the explorers, traders, mis-
       sionaries, settlers and government diplo-
       mats and soldiers seeking dominion over
       their ancient homeland.
       OCLC # 3543613

2273   Native American and Energy Development.
       Joseph G. Jorgensen; pref. by Harris
       Arthur, photos by Lillian Kemp. Cam-
       bridge, MA., Anthropology Resource
       Center, 1978.
       Essays in this collection are also listed
       individually and refer to this citation.
       OCLC # 4834202

2274   Native Americans and Energy Development II.
       Edited by Joseph J. Jorgensen with the
       assistance of Sally Swenson; foreword by
       Daniel Bomberry; afterword by John Mohawk.
       2nd and fully expanded ed. Boston, MA.,
       Anthropology Resource Center, Seventh Gen-

eration Fund, 1984.
Essays in this collection are also listed
individually and refer to this citation.
OCLC # 10895234

2275 Native American on Film and Video. Edited by
Elizabeth Weatherford with Emelia Seubert.
New York, Museum of the American Indian,
Heye Foundation, 1981.
OCLC # 8298119

2276 Native Californians: A Theoretical Retro-
spective. Edited by Lowell J. Bean and
Thomas C. Blackburn. Ramona, CA., Ballena Press, 1976.
Essays in this collection are also listed
individually and refer to this citation.
OCLC # 2325760

2277 Native Languages of the Americas. Edited by
Thomas Sebeok. New York, Plenum Press,
1976, 1977.
OCLC # 2388194

2278 Native North American Cultures: Four Cases.
Edited by George and Louise Spindler. New
York, Holt, Rinehart, and Winston, 1977.
OCLC # 2331979

2279 Native North American Spirituality of the
Eastern Woodlands: Sacred Myths, Dreams,
Visions, Speeches, Healing Formulas,
Rituals and Ceremonies. Edited by Eliza-
beth Tooker. Preface by William C. Stur-
tevant. New York, Paulist Press, 1979.
The classics of western spirituality
OCLC # 5670465

2280 Nawpa Pacha. 1- . Berkeley, CA., 1963.
Issued by the Institution of Andean
Studies, Berkeley, CA.,
An International Series for Andean Arche-
ology. Library has v. 9-12 only.
OCLC # 1605919

Naylor, Maria see 0146

2281 Neely, Sharlotte. Acculturation and Persistence Among North Carolina's Eastern

Band of Cherokee Indians. In 2930, pp. 154-173.

2282 Neighbors and Intruders: An Ethnohistorical Exploration of the Indians of Hudson's River. Editors: Laurence M. Hauptman and Jack Campisi. Ottawa, National Museums of Canada, 1978. Essays in this collection are also listed individually and refer to this citation. Mercury Series, Canada, National Museum of Man, Canadian Ethnology Service. Paper 39. OCLC # 4601722

2283 Neihardt, John Gneisenau, 1881-1973. The Sixth Grandfather: Black Elk's Teachings Given to John G. Neihardt. Edited and with an introd. by Raymond J. DeMallie; foreword by Hilda Neihardt Petri. Lincoln, University of Nebraska Press, 1984. OCLC # 9762083

_____. see also 0288

Nellermoe, John. see 3432

Nelson, Ralph. see 2494

2284 Nelson, Richard K. Make Prayers to the Raven: A Koyukon View of the Northern Forest. Chicago, University of Chicago Press, 1983. OCLC # 8475556

2285 Nespor, Robert Paschal, 1951- . The Evolution of the Agricultural Settlement Pattern of the Southern Cheyenne Indians in Western Oklahoma, 1876-1930. Ann Arbor, MI., University Microfilms International, 1984. Microfilm - PhD Thesis - University of Oklahoma

2286 Netting, Robert McC. Maya Subsistence: Mythologies, Analogies, Possibilities. In 2378, pp. 299-333.

2287 Neuman, Robert W. An Introduction To Louisiana Archaeology. Baton Rouge, Louisiana

State University Press,   1984.
OCLC # 10021922

2288   Neusius,   Sarah Ward,   1951- .   Early Middle
        Archaic Subsistence Strategies: Changes in
        Faunal Exploitation at the Koster Site.
        Ann Arbor,   MI.,   University Microfilms
        International,   1982.
        Microfilm - PhD Thesis - Northwestern
        University
        OCLC # 11492113

2288.5 Neuwirth,   Steven Douglas.   The Imagined
        Savage: The American Indian and the New
        England Mind,   1620-1675.   Ann Arbor,   MI.,
        University Microfilms International,   1982.
        PhD Thesis - Washington University
        OCLC # 11299350

2289   New Light on Chaco Canyon.   Edited by David
        Grant Noble.   Santa fe,   NM.,   School of
        American Research Press,   1984.
        Essays in this collection are also listed
        individually and refer to this citation.
        Special volume in the School of American
        Research Exploration Series.
        OCLC # 10780064

        New Orleans Museum of Art.   see   0092

2290   New York Public Library.   Papers Pertaining
        to Indian Affairs (1709;   1750-1775;   1710-
        1797).   Originals in New York Public Li-
        brary.   One reel microfilm provided by
        American Philosophical Society,   Phila-
        delphia.
        For detailed description see the Freeman
        guide #233.

        New York State Archaeological Association.
        Bulletin.   see   0596

2291   New York (state) Interdepartmental Committee
        on Indian Affairs.   Annual Report.   1974-
        75.

2292   New York (State).   Legislature.   Assembly.
        Committee on Governmental Operations.   Sub-
        committee on Indian Affairs.   Report of the
        Assembly Subcommittee on Indian Affairs to

the Standing Committee on Governmental Operations. Albany,   1971.
OCLC # 1351479

2293 New York (State). Legislature. Assembly.
Special Committee to Investigate the Indian
Problem. Report of the Special Committee
to Investigate the Indian Problem of the
State of New York: Appointed by the As-
sembly of 1888. Transmitted to the Legis-
lature Feb. 1, 1889. Albany, Troy Press
Co., 1889.
State of New York, no. 51. In Assembly
Feb. 1, 1889
OCLC # 4709377

2294 New York (State). Office of Planning Ser-
vices. Final Report of the Pilot Planning
Program for the Indians in New York State
(Indian Needs Planning Project) N. Y.
P-239. Albany, The Office, 1974.
OCLC # 1196342

2295 New York (State). State Interdepartmental
Committee on Indian Affairs. Annual Report
- New York State Interdepartmental Commit-
tee on Indian Affairs. Albany.
Report year ends June 30. Library has
1967-1971
OCLC # 1793456

2296 _____. The Indian Today in New York State.
6th ed. Albany, 1969
OCLC # 125206

2297 Newcomb, William Wilmon, 1921- . Culture
and Acculturation of Delaware Indians. Ann
Arbor, MI., University of Michigan,
1956.
Anthropological Papers, Museum of Anthropology, University of Michigan no. 10.
OCLC # 627487

2298 _____. Pecos River Pictographs: The Development of an Art Form. In 0710, pp. 175-
190.

2299 Newell, H. Perry. The George C. Davis
Site, Cherokee County, Texas. ... and
Alex D. Krieger. Menasha, WI., Pub.

NEWHOUSE 328

jointly by the Society for American Archaeology and the University of Texas Press, 1949. Millwood, NY., Kraus Reprint, 1974.
Memoirs of the Society for American Archaeolgy no. 5. Supplement to American Antiquity v. 14, no. 4, pt. 2, April 1949.
Bound with Bennett, Wendell Clark, A Reappraisal of Peruvian Archaeology.
OCLC # 1185893

2300 Newhouse, Seth (Da-yo-de-ka-ne). Traditional History and Constitution of the Iroquois Confederacy, 1885. One reel of microfilm, provided by the American Philosophical Society, Philadelphia.
Note from Freeman guide A129 - Copy of original, formally in possession of Ray Fadden, St. Regis Mohawk Reservation, Hogansburg, NY., now in possession of the Mohawk Tribe. Title - Cosmography of De-ka-na-wi-das' Government.

2301 Newson, Linda A. Aboriginal and Spanish Colonial Trinidad: A Study in Culture Contact. New York, Academic Press, 1976.
OCLC # 2644018

2302 Niatum, Duane, 1938- . Carriers of the Dream Wheel: Contemporary Native American Poetry. New York, Harper & Row, 1975.
Authors included are Liz Sohappy Bahe; Jim Barnes; Joseph Bruchac; Gladys Cardiff; Lance Henson; Roberta Hill; N. Scott Momaday; Dana Naone; Duane Niatum; Simon J. Ortiz; Anita Endrezze Probst; W. M. Ransom; Wendy Rose; Leslie Silko; James Welch and Ray A. Young Bear.
OCLC # 1054122

Nicholas, Thomas. b. ca. 1532. see 1220

2303 Nichols, David A., 1939- . Lincoln and the Indians: Civil War Policy and Politics. Columbia, University of Missouri Press, 1978.
OCLC # 3240588

Nichols, John D. see 1710

2304 Nichols, Roger L. <u>The American Indian:</u>
      <u>Past and Present</u>. Edited by ... and Geroge
      R. Adams. Waltham, MA., Xerox College
      Pub., 1971.
      Essays in this collection are also listed
      individually and refer to this citation.
      OCLC # 135676

2305 Nichols, William. <u>Badger and Coyote Were</u>
      <u>Neighbors': Comic Reconciliation in a</u>
      <u>Clackamas Chinook Myth</u>. In 2904, pp.
      301-308.

2306 _____. <u>Black Elk's Truth</u>. In 2904, pp.
      334-343.

2307 Nicholson, Henry B. and Clement W.
      Meighan. <u>The UCLA Department of Anthrop-</u>
      <u>ology Program in West Mexican Archaeology-</u>
      <u>Ethnohistory, 1956-1970</u>. In 0231, pp.
      6-18.

2308 _____. <u>Western Mesoamerica: A. D. 900-</u>
      <u>1520</u>. In 0377, pp. 285-329.

      _____. see also 2520

2309 Nicholson, Irene. <u>Mexican and Central Amer-</u>
      <u>ican Mythology</u>. New rev. ed. New York,
      Bedrick Books, 1985.
      Library of the World's Myths and Legends
      OCLC # 11518593

2310 Nickeson, Steve. <u>The Structure of the</u>
      <u>Bureau of Indian Affairs</u>. In 0087, pp.
      61-76.

2311 Nicolett, J. N. (Joseph Nicholas), 1786-
      1843. <u>Joseph N. Nicolett on the Plains</u>
      <u>and Prairies: The Expeditions of 1838-39,</u>
      <u>with Journals, Letters and Notes on the</u>
      <u>Dakota Indians</u>. Trans. from the French
      and edited by Edmund C. Bray and Martha
      Coleman Bray. St. Paul, Minnesota His-
      torical Society, 1976.
      Publications of the Minnesota Historical
      Society
      OCLC # 2072714

2312 _____. <u>The Journal of Joseph N. Nicolett:</u>

*A Scientist on the Mississippi Headwaters,
with Notes on Indian Life, 1836-37.*
Trans. from the French by Andre Fertey.
Edited by Martha Coleman Bray. St. Paul,
Minnesota Historical Society, 1970.
Publications of the Minnesota Historical
Society. Includes a trans. of selected
manuscripts on deposit at the Library of
Congress dealing with the author's first
visit to what is now Minnesota.
OCLC # 118409

2313 Niemczycki, Mary Ann Palmer. *The Origin and
Development of the Seneca and Cayuga Tribes
of New York State.* Ann Arbor, MI., Uni-
versity Microfilms International, 1983.
Microfilm - PhD Thesis - S. U. N. Y. at
Buffalo
OCLC # 10713519

2314 Neitzel, Jill E. *The Regional Organization
of the Hohokam in the American Southwest:
A Stylistic Analysis of Red-on-Buff Pot-
tery.* Ann Arbor, MI., University Micro-
films International, 1984.
Microfilm - PhD Thesis - Arizona State
University
OCLC # 12580736

Nilta' Alchini Ba Educational Center
(Shiprock, NM.). see 3499

2315 Nissen, Karen M. *Images from the Past: An
Analysis of Six Western Great Basin Petro-
glyph Sites.* Ann Arbor, MI., University
Microfilms International, 1982.
Microfilm - PhD Thesis - University of
California - Berkeley
OCLC # 10395866

2316 Noble, David Grant. *Ancient Ruins of the
Southwest: An Archaeological Guide.* Flag-
staff, AZ., Northland Press, 1981.
OCLC # 7396625

_____. see also 2289

2317 Noble, W. C. *An Unusual Neutral Iroquois
House Structure.* New York State Archeological Association Bulletin 48, March 1970,

pp. 14-15. Millwood, NY., Kraus Reprint, 1976.

2318 Noguera, Eduardo. Excavations at Tehuacan.
In 2105, pp. 306-319.

2319 Nohl, Lessing H. Mackenzie Against Dull
Knife: Breaking the Northern Cheyennes in
1876. In 0638, pp. 86-92.

2319.5 Noley, Grayson. Choctaw Bilingual and
Bicultural Education in the 19th Century.
In 2238.5, pp. 25-39.

2320 _____. A Description of Graduate Training
Requirements for Future Administrators of
Education for American Indians. In 2962,
pp. 67-81.

2320.5 _____. Summary and Critique of the Report
on Indian Education of the American Indian
Policy Review Commission. In 2961.5, pp.
57-73.

2321 Noonan, Karen K. Witchs Walk #1: A Pre-
liminary Site Report. New York State
Archeological Association Bulletin 52,
July 1971, pp. 22-38. Millwood, NY.,
Kraus Reprint, 1976.

2322 Nordenskiold, Erland, friherre, 1877-1932.
The Changes in the Material Culture of Two
Indian Tribes Under the Influence of New
Surroundings. New York, AMS Press, 1979.
Reprint of the 1920 ed. pub. by Pehrssons
forlog, Goteborg, Sweden, which was is-
sued as v. 2 of Comparative Ethnographical
Studies.
OCLC # 3914714

2323 _____. The Copper and Bronze Ages in South
America, With Two Appendixes by Axel Hult-
gren. New York, AMS Press, 1979.
Reprint of the 1921 ed. pub. by Pehrssons
forlag, Goteborg, Sweden, which was is-
sued as v. 4 of Comparative Ethnographical
Studies.
OCLC # 3934666

2324 _____. Deductions Suggested by the Geo-

graphical Distribution of Some Post-Co-
lumbian Words Used by the Indians of South
America. New York, AMS Press, 1979.
Reprint of the 1922 ed. pub. by Pehrssons
forlag, Goteborg, Sweden, which was is-
sued as v. 5 of Comparative Ethnographical
Studies.
OCLC # 3914711

2325 _____. An Ethno-Geographical Analysis of
the Material Culture of Two Indian Tribes
in the Gran Chaco. New York, AMS Press,
1979.
Reprint of the 1919 ed. pub. by the
author, Goteborg, Sweden, which was is-
sued as v. 1 of Comparative Ethnographical
Studies. Trans. of Eine Geographische und
Ethnographische Analyse der Materiellen
Kultur Zweier Indianerstamme in El Gran
Chaco (Sudamerika).
OCLC # 3934667

2326 _____. The Ethnography of South America
Seen From Mojos in Bolivia. New York, AMS
Press, 1979.
Reprint of the 1924 ed. pub. by Pehrssons
forlag, Goteborg, Sweden, which was is-
sued as v. 3 of Comparative Ethnographical
Studies.
OCLC # 3914712

2327 _____. An Historical and Ethnological
Survey of the Cuna Indians. ... in collab-
oration with the Cuna Indians, Ruben Perez
Kantule; arranged and edited from the
posthumous ms. and notes, and original
Indian documents at the Gothenburg Ethno-
graphical Museum by Henry Wassen. New
York, AMS Press, 1979.
Reprint of the 1938 ed. pub. by Goteborgs
Museum, Etnografiska avdelningen, Gote-
borg, Sweden, which was issued as v. 10
of Comparative Ethnographical Studies.
OCLC # 3914706

2328 _____. Modifications in Indian Culture
Through Inventions and Loans. New York,
AMS Press, 1979.
Reprint of the 1930 ed. pub. by Pehrssons
forlag, Goteborg, Sweden, which was is-

sued as v. 8 of Comparative Ethnographical
Studies.
OCLC # 3914709

2329 _____. Origin of the Indian Civilizations
in South America. An Arrow Poison With
Cardiac Effects from the New World by C.
G. Santersson. The Ancient Peruvian Aba-
cus by Henry Wassen. New York, AMS
Press, 1979.
Reprint of the 1931 ed. pub. by Pehrssons
forlag, Goteborg, Sweden, which was is-
sued as v. 9 of Comparative Ethnographical
Studies.
OCLC # 3914708

2330 _____. The Secret Peruvian Quipus. New
York, AMS Press, 1979.
Reprint of the 1925 ed. pub. in 2 vols.
by Pehrssons forlag, Goteborg, Sweden,
which was issued as v. 6 of Comparative
Ethnographical Studies.
OCLC # 4006792

_____. see also 2475

Noreau-Hébert, Micheline see 0858

2331 Norick, Sylvester. Outdoor Life in the
Menominee Forest. Chicago, Franciscan
Herald Press, 1980.
OCLC # 4664350

Norman, Howard A. see 3397

2332 North American Indians: A Dissertation
Index. Ann Arbor, MI., University
Microfilms International, 1977.
Listing of doctoral dissertations written
between 1904 and 1976 concerning all
American Indian groups within the North
American continent.
OCLC # 3087000

North Carolina. Division of Archives and
History. see 0466

2333 Northern Athapaskan Conference, 1st,
Ottawa, Ont., 1971. Proceedings, Northern Athapaskan Conference. Edited by A.

McFadyen Clark. Ottawa, National Museums
of Canada, 1975.
2 vols. Paper - Canadian Ethnology
Service, no. 27, Mercury Series.
Summaries in French.
OCLC # 2320668

2334   Northern Iroquoian Texts. Edited by Marianne
       Mithun and Hanni Woodbury. Chicago, Uni-
       versity of Chicago Press, Ann Arbor, MI.,
       distributed by University Microfilms Inter-
       national, 1980.
       IJAL - NATS monograph no. 4.
       OCLC # 6086454

       Northlight Gallery. see 1499

2335   Northrop, Henry Davenport, 1836-1909.
       Indian Horrors, or, Massacres by the Red
       Men: Being a Thrilling Narrative of Bloody
       Wars With...Savages, Including a Full Ac-
       count of the Daring Deeds and Tragic Death
       of...Sitting Bull, With Startling Descrip-
       tions of Fantastic Ghost Dances, Myster-
       ious Medicine Men...Scalping of Helpless
       Settlers...etc., the Whole Comprising a
       Fascinating History of the Indians from the
       Discovery of America to the Present Time.
       Philadelphia, National Pub. Co., 1891.
       Spine title - Wild Indians and Their Daring
       Deeds. Most plates printed on both sides.
       OCLC # 7700381

2336   Norton, John, 1715-1778. The Redeemed
       Captive. New York, Garland Pub. Co.,
       1977.
       Garland Library of narratives of North
       American Indian captivities, v. 6.
       Reprint of the 1748 ed. printed and sold
       by S. Kneeland, Boston. Issued with the
       reprint of the 1728 ed. of E. Hanson
       God's Mercy Surmounting Man's Cruelty.
       OCLC # 3104353

2337   Norton, Thomas E. Iroquois Diplomacy and
       the New York Fur Trade. In 1583, pp. 13-
       23.

2338   Nunez A., Lautaro. Northern Chile. In
       0577, pp. 483-511.

2339 Nute, Grace Lee, 1895- . <u>Caesars of the</u>
      <u>Wilderness: Medard Chouart, Sieur des</u>
      <u>Groseillier's and Pierre Esprint Radisson,</u>
      <u>1618-1710.</u> St. Paul, Minnesota His-
      torical Society Press, 1978, 1943.
      Reprint of the 1943 ed. published by
      Appleton-Century, New York.
      OCLC # 3627470

2340 Nutini, Hugo G. <u>The Demographic Functions</u>
      <u>of Compadrazgo in Santa Maria Belen Azit-</u>
      <u>zimititlan and Rural Tlaxcala</u>. In 0958,
      pp. 219-236.

2341 _____. <u>Introduction: The Nature and</u>
      <u>Treatment of Kinship in Mesoamerica</u>. In
      0958, pp. 3-27.

2342 _____. <u>Ritual Kinship</u>. ... Betty Bell,
      Princeton, NJ., Princeton University
      Press, c1980 - c1984.
      v. 1. The structure and historical
      development of the compadrazgo system in
      rural Tlaxcala. v. 2. Ideological and
      structural integration of the compadrazgo
      system in rural Tlaxcala.
      OCLC # 5726407

      _____. <u>see also</u> 0958

2343 Nuttall, Thomas, 1786-1859. <u>Journal of</u>
      <u>Travels Into the Arkansa Territory, During</u>
      <u>the Year 1819</u>. Edited by Savoie Lottin-
      ville. University of Oklahoma Press,
      1980.
      The American Exploration and Travel Series
      v. 66. First published in 1821 by T. H.
      Palmer in Philadelphia under title <u>A Jour-</u>
      <u>nal of Travels Into the Arkansa Territory</u>
      <u>During the Year 1819</u>.
      OCLC # 5310451

      Nuttall, Zelia, 1858-1933. <u>see</u> 0329,
      0598

2343.5 Oandasan, William. <u>Surrealism and</u>
      <u>Primalism: A Comparative Analysis and</u>
      <u>Extrapolation of the Psycho-Esthetics</u>. In
      2831.5, pp. 185-198.

OBENAUF

336

2344 Obenauf, Margaret Senter. A History of
Research on the Chacoan Roadway System. In
0711, pp. 123-167.

2345 Oberg, Kalervo, 1901-1973. Indian Tribes
of Northern Grosso, Brazil. New York,
AMS Press, 1979.
Reprint of the 1953 ed. pub. by U. S.
Govt. Print. Off., which was issed as
publication no. 15 of Smithsonian Insti-
tution, Institute of Social Anthropology.
OCLC # 4500117

2346 _____. The Terena and the Caduveo of South-
ern Mato Grosso, Brazil. Prepared in co-
operation with the United States Dept. of
State as a project of the Interdepartmental
Committee on Scientific and Cultural Co-
operation. New York, AMS Press, 1980.
Reprint of the 1949 ed. pub. by U. S.
Govt. Print. Off., which was issued as
Publication no. 9 of the Smithsonian In-
stitution, Institute of Social Anthrop-
ology.
OCLC # 5891057

2347 O'Brien, Michael J. and Robert E. Warren.
An Archaic Projectile Point Sequence from
the Southern Prairie Peninsula: The Pigeon
Roost Creek Site. In 0124, pp. 71-98.

2348 O'Brien, Patricia J. Steed-Kisker: A Western Mississippian Settlement System. In
2172, pp. 1-19.

Occom, Samson, 1723-1792. see 2632

2349 O'Connell, Barbara Lucille Heminger.
Fluctuating Asymmetry as a Measure of De-
velopmental Stability in Illinois Woodland
Population. Ann Arbor, MI., University
Microfilms International, 1983.
Microfilm - PhD Thesis - Northwestern
University

O'Connell, James F. see 0470

2350 O'Donnell, James. Joseph Brant. In 0081,
pp. 21-40.

2351 O'Donnell, James H., 1937- . Southeastern
      Frontiers: Europeans, Africans and Ameri-
      can Indians, 1513-1840; A Critical Bib-
      liography. Bloomington, Published for the
      Newberry Library by Indiana University
      Press, 1982.
      Bibliographical Series, The Newberry
      Library Center for the History of the
      American Indian
      OCLC # 7975987

2352 _____. The Southern Indians in the War for
      American Independence, 1775-1783. In
      1099, pp. 46-64.

2353 Officer, James E. The Indian Service and
      its Evolution. In 0034, pp. 59-103.

      _____. see also 1725

2354 Offner, Jerome A. Household Organization in
      the Texcocan Heartland. In 0978, pp.
      127-146.

2355 _____. Law and Politics in Aztec Texcoco.
      New York, Cambridge University Press,
      1983.
      Cambridge Latin American Studies v. 44.
      OCLC # 8388192

      O'Flynn, Donnel. see 3453

      Oklahoma Museum of Art. see 0092, 2851

2356 Olafson, Sigfus. Bannerstones in the Lower
      Hudson Valley. New York State Archeologi-
      cal Association Bulletin 20, Nov. 1960,
      pp. 6-9. Millwood, NY., Kraus Reprint,
      1976.
      Paper presented at the annual meeting April
      2, 1960.

2357 Olden, Sarah Emilia. Shoshone Folk Lore,
      as Discovered from the Rev. John Roberts,
      a Hidden Hero, on the Wind River Indian
      Reservation in Wyoming. Milwaukee, WI.,
      Morehouse Publishing Co., 1923.
      OCLC # 4380615

      O'Leary, Marilyn. see 0881

O'Leary, Timothy J. see 2241

2358 Olexer, Barbara, 1942- . Enslavement of
      the American Indian. With an introduction
      by Stephen paul DeVillo. Monroe, NY.,
      Library Research Associates, 1982.
      OCLC # 8866739

2359 Olivera, Mercedes. The Barrios of San
      Andrés Cholula. In 0958, pp. 65-95.

2360 Oliveros, Jose Arturo. Nuevas Exploraciones
      en El Opeño, Michoacán. In 0231, pp.
      182-201.

      Olney, Orville A. see 2263

2361 Olsen, Angmalortok. Processes of the Dis-
      solution of the Greenlandic Societies and
      Necessities and Possibilities in Rebuilding
      a New Greenlandic Society. In 1875, pp.
      431-459.

2362 Olsen, Fred, 1891- . Indian Creek;
      Arawak Site on Antigua, West Indies. 1973
      excavation by Yale University and the Anti-
      gua Archeological Society. Norman, Uni-
      versity of Oklahoma Press, 1974.
      OCLC # 1365878

2363 _____. On the Trail of the Arawaks. With a
      foreword by George Kubler and an introduct-
      ory essay by Irving Rouse. Norman, Uni-
      versity of Oklahoma Press, 1974.
      Civilization of the American Indian Series
      OCLC # 865922

2364 Olsen, Stanley John, 1919- . An Osteology
      of Some Maya Mammals. Cambridge, MA.,
      Peabody Museum of Archaeology and Ethnol-
      ogy, Harvard University. Distributed by
      Harvard University Press, 1982.
      Papers of the Peabody Museum of Archaeology
      and Ethnology v. 73.
      OCLC # 8235169

2365 _____. Prehistoric Environmental
      Reconstruction by Vertebrate Faunal Analy-
      sis, Grasshopper Pueblo. In 2239, pp.
      63-72.

2366   _____. Water Resources and Aquatic Fauna at
        Grasshopper Pueblo. In 2239,   pp.   61-62.

        _____. see also 0324

2367   Olson,   Paul A.   "Black Elk Speaks" as Epic
        and Ritual Attempt to Reverse History.   In
        3275,   pp.   3-25.

2367.5 O'Neil,   Floyd A.   The Mormons,   the
        Indians,   and George Washington Bean.   In
        0578.5,   pp.   77-107.

2367.7 _____. Multiple Sources and Resources for
        the Development of Social Studies Curricu-
        lum for the American Indian.   In 2238.5,
        pp.   153-156.

2368   _____. Southwest Indians: A Brief History.
        In 1556,   pp.   68-71.

2369   _____. 'They Come to Do Good and They Do
        Well".   In 1556,   pp.   18-19.

        _____. see also 0578.5

2370   O'Neil,   John D.,   1951- .   Is It Cool To Be
        an Eskimo?:   A Study of Stress Identity,
        Coping and Health Among Canadian Inuit
        Young Adult Men.   Ann Arbor,   MI.,
        University Microfilms International,   1984.
        Microfilm - PhD Thesis - University of
        California-San Francisco
        OCLC # 12126949

        Onondaga County (N.Y.) - Dept.   of Parks and
        Recreation.   see 3483.5

2371   Opler,   Morris Edward,   1907- .   Dirty Boy:
        A Jicarilla Tale of Raid and War.   New
        York,   Kraus Reprint,   1969.
        Memoirs of the American Anthropological
        Association no.   52,   1938.
        OCLC # 676802

2372   Opperman,   Renee.   The Olmec-Chavin   Connec-
        tion.   In 0121,   pp.   121-130.

2373   _____. Prehistoric Cosmology in Mesoamerica
        and South America.   Greeley,   Museum of

Anthropology,   University of Northern
Colorado Press.
University of Northern Colorado,   Museum of
Anthropology,   Occasional Publications in
Anthropology,   Archaeological Series no.
27.
OCLC # 1541399

2374   Orchard,   WIlliam C.   Beads and Beadwork of
the American Indians: A Study Based on
Specimens in the Museum of the American
Indian, Heye Foundation.   2n ed. ,   New
York,   The Museum,   1975.
Contributions from the Museum of the
American Indian,   Heye Foundation v. 11.
OCLC # 2034679

2375   Order of Indian Wars.   The Papers of the
Order of Indian Wars.   Introd.   by John M.
Carroll;   preface by George S.   Pappas.
Ft. Colins,   CO. ,   The Old Army Press,
1975.
OCLC # 1741707

2376   O'Reilly,   Henry J. ,   1806-1886.   Papers re-
lating to the Six Nations, 1784-1820.
Originals - New York Historical Society.
Selections from v.   6-15 with some docu-
ments from the American State Papers.
Letters.   One reel microfilm provided by
American Philosophical Society,   Philadel-
phia.
For detailed description see the Freeman
guide #234.

2377   _____.   Notices of Sullivan's Campaign: Or,
the Revolutionary Warfare in Western New
York: Embodied in the Addressess and Docu-
ments Connected with the Funeral Honors
Rendered to Those Who Fell With the Gallant
Boyd in the Genesee Valley, Including the
Remarks of Gov.   Seward at Mount Hope.
Port Washington,   NY. ,   Kennikat Press,
1970.
Kennikat American Bicentennial Series.
Reprint of the 1842 edition.
OCLC # 94435

2378   The Origins of Maya Civilization.   Edited by
Richard E.   W.   Adams.   Albuquerque,   Uni-

versity of New Mexico Press, 1977.
School of American Research Advanced
Seminar Series. Seminar held Oct. 14-18,
1974 in Santa Fe.
OCLC # 2984416

2378.5   Orr, Charles, 1862- . History of the
Pequot War: The Contemporary Accounts of
Mason, Underhill, Vincent and Gardener.
Reprint from the collections of the Mas-
sachusetts Historical Society, with addi-
tional notes and an introd. by Charles
Orr... Cleveland, The Helman-Taylor Com-
pany, 1897.
The first three accounts have special title
pages. CONTENTS: A Brief History of the
Pequot War by Major Iohn Mason... Boston,
1736. Nevves from America by Captaine Iohn
Underhill... London. 1638. A Trve Relation
of the Late Battell Fought in New England
Between the English and the Pequet Salvages
by Philip Vincent, London, 1638. Leift
Lion Gardener, His Relation of the
Pequot Warres.
OCLC # 1651227

2379   Ortiz, Roxanne Dunbar. The Context of Colonialism in Writing American Indian History. In 2962, pp. 159-165.

2380   _____. Indians of the Americas: Human
Rights and Self-Determination. New York,
Praeger, 1984.
OCLC # 11463386

2380.5   Ortiz, Roxanne Dunbar. Roots of Resist-
ance: Land Tenure in New Mexico, 1680-
1980. Chicano Studies Research Center
Publications, University of California,
Los Angeles; American Indian Studies Cen-
ter, University of California, Los
Angeles, 1980.
Monograph - Chicano Studies Research
Center Publications, University of Cal-
ifornia, v. 10.
OCLC # 6532780

2381   Ortiz de Montellano, Bernard. Empirical
Aztec Medicine. In 0154, pp. 65-70.
Reprinted from Science v. 188, (4185),

April 18, 1975, pp. 215-220.

2382 _____. The Rational Causes of Illnesses
Among the Aztecs. In 0154, pp. 43-64.
Presented at symposium The Concept of
Illness of Mesoamerica, XLII, Interna-
tional Congress of Americanists, Paris,
France, September 1976..

2383 Osage Nation. Constitution. The Constitution and Laws of the Osage Nation, Passed
at Pawhuska, Osage Nation, in the Years
1881 and 1882; Constitution and Laws of
the Sac and Fox Nation, Indian Territory.
Wilmington, DE., Scholarly Resources,
1975.
Constitutions and laws of the American Indian tribes, series 2, v. 31. Reprint of
the 1888 ed. pub. by A. Gast Bank Note
and Litho Co., St. Louis.
OCLC # 1526622

2384 Osgood, Cornelius, 1905- . The Ethno-
graphy of the Tanaina. New Haven, Human
Relations Area Files, 1966.
Yale University Publications in Anthro-
pology no. 16. Reprint of the 1937 ed.
OCLC # 497052

2385 Ossa, Paul P. Paiján in Early Andean Prehistory: The Moche Valley Evidence. In
0902, pp. 290-295.

2386 Oswalt, Wendell H. Alaskan Eskimos. San
Francisco, Chandler Pub. Co., distributors: Science Research Assoc., Chicago,
1967.
OCLC # 419694

2387 Otis, Morgan George. Native Americans in
Higher Education: Rationale and Retention.
In 2962, pp. 59-65.

2388 Ottaway, Lucretia Vickery. Some Architect-
ural Features Characteristic of the Taos,
New Mexico Area: Early Manifestations at
TA-26. In 0622, pp. 407-436.

Otto, Eberhard, 1913-1974. see 0501,
1922

343 OURADA

2389 Ourada, Patricia K., 1926- . The Menominee Indians: A History. With a foreword
by Donald J. Berthrong. Norman, University of Oklahoma Press, 1979.
Civilization of the American Indian Series
no. 146.
OCLC # 3844621

2390 Overstreet, David F. Oneota Settlement Patterns in Eastern Wisconsin: Some Consider-
ations of Time and Space. In 2172, pp.
21-52.

2391 Owens, Nancy J. Can Tribes Control Energy
Development. In 2274, pp. 49-62.

2392 Packer, Rhonda, 1949- . Sorcerers, Med-
icine-Men, and Curing Doctors: A Study of
Myth and Symbol in North American Shaman-
ism. Ann Arbor, MI., University Micro-
films International, 1983.
Microfilm - PhD Thesis - University of
California - Los Angeles
OCLC # 11277715

Page, Jake. see 2393

2393 Page, Susanne. Hopi. ... and Jake Page.
New York, Abrams, 1982.
OCLC # 7924708

2394 Page, William D. The Geology of the El
Bosque Archaeological Site, Nicaragua. In
0902, pp. 231-260.

2395 Page, William R. A Preliminary Bibliography
of Hopewell Archaeology. Greeley, Univer-
sity of Northern Colorado, Museum of
Anthropology, 1976.
University of Northern Colorado, Museum of
Anthropology, Misc. Series no. 21, Dec.
1976.
OCLC # 3518714

2396 Pailes, Richard A. The Rio Sonora Culture
in Prehistoric Trade Systems. In 0014,
pp. 134-143.

2397 Paillés, Maricruz. The Process of Transformation at Pajón: A Preclassic Society

Located in an Estuary in Chiapas, Mexico.
In 2524, pp. 81-100.

Paine, John, 1632-1675. see 2898

2398 Palkovich, Ann M. Tuberculosis Epidemiology
in Two Arikara Skeletal Samples: A Study
of Disease Impact. In 2526, pp. 161-175.

2399 Palmatary, Helen Constance. Archaeology of
the Lower Tapajos Valley, Brazil. Philadelphia, American Philosophical Society,
1960.
Transactions of the American Philosophical
Society. New Series v. 50, pt. 3.
OCLC # 656308

2400 Pandey, Triloki Nath. Flora Zuñi: A Portrait Zuni 1879-. In 0080, pp. 217-225.

2401 _____. Images of Power in a Southwestern
Pueblo. In 0111, pp. 195-215.

2402 Papers Pertaining to Indian Affairs 1665-
1775. 3 reels microfilm. Originals in
Mass. Archives. Film provided by American
Philosophical Society, Philadelphia.
CONTENTS: reel 1, v. 1-28. reel 2, v.
28-38. reel 3, v. 51-287.

2403 Papovich, John. I. Spin the Names of Earth
and Sky: Native American Landscape Tradi-
tions and the Way to Rainy Mountain. II.
Teaching Homeric Poems in Translation:
Seeing Homeric Value. Ann Arbor, MI.,
University Microfilms International, 1984.
Microfilm - PhD Thesis - University of
Virginia
OCLC # 11740291

Pappas, George S. see 2375

Papworth, Mark L. see 0267

2404 Paredes, J. Anthony (James Anthony), 1939-
Back From Disappearance: The Alabama
Creek Indian Community. In 2930, pp.
123-141.

2405. The Folk Culture of the Eastern Creek In-

dians: Synthesis and Change.   In 1282,
pp. 93-111.

2406 Parezo,   Nancy J.   Navajo Sandpaintings:
From Religious Act to Commercial Art.
Tucson,   University of Arizona Press,
1983.
OCLC # 9575958

Parins,   James W.   see   1924,   1924.5

2407 Parker,   Ann.   Molas Folk Art of the Cuna
Indians. ... and Avon Neal.   Photos by Ann
Parker.   Barre, MA.,   Barre Pub.,   New
York,   distributed by Crown Pub.,   1977.
OCLC # 3169218

2408 Parker,   Arthur Caswell,   1881-1955.
Champlain's Assault on the Fortified Town
of the Oneidas.   In New York State Museum
Bulletin 207-208,   1917, pp. 165-174.

2409 _____.   Report of the Archeologist.   In New
York State Museum Bulletin 164,   1912, pp.
45-57.

2410 _____.   Report of the Archeologist.   In New
York State Museum Bulletin 173,   1914, pp.
93-102.

2411 _____.   Report of the Archeologist.   In New
York State Museum Bulletin 196,   1917, pp.
67-75.

2412 _____.   Report on Archeology.   In New York
State Museum Bulletin 158,   1911, pp. 61-
84.

2413 _____.   Report on the Division of Archeology
and Ethnology.   In New York State Museum
Bulletin 177,   1915, pp. 63-73.

2414 _____.   Rumbling Wings and Other Indian
Tales.   Illus.   by Will Crawford.   Garden
City,   NY.,   Doubleday,   Doran & Co.,
Inc.,   1928.
OCLC # 2438019

_____.   see also 1332

2415   Parker, Ely Samuel, 1828-1895. Papers
        (1794-1946), Collected by Arthur C. Park-
        er, of Ely S. Parker and Other Members of
        the Family. 3 reels microfilm provided by
        American Philosophical Society, Philadel-
        phia.
        CONTENTS: reel 1 - 1794-1858, reel 2 -
        1858-1946, and n.d. and Asher Wright Lin-
        guistic materials. reel 3 - Asher Wright
        Linguistic materials. For detailed des-
        cription see the Freeman Guide #135.

2416   Parks, Douglas R. James R. Murie, Pawnee
        Ethnographer, Pawnee, 1862-1921. In
        0080, pp. 75-89.

2417   _____, Margot Liberty and Andrea Ferenci.
        Peoples of the Plains. In 0112, pp. 284-
        295.

        _____. see also 1485

        Parmalee, P. W. see 1279

2418   Parman, Donald L. The Navajos and the New
        Deal. New Haven, Yale University Press,
        1976.
        Yale Western Americana no. 27.
        OCLC # 2054678

2419   Parsons, Elsie Worthington Clews, 1875-
        1941. Hopi and Zuñi Ceremonialism. New
        York, Kraus Reprint, 1964.
        Memoirs of the American Anthropological As-
        sociation, no. 39, 1933.
        OCLC # 676799

2420   _____. Notes on the Caddo. New York,
        Kraus Reprint, 1969.
        Memoirs of the American Anthropological As-
        sociation, no. 57. Suppl. to American
        Anthropologist v. 43, no. 3, pt. 2,
        1941.
        OCLC # 653496

2421   _____. A Pueblo Indian Journal: 1920-1921.
        Introd. and notes by Elsie Clews Parsons.
        Millwood, NY., Kraus Reprint, 1974.
        Memoirs of the American Anthropological As-
        sociation, no. 32. Reprint of the 1925

ed.
OCLC # 1313994

2422 _____. The Scalp Ceremonial of Zuñi. New
     York, Kraus Reprint, 1964.
     Memoirs of the American Anthropological As-
     sociation, no. 31, 1924.
     OCLC # 1852528

2423 _____. The Social Organization of the Tewa
     of New Mexico. New York, Kraus Reprint,
     1964.
     Memoirs of the American Anthropological As-
     sociation, no. 36, 1929.
     OCLC # 664681

     _____. see also 0880

2424 Parsons, Jeffrey R. The Role of Chinampa
     Agriculture in the Food Supply of the Aztec
     Tenochtitlan. In 0710, pp. 233-257.

2425 _____. Settlement of Population History of
     the Basin of Mexico. In 3237, pp. 69-
     100.

     _____. see also 2744

2426 Pastore, Ralph Thomas, 1941- . The Board
     of Commissioners for Indian Affairs in the
     Northern Department and the Iroquois In-
     dians, 1775-1778. Ann Arbor, MI., Uni-
     versity Microfilms International, 1972.
     Microfilm - PhD Thesis - University of
     Notre Dame
     OCLC # 765500

2427 _____. Indian Summer: Newfoundland Micmacs
     in the Nineteenth Century. In 0479, pp.
     167-178.

2428 Pasztory, Esther. Aztec Art. New York,
     Abrams, 1983.
     OCLC # 8627850

2429 Pathways to Self-determination: Canadian
     Indians and the Canadian State. Edited by
     Leroy Little Bear, Menno Boldt, J. An-
     thony Long. Toronto, Buffalo, University

of Toronto Press,   1984.
OCLC # 10607835

2430 Patterson,   Andrew M.   The John Collier Pa-
      pers, 1922-1968: A Guide to the Microfilm
      Edition.   Edited by ... and Maureen Brod-
      off.   Sanford,   NC.,   Microfilming Corp.
      of America,   1980.
      OCLC # 7813568

2431 Pattie,   James O.   (James Ohio),   1804?-1850?
      The Personal Narrative of James O. Pattie.
      Edited by Timothy Flint.   Lincoln,   Univer-
      sity of Nebraska Press,   1884.
      Reprinted,   originally published: The
      Personal Narrative of James O. Pattie of
      Kentucky,   J. H. Wood,   1831.
      OCLC # 10324968

2432 Peabody Museum of Archaeology and Ethnology.
      Historic Hopi Ceramics: The Thomas V.
      Keam Collection of the Peabody Museum of
      Archaeology and Ethnology, Harvard Univer-
      sity. Catalog. Edwin L. Wade and Lea S.
      McChesney. Cambridge, MA., Peabody
      Museum Press,   Distributed by Harvard Uni-
      versity Press,   1981.
      OCLC # 8532937

      Peabody Museum Upper Gila Expedition,   1947-
      see 2011

2433 Peale,   Arthur L.   Memorials and Pilgrimages
     in the Mohegan Country.   The Bulletin Co.,
     Norwich,   CT.,   1930.

2434 Pearson,   Charles E.   Analysis of Late Mis-
      sissippian Settlements on Ossabaw Island,
      Georgia.   In 2172,   pp. 53-80.

2435 Pechuman,   L. L.   Another Radio-carbon Date
      for New York State.   The Oakfield Site,
      Genesee County.   New York State Archeolog-
      ical Association Bulletin 14,   Nov. 1958,
      pp. 2-4. Millwood, NY., Kraus Reprint,
      1976.
      Paper presented at annual meeting April 12,
      1958

      Peck,   Edmund James.   see 0309

Peckham, Howard Henry, 1910- . see 0144

2436 Peckman, Barbara A. Pueblo IV Murals at
Mound 7. In 1387, pp. 15-38.

2437 Peebles, Christopher S. Biocultural Adaptation in Prehistoric America: An Archae-
ologists Perspective. In 0270, pp. 115-
130.

2438 _____. Determinats of Settlement Size and
Location in the Moundville Phase. In 2172,
pp. 369-416.

2439 _____. Moundville: Later Prehistoric
Sociopolitical Organization in the Southeastern United States. In 0796, pp. 183-
198.

Pelzer, Louis, 1879-1946. see 0485

2440 Pendergast, James F. Ceramic Motif
Mutations at Glenbrook. In 1585, pp.
133-146.

2441 Pendleton, Lorann S. A. The Fort Sage
Drift Fence, Washoe County, Nevada. ...
and David Hurst Thomas. New York, Ameri-
can Museum of Natural History, 1983.
Anthropological Papers of the American
Museum of Natural History, v. 58, pt.
2.
OCLC # 9814026

2442 Penhallow, Samuel, 1665-1726. Penhallow's
Indian Wars: A Facsimile Reprint of the
First Ed. Printed in Boston in 1726, With
the Notes of Earlier Editors and Additions
for the Original Manuscript. Notes, index
and introd. by Edward Wheelock. Williams-
town, MA., Corner House Pub., 1973.
1726 ed. title The History of the Wars of
New England, With the Eastern Indians.
Reprint of the 1924 ed.
OCLC # 909553

2443 Penn, WIlliam. Penn Letters and Ancient
Documents Relating to Pennsylvania and New
Jersey, 1665-1819. One reel microfilm,

provided by American Philosophical Society, Philadelphia.

Pennacook/Sokoki Intertribal Nation. <u>see</u> 1461

Penrose, Maryly Barton. <u>see</u> 1561

2444 Pentland, David H. <u>Diminutive Consonant Symbolism in Algonquian</u>. In 0068, pp. 237-352.

2445 Pepper, George Hubbard, 1873-1924. <u>An Hidatsa Shrine and the Beliefs Respecting it</u>. ... and Gilbert L. Wilson . New York, Kraus Reprint, 1964.
Memoirs of the American Anthropological Association, no. 2, pt. 4, 1908
OCLC # 2576505

Percy, George W. <u>see</u> 0400

2446 Perdue, Theda, 1949- . <u>Cherokee Planters: The Development of Plantation Slavery Before Removal</u>. In 0547, pp. 110-128.

2447 _____. <u>Slavery and the Evolution of Cherokee Society, 1540-1866</u>. Knoxville, University of Tennessee Press, 1979.
OCLC # 4036878

_____. <u>see also</u> 0337, 2269

2448 Peregoy, Robert M. <u>The Role of University Native American Studies Programs in Facilitating Tribal Educational and Economic Development</u>. In 2962, pp. 35-49.

Perez, Kantule, Ruben, 1907- . <u>see</u> 2327

2449 Perkins, V. F. <u>Cheyenne Autumn</u>. In 2533, pp. 152-155.
Reprinted from <u>Movie</u> v. 12, Spring 1965, pp. 36-37.

2450 Peroff, Nicholas A. <u>Menominee Drums: Tribal Termination and Restoration, 1954-1974</u>. Norman, University of Oklahoma Press, 1982.
OCLC # 7998605

2451 Persico, V. Richard, Jr. Early Nineteenth
      Century Cherokee Political Organization.
      In 0547, pp. 92-109

2451.5 Perzigian, Anthony J. Teeth as Tools for
        Prehistoric Studies. In 0270, pp. 101-
        114.

        _____. see also 3426

2452 Petersen, James Brant. The Winooski Site
      and the Middle Woodland Period in the
      Northeast. Ann Arbor, MI., University
      Microfilms International, 1983.
      Microfilm - PhD Thesis - University of
      Pittsburgh
      OCLC # 10978733

2453 Peterson, Drexel A. The Introduction, Use,
      and Technology of Fiber-Tempered Pottery in
      the Southeastern United States. In 0905,
      pp. 363-372.

2454 Peterson, Jacqueline and John Anfinson. The
      Indian and the Fur Trade. In 2789, pp.
      223-257.

2455 _____. The People in Between: Indian-White
      Marriage and the Genesis of a Metis Soci-
      ety and Culture in the Great Lakes Region,
      1680-1830. Ann Arbor, MI., University
      Microfilms International, 1983.
      OCLC # 10362514

2456 Peterson, Jim. The Olcott Site and Pali-
      sades. New York State Archeological As-
      sociation Bulletin 18, March 1960, pp.
      6-12. Millwood, NY., Kraus Reprint,
      1976.

2457 Peterson, John. The Efforts of Past Indian-
      White Contracts on Contemporary Indian
      Studies. In 1282, pp. 51-64.

2458 Peterson, John H. Louisiana Choctaw Life at
      the End of the Nineteenth Century. In
      1099, pp. 101-112.

2459 _____. Three Efforts at Development Among

the Choctaws of Mississippi. In 2930, pp.
142-153.

2460 Peterson, Susan (Susan Harnly). The Living
      Tradition of Maria Martínez. New York,
      Harper and Row, 1977.
      OCLC # 3452099

2461 _____. Lucy M. Lewis, American Indian
      Potter. Design by Dana Levy. Toyko, New
      York: Kodansha International. Distributed
      in the U. S. by Kodansha International-
      /USA through Harper and Row, 1984.
      OCLC # 10923883

      Petrone, Penny. see 1053

      Petter, Rodolphe. see 2192

2462 Pettipas, Leo. Early Man in Manitoba. In
      1467, pp. 5-28.

2463 Phelan, John Leddy, 1924- . The Millenni-
      al Kingdom of the Franciscans in the New
      World. 2d ed. rev. Berkeley, University
      of California Press, 1970.
      OCLC # 88926

2464 Philbrook Art Center. Native American Art at
      Philbrook, August 17-September 21, 1980.
      (Preparation of catalogue entre data, John
      Mahey, Isabel McIntosh, photography,
      Ronda Kasl). Tulsa, OK., Philbrook Art
      Center, 1980?
      OCLC # 7007812

      _____. see also 0384, 3289

2465 Philip, Kenneth R., 1941- . John Collier
      and the Controversy Over the Wheeler-Howard
      Bill. In 2265, pp. 171-206.

2466 _____. John Collier's Crusade for Indian
      Reform. 1920-1954. With a foreword by
      Francis Paul Prucha. Tucson, University
      of Arizona Press, 1977.
      OCLC # 2905614

2467 Philips, Susan Urmston. The Invisible
      Culture: Communication in Classroom and

Community on the Warm Springs Indian Reservation. New York, Longmans, 1982.
OCLC # 8034653

2468 Phillips, David A. and William Rathje.
Streets Ahead: Exchange Values and the
Rise of the Classic Maya. In 2920, pp.
103-112.

2469 Phillips, James L. The Labras Lake Site and
the Paleogeographic Setting of the Late Archaic in the American Bottom. In 0124,
pp. 197-218.

2470 Phillips, Philip, 1906- . Middle American
Influences on the Archaeology of the Southeastern United States. In 2105, pp. 349-
367.

2471 Pickering, Robert B. A Preliminary Report
on the Osteological Remains from Alta
Vista, Zacatecas. In 0231, pp. 240-248.

2472 Pickering, Timothy, 1745-1829. Papers Pertaining to Indian Affairs (1790-1795) ca.
From Pickering papers in the Essex Institute, Salem, MA. Three reels microfilm
provided by American Philosophical Society,
Philadelphia.
CONTENTS: Reel 1, v. 6-60. Reel 2, v.
61-62. Reel 3, v. 12 to Misc. Mss and v.
17, 1784-1796.

2473 _____. Papers Pertaining to Indian Affairs
(1790-1795). Manuscript. Originals in
Pickering Papers, Massachusetts Historical
Society. One reel microfilm provided by
American Philosophical Society, Philadel-
phia.
For additional information consult the
Freeman Guide #239, #240.

2474 Pickersgill, Barbara. Migration of Chili
Peppers, Capsicum spp., in the Americas.
In 2541, pp. 105-123.

2475 Picture Writings and Other Documents. Nele
and Ruben Perez Kantule. New York, AMS
Press, 1979.

Part 2 by Nele, C. Slater, C. Nelson
and other Cuna Indians. Reprint of the
1928-1930 ed. pub. in 2 v. by E. Nordenskiold, Goteborg. Sweden, which was
issued as v. 7 of Comparative Ethnological
Studies.
OCLC # 3914710

2476 Pinxten, Rik. The Anthropology of Space:
Exploration Into the Natural Philosophy and
Semantics of the Navajo. ... and Ingrid van
Dooren, Frank Harvey. Philadelphia, Uni-
versity of Pennsylvania Press, 1983.
OCLC # 9082238

2477 Pittier, Henri., 1857-1950. Ethnographic
and Linguistic Notes on the Paez Indians of
Tierra Adentro, Cauca, Colombia. New
York, Kraus Reprint, 1964.
Reprint of the New Era Printing Co., 1907.
Memoirs of the American Anthropological As-
sociation, v. 1, pt. 5.
OCLC # 1855383

2478 Pjettursson, Jorgen. Bilingualism in Greenland and its Resulting Problems. In 1875,
pp. 534-551.

2479 1877: Plains Indian - Sketch Books of Zo-tom
& Howling Wolf. With an introd. by
Dorothy Dunn. Flagstaff, AZ., Northland
Press, 1969.
OCLC # 5084328

2480 The Plains Indians of the Twentieth Century.
Edited with an introd. by Peter Iverson.
Norman, University of Oklahoma Press,
1985.
OCLC # 12215503

2481 Plog, Fred and Steadman Upham. The Analysis
of Prehistoric Political Organization. In
0796, pp. 199-213.

2482 Plowman, Timothy. The Origin, Evolution,
and Diffusion of Coca, Erythroxylum spp.,
in South and Central America. In 2521,
pp. 125-163.

2483 Polhemus, Richard R. Tennessee Bead Seria-
      tion (Abstract). In 1204, pp. 145-146.

2484 The Politics of Indian Affairs. In 0137,
      pp. 164-187.
      Abridged from chapter 17 of A Survey of
      Contemporary Indians of Canada, part 1,
      edited by H. B. Hawthorn, Ottawa, 1966.

2485 The Politics of Indianness: Case Studies of
      Native Ethnopolitics in Canada. St.
      John's, Newfoundland, Canada. Institute
      of Social and Economic Research, Memorial
      University of Newfoundland, 1983.
      Essays in this collection are also listed
      individually and refer to this citation.
      Social and Economic Papers no. 12.
      OCLC # 10613840

2486 Pollak-Eltz, Angelina. Masks and Masquer-
      ades in Venezuela. In 2502, pp. 174-192.

2487 Pollard, John Garland, 1871-1937. The Pa-
      munkey Indians of Virginia. Washington,
      U. S. Govt. Print. Off., 1894.
      U. S. Bureau of American Ethnology
      Bulletin no. 17.
      OCLC # 962336

2488 Pollard, Gordon C. Identification of Domes-
      tic Lama sp. from Prehispanic Northern
      Chile Using Microscopy. In 0873, pp.
      116-119.

2489 Pollock, H. E. D. (Harry Evelyn Door),
      1900- . The Puuc: An Architectural Sur-
      vey of the Hill Country of Yucatan and
      Northern Campeche, Mexico. Cambridge,
      MA., Peabody Museum of Archaeology and
      Ethnology, Harvard University, 1980.
      Memoirs of the Peabody Museum v. 19.
      OCLC # 6367057

2490 _____. Sources and Methods in the Study of
      Maya Architecture. In 2105, pp. 179-201.

2491 Poma de Ayala, Felipe Guaman, fl. 1613.
      Letter to a King: A Peruvian Chief's Ac-
      count of Life Under the Incas and Under
      Spanish Rule. Arr. and edited with an

introd. by Christopher Dilke and trans.
New York, E. P. Dutton, 1978.
OCLC # 4330079

2492 Ponting, J. Rick. <u>Out of Irrelevance: A
Socio-political Introduction to Indian Af-
fairs in Canada.</u> ... and Roger Gibbins,
with a contribution by Andrew J. Siggner.
Toronto, Butterworths, 1980.
OCLC # 7152579

2493 Popol vuh. English. <u>Popol vuh.: The Defin-
itive Edition of the Mayan Book of the Dawn
of Life and the Glories of Gods and Kings.</u>
Trans. by Dennis Tedlock. New York,
Simon and Schuster, 1984.
OCLC # 11467786

2494 _____. <u>Popol vuh: The Great Mythological
Book of the Ancient Maya.</u> Newly trans.
with an introd. by Ralph Nelson. With
drawings from the Codices Mayas. Boston,
Houghton Mifflin, 1976.
OCLC # 3103560

2494.5 Porter, Frank W., 1947- . <u>In Pursuit of
the Past: An Anthropological and Biblio-
graphic Guide to Maryland and Delaware.</u>
Metuchen, NJ., Scarecrow Press, 1986.
Native American Bibliography Series no. 8.
OCLC # 12107373

2495 _____. <u>Indians in Maryland and Delaware: A
Critical Bibliography.</u> Bloomington, Pub-
lished for the Newberry Library by Indiana
University Press, 1979.
OCLC # 5498914

2496 Porter, Harry Culverwell. <u>The Inconstant
Savage: England and the North American In-
dian, 1500-1660.</u> London, Duckworth,
Dallas, distributed in the U. S. by
Southwest Book Service, 1979.
OCLC # 4737012

Porter, James W. (James Warren). <u>see</u> 0077

2497 Porter, Joseph C., 1946- . <u>John Gregory
Bourke, Biographical Notes: A Military
Officer Among the Apache.</u> Greeley, CO.,

University of Northern Colorado,   Museum of
Anthropology, 1984.
University of Northern Colorado,   Museum of
Anthropology, Misc. Series no. 54.
OCLC # 10569784

_____. see also 1212

2498 Potter, L. D. Aerial Photointerpretation
      of Vegetation of Chaco Canyon National Mon-
      ument. In 0711, pp. 87-104.

2499 Powell, J. V. Quileute: An Introduction
      to the Indians of La Push. Prepared for
      the Quileute Tribe by ... and Vickie Jen-
      sen. Seattle, University of Washington
      Press, 1976.
      OCLC # 2224773

2500 Powell, Peter J., 1928- . The Cheyennes,
      Mahoe's People: A Critical Bibliography.
      Bloomington, Published for the Newberry
      Library by Indiana University Press, 1980.
      OCLC # 6891160

2501 _____. People of the Sacred Mountain: A
      History of the Northern Cheyenne Chiefs and
      Warrior Societies, 1830-1879; With an Ep-
      ilogue 1969-1974. San Francisco, Harper
      and Row, 1981.
      OCLC # 8239387

      Power, Marjory W., 1930- . see 1375

2502 The Power of Symbols: Masks and Masquerade
      in the Americas. Edited by N. Ross Crum-
      rine and Marjorie Halpin. Vancouver, Uni-
      versity of British Columbia, 1983.
      Essays in this collection are also listed
      individually and refer to this citation.
      OCLC # 10076741

2503 Powers, Mabel. The Indian as Peacemaker.
      By ... (Yehsennohwehs). New York, Fleming
      H. Revell Company, 1932.
      OCLC # 1403056

2503.5 Powers, Marla N. Oglala Women: Myth,
        Ritual, and Reality. Chicago, University
        of Chicago Press, 1986.

Women in Culture and Society
OCLC # 12664051

2504   Powers, Robert P., 1952- . <u>Outlier</u>
        <u>Survey: A Regional View of Settlement in</u>
        <u>the San Juan Basin</u>. By ... and William B.
        Gillespie, Stephen H. Lekson. Albuquer-
        que, NM., Division of Cultural Research,
        National Park Service, U. S. Dept. of
        the Interior, 1983.
        Reports of the Chaco Center no. 3.
        OCLC # 9416843

2505   _____. <u>Outliers and Roads in the Chaco</u>
        <u>System</u>. In 2289, pp. 45-58.

2506   Powers, Stephen. <u>Tribes of California</u>.
        With an introd. and notes by Robert F.
        Heizer. Berkeley, University of Califor-
        nia Press, 1976.
        Reprint of the 1877 ed. published by
        U. S. Govt. Print. Off., v. 3 of
        Contributions to North American Ethnology
        OCLC # 2666295

2507   Powers, William K. <u>Oglala Religion</u>. Lin-
        coln, University of Nebraska Press, 1977.
        OCLC # 2645401

2508   _____. <u>Plains Indian Music and Dance</u>. In
        0113, pp. 212-229.

2508.5 _____. <u>Sacred Language: The Nature of</u>
        <u>Supernatural Discourse in Lakota</u>. Norman,
        University of Oklahoma Press, 1986.
        Civilization of the American Indian Series
        v. 179.
        OCLC # 13821042

2509   _____. <u>Yuwipi, Vision and Experience in</u>
        <u>Oglala Ritual</u>. Lincoln, University of
        Nebraska Press, 1982.
        OCLC # 7573144

2510   Powers, William Roger and Thomas D. Ham-
        ilton. <u>Dry Creek: A Late Pleistocene Hu-</u>
        <u>man Occupation in Central Alaska</u>. In 0902,
        pp. 72-77.

2511   Pozorski, Shelia Griffis. <u>The Significance</u>

of the Casma Valley in Understanding Early
State Formation. In 0121, pp. 154-163.

2512 Pozorski, Thomas George. The Role of
Irrigation Agriculture Within the Chimu
State. In 0121, pp. 131-146.

2513 Prance, Ghillean T., 1937- . The Peji-
baye, Guilielma Gasipaes (HBK) Bailey,
and the Papaya, Carica Papaya L. In 2521,
pp. 85-104.

2514 Pratt, Marjorie K. The Saint Lawrence Iroquois Conference - Some Lessons to be
Learned. In 1585, pp. 31-32.

2515 Pratt, Peter P. Archaeology of the Oneida
Iroquois. George's Mills, NH., Man in
the Northeast, Inc., 1976.
Occasional Publicatgions in Northeastern
Anthropology no. 1.
OCLC # 2438397

2516 _____. Glass Trade Beads Among the Iroquois: A Perspective. In 1204, pp. 213-
217.

2517 _____. Oneida Iroquois Pottery Typology.
In 1585, pp. 35-49.

2518 _____. A Perspective on Oneida Archaeology.
In 0712, pp. 51-69.

Pray, Mrs. Mary, 1630?-1686. see 2898

2519 Pre-Columbian Art from Mesoamerica and Ecua-
dor: Selections from Distinguished Private
Collections: The Lowe Art Museum, Oct. 9
Through Nov. 30, 1980. Exhibition organ-
ized by Peter David Joralemon; essay by
Elizabeth P. Benson. Coral Gables, FL.,
The Museum, 1980.
OCLC # 7503105

2520 Pre-Columbian Art from the Land Collection.
H. B. Nicholson, Alana Cordy-Collins;
edited by L. K. Land. San Francisco,
California Academy of Sciences, 1979.
Catalog of the exhibition prepared for the
dedication of the Wattis Hall of Man, Cal-

ifornia Academy of Sciences,   June 1976 –
Oct. 1977.
OCLC # 5102888

2521   Pre-Columbian Plant Migration Symposium
       (1982:   Manchester,   Greater Manchester).
       Pre-Columbian Plant Migration: Papers Pre-
       sented at the Pre-Columbian Plant Migration
       Symposium,   44th International Congress of
       Americanists,   Manchester,   England.   Edit-
       ed by Doris Stone,   with contributions by
       Robert McK Bird. ... et al.   Cambridge,
       MA. Peabody Museum of Archaeology and
       Ethnology,   Harvard University,   Distribut-
       ed by Harvard University Press,   1984.
       Essays in this collection are also listed
       individually and refer to this citation.
       Papers of the Peabody Museum of Archaeology
       and Ethnology v.   76.
       OCLC # 11417467

2522   Prehispanic Maya Agriculture.   Edited by
       Peter D.   Harrison and B.   L.   Turner.
       Albuquerque,   University of New Mexico
       Press,   1978.
       OCLC # 4003706

2523   Prehispanic Mexican Art.   By Paul Westheim
       and others.   New York,   Putnam,   1972.
       OCLC # 507842

2524   Prehistoric Coastal Adaptation: The Economy
       and Ecology of Maritime Middle America.
       Edited by Barbara L.   Stark,   Barbara
       Voorhies.   New York,   Academic Press,
       1978.
       Studies in Archeology
       OCLC # 3771810

2525   Prehistoric Man and His Environments: A Case
       Study in the Ozark Highland.   Edited by W.
       Raymond Wood and R.   Bruce McMillan.   New
       York,   Academic Press,   1975.
       Studies in Archeology.   Contains contribu-
       tions 9-24... of the Archaeological and
       Quarternary Studies program,   Illinois
       State Museum
       OCLC # 1622030

2526   Prehistoric Tuberculosis in the Americas.

Edited by Jane E. Buikstra. Evanston,
IL., Northwestern University Archeological
Program, 1981.
Scientific Papers - Northwestern University Archeological Program, v. 5.
Papers presented at a Symposium organized for the
annual meeting of the American Association
of Physical Anthropologists, held April
12-15, 1978, in Toronto, in Association
with the annual meeting of the Paleopathol-
ogy Association
Essays in this collection are also listed
individually and refer to this citation.
OCLC # 7197014

2527 Prem, Hanns J., 1941- . Early Spanish
Colonization and Indians in the Valley of
Atlixco, Puebla. In 0978, pp. 205-228.

        _____. see also 0978

2528 Presbyterian Historical Society. User's
Guide to American Indian Correspondence:
The Presbyterian Historical Society Collec-
tion of Missionaries Letters, 1833-1893.
Presbyterian Historical Society, Westport,
CT., Greenwood Press, 1979?
OCLC # 4949289

2529 Press, Irwin. Historical Dimensions of
Orientation to Change in a Yucatec Peasant
Community. In 0109, pp. 275-288.
Reprinted from Tradition and Adaptation:
Life in a Modern Yucatan Maya Village,
Greenwood Press, Sept. 1975.

2530 _____. Tradition and Adaptation: Life in a
Modern Yucatan Maya Village. Irwin Press,
Westport, CT., Greenwood Press, 1975.
OCLC # 1504648

2531 Preston, Richard Joseph., 1931- . Cree
Narrative: Expressing the Personal Meaning
of Events. Ottawa, National Museums of
Canada, 1975.
National Museum of Man Mercury Series.
Paper - Canadian Ethnology Service no. 30.
OCLC # 2561279

2532 _____. Eastern Cree Community in Relation

to Fur Trade Post in the 1830's: The Background of Posting Process.   In 0068,   pp.
324-335.

_____. see also 0480

2533 The Pretend Indians: Images of Native Ameri-
cans in the Movies. Edited by Gretchen M.
Bataille,   Charles L.   P.   Silet.   Ames,
Iowa State University Press,   1980.
OCLC # 5941472

2534 Price,   Barbara J.   A Chronological Framework
for Cultural Development in Mesoamerica.
In 3237,   pp.   13-21.

2535 Price,   James E.   The Settlement Pattern of
the Powers Phase.   In 2172,   pp.   201-231.

2536 Price,   John A.,   1933-   .   The Sterotyping
of North American Indians in Motion Pictures.   In 2533,   pp.   75-93.
Reprinted from Ethnohistory v.   20,   Spring
1973,   pp.   153-171.

2537 Price,   Monroe Edwin,   1938-   .   and Gary D.
Weatherford.   Indian Water Rights in Theory
and Practice: Navajo Experience in the
Colorado River Basin.   In 0087,   pp.   97-
131.

Price,   Richard,   1942-   . see 2959

2538 Price,   T.   Douglas (Theron Douglas).
Kaminaljuyu Test Trench 46-23-072.   In
2825,   pp.   591-618.

Princeton.   University.   Art Museum. see
0602

2539 Pring,   D.   C.   Influence or Intrusion?   The
"Protoclassic" in the Maya Lowlands.   In
2920,   pp.   135-165.

2540 Prisch,   Betty Coit.   Aspects of Change in
Seneca Iroquois Ladles, A. D. 1600-1900.
Rochester,   NY.,   Research Division,
Rochester Museum and Science Center,   1982.
Research records/the research division,

Rochester Museum and Science Center v. 15.
OCLC # 9612406

2541   Proctor, Samuel. The Southeastern Indian
        Oral History Program at the University of
        Florida. In 1282, pp. 1-5.

2543   _____. Taping Indian Past: The University
        of Florida's Oral History Project. In
        3071, pp. 194-201.

        _____. see also 3071

2543   Protsch, Reiner R. R., d. 1939. Catalog
        of Fossil Hominids of North America. New
        York, G. Fischer, 1978.

2544   Proulx, Donald A., 1939- . The Early Ho-
        rizon of North Coastal Peru: A Review of
        Recent Developments. In 0121, pp. 11-25.

2545   Prucha, Francis Paul. American Indian Pol-
        icy in Crisis: Christian Reformers and the
        Indian, 1865-1900. Norman, University of
        Oklahoma Press, 1975.
        OCLC # 2547338

2546   _____. Bibliographical Guide to the History
        of Indian-White Relations in the United
        States. Chicago, University of Chicago
        Press, 1977.
        OCLC # 2213250

2547   _____. The Churches and the Indian Schools,
        1888-1912. Lincoln, University of Nebras-
        ka Press, 1979.
        OCLC # 4858068

2548   _____. Documents of the United States In-
        dian Policy. Lincoln, University of Ne-
        braska Press, 1975.
        OCLC # 1174388

2549   _____. Doing Indian History. In 2265, pp.
        1-10.

2550   _____. The Great Father: The U. S. Gov-
        ernment and the American Indian. Lincoln,
        University of Nebraska Press, 1984.
        OCLC # 9918967

2551   _____. Indian Peace Medals in American His-
        tory. Lincoln, University of Nebraska
        Press, 1971.
        Reprint of the ed. pub. by State Histori-
        cal Society of Madison, WI.
        OCLC # 2048192

2552   _____. Indian Policy in the United States:
        Historical Essays. Lincoln, University of
        Nebraska Press, 1981.
        OCLC # 7273611

2553   _____. Indian-White Relations in the United
        States: A Bibliography of Works Published
        1975-1980. Lincoln, University of Nebras-
        ka Press, 1982.
        Supplement to A Bibliographical Guide to
        the History of Indian-White Relations in
        the United States.
        OCLC # 7773562

2554   _____. Indians in American Society: From
        the Revolutionary War to the Present.
        Berkeley, University of California Press,
        1985.
        Quantum Books. Essays presented as the
        Gasson Lectures at Boston College on Nov.
        30, 1983, March 14, 1984, Nov. 7,
        1984, March 13, 1985.
        OCLC # 11728329

2555   _____. United States Indian Policy: A
        Critical Bibliography. Bloomington, Pub-
        lished for the Newberry Library by Indiana
        University Press, 1977.
        Bibliographical Series
        OCLC # 3072186

        _____. see also 0966

2556   Psychological Research on American Indian and
        Alaska Native Youth: An Indexed Guide to
        recent Dissertations. Compiled by Spero M.
        Manson. Westport, CT., Greenwood Press,
        1984.
        OCLC # 10695359

2557   Puleston, Dennis Edward, 1940-1978. The
        Art and Archaeology of Hydraulic Agricul-

ture in the Maya Lowlands. In 2920, pp. 449-467.

2558 _____. An Epistemological Pathology and the Collapse, or Why the Maya Kept the Short Count. In 0472, pp. 63-71.

2559 _____. Terracing, Raised Fields, and Tree Cropping in the Maya Lowlands: A New Perspective on the Geography of Power. In 2522, pp. 225-245.

Pulling, Albert van Sicler. see 2560

2560 Pulling, Pierre, 1891- . Canoeing the Indian Way: Straight Talk for Modern Paddlers from the Dean of American Canoeists. New York, McKay, 1979. OCLC # 5652029

2561 Puniello, Anthony J. Iroquois Series Ceramics in the Upper Delaware Valley, New Jersey and Pennsylvania. In 1585, pp. 147-155.

Punley, Randolph J. see 1112

2562 Puritans Among the Indians: Accounts of Captivity and Redemption, 1676-1724. Edited by Alden T. Vaughan and Edward W. Clark. Cambridge, MA., Belknap Press, 1981. Essays in this collection are also listed individually and refer to this citation. John Harvard Library OCLC # 6916398

2563 Puritans, Indians, and Manifest Destiny. Charles M.. Segal and David C. Stineback. Foreword by Sacvan Bercovitch. New York, Putnam, 1977. OCLC # 3434885

2564 Pyle, Jane. A Reexamination of Aboriginal Population Estimates for Argentina. In 0779, pp. 181-204.

2565 Quaife, Milo Milton, 1880-1959. The Siege of Detroit in 1763: The Journal of Pontiac's Conspiracy and John Rutherfurd's Narrative of a Captivity. Chicago, R. R.

Donnelley, 1958.
Lakeside Classics,   no.   56.
OCLC # 1140002

_____.   see also   0464,   0634

2566 Quetzalcoatl in Myth,   Archeology and Art.
      Lose Lopez Portillo,   Demetrio Sodi,   Fer-
      nando Diaz Infante.   New York,   Continum,
      1982.
      Translation of Quetzalcoatl
      OCLC # 8171135

2567 Quigg, J. Michael. Archaeological Recon-
      naissance in Colorado City and the Other
      Three R-Ranch Area. Preliminary Report -
      1970. Greeley,   University of Northern
      Colorado,   1971.
      University of Northern Colorado,   Museum of
      Anthropology,   Misc. Series no.   29,
      April 1971.
      OCLC # 261973

2568 The Quijotoa Valley Project. E.   Jane
      Rosenthal... (et al.);   with appendices by
      Richard S. White... (et al.).   Tucson,
      AZ.,   Cultural Resources Management Center,
      National Park Service,   1978.
      OCLC # 4097105

      Quimby,   George Irving,   1913- . see 2075

2569 Quinten, B. T. Oklahoma Tribes,   the Great
      Depression and the Indian Bureau. In 2304,
      pp. 243-254.
      Reprinted from Mid-America v.   49,   no.   1,
      Jan. 1967, pp. 29-43.

2570 Quirarte,   Jacinto,   1931- . Early Art
      Styles of Mesoamerica and Early Classic
      Maya Art. In 2378, pp. 249-283.

2571 _____.   The Representation of Underworld
      Processions in Maya Vase Painting: An
      Iconographic Study. In 0472, pp. 116-
      148.

2572 Rabiela,   Teresa Rojas. Agricultural
      Implements in Mesoamerica. In 0978, pp.
      175-204.

2573 Rachlin, Carol K. The Historic Position of
      the Proto-Cree Textiles in the Eastern
      Fabric Complex, an Ethnological-Archae-
      ological Correlation. In National Museum
      of Canada Bulletin no. 167, Contributions
      to Anthropology, 1958. Ottawa, Dept. of
      Northern Affairs and National Resources,
      1960, pp. 80-89.

      _____. see also 2068

2574 Radell, David R. The Indian Slave Trade and
      Population of Nicaragua During the Six-
      teenth Century. In 0779, pp. 67-76.

2575 Radin, Paul, 1883-1959. Religion of the
      North American Indians. In 0110, pp.
      259-305.

2576 _____. The Social Organization of the
      Winnebago Indians: An Interpretation. Ot-
      tawa, Government Printing Bureau, 1915.
      Canada. Geological Survey. Museum Bulle-
      tin no. 10. Anthropological Series no.
      5.
      OCLC # 4239565

2577 Radloff, Ralph Mark, 1928- . Moravian
      Mission Methods Among the Indians of Ohio.
      Ann Arbor, MI., University Microfilms
      International, 1973.
      Microfilm - PhD Thesis - University of Iowa
      OCLC # 3726065

2578 Raemsch, Bruce E. Some Early Man Cultures
      of the Catskill Region. In 3519, pp. 1-
      13.

2579 Rainey, Froelich. Significance of Recent
      Archaeological Discoveries in Inland
      Alaska. In 0076, pp. 43-46.

2580 Ralbovsky, Marty. An Indian Affair: Ameri-
      can Indian Students Concerned About Nick-
      names, Mascots in Sports. In 1456, pp.
      212-214.
      Reprinted from The New York Times nov. 14,
      1971, pp. 9.

2581 Ramenofsky, Ann Felice, 1942- . The

Archaeology of Population Collapse: Native
American Response to the Introduction of
Infectious Disease.   Ann Arbor, MI., Uni-
versity Microfilms International, 1983.
Microfilm - PhD Thesis - University of
Washington
OCLC # 12515413

2582   Ramsey,   Jarold.   'The Hunter who had an Elk
       for a Guardian Spirit'   and the Ecological
       Imagination.   In 2904,   pp.   309-322.

2583   Rands,   Robert L.   The Rise of Classic Maya
       Civilization in the Northwestern Zone:
       Isolation and Integration.   In 2378,   pp.
       159-180.

2584   Ranere,   Anthony J.   and Pat Hansell.   Early
       Subsistence Patterns Along the Pacific
       Coast of Central Panama.   In 2524,   pp.
       43-59.

       Ranney,   Edward.   see   1411

2585   Rapp,   Susan Power,   1944-   .   Southeast
       Indian Art and Culture: Implications for
       Education.   Ann Arbor, MI.,   University
       Microfilms International,   1982.
       Microfilm - PhD Thesis - University of
       Georgia
       OCLC # 12011708

2586   Rasmussen,   Knud Johan Victor,   1879-1933.
       Iglulik and Caribou Eskimo Texts.   Trans.
       by W.   Worster and W.   E.   Calvert.   New
       York,   AMS Press,   1976.
       Reprint of the 3d pt.   of the 3 vol.   work
       Intellectual Culture of the Hudson Bay Es-
       kimos pub.   in 1930 by Gyldendal,   Copen-
       hagen,   originally issued as v.   7,   no.   2
       of Report of the 5th Thule Expedition 1921-
       24.
       OCLC # 2332320

2587   _____.   Intellectual Culture of the Copper
       Eskimos.   Trans.   by W.   E.   Calvert.   New
       York,   AMS Press,   1976.
       Reprint of the 1932 ed.   pub.   by
       Gyldendal,   Copenhagen,   which was issued
       as v.   9 of the Report of the Fifth Thule

Expedition, 1921-24.
OCLC # 2331394

2588   _____. Intellectual Culture of the Iglulik
         Eskimos. Trans. by W. Worster from the
         Danish original. New York, AMS Press,
         1976.
         Reprint of the 1st part of the 3 vol. work
         Intellectual Culture of the Hudson Bay
         Eskimo pub. in 1929 by Gyldendal, Copen-
         hagen, originally issued as v. 7, no. 1
         of Report of the Fifth Thule Expedition
         1921-24.
         OCLC # 2644947

2589   _____. Netsilik Eskimos, Social Life and
         Spiritual Culture. Trans. by W. E. Cal-
         vert from the Danish original. New York,
         AMS Press, 1976.
         Reprint of the 1931 ed. pub. by Gylden-
         dal, Copenhagen, which was issued as v.
         8, no. 1-2 of Report of the Fifth Thule
         Expedition, 1921-24.
         OCLC # 3921428

2590   _____. Observations on the Intellectual
         Culture of the Caribou Eskimos. New York,
         AMS Press, 1976.
         Reprint of the 2nd pt. of a 3 vol. work
         Intellectual Culture of the Hudson Bay
         Eskimos pub. in 1930 by Gyldendal, Copen-
         hagen, originally issued as v. 7 no. 2
         of Report of the Fifth Thule Expedition
         1921-24.
         OCLC # 2331534

2591   Rathje, William L. The Tikal Connection.
         In 2378, pp. 373-382.

         Raudot, Antoine Denis, 1679-1737. see
         1765

         Raup, Hugh Miller, 1901- . see 1643

2592   Rawls, James J. Indians of California: The
         Changing Image. Norman, University of
         Oklahoma Press, 1984.
         OCLC # 10046361

2593   Ray, Arthur J. "Give Us Good Measure": An

Economic Analysis of Relations Between Indians and the Hudson's Bay Company Before
1763. ... and Donald B. Freeman. Toronto,
Buffalo, University of Toronto Press,
1978.
OCLC # 5076476

2594 _____. Periodic Shortages, Native Welfare,
and the Hudson's Bay Company, 1670-1930.
In 3047, pp. 1-20.

_____. see also 1398

2595 Ray, Dorothy Jean. Eskimo Art: Tradition
and Innovation in North Alaska. Seattle,
Pub. for Henry Art Gallery by the University of Washington Press, 1977.
Index of Art in the Pacific Northwest v.
11.
OCLC # 2346032

2596 _____. The Eskimos of Bering Strait 1650-
1898. Seattle, University of Washington
Press, 1975.

Ray, Verne Frederick, 1905- . see 0078

2597 Reaves, Roy W. III. A Case for Limited
Problem-oriented Research. In 0622, pp.
437-453.

2598 Reck, Gregory G., 1944- . In the Shadow
of Tlaloc: Life in a Mexican Village.
Harmondsworth, Eng., New York, Penguin
Books, 1978.
OCLC # 3630991

2599 Records of the British Colonial Office,
Class 5 (Microfilm). Edited by Randolph
Boehm; guide compiled by Linda Womaski.
Frederick, MD., University Publications
of America, 1981?
26 reels microfilm reproduced from the
collection of the Manuscript Division, Li-
brary of Congress. CONTENTS: Pt. 1.
Westward Expansion 1700-1783. pt. 2.
Board of Trade, 1660-1782. pt. 3.
French and Indian War, 1754-1764.
OCLC # 9470958

2600   Red and White: Indian Views of the White
        Man, 1492-1982.   Collected by Annette
        Rosenstiel.   New York,   Universe Books,
        1983.
        OCLC # 9082997

2601   The Red Man.   (Periodical),   v. 1-9,   1909-
        1917.   Microfilm copy.

2602   Red Men and Hat-Wearers: A Viewpoint in
        Indian History: Papers from the Colorado
        State University Conference on Indian His-
        tory, August 1974.   Edited by Daniel Ty-
        ler,   Boulder,   CO.,   Pruett Pub.   Co.,
        1976.
        Essays in this collection are also listed
        individually and refer to this citation.
        OCLC # 2121648

2603   The Red Swan: Myths and Tales of the Ameri-
        can Indian.   John Bierhorst,   New York,
        Farrar,   Straus and Giroux,   1976.
        OCLC # 2822756

2603.5 Rediscovered Masterpieces of Mesoamerica:
        Mexico-Guatemala-Honduras.   Boulogne,
        France,   Editions Arts,   1985.
        Rediscovered masterpieces series.   Produced
        by Gerald Berjonneau,   Emile Deletaille and
        Jean-Louis Sonnery.
        OCLC # 13186418

2604   Reed,   Erik Kellerman,   1914- . Human
        Skeletal Material from the Gran Quivira
        District.   In 1387,   pp.   75-118.

2605   Reed,   Gerard.   Postremoval Factionalism in
        the Cherokee Nation.   In 0547,   pp.   148-
        163.

        Reed,   Mabel.   see   0134

2606   Reeves,   Brian O.   K.   Cultural Dynamics in
        the Manitoba Grasslands 1000 B.   C.   - A.
        D.   700.   In 1467,   pp.   153-174.

2607   _____.   Fractured Cherts from Pleistocene
        Fossiliferous Beds at Medicine Hat,
        Alberta.   In 0905,   pp.   83-98.

2608   Reference Encyclopedia of the American
       Indian. Barry Klein, editor. 3rd ed.,
       Rye, NY., Todd Publications, 1978.
       2 vols. V. 2. Who's Who.
       OCLC # 3778069

2608.5 Reference Encyclopedia of the American
       Indian. Barry T. Klein, editor. 4th
       ed., New York, Todd Publications, 1986.
       v. 1. Includes bibliographies. v. 2.
       Who's Who
       OCLC # 13411320

2609   Reichard, Gladys Amanda, 1893-1955. Navaho
       Religion: A Study of Symbolism. Tucson,
       University of Arizona Press, 1983.
       Reprint, originally published 2n ed.
       Princeton, Princeton University Press,
       1974.
       OCLC # 9646623

2610   Reid, J. Jefferson and Izumi Shimada.
       Pueblo Growth at Grasshopper: Methods and
       Models. In 2239, pp. 12-18.

2611   _____. Responses to Stress at Grasshopper
       Pueblo, Arizona. In 0822, pp. 195-213.

2612   Reid, John Phillip. A Better Kind of Hat-
       chet: Law, Trade and Diplomacy in the
       Cherokee Nation During the Early Years of
       European Contact. University park, Penn-
       sylvania State University Press, 1976.
       OCLC # 1364165

2613   _____. The Perilous Rule" The Law of
       International Homicide. In 0547, pp. 33-
       45.

2614   Reid, Kenneth C. The Nebo Hill Phase: Late
       Archaic Prehistory in the Lower Missouri
       Valley. In 0124, pp. 11-39.

2614.5 Reid, William, 1920- . The Raven Steals
       the Light. Drawings by Bill Reid; with
       stories by Bill Reid and Robert Bringhurst.
       Vancouver, Douglas & McIntyre; Seattle,
       University of Washington Press, 1984.
       OCLC # 11563296

_____. see also 2999

2615 Reid, W. Max (William Max), 1839-1911.
      The Mohawk Valley, It's Legends and It's
      History. With illus. from photos by J.
      Arthur Maney. Harrison, NY., Harbor Hill
      Books, 1979.
      Reprint of the 1901 ed. pub. by Putnam,
      New York.
      OCLC # 5101876

2616 Reina, Ruben E. The Traditional Pottery of
      Guatemala. ... and Robert M. Hill II.
      Austin, University of Texas Press, 1978.
      Texas Pan American Series
      OCLC # 3433300

2617 Remington, Judith A. Current Astronomical
      Practices Among the Maya. In 2270, pp.
      75-88.

      Rempe, Melissa. see 1346

      Reno, Marcus A. (Marcus Albert), 1835-
      1889. see 3252

      Reno Court of Inquiry. see 3252

      Renwick Gallery. see 0973

2618 The Returned Captive. New York, Garland
      Pub. Co., 1978.
      Garland Library of narratives of North
      American Indian captivities, v. 18.
      Reprint of the 1787 ed. printed by Ashbel
      Stoddard, Hudson. Issued with the reprint
      of the 1787 ed. of J. Graham, John
      Graham's Address to the Master and Worthy
      Family of this House and Others.
      OCLC # 3543298

2619 Reyman, Jonathan E. Pochteca Burials at
      Anasazi Sites? In 0014, pp. 242-259.

2620 Reynolds, John D., 1943- . Residential
      Architecture at Kaminaljuyu. In 2825, pp.
      223-275.

2621 Reynolds, Quentin James, 1902-1965.
      Custer's Last Stand. Illus. by Frederick

T. Chapman, New York, Randon House,
1951.
OCLC # 471618

2622 Rice, Don S. Population Growth and Sub-
      sistence Alternatives in a Tropical La-
      custrine Environment. In 2522, 35-61.

2623 Rice, Prudence M. Ceramic Continuity and
      Change in the Valley of Guatemala. In
      0531, pp. 401-510.

2624 _____. Clear Answers to Vague Questions:
      Some Assumptions of Provenience Studies of
      Pottery. In 0531, pp. 511-542.

      _____. see also 0132

2625 Rice, Susan, And Afterwards, Take Him to a
      Movie. In 2533, pp. 143-148.
      Reprinted from Media and Methods v. 7,
      April 1971, pp. 43-44, 71.

2626 Rice, William H. A Pre-Pottery Site in
      Northern Saratoga County, NY. New York
      State Archeological Association Bulletin v.
      9, March 1957, pp. 2-4.
      Paper presented at annual meeting April 14,
      1956.

2627 Richards, Cara B. Matriarchy or Mistake:
      The Role of Iroquois Women Through Time.
      In 0078, pp. 36-46.

2628 Richardson, Boyce. Strangers Devour the
      Land: A Chronicle of the Assault Upon the
      Last Coherent Hunting Culture in North
      America, The Cree Indians of Northern Que-
      bec, and Their Vast Primeval Homelands.
      New York, Knopf, distributed by Random
      House, 1976, c1975.
      OCLC # 1502218

2629 Richardson, Francis B. Non-Maya Monumental
      Sculpture of Central America. In 2105,
      pp. 395-416.

2630 Richardson, James B. Early Man on the Peru-
      vian North Coast, Early Maritime Exploita-

tion and the Pleistocene and Holocene
Environment. In 0905, pp. 274-289.

2631   _____. The Impact of European Contact on
Northeastern Iroquois and Algonkian Art
Styles. In 0712, pp. 113-119.

2632 Richardson, Leon Burr, 1878- . An Indian
Preacher in New England; Being Letters and
Diaries Relating to the Mission of the Reverend Samson Occom and the Reverend Nathaniel Whitaker to Collect Funds in England
for the Benefit of Eleazar Wheelock's Indian Charity School, from Which Grew Dartmouth College. Edited from the originals
by Leon Burr Richardson. Hanover, NH.,
Dartmouth College, 1933.
Dartmouth College Manuscript series no. 2.
OCLC # 583419

2633 Richling, Barnett. Labrador Nalujuk: The
Transformation of an Aboriginal Inuit Ritual Complex in a Post-Contact Setting. In
2502, pp. 21-29.

2634 Rick, John W. Prehistoric Hunters of the
High Andes. New York, Academic Press,
1980.
Studies in Archaeology
OCLC # 5831285

2635   _____. Heat-altered Cherts of the Lower
Illinois Valley: An Experimental Study in
Prehistoric Technology. ... assisted by
David L. Asch. Evanston, IL. Northwest-
ern University Archeological Program,
1978.
Prehistoric Records v. 2.
OCLC # 5077942

Rickard, Vincent. see 1314

2636 Ricketson, Oliver G. An Outline of Basic
Physical Factors Affecting Middle America.
In 2105, pp. 10-31.

2637 Ricklis, Robert. Excavation of a Probable
Late Prehistoric Onondaga House Site. New
York State Archeological Association Bulle-

tin 39, March 1967, pp. 15-17.
Millwood, NY., Kraus Reprint, 1976.

2638 Riebeth, Carolyn Reynolds, 1898- . J. H.
Sharp: Among the Crow Indians, 1902-1910:
Personal Memories of His Life and Friend-
ships on the Crow Reservation in Montana.
Introd. by Richard Upton. El Segundo,
CA., Upton & Sons, 1985.
Montana and the West series v. 2
OCLC # 12755141

2639 Riley, Carroll L. Early Accounts of the
South and Central American Blowgun. In
1430, pp. 78-89.

2640 _____. The Frontier People: The Greater
Southwest in the Protohistoric Period.
Carbondale, IL., Southern Illinois Uni-
versity at Carbondale, 1982.
Occasional paper/ Center for Archaeologi-
cal Investigations v. 1.
OCLC # 8785862

2641 _____. Pecos and Trade. In 0014, pp. 53-
64.

2642 _____. Pueblo Indians in Mesoamerica: The
Early Historic Period. In 0622, pp. 454-
462.

2643 _____. A Survey of Navajo Archaeology. In
1430, pp. 45-60.

_____. see also 0014

2644 Riley, Glenda, 1938- . Women and Indians
on the Frontier, 1825-1915. Albuquerque,
University of New Mexico Press, 1984.
OCLC # 10837954

Ringheim, Melissa M. see 3018

2645 Rinnander, Elizabeth Ann, 1947- . The BIA
Higher Education Program in Southern California. In 2962, pp. 101-113.

2646 Ritchie, William Augustus, 1903- .
Archaeology of New York State. Rev. ed.
2d. printing with minor corrections. Har-

rison, NY., Harbor Hill Books, 1980.
OCLC # 6195540

2647 _____. The Archaic in New York. New York
State Archeological Association Bulletin
52, July 1971, pp. 2-12. Millwood,
NY., Kraus Reprint, 1976.

2648 _____. Arthur Caswell Parker. New York
State Archeological Association Bulletin 3,
March 1955, pp. 1-3. Millwood, NY.,
Kraus Reprint, 1976.

2649 _____. The Eastern Dispersal of Adena. ...
and Don W. Dragoo, asst. curator, Section of Man, Carnegie Museum, Albany,
University of the State of New York, 1960.
New York State Museum Bulletin no. 379,
1960
OCLC # 888961

2650 _____. The KI Site, the Vergennes Phase
and the Laurentian Tradition. New York
State Archeological Association Bulletin
42, March 1968. Millwood, NY., Kraus
Reprint, 1976.
Paper presented at the annual meeting,
April 29, 1967.

2651 _____. The Perch Lake Mounds. New York
State Archeological Association Bulletin
46, March 1969, pp. 1-10. Millwood,
NY., Kraus Reprint, 1976.

2652 _____. Recent Discoveries Suggesting an
Early Woodland Burial Cult in the North-
east. Albany, The University of the State
of New York, 1955.
Circular - New York State Museum and
Science Service, 40.
OCLC # 2635270

2653 _____. The Stony Brook Site and it's Relation to Archaic and Transitional Cultures
on Long Island. Albany, University of the
State of New York, 1959.
New York State Museum Bulletin no. 372,
1959. Reprinted 1965.
OCLC # 830106

_____. see also 0712

Ritzenthaler, Pat. see 2654

2654 Ritzenthaler, Robert Eugene, 1911- . The
      Woodland Indians of the Western Great
      Lakes. ... and Pat Ritzenthaler. Milwau-
      kee, WI., Milwaukee Public Museum, 1983.
      OCLC # 10408699

2655 Rivard, Jean-Jacques. A Hierophany at
      Chichen Itza and Pictures Can Be Glyphs.
      Greeley, University of Northern Colorado,
      Museum of Anthropology, 1971.
      University of Northern Colorado. Museum
      of Anthropology, Misc. Series no. 26,
      March 1971
      OCLC # 311434

2656 Rivet, Paul, 1876-1958. Los Origenes del
      Hombre Americano. Mexico, Fondo de Cul-
      tura Economica, 1966, c1960.
      OCLC # 4540519

2657 Robbins, Louise M. The Prehistoric People
      of the Fort Ancient Culture of the Central
      Ohio Valley. ... and Georg K. Neumann.
      Ann Arbor, MI., University of Michigan,
      1972.
      University of Michigan. Museum of Anthrop-
      ology. Anthropological Papers no. 47.
      OCLC # 669642

2658 _____. The Story of Life Revealed by the
      Dead. In 0270, pp. 10-26.

2659 Robbins, Lynn A. CERT 1981, Doing Business
      with Indian Tribes: A Report of the Pro-
      ceedings. In 2274, pp. 52-53.

2660 _____. Energy Developments and the Navajo
      Nation. In 2273, pp. 35-48.

2661 _____. Energy Developments and the Navajo
      Nation: An Update. In 2273, pp. 116-
      145.

2662 Robert-Lamblin, Joelle. Endogamy and Exo-
      gamy in Two Arctic Communities: Aleut and

East Greenlandic Eskimos. In 1052, pp.
293-307.

2663   Roberts, Dan L. A Calendar of Eastern
       Pueblo Indian Ritual Dramas. In 2931, pp.
       103-124.

2664   Roberts, Frank H. H. (Frank Harold Hanna),
       1897-1966. Pre-pottery Horizon of the An-
       asazi and Mexico. In 2105, pp. 331-340.

       Roberts, John. see 2357

2664.5 Roberts, Kenneth G. The Canoe: A History
       of the Craft from Panama to the Arctic. ...
       and Philip Shackleton. Toronto, Macmillan
       of Canada, 1983.
       OCLC # 10262091

2665   Roberts, Lance W. Becoming Modern - Some
       Reflections on Iniut Social Change. In
       0137, pp. 299-314.

2666   Robertson, Merle Greene. Painting Practices
       and Their Change Through Time of the Palen-
       que Stucco Sculptures. In 2920, pp. 297-
       326.

2667   _____. The Sculpture of Palenque. Prince-
       ton, NJ., Princeton University Press,
       1983.
       OCLC # 8171896

2668   _____. A Sequence for Palenque Painting
       Techniques. In 0472, pp. 149-172.

2669   Robicsek, Francis. The Maya Book of the
       Dead: The Ceramic Codex; the Corpus of
       Codex Style Ceramics of the Late Classic
       Period. With comments on the hieroglyphic
       text by Donald M. Hales; foreword by Mi-
       chael D. Coe. Charlottesville, VA.,
       University of Virginia Art Museum, Norman,
       University of Oklahoma Press, 1981.
       OCLC # 9073379

2670   _____. The Smoking Gods: Tobacco in Maya
       Art, History and Religion. Foreword by
       Michael D. Coe and Barbara A. Goodnight,
       photos by the author. Norman, University

of Oklahoma Press, 1978.
OCLC # 4647021

2671 _____. A Study in Mayan Art and History:
The Mat Symbol. Foreword by Michael D.
Coe, photos by the author and Steven A.
Robicsek. New York, Museum of the Ameri-
can Indian, Heye Foundation, 1975.
OCLC # 2474230

Robinson, William J. see 0743

2672 Rocca-Arvay, Marie L. Assimilation and Re-
sistance of the Yaqui Indians of Northern
Mexico During the Colonial Period. Ann
Arbor, MI., University Microfilms Inter-
national, 1981.
Microfilm - PhD. Thesis - Columbia
University
OCLC # 11731548

Rochester Museum and Science Center. see
2699

2673 Rock, Howard. Arctic Survival - Inaccurate
Textbooks Create Igloo Myths in Alaska. In
1456, pp. 138-143.
Reprinted from Tundra Times Nov. 19, 1962
and Tundra Times Jan. 23, 1974, pp. 7.

2674 Rock, Roger O. The Native Americans in
American Literature: A Selectively An-
notated Bibliography. Westport, CT.,
Greenwood Press, 1985.
Bibliographies and indexes in American
Literature no. 3.
OCLC # 11531626

2675 Rodman, Selden, 1909- . A Short History
of Mexico. New York, Stein and Day,
1982.
Previously published as The Mexican
Traveler
OCLC # 7273141

2676 Rodnick, David, 1908- . The Fort Belknap
Assiniboine of Montana: A Study in Culture
Change. New York, AMS Press, 1978.
Reprint of the 1938 ed. pub. in New

Haven,   CT.
OCLC # 4137421

Rodrigues O.,   Jaime E.,   1940- . see 2024

2677   Rods, Bundles and Stitches: A Century of
       Southern California Basketry. Edited by
       Raul A. Lopez and Christopher L. Moser.
       Riverside, CA., Riverside Museum Press,
       1981.
       Essays in this collection are also listed
       individually and refer to this citation.
       OCLC # 8369765

2678   Roe,   Peter G.   The Cosmic Zygote: Cosmology
       in the Amazon Basin. New Brunswick,   NJ.,
       Rutgers University Press,   1982.
       OCLC # 7172681

2679   _____.   Recent Discoveries in Chavin Art:
       Some Speculations on Methodology and Sig-
       nificance in the Analysis of a Figural
       Style. In 0120, pp.   49-89.

2680   Roemer,   Kenneth M.   Native American Oral
       Narratives: Context and Continuity. In
       2904, pp. 39-54.

2681   Rogers, Anne Frazer. An Interpretation of a
       Late Archaic Period Site in Piedmont Geor-
       gia. Ann Arbor, MI., University Micro-
       films International, 1982.
       Microfilm - PhD Thesis - University of
       Georgia
       OCLC # 10346285

2682   Rogers, Edward S. The Hunting Group -
       Huntington Territory Complex Among the
       Mistassini Indians. Ottawa, Dept. of
       Northern Affairs and National Resources,
       1963.
       National Museums of Canada Bulletin no.
       195, Anthropological Series no. 63.
       OCLC # 2018365

2683   _____. and Jean H. Rogers. The Individual
       in Mistassini Society from Birth to Death.
       In National Museum of Canada Bulletin no.
       10. Contributions to Anthropology, 1960,
       pt. 2. Ottawa, Dept. of Northern Af-

fairs and National Resources, 1963, pp.
14-36.

2684   _____.   The Material Culture of the
        Mistassini. Ottawa, The Queen's Printer,
        1967.
        National Museum of Canada Bulletin no.
        218, Anthropological Series no. 80.
        OCLC # 455978

2685   _____.   The Quest for Food and Furs: The
        Mistassini Cree, 1953-1954. National
        Museums of Canada, 1973.
        Publications in Ethnology no. 5. Summary
        in French
        OCLC # 822040

2686 Rogers, George William, 1917- . Native
      Pauperization and Social Segregation in
      Alaska. In 1875, pp. 90-110.

2687 Rogers, Jean H. Notes on Mistassini Pho-
      nemics and Morphology. In National Museum
      of Canada Bulletin no. 167. Contributions
      to Anthropology, 1958. Ottawa, Dept. of
      Northern Affairs and National Resources,
      1960, pp. 90-113.

2688   _____.   Survey of Round Lake Ojibwa Phonol-
        ogy and Morphology. In National Museum of
        Canada Bulletin no. 194, Contributions to
        Anthropology, 1961-62, pt. 2. Ottawa,
        Dept. of the Secretary of State, 1964,
        pp. 92-154.

        _____.   see also 2683

2689 Rogers, John, Chippewa Chief. Red World
      and White: Memories of a Chippewa Boyhood.
      Foreword by Joseph W. Whitecotton. Nor-
      man, University of Oklahoma Press, 1974.
      Civilization of the American Indian Series.
      Pub. in 1957 under title A Chippewa Speaks
      OCLC # 698447

2690 Rogers, Robert, 1731-1795. A Concise
      Account of North America. Yorkshire,
      Eng., S. R. Publishers, New York,
      Johnson Reprint, 1966.
      OCLC # 1065054

2691 Rohn, Arthur H., 1929- . American South-
      west. In 0577, pp. 201-222.

2692 _____. Cultural Change and Continuity on
      Chapin Mesa. Laurence, Regents Press of
      Kansas, 1977.
      OCLC # 2868662

      Rojas Rabiela, Theresa. see 2572

2693 Rolingson, Martha Ann. The Bartholomew
      Phase: A Plaquemine Adaptation in the Mis-
      sissippi Valley. In 0710, pp. 99-119.

2694 Rome, Jesus. Life of the Incas in Ancient
      Peru. ... and Lucienne Rome. Barcelona,
      Spain, Productions Liber, 1978.
      OCLC # 5384699

      Rome, Lucienne. see 2694

2695 Ronda, James P., 1943- . Indian Missions:
      A Critical Bibliography. ... and James
      Axtell. Bloomington, Pub. for the New-
      berry Library by Indiana University Press,
      1978.
      Bibliographical Series
      OCLC # 4004974

2696 _____. Lewis and Clark Among the Indians.
      Lincoln, University of Nebraska Press,
      1984.
      OCLC # 10457420

      _____. see also 0937

      Ronnefeldt, Karin. see 3427

2697 Roosevelt, Anna. Problems Interpreting the
      Diffusion of Cultivated Plants. In 2521,
      pp. 1-18.

      Roosevelt, Anna Curtenius. see 2251

2697.5 Root, Dolores, 1950- . Material Dimen-
      sions of Social Inequality in Non-Stratif-
      ied Societies - An Archaeological Perspect-
      ive. Ann Arbor, MI., University Micro-
      films International, 1984.
      Microfilm - PhD Thesis - University of

Massachusetts at Amherst
OCLC # 11452105

2698 Root, Elihu. The Iroquois and the Struggle
      for America. In New York State Museum Bul-
      letin no. 140, June 15, 1910, pp. 204-
      212. Text of speech in Plattsburgh, July
      7, 1909.

      Rosaldo, Renato. see 1557

2699 Rose, Richard, 1937- . Face to face: En-
      counters With Identity. Photography by
      Earl W. Kage. Rochester, NY., Rochester
      Museum and Science Center, 1983.
      Catalog of an exhibition held at the Ro-
      chester Museum and Science Center from Dec.
      17, 1983 for a period of about 5 years.
      OCLC # 10366431

2700 Rosenblat, Angel. The Population of His-
      paniola at the Time of Columbus. In 0779,
      pp. 43-66.
      Reprinted from La Poblacion de America en
      1492: Viejos y Nuevos Calculos. El
      Colegio de Mexico, Mexico, 1969, pp. 7-
      23, 82-84. Trans. by William M. Denevan
      and Elizabeth Lopez Noel.

2701 Rosenfelt, Daniel M. Toward a More Coherent
      Policy for Funding Indian Education. In
      0087, pp. 190-223

2702 Rosenzweig, Mark Samuel. Late Archaic Oc-
      cupations of the Niagara Frontier. Ann
      Arbor, MI., University Microfilms Inter-
      national, 1983.
      Microfilm - PhD Thesis - S. U. N. Y. at
      Buffalo
      OCLC # 9634853

2703 Ross, John, Cherokee Chief, 1790-1866.
      Letter from John Ross, the Principal Chief
      of the Cherokee Nation, to a Gentleman in
      Philadelphia. Job R. Tyson, 1838.
      Library has a photocopy

2704 _____. The Papers of Chief John Ross. Ed-
      ited by and with an introd. by Gary E.
      Moulton. Norman, University of Oklahoma

Press, 1985.
OCLC # 11316121

Ross, Norman A., 1942- . see 1559, 1560

2705 Ross, William Gillies, 1933- . Whaling
and Eskimos: Hudson's Bay 1860-1915. Ottawa, National Museums of Canada, 1975.
Pubs. in Ethnology no. 10.
OCLC # 2307254

2705.5 Rosson, Robert W. Values and American Indian Leadership Styles. In 2238.5, pp.
117-127.

2706 Rothchild, Nan A., 1937- . The Recogni-
tion of Leadership in Egalitarian Societies
of the Northeast. In 0796, pp. 165-182.

Rothhammer, Francisco. see 2796

2707 Rothovius, Andrew E. A Possible Megalithic
Settlement Complex at North Salem, NH.:
And Apparently Related Structures Elsewhere
in New England. New York State Archeological Association Bulletin 27, March 1963,
pp. 2-13.

2708 Rotstein, Abraham. Fur Trade and Empire:
An Institutional Analysis. Toronto: s.
n., 1967.
Thesis, University of Toronto, microfilm
copy. Ottawa, Central Microfilm Unit Pub-
lic Archives of Canada, 1972. Canadian
Thesis on Microfilm no. 13806
OCLC # 2686745

2709 Rouillard, John. American Indian Studies
and the Future. In 2962, pp. 187-191.

2710 Roundtree, Helen C. The Indians of Virginia: A Third Race in a Biracial State. In
2931, pp. 27-48.

2711 Rouse, Irving and Louis Allaire. Caribbean.
In 0577, pp. 432-481.

2712 Rovner, Irwin, 1941- . A Method of Deter-
mining Obsidian Trade Patterns in the Maya
Lowlands. In 2208, pp. 33-41.

2713 Rowlandson, Mary White, ca.1635-ca.1678.
The Sovereignty and Goodness of God. In
2562, pp. 29-75.

2714 _____. A True History of the Captivity and
Restoration of Mary Rowlandson. New York,
Garland Pub. Co., 1977.
Garland Library of narratives of North
American Indian captivities, v. 1.
Reprint of the 1682 London ed. originally
printed under title The Soveraignty and
Goodness of God. Issued with the reprint
of the 1697 ed. of Cotton Mather Humilia-
tions follow'd with Deliverances. New
York, 1977.
OCLC # 2874463

Royce, John Q. see 1043

2715 Ruby, Robert H. The Cayuse Indians: Im-
perial Tribesmen of Old Oregon. ... and
John A. Brown. Foreword by Clifford M.
Drury. Norman, University of Oklahoma
Press, 1972.
Civilization of the American Indian Series
v. 120.
OCLC # 293017

2716 _____. Chinook Indians. Norman, University of Oklahoma Press, 1976.
Civilization of the American Indian Series
v. 138
OCLC # 1958350

2717 _____. Indians of the Pacific Northwest: A
History. ... and John A. Brown. With a
foreword by Alvin M. Josephy, Jr. Norman, University of Oklahoma Press, 1981.
Civilization of the American Indian Series
v. 158
OCLC # 7272798

2718 Rule, Pamela A. The Development of Regional
Subtraditions in Clovis Culture. Ann
Arbor, MI., University Microfilms Inter-
national, 1983.
Microfilm - PhD Thesis - University of
Arizona
OCLC # 11691728

2718.5 Running, John. Honor Dance: Native American Photographs. Foreword by William Albert Allard. Reno, University of Nevada
Press, 1985.
OCLC # 12344717

2719 Ruppert Karl. A Special Assemblage of Maya
Structures. In 2105, pp. 222-231.

2720 Russell, Donald B., 1899- . The Lives and
Legends of Buffalo Bill. Norman, Univer-
sity of Oklahoma Press, 1960.
OCLC # 186887

2721 Russell, Frank, 1868-1903. The Pima In-
dians. Rededition with introd. citation
sources, and bibliography by Bernard L.
Fontana. Tucson, University of Arizona
Press, 1975.
Originally pub. as part of the Bureau of
American Ethnology, 26th Annual Report,
1904-05.
OCLC # 1865091

2722 Russell, Howard S. Indian New England Before the Mayflower. Hanover, NH., University Press of New England, 1980.
OCLC # 6534431

Rutherfurd, John, 1746-1830. see 2565

2723 Rutsch, Edward S. An Analysis of the Lithic
Materials Used in the Manufacture of Pro-
jectile Points in Central New York. New
York State Archeological Association Bulle-
tin 49, July 1970, pp. 1-12. Millwood,
NY., Kraus Reprint, 1976.

2724 Ruttenber, Edward Manning, 1825-1907. His-
tory of the Indian Tribes of the Hudson's
River: Their Origin, Manners and Customs,
Tribal and subtribal Organizations, Wars,
Treaties, etc. Albany, NY., Munsell,
1872.
OCLC # 4709555

2725 Ruz Lhuillier, Alberto, 1906- . Geronto-
cracy at Palenque? In 2920, pp. 287-295.

2726 Ryan, Carmelita S. Special Study of the Ap-

praisal of Indian records.   In 2265,   pp.
33-42.

2727   Ryder,   James W.   Internal Migration in Yucatan: Interpretation of Historical Demography and Current Patterns.   In 0109,   pp.
191-231.

Sabloff,   Jeremy A.   see   0122,   3436

Sabloff,   Paula L.   W.   see   0114

2728   Sagard,   Gabriel.   The Long Journey to the
Country of the Hurons.   Edited with introd.
and notes by George M.   Wrong and trans.
into English by H.   H.   Langton,   New York,
Greenwood Press,   1968.
Champlain Society Pub.   25.   Trans.   of Le
Grand Voyage du Pays des Hurons.   with
French text of the original 1632 ed.
OCLC # 21657

2729   Sahagun,   Bernardino de,   d.   1590.   General
History of the Things of New Spain.   Trans.
from the Aztec into English,   with notes
and illus.   by Arthur J.   O.   Anderson and
Charles E.   Dibble.   2d ed.,   rev.   Santa
Fe,   NM.,   School of American research,
1970.
Monograph of the School of American Re-
search no.   14,   pts. 2-13.   Florentine
Codex.   Library has bks. 1,   6,   7,   9-12.
CONTENTS: bk.   1.   The Gods.   Bk.   6.
Rhetoric and Moral Philosophy.   Bk.   7.
The Sun,   Moon,   and Stars,   and the Bind-
ing of the Years.   Bk.   9.   The Merchants.
Bk.   10.   The People.   Bk.   11.   Earthly
Things.   Bk.   12.   The Conquest of Mexico.
OCLC # 197184

2730   _____.   The War of Conquest: How it Was
Waged Here in Mexico: The Aztecs Own
Story/   As Given to Bernardino de Sahagun;
rendered into modern English by Arthur J.
O.   Anderson and Charles E.   Dibble.   Salt
Lake City,   University of Utah Press,
1978.
A modernized translation of Book 12,   His-
toria de la Conquista de Mexico of Historia

General de las Cosas de Nueve Espana.
OCLC # 4578934

2730.5 St. Pierre, Mark. The Status of
Contemporary Lakota Tribal Arts. In
2831.5, pp. 13-23.

2731 Saler, Benson. Spiritual Power in Santiago
el Palmar. In 0111, pp. 287.

2732 Salisbury, Neal Emerson, 1940- . Conquest
of the "Savage": Puritans, Puritan Mis-
sionaries and the Indians, 1620-1680. Los
Angeles, CA., Salisbury, 1972. Ann
Arbor, MI., University Microfilms Inter-
national, 1972.
Microfilm - PhD Thesis - University of
California
OCLC # 17141983

2733 _____. The Indians of New England: A Critical Bibliography. Bloomington, Published for the Newberry Library by Indiana University Press, 1982.
Bibliographical Series
OCLC # 7946809

2734 _____. Manitou and Providence: Indians,
Europeans, and the Making of New England,
1500-1643. New York, Oxford University
Press, 1982.
OCLC # 7671306

2735 _____. Prospero in New England: The Puritan Missionary as Colonist. In 0068, pp.
253-273.

2735.5 Salomon, Frank. Native Lords of Quito in
the Age of the Incas: The Political Economy of North Andean Chiefdoms. New York,
Cambridge University Press, 1986.
Cambridge Studies in Social Anthropology
no. 59.
OCLC # 11840258

2736 Salomon, Julian Harris, 1896- . Indians
of the Lower Hudson Region. Munsee, New
York, Historical Society of Rockland
County, 1982.
OCLC # 7977107

2737 Salovesh, Michael. <u>Postmarital Residence in
      San Bartolome de los Llanos, Chiapas</u>. In
      0958, pp. 207-217.

2738 Salwen, Bert and Sarah T. Bridges.
      <u>Cultural Differences and the Interpretation
      of Archeological Evidence: Problems with
      Dates</u>. In 0711, pp. 165-173.

3739 Salz, Beate R. <u>The Human Element in Indus-
      trialization: A Hypothetical Case Study of
      Ecuadorean Indians</u>. Millwood, NY., Kraus
      Reprint, 1974.
      Memoirs of the American Anthropological As-
      sociation, no. 85. Suppl. to <u>American
      Anthropologist</u> v. 57, no. 6, pt. 2,
      1955. Economic development and cultural
      change v. 4, no. 1, pt. 2, Oct.
      1955.
      OCLC # 824557

3740 <u>Sampling in Archaeology</u>. Collaborating
      authors David L. Asch... et al. James W.
      Mueller, editor. Tucson, University of
      Arizona Press, 1975.
      OCLC # 1735255

3741 Samuels, Gertrude. <u>Vistas in Navajoland</u>.
      In 3335, pp. 131-147.
      Source - <u>New York Times</u> Aug. 11, 1968

      San Juan Valley Archaeological Project. <u>see</u>
      0019

      Sanchez, Lynda. <u>see</u> 0163

      Sandefur, Gary D., 1951- . <u>see</u> 3120

2742 Sanders, Ronald. <u>Lost Tribes and Promised
      Lands: The Origins of American racism</u>.
      Boston, Little, brown, 1978.
      OCLC # 3481587

2743 Sanders, Thomas Edward, 1926- .
      <u>Literature of the American Indians</u>. ... and
      Walter W. Peek. New York, Academic
      Press, 1973.
      OCLC # 658106

2744   Sanders, William T. The Agricultural
        History of the Basin of Mexico. In 3237,
        pp. 101-159.

2745   _____. The Basin of Mexico: Ecological
        Processes in the Evolution of a Civiliza-
        tion. ... and Jeffrey R. Parsons and Rob-
        ert S. Santley. New York, Academic
        Press, 1979.
        Studies in Archaeology
        OCLC # 658106

2746   _____. Ecological Adaptation in the Basin
        of Mexico: 23,000 B. C. to Present. In
        0122, pp. 147-197.

2747   _____. Environmental Heterogeneity and the
        Evolution of Lowland Maya Civilization. In
        2378, pp. 287-297.

2748   _____. Ethnographic Analogy and the Teoti-
        huacan Horizon Style. In 3096, pp. 397-
        410.

2749   _____. The Lowland Huasteca Archaeological
        Survey and Excavation" 1957 Field Season.
        Columbia, Dept. of Anthropology, Univer-
        sity of Missouri - Columbia, 1978.
        University of Missouri Monographs in
        Anthropology no. 4.
        OCLC # 4877323

2750   _____. The Natural Environment of the Basin
        of Mexico. In 3237, pp. 59-67.

2751   _____. The Population of the Central Mex-
        ican Symbiotic Region, the Basin of Mex-
        ico, and the Teotihuacan Valley in the
        16th Century. In 0779, pp. 85-150.
        Reprinted from ... and Kovar, A., Charl-
        ton, T., and Diehl, R. A. The Teoti-
        huacan Valley Project, Final Report, Vol-
        ume 1: The Natural Environment, Contem-
        porary Occupation and 16th Century Popula-
        tion of the Valley. Occasional Papers in
        Anthropology no. 3, Dept. of Anthropol-
        ogy, Pennsylvania State University, Uni-
        versity Park, 1970, pp. 385-457.

        _____. see also 3096

2752 Sando, Joe S., 1923- . Nee Hemish, a
      History of Jemez Pueblo. Foreword by
      Alfonso Ortiz. Albuquerque, University of
      New Mexico Press, 1982.
      OCLC # 8728895

2753 Sandoz, Mari, 1896-1966. The Battle of the
      Little Bighorn. Lincoln, University of
      Nebraska Press, 1978. c1966.
      A Bison Book. Reprint of the ed. pub. by
      Lippincott, Philadelphia.
      OCLC # 6794289

2754 _____. Crazy Horse; The Strange Man of the
      Oglalas, a Biography. Lincoln, Univer-
      sity of Nebraska Press, 1961, 1942.
      A Bison Book
      OCLC # 3303932

2755 _____. These were the Sioux. Lincoln,
      University of Nebraska Press, 1985,
      c1961.
      A Bison Book. Reprint. Originally pub.
      New York, Hastings House, 1961.
      OCLC # 1181470

      Sands, Kathleen M. see 0199

2756 Sandstrom, Alan R. The Image of Disease:
      Medical Practices of Nahua Indians of the
      Huasteca. Columbia. Dept. of Anthropol-
      ogy, University of Missouri - Columbia,
      1978.
      University of Missouri Monographs in
      Anthropology v. 3.
      OCLC # 4513693

      Santa Fe, NM., Laboratory of Anthropology.
      see 2170

2757 Santeford, Lawrence Gene. Mississippian
      Political Organization and Chipped Stone
      Artifacts: A Typological Model for the
      Study of a Prehistoric Society in Southern
      Illinois. Ann Arbor, MI., University
      Microfilms International, 1982.
      Microfilm - PhD Thesis - Southern Illinois
      University at Carbondale
      OCLC # 10067537

Santesson, C. G. (Carl Gustof), 1862-
1939. see 2329

Santley, Robert S., see 2745

2758 Sapir, Edward, 1884-1939. Native Accounts
of Nootka Ethnography. ... and Morris Swad-
esh. New York, AMS Press, 1978.
Reprint of 1955 ed. pub. by Indiana
University Research Center in Anthropology,
Folklore and Linguistics, which was issued
as v. 1 of pubs. of Indiana University
Research Center in Anthropology, Folklore
and Linguistics and as v. 21, no. 4,
pt. 2 of International Journal of American
Linguistics.
OCLC # 4137397

2759 Sauer, Carl Ortwin, 1889- . Seventeenth
Century North America. Berkeley, Turtle
Island, 1980.
OCLC # 7061103

2760 Saunders, Charles, fl. 1763. Horrid
Cruelty of the Indians. New York, Garland
Pub. Co., 1977.
Garland Library of narratives of North
American Indian captivities, v. 10. Re-
print of the 1763 ed. printed by T. War-
ren, Birmingham.
OCLC # 2798653

2761 Satz, Ronald N. Tennessee's Indian People:
From White Contact to Removal, 1540-1840.
Knoxville, University of Tennessee Press,
1979.
OCLC # 3205532

2761.5 Saum, Lewis O., The Fur Trade and the In-
dians. Seattle, University of Washington
Press, 1965.
OCLC # 245101

Savage, William W. see 1566

2762 Savelle, Max, 1896- . Empires to Nations
in America, 1713-1824. Minneapolis, University of Minnesota Press, 1974.
OCLC # 1093826

2763 Savery, William, 1750-1804. _Journal_.
     1844. Microfilm provided by American Phil-
     osophical Society, Philadelphia. For de-
     tailed description see Freeman's Guide
     #239.

     Saville, Marshall Howard, 1867-1935. <u>see</u>
     2259

2764 Savishinsky, Joel S. <u>The Trail of the Hare:</u>
     <u>Life and Stress in an Arctic Community</u>.
     New York, Gordon and Breach, 1974.
     Library of Anthropology, v. 2.
     OCLC # 1194863

     Sayers, Robert. <u>see</u> 0938

2765 Sayles, E. B. (Edwin Booth), 1892-1977.
     <u>Archaeological Analysis</u>. In 2768, pp.
     48-81.

2766 _____. <u>Cazador State</u>. In 2768, pp. 90-
     113.

2767 _____. <u>Chiricahua Stage</u>. In 2768, pp.
     114-124.

2768 _____. <u>The Cochise Cultural Sequence in</u>
     <u>Southeastern Arizona</u>. With collaboration
     of Ernst Antevs, Tucson, University of
     Arizona Press, 1983.
     Essays in this collection are also listed
     individually and refer to this citation.
     Anthropological Papers of the University of
     Arizona, no. 42.
     OCLC # 9196397

2769 _____. <u>Correlation of Cochise Geological-</u>
     <u>Archaeological Records with Radiocarbon</u>
     <u>Dating-Pollen Records</u>. In 2768, pp. 136-
     157.

2770 _____. <u>Early Pottery Horizon</u>. In 2768,
     pp. 132-1356.

2771 _____. <u>San Pedro Stage</u>. In 2768, pp.
     125-131.

2772 _____. <u>Sulphur Springs Stage</u>., In 2768,
     pp. 82-89.

2773   Sayre,   Robert F.   Thoreau and the American
       Indian.   Princeton,   NJ.,   Princeton Uni-
       versity Press,   1977.
       OCLC # 2985480

2774   Scaglion,   Richard.   The Plains Culture Area
       Concept.   In 0113,   pp.   23-34.

2775   Scarry,   John Francis.   Fort Walton Develop-
       ment: Mississippian Chiefdoms in the Lower
       Southeast.   Ann Arbor,   MI.,   University
       Microfilms International,   1984.
       Microfilm - PhD Thesis - Case Western Re-
       serve University
       OCLC # 10649880

2776   Schaafsma,   Polly.   Indian Rock Art of the
       Southwest.   Santa Fe,   School of American
       Research,   1980.
       Southwest Indian Art Series
       OCLC # 5101947

2777   _____.   Rock Art in Chaco Canyon.   In 2289,
       pp.   59-64.

2778   Scheick,   William J.   The Half Blood: A
       Cultural Symbol in 19th Century American
       Fiction.   Lexington,   University of Ken-
       tucky Press,   1979.
       OCLC # 5219793

2779   Schela,   Linda.   Palenque: The House of the
       Dying Son.   In 2270,   pp.   42-56.

       Schell,   Lawrence M.   see   1653

2780   Schickel,   Richard.   Why Indians Can't Be
       Villains Any More.   In 2533,   pp.   149-181.

2781   Schiffer,   Michael B.   Chipped Stone and
       Human Behavior at the Joint Site.   In 0822,
       pp.   141-163.

2782   _____.   A Synthetic Model of Archaeological
       Inference.   In 0822,   pp.   123-139.

2783   Schlak,   Arthur Edmund.   The Venus Gods: A
       Study in Mesoamerican Astronomy,   Archaeol-
       ogy,   Art History,   Symbol,   Religion and
       Thought.   Ann Arbor,   MI.,   University

Microfilms International, 1983.
Microfilm - PhD Thesis - Yale University
OCLC # 11486873

Schlenker, Jon A. see 2016

2784 Schneider, Mary Janes. Plains Indian Art.
In 0113, pp. 197-211.

2785 _____. Women's Work: An Examination of Women's Roles in Plains Indian Arts and
Crafts. In 1438, pp. 101-121.

2786 Schnell, Frank T. Cemochechobee: Archaeol-
ogy of a Mississippian Ceremonial Center on
the Chattahoochee River. ... Vernon J.
Knight, Jr. and Gail S. Schnell. With
contributions by Mary E. Dunn ... et al.
Gainesville, University Presses of
Florida, 1981.
Ripley P. Bullen monograph in anthropology
and history no. 3.
OCLC # 7876062

2787 Schnell, Gail Schroeder. Hotel Plaza: An
Early Historic Site with a Prehistory.
With appendix by Paul W. Parmalee.
Springfield, Illinois State Museum, 1974.
Reports of investigations - Illinois State
Museum no. 29.
OCLC # 1530296

_____. see also 2786

2788 Schoff, Harry. A Recent Find at Factory
Hollow. New York State Archeological Association Bulletin 14, Nov. 1958, pp.
9-10. Millwood, NY., Kraus Reprint,
1976.

2789 Scholars and the Indian Experience: Critical
Reviews in the Social Sciences. Edited by
W. R. Swagerty. Bloomington, Pub. for
D'Arcy McNickle Center for the History of
the American Indian, Newberry Library by
Indiana University Press, 1984.
Essays in this collection are also listed
individually and refer to this citation.
Bibliographical Series
OCLC # 10459087

2789.5 Scholder, Fritz, 1937- . The Native
American and Contemporary Art: A Dilemma.
In 2831.5, pp. 61-63.

2790 Scholes, France V. and Eric Thompson. The
Francisco Perez 'Probanza' of 1654-1656 and
the 'Matricula' of Tipu (Belize). In 0109,
pp. 43-68.

2791 Schondube, Otto and L. Javier Galvan. Salvage Archaeology at El Grillo-Tabachines,
Zapopan, Jalisco, Mexico. In 0014, pp.
144-164.

School of American Research (santa Fe, NM.)
see 0123

2792 Schoolcraft, Henry Rowe, 1793-1864. Indian
and His Wigwam: Or, Characteristics of
the Red Race of America: From Original
Notes and Manuscripts. New York, AMS
Press, 1978.
Originally issued 1844-1845, in eight num-
bers with paper covers bearing title
Oneota; or the Red Race of America...
afterwards pub. under various titles: The
Red Race of America; The Indian in His
Wigwam; The American Indians; Western
Scenes and Reminiscences. cf. Sabin. Re-
print of the 1848 ed. pub. by W. H.
Graham, New York.
OCLC # 3446093

2793 _____. Personal Memoirs of a Residence of
Thirty Years With the Indian tribes. New
York, AMS Press, 1978.
Reprint of the 1851 ed. pub. by Lippin-
cott, Grambo, Philadelphia.
OCLC # 3432305

2794 _____. Travels in the Central Portions of
the Mississippi Valley: Comprising Observations on its Mineral Geography, Internal
Resources and Aboriginal Population. Millwood, NY., Kraus Reprint, 1975.
Reprint of the 1825 ed. pub. by Collins
and Hannay, New York
OCLC # 1257092

2795 Schrabisch, Max. Indian Rock-Shelters in

Northern New Jersey and Southern New York.
In 3469,   pp.   139-165.

2796   Schull,   William J.   and Francisco Rothhammer.   Analytic Methods for Genetic and
Adaptational Studies.   In 1025,   pp.   241-
255.

2797   Schulter,   Steven C.   (Steven Christopher).
Indian and White Politics in the Modern
West: Sioux and White Leadership in South
Dakota, 1920-1965.   Ann Arbor,   MI.,   Uni-
versity Microfilms Iternational,   1984.
Microfilm - PhD Thesis - University of
Wyoming
OCLC # 12488108

2798   Schultes,   Richard Evans.   Amazonian Cult-
igens and Their Northward and Westward Migrations in Pre-Columbia Times.   In 2521,
pp.   19-37.

2799   Schultz,   George A.,   1925- .   An Indian
Canaan: Isaac McCoy and the Vision of an
Indian State.,   Foreword by Robert E.
Bell.   Norman,   University of Oklahoma
Press,   1972.
Civilization of the American Indian Series
v.   12.
OCLC # 323784

2800   Schultz,   James Willard,   1859-1947.   My Life
as an Indian: The Story of a Red Woman and
a White Man in the Lodges of the Blackfeet.
Illus.   from photographs,   mostly by George
Bird Grinnell.   New York,   Doubleday,   Page
and Co.,   1907.
Originally pub.   serial in Field and Stream
under title In the Lodges of the Blackfeet
and over pseudonym W.   B.   Anderson.
OCLC # 946852

2802   _____.   With the Indians in the Rockies.
Illus.   with photographs by Roland Reed.
Lewiston,   ID.,   Confluence Press,   1984.
OCLC # 11247831

2801   _____.   The Squawman Fought Their Battles.
In 1566,   pp.   209-230.
Reprinted from My Life as an Indian: The

Story of a Red Woman and a White Man in the
Lodges of the Blackfeet, New York, Doubleday, Page and Co., 1907, pp. 411-
426.

2803 Schultz, John L. White Medicine, Indian
Lives...As Long As the Grass Shall Grow.
Ft. Collins, Colorado State University
Press, 1976.
OCLC # 2568045

2804 Schusky, Ernest Lester, 1931- . The Forgotten Sioux: An Ethnohistory of the Lower
Brule Reservation. Chicago, Nelson-Hall,
1975.
OCLC # 1230511

2805 Schuster, Helen H. The Yakimas: A Critical
Bibliography. Bloomington, Published for
the Newberry Library by Indiana University
Press, 1982.
Bibliographical Series
OCLC # 7976006

Science Museums of Minnesota. see 3018

2806 Sciulli, P. W. Human Remains from Meadowcroft Rockshelter, Washington County,
Southwestern Pennsylvania, In 2111, pp.
175-185.

2807 Scollon, Ronald, 1939- . The Context of
the Informant Narrative Performance: From
Sociolinguistics to Ethnolinguistics at
Fort Chipewyan, Alberta. Ottawa, Nation-
al Museums of Canada, 1979.
Paper - Canadian Ethnology Service, no.
52. Mercury Series
OCLC # 5301663

2808 Scott, Catherine J., 1950- . The Evolution of Mimbres Pottery. In 0391, pp.
39-68.

_____. see also 0391

2809 Scott, G. Richard. A Stature Reconstruction of the Gran Quivira Skeletal Population. In 1387, pp. 129-137.

2810   Scott,   H.   L. ,   Captain 7th Cavalry,   U.   S.
       Army.   The Sign Language of the Plains In-
       dian.   In 0008,   pp.   53-67.
       Reprinted from the International Folk-lore
       Congress of the World's Columbian Exposi-
       tion,   (Chicago,   1893)   Archives of the
       International Folk-lore Association,   v.
       1,   1898,   pp.   206-220.

2811   Scott,   Stuart D.   Archaeology and the Estu-
       ary: Researching Prehistory and Paleoecol-
       ogy in the Marsimas Nacionales,   Sinaloa
       and Nayarit,   Mexico.   In 0231,   pp.   51-
       56.

2812   Scully,   Vincent Joseph,   1920- .   Pueblo:
       Mountain,   Village,   Dance.   New York,
       Viking Press,   1975.
       OCLC # 1708531

       Sears,   Elsie O'R.   see   2813

2813   Sears,   William H.   (William Hulse),   1920- .
       Fort Center: An Archaeological Site in the
       Lake Okeechobee Basin.   With contributions
       by Elsie O'R Sears and Karl T.   Steinen.
       Gainesville,   University Presses of
       Florida,   1982.
       Ripley P.   Bullen monographs in anthropol-
       ogy and history v.   4.
       OCLC # 8627338

2814   Seary,   E.   R.   The Avalon Peninsula of New-
       foundland and Ethnolinguistic Study.   ...
       and G.   M.   Story and W.   J.   Kirwin.   Ot-
       tawa,   Queens Printer,   1968.
       National Museums of Canada Bulletin no.
       219,   Anthropological Series no.   81.
       OCLC # 27672

       Seattle Art Museum.   see   1486

       Sebiok,   Thomas Albert,   1920- .   see   0008,
       2277

2815   The Second Coastal Archaeology Reader: 1900
       to the Present.   Edited by James E.   Truex.
       Stony Brook,   NY. ,   Suffolk County Archae-
       ological Association,   Lexington,   MA. ,
       Ginn Custom Pub. ,   1981.

Readings in Long Island Archaeology and
Ethnohistory v. 5.
OCLC # 9018721

2816 Seeger, Anthony. <u>Nature and Society in Central Brazil: The Suya Indians of Mato-
Grosso</u>. Cambridge, MA., Harvard University Press, 1981.
Harvard Studies in Cultural Anthropology,
v. 4.
OCLC # 6532277

2817 <u>Seeing Castaneda: Reactions to the "Don
Juan" Writings of Carlos Castaneda</u>. Edit-
ed, selected and with introd. by Daniel
C. Noel. New York, Putnam, 1976.
OCLC # 1582614

2818 <u>Seeing with a Native Eye: Essays on Native
American Religion</u>. By Ake Hultkrantz, et
al., edited by Walter Holden Cappes, as-
sisted by Ernst F. Tonsing. New York,
Essays in this collection are also listed
individually and refer to this citation.
Harper and Row, 1976.
A Harper Forum Book
OCLC # 2388018

Segal, Charles M. <u>see</u> 2563

2819 Seguin, Margaret, 1945- . <u>Lest There Be
No Salmon: Symbols in Traditional Tsimshian Potlatch</u>. In 3162, pp. 110-133.

2820 Sejourne, Laurette. <u>Burning Water: Thought
and Religion in Ancient Mexico</u>. Introd.
by Jose A. Arguelles. Berkeley, CA.,
Shambhala; New York, distributed by Ran-
dom House, 1976.
OCLC # 2567241

2821 Sekaquaptewa, Emory. <u>Hopi Indian Ceremon-
ies</u>. In 2818, pp. 35-43.

2822 Selby, Henry A. <u>The Study of Social Organization in Traditional Mesoamerica</u>. In
0958, pp. 29-43.

2823 Sempowski, Martha Lou, 1942- . <u>Mortuary
Practices at Teotihuacan, Mexico: Their</u>

Implications for Social Status. Ann Arbor,
MI., University Microfilms International,
1983.
Microfilm - PhD Thesis - University of
Rochester
OCLC # 10562508

Seneca Nation. see 2197

2824 Servies, James A. Notes on the Literature
      of the Gulf Coast Indians. In 1282, pp.
      6-24.

2825 Settlement Pattern Excavations at Kaminal-
      juyu, Guatemala. Edited by Joseph W. Mi-
      chels. University Park, Pennsylvania
      Press, 1979.
      Essays in this collection are also listed
      individually and refer to this citation.
      University of Pennsylvania Press monograph
      series on Kaminaljuyu
      OCLC # 5265309

2826 Sevareid, Eric, 1912- . Canoeing With the
      Cree. St. Paul, Minnesota Historical
      Society, 1968.
      Reprint, publications of the Minnesota
      Historical Society
      OCLC # 454079

      Sexton, James D. see 0284, 0285

2827 Seymour, Flora Warren (Smith), 1888- .
      Lords of the Valley, Sir William Johnson
      and His Mohawk Brothers. London, New
      York, Longmans, Green and Co., 1930.
      First edition

2828 Seymour, Peter J. The Golden Woman: The
      Colville Narrative of Peter J. Seymour.
      Edited by Anthony Mattina; trans. by
      Anthony Mattina and Madeline deSautel.
      Tucson, University of Arizona Press,
      1985.
      OCLC # 11815714

      Shackleton, Philip. see 2664.5

2829 Shadomy, H. Jean. The Differential Diag-
      nosis of Various Pathogens and Tuberculosis

in the Prehistoric Indians. In 2625, pp.
25-34.

2830 Shane, Audrey. Power in Their Hands: The
Gitsontk. In 3162, pp. 160-173.

Shankman, Arnold M., 1945- . see 0546

2831 Sharer, Robert J. The Maya Collapse Revisited: Internal and External Perspectives. In 2920, pp. 531-552.

_____. see also 2215

2831.5 Sharing a Heritage. Los Angeles, American
Indian Studies Center, University of Cal-
ifornia, 1984.
Contemporary American Indian Issues series
v. 5. Published results of the American
Indian Studies Center's Sixth Annual Spring
Conference on Contemporary American Indian
Issues, held in 1982 at the University of
California, Los Angeles, and co-sponsored
by the Malki Museum. Essays in this col-
lection are also listed individually and
refer to this citation.
OCLC # 11468512

2831.7 Shaughnessy, Timothy F. and Eddie F.
Brown. Developing Indian Content in Social
Work Education: A Community Based Curricu-
lum Model. In 2238.5, pp. 157-169.

2832 Shaw, Dennis Edward. The Battle of Wounded
Knee: Myths Versus Reality. Ann Arbor,
MI., University Microfilms International,
1984.
Microfilm - PhD Thesis - University of
Miami
OCLC # 8860788

2833 Shaw, Helen Louise. British Administration
of the Southern Indians, 1756-1783. New
York, AMS Press, 1981.
Originally presented as the author's
thesis, Bryn Mawr College, 1929. Reprint
of the 1931 ed. pub. by Lancaster Press,
Lancaster, PA.
OCLC # 6737156

2834   Shea,   David E. <u>A Defense of Small Popula-
       tion Estimates for the Central Andes in
       1520</u>. In 0779,   pp.   157-180.

       Shea,   John Dawson Gilmary,   1824-1892. <u>see</u>
       1380

2835   Sheehan,   Bernard W. <u>Savagism and Civility:
       Indians and Englishmen in Colonial Virgin-
       ia</u>.   Cambridge;   New York,   Cambridge Uni-
       versity Press,   1980.
       OCLC # 5239471

2836   Sheldon,   Elisabeth Shepard.   <u>Continuity and
       Change in Plant Usage for the Mississip-
       pian to the Historic Period</u>.   Ann Arbor,
       MI.,   University Microfilms International,
       1982.
       Microfilm - PhD Thesis - University of
       Alabama
       OCLC # 9744373

2837   Shenkel,   J.   Richard.   <u>Quantitative Analysis
       and Population Estimates of the Shell
       Mounds of the Marismas Nacionales,   West
       Mexico</u>.   In 0231,   pp.   57-67.

2838   Shepardson,   Mary.   <u>Navajo Ways in Govern-
       ment: A Study in Political Process</u>.   Mill-
       wood,   NY.,   Kraus Reprint,   1974.
       Memoirs of the American Anthropological As-
       sociation no.   96.   Supplement to <u>American
       Anthropologist</u> v.   65,   no.   3,   pt.   2,
       1963.
       OCLC # 1314111

       Shepaug Valley Archaeological Society,   Wash-
       ington,   D. C. <u>see</u> 3066

2839   Sherman,   William L.   <u>Forced Native Labor in
       Sixteenth-Century Central America</u>.   Lin-
       coln,   University of Nebraska Press,   1979.
       OCLC # 4136283

2840   Sherzer,   Joel.   <u>Kuna Ways of Speaking: An
       Ethnographic Perspective</u>.   Austin,   Univer-
       sity of Texas Press,   1983.
       Texas Linguistic Series
       OCLC # 9280596

Shimada, Izumi. <u>see</u> 2610

2841 Shimony, Annemarie. <u>Alexander General,</u>
      <u>"Deskahe", Cayuga-Oneida, 1889-1965.</u>
      In 0080, pp. 159-175.

2842 _____. <u>Conflict and Continuity: An Anal-</u>
      <u>ysis of an Iroquois Uprising.</u> In 0979,
      pp. 153-164.

2843 <u>The Shinnecock Indians, A Cultural History.</u>
      Edited by Gaynell Stone. Stony Brook,
      NY., Suffolk County Archaeological Assoc-
      iation, Lexington, MA., Ginn Custom
      Pub., 1983.
      Readings in Long Island Archaeology and
      Ethnohistory v. 6.
      OCLC # 11037723

2844 Shirley, Glenn. <u>Pawnee Bill: A Biography</u>
      <u>of Major Gordon W. Lillie.</u> Albuquerque,
      University of New Mexico Press, 1958.
      OCLC # 361807

2845 Shkilnyk, Anastasia M., 1945- . <u>A Poison</u>
      <u>Stronger Than Love: The Destruction of an</u>
      <u>Ojibwa Community.</u> Foreword by Kai Erikson,
      photographs by Hiro Miyamatsu. New Haven,
      Yale University Press, 1985.
      OCLC # 10778760

2846 <u>A Shot Was Fired and Carnage Ensued.</u> In
      1566, pp. 249-265.
      Reprinted from <u>16th Annual Report of the</u>
      <u>Commissioner of Indian Affairs to the Sec-</u>
      <u>retary of the Interior, 1891,</u> Washington,
      Govt. Print. Off., 1891, pp. 123-135.

2847 Shutler, Richard, 1921- . <u>The Australian</u>
      <u>Parallel to the Peopling of the New World.</u>
      In 0902, pp. 43-45.

      Sibbick, John. <u>see</u> 3488

2847.5 Sider, Gerald M. <u>Culture and Class in</u>
      <u>Anthropology and History: A Newfoundland</u>
      <u>Illustration.</u> New York, Cambridge Univer-
      sity Press, 1986.
      Cambridge Studies in Social Anthropology v.

60.
OCLC # 12217306

2848   Sideroff, Maria Louise. Pottery Replica-
       tion. In 1585, pp. 179-194.

2849   Siegel, Sanford J., 1951- . The Emerging
       Influence of Pan-Indian Elements on the
       Tribal Identity of the Gros Ventre of North
       Central Montana. Ann Arbor, MI., Univer-
       sity Microfilms International, 1983.
       Microfilm - PhD Thesis - Ohio State
       University
       OCLC # 11542988

2850   Siemens, Alfred H. Karst and the Prehispan-
       ic Maya in the Southern Lowlands. In 2522,
       pp. 117-143.

       Siggner, Andrew J. see 2492

2851   Silberman, Arthur. 100 Years of Native
       American Painting, March 5 - April 16,
       1978, the Oklahoma Museum of Art, Okla-
       homa City: Exhibition Catalogue. Introd.
       by Jamake Highwater; text by Arthur Sil-
       berman. Oklahoma City, The Museum, 1978.
       OCLC # 4884341

       Silet, Charles L. P. see 2533

2852   Silverberg, Robert. Mound Builders of An-
       cient America; The Archaeology of a Myth.
       Greenwich, CT., New York Graphic Society,
       1968.
       OCLC # 186113

       Silverman, Sydel. see 3139

       Simmons, Cheryl L. see 1055

       Simmons, William Scranton, 1938- . see
       1055

       Simon Fraser University. see 1562

2853   Simpson, Allan A. The Manitoba Escarpment
       Cultural Sequence. In 1467, pp. 139-151.

2854   Simpson, D. W. and K. Bowles. Integra-

tion of Eskimo Manpower Into Industrial
Society: Difficulties - Programs -
Attitudes. In 1875,   pp. 349-367.

2855   Simpson, Ruth Dee. The Calico Mountains
       Archaeological Site. In 0902, pp. 218-
       220.

2856   _____. Calico Mountains Site: Pleistocene
       Archaeology in the Mojave Desert, Califor-
       nia. In 0905, pp. 7-20.

2857   Sipe, C. Hale (Chester Hale), 1880- .
       Indian Chiefs of Pennsylvania. New York,
       Arno Press and the New York Times, 1971.
       The First American Frontier
       OCLC # 1100966

2858   Siskin, Edgar E., 1907- . Washo Shamans
       and Peyotists: Religious Conflict in an
       American Indian tribe. Salt Lake City,
       University of Utah Press, 1983.
       OCLC # 9785183

2859   Siskind, Janet. To Hunt in the Morning.
       London; New York, Oxford University
       Press, 1975, c1973.
       A Galaxy Book v. GB 430
       OCLC # 7473095

2860   Skinner, Alanson Buck, 1886-1925. Archae-
       ology of Manhattan Island. In 3469, pp.
       111-121.

2861   _____. Archaeology of the New York Coastal
       Algonkin. In 3469, pp. 211-235.

2862   _____. Kansa Organizations. In 3473, pp.
       741-775.
       American Museum of Natural History.
       Anthropological Papers v. 11, pt. 9.

2863   _____. The Lenapé Indians of Staten Island.
       In 3469, pp. 1-62.

2864   _____. The Manhattan Indians. In New York
       State Museum Bulletin no. 158, pp. 199-
       212.

2865   _____. Notes on Iroquois Archaeology. New

York, AMS Press, 1978.
Reprint of the 1921 ed. pub. by Museum of
the American Indian, Heye Foundation, New
York, which was issued as no. 18 of its
Indian Notes and Monographs.
OCLC # 4500139

2866 _____. Political and Ceremonial Organizations of the Plains Ojibway. In 3473, pp.
475-511.
American Museum of Natural History,
Anthropological Papers v. 11, pt. 6.

2867 _____. Political Organization, Cults and
Ceremonies of the Plains - Cree. In 3473,
pp. 513-541.
American Museum of Natural History.
Anthropological Papers v. 11, pt. 6.

2868 _____. Ponca Societies and Dances. In
3473, pp. 777-801.
American Museum of Natural History.
Anthropological Papers, v. 11, pt. 9.

2869 _____. Societies of the Iowa. In 3473,
pp. 679-739.
American Museum of Natural History.
Anthropological Papers, v. 11, pt. 9.

2870 Skirboll, E. Analysis of Constant Volume
Samples From Meadowcroft Rockshelter,
Washington County, Southwestern Pennsylva-
nia. In 2111, pp. 221-240.

2871 Slade, Doren L. Kinship in the Social Organization of a Nahuat-speaking Community
in the Central Highlands. In 0958, pp.
155-185.

2871.5 Slagle, Al Logan. The American Indian
Policy Review Commission: Repercussions
and Aftermath. In 2961.5, pp. 115-132.

Slotkin, Richard, 1942- . see 2919

Slover, John, fl. 1773-1782. see 0343

2872 Smethurst, Gamaliel. A Narrative for an
Extraordinary Escape. New York, Garland
Pub., 1977.

The Garland Library of Narratives of North
American Indian Captivities, v. 10. Issued with the reprint of the 1764 ed. of
C. Saunders <u>The Horrid Cruelty of the In-
dians</u>. Reprint of the 1774 ed. printed by
the author, London.
OCLC # 2969473

2873 Smiley Terah L. (Terah LeRoy), 1914- .
<u>Paleo-ecological Evidence</u>. In 2768, pp.
20-25.

2874 _____. <u>The Corbeled Arch in the New World</u>.
In 2105, pp. 202-221.

2875 Smith, A. Ledyard. <u>Patolli at the Ruins of
Seibal, Peté, Guatemala</u>. In 2920, pp.
349-363.

2876 Smith, Betty Anderson. <u>Distribution of 18th
Century Cherokee Settlements</u>. In 0547,
pp. 46-60.

2877 Smith, Bradford, 1909- . <u>Captain John
Smith, His Life and Legend</u>. 1st ed.,
Philadelphia, Lippincott, 1953.
OCLC # 1276187

2878 Smith, Bruce D. <u>Prehistoric Patterns of Hu-
man Behavior: A Case Study in the Missis-
sippi Valley</u>. With a contribution by Wilma
A. Wetterstrom. New York, Academic
Press, 1978.
Studies in Archaeology
OCLC # 3650979

2878 _____. <u>"Twitching": A Minor Ailment Affecting Human Paleoecological Research</u>. In
0710, pp. 275-292.

2880 _____. <u>Variation in Mississippian Settlement Patterns</u>. In 2172, pp. 479-503.

_____. <u>see also</u> 2172

2880.5 Smith, Donald B. <u>Long Lance, the True
Story of an Impostor</u>. Lincoln, University
of Nebraska Press, 1983, c1982.
A Bison Book
OCLC # 9488721

Smith, Dwight LaVern, 1918- . see 1576

2881 Smith, E. B. Indian Tribal Claims: De-
      cided in the Court of Claims of the United
      States, Briefed and Compiled to June 30,
      1947. Washington, D. C., University
      Publications of America, 1976.
      Originally compiled in 1947 by E. B.
      Smith, chief Indian claims section, Unit-
      ed States General Accounting Office
      OCLC # 2663373

2882 Smith, Gerald A. (Gerald Arthur), 1915- .
      Indian Rock Art of Southern California With
      Selected Petroglyphs. ... and Wilson G.
      Turner. Redlands, CA., San Bernardino
      County Museum Association, 1975.
      OCLC # 2979582

2883 _____. The Sundry Uses of Basketry. In
      2677, pp. 52-81.

2884 Smith, Hale G. and Mark Gottlob. Spanish -
      Indian Relationships: Synoptic History and
      Archeological Evidence, 1500-1763. In
      3071, pp. 1-18.

2885 Smith, Henry Nash. American Emotional and
      Imaginative Attitudes Toward the Great
      Plains and Rocky Mountains, 1803-1850.
      Cambridge, MA., 1940.
      Microfilm - PhD Thesis - Harvard University
      Harvard University Library, Microreproduc-
      tion Dept., 1966.

2886 Smith, Huron Herbert, 1833-1933. Ethnobot-
      any of the Menomini Indians; Ethnobotany
      of the Meskwaki Indians. New York, AMS
      Press, 1978.
      Reprint of 2 works pub. by order of the
      Board of Trustees of the Public Museum of
      the City of Milwaukee in 1923 and 1928,
      respectively, which were issued as v. 4,
      no. 1-2 of its Bulletin.
      OCLC # 4659587

2887 _____. Ethnobotany of the Meskwaki Indians.
      New York, AMS Press, 1978.
      Reprint of Bulletin of Public Museum of the
      City of Milwaukee, v. 4, no. 1, Dec.

10, 1923, pp. 1-74
Bound with 2886

2888   Smith, Ira F. III. Schultz Site Settlement
       Patterns and External Relations: A Prelim-
       inary Discussion and Possible Interpreta-
       tion. New York State Archeological Assoc-
       iation Bulletin 50, Nov. 1970, pp. 27-
       35. Millwood, NY., Kraus Reprint, 1976.

2889   Smith, James G. E. Leadership Among the
       Southwestern Ojibwa. Ottawa, National
       Museum of Canada, 1973.
       Publications in Ethnology no. 7.
       OCLC # 1057448

       _____. see also 2251

       Smith, Jane F. se 2265

2890   Smith, John. The Generall Historie, 1624.
       In 3413, pp. 14-20.
       Reprinted from The Generall Historie of
       Virginia, New-England and the Summer
       Isles. London, 1624, pp. 46-49.

2891   Smith, M. Estellie, 1935- . Pueblo
       Councils: An Example of Stratified Egal-
       itarianism. In 0796, pp. 32-44.

2892   Smith, Marian. The War Complex of the
       Plains Indians. In 2304, pp. 146-155.
       Abridged and reprinted from American Philo-
       sophical Society Proceedings v. 78, no.
       3, 1937, pp. 425-461.

2893   Smith, Marian Wesley, 1907-1961. Archae-
       ology of the Columbia - Fraser Region.
       Millwood, NY., Kraus Reprint, 1974.
       Reprint of the 1950 ed. pub. by the Soc-
       iety for American Archaeology, Menasha
       WI., which was issued as the Memoirs of
       the Society no. 2. and suppl. to American
       Antiquity v. 15, no. 4, pt. 2, April
       1950.
       OCLC # 2571235

2894   Smith, Marvin T. Chronology from Glass
       Beads: The Spanish Period in the South-

SMITH   412

east, c. A. D. 1513-1670. In 1204,
pp. 147-158.

2895 _____. Early 16th Century Glass Beads in

the Spanish Colonial Trade. ... and Mary
Elizabeth Good. Greenwood, MS.,   Cotton-
landia Museum Publications, 1982.
OCLC # 8893765

2896 Smith, Ralph A. The Scalp Hunter in the
Borderlands, 1835-1850. In 2304, pp.
156-167.
Abridged and reprinted from Arizona and the
West v. 6, no. 1, Spring 1964, pp. 5-
22.

2897 Smith, Rex Allen. Moon of the Popping
Trees. New York, Reader's Digest Press,
distributed by Crowell, 1975.
OCLC # 1341423

2898 Smith, Richard, 1630?-1692. Further Let-
ters on King Philips War. ...Mr. John
Paine, the Commissioners of the United
Colonies, Mrs. Mary Pray. Issued at the
General Court of the Society of Colonial
Wars in the State of Rhode Island and Pro-
vidence Plantations by its Governor William
Bates Greenough...and the Council of the
Society, Dec. 29, 1923. Providence,
printed for the Society by the E. L.
Freeman Co., 1924.
OCLC # 8459857

2899 Smith, Robert E. Ceramics of the Peten. In
2105, pp. 242-249.

2900 Smith, Robin Laurie. Coastal Mississippian
Period Sites at Kings Bay, Georgia: A
Model - Based Archaeological Analysis. Ann
Arbor, MI., University Microfilms Inter-
national, 1982
Microfilm - PhD Thesis - University of
Florida
OCLC # 10346340

2901 Smith, Sherry Lynn, 1951- . "Civilization's Guardians": Army Officers' Reflections on Indians and the Indian Wars in the

Trans-Mississippian West, 1848-1890. Ann
Arbor, MI., University Microfilms Inter-
national, 1984.
Microfilm - PhD Thesis - University of
Washington
OCLC # 12532944

2902 Smith, Thomas R. A Choctaw's Honor. Ven-
tura, CA., Aazunna Publishing, 1981.
Library's copy signed by the author on
title page
OCLC # 7805520

2903 Smith, Watson, 1897-   . Prehistoric Kivas
of Antelope Mesa, Northeastern Arizona.
Cambridge, MA., Peabody Museum of Archaeology and Ethnology, Harvard University,
1972.
Papers of the Peabody Museum of Archaeology and Ethnology, Harvard University v.
39, no. 1. Reports of the Awatovi Expedition no. 9.
OCLC # 613761

_____. see also 1185

Smithsonian Institution. Traveling Exhibition Service. see 1982

2904 Smoothing the Ground: Essays on Native Amer-
ican Oral Literature. Edited by Brian
Swann. Berkeley, University of California
Press, 1983.
Essays in this collection are also listed
individually and refer to this citation.
OCLC # 8729070

2905 Snider, John Michael. The Treatment of
American Indians in Selected American Lit-
erature: A Radical Criticism. Ann Arbor,
MI., University Microfilms International,
1983.
Microfilm - PhD Thesis - University of
Illinois at Urbana-Champaign
OCLC # 11078057

Snow, Charles Ernest, 1910- . see 3342

2906 Snow, David H. The Identification of Puaray
Pueblo. In 0622, pp. 463-480.

2907 Snow, Dean R. <u>Archaeology and Ethnohistory</u>
      <u>in Eastern New York</u>. In 0712, pp. 107-
      112.

2908 _____. <u>The Archaeology of New England</u>. New
      York, Academic Press, 1980.
      New World Archaeological Record
      OCLC # 6734931

2909 _____. <u>The Archaeology of North America</u>.
      Photos by Werner Forman, New York, Viking
      Press, 1976.
      OCLC # 2123582

2910 _____. <u>The Archaeology of North America:</u>
      <u>American Indians and Their Origins</u>. Photos
      by Werner Forman. 1st pbk ed. with re-
      visions. New York, Thames and Hudson,
      1980, c1976.
      OCLC # 6759865

2911 _____. <u>Iroquois Prehistory</u>. In 0979, pp.
      241-257.

2912 _____. <u>:Keepers of the Game: and the Nature</u>
      <u>of Explanation</u>. In 1574, pp. 59-71.

2913 _____. <u>Native American Prehistory</u>. In
      2789, pp. 1-16.

2914 _____. <u>Native American Prehistory: A Crit-</u>
      <u>ical Bibliography</u>. Bloomington, Published
      for the Newberry Library by Indiana Univer-
      sity Press, 1979.
      Bibliographical Series
      OCLC # 5102117

      _____. <u>see also</u> 1098

2915 Snyder, Charles McCool. <u>Red and White on</u>
      <u>the New York Frontier: A Struggle for Sur-</u>
      <u>vival: Insights from the Papers of Erastus</u>
      <u>Granger, Indian Agent, 1807-1819</u>. Ed.
      with an intro. by Charles M. Snyder.
      Harrison, NY., Harbor Hill Books, 1978.
      OCLC # 4135919

2916 Snyder, Gary. <u>He Who Hunted Birds in His</u>
      <u>Father's Village: The Dimensions of a</u>
      <u>Haida Myth</u>. With a preface by Nathaniel

Tarn. Bolinas, CA., Grey Fox Press,
1979.
OCLC # 4004167

2917 Snyder, Joan. The Changing Context of an
      Andean Community. In 0078, pp. 20-29.

2918 Snydermen, George Simon, 1908- . Behind
      the Tree of Peace: A Sociological Analysis
      of Iroquois Warfare. New York, AMS Press,
      1979.
      Reprint of the author's thesis, University
      of Pennsylvania, 1948.
      OCLC # 4908090

2919 So Dreadful a Judgement: Puritan Responses
      to King Philip's War, 1676-1677. Edited
      by Richard Slotkin and James K. Folsom.
      Middletown CT., Wesleyan University
      Press, 1978.
      OCLC # 5449353

2920 Social Process in Maya Prehistory: Studies
      in Honor of Sir Eric Thompson. Edited by
      Norman Hammond, London, New York, Acad-
      emic Press, 1977.
      Essays in this collection are also listed
      individually and refer to this citation.
      OCLC # 4005796

2921 Society for American Archaeology. Seminars
      in Archaeology. Organized and edited by
      Robert Wauchope, Chairman Richard K.
      Beardsley et al. Salt Lake City, Society
      for American Archaeology. Millwood, NY.,
      Kraus Reprint, 1974.
      Memoirs of the Society for American Archae-
      ology no. 1. Suppl. to American Antiquity
      v. 22, no. 2, pt. 2, 1956. Reprint
      of the 1956 ed. CONTENTS: 1. An Archae-
      ological Classification of Cultural Contact
      Situations. 2. An Archaeological Approach
      to the Study of Cultural Stability. 3.
      The American Southwest: A Problem in Cult-
      ural isolation. 4. Functional and Evolu-
      tionary Implications of Community Pattern-
      ing
      OCLC # 1209657

      _____. see also 3071

2921.5   Society for the Propagation of the Gospel
          in New England. _A Further Manifestation of_
          the Progress of the Gospel Among the In-
          dians of New England. The Society, New
          York, Reprinted for J. Sabin, 1865.
          OCLC # 4945675

          _____.   see also 1713

          Society of Colonial Wars. Rhode Island. see
          2898

2922   Solecki, Ralph S. _Program for Archeological_
          Research on Western Long Island. New York
          State Archeological Association Bulletin 7,
          Aug. 1956, pp. 5-7. Millwood, NY.,
          Kraus Reprint, 1976.

2923   _Songs From This Earth on Turtle's Back: Con-_
          temporary American Indian Pottery. Edited
          by Joseph Bruchac. Greenfield Center,
          NY., Greenfield Review Press, 1983.
          OCLC # 10089966

          Sonnery, Jean-Louis. see 2603.5

2924   Sorkin, Alan L. _The Urban American Indian_.
          Lexington, MA., Lexington Books, 1978.
          OCLC # 4137396

2925   Sosin, Jack M. _The Use of Indians in the_
          War of the American Revolution: A Re-
          assessment of Responsibility. In 2304,
          pp. 96-110.
          Abridged and reprinted from _Canadian His-_
          torical Review v. 46, no. 2, June 1965,
          pp. 101-121.

2926   Sotheby, Parke Bernet New York. _Fine Amer-_
          ican Indian Art: Property of Various Own-
          ers Including the University of the Pacif-
          ic, California, A Canadian Private Col-
          lector. Sotheby Parke Bernet, Inc., NY.,
          Sotheby Parke Bernet, 1981.
          Exhibition from Sunday Oct. 18, 1981 to 3
          p. m. on Thursday, OCt. 22, 1981.
          Public Auction, Friday Oct 23, 1981 at
          10:15 a. m. and 2 p. m.
          OCLC # 8383560

2927   Soustelle,   Jacques,   1912- . The Olmecs:
       The Oldest Civilization in Mexico.   Trans.
       from the French by Helen R.   Lane.   Garden
       City,   NY.,   Doubleday,   1984.
       OCLC # 9082891

2928   South Carolina (Colony).   Documents Relating
       to Indian Affairs.   Edited by William L.
       McDowell,   Jr.,   Columbia,   South Carolina
       Archives Dept.,   1958-1970.
       2 v.   The Colonial Records of South Carol-
       ina Series 2,   The Indian Books.   CONTENTS"
       v.   1.   May 21,   1750 - Aug.   7,   1754.   v.
       2.   1754-1765.
       OCLC # 270726

2929   South Carolina (Colony).   Board of Commis-
       sioners of the Indian Trade.   Journals of
       the Commissioners of the Indian Trade,
       Sept.   20,   1710 - Aug.   29,   1718.   Edited
       by W.   L.   McDowell.   Columbia,   South
       Carolina Archives Dept.,   1955.
       OCLC # 2234206

2930   Southeastern Indians Since the Removal Era.
       Edited by Walter L.   Williams.   Athens,
       University of Georgia Press,   1979.
       OCLC # 4496245

       Southern Anthropological Society.   see   1133

       Southwest Parks and Monuments Association.
       see   1918

2931   Southwestern Indian Ritual Drama.   Edited by
       Charlotte J.   Frisbie.   Albuquerque,   Uni-
       versity of New Mexico Press,   1980.
       School of American Research based on an
       advanced seminar sponsored by the School of
       American Research,   April 3-8,   1978.
       OCLC # 5940836

2932   Spaulding,   ALbert C.   Multifactor Analysis
       of Association: An Application to Owasco
       Ceramics.   In 0710,   pp.   59-68.

2933   Spaulding,   John M.,   1944- . The Percep-
       tion of Mental Disorder among the Yaqui
       Indians of Tucson,   Arizona: An Explorat-
       ory Study.   Ann Arbor,   MI.,   University

Microfilms International, 1983.
Microfilm - PhD Thesis - University of
Arizona
OCLC # 11282499

2934 Spalding, Phinizy. Oglethorpe in America.
Chicago, University of Chicago Press,
1977.
OCLC # 2372461

2835 Speck, Frank Gouldsmith, 1881-1950. Beothuk and Micmac. New York, AMS Press,
1981.
Reprint of the 1922 ed. pub. by the
Museum of the American Indian, Heye Foundation, NY., which was issued as no. 22
of Indian Notes and Monographs, Misc.
OCLC # 6737157

2936 _____. Cherokee Dance and Drama. ... and
Leonard Broom, in collaboration with Will
West Long. Norman, University of Oklahoma
Press, 1983.
Civilization of the American Indian Series
OCLC # 9371427

2937 _____. Ethnology of the Yuchi Indians. New
York, AMS Press, 1980.
Reprint of the 1909 ed. pub. by Univer-
sity Museum, Philadelphia, which was is-
sued as v. 1, no. 1 of Anthropological
publications of the University Museum,
University of Pennsylvania
OCLC # 6737158

2938 _____. Family Hunting Territories and Soc-
ial Life of various Algonkian Bands of the
Ottawa Valley. Ottawa, Government Print-
ing Bureau, 1915.
Canada. Geological Survey. Memoir 70.
Anthropological Series no. 8
OCLC # 4160362

2939 _____. Myths and Folklore of the Timiskam-
ing Algonquin and Timagami Ojibwa. Ottawa,
Government Printing Bureau, 1915.
Canada. Geological Survey. Memoir 71.
Anthropological Series no. 9
OCLC # 4267235

2940 _____. The Nanticoke Community of Delaware.
New York, AMS Press, 1981.
Reprint of the 1915 ed. pub. by the
Museum of the American Indian, Heye Found-
ation, NY., which was issued as v. 2,
no. 4 of Contributions from the Museum of
the American Indian, Heye Foundation
OCLC # 7167701

2941 _____. Notes on the Mohegan and Niantic
Indians. In 3469, pp. 181-210.

2941.5 _____. Penn Wampum Belts., New York,
DeVinne Press, 1925.
Leaflets of the Museum of the American
Indian, Heye Foundation, no. 4. The
Technique of the belts, signed by W. C.
Orchard, pp. 17-20.
OCLC # 2809995

2942 _____. Penobscot Shamanism. New York,
Kraus Reprint, 1964.
Memoirs of the American Anthropological As-
sociation, v. 6, no. 4, 1919
OCLC # 1280800

2943 Speck, Gordon. Breeds and Half-breeds. New
York, C. N. Potter; distributed by
Crown Publishers, 1969.
OCLC # 88378

2944 Spector, Janet. Male/Female task Differentiation Among the Hidatsa: Toward the Development of an Archaeological Approach to
the Study of Gender. In 1438, pp. 77-99.

2945 Spielmann, Katherine Ann. Inter-Societal
Food Acquisition Among Egalitarian Societ-
ies: An Ecological Study of Plains/Pueblo
Interaction in the American Southwest. Ann
Arbor, MI., University Microfilms Inter-
national, 1982.
Microfilm - PhD Thesis - University of
Michigan
OCLC # 11543256

2946 Spence, Michael W. A Cultural Sequence from
the Sierra Madre of Durango, Mexico. In
0014, pp. 165-189.

2947   Spencer,   Robert Francis,   1917- . The
       Native Americans: Ethnology and Back-
       grounds of the North American Indians.   ...
       and Jesse D.   Jennings,   et al.   2nd ed.,
       New York,   Harper and Row,   1977.

       OCLC # 2525240

2948   _____.   Shamanism in Northwestern North
       America.   In 0111,   pp.   351-363.

       Spencer,   Virginia E.   see   1628

       Sperlich,   Elizabeth Katz,   1944- . see
       2949

2949   Sperlich,   Norbert,   1938- . Guatemalan
       Backstrap Weaving.   ... and Elizabeth Katz
       Sperlich;   with photos and drawings by the
       authors.   Norman,   University of Oklahoma
       Press,   1980.
       OCLC # 5846635

2950   Speth,   John D.   Bison Kills and Bone Counts:
       Decision Making by Ancient Hunters.   Chic-
       ago,   University of Chicago Press,   1983.
       Prehistoric Archaeology and Ecology
       OCLC # 8975384

2951   _____ and Gregory A.   Johnson.   Problems in
       the Use of Correlation for the Investiga-
       tion of Tool Kits and Activity Areas.   In
       0710,   pp.   35-57.

2952   Spicer,   Edward Holland,   1906- . European
       Expansion and the Enclavement of Southwest-
       ern Indians.   In 2304,   pp.   86-95.
       Abridged and reprinted from Arizona and the
       West v.   1,   no.   2,   Summer 1959,   pp.
       132-145.

2953   _____.   Political Incorporation and Cultural
       Change in New Spain: A Study in Spanish-
       Indian Relations.   In 0144,   pp.   107-135.

2954   _____.   Potam: A Yaqui Village in Sonora.
       Millwood, NY.,   Kraus Reprint,   1974.
       Memoirs of the American Anthropological As-
       sociation,   no.   77.   Suppl. to American
       Anthropologist v.   56,   no.   4,   pt.   2,

1954.
OCLC # 2748620

2955   Spicer, Edward Holland, 1906- . The
        Yaquis, a Cultural History. Tucson, Uni-
        versity of Arizona Press, 1980.
        OCLC # 5894371
2956   Spiess, Arthur E. Reindeer and Caribou
        Hunters. New York, Academic Press, 1979.
        Studies in Archaeology
        OCLC # 5239880

_____. see also 3456

Spiess, Fritz. see 0501

2957   Spinden, Herbert J. Diffusion of Maya As-
        tronomy. In 2105, pp. 162-178.

Spindler, George Dearborn. see 2278

2958   Spindler, Louise S. Menomini Women and
        Culture Change. Millwood, NY., Kraus
        Reprint, 1974
        Memoirs of the American Anthropologists
        Association no. 91. Suppl. to American
        Anthropologist v. 64, no. 1, pt. 2,
        1962.
        OCLC # 1627330

_____. see also 2278

2959   The Spirit of the Alberta Indian Treaties.
        Edited by Richard Price. Montreal: Insti-
        tute for Research on Public Policy; Toron-
        to: distributed by Butterworth & Co.,
        (Canada), 1979.
        OCLC # 6489577

2960   Spiro, Melford E. Ojibwa Culture and World
        View. In 1318, pp. 353-474.

2961   Sprague, Roderick. Tile Bead Manufacturing.
        In 1204, pp. 167-172.

2961.5 Spring Conference on Contemporary American
        Indian Issues, (2nd: 1978: University of
        California, Los Angeles). New Directions
        in Federal Indian Policy: A Review of the
        American Indian Policy Review Commission.

Los Angeles, American Indian Studies Center, University of California, 1979.
Contemporary American Indian Issues Series
v. 1. Originally presented as papers at a
conference sponsored by the American Indian
Studies Center, UCLA...in 1978. Essays in
this collection are also listed individually and refer to this citation.
OCLC # 6469833

2962 Spring Conference on Contemporary American
Indian Issues (4th: 1980: University of
California, Los Angeles). American Indian
Issues in Higher Education. American In-
dian Studies Center, Los Angeles, CA.,
American Indian Studies Center, 1981.
Contemporary American Issues Series no. 3
Essays in this collection are also listed
individually and refer to this citation.
OCLC # 7576796

2963 Spry, Irene M. The Tragedy of the Loss of
the Commons in Western Canada. In 0137,
pp. 203-228.
Revised and reprinted from C. P. R. C.
publication no. 6, Man on the Prairies
edited by Richard Allen.

2964 Spuhler, James N. Genetic Distances, Trees
and Maps of North American Indians. In
1052, pp. 135-183.

2965 Squier, E. G. (Ephraim George), 1821-
1888. The Serpent Symbol and the Worship
of the Reciprocal Principles of Nature in
America. Millwood, NY., Kraus Reprint,
1975.
Reprint of the 1851 ed. pub. by Putnam,
New York, which was issued as no. 1 of
American Archaeological Researches
OCLC # 1273395

2966 Stagg, Ronald M., William W. Vernon and
Bruce E. Raemsch. Wisconsin and Pre-
Wisconsin Stone Industries of New York
State and Related Tools from a Shop Site
Near Tula, Mexico. In 0905, pp. 41-67.

2967 Stanbury, W. T. Success and Failure: Indians in Urban Society. assisted by Jay H.

Siegel, Vancouver, University of British
Columbia Press, 1975.
OCLC # 1496129

2968 Standing Bear, Luther, Dakota Chief, 1868-
      1939. *My People the Sioux*. Edited by E.
      A. Brininstool, with an introd. by Rich-
      ard N. Ellis. Lincoln, University of
      Nebraska Press, 1975.
      OCLC # 1363618

2969 Stands in Timber, John, 1884-1967. *Chey-
      enne Memories*. ... and Margot Liberty,
      with the assistance of Robert M. Utley.
      New Haven, Yale University Press, 1967.
      Yale Western Americana Series v. 17
      OCLC # 946250

2970 Stanford, Dennis J. *Pre-Clovis Occupation
      South of the Ice Sheets*. In 0903, pp.
      65-72.

      _____. see also 1126

2971 Stanley, George Francis Gilman. *As Long As
      the Sun Shines and Water Flows: An Histor-
      ical Comment*. In 0137, pp. 1-26.

2972 Stanley, Henry M. (Henry Morton), 1841-
      1904. *My Early Travels and Adventures in
      America*. Lincoln, University of Nebraska
      Press, 1982.
      Reprint. Originally pub. *My Early Travels
      and Adventures in America and Asia* v. 1.
      London, S. Low, Marston, 1895.
      OCLC # 7924732

2973 Stanley, Sam. *American Indian Power and
      Powerlessness*. In 0111, pp. 237-242.

2974 Stanton, Max E. *Southern Louisiana Survi-
      vors: The Houma Indians*. In 2930, pp.
      90-109.

2975 Starbuck, David R. *The Middle Archaic in
      Central Connecticut: The Excavation of the
      Lewis-Walpole Site*. In 0901, pp. 5-37.

      _____. see also 0901

2976   Stark,   Barbara L.   An Ethnohistoric Model
       for Native Economy and Settlement Patterns
       in Southern Veracruz, Mexico.   In 2524,
       pp.   211-238.

2977   _____.   The Rise of Sedentary Life.   In
       0122,   pp.   345-372.

       _____.   see also   2524

       Starkman,   Neal.   see   1575

2978   Starna,   William A.   Late Archaic Lifeways
       and Archaeological Variation.   In 2519,
       pp.   74-83.

       State Historical Society of Wisconsin.   see
       0723

       Staubitz,   W.   W.   (Ward W.).   see   2197

2978.5 Stauss,   Joseph H.   A Critique of the Task
       Force Eight,   Final Report to the American
       Indian Policy Review Commission: Urban and
       Rural Non-Reservation Indians.   In 2961.5,
       pp.   87-98.

2979   Stearns,   Mary Lee.   Haida Culture in Cus-
       tody: the Massett Band.   Seattle,   Univer-
       sity of Washington Press;   a Vancouver,
       Douglas & McIntyre,   1981.
       Based on author's thesis,   UCLA,   1973
       OCLC # 7173366

2980   Steck,   Francis Borgia,   1884- .   The
       Jolliet-Marquette Expedition, 1673.   Glen-
       dale,   CA.,   for sale by A.   H.   Clark Co.,
       1928.   New York,   AMS Press,   1974.
       Also issued as Catholic University of Amer-
       ica.   Studies in American Church History v.
       6
       OCLC # 754356

2981   Stedman,   Raymond William.   Shadows of the
       Indian: Stereotypes in American Culture.
       Foreword by Rennard Strickland.   Norman,
       University of Oklahoma Press,   1982.
       OCLC # 8554267

2982   Steele,   William O.,   1917- .   The Cherokee

Crown of Tannassy. Winston-Salem, NC.,
J. F. Blair Publisher, 1977.
While attempting to charm the Cherokees
into loyalty to England, Sir Alexander
Cuming is offered by them the crown of the
Cherokee kingdom
OCLC # 3380342

2983 Steffan, Jerome O., 1942- . William
     Clark: Jeffersonian Man on the Frontier.
     Norman, University of Oklahoma Press,
     1977.
     OCLC # 2202488

2984 Stefon, Frederick Joseph. Native American
     Education and the New Deal. Ann Arbor,
     MI., University Microfilms International,
     1983.
     Microfilm - EdD Thesis - Pennsylvania State
     University
     OCLC # 13536566

2985 Stein, William W. Outside Contact and
     Cultural Stability in a Peruvian Highland
     Village. In 0078. pp. 15-19.

2986 Steinbring, Jack. Evidences of Old Copper
     in a Northern Transitional Zone. In 1467,
     pp. 47-75.

2987 _____. The Tie Creek Boulder Site of South-
     eastern Manitoba. In 1467, pp. 223-268.

     Steiner, Karl T. see 2813

2988 Steiner, Stanley. The Vanishing White Man.
     Drawings by Maria Garza. New York, Harper
     and Row, 1976.
     OCLC # 2224693

2989 Steltzer, Ulli. A Haida Potlatch. Foreword
     by Marjorie Halpin. Seattle, University
     of Washington Press, 1984.
     OCLC # 10779534

2990 Stenholm, Nancy A. Identification of House
     Structures in Mayan Archaeology: A Case
     Study in Kaminaljuku. In 2825, pp. 31-
     182.

Stephens, Christopher. <u>see</u> 3343

2991   Steponaitis, Vincas P. <u>Ceramics, Chron-</u>
       <u>ology, and Community Patterns: An Archae-</u>
       <u>ological Study at Moundville</u>. New York,
       Academic Press, 1983.
       Studies in Archaeology
       OCLC # 7947829

2992   _____. <u>Location Theory and Complex Chief-</u>
       <u>doms: A Mississippian Example</u>. In 2172,
       pp. 417-453.

2993   Sterud, Eugene L. <u>The Application of Small</u>
       <u>Site Methodology to the New York Archaic</u>.
       In 2519, pp. 53-73.

2994   Stevens, Alden. <u>Voice of the Native: Ari-</u>
       <u>zona's and New Mexico's Redskins Could</u>
       <u>Swing the Election in Those Two States</u>. In
       3335, pp. 90-92.
       Source - <u>New York Times</u>, Nov. 2, 1952

2995   Stevens, Paul Lawrence. <u>His Majesty's Sav-</u>
       <u>age Allies: British Policy and the North-</u>
       <u>ern Indians During the Revolutionary War,</u>
       <u>The Carleton Years, 1774-1778</u>. Ann Arbor,
       MI., University Microfilms International,
       1984.
       Microfilm - PhD Thesis - SUNY at Buffalo
       OCLC # 11047616

2996   Stevenson, A. <u>The Changing Canadian</u>
       <u>Eskimos</u>. In 1875, pp. 180-196.

2997   Stewart, Edgar Irving. <u>Custer's Luck</u>.
       Norman, University of Oklahoma Press,
       1955.
       1971 printing
       OCLC # 418228

2998   Stewart, Hilary. <u>Artifacts of the Northwest</u>
       <u>Coast Indians</u>. Written and illus. by Hil-
       ary Stewart. Saanichton, B. C., Hancock
       House Publishers, 1973.
       OCLC # 2722276

2999   _____. <u>Cedar: Tree of Life to the</u>
       <u>Northwest Coast Indians</u>. With drawings by
       the author. Vancouver, B. C., Douglas &

McIntyre: Seattle,   University of
Washington Press,   1984.
OCLC # 10950356

3000 Stewart,   Marilyn C.   Pits in the Northeast:
A Typological Analysis.   In 0712,   pp.
149-164.

3001 Stewart,   Omer Call,   1908- .   The Ghost
Dance.   In 0113,   pp.   179-187.

3002 _____.   Indians of the Great Basin.   Bloomington,   Published for the Newberry Library
by Indiana University Press,   1982.
Bibliographical Series
OCLC # 7975981

3003 _____.   The Native American Church.   In
0113,   pp.   188-196.

3004 _____.   Ute Peyotism;   a Study of a Cultural
Complex.   Boulder,   University of Colorado
Press,   1948.   New York,   Kraus Reprint
Corp.,   1972.
University of Colorado Studies.   Series in
Anthropology no.   1
OCLC # 552589

_____.   see also   0004

3005 Stewart,   T.   Dale.   Patterning of Skeletal
Pathologies and Epiderminology.   In 1052,
pp.   257-274.

3006 Stierlin,   Henri.   Art of the Aztecs and its
Origins.   New York,   Rizzoli,   1982.
Trans.   of L'art Azteque et Ses Origines
OCLC # 9118138

3007 _____.   Art of the Incas and its Origins.
New York,   Rizzoli,   1984.
Trans.   of L'art Inca et Ses Origines: de
Valdivia a Machu Picchu by Betty and Peter
Ross
OCLC # 10185554

3008 _____.   Art of the Maya: From the Olmecs to
the Toltec-Maya.   Trans.   from the French
by Peter Graham.   New York,   Rizzoli,
1981.

Trans. of L'art Maya
OCLC # 7913996

3009   Stile, T. E. Perishable Artifacts from
       Meadowcroft Rockshelter, Washington
       County, Southwestern Pennsylvania. In
       2111, pp. 130-141.

       Stinebeck, David C. see 2563

       Stirling, Matthew William, 1896-1975. see
       2266

3010   Stites, Sara Henry, 1877- . Economics of
       the Iroquois. New York, AMS Press, 1978.
       Originally presented as the author's the-
       sis, Bryn Mawr, 1904. Reprint of the
       1905 ed. printed by Press of New Era Print
       Co., Lancaster, PA., which was issued as
       v. 1, no. 3 of Bryn Mawr College mono-
       graphs, Monograph series.
       OCLC # 4500137

3011   Stocks, Anthony. Cocamilla Fishing: Patch
       Modification and Environmental Buffering in
       the Amazon Varzea. In 0023, pp. 239-267.

3012   Stoltman, James B., 1935- . Groton Plant-
       ation: An Archaeological Stufy od a South
       Carolina Locality. Cambridge, MA., Pea-
       body Museum of Archaeology and Ethnology,
       Harvard University, 1974.
       Peabody Museum Monographs no. 1
       OCLC # 1085955

       _____. see also 0443

3013   Stone, Doris, 1909- . Pre-Columbian
       Migration of Theobroma Cacao Linnaeus and
       Manihot Esculenta Crantz from Northern
       South America into Mesoamerica: A Partic-
       ally Hypothetical View. In 2521, pp. 67-
       83.

3014   _____. Pre-Columbian Man in Costa Rica.
       Cambridge, MA., Peabody Museum, 1977.
       OCLC # 3934529

3015   _____. The Ulua Valley and Lake Yojoa. In
       2105, pp. 386-394.

_____. see also 0123, 2521

Stone, Gaynell. see 2843

3016 Stone, Lyle M. Fort Michilimackinac, 1715-
      1781: An Archaeological Perspective on the
      Revolutionary Frontier. East Lansing, The
      Museum, Michigan State University, 1974.
      Anthropological Series v. 2. Pub. of
      Museum, Michigan State University
      OCLC # 1611551

3017 Storm, Hyemeyohsts. Song of Heyoehkah. San
      Francisco, Harper and Row, 1981.
      OCLC # 7202972

      Story, G. M. (George Morley), 1927- .
      see 2814

3018 Straight Tongue: Minnesota Indian Art from
      the Bishop Whipple Collections: An Exhibi-
      tion at the Science Museum of Minnesota,
      St. Paul, MN., October 17, 1980 - April
      30, 1981. Catalogue text, Louise B.
      Casagrande, Melissa M. Ringheim; photo-
      graphy Gary Mortenson, St. Paul, MN.,
      Science Museum of Minnesota, 1980.
      OCLC # 7573559

3019 Strausfeld, David M. Reformers in Conflict:
      The Pueblo Dance Controversy. In 0034,
      pp. 19-43.

      Street, Matthew H. see 0206

      Strickland, Edward Dinwoodie. see 0432

3020 Strickland, Rennard and Jack Gregory. Emmet
      Starr: Heroic Historian, Cherokee, 1870-
      1930. In 0080, pp. 105-114.

3021 _____. Fire and the Spirits: Cherokee Law
      from Clan to Court. Foreword by Neill H.
      Alford, Jr. Norman, University of Okla-
      homa Press, 1975.
      Civilization of the American Indian Series
      v. 133.
      OCLC # 1103010

3022 _____. Indians in Oklahoma. Norman, Uni-

versity of Oklahoma Press,   1980.
OCLC # 5799613

_____.   see also 0615,   3289

3023   Strong,   William Duncan,   1899-1962.   Anthro-
       pological Problems in Central America.   In
       2105,   pp.   377-385.

3024   _____.   Paracas, Nazca and Tiahuanacoid
       Cultural Relationships in South Coastal
       Peru.   Salt Lake City,   Society for Ameri-
       can Archaeology,   1957.   Millwood,   NY.,
       Kraus Reprint,   1974.
       Memoirs of the Society for American Archae-
       ology no.   13.   Suppl. to American Antiqu-
       ity v.   22,   no.   4,   pt.   2.   Bound with
       Society for American Archaeology Seminars
       in Archaeology,   1955.
       OCLC # 1428223

3025   Stross,   Brian.   Tzeltal Conceptions of
       Power.   In 0111,   pp.   271-285.

3026   _____.   Tzeltal Tales of Demons and Mon-
       sters.   Columbia Museum of Anthropology,
       Universisty of Missouri - Columbia,   1978.
       Museum Briefs no.   24.   English and Tzeltal
       OCLC # 4435631

       _____.   see also 1954

3027   Struever,   Stuart.   Koster: Americans in
       Search of their Prehistoric Past.   ... and
       Felicia Antonelli Holton,   Garden City,
       NY.,   Anchor Press/Doubleday,   1979.
       OCLC # 4195390

3028   Struggle and Survival in Colonial America.
       Edited by David G.   Sweet and Gary B.
       Nash.   Berkeley,   University of California
       Press,   1981.
       OCLC # 6250866

3029   Stryd,   Arnoud.   Prehistoric Mobile Art from
       the Mid-Fraser and Thompson River Areas.
       In 1562,   pp.   167-181.

3030   Stuart,   Josefa.   Images of American Indian
       Art.   ... and Robert H.   Ashton,   Jr.   New

York,   Walker & co.,   1977.
A Walker Gallery Book
OCLC # 3598988

3031 Stuart, Paul, 1943- . The Indian Office:
      Growth and Development of American Institu-
      tion, 1865-1900. Ann Arbor, MI.,   Uni-
      versity Microfilms International Research
      Press,   1979.
      Studies in American History and Culture no.
      12.
      OCLC # 5726706

3032 Stuckenrath, R. The Stratigraphy,   Cultural
      Features and Chronology at Meadowcroft
      Rockshelter, Washington County,   South-
      western Pennsylvania. In 2111, pp.   69-
      90.

3033 Studies in American Indian Literature:
      Critical Essays and Course Designs. Edited
      by Paula Gunn Allen, New York, Modern
      Language Association, 1983.
      OCLC # 8628563

3034 Studies of Ancient Tollan: A Report of the
      University of Missouri Tula Archaeological
      Project. Edited by Richard A. Diehl.
      Columbia, Dept. of Anthropology, Univer-
      sity of Missouri - Columbia, 1974.
      University of Missouri Monographs in An-
      thropology no. 1.
      OCLC # 1342388

3035 Studies on Iroquoian Culture. Edited by
      Nancy Bonvillain. Redge, NH., Pierce
      College, 1980.
      Occasional Publications in Northeastern
      Anthropology no. 6.
      OCLC # 6365755

3036 Sturgis, Thomas. Common Sense View of the
      Sioux War, With True Method of Treatment,
      as Opposed to Both the Exterminative and
      the Sentimental Policy. Cheyenne, WY.,
      Leader Stream Book and Job Printing House,
      1877.
      One reel microfilm - Library of Congress,
      Class E - Misc. monographs and Pamphlets,

         Shelf #44140-44175,   #44143.
         OCLC # 13933878

3037   Sturtevant, William C. _Animals and Disease
       in Indian Belief_. In 1574, pp. 177-188.

3038   _____.   _The Cherokee Frontiers, the French
       Revolution and William Augutus Bowles_. In
       0547, pp. 61-91.

3039   _____.   _The Last of the South Florida Abo-
       rigines_. In 3071, pp. 141-162.

3040   _____.   _Seneca Masks_. In 2502, pp. 39-47.

3041   _____.   _A Structural Sketch of Iroquois
       Ritual_. In 0979, pp. 133-152.

3042   _____.   _Tribe and State in the 16th and 20th
       Centuries_. In 0796, pp. 3-16.

       _____.   see also 1330

3043   Styles, Bonnie Wharley, 1950- . _Faunal
       Exploitation and Resource Selection: Early
       Late Woodland Subsistence in the Lower Il-
       linois Valley_. Evanston, IL., Northwest-
       ern University Archeological Program,
       1981.
       Scientific Paper - Northwestern University
       Archeological Program, v. 3.
       OCLC # 7169361

3044   _____.   _Modoc Rock Shelter Revisited_. In
       0124, pp. 261-297.

3045   Stymeist, David. _Migration and a Local
       Social System_. In 0479, pp. 371-386.

3046   Suarez, Jorge A. _Mesoamerican Indian Lan-
       guages_. New York, Cambridge University
       Press, 1983.
       Cambridge Language Surveys
       OCLC # 8034800

3047   _The Subarctic Fur Trade: Native Social and
       Economic Adaptations_. Edited by Shepard
       Krech III. Vancouver, University of Brit-
       ish Columbia, 1984.
       Essays in this collection are also listed

individually and refer to this citation.
OCLC # 11143556

3048   Sublett, Audrey J. The Sawmill Road Ossu-
       ary, Clarence, New York. New York State
       Archeological Association Bulletin 41,
       Nov. 1967, pp. 17-22. Millwood, NY.,
       Kraus Reprint, 1976.

3049   _____. Some Examples of Accidental and De-
       liberate Human Skeletal Modification in the
       Northeast. New York State Archeological
       Association Bulletin 50, Nov. 1970, pp.
       14-26. Millwood, NY., Kraus Reprint,
       1976.

3050   Such, Peter. Vanished Peoples: The Archaic
       Dorset and Beothuk People of Newfoundland.
       Toronto, NC Press, 1978.
       OCLC # 4281134

       Sudbury, Byron. see 1460

       Suffolk County Archaeological Association.
       see 0596, 0906, 2815

3050.5 Sugden, John, 1947- . Tecumseh's Last
       Stand. Norman, University of Oklahoma
       Press, 1985.
       OCLC # 12163188

3051   Sullivan, Thomas. Journal of the Operations
       of the American War, 1778. Manuscript in
       American Philosophical Society Library,
       Philadelphia, PA. One reel microfilm pro-
       vided by American Philosophical Society.
       For detailed description see the Freeman
       Guide item #173.

       Sullivan Centennial, Seneca Co., NY. see
       3331

3052   Sun, Pao-Kong. SCAPULA System: A Comput-
       erized Retrieval System for Archaeological
       Data from the Upper Wabash Drainage. Ann
       Arbor, MI., University Microfilms Inter-
       national, 1984.
       Microfilm - PhD Thesis - Ball State
       University
       OCLC # 11787893

Sun Valley Center for the Arts and
Humanities. see 1556

3053 Surtees, Robert J., 1941- . Canadian
Indian Policy: A Critical Bibliography.
Bloomington, Published for the Newberry
Library Center for the History of the Amer-
ican Indian, 1982.
Bibliographical Series
OCLC # 7975996

3054 _____. Indian Land Cessions in Upper Canada, 1815-1830. In 0137, pp. 65-84.

3055 _____. The Iroquois in Canada. In 1463,
pp. 67-83.

3056 Sutherland, Janet Lynn, 1948- . Aufgeh-
obene Welten: Orality and World View in
the Fictional Works on N. Scott Momaday,
Leslie Marmon-Silko and James Welch. Ann
Arbor, MI., University Microfilms Inter-
national, 1984.
Microfilm - PhD Thesis - University of
Oregon
OCLC # 11568004

3057 Suttles, Wayne. Productivity and its Con-
straints: A Coastal Salish Case. In 1562,
pp. 67-87.

3058 Sutton, Imre, 1928- . Indian Land Tenure:
Bibliographical Essays and a Guide to the
Literature. New York, Clearwater Pub.
Co., 1975.
The Library of Indian Affairs
OCLC # 1582392

3059 Svaldi, David Paul, 1948- . Symbols of
Sand Creek: A Case Study in the Rhetoric
of Extermination. Ann Arbor, MI., Uni-
versity Microfilms International, 1983.
Microfilm - PhD Thesis - Northwestern
University
OCLC # 11658377

3060 Svingen, Orlan J. The Administrative History of the Northern Cheyenne Indian Reservation, 1877-1900. Ann Arbor, MI., University Microfilms International, 1982.

Microfilm - PhD Thesis - University of
Toledo
OCLC # 9930589

Swadesh, Morris, 1909-1967. <u>see</u> 2758

3061 Swaggerty, William Royce, 1951- . <u>Beyond
Bimini: Indian Responses to European In-
cursions into the Spanish Borderlands,
1513-1600</u>. Ann Arbor, MI., University
Microfilms International, 1981.
Microfilm - PhD Thesis - University of
California - Santa Barbara
OCLC # 9564945

3062 _____. <u>Spanish - Indian Relations, 1513-
1821</u>. In 2789, pp. 36-78.

_____. <u>see also</u> 0831

3063 Swanton, John Reed, 1873-1958. <u>An Early
Account of the Choctaw Indians</u>. New York,
Kraus Reprint, 1964.
Memoirs of the American Anthropological As-
sociation, v. 5, 1918 no. 22.
OCLC # 554876

3064 _____. <u>Primitive American History</u>. In
0110, pp. 5-41.

Swarm, Michael. <u>see</u> 2831.5

Sweet, David G. <u>see</u> 3028

3065 Sweetman, Rosemary. <u>Prehistoric Pottery
from Coastal Sinaloa and Nayarit</u>. In 0231,
pp. 68-82.

3066 Swigart, Edmund K. <u>The Prehistory of the
Indians of Western Connecticut. Part 1,
9000-1000 B. C.</u> Washington, CT., Shep-
aug Valley Archaeological Society, 1974.
A Research Report of the Shepaug Valley
Archaeological Society
OCLC # 2028146

Swizter, Ronald R. <u>see</u> 1986

3066.5 Sword, Wiley. <u>President Washington's Indian War: The Struggle for the Old North-</u>

west,   1790-1795.   Norman,   University of
Oklahoma Press,   1985.
OCLC # 12215505

3067   Sylvester,   Nathaniel Bartlett,   1825-1894.
       Historical Sketches of Northern New York
       and the Adirondack Wilderness.   Harrison,
       NY.,   Harbor Hill Books,   1973.
       Reprint of the 1877 ed.   pub.   by William
       H. Young,   Troy,   NY.
       OCLC # 618380

3068   Symposium on Andean Kinship and Marriage,
       Toronto,   Ont.,   1972.   _Andean Kinship and_
       Marriage.   Edited by Ralph Bolton and Enri-
       que Mayer.   Washington,   American Anthropo-
       logical Association,   1977.
       American Anthropological Association
       Special Pub.   no.   7.
       OCLC # 3608157

3069   Syms,   Leigh.   _The McKean Complex in_
       Manitoba.   In 1467,   pp.   123-138.

3070   Szathmary,   Emoke J.   E.   _Blood Groups of_
       Siberians,   Eskimos and Subarctic and
       Northwest Coast Indians: The Problems of
       Origins and Genetic Relationships.   In
       1052,   pp.   185-209.

3071   _Tacachale: Essays on the Indians of Florida_
       and Southeastern Georgia During the Histor-
       ic Period.   Edited by Jerald Milanich and
       Samuel Proctor.   Gainesville,   University
       Presses of Florida,   1978.
       Ridley P.   Bullen Monographs in Anthropol-
       ogy and History no.   4.   Papers presented
       in abbreviated form at a symposium held as
       part of the 38th annual meeting of the Soc-
       iety for American Archaeology,   San Fran-
       cisco,   May 1973;   with one additional pap-
       er.   Essays in this collection are also
       listed individually and refer to this cita-
       tion.
       OCLC # 3380362

3071.5   Tacheenie-Campoy,   Glory.   _The Ethnics of_
         Portraying Navajo Religious Themes in Sand-
         painting as Art.   In 2831.5,   pp.   153-157.

3072 Taggart, James M., 1941- . <u>Action Group</u>
      <u>Recruitment: A Nahuat Case</u>. In 0958,
      pp. 137-153.

      _____. <u>see also</u> 0958

3073 Talbot, Steve. <u>Roots of Oppression: The</u>
      <u>American Indian Question</u>. New York, In-
      ternational Publishers,   1981.
      OCLC # 7576005

3074 Tanner, Adrian, 1937- . <u>Bringing Home</u>
      <u>Animals: Religious Ideology and Mode of</u>
      <u>Production of the Mistassini Cree Hunters</u>.
      New York, St. Martin's Press, 1979.
      OCLC # 4832552

3075 _____. <u>Canadian Indians and the Policy of</u>
      <u>Dependency</u>. In 2485, pp. 1-35.

3076 _____. <u>The Hidden Feast: Eating and Ideol-</u>
      <u>ogy Among the Mistassine Cree</u>. In 0068,
      pp. 291-313.

      _____. <u>see also</u> 2485

3077 Tanner, Clara Lee. <u>Apache Indian Baskets</u>.
      Tucson, University of Arizona Press,
      1982.
      OCLC # 8451669

3078 _____. <u>Indian Baskets of the Southwest</u>.
      Tucson, University of Arizona Press,
      1983.
      OCLC # 9646350

      _____. <u>see also</u> 2057

3079 Tanner, Helen Hornbeck. <u>The Ojibwas: A</u>
      <u>Critical Bibliography</u>. Bloomington, Pub-
      lished for the Newberry Library by Indiana
      University Press,   1976.
      Bibliographical Series
      OCLC # 2331655

3080 Tantaquidgeon, Gladys. <u>A Study of Delaware</u>
      <u>Indian Medicine Practice and Folk Beliefs</u>.
      New York, AMS Press, 1980.
      Reprint of the 1942 ed. pub. by Penn-

sylvania Historical Commission,   Harrisburg
OCLC # 6737160

3081   Tarn,   Nathaniel.   Robert Redfield.   In 3139,
       pp.   255-286.

3081.5 Tate,   Michael L.   The Indians of Texas:
        An Annotated Research Bibliography.
        Metuchen,   NJ.,   Scarecrow Press,   1986.
        Native American Bibliography Series no.   9.
        OCLC # 12557377

3082   Taylor,   Allan Ross.   Non-verbal Communica-
       tion in Aboriginal North America: The
       Plains Sign Language.   In 0008,   pp.   223-
       244.

3083   Taylor,   Graham D.,   1944- . The New Deal
       and American Indian Tribalism: The Admin-
       istration of the Indian Reorganization Act,
       1934-35.   Lincoln,   University of Nebraska
       Press,   1980.

3084   Taylor,   Lyda Averill Paz.   Plants Used as
       Curatives by Certain Southeastern Tribes.
       New York,   AMS Press,   1978.
       Reprint of the 1940 ed.   pub.   by the Bot-
       anical Museum of Harvard University,   Cam-
       bridge,   MA.
       OCLC # 4196109

3085   Taylor,   R.   E.   (Royal Ervin),   1938- .
       Archaeometric Studies in West Mexican
       Archaeology.   In 0231,   pp   215-224.

3086   _____.   Dating Methods in New World
       Archaeology.   In 0577,   pp.   1-27.

       _____.   see also 0577

3087   Taylor,   Theodore W.   American Indian Policy.
       Mt.   Airy,   MD.,   Lomond Publications,
       1983.
       OCLC # 10116699

3088   _____.   The Bureau of Indian Affairs.   Fore-
       word by Phillip Martin.   Boulder,   CO.,
       Westview Press,   1984.
       Westview Library of Federal Departments,

Agencies and Systems
OCLC # 9323645

Taylor, William E. Jr. see 1844

3089   Tedlock, Barbara. Songs of the Zuñi Kachina
       Society: Composition, Rehearsal, and
       Performance. In 2931, pp. 7-35.

3090   Tedlock, Dennis, 1939- . Finding the Cen-
       ter; Narrative Poetry of the Zuñi Indians.
       Trans. by Dennis Tedlock. From perform-
       ances in the Zuni by Andrew Peynetsa and
       Walter Sanchez. New York, Dial Press,
       1972.
       OCLC # 278003

3091   _____. On the Translation of Style in Oral
       Narrative. In 2904, pp. 57-77.
       Reprinted from Journal of American Folklore
       v. 84, no. 331, 1971, pp. 114-133.

       _____. see also 2493

3092   Teeter, Karl V. American Indian Linguist-
       ics. In Annual Review of Anthropology v.
       1, 1972, pp. 411-424.

3093   Tehanetorens. Tales of the Iroquois. Roose-
       veltown, NY., Akwesasne Notes, 1976.
       Six Nations Indian Museum Series. Many of
       the folktales in this collection are also
       available individually in the college's
       collection, most authored by Aren Akweks.
       OCLC # 3658775

3094   Teit, James Alexander, 1864- . Sign Lan-
       guage of the Salishan Tribes of the Western
       Plateaus. In 0008, pp. 77-90.
       Reprinted from U. S. Bureau of American
       Ethnology, 45th Annual Report, Smithson-
       ian Press, 1930, pp. 135-150, 261,
       373, 396.

3095   _____. Traditions of the Thompson River
       Indians of British Columbia. Collected and
       annotated by James Teit; with introd. by
       Franz Boas. Boston, Published for the
       American Folk-Lore Society by Houghton
       Mifflin Co., 1898. New York, Kraus Re-

print Co., 1969.
Memoirs of the American Folk-Lore Society
v. 6
OCLC # 1847411

3096 Teotihuacan and Kaminaljuhu: A Study of Pre-
      historic Culture, Contact. Edited by
      William T. Sanders and Joseph W. Michels.
      University Park, Pennsylvania State Uni-
      versity Press, 1977.
      Pennsylvania State University Press Mono-
      graph Series on Kaminaljuyu. Essays in
      this collection are also listed individual-
      ly and refer to this citation.
      OCLC # 3327234

      Terrell, Donna M. see 3098

3097 Terrell, John Upton, 1900- . The Arrow
      and the Cross: A History of the American
      Indian and the Missionaries. Santa Bar-
      bara, CA., Capra Press, 1979.
      OCLC # 5101803

3098 _____. Indian Women of the Western Morning;
      Their Life in Early America. ... and Donna
      M. Terrell. New York, Dial Press, 1974.
      OCLC # 934719

3099 _____. Land Grab: The Truth About "The
      Winning of the West". New York, Dial
      Press, 1972.
      OCLC # 329000

3100 _____. The Plains Apache. New York,
      Crowell, 1975.
      OCLC # 1288353

      Terry, Alfred Howe, 1827-1890. see 0158

3101 Terry, Rhonda Dale. Diet, Anthropometric
      Characteristics, and Diabetes Related At-
      titudes and Knowledge Among Women Residing
      in the Eastern Cherokee Township of Snow-
      bird. Ann Arbor, MI., University Micro-
      films International, 1982.
      Microfilm - PhD Thesis - University of Ten-
      nessee, Knoxville
      OCLC # 9148665

3102 Theler, James Louis. <u>Woodland Tradition
      Economic Strategies: Animal Resource Util-
      ization in Southwestern Wisconsin and
      Northeastern Iowa</u>. Ann Arbor, MI., Uni-
      versity Microfilms International, 1983.
      Microfilm - PhD Thesis - University of
      Wisconsin - Madison
      OCLC # 10199465

      Thomas, Alfred Barney. <u>see</u> 0697

3103 Thomas, David Hurst. <u>The Archaeology of
      Hidden Cave, Nevada</u>. With contributions
      by Nancy K. Bernstein. illus. by Dennis
      O'Brien and Nicholas Amorosi. New York,
      American Museum of Natural History, 1985.
      Anthropological Papers of the American Mus-
      eum of Natural History, v. 61, pt. 1.
      OCLC # 12284050

3104 _____. <u>The Archaeology of Monitar Valley</u>.
      With contributions by Robert R. Kautz, et
      al. New York, American Museum of Natural
      History, 1983.
      Anthropological Papers of the American Mus-
      eum of Natural History v. 58, pt. 1, v.
      59, pt. 1.
      OCLC # 10046207

3105 _____. <u>On Steward's Models of Shoshonean
      Sociopolitical Organizations: A Great
      Bias in the Basin?</u> In 0796, pp. 59-68.

3106 _____. <u>Prehistoric Pinon Ecotone Settle-
      ments of the Upper Reese River Valley,
      Central Nevada</u>. ... and Robert L. Bett-
      inger with contributions by Brian W. Hat-
      off. New York, American Museum of Natural
      History, 1976.
      Anthropological Papers of the American Mus-
      eum of Natural History v. 53, pt. 3
      OCLC # 2865310

      _____. <u>see also</u> 0112, 1850, 2441

3107 Thomas, David John, 1945- . <u>Order Without
      Government: The Society of the Pemon In-
      dians of Venezuela</u>. Urbana, University of
      Illinois Press, 1982.
      OCLC # 7274681

Thomas,   Davis.   see   3427

3108   Thomas,   Peter A.   The Riverside District,
        the Wmeco Site,   and Suggestions for Arche-
        ological Modeling.   In 0901,   pp.   73-95.

3109   Thomas Gilcrease Institute of American His-
        tory and Art.   Treasures of the Old West:
        Painting and Sculpture from the Thomas Gil-
        crease Institute of American History and
        Art.   Peter H.   Hassrick.   New York,
        Abrams,   1984.
        Published in connection with an exhibition
        in 1984 at the Denver Art Museum and the
        Buffalo Bill Historical Center in Cody,
        Wyoming.
        OCLC # 9830896

3110   Thompson,   David,   1770-1857.   Narrative.   A
        Fascim.   ed.   New York,   Greenwood Press,
        1968.
        Reprint of the 1916 ed.   under title David
        Thompson's Narrative of his Explorations in
        Western America,   1784-1812.   Champlain
        Society Pub.   no.   12.
        OCLC # 21648

3111   Thompson,   Gerald.   The Army and the Navajo.
        Tucson,   University of Arizona Press,
        1976.
        OCLC # 2146459

3112   Thompson,   John Eric Sidney,   Sir,   1898-
        1975.   Archaeological Problems of the Low-
        land Maya.   In 2105,   pp.   126-138.

3113   _____.   Maya History and Religion.   Norman,
        University of Oklahoma Press,   1970.
        OCLC # 177832

3114   _____.   A Proposal for Constituting a Maya
        Subgroup,   Cultural and Linguistic in the
        Peten and Adjacent Regions.   In 0109,   pp.
        3-42.

        _____.   see also   2790,   2920

3114.5 Thompson,   Mark.   Nurturing the Forked
        Tree: Conception and Formation of the

American Indian Policy Review Commission.
In 2961.5 pp.   5-18.

3115 Thompson, Neil B., 1921- . Crazy Horse
      Called them Walk-a-Heaps: The Story of the
      Foot Soldiers in the Prairie Indian Wars.
      St.   Cloud, MN.,   North Star Press, 1979.
      OCLC # 5454451

3116 Thornton, Russell. American Indian Studies
      as an Academic Discipline: A Revisit. In
      2926, pp. 3-10.

3117 _____. Bibliography of Social Science Re-
      search and Writings on American Indians.
      ... and Mary K. Grasmick. Minneapolis,
      Center for Urban and Regional Affairs,
      University of Minnesota, 1979.
      Publication/Center for Urban and Regional
      Affairs, no. 79-1
      OCLC # 4194524

3118 _____. Contemporary American Indians. In
      2789, pp. 162-178.

3119 _____. Sociology of American Indians: A
      Critical Bibliography. ... and Mary K.
      Grasmick. Bloomington, Published for the
      Newberry Library by Indiana University
      Press, 1980.
      OCLC # 6891162

3120 _____. The Urbanization of American In-
      dians: A Critical Bibliography. ... and
      Gary D. Sandefur, Harold G. Grasmick.
      Bloomington, Published for the Newberry
      Library by Indiana University Press, 1982.
      Bibliographical Series
      OCLC # 7975991

3121 Thrapp, Dan L. The Conquest of Apacheria.
      Norman, University of Oklahoma Press,
      1967.
      OCLC # 418627

3122 Thwaites, Reuben Gold, 1853-1913. How
      George Rogers Clark Won the Northwest: And
      Other Essays in Western History. Williams-
      town, MA., Corner House, 1978.
      Reprint of the 1930 ed.

OCLC # 6032857

2123   Tiger, Peggy, 1943- . <u>The Life and Art of</u>
       <u>Jerome Tiger: War to Peace, Death to</u>
       <u>Life</u>. ... and Molly Babock; foreword by
       Paul A. Rossi. Norman, University of
       Oklahoma Press, 1980.
       This volume contains many color reproduc-
       tions of the artists works
       OCLC # 6555815

3124   <u>Tijeras Canyon: Analysis of the Past</u>. Edit-
       ed by Linda S. Cordell, Albuquerque,
       Maxwell Museum of Anthropology, University
       of New Mexico Press, 1980.
       Maxwell Museum of Anthropology Publication
       series
       OCLC # 6790566

3125   Tiller, Veronica E. Velarde. <u>The Jicarilla</u>
       <u>Apache Tribe, A History, 1846-1970</u>. Lin-
       coln, University of Nebraska Press, 1983.
       OCLC # 8389799

3126   Tillett, Leslie, 1915- . <u>Wind on the Buf-</u>
       <u>falo Grass: The Indians' Own Account of</u>
       <u>the Battle of the Little Big Horn, and the</u>
       <u>Death of Their Life on the Plains</u>. Col-
       lected and edited by ..., New York, Cro-
       well, 1976.
       OCLC # 2089495

3127   Timberlake, Henry, d. 1765. <u>Memoirs of</u>
       <u>Lieut. Henry Timberlake</u>. New York, Arno
       Press, 1971, c1927.
       First published in 1765 as <u>The Memoirs of</u>
       <u>Lieut. Henry Timberlake</u>, reprinted in
       1927 with the title <u>Lieut. Henry Timber-</u>
       <u>lake's Memoirs</u>. The First American
       Frontier
       OCLC # 267394

       Timberlake, Janice. <u>see</u> 1346

3128   Tixier, Jacques. <u>Glossary for the Descrip-</u>
       <u>tion of Stone Tools: With Special Refer-</u>
       <u>ence to the Epipalaeolithic of the Maghreb</u>.
       Trans. by M. H. Newcomer. Pullman,
       WA., Newsletter of Lithic Technology,
       Washington State University Press, 1974.

Newsletter of Lithic Technology: a special
publication no.   1.   First appeared in
Typologie de L'espipaleolithique du Maghreb
1963.
OCLC # 4426198

3129 Tobias,   John L.   Protection,   Civilization,
      Assimilation: An Outline History of Can-
      ada's Indian Policy.   In 0137,   pp.   39-55.
      Reprinted from Western Canadian Journal of
      Anthropology v.   6,   no.   2,   1976.

3130 Todd,   Lawrence C.,   1954- .   The Honer
      Site: Taphonomy on an Early Holocene Bison
      Bonebed.   Ann Arbor,   MI.,   University
      Microfilms International,   1983.
      Microfilm - PhD Thesis - University of New
      Mexico
      OCLC # 11227152

3131 Toelken,   Barre.   How Many Sheep Will it
      Hold?   In 2818,   pp.   9-24.

3132 Tooker,   Elisabeth.   Eighteenth Century Pol-
      itical Affairs and the Iroquois League.   In
      1583,   pp.   1-12.

3133 _____.   Ely S.   Parker,   Seneca,   1828-1895.
      In 0080,   pp.   15-30.

3134 _____.   The Indians of the Northeast,   a
      Critical Bibliography.   Bloomington,   Pub-
      lished for the Newberry Library by Indiana
      University Press,   1978.
      Bibliographic Series
      OCLC # 4004975

3135 _____.   The Iroquois Ceremonial of Midwint-
      er.   Syracuse,   Syracuse University Press,
      1970.
      OCLC # 88494

3136 _____.   The Many Faces of Masks and Masking:
      Discussion.   In 2502,   pp.   12-20.

3137 _____.   Women in Iroquois Society.   In 0979,
      pp.   109-123.

      _____.   see also   0796,   2279

3138 Tolstoy, Paul. Western Mesoamerica Before
A. D. 900. In 0577, pp. 241-284.

Toole, Kenneth Ross, 1920- . see 0638

3139 Totems and Teachers: Perspectives on the
History of Anthropology. Sydel Silverman,
editor. New York, Columbia University
Press, 1981.
Essays in this collection are also listed
individually and refer to this citation.
OCLC # 6487253

3140 Toulouse, Carmie Lynn. Notes on the Summer
Migration of Eastern Reservation Navajos.
In 0622, pp. 481-489.

3141 Townsend, Joan B. Pre-contact Political
Organization and Slavery in Aleut Societies. In 0796, pp. 120-132.

3142 Tozzer, Alfred M. (Alfred Marston), 1877-
1954. A Comparative Study of the Mayas and
the Lacandones. New York, AMS Press,
1978.
Reprint of the 1907 ed. pub. for the
Archaeological Institute of America by
Macmillan, New York, as the 1902-1905 Report of the Fellow in American Archaeology
OCLC # 3914104

3143 _____. Preliminary Study of the Ruins of
Tikal, Guatemala; A Report of the Peabody
Museum Expedition, 1909-1910. With 54
illus. in the text and twenty-three
plates. Cambridge, MA., The Museum,
1913. New York, Kraus Reprint, 1976.
Harvard University. Peabody Museum of
American Archaeology and Ethnology Memoirs
v. 5, no. 3.
OCLC # 125476

3144 Traditional Literature of the American Indian: Texts and Interpretations. Compiled
and edited by Karl Kroeber. Lincoln, University of Nebraska Press, 1981.
OCLC # 6487141

3145 Trafzer, Clifford E. The Kit Carson Campaign: The Last Great Navajo War. Norman,

University of Oklahoma Press, 1982.
OCLC # 7924967

3146 **Transition to Statehood in the New World**.
Edited by Grant D. Jones, Robert R.
Kautz. New York, Cambridge University
Press, 1981.
New Directions in Archaeology. Based on
papers presented at a conference held at
Hamilton College, Clinton, NY., Jan.
19-21, 1979.
OCLC # 7278205

3147 Trautmann, Wolfgang. **The Impact of Spanish
Conquest on the Development of the Cultural
Landscape in Tlaxcala, Mexico**. In 0978,
pp. 253-276.

3148 **Treaties, Land Cessions and Other U. S.
Congressional Documents Relative to Ameri-
can Indian Tribes. Treaties Between the
Tribes of the Great Plains and the United
States of America: The Crow, 1825-1912**.
Assembled by George E. Fay. Greeley,
CO., University of Northern Colorado,
Museum of Anthropology, 1982.
University of Northern Colorado, Museum of
Anthropology, Occasional Papers in Anthro-
pology. Ethnology Series no. 23.
OCLC # 8875976

3149 **Treaty Held With the Ohio Indians at Carlisle
in October, 1753**. One reel microfilm provided by American Philosophical Society,
Philadelphia, 16pps. For detailed description see the Freeman Guide #176.

3150 Trelease, Allen W. **Dutch Treatment of the
American Indians, With Particular Reference to New Netherland**. In 0144, pp. 47-
59.

3151 Trennert, Robert A. **Indian Traders on the
Middle Border: The House of Ewing, 1827-
54**. Lincoln, University of Nebraska
Press, 1981.
OCLC # 6891401

3152 Trento, Salvatore Michael. **The Search for
Lost America: Mysteries of the Stone Ruins**

in the U. S. Harmondsworth, Eng., New
York, Penguin Books, 1979.
OCLC # 4933091

3153 **Tribes of the Amazon Basin in Brazil 1972:
Report for Aborigines Protection Society.**
Edwin Brooks, et al., London, C.
Knight, 1973.
OCLC # 944147

3154 Trigger, Bruce G. **The Children of Aataents-
ic: A History of the Huron People to 1660.**
Montreal, McGill Queen's University Press,
1976.
OCLC # 3344685

3155 _____. **Indian and White History: Two
Worlds or One?** In 0979, pp. 17-33.

3156 _____. **Natives and Newcomers: Canada's
"Heroic Age" Reconsidered.** Kingston,
McGill Queen's University Press, 1985.
OCLC # 12728383

3157 _____. **Ontario Native People and the Epi-
demics of 1634-1640.** In 1574, pp. 19-38.

3158 Trowbridge, C. C. (Charles Christopher),
1800-1883. **Shawnese Traditions, C. C.
Trowbridge's Account.** Edited by Vernon
Kinietz and Erminie W. Voegelin. New
York, AMS Press, 1980.
Reprint of the 1939 ed. pub. by Univer-
sity of Michigan Press, Ann Arbor, which
was issued as no. 9 of Occasional Contrib-
utions of the Museum of Anthropology,
University of Michigan.
OCLC # 6737162

3159 Trubowitz, Neal L. **Highway Archaeology and
Settlement Study in the Genesee Valley.**
George's Mills, NH., OPNEA, 1983.
Occasional Publications in Northeastern
Anthropology no. 8
OCLC # 10560989

3160 _____. **A Statistical Examination of the
Social Structure of Frontenac Island.** In
0712, pp. 123-147.

Trudeau,   Robert S.   (Robert Sanderson),
1945- . see 0859

Truex,   James E.   see 2815

3161   Trumbull,   James Hammond,   1821-1897.   Natick
Dictionary.   Washington,   U. S. Govt.
Print. Off., 1903.
Bureau of American Ethnology Bulletin no.
25.   Also issued as House Doc.   455,   57th
Congress,   2nd Session.   Introd.   by Edward
Everett Hale.
OCLC # 561095

3162   The Tsimshian: Images of the Past, Views
for the Present.   Edited by Margaret
Seguin.   Vancouver,   University of British
Columbia Press,   1984.
Essays in this collection are also listed
individually and refer to this citation.
OCLC # 12422540

3163   Tuck,   James A.   A Look at Laurentian.   In
0712,   pp.   31-40.

3164   _____.   Paleoeskimo Cultures of Northern
Labrador.   In 0908,   pp.   89-102.

Tullberg,   Steven M.   see 0669

3165   Turnbaugh,   William A.   Early and Middle Archaic Elements in Southern Rhode Island.
In 0901,   pp.   59-71.

3166   Turner,   Billie Lee.   Ancient Agricultural
Land Use in the Central Maya Lowlands.   In
2522,   pp.   163-183.

3167   _____.   The Development and Demise of the
Swidden Thesis of Maya Agriculture.   In
2522,   pp.   13-22.

3168   _____.   Implications from Agriculture for
Maya Prehistory.   In 2522,   pp.   337-373.

3169   _____.   Prehispanic Terracing in the Central Maya Lowlands: Problems of Agricultural Intensification.   In 0472,   pp.
103-115.

_____. see also 2522

3170 Turner,   Christy G.   III.   The Arizona State
      University Study of Gran Quivira, Physical
      Anthropology. In 1387, pp. 119-121.

3171 _____. Dental Evidence for the Peopling of
      the Americas. In 0903, pp. 147-157.

3172 _____. and Joseph Katich. Tympanic Plate
      Dehiscences in Gran Quivira Crania. In
      1387, pp. 145.

      _____. see also 0447

3172.5 Turner,   Frederick Jackson,   1861-1932.
      Rise of the New West, 1819-1829. Glou-
      cester, MA., P. Smith, 1961, c1906.
      The American Nation: A History v. 14
      OCLC # 1636421

3173 Turner, John W., 1912- . Little Big Man:
      The Novel and the Film. In 2533, pp.
      156-162.
      Reprinted from Literature/Film Quarterly v.
      5, Spring 1977, pp. 154-163.

3174 Turner, Lucy W. Naskapi Trance: Counter
      Balance to the Mask. In 2485, pp. 30-38.

      Turner, Wilson G. see 2882

3175 Tussing, Arlon and Robert D. Arnold. Eski-
      mo Population and Economy in Transition:
      Southwest Alaska. In 1875, pp. 123-169.

3176 Tyler, Daniel. The Indian Weltanschauung:
      A Summary of Views Expressed by Indians at
      the "Viewpoints in Indian History" Confer-
      ence, August 1974, Colorado State Univer-
      sity. In 2602, pp. 135-139.

3177 Tyler, Hamilton A. Pueblo Birds and Myths.
      Illus. by Donald Phillips. Norman, Uni-
      versity of Oklahoma Press, 1979.
      Civilization of the American Indian Series
      v. 147
      OCLC # 4193226

3178 Tyler, S. Lyman (Samuel Lyman), 1920- .

A History of Indian Policy. Washington,
Bureau of Indian Affairs,   U.   S.   Govt.
Print.   Off.,   1973
OCLC # 3187576

3179   Tyrrell,   Joseph Burr,   1858-1957.   Documents
Relating to the Early History of Hudson
Bay.   Edited,   with introd.   and notes by
J.   B.   Tyrrell.   A Facsim.   ed.   New York,
Greenwood Press,   1968.
The works of Silvy,   Marest,   and Bacque-
ville de la Potherie are given in English
and French.   Reprint of the 1931 ed.   pub.
by Champlain Society,   Toronto,   which was
issued as Champlain Society Publication 18.
OCLC # 45479

3180   UCLA Conference on American Folk Medicine
(1973).   American Folk Medicine: A Symposium.   Edited with an introd.   by Wayland
D.   Hand.   Berkeley,   University of California Press,   1976.
Publications of UCLA Center for the Study
of Comparative Folklore and Mythology
OCLC # 2406063

3181   Ubelaker,   Douglas H.   The Sources and Methodology for Mooney's Estimates on North
American Indian Populations.   In 0779,   pp.
243-288.

3182   Uhler,   Sherman P.   Pennsylvania Indian Relations to 1754.   New York,   AMS Press,
1984.
Reprint,   originally pub.   Allentown,   PA.,
1951,   Ph D Thesis,   Temple University,
1950.
OCLC # 10072384

Umiker-Sebeok,   Donna Jean.   see   0008

Underhill,   Lonnie E.   see   1162

3183   Underhill,   Ruth Murray,   1884-   .   The Autobiography of a Papago Woman.   New York,
Kraus Reprint,   1969.
Memoirs of the American Anthropological Association,   no.   46,   1936.   "The narrator
of the following autobiography was Maria

Chona".
OCLC # 3951834

3184 _____. **Papago Women**. New York, Holt,
Rinehart and Winston, 1979.
Case Studies in Cultural Anthropology. Pt.
2 originally published in 1936 as Memoirs
of the American Anthropological Association, no. 36.
OCLC # 4638175

_____. **see also** 0520

United Colonies of New England. Commissions.
see 2898

United Indians of All Tribes Foundation (U.
S.). **see** 1575

3185 United States. **American Indian Treaty**
Series. Prepared and produced by Institute
for the Development of Indian Law, Inc.,
Washington, Institute for the Development
of Indian Law, 1973-75.
9 vols. CONTENTS: A Chronological List of
Treaties and Agreements Made by Indian
Tribes with the United States. Treaties
and Agreements and the Proceedings of
Treaties and Agreements of the Tribes and
Bands of the Sioux Nation. Treaties and
Agreements of the Indian tribes of the Pac-
ific Northwest. Treaties and Agreements of
the Indian tribes of the Northern Plains.
Treaties and Agreements of the Eastern
Oklahoma Indians. Treaties and agreements
of the Indian Tribes of the Southeast (in-
cluding western Oklahoma). Treaties and
Agreements of the Chippewa Indians. Treat-
ies and Agreements of the Indian tribes of
the Great Lakes.
OCLC # 4376950

3186 _____. American Indian Policy Review
Commission. Task Force Three. **Report on**
Federal Administration and Structure of In-
dian Affairs: Final Report to the American
Indian Policy Review Commission/Task Force
Three. Federal Administration and Struc-
ture of Indian Affairs. Washington,

U. S.   Govt.   Print.   Off.,   1976.
OCLC # 2939239

_____.   Archives.   see   1445

3187   _____.   Army.   Corps of Topographical Engineers.   (Message from the President of the
United States...Communicating a Report of
an Expedition Led by Lieutenant Albert on
the Upper Arkansas)/Through the Country of
the Comanche Indians in the Fall of the
Year 1845:   The Journal of a U.   S.   Army
Expedition Led by Lieutenant James W.   Albert of the Topographical Engineers,   Art-
ist Extraordinary Whose Paintings of Indians and their Wild West Illustrate This
Book.   Edited by John Galvin.   San Francisco,   J.   Howell,   1970.
First Published in 1846 under title Message
from the President of the United States...
Communicating a Report of an Expedition Led
by Lieutenant Albert on the Upper Arkansas.
OCLC # 91013

_____.   Bureau of American Ethnology. Annual
reports.   see   0146,   2263

3188   _____.   Bureau of the Census.   Indian Popul-
ation in the United States and Alaska 1910.
Washington,   U.   S.   Govt.   Print.   Off.,
1915.
Prepared under the supervision of William
C.   Hunt,   Chief Statistician for Popula-
tion,   by Dr.   Roland B.   Dixon and Dr.   F.
A.   McKenzie expert special agents.
OCLC # 420142

3189   _____.   Bureau of Indian Affairs.   Agencies
Under the Jurisdiction of the Office of In-
dian Affairs by Reservation or Area and
County,   April 1,   1941.
Photocopy of a list

3190   _____.   Commission on Civil Rights.   Indian
Tribes: A Continuing Quest for Survival:
A Report of the United States Commission on
Civil Rights.   Washington,   The Commission,
U.   S.   Govt.   Print.   Off.,   1981.
OCLC # 7754560

3191   _____. _____. The Navaho Nation: An
        American Colony: A Report of the U. S.
        Commission on Civil Rights. Washington,
        The Commission,   1975.
        OCLC # 3035112

3192   _____. Commission to the Five Civilized
        Tribes. The Final Rolls of Citizens and
        Freedman of the Five Civilized Tribes in
        Indian Territory. Prepared by the Commis-
        sion and the Commissioner to the Five Civ-
        ilized Tribes, and Approved by the Secret-
        ary of the Interior on or prior to March 4,
        1907. Arlington, Va., University
        Publications of America, 1979.
        Three reel, 35mm microfilm. Compiled and
        printed under authority conferred by the
        Act of Congress and approved June 21, 1906.
        OCLC # 2015511

3193   _____. Congress. American Indian Policy
        Review Commission. Task Force Eight. Re-
        port on Urban and Rural Non-Re-servation
        Indians: Final Report to the American In-
        dian Policy Review Commission., Task Force
        Eight. Urban and Rural Non-Reservation In-
        dians. Washington, U. S. Govt. Print.
        Off., 1976.
        OCLC # 2692440

3194   _____. _____. Committee on Interior and
        Insular Affairs. Providing for Settlement
        of the Land Claims of the Cayuga Indian Na-
        tion in the State of New York, and for
        Other Purposes: Report Together with Dis-
        senting Views to Accompany H. R. 6631.
        Washington, U. S. Govt. Print. Off.,
        1980.
        House Report - 96th Congress, 2d Session;
        no. 96-827
        OCLC # 6260484

3195   _____. _____. House. Committee on In-
        dian Affairs. Hearings Before the Commit-
        tee on Investigation of Indian Service.
        House of Representatives, Washington, U.
        S. Govt. Print. Off., 1917.
        C. D. Carter, Chairman. One reel
        microfilm, Library of Congress, Class E -

Misc. Monographs and Pamphlets, shelf
#44140-44175, #44144. CONTENTS v. 1.
Condition of the Florida Seminoles, March
12-14, 1979. v. 2. Condition of the
Mississippi Choctaws, Union, MS., March
16, 1917. v. 3. Condition of the Indians of Oklahoma, March 19-21, 23,
1917.

3196   _____. _____. _____. _____. Indian
Claims Commission. New York, AMS Press,
1976.
Reprint of the 1935 ed, pub. by U. S.
Govt. print. Off., Hearings before the
Committee on Indian Affairs, H. R. 74th
Congress, 1st session, on HR 7838...May
22, 1935.
OCLC # 2164537

3197   _____. _____. _____. Committee on the
Conduct of the War. Massacre of the Cheyenne Indians. Washington, Committee on
the Conduct of the War, 1865.
38th Congress, 2nd Session. In the House
of Representatives, Jan. 10, 1865.
OCLC # 7987419

3197.5   _____. _____. _____. Committee on
Interior and Insular Affairs. Settlement
of the Catawba Indian Land Claims: Hearings Before the Committee on Interior and
Insular Affairs, House of Representatives,
96th Congress, 1st Session, on HR 3274.
Washington, U. S. Govt. Print. Off.,
1979.
OCLC # 6627713

3198   _____. _____. Senate. Committee on In-
dian Affairs. Appeals from Judgments or
Decrees of the Court of Claims. Hearings
Before the Committee on Indian Affairs, U.
S. Senate, on the Bill S. 8245, to Au-
thorize Appeals to be Taken from the Judg-
ments of the Court of Claims to the Supreme
Court...in Certain Cases Now Pending...Jan.
21, 1909. Washington, U. S. Govt.
Print. Off., 1909.
One reel microfilm - Library of Congress
Class E - misc. Monographs and Pamphlets,
Shelf #44140-44175, #44145. Land Cessions

of Choctaw and Chickasaw Indians

3199 _____. _____. _____. _____. Indian
Appropriation Bill. Hearings Before the
Committee on Indian Affairs, U. S. Sen-
ate, 63rd Congress, 3rd Session, on H.
R. 20150, an Act Making Appropriations
for the Current and Contingent Expenses of
the Bureau of Indian Affairs, Fulfilling
Treaty Stipulations with Various Indian
Tribes and for other Purposes, for the
Fiscal Year Ending June 30, 1916... Jan.
16-Feb. 22, 1915. U. S. Govt. Print.
Off., 1915.
One reel microfilm, Library of Congress -
Class E - Misc. Monographs and Pamphlets,
shelf #44140-44175, #44146

3200 _____. _____. _____. _____. Survey of
Conditions of the Indians in the United
States. Hearings Before the Subcommittee
of the Committee on Indian Affairs, United
States Senate 1929-1943. Arlington, VA.,
University Publications of America, 1975.
Eight reels microfilm, 35mm. U. S. 70th
Congress, 2d Session, 1929. Senate -
78th Congress, 1st Session, 1934. Senate
Res. 79, 230, 241, 263, 232, 416.
Each session has a separate index. Accom-
panied by a guide (printed) for the con-
tents of the film.
OCLC # 3127728

3201 _____. _____. Committee on the Judiciary.
Subcommittee to Investigate the Administration of the Internal Security Act and Other
Internal Security laws. Revolutionary Act-
ivity Within the U. S.: The American Indian Movement" Report of the Subcommittee
to Investigate the Administration of the
Internal Security Act and Other Internal
Security Laws of the Committee on the Judiciary, U. S. Senate, 94th Congress,
2nd Session. Washington, U. S. Govt.
Print. Off., 1976.
OCLC # 2819400

3202 _____. _____. _____. _____. _____.
Revolutionary Activities Within the U. S.
Indian Movement: Hearings Before the Sub-

committee to Investigate the Administration
of the Internal Security Act and Other Internal Security Laws of the Committee on
the Judiciary, U. S. Senate, 94th Congress, 2nd Session, April 6, 1976.
Washington, U. S. Govt. Print. Off.,
1976.
OCLC # 2455946

3203   _____. _____. _____. Statute of Limit-
ations Extension for Indian Claims: Hear-
ings Before the U. S. Senate, Select
Committee on Indian Affairs, on S. 1377
...May 3 and 16, 1977. Washington, U. S.
Govt. Print. Off., 1977.
OCLC # 3378456

        _____. Court of Claims. see 2881

        _____. Customs House (New York, NY.).
        see 2251

        _____. General Accounting Office. see
        2881

        _____. Indian Claims Commission. see
        1559, 1560, 3394

3204   _____. Indian Peace Commission. Proceedings of the Great Peace Commission of 1867-
1868. With an introd. by Vine Deloria and
Raymond DeMallie. Washington, Institute
for the Development of Indian Law, 1975.
OCLC # 2337499

        _____. Interdepartmental Committee on Sci-
entific and Cultural Cooperation. see
2346

3205   _____. Laws, Statutes, etc. Gen eral
Allotment Act and Amendments... Washington, U. S. Govt. Print. off., 1909.
Act of Feb. 8, 1887, "To provide for the
allotment of lands in severalty to Indians
on the various reservations and to extend
the protection of the laws of the U. S.
and the territories over the Indians". One
reel microfilm - Library of Congress -
Class E - Misc. Monographs and Pamphlets,
shelf #44140-44175, #44147.

3206 _____. National Advisory Council on Indian
Education. Annual Report to the Congress
of the United States from the National Advisory Council on Indian Education. Washington, The Council, U. S. Govt.
Print. Off., Began with first, 1973/73.
OCLC # 1793008

3207 _____. _____. Indian Education: The
Right to Be Indian. The Council, Washington, U. S. Govt. Print. Off.,
1976.
3rd annual report to Congress
OCLC # 3537506

3208 _____. National Archives. List of Docu-
ments Concerning the Negotiations of Ratif-
ied Indian Treaties, 1801-1869. Millwood,
NY., Kraus Reprint, 1975.
Reprint of the 1949 ed. pub. by National
Archives, Washington as its Special List
no. 6 and its publication no. 49-31.
OCLC # 1288306

3209 _____. _____. American Indians: A Select
Catalog of National Archives Microfilm Pub-
lications. Washington, National Archives
Trust Fund Board, General Services Admin-
istration, 1984.
Rev. ed. of The American Indian 1972
OCLC # 9783823

_____. National Park Service. see 1387

_____. _____. Cultural Resources Manage-
ment Division. see 0711, 2504

3210 _____. Office of Education. Indian Education and Civilization; A Report Prepared
in Answer to Senate Resolution of Feb. 23,
1885. By Alice C. Fletcher, under direc-
tion of the Commissioner of Education,
Washington, U. S. Govt. Print. Off.,
1888. Millwood, NY., Kraus Reprint,
1973.
Original ed. issued as Executive Doc. no.
95 of 48th Congress, 2nd Session. Senate
OCLC # 538926

3211   _____.   Office of Indian Affairs. <u>Agencies</u>
<u>Under Jurisdiction of the Office of Indian</u>
<u>Affairs by Reservation and County</u>. Wash-
ington?,   1938.
One reel microfilm - Library of Congress -
Class E - Misc. Monographs and Pamphlets
Shelf #44140-44175,   #44148.

3212   _____.   _____.   <u>General Accounting for the</u>
<u>United States Indian Service</u>. <u>Effective</u>
<u>July 1,   1919</u>. Washington,   U.   S.   Govt.
Print. Off.,   1919.
One reel microfilm - Library of Congress -
Class E - Mics. Monographs and Pamphlets,
Shelf #44140-44175,   #44150

3213   _____.   _____.   <u>Indian and Pioneer Stories</u>
<u>Suitable for Children</u>. Washington? 1923.
One reel microfilm - Library of Congress -
Class E - Misc. Monographs and pamphlets,
Shelf #44140-44175,   #44149.
Its Bulletin 13,   1923,   typewritten copy

3214   _____.   President. <u>Executive Orders Relat-</u>
<u>ing to Indian Reservations,   1885-1922</u>.
Washington,   U.   S.   Govt.   Print.   Off.,
1912-1922.   Wilmington,   Scholarly Resources Inc.,   1975.
OCLC # 1736718

3215   _____.   Presidential Commission on Indian
Reservation Economies. <u>Report and Recom-</u>
<u>mendations to the President of the United</u>
<u>States</u>. Washington,   Presidential Commis-
sion on Indian Reservation Economies,   U.
S.   Govt.   Print.   Off.,   1984.   Nov.   1984
OCLC # 12051334

3216   _____.   Treaties,   etc. <u>Treaties Be tween</u>
<u>the Oneida Indians and the United States of</u>
<u>America: 1784-1838</u>. Assembled by George
E.   Fay.   Greeley,   CO.,   University of
Northern Colorado,   Museum of Anthropology,
1978.
University of Northern Colorado,   Museum of
Anthropology,   Misc.   Series no.   40,   1978
OCLC # 4473955

3217   _____.   _____.   <u>Treaties Between the Pota-</u>
<u>watomi Tribe of Indians and the United</u>

States of America, 1789-1867. Assembled/ edited by George E. Fay. Greeley, CO., University of Northern Colorado, Museum of Anthropology, 1971. University of Northern Colorado, Museum of Anthropology, Occasional Publications in Anthropology. Ethnology Series no. 19 OCLC # 979922

3218 _____. _____. Treaties Between the Stockbridge-Munsee Tribe(s) of Indians and the United States of America, 1805-1871. Assembled by George E. Fay. Greeley, CO., University of Northern Colorado, Museum of Anthropology, 1970. University of Northern Colorado, Museum of Anthropology, Misc. Series no. 18, July 1970. OCLC # 1341299

3219 _____. _____. Winnebago Indians. Treaties Between the Winnebago Indians and the United States of America, 1817-1856. Compiled by George E. Fay. Greeley, CO., University of Northern Colorado, Museum of Anthropology, 1967. University of Northern Colorado, Museum of Anthropology, Misc. Series no. 1, April 1967 OCLC # 454885

_____. Women's Bureau. see 1025

University League for Social Reform, Toronto. see 0777

3220 University of Alaska. Dept. of Education, College, Alaska. Misrepresentations of the Alaskan Natives in Social Studies Texts Currently in Use in the United States Including Alaska. In 1456, pp. 111-120. Reprinted from the hearings before the Subcommittee on Indian Education of the Committee on Labor and Public Welfare, U. S. Senate, 91st Congress, 1969

University of California, Los Angeles. American Indian Studies Center. see 2238.5, 2831.5, 2961.5

461 UNIVERSITY

University of Cambridge. Center for Latin
American Studies. see 0473

3221 Unrau, William E., 1929- . The Emigrant
Indians of Kansas: A Critical Biblio-
graphy. Bloomington, Published for the
Newberry Library by Indiana University
Press, 1979.
Bibliographical Series
OCLC # 4983585

3221.5 _____. The Kansa Indians: A History of
the Wind People, 1673-1873. Foreword by
R. David Edmunds. Norman, University of
Oklahoma Press, 1986, 1971.
Civilization of the American Indian Series
v. 114.
OCLC # 12839335

3222 _____. Tribal Dispossession and the Ottawa
Indian University Fraud. ... and H. Craig
Miner. Norman, University of Oklahoma
Press, 1985.
OCLC # 11114657

_____. see also 1647

3223 Upham, Steadman. Politics and Power: An
Economic and Political History of the West-
ern Pueblo. New York, Academic Press,
1982.
Studies in Archaeology
OCLC # 8168686

_____. see also 2481

3224 Upton, Helen M. The Everett Report in His-
torical Perspective: The Indians of New
York. New York State American Revolution
Bicentennial Commission, 1980.
OCLC # 6334964

3225 Upton, Leslie Francis Stokes. Micmacs and
Colonists: Indian-White Relations in the
Maritimes, 1713-1867. Vancouver, Univer-
sity of British Columbia Press, 1979.
OCLC # 5857082

Upton, Richard, 1933- . see 1563

3226 The Upward Moving and Emergence Way: The
      Gishin Biye Version. Recorded by Berard
      Haile; Karl W. Luckert, editor; Navajo
      Orthography by Irvy W. Goossen. Lincoln,
      University of Nebraska Press, 1982.
      American Tribal Religions v. 7. A Bison
      Book
      OCLC # 7554393

3227 Urssenbacher, Abraham. Erzenhlung eines
      Unter den Indianern Gewesener Gefangenen _
      Captivity of Abraham Urssenbacher. New
      York, Garland Pub., 1978.
      Garland Library of narratives of North
      American Indian captivities, v. 8. Re-
      printed from Neu - Einerichteter Amerikan-
      ischer Geschichts - und Haus - Calendar,
      1762. Issued with the reprint of the 1756
      ed. of W. A. Fleming, A Narrative of
      Sufferings and Deliverance.
      OCLC # 3871843

3228 Urton, Gary, 1946- . At the Crossroads of
      the Earth and the Sky: An Andean Cosmol-
      ogy. Austin, University of Texas Press,
      1981.
      Latin American Monographs, University of
      Texas at Austin. Institute of Latin Ameri-
      can Studies v. 55
      OCLC # 7329475

3229 Utley, Robert Marshall, 1929- . The Amer-
      ican Heritage History of the Indian Wars.
      ... and Wilcomb E. Washburn. Editors Ann
      Moffat and Richard F. Snow. New York,
      American Heritage Pub. Co., book trade
      distribution by Simon and Schuster, 1977.
      OCLC # 3089828

3230 _____. The Celebrated Peace Policy of
      General Grant. In 2304, pp. 183-199.

3231 _____. A Clash of Cultures: Fort Bowie and
      the Chiricahua Apaches. Washington, Of-
      fice of Publications, National Park Ser-
      vice, 1977.
      Sup. Doc. No. I 29. 2: F776/2
      OCLC # 1736238

3232 _____. Custer and the Great Controversy:

The origin and Development of a Legend.
Los Angeles, Westernlorn Press, 1962.
Great West and Indian Series 22.
OCLC # 476447

3233 _____. The Frontier Army: John Fordor
Arthur Penn? In 2265, pp. 133-145.

3234 _____. The Indian Frontier of the American
West, 1846-1890. Albuquerque, University
of New Mexico Press, 1984.
Histories of the American Frontier
OCLC # 9685353

3234.5 _____. Indian Soldiers and Settlers: Experiences in the Struggle for the American
West. St. Louis, MO., Jefferson National Expansion Historical Association, 1979.
OCLC # 6303405

Utton, Albert E., 1931-   . see 0881

3235 Vaillant, George Clapp, 1901-1945. Patterns in Middle American Archaeology. In
2105, pp. 295-305.

3236 Valdman, Albert. Basic Course in Haitian
Creole. Bloomington, Indiana University
Press, 1971.
Indiana University Publications. Language
Science Monographs v. 5
OCLC # 158371

3237 The Valley of Mexico: Studies in Pre-Hispanic Ecology and Society. Edited by Eric
R. Wolf. Albuquerque, University of New
Mexico Press, 1976.
Advanced Seminar Series. Papers based on
a seminar held in Santa Fe, NM., April 3-
8, 1972. Essays in this collection are
also listed individually and refer to this
citation.
OCLC # 2188435

3238 Van den Berghe, Pierre L. Inequality in the
Peruvian Andes: Class and Ethnicity in
Cuzco. ... and George P. Primov, with the
assistance of Gladys Becerra Velazque,
Narcisco Ccahuana Ccohuate. Columbia,

University of Missouri Press, 1977.
OCLC # 2523378

3239 Van der Beets, Richard. The Indian Captivity Narratives: An American Genre. Lanham, MD., University Press of America, 1984.
OCLC # 10045474

3240 Van der Donck, Adriaen. A Description of the New Netherlands. In Collections of the New York State Historical Society, 2nd series, v. 1, pp. 129-242. Reprint of book published 1653.

3241 Vanderlaan, Stanley. A Fishing Village on Oak Orchard Creek - Ood 6-3. New York State Archeological Association Bulletin 22, July 1961, pp. 14-16. Millwood, NY., Kraus Reprint, 1976.

3242 _____. Fording Places Ood 2-3. New York State Archeological Association Bulletin 25, July 1962, pp. 15-22. Millwood, NY., Kraus Reprint, 1976.

3243 _____. The Granshaw Site (MDA 3-4). New York State Archeological Association Bulletin 35, Nov. 1965, pp. 3-19. Millwood, NY., Kraus Reprint, 1976.

3244 _____. The Nok Site (MDA 9-4). New York State Archeological Association Bulletin 26, Nov. 1962, pp. 15-18. Millwood, NY., Kraus Reprint, 1976.

3245 _____. The Oakfield Phase - Western New York. In 1585, pp. 95-98.

3246 _____. The Wilkins Site. New York State Archeological Association Bulletin 18, March 1960, pp. 5-6. Millwood, NY., Kraus Reprint, 1976.

Van Dooren, Ingrid. see 2476

3247 Van Dusen, C. The Indian Chief: An Account of the Labours, Losses, Sufferings and Oppression of Ke-zig-ko-e-ne-ne (David Sawyer) a Chief of the Ojibbeway Indians in

Canada West. by Enemikeese, London,
Printed by W. Nichols, 1867.
OCLC # 3981378

3248 Van Every, Dale, 1896- . A Company of
Heroes: The American Frontier, 1775-1783.
New York, Arno Press, 1977, c1962.
Reprint of the ed. pub. by Morrow, New
York. The second vol. of the author's
work The Frontier People of America; the
other vols. are Forth to the Wilderness,
Ark of Empire and The Final Challenge.
OCLC # 2807947

3249 _____. Forth to the Wilderness: The First
American Frontier, 1754-1774. New York,
Arno Press, 1977, c1961.
Reprint of the ed. pub. by Morrow, New
York. Vol. 1 of the author's work The
Frontier People of America.
OCLC # 2119315

3250 _____. The Final Challenge: The American
Frontier, 1804-1845. New York, Morrow,
1966, 1964.
Vol. 4 of the author's work The Frontier
People of America
OCLC # 478971

3251 Van Hoesen, Paul. The (De-U-No-Dil-Lo)
Fluted Culture from Ten Thousand Years
Along the Unadilla. New York State Archeo-
logical Association Bulletin 20, Nov.
1960, pp. 14-16. Millwood, NY., Kraus
Reprint, 1976.

Van Stone, James W. see 0616

3252 Varnum, Charles Albert, 1849-1936. I,
Varnum, Autobiographical Reminiscences of
Custer's Chief of Scouts: Including His
Testimony at the Reno Court of Inquiry.
Edited by John M. Carroll. Intro. and
biographical chronology by Charles K.
Mills. Glendale, CA., A. H. Clark,
1982.
Hidden Springs of Custeriana v. 7
OCLC # 8879841

3253 Vaughan, Alden T., 1929- . Narratives of

North American Indian Captivity: A Se-
lective Bibliography. New York,   Garland
Pub.   Co.,   1983.
Garland Reference Library of the Humanities
v.   370
OCLC # 9045135

3254   _____.   Pequots and Puritans: The Causes of
the War of 1637.   In 2304,   pp.   61-73.
Reprinted from William and Mary Quarterly
3rd series v.   21,   no.   2,   April 1964,
pp.   256-269.

       _____.   see also   0900,   2652

3255   Vecsey,   Christopher.   American Indian Environmental Religions.   In 0079,   pp.   1-37.

3256   _____.   Traditional Ojibwa Religion and its
Historical Changes.   Philadelphia,   Ameri-
can Philosophical Society,   1983.
Memoirs series v.   152
OCLC # 10061919

       _____.   see also   0079,   0955,   1535

3257   Veeder,   William H.   Water Rights in the Coal
Fields of the Yellowstone River Basin.   In
0087,   pp.   77-96.

3258   Velie,   Alan R.,   1937- .   Four American Indian Literary Masters: N.   Scott Momaday,
James Welch,   Leslie Marmon Silko and Gerald Vizenor.   Norman,   University of Oklahoma Press,   1982.
OCLC # 8033389

       _____.   see also   0082

3259   Venables,   Robert W.   The Indians' Revolutionary War in the Hudson Valley,   1775-
1783.   In 2282,   pp.   224-241.

3260   _____.   Iroquois Environments and "We the
People of the United States":   Gemeinschaft
and Gesellschaft in the Apposition of Iroquois,   Federal and New York State Sover-
eignties.   In 0079,   pp.   81-127.

3261   _____.   Victim Versus Victim: The Irony of

the New York Indian's Removal to Wisconsin.
In   0079,   pp.   140-151.

_____.   see also   0079

3262   Vennum,   Thomas.   Ojibwa Dance Drum: Its
       History and Construction.   Washington,
       Smithsonian Institution Press,   1982.
       Smithsonian Folklife Studies no.   2
       OCLC # 9131584

3262.5   _____.   Who Should Have Access to Indian
         Music in Archives.   In 2831.5,   pp.   137-
         146.

3263   Vento,   F.   J.   Lithic Raw Material Utiliza-
       tion at Meadowcroft Rockshelter and in the
       Cross Creek Drainage.   In 2111,   pp.   112-
       129.

3264   Vernon,   Howard.   The Dutch,   the Indians and
       the Fur Trade in the Hudson Valley,   1609-
       1664.   In   2282,   pp.   197-209.

3265   Vernon,   William W.   Geology and Chronology
       of the Timlin Site.   In 3519,   pp.   17-24.

3266   Vestal,   Stanley,   1887-1959.   Happy Hunting
       Grounds.   Introd.   by Peter J.   Powell.
       Illus.   by Frederick Weygold.   Norman,
       University of Oklahoma Press,   1975.
       OCLC # 1272426

3267   _____.   The Hollywooden Indian.   In 2433,
       pp.   63-67.
       Reprinted from Southwest Review   v.   21,
       1936,   pp.   418-423.

3268   Vetromile,   Eugene,   1819-1881.   The Abnakis
       and Their History.   New York,   AMS Press,
       1984.
       Reprint - originally pub.   New York,   J.
       B.   Kirker,   1886
       OCLC # 10484634

3269   Vickers,   William T.   The Territorial Dimen-
       sions of Siona-Secoya and Encabellado
       Adaptation.   In 0023,   pp.   451-478.

_____.   see also   0023

3270   Victor, Frances Fuller, 1826-1902. The
       River of the West: The Adventure of Joe
       Meek. Missoula, Mountain Press Pub.
       Co., 1983.
       Originally pub. Hartford, CT., R. W.
       Bliss, 1870
       OCLC # 9576271

       Victoria, B. C. Art Gallery of Greater
       Victoria. see 0878

3271   Vincent, Joseph E. How to Pronounce and
       Understand Nahuatl Names. In 0145, pp.
       95-100.

3272   Viola, Herman J. Diplomats in Buckskin: A
       History of Indian Delegations in Washington
       City. Washington, Smithsonian Institution
       Press, 1981.
       OCLC # 6889850

3273   _____. From Civilization to Removal: Early
       American Indian Policy. In 2265, pp. 45-
       56.

3274   _____. The Indian Legacy of Charles Bird
       King. Washington, Smithsonian Institution
       Press, 1976.
       Smithsonian Institution Press Pub. #6256
       OCLC # 2224980

       _____. see also 0631, 2264

3275   Vision and Refuge: Essays on the Literature
       of the Great Plains. Edited by Virginia
       Faulkner with Frederick C. Luebke. Lin-
       coln. Published by the University of Ne-
       braska Press for the Center for Great
       Plains Studies, University of Nebraska,
       Lincoln, 1982.
       Essays in this collection are also listed
       individually and refer to this citation.
       OCLC # 7572579

3276   Vivan, R. Gwinn. Wooden Ritual Artifacts
       from Chaco Canyon, New Mexico. Tucson,
       University of Arizona Press, 1978.
       Chaco Center Contributions from Chaco Cen-
       ter no. 11. Arizona University Anthropo-

logical Papers no. 32.
OCLC # 4356328

3277 Vizenor, Gerald Robert, 1934- . The Ever-
      lasting Sky; A New Voice from the People
      Named the Chippewa. New York, Crowell -
      Collier Press, 1972.
      OCLC # 488170

3278 _____. People Names the Chippewa: Narrat-
      ive Histories. Minneapolis, University of
      Minnesota Press, 1984.
      OCLC # 9971255

3279 Vlcek, David T. Contemporary Farming and
      Ancient Maya Settlements: Some Disconcert-
      ing Evidence. In 2522, pp. 211-223.

3280 Voegelin, Carl F. Sign Language Analysis,
      on One Level or Two? In 0008, pp. 205-
      211.
      Reprinted from International Journal of
      American Linguistics, v. 24, 1958, pp.
      71-77.

3281 _____ and Voegelin, F. M. Some recent
      (and not so Recent) Attempts to Interpret
      Semantics of Native Languages of North
      America. In 1902, pp. 75-104.

      Voegelin, Ermine Wheeler, 1908- . see
      1903, 3158

      Voegelin, F. M. see 3281

3282 Vogel, Virgil J. American Indian Foods Used
      as Medicine. In 3180, pp. 125-141.

3283 Voget, Fred W. American Indian Reformations
      and Acculturation. In National Museum of
      Canada Bulletin no. 10. Contributions to
      Anthropology 1960, pt. 2. Ottawa, Dept.
      of Northern Affairs and National Resources,
      1963, pp. 1-13.

3284 _____. Anthropological Theory and Iroquois
      Ethnography: 1850-1970. In 0979, pp.
      343-357.

3285 _____. The Shoshoni-Crow Sun Dance. Nor-

man,   University of Oklahoma Press,   1984.
Civilization of the American Indian Series
no.   170
OCLC # 10727363

3286   Voohies,   Barbara.   Previous Research on
       Nearshore Coastal Adaptations in Middle
       America.   In 2524,   pp.   5-21.

       _____.   see also   2524

3287   Wachtel,   David.   The Use of Discretion by
       Navaho Indian Police Officers.   Ann Arbor,
       MI.,   University Microfilms International,
       1983.
       Microfilm - PhD Thesis - SUNY at Buffalo
       OCLC # 1062557

3288   Wachtel,   Nathan.   Vision of the Vanquished:
       The Spanish Conquest of Peru Through Indian
       Eyes,   1530-1570.   Trans.   by Ben and Sian
       Reynolds.   New York,   Barnes and Noble,
       1977.
       Trans.   of La Vision des Vaincus
       OCLC # 3018990

3289   Wade,   Edwin L.   Magic Images: Contemporary
       Native American Art.   ... and Rennard
       Strickland.   Norman,   Philbrook Art Center,
       University of Oklahoma,   1982.
       OCLC # 8283079

3290   Wade,   Mason,   1913- .   Francis Parkman,
       Heroic Historian.   Hamden,   CT.,   Archon
       Books,   1972,   1942.
       OCLC # 379422

3291   _____.   The French and the Indians.   In
       0144,   pp.   61-80.

3292   Wagley,   Charles,   1913- .   The Social and
       Religious Life of a Guatemalan Village.
       Millwood,   NY.,   Kraus Reprint,   1974.
       Memoirs of the American Anthropological As-
       sociation,   no.   71.   Suppl.   to American
       Anthropologist v.   51,   no.   4,   pt.   2,
       1949.
       OCLC # 1203629

3293   Wagner,   Erika.   The Prehistory and Ethno-

history of the Carache Area of Western
Venezuela. New Haven, Dept. of
Anthropology, Yale University, 1967.
Yale University Publications in Anthro-
pology no. 71
OCLC # 468862

3293.5 Waheenee, 1839?- . Waheenee, an Indian
Girl's Story; Told by Herself to Gilbert
L. Wilson. Introd. by Jeffrey R. Han-
son; illus. by Frederick N. Wilson.
Lincoln, University of Nebraska Press,
1981.
First Bison Book Printing. Originally pub.
St. Paul, Webb Pub. Co., 1921.
OCLC # 7462800

3294 Wahrhaftig, Albert L. Institution Building
Among Oklahoma's Traditional Cherokees. In
1099, pp. 132-147.

3295 _____ and Jane Lukens-Wahrhaftig. New Mil-
itants or Resurrected State? The Five
County Northeastern Oklahoma Cherokee Organization. In 0547, pp. 223-246.

3296 _____ and Jane Lukens-Wahrhaftig. The
Thrice Powerless; Cherokee Indians in
Oklahoma. In 0111, pp. 225-236.

3297 Waldman, Carl. Atlas of the North American
Indian. Maps and illus. by Molly Braun.
New York, Facts on File, 1985.
OCLC # 9575580

3298 Waldram, James B. (James Burgess). The Im-
pact of Hydro-electric Development Upon a
Northern Manitoba Native Community. Ann
Arbor, MI., University Microfilms Inter-
national, 1983.
Microfilm - PhD Thesis - University of
Connecticut
OCLC # 11017569

3299 Walens, Stanley, 1948- . Analogic Caus-
ality and the Power of Masks. In 2502,
pp. 70-78.

3300 _____. Feasting With Cannibals: An Essay
on Kwakiutl Cosmology. Princeton, NJ.,

Princeton University Press,   1981.
OCLC # 7554742

3301   Walker,   Alexander,   1764-1831.   An Account
       of a Voyage to the North West Coast of
       America in 1785 and 1786.   Edited by Robin
       Fisher and J.   M.   Bumsted.   Vancouver,
       Douglas & McIntyre,   Seattle,   University
       of Washington Press,   1982.
       Reproduced from the unpublished manuscript
       in the National Library of Scotland (Ms.
       13780)
       OCLC # 8283163

       Walker,   Elkanah,   1805-1877.   see   0872

3302   Walker,   J.   R.   (James R.).   Lakota Belief
       and Ritual.   Edited by Raymond J.   DeMallie
       and Elaine A.   Jahner.   Lincoln,   Univer-
       sity of Nebraska Press,   1980.
       OCLC # 5310088

3303   _____.   Lakota Myth.   Edited by Elaine A.
       Jahner.   Lincoln,   University of Nebraska
       Press,   1983.
       Pub.   in cooperation with the Colorado
       Historical Society.   A Bison Book
       OCLC # 9324144

3304   _____.   Lakota Society.   Edited by Raymond
       J.   DeMallie.   Lincoln,   University of
       Nebraska Press,   1982.
       Pub.   in cooperation with the Colorado
       Historical Society
       OCLC # 7773119

3305   Walker,   James W.   St.   G.,   1940-   .   The
       Indian in Canadian Historical Writing,
       1971-1981.   In 0137,   pp.   340-357.

3306   Walker,   Jerell R.   The Sign Language of the
       Plains Indians of North America.   In 0008,
       pp.   175-184.
       Reprinted from Chronicles of Oklahoma v.
       31,   no.   2,   1953-54,   pp.   168-177.

3307   Walker,   Stanley.   Let the Indian Be the
       Hero.   In 3335,   pp.   107-111.
       Source - New York Times April 24,   1960.

3308   Walker,   Willard.   The Proto-Algonquians.
       Lisse,   Belgium,   Peter de Rider,   1975.
       PdR Press Publication in North American
       Linguistic Prehistory v.   1.   The text of
       this article is reprinted from Linguistics
       and Anthropology: In Honor of C.   F.
       Voegelin...
       OCLC # 7890998

3309   Wallace,   Anthony F.   C.,   1923-   .   Death
       and Rebirth of the Seneca.   With the as-
       sistance of Sheila C.   Steen.   New York,
       Knopf,   1973.
       Pub.   1970,   reprinted 1973
       OCLC # 76618

3310   _____.   Prelude to Disaster;   The Course of
       Indian-White Relations Which Led to the
       Black Hawk War of 1832.   Springfield,   Il-
       linois State Historical Library,   1970.
       Reprinted from Introduction to the Black
       Hawk War,   1831-1832,   compiled and edited
       by Ellen M.   Whitney and pub.   as vol.   35
       of the Collections of the Illinois State
       Historical Library.
       OCLC # 1016675

3311   Wallace,   Ernest.   The Comanches: Lords of
       the South Plains.   ...   and E.   Adamson
       Hoebel.   Norman,   University of Oklahoma
       Press,   1952.
       Civilization of the American Indian Series
       no.   34
       OCLC # 1175397

3312   Wallas,   James,   1907-   .   Kwakiutl Legends
       as Told to Pamela Whitaker by Chief James
       Wallas.   North Vancouver,   British Colum-
       bia,   Hancock House,   1981.
       OCLC # 8998032

3313   Wallis,   Wilson D.   Historical Background of
       the Micmac Indians of Canada.   In National
       Museum of Canada Bulletin 173,   Anthro-
       pological Series no.   50.   Contributions to
       Anthropology,   1959.   Ottawa,   Dept.   of
       Northern Affairs and National Resources,
       1961,   pp.   42-63.

3314   Walsh,   Jame MacLaren.   John Peabody Harring-

ton,   the Man and His California Indian
Field Notes.   With a foreword by Lowell
John Bean.   Ramona,   CA.,   Ballena Press,
1976.
Ballena Press Anthropological Papers no.   6
OCLC # 2912968

3315   Walthall,   John A.   Prehistoric Indians of
the Southeast: Archaeology of Alabama and
the Middle South.   University,   University
of Alabama Press,   1980.
OCLC # 4982934

3316   Walton,   George H.   Fearless and Free: The
Seminole Indian War,   1835-1842.   Indiana-
polis,   Bobbs-Merrill,   1977.
OCLC # 3089203

3317   Walton,   William,   1740-1824.   A Narrative of
the Captivity and Suffering of Benjamin
Gilbert.   New York,   Garland Pub.,   1975.
The Garland Library of Narratives of North
American Indian Captivities,   v.   15.   Re-
print of the 1784 ed.   printed and sold by
J.   Crukshank,   Phila.   under title A Nar-
rative of the Captivity and Sufferings of
Benjamin Gilbert and His Family.   Issued
with the reprint of the 3rd ed.,   rev.   and
enl. 1848,   printed by J.   Richards,
Phila.
OCLC # 1531880

3317.5   Wapp,   Edward.   The American Indian Court-
ing Flute: Revitalization and Change.   In
2831.5,   pp.   49-59.

3318   Wardell,   Morris L.,   1889-   .   A Political
History of the Cherokee Nation,   1838-1907;
In Search of Cherokee History.   A biblio-
graphical foreword to the second printing
by Rennard Strickland.   Norman,   University
of Oklahoma Press,   1977.
Reprint of the 1938 ed.   pub.   by the
University of Oklahoma Press,   Norman,
which was issued as Civilization of the
American Indian Series no.   17.
OCLC # 2984023

Warden,   Dorothy M.   see   1166

Waring, Antonio J. see 0688

3319 Warren, A. Helene. **A Petrographic Study of
the Pottery of Gran Quivira**. In 1387, pp.
57-73.

_____. **see also** 1388

3319.5 Warren, Dave. **American Indian Challenge
and Opportunity of a New Century**. In
2831.5, pp. 3-9.

3320 Warren, Kay B., 1947- . **The Symbolism of
Subordination: Indian Identity in a Guate-
malan Town**. Austin, University of Texas
Press, 1978.
Texas Pan American Series
OCLC # 3912565

3321 Washburn, Dorothy Koster. **A Symmetry Analysis of Upper Gila Area Ceramic Design**.
Illus. by Sarah Whitney Powell and Barbara
Westman. Cambridge, MA., Peabody Museum
of Archaeology and Ethnology, Harvard University, 1977.
Papers of the Peabody Museum of Archaeology
and Ethnology, Harvard University v. 68
OCLC # 3242978

3322 _____. **A Symmetry Classification of Pueblo
Ceramic Design**. In 0822, pp. 101-121.

_____. **see also** 0938, 1498

3323 Washburn, Wilcomb E. **Cultural Change**. In
1318, pp. 477-529.

3324 _____. **The Historical Context of American
Indian Legal Problems**. In 0087, pp. 12-
24.

3325 _____. **Indian Policy Since the 1880's**. In
0034, pp. 45-57.

_____. **see also** 3229

3326 Washburne, Heluiz Chandler, 1892- . **Land
of the Good Shadows: The Life Story of
Anauta, an Eskimo Women**. New York, AMS
Press, 1976

Reprint of the 1940 ed.
OCLC # 2545014

3327 Wasley, William Warick, 1919- . Environmental Setting. In 2768, pp. 6-19.

3328 _____ and E. B. Sayles. Radiocarbon
Dating. In 2768, pp. 44-57.

3329 _____. Salvage Archaeology in Pointed Rocks
Reservoir, Western Arizona. ... and Al-
fred E. Johnson, with appendices by Hugh
C. Cutler, Mary Elizabeth King. Tucson,
University of Arizona Press, 1965.
University of Arizona. Anthropological
Papers no. 9
OCLC # 1141393

Wassben, Henry, 1908- . see 2329

3330 Wassell, William H. The Indian Sign
Language. In 0008, pp. 37-41.
Reprinted from Chataquan v. 23, 1896,
pp. 581-585.

Wasserman, Mark, 1946- . see 1708

3331 Waterloo Library and Historical Society,
Waterloo, NY. The Centennial Celebration
of General Sullivan's Campaign Against the
Iroquois in 1779, Held at Waterloo, September 2nd, 1879. Prepared by Diedrick
Willers, Jr. To which is prefixed a
sketch of the Waterloo Library and Historical Society, by Rev. S. H. Gridley, D.
D. published under the auspices of the Waterloo Library and Historical Society. Waterloo, NY., Observer Steam Print, 1880.
OCLC # 3486908

Waters, Frank. see 0965

Watkins, Mel. see 0777

3332 Watson, James B. (James Bennett), 1918- .
Cayua Culture Change: A Study in Accult-
uration and Methodology. Millwood, NY.,
Kraus Reprint, 1974.
Memoirs of the American Anthropological
Association no. 73. Suppl. to American

<u>Anthropologist</u> v. 54, no. 2, pt. 2, 1952.
OCLC # 1950945

Watson, Thomas D. <u>see</u> 0616.5

3333 Waugh, Frederick Wilkerson. <u>Iroquis (sic)</u>
<u>Foods and Food Preparation</u>. Ottawa, Gov-
ernment Printing Bureau, 1916
Canada. Dept. of Mines. Geological Survey. Memoir 86. Reprint of the 1916   ed.
OCLC # 3920494

3334 Wauchope, Robert, 1909- . <u>Domestic Ar-</u>
<u>chitecture of the Maya</u>. In 2105, pp.
232-241.

3335 Wax, Murray Lionel, 1922- . <u>Solving "The</u>
<u>Indian Problem", the White Man's Burden-</u>
<u>some Business</u>. Edited by ... and Robert W.
Buchanan. New York, New View Points,
1975.
Essays in this collection are also listed
individually and refer to this citation.
OCLC # 948141

3336 Way, Royal B. <u>The United States Factory</u>
<u>System for Trading with the Indians, 1796-</u>
<u>1822</u>. In 2304, pp. 111-119.
Abridged and reprinted from <u>Mississippi</u>
<u>Valley Historical Review</u> v. 6, no. 2,
Sept. 1919, pp. 220-235.

Weatherford, Gary D. <u>see</u> 2537

3337 Weaver, Sally M. <u>Making Canadian Indian</u>
<u>Policy: The Hidden Agenda, 1968-70</u>. To-
ronto, University of Toronto Press, 1981.
Studies in the Structure of Power, Deci-
sion-making in Canada, v. 9
OCLC # 7783590

3338 _____. <u>Medicine and Politics Among the</u>
<u>Grand River Iroquois; A Study of the Non-</u>
<u>Conservatives</u>. Ottawa, National Museums
of Canada, 1972.
Pubs. in Ethnology no. 4. Summary in
French
OCLC # 689754

3339   _____.   Seth Newhouse and the Grand River
        Confederacy at Mid-Nineteenth Century. In
        0979, pp. 165-182.

3340   Webb,   George Washington, 1856-1938. Chron-
        ological List of Engagements Between the
        Regular Army of the United States and Var-
        ious Tribes of Hostile Indians Which Oc-
        curred During the Years 1790 to 1898, In-
        clusive. New York,   AMS Press,   1976.
        Reprint of the 1939 ed. pub.   by Wing
        Print. and Pub. Co., St. Joseph, MO.
        OCLC # 2237510

3341   Webb,   Walter Prescott, 1888-1963. The
        Sign Language of the Plains Indians. In
        0008, pp. 91-107.
        Reprinted from The Great Plains, Boston,
        Ginn and Co., 1931, pp. 68-84.

3342   Webb,   William Snyder, 1882-1964. The Adena
        People. ... and Charles E. Snow. With a
        Chapter on Adena pottery and a foreword to
        the new ed. by James B. Griffin. Knox-
        ville,   University of Tennessee Press,
        1974.
        Reprint of the 1945 ed. pub.   by Univer-
        sity of Kentucky, Lexington,   which was
        issued as v. 6 of its Dept. of Anthropol-
        ogy and Archaeology Reports in Anthropology
        and Archaeology
        OCLC # 940632

3343   Webber,   Mark,   Christopher Stephens and
        Charles Laughlin Jr. The Masks: A Re-
        examination, or Masks? You mean They
        Effect the Brain? In 2502, pp. 204-218.

3344   Webster,   David L. Warfare and the Evolution
        of Maya Civilization. In 2378, pp. 335-
        372.

3345   _____.   Warfare and Evolution of the State:
        A Perspective from the Maya Lowlands. In
        2208, pp. 12-30.

3346   _____.   Warfare and the Evolution of the
        State: A Perspective from the Maya Low-
        lands. Greeley,   University of Northern
        Colorado,   Museum of Anthropology,   1976.

University of Northern Colorado. Museum of
Anthropology. Misc. Series 19, 1976.
OCLC # 3518753

3347 Webster, Gary S. Northern Iroquoian Hunt-
ing: An Optimization Approach. Ann Arbor,
MI., University Microfilms International,
1983.
Microfilm - PhD Thesis - Pennsylvania State
University
OCLC # 12685276

3348 Wedel, Mildred Mott and Raymond J. DeMal-
lie. The Ethnohistorical Approach in
Plains Area Study. In 0113, pp. 110-128.
This paper has an extensive bibliography

3349 Wedel, Waldo Rudolph, 1908- . Native Astronomy and the Plains Caddoans. In 2270,
pp. 131-145.

3350 _____. The Prehistoric Plains. In 0097,
pp. 203-241.

3351 Weeks, Alvin Gardner, 1966- . Massossoit
of the Wampanoags: With a Brief Commentary
on Indian Character; And Sketches of Other
Great Chiefs, Tribes and Nations; Also a
Chapter on Samoset, Squanto and Hobamock,
Three Early Native Friends of the Plymouth
Colonists. Fall River, MA., Priv.
Print., The Plimpton Press, 1920, c1919.
OCLC # 1138890

Weeks, Stephen Beauregard, 1865-1918. see
1377

3352 Weick, E. R.; Armstrong, G. T.; Mathur-
ian, D. C. E. and MacBain, S. K. Economic Development of the Canadian North
and Its Consequences for the Canadian Eskimo Society. In 1875, pp. 197-208.

Weidman, Bette S. see 3413

3353 Weigand, Phil C. The Ahualulco Site and the
Shaft-tomb Complex of the Etzalan Area. In
0231, pp. 120-131.

3354 Weinman, Paul L. The Denham Site (Glf 21-

1). New York Archeological Association
Bulletin 40,   July 1967,   pp.   3-4.   Millwood, NY.,   Kraus Reprint,   1976.

3355   _____.   The Fred Young Site - A River Phase
Component.   New York Archeological Associa-
tion Bulletin 43,   July 1968,   pp.   1-6.
Millwood,   NY.,   Kraus Reprint,   1976.
Paper presented at the annual meeting
April 20,   1968

3356   _____.   The Hammerstone Rockshelter.   New
York Archeological Association Bulletin 53,
Nov.   1971,   pp.   22-24.   Millwood,   NY.,
Kraus Reprint,   1976.

3357   _____.   The Hound Dog Rockshelter.   New York
Archeological Association Bulletin 47,
Nov.   1969,   pp.   12-15.   Millwood,   NY.,
Kraus Reprint,   1976.

3358   _____.   The John Himmer Rockshelter.   New
York Archeological Association Bulletin 48,
March 1970,   pp.   19-23.   Millwood,   NY.,
Kraus Reprint,   1976.

3359   _____.   The Moonshine Rockshelter.   New York
Archeological Association Bulletin 46,
July 1969,   pp.   11-15.   Millwood,   NY.,
Kraus Reprint,   1976.

3360   _____.   The Parrish Site - A Vergennes Com-
ponent.   New York Archeological Association
Bulletin 49,   July 1970,   pp.   30-32.
Millwood,   NY.,   Kraus Reprint,   1976.

3361   _____.   Two Recent Excavations.   New York
Archeological Association Bulletin 41,
Nov.   1967,   pp. 14-16.   Millwood,   NY.,
Kraus Reprint,   1976.

3362   _____.   Two Small Stratified Sites on Lake
George.   New York Archeological Association
Bulletin 34,   July,   1965,   pp.   6-10.
Millwood,   NY.,   Kraus Reprint,   1976.

Weinman,   Thomas P. see 1146,   1147,   3354-
3361

3363 Weinstein,   Laurie Lee.   Indians vs Col-

onists: Competition for Land in 17th Cent-
ury Plymouth Colony. Ann Arbor, MI.,
University Microfilms International,   1983.
Microfilm - PhD Thesis - Southern Methodist
University
OCLC # 11098041

3364   Weiss,   Gerald.   Campa Cosmology: The World
       of a Forest Tribe in South America.   New
       York,   American Museum of Natural History,
       1975.
       Anthropological Papers of the American
       Museum of Natural History v.   52,   pt.   5
       OCLC # 2011549

3365   Weiss,   Lawrence David.   Development of Cap-
       italism in the Navaho Nation: A Political-
       Economic History.   Minneapolis,   MEP Pub-
       lication,   1984.
       Studies in Marxism   v.   15
       OCLC # 9895486

3366   Weist,   Katherine M.   Beasts of Burden and
       Menial Slaves: 19th Century Observations
       of Northern Plains Indian Women.   In 1438,
       pp.   29-52.

3367   _____.   Plains Indian Women: An Assessment.
       In 0113,   pp.   255-271.

3368   Weitzner,   Bella.   Notes on the Hidatsa In-
       dians Based on Data Recorded by the Late
       Gilbert L.   Wilson.   New York,   American
       Museum of Natural History,   1979.
       American Museum of Natural History.   An-
       thropological Papers,   v.   56,   pt.   2
       OCLC # 6091321

3369   Welch,   James,   1940- .   Winter in the
       Blood.   New York,   Harper and Row,   1981.
       Perennial Library
       OCLC # 7150821

3370   Wellmann,   Klaus F.   North American Indian
       Rock Art.   New York State Journal of Med-
       icine v.   79,   June 1979,   pp.   1094-1105.
       Reprint copy

3370.5 Welsch,   Roger L.   Omaha Tribal Myths and
       Trickster Tales.   Chicago,   Sage Books,

1981.
OCLC # 6788857

3371 Welsh, Michael E. The Road to Assimilation:
      The Seminoles in Oklahoma, 1939-1936. Ann
      Arbor, MI., University Microfilms Inter-
      national, 1983.
      Microfilm - PhD Thesis - University of New
      Mexico
      OCLC # 11765640

3372 Werner, Dennis. Why Do the Mekranoti Trek?
      In 0023, pp. 225-238.

3373 Weslager, C. A. (Clifton Alfred), 1909- .
      The Delawares: A Critical Bibliography.
      Bloomington, Published for the Newberry
      Library by Indiana University Press, 1978.
      Bibliographical Series
      OCLC # 4004976

3374 _____.   The Nanticoke Indians (A Refugee
      Tribal Group of Pennsylvania). New York,
      AMS Press, 1983.
      Reprint. Originally pub. Harrisburg,
      Pennsylvania Historical and Museum Commis-
      sion, 1948
      OCLC # 9853779

3375 _____.   The Nanticoke Indians: Past and
      Present. Newark, University of Delaware
      Press, London, Associated University
      Press, 1983.
      Based in part on the author's Delaware's
      Forgotten Folk, 1943 and The Nanticoke
      Indians, 1948.
      OCLC # 9441284

      _____. see also 2059

3376 Wesler, Kit W. Towards a Synthetic Approach
      to the Chesapeake Tidewater: Historic
      Site Patterning in Temporal Perspective.
      Ann Arbor, MI., University Microfilms In-
      ternational, 1982.
      Microfilm - PhD Thesis - University of
      North Carolina at Chapel Hill
      OCLC # 10248601

3376.5 West, Frederick Hadleigh. The Archaeology

of Beringia. New York, Columbia University Press, 1981.
OCLC # 7552168

3377 _____. Late Paleolithic Cultures in Alaska.
In 0905, pp. 161-187.

3378 West, John, 1779?-1845. The Substance of a
Journal During A Residence at the Red River
Colony. East Ardsley, Yorkshire, Eng-
land. S. R. Publishers, New York,
Johnson Reprint Corp., 1966.
Canadiana before 1867
OCLC # 748297

West, W. Richard Jr. see 1851

Westheim, Paul. see 2523

3379 Weston, Warren. Freedom of Religion and the
American Indian. In 2304, pp. 263-268.
Reprinted from Rocky Mountain Social Science Journal v. 2, no. 1, March 1965,
pp. 1-6.

3380 Wetherington, Ronald K. Ceramic Analysis:
The Methodology of the Kaminaljuyu Project.
In 0531, pp. 3-50.

3381 _____. The Ceramic Chronology of
Kaminaljuyu. In 0531, pp. 115-149.

3382 _____. Ceramic Figurines at Kaminaljuyu.
In 0531, pp. 299-324.

3383 _____. Descriptive Taxonomy of Kaminaljuyu
Ceramics. In 0531, pp. 51-114.

3384 _____. Postclassic Ceramics at Beleh. In
0531, pp. 173-184.

3385 _____. The Spatial Distribution of Kaminaljuyu Ceramics. In 0531, pp. 185-222.

_____. see also 0752, 2132

3386 Wetmore, Ruth Y. First on the Land: The
Northern Carolina Indians. Winston-Salem,
NC., J. F. Blair, 1975.
OCLC # 1831268

3387   Wettersten,   Vernon Herbert.   A Study of Late
        Woodland Cultural Change in the Lower Illi-
        nois River Valley.   Ann Arbor,   MI.,   Uni-
        versity Microfilms International,   1983.
        Microfilm - PhD Thesis - Northwestern
        University

3388   Weyler,   Rex,   1947-   .   Blood of the Land:
        The Government and Corporate War Against
        the American Indian Movement.   New York,
        Everest House,   1982.
        OCLC # 8280425

3389   Whallon,   Robert.   On the Monothetic Nature
        of "Traditional"   Types.   A Contribution
        from Analysis of Owasco and Iroquois Cer-
        amics.   In 1585,   pp.   9-20.

3390   Wheat,   Joe Ben.   Kroeber's Formulation of
        the Southwest Culture Area.   In 1430,   pp.
        23-44.

3391   _____.   Mogollon Culture Prior to A. D.
        1000.   Millwood,   NY.,   Kraus Reprint,
        1974.
        Memoirs of the American Anthropological
        Association no.   82.   Suppl. to American
        Anthropologist v.   57,   no.   2,   pt.   3,
        1955.   Society for American Archaeology
        Memoir no.   10
        OCLC # 1204434

3392   _____.   A Preliminary Test of Herskovit's
        Hypothesis of Cultural Focus in Relation to
        Cultural Change.   In 1430,   pp.   61-77.

        _____.   see also   0491,   2057

3393   Wheeler,   C.   J.   and A.   P.   Brickner.   Rock
        Art: A Metalinguistic Interpretation of
        the Algonkian Word for Stone.   In 0068,
        pp.   362-371.

        Wheeler,   Richard Page.   see   0324 0527

3394   Wheeler-Voegelin,   Erminie,   1903-   .   An
        Ethnohistorical Report on the Wyandot,
        Potawatomi,   Ottawa,   and Chippewa of
        Northern Ohio.   New York,   Garland Pub.
        Co.,   1974.

American Indian Ethnohistory: Northcentral
and Northeastern Indians.   Before the Indian Claims Commission,   Docket nos.   13-F,
et al.
OCLC # 828283

3395   _____.   Mortuary Customs of the Shawnee and
Other Eastern Tribe.   New York,   AMS Press,
1980.
Reprint of the 1944 ed.   pub.   by the Indiana Historical Society,   Indianapolis,
which was issued as v.   2 no.   4 of Prehistory Research Series
OCLC # 6790644

3396   Wheelock,   Jaime.   Raices Indigenas de la
Lucha Anticolonialista en Nicaragua,   de
Gil Gonzales a Joaquin Zavala,   1523 a
1881.   Mexico,   Siglo Veintiuno,   1974.
OCLC # 1746922

3397   Where the Chill Came From: Cree Windigo
Tales and Journeys.   Gathered and trans.
by Howard Norman.   San Francisco,   North
Point Press,   1982.
OCLC # 8265648

Whitaker,   Nathaniel,   1732-1795.   see   2632

Whitaker,   Pamela.   see   3312

White,   Anta M.   see   2187-2189

3398   White,   Jack Chapman.   American Indian Youth
Alcohol Abuse and Alcoholism Prevention
Project.   Ann Arbor,   MI.,   University
Microfilms International,   1982.
Microfilm - PhD Thesis - Union for Experi-
menting College and Universities
OCLC # 13465029

3399   White,   Jay Vincent,   1945-   .   Taxing Those
They Found Here: An Examination of the Tax
Exempt Status of the American Indian.
Washington,   Institute for the Development
of Indian Law,   1972.
OCLC # 572242

3400   White,   John,   fl.   1575-1593.   America 1585:
The Complete Drawings of John White.

Chapel Hill,   University of North Carolina
Press,   a British Museum Publication,
1984.
OCLC # 10505120

_____.   see also 1247

3401 White,   John Kinnardh.   Pottery Techniques of
      Native North America: An Introduction to
      Traditional Technology.   Photos by Stewart
      J. MacLeod.   Chicago,   University of
      Chicago Press,   1976.
      OCLC # 2137142

3402 White,   John Ewbank Manchip,   1924- .   Eve-
      ryday Life of the American Indian.   New
      York,   Holmes and Meier Publishers,   1979.
      OCLC # 4591585

3403 White,   Leslie A.,   1900-1975.   The Pueblos
      at San Felipe.   New York,   Kraus Reprint,
      1964.
      Memoirs of the American Anthropological As-
      sociation,   no.   38,   1932
      OCLC # 581457

3404 _____.   The Pueblos of Santa Ana, New
      Mexico.   New York,   Kraus Reprint,   1969.
      Memoirs of the American Anthropological As-
      sociation,   no.   60.   Suppl.   to American
      Anthropologist v.   44,   no.   4,   pt.   2,
      1942.
      OCLC # 1949160

3405 _____.   The Pueblo of Santo Domingo, New
      Mexico.   New York,   Kraus Reprint,   1964.
      Memoirs of the American Anthropological As-
      sociation,   no.   43,   1935.   Suppl.   to
      American Anthropologist v.   37,   no.   2,
      pt.   2.
      OCLC # 653366

_____.   see also 0171

3406 White,   Marian E.   (Marian Emily),   1921-
      1975.   Dating the Niagara Frontier Iroquois
      Sequence.   New York State Archeological As-
      sociation Bulletin 14,   Nov.   1958,   pp.
      4-9.   Millwood,   NY.,   Kraus Reprint,
      1976.

Paper presented at annual meeting April 2,
1958

3407 _____. The Orchid Site Ossuary, Fort Erie,
Ontario. New York State Archeological Association Bulletin 38, Nov. 1966, pp.
1-35. Millwood, NY., Kraus Reprint,
1976.

3408 _____. The Shelby Site Reexamination. In
0712, pp. 85-91.

_____. see also 3048

3409 White, Raymond. Religion and its Role Among
the Luiseño. In 2276, pp. 355-378.

3410 White, Richard, 1947- . Native Americans
and the Environment. In 2789, pp. 179-
204.

3411 _____. The Roots of Dependency: Subsist-
ance, Environment, and Social Change
Among the Choctaws, Pawnees, and Navajos.
Lincoln, University of Nebraska Press,
1983.
OCLC # 8553053

3412 White, William Henry, 1851-1938. Custer,
Cavalry and Crows, Being the Thrilling Ac-
count of the Western Adventures of William
White...: The Story of William White as Told
to Thomas Marquis. Fort Collins, CO.,
The Old Army Press, 1975.
Source Custeriana Series v. 6
OCLC # 2332471

White Cloud Center. see 1731

White Moon, 1897- . see 2420

3413 White on Red: Images of the American Indian.
Edited by Nancy B. Black and Bette S.
Weidman. Port Washington, NY., Kennikat
Press, 1976.
Some essays in this collection are also
listed individually and refer to this
citation.
OCLC # 2238321

3414   Whitecotton, Joseph W., 1937- . The Zap-
        otecs Princes, Priests and Peasants. Nor-
        man, University of Oklahoma Press, 1977.
        Civilization of the American Indian Series
        OCLC # 2633138

3415   Whitehead, Ruth Olmes. Micmac Porcupine
        Quillwork. In 0479, pp. 157-166.

3416   Whiting, Alfred F. Havasupai Habitat: A.
        F. Whiting's Ethnography of a Traditional
        Indian Culture. Edited by Steven A. Weber
        and P. David Seaman. Tucson, University
        of Arizona Press, 1985.
        OCLC # 11523712

3417   Whitney, Ellen M. Black Hawk War, 1831-
        1832. Compiled and edited by ..., with an
        introd. by Anthony F. C. Wallace.
        Springfield, Illinois State Historical
        Library, 1970.
        Collections of the Illinois State Histor-
        ical Library v. 35. CONTENTS: v. 1.
        Illinois Volunteers. v. 2. Letters and
        Papers, pt. 1, April 30, 1831 - June
        23, 1832. pt. 2. June 24, 1832 - Oct.
        14, 1834.
        OCLC # 128655

        _____. see also 3310

3418   Whitney, Theodore. The Buyea Site OND 13-3.
        New York State Archeological Association
        Bulletin 50, Nov. 1970, pp. 1-14.
        Millwood, NY., Kraus Reprint, 1976.

3419   Whittaker, John Charles. Arrowheads and
        Artisans: Stone Tool Manufacture and In-
        dividual Variation at Grasshopper Pueblo.
        Ann Arbor, MI., University Microfilms
        International, 1984.
        Microfilm - PhD Thesis - University of
        Arizona
        OCLC # 12729220

3420   Whitten, Norman E. Ecuadorian Ethnocide and
        Indigenous Ethnogenesis: Amazonian Resurg-
        ence Amidst Andean Colonialism. Copenhag-
        en, IWGIA, 1976.
        OCLC # 3541409

3421 _____. Sacha Runa: Ethnicity and Adapta-
      tion of Ecuadorian Jungle Quichua. With
      the assistance of Marcelo Naranjo, Marcelo
      Santi Simbana, Dorothea S. Whitten. Urb-
      ana, University of Illinois Press, 1976.
      OCLC # 1637928

3422 _____. Sicuanga Runa: The Other Side of
      Development in Amazonian Equador. Urbana,
      University of Illinois Press, 1985.
      OCLC # 10483770

3423 Whittlesey, Stephanie W.,   Eric Arnould and
      William Reynolds. Archaeological Sedi-
      ments: Discourse, Experiment and Applica-
      tion. In 2239, pp. 28-35.

3424 Wrant, Michael D.,   1949- . Napoleon Hol-
      low and Koster Site Stratigraphy: Implica-
      tions for Holocene Landscape Evolution and
      Studies of Archaic Period Settlement Pat-
      terns in the Lower Illinois River Valley.
      In 0124, pp. 147-164.

3425 Wickwire, Wendy C. Cultures in Contact:
      Music, the Plateau Indian and the Western
      Encounter. Ann Arbor, MI., University
      Microfilms International, 1982.
      Microfilm - PhD Thesis - Wesleyan
      University
      OCLC # 11509315

3426 Widmer, Lee and Anthony J. Perzigian. The
      Ecology and Etiology of Skeletal Lesions in
      Late Prehistoric Populations of Eastern
      North America. In 2526, pp. 99-113.
      This is an expanded version of a paper pub-
      lished in Journal of the American Medical
      Association v. 241, 1979, pp. 2643-2646.

3427 Wied, Maximilian, Prinz von, 1782-1867.
      People of the First Man: Life Among the
      Plains Indians in their Final Days of
      Glory: The Firsthand Account of Prince
      Maximilian's Expedition up the Missouri
      River, 1833-34. Edited and designed by
      Davis Thomas and Karin Ronnefeldt; water-
      colors by Karl Bodmer. New York, Dutton,
      1976.
      OCLC # 2213355

3428 Wiget,   Andrew.   Native American Literature.
      Boston,   Twayne Publishers,   1985.
      Twayne's United States authors series;
      TUSA 467
      OCLC # 11188180

3429 Wilbur,   C.   Keith,   1923-   .   The New Eng-
      land Indians.   Chester,   CT.,   Globe Pequot
      Press,   1978.
      OCLC # 4530011

3430 Wilcocke,   Samuel Hull,   1766?-1833.   A Nar-
      rative in the Indian Country of North Amer-
      ica.   East Ardsley,   Wakefield,   Yorkshire,
      England.   S.   R.   Publishers,   New York,
      Johnson Reprint Corp.,   1968.
      Facsimile reprint of 1817 ed.   Canadiana
      Before 1867.
      OCLC # 654538

3431 Wilcox,   David.   A Set-Theory Approach to
      Sampling Pueblos: The Implications of
      Room-set Additions at Grasshopper Pueblo.
      In 2239,   pp.   19-27.

3432 Wildenhain,   Marguerite.   That We Look and
      See: An Admirer Looks at the Indians.   Ed-
      ited by John Nellermoes,   photos by David
      Stone.   Decorah,   IO.,   South Bear Press,
      1979.
      OCLC # 5678387

3433 Wildschut,   William.   Crow Indian Medicine
      Bundles.   Edited by John C.   Ewers.   New
      York,   Museum of the American Indian,   Heye
      Foundation,   1975.
      Contributions from the Museum of the
      American Indian,   Heye Foundation,   v.   17.
      OCLC # 1339043

3433.5 Wilkins,   Thurman.   Cherokee Tragedy: The
      Ridge Family and the Decimation of a Peo-
      ple.   2d ed.   rev.,   Norman,   University of
      Oklahoma Press,   1986.
      Civilization of the American Indian Series
      v.   169
      OCLC # 12552865

      Willers,   Diedrick,   1833-1908.   see 3331

3434 Willey, Gordon Randolph, 1913- . Exca-
vations at Seibal: Dept. of Peten,
Guatemala. Cambridge, MA., Harvard Uni-
versity, Peabody Museum of Archaeology and
Ethnology, 1975.
Peabody Museum of Archaeology and Ethnology
Memoirs v. 13, no. 1, 2. CONTENTS:
no. 1. Intro. The Site and Its Setting.
no. 2. Ceramics
OCLC # 1970308

3435 _____. External Influence on the Lowland
Maya: 1940 and 1975 Perspectives. In
2920, pp. 58-75.

3436 _____. A History of American Archaeology.
... and Jeremy A. Sabloff, 2d ed. San
Francisco, W. H. Freeman, 1980.
OCLC # 5564980

3437 _____. Prehispanic Maya Agriculture: A
Contemporary Summation. In 2522, pp.
325-335.

3438 _____ and Richard M. Leventhal. Prehistoric Settlement at Copan. In 0472, pp. 75-
102.

3439 _____. Recent Researches and Perspectives
in Mesoamerican Archaeology: An Introduct-
ory Commentary. In 0122, pp. 3-27.

3440 _____. The Rise of Classic Maya Civilization: A Pasion Valley Perspective. In
2378, pp. 133-157.

3441 _____. The Rise of Maya Civilization: A
Summary View. In 2378, pp. 383-423.

_____. see also 0472, 1085

3442 Willey, Lorraine Mary. Instruction in North
American Arechaeology: The Design of
Course Aligned Museum Displays. Ann Arbor,
MI., University Microfilms International,
1983.
Microfilm - EdD Thesis - Pennsylvania State
University

3443 Williams, Barbara J. Mexican Pictorial

Cadastral Registrers. In 0978, pp. 103-125.

3444 Williams, John, 1664-1729. The Redeemed Captive Returning to Zion. In 2562, pp. 165-226.
First published in 1707

3445 Williams, John Mark, 1948- . The Joe Bell Site: Seventeenth Century Lifeways on the Oconee River. Ann Arbor, MI., University Microfilms International, 1983.
Microfilm - PhD Thesis - University of Georgia
OCLC # 10134250

3446 Williams, Stephen, 1926- . Excavations at the Lake George Site: Yazoo County, Mississippi, 1958-1960. ... and Jeffrey P. Brain. Cambridge, MA., Peabody Museum of Archaeology and Ethnology, Harvard University, Distributed by Harvard University Press, 1983.
Papers of the Peabody Museum of Archaeology and Ethnology v. 74.
OCLC # 12544852

3447 Williams, Stephen Guion, 1942- . In the Middle, Qitinganituk: The Eskimo Today. Introd. by Edmund Carpenter. Boston, MA., D. R. Godine, 1983.
OCLC # 9080962

3448 Williams, Terry Tempest. Pieces of White Shell, a Journey to Navajoland. Illus. by Clifford Bryceka. New York, Scribners, 1984.
OCLC # 10823592

3449 Williams, Walter L., 1948- . and Thomas French. Bibliographic Essay. In 2930, pp. 211-241.

3450 _____. Patterns in the History of the Remaining Southeastern Indians, 1840-1975. In 2930, pp. 193-207.

3451 _____. Southeastern Indians Before Removal: Prehistory, Contact, Decline. In 2930, pp. 3-24.

_____. see also 2930

3452 Williamson, R. G. **Eskimo Value Persistence in Contemporary Acculturation**. In 1875, pp. 265-288.

3453 Williamson, Ray A., 1938- ; Howard J. Fisher and Donnel O'Flynn. **Anasazi Solar Observations**. In 2270, pp. 203-217.

3454 _____. **Living Sky: The Cosmos of the American Indian**. Line illus. by Snowden Hodges. Boston, Houghton Mifflin, 1984. OCLC # 10558156

_____. see also 0354

3455 Willis, William S. **Divide and Rule: Red, White and Black in the Southeast**. In 2304, pp. 74-85. Abridged and reprinted from **Journal of Negro History** v. 48, no. 3, July 1963, pp. 157-176.

3456 Willoughby, Charles Clark, 1857-1943. **Indian Antiquities and the Kennebec Valley**. With a foreword and notes by Arthur E. Spiess. Augusta, ME., Maine Historic Preservation Commission, Maine State Museum, 1980. Occasional Publication in Maine Archaeology v. 1 OCLC # 7046565

Willis, W. H. see 0930

Wilson, Gilbert Livingstone, 1868-1930. see 2445, 3293.5

3457 Wilson, Jack Hubert. **A Study of the Late Prehistoric Protohistoric and Historic Indians of the Carolina and Virginia Piedmont**. Ann Arbor, MI., University Microfilms International, 1983. Microfilm - PhD Thesis - University of North Carolina - Chapel Hill OCLC # 12672703

3458 Wilson, Raymond, 1945- . **Ohiyesa: Charles Eastmen, Santee Sioux**. Urbana,

University of Illinois Press,   1983.
OCLC # 8346682

3458.5   Wilson,   Terry P.,   1941- .   Bibliography
         of the Osage.   Metuchen,   NJ.,   Scarecrow
         Press,   1985.
         Native American Bibliography Series v.   6
         OCLC # 11815724

3459   _____.   The Underground Reservation: Osage
         Oil.   Lincoln,   University of Nebraska
         Press,   1985.
         OCLC # 11497893

3460   Winchell,   Dick Glenn.   Space and Place of
         the Yavapai.   Ann Arbor,   MI.,   University
         Microfilms International,   1982.
         Microfilm - PhD Thesis - Arizona State
         University
         OCLC # 10621398

         Winders,   Thomas C.   see   1385

3461   Wing,   Elizabeth S.   Use of Dogs for Food:
         An Adaptation to the Coastal Environemnt.
         In 2524,   pp.   29-41.

         Wingerson,   Roberta.   see   0370

3462   Wingert,   John L.   Inhalant Used Among Native
         American Adolescents: A Comparison of
         Users and Non-users at Intermountain Inter-
         tribal School.   Ann Arbor,   MI.,   Univer-
         sity Microfilms International,   1982.
         Microfilm - PhD Thesis - Utah State
         University
         OCLC # 8903858

         Winkler,   James.   see   0728

3463   Winter,   Keith John,   1935- .   Shananditti:
         The Last of the Beothucks.   Vancouver,   J.
         J.   Douglas,   1975.
         OCLC # 2117819

         Wirth,   John D.   see   1557

3464   Wisdom of the Seneca.   Albany,   State Educa-
         tion Dept.,   Bureau of Bilingual Education,
         1979.

OCLC # 6383939

3465 Wiseman, Frederick M. Agricultural and His-
      torical Ecology of the Maya Lowlands. In
      2522, pp. 63-115.

3466 Wishart, David J., 1946- . The Fur Trade
      of the American West, 1807-1840: A Geo-
      graphical Synthesis. Lincoln, University
      of Nebraska Press, 1979.
      OCLC # 4135800

3467 Wissler, Clark, 1870-1947. Costumes of the
      Plains Indians Together with Structural Ba-
      sis to the Decoration of Costumes Among the
      Plains Indians. New York, AMS Press,
      1975.
      Reprint of the 1915 and 1916 ed. pub. by
      order of the Trustees of the American Mus-
      eum of Natural History, New York, which
      was issued as v. 17, pt. 2 and pt. 3 of
      the Museum's Anthropological papers.
      OCLC # 1582330

3468 _____. General Discussion of Shamanistic
      and Dancing Societies. In 3473, pp. 853-
      875.
      Anthropological Papers of the American
      Museum of Natural History v. 11, pt. 12.

3469 _____. Indians of Greater New York and the
      Lower Hudson. New York, AMS Press, 1975.
      Reprint of 1909 ed. Anthropological Papers
      of the American Museum of Natural History
      v. 3. Essays in this collection are also
      listed individually and refer to this cita-
      tion.
      OCLC # 1551052

3470 _____. Material Cultures of the North
      American Indians. In 0110, pp. 76-134.

3471 _____. Societies and Ceremonial Associa-
      tions in the Oglala Division of the Teton-
      Dakota. In 3473, pp. 1-99.
      Anthropological Papers of the American
      Museum of Natural History v. 11, pt. 1.

3472 _____. Societies and Dance Associations of
      the Blackfoot Indians. In 3473, pp. 359-

459.
Anthropological Papers of the American
Museum of Natural History v. 11, pt. 4.

3473 _____. Societies of the Plains Indians.
New York, AMS Press, 1975.
Anthropological Papers of the American Museum of Natural History, pub. in 13 parts
from 1912-1916. Anthropological Paper v.
11.
OCLC # 1601810

3474 Witherspoon, Gary. The Central Concepts of
Navajo World View. Lisse, Peter de Ridder
Press, 1975.
Reprinted from Linguistics and Anthropol-
ogy: In Honor of C. F. Voegelin, pub.
by Peter de Ridder Press, 1975, pp. 701-
720.
OCLC # 3758275

3475 _____. The Language and Art in the Navajo
Universe. Ann Arbor, MI., University of
Michigan Press, 1977.
OCLC # 2837039

3476 Witt, Shirley Hill. A Cherokee Story. In
1556, pp. 24.

3477 _____. Northeast Indians: The Iroquois
Confederacy and Matrilineal Society. In
1556, pp. 62-66.

3478 _____. Prior Use. In 1556, pp. 31.

3479 _____. The Right Remains. In 1556, pp.
10-12.

3480 Witthoft, John. Green Corn Ceremonialism in
the Eastern Woodlands. Ann Arbor, MI.,
University of Michigan Press, 1949.
Occasional Contributions from the Museum of
Anthropology of the University of Michigan
no. 13.
OCLC # 653668

3481 _____. Notes on the Archaic Cultures of the
Appalachian Mountain Region. New York
State Archeological Association Bulletin

21, March 1961, pp. 7-16. Millwood,
NY., Kraus Reprint, 1976.

3482 _____. Observations on Social Change Among
the Eastern Cherokees. In 0547, pp. 202-
222.

3483 _____. Some Sources of Uncertainity in
Radio-carbon Dating. New York State
Archeological Association Bulletin 12,
March 1958, pp. 1-4. Millwood, NY.,
Kraus Reprint, 1976.

3483.5 Wolcott, Fred Ryther, 1862-1946. Onon-
daga: Portrait of a Native People. Pre-
face by Dennis J. Connors; Foreword by
Laurence M. Hauptman; Introd. by Ray
Gonyea; Photos by Fred R. Wolcott; On-
ondaga County Dept. of Parks and Recrea-
tion. Syracuse, NY., Syracuse University
Press in Association with Everson Museum of
Art, 1986.
OCLC # 12840169

3484 Wolf, Carolyn E., 1941- . Indians of
North and South America: A Bibliography
Based on the Collection at the Willard E.
Yager Library-Museum, Hartwick College,
Oneonta, NY., Metuchen, NJ., Scarecrow
Press, 1977.
OCLC # 2818411

3485 Wolf, David J. Middle Mississippean: A
Prehistoric Cultural System Viewed From a
Biological Perspective. In 0270, pp. 27-
44.

3486 Wolf, Eric R. Alfred L. Kroeber. In
3139, pp. 35-65.

Womanski, Linda. see 1277

3487 Wood, Alice. Historic Burials at the
Boughton Hill Site (CAN 2-2), Victor TWP.,
Ontario County, NY., New York State
Archeological Association Bulletin 32,
Nov. 1964, pp. 6-16. Millwood, NY.,
Kraus Reprint, 1976.

3488 Wood, Marion. Spirits, Heroes and Hunters

for North American Indian Mythology.
Illus. by John Sibbick, New York,
Schocken Books, 1982.
World Mythology Series. A Collection of
American Indian myths and legends illus-
trating the customs and values of the trad-
itional Indian way of life.
OCLC # 7835791

3489 Wood, Nancy C. When Buffalo Free the Moun-
tains. Photos by the author. Garden City,
NY., Doubleday, 1980.
OCLC # 6486329

3490 Wood, W. Raymond. Plains Trade in Prehistoric and Protohistoric Intertribal Relations. In 0113, pp. 98-109.

_____. see also 0113, 1635, 2525

3491 Woodbury, Hanni. Translation Glosses and
Semantic Description. In 0979, pp. 209-
227.

_____. see also 2334

3492 Woodcock, George, 1912- . Peoples of the
Coast: The Indians of the Pacific North-
west. Bloomington, Indiana University
Press, 1977.
OCLC # 3088985

3493 Wooden Leg, Cheyenne Indian, 1858- .
Wooden Leg, a Warrior Who Fought Custer.
Interpreted by Thomas B. Marquis. Lin-
coln, University of Nebraska Press, 1962,
c1957.
A Bison Book. Originally published in 1931
as A Warrior Who Fought Custer
OCLC # 704399

3494 Woodruff, Anne Schillingsburg and F. Alan
Palmer. The Unalachtigo of New Jersey,
the Original People of Cumberland County.
Cumberland County Historical Society,
1973.

3495 Woods, Patricia Dillon, 1948- . French-
Indian Relations on the Southern Frontier,
1699-1762. Ann Arbor, MI., University

Microfilms International Research
Press, 1980.
Studies in American History and Culture no.
18. Originally published in 1978 under
title <u>The Relations Between the French of
Colonial Louisiana and the Choctaw, Chick-
asaw, and Natchez Indians, 1699-1762</u>.
OCLC # 6423032

Woods, Willis F. <u>see</u> 1891

3496   Woodward, Ashbel, 1804-1885. <u>Wampum, a
Paper Presented to the Numismatic and Anti-
quarian Society of Philadelphia</u>. Albany,
J. Munsell, printer, 1878.
OCLC # 2765823

3497   Worcester, Donald Emmet, 1915- . <u>The
Apaches; Eagles of the Southwest</u>. Norman,
University of Oklahoma Press, 1979.
Civilization of the American Indian Series
v. 149
OCLC # 4935343

3498   _____. <u>Santanta</u>. In 0081, pp. 107-130.

3499   Workshop for American Indian Educators on the
Learning Potential Assessment Devices and
Instrumental Enrichment Programs (1982:
Shiprock, NM.) <u>To Sing Our Own Songs:
Cognition and Culture in Indian Education:
Report from a Workshop for American Indian
Educators on the Learning Potential Assess-
ment Device and Instrumental Enrichment
Programs, Shiprock, Navaho Nation, New
Mexico</u>. New York, Association on American
Indian Affairs, 1985.
Conference held in Aug. 1982. Pub. in
cooperation with the NiHa'Alchini Ba Educa-
tional Center, Shiprock, NM.
OCLC # 11289245

3500   <u>World of the American Indian</u>. Washington,
National Geographic Society, 1974.
Story of Man Library
OCLC # 1149014

3501   Wormington, H. Marie. <u>Early Man in the New
World: 1970-1980</u>. In 0903, pp. 191-195.

3502   Worsley,   Peter.   <u>Groote Eylandt Totemism and</u>
       <u>Le Totemisme Aujourd'hui</u>.   In 3547 (of
       original vol.),   pp.   141-159.

3503   Worth,   Sol.   <u>Through Navajo Eyes,   an Ex-</u>
       <u>ploration in Communication and Anthropol-</u>
       <u>ogy</u>.   ... and John Adair.   Bloomington,
       Indiana University Press,   1972.
       OCLC # 533404

3504   Wray,   Charles F.   <u>Archeological Evidence of</u>
       <u>the Mask Among the Seneca</u>.   New York State
       Archeological Association Bulletin 7,   Aug.
       1956,   pp.   7-8.   Millwood,   NY.,   Kraus
       Reprint,   1976.
       Abstract of paper presented at the annual
       meeting April 14,   1956

3505   _____.   <u>New Discoveries on an Old Site:</u>
       <u>The Bunce Site</u>.   New York State Archeologi-
       cal Association Bulletin 18,   March 1960,
       pp.   1-4.   Millwood,   NY.,   Kraus Reprint,
       1976.

3506   _____.   <u>Seneca Glass Trade Beads,   c.   A.</u>
       <u>D.   1550-1820</u>.   In 1204,   pp.   41-49.

3507   _____.   <u>Seneca Tobacco Pipes</u>.   New York
       State Archeological Association Bulletin 6,
       March 1956,   pp.   15-16.   Millwood,   NY.,
       Kraus Reprint,   1976.
       Abstract of paper presented at the annual
       meeting April 16,   1955

       _____.   <u>see also</u>   3049

3508   Wright,   Albert Hazen,   1879- .   <u>Sullivan</u>
       <u>Expedition of 1779,   Contemporary Newspaper</u>
       <u>Comment</u>.   Ithaca,   NY.,   A.   H.   Wright,
       1943.
       4 parts in 1.   His Studies in History no.
       5,   6,   7,   and 8.   Each part has subtitle
       <u>Contemporary Newspaper Comment and Letters</u>.
       Pt.   1.   Preliminary Correspondence and
       Raids.   Pt.   2.   Indian Participants.
       Broadhead's Expedition.   Battle of Chemung.
       Pt.   3.   Battle of Newtown.   Genesee -
       Return.   Pt.   4.   Conclusions.
       OCLC # 1827984

3509   Wright,   Asher,   1803-1875.   Diu'hsawahgwah,
       Gayadoshah.   Boston,   Nadigve'hjihsh-vohvoh
       Dodisdoyagvoh,   1836.
       Elementary reading book in the Seneca
       language
       OCLC # 656335

3510   Wright,   Gary A.   and Susanne J.   Miller.
       Prehistoric Hunting of New World Wild
       Sheep: Implications for the Study of Sheep
       Domestication.   In 0710,   pp.   293-312.

3511   Wright,   J.   Leitch (James Leitch),   1929- .
       The Only Land They Knew: The Tragic Story
       of the American Indians in the Old South.
       New York,   Free Press,   London,   Collier
       Macmillian,   1981.
       OCLC # 6982151

3512   Wright,   J.   V.   (James Valliere),   1932- .
       The Shield Archaic in Manitoba - a Prelim-
       inary Statement.   In 1467,   pp.   29-45.

3513   _____.   The Cultural Continuity of the
       Northern Iroquoian-Speaking Peoples.   In
       0979,   pp.   283-299.

3514   _____.   The Role of Attribute Analysis in
       the Study of Iroquoian Prehistory.   In
       1585,   pp.   21-26.

3515   Wright,   Peter M.   Washakie.   In 0081,   pp.
       131-151.

       Wrong,   George McKinnon.   see   2728

       Wyckoff,   Don G.   see   0410

3516   Wyman,   Leland Clifton,   1897- .   The
       Mountainway of the Navajo;   With a Myth of
       the Female Branch.   Recorded and trans.   by
       Berard Haile.   Tucson,   University of
       Arizona Press,   1975.
       OCLC # 1983268

3517   _____.   Navajo Indian Medical Ethnobotany.
       ... and Stuart K.   Harris.   New York,   AMS
       Press,   1979.
       Reprint of the 1941 ed.   pub.   in series,
       The University of New Mexico Bulletin,   An-

thropological Series v. 3, no. 5, whole
no. 366.
OCLC # 4956635

3518 _____. Southwest Indian Drypainting. Santa
Fe, School of American Research, Albuquerque, University of New Mexico Press,
1983.
OCLC # 9082993

3519 Yager Conference on Archaeology and Geo-
chronology, Hartwick College, 1976.
Archaeology and Geochronology of the Sus-
quehanna and Schoharie Regions: Proceed-
ings of the Yager Conference at Hartwick
College, 6 Nov., 1976. Edited by John R.
Cole and Laurie R. Godfrey. Oneonta,
NY., Hartwick College, 1977.
Essays in this collection are also listed
individually and refer to this citation.
OCLC # 3670875

3520 Yalman, Nur. "The Raw: The Cooked::
Nature::Culture" - Observations on Le Cru
et le Cuit. In 3547 (of the original
vol.), pp. 71-89.

3521 Yarnell, Richard A. Early Plant Husbandry
in Eastern North America. In 0710, pp.
265-273.

3522 Yost, James A. and Patricia M. Kelley.
Shotguns, Blowguns, and Spears: The
Analysis of Technological Efficiency. In
0023, pp. 189-224.

3523 Yost, Nellie Irene Snyder. Medicine Lodge:
The Story of a Kansas Frontier Town.
Introd. by Don Russell. Chicago, Sage
Books, 1970.
OCLC # 100886

Young, Jon Nathan. see 1388

3524 Young, Mary E. Indian Removal and Land Allotment: The Civilized Tribes and Jackson-
ian Justice. In 2304, pp. 132-145.
Reprinted from American Historical Review
v. 64, no. 1. Oct. 1958, pp. 31-45.

3525   _____. Indian Removal and the Attack on
Tribal Autonomy: The Cherokee Case.   In
1282, pp.   125-142.

Younger,   Erin. see 1499

3526 Zanger,   Martin.   Red Bird.   In 0081,   pp.
64-87.

3526.5   _____. "Straight Tongue's Heathen Wards":
Bishop Whipple and the Episcopal Mission to
the Chippewas.   In 0578.5,   pp.   177-214.

3527 Zawacki,   April Allison.   Early Vegetation of
the Lower Illinois Valley: A Study of the
Distribution of Floral Resources with Reference to Prehistoric Cultural-Ecological
Adaptation. ... and Glenn Hausfater,   assisted by J.   Thomas Meyers.   Springfield,
IL.,   1969.
Illinois State Museum.   Reports of Investigations v.   17.   Illinois Valley Archaeological Program Research papers v.   1.
OCLC # 649839

3528 Zeilik,   Michael.   Archaeoastronomy of Chaco
Canyon.   In 2289,   pp.   65-72.

3529 Zeisberger,   David,   1721-1808.   Grammar of
the Language of the Lenni Lenape or Dela-
ware Indians.   Trans.   from the German
manuscript of the author by Peter Stephen
DuPonceau.   New York,   AMS Press,   1980.
Reprint of the 1827 ed.   printed by J.
Kay,   Philadelphia.
OCLC # 5500179

3530 Zeitlin,   Judith Francis.   Changing Patterns
of Resource Exploitation,   Settlement Distribution and Demography on the Southern
Isthmus of Tehuantepec,   Mexico.   In 2524,
pp.   151-177.

3531 Zeitlin,   Robert Norman.   Long Distance Exchange and the Growth of a Regional Center
on the Southern Isthmus of Tehuantepec,
Mexico.   In 2524,   pp.   183-210.

3532 Zenk,   henry Benjamin,   1944- .   The Chinook
Jargon and Native Cultural Persistence in

the Grand Ronde Indian Community, 1856-
1907: A Special Case of Creolization. Ann
Arbor, MI., University Microfilms Inter-
national, 1984.
Microfilm - PhD Thesis - University of
Oregon
OCLC # 12231068

3533 Zimmerly, David W., 1938- . Museocinema-
tography: Ethnographic Film Programs of
the National Museum of Man, 1913-1973.
Ottawa, National Museums of Canada, 1974.
Paper - Ethnology Division no. 11. Mer-
cury Series. Abstract in English and
French
OCLC # 1419172

3534 Zimmerman, Albright Gravenor. Indian Trade
of Colonial Pennsylvania. Ann Arbor, MI.,
University Microfilms International, 1966.
Microfilm - PhD Thesis - University of
Delaware
OCLC # 275568

3534.5 Zimmerman, Bill. Airlift to Wounded Knee.
Chicago, Swallow Press, 1976.
OCLC # 2503893

3535 Zimmerman, Michael R. The Diagnosis of
Granulomatous Disease in Mummies. In 2526,
pp. 63-68.

3536 Ziontz, Alvin J. Indian Litigation. In
0034, pp. 149-183.

3537 Zitkala-Sa, 1876-1938. Old Indian Legends.
Retold by Zitkala-Sa. With illus. by
Angel DeCora. Foreword by Agnes M. Pic-
otte. Lincoln, University of Nebraska
Press, 1985.
A Bison Book. reprint. Originally pub.
Boston, Ginn, 1901
OCLC # 12104125

3538 Zitzow, Darry, and George Estes. The Heritage Consistency Continuum in Counseling Native American Students. In 2962, pp.
133-139.

Zo-Tom. see 2479

3539 Zolbrod, Paul G. Poetry and Culture: The
      Navaho Example. In 2904, pp. 221-224.
      Reprinted from Shantih v. 4, no. 2,
      1979, pp. 10-14.

      _____. see also 0817

3540 Zubrow, Ezra B. W. New World Archaeology:
      Theoretical and Cultural Transformations.
      Readings from Scientific American, select-
      ed and with introd. by ... and Margaret C.
      Fritz and John M. Fritz. San Francisco,
      W. H. Freeman, 1974.
      OCLC # 874256

3541 Zuidema, R. T. The Inca Calendar. In
      2270, pp. 219-259.

3542 _____. Masks in the Incaic Solstice and
      Equinoctial Rituals. In 2502, pp. 149-
      156.

TITLE INDEX

507

589   Series Index

0147, 0148, 1358, 2957
Athapascan Indians 0099,
   0651, 1028, 1407, 1783,
   1784, 2267, 2333
Atlantic States 0932,
   1585
Atopula Site, Mex. 1413
Atsina Indians 2849
Atsugewi Indians 1165
Atwell Fort Site,
   Onondaga Co., NY 2637
Authors, Canadian 1713.5
Autonomy 0372
Avent, Carrie 2895
Avery Site, Manitoba 1679
Aztec Language 0154, 1776
Aztecs 0154, 0170, 0241,
   0329, 0431, 0503, 0666,
   0730, 0986, 1195, 1557,
   1707, 1708, 2013, 2024,
   2065, 2206, 2209, 2211,
   2381, 2382, 2259, 2953,
   3271
Aztecs--Art 2205, 2428,
   3006
Aztecs--Calendar 0329,
   0330
Aztecs--History 0729,
   2209, 2428, 2730
Aztecs--Religion and
   Mythology 0329, 0330,
   0430, 0503, 2820

BBB Motor Site, IL 0944.5
Baldwin Rock Shelter
   Site, NY 3361
Bandelier, Adolph Francis
   Alphonse, 1840-1914
   0171, 1821
Bannock Indians 1551,
   2126
Barasana Indians 1600
Bari Indians see Motilon
   Indians
Barium 2197
Barnes, Will C., 1858-
   1936 0180
Baritz, Albert 0182
Barnitz, Jennie 0182
Barrow, Robert d. 1697
   0805

Barton Ramie Site, Belize
   1183, 1186
Basketmaker Indians 0094,
   0240, 0252, 0452, 0893,
   2190, 2217, 2664
Basketmaking 0027, 0195,
   0467, 1786, 1812, 1990,
   2229, 2230, 2677, 2077,
   3077
Beads 0070, 0238, 0345,
   1108, 1222, 1324, 1528,
   1695, 1743, 2143, 2483,
   2516, 2894, 2961, 3506
Beads (as Money) 1125
Beadword 0207, 2374,
   2941.5
Bean, George Washington
   2367.5
Beavers 3240
Belek Site, Guatemala
   3384
Bella Coola 0671
Benedict, Ruth 2165
Beothuk Indians 1515,
   1620, 2935, 3050, 3463
Beothuk Language 1515
Bering Land Bridge 3376.5
Bering Strait 2596
Bet Helicker's Cave Site
   1350
Beynon, William, Toim-
   shian, 1888-1959 1322
Bibliography 0086, 0199,
   0294, 0382, 0427, 0513,
   0586, 0658, 0736, 0820,
   0828, 0829, 1166, 1257,
   1293, 1399, 1401, 1407,
   1470, 1576, 1594, 1650,
   1757, 1798.5, 1924,
   1924.5, 2017, 2100,
   2119, 2163, 2182, 2241,
   2351, 2357, 2395,
   2494.5, 2495, 2500,
   2556, 2608, 2608.5,
   2674, 2695, 2733, 2789,
   2824, 2910, 2913, 3079,
   3117-3120, 3134, 3208,
   3213, 3305, 3314, 3449,
   3484
Biblioteca Nazionale Cen-
   trale di Firenze.

Dann Site, Monroe Co., NY
0662, 2410
Dartmouth College 2632
Data Processing 2236,
3052
Dating in Archaeology see
Archaeology (Methodol-
ogy)
Davidson, Florence Eden-
shaw, 1896-. 0290
Davis Site, Margarets-
ville, NY 1596
Dawes Act (Feb. 8, 1887)
(see also Land Tenure)
1303, 2353
Dearborn, Henry Alexander
Scammet, 1783-1851.
0744
DeCalves, Alfonso, pseud.
0750
Deer Dance (see also
Dances) 0408
DeLaguna, Fredrica, 1906-
. 0757
Delaware 0717, 0846,
2494.5, 2495
Wilmington 0846
Delaware Indians 0758,
0957, 1208, 1349, 1393,
1484, 1546, 1827, 1877,
2297, 3080, 3373, 3480
Delaware Language 3529
Delaware River Valley
(NY-DE and NJ) 0001,
0102, 0932, 1208, 1596,
1766, 1781, 1845, 1879,
2561
DeMange Site, IL 2157
Demography 0829
Dendrochronology (Tree
Rings) 0743
Denham Site, NY 3354
Dennis Site, Albany Co.,
NY 1139
Dentition 0674, 1333,
2039, 2218, 3171
Denver Art Museum 0639,
0788
Dept. of Indian Affairs
(Canada) 1312
Detroit--Siege of, 1763.

2565
Devil's Tower Reservation
2056
Diabetes (see also
Diseases) 3101
Dickinson, Johathan 1663-
1722. 0805
Dickson Mounds 1815
Directories 0210, 0223,
0658, 1112, 2608,
2608.5
Discovery and Explor-
ation--America (see
also Explorers; names
of explorers and ex-
peditions) 0136, 0177,
1878, 1889, 2311, 2790,
2884
Diseases (see also Health
and Hygiene; names of
individual diseases)
0072, 0209, 0252, 0280,
0636, 0675, 1136, 1369,
1795, 1815, 1937, 2526,
2966, 3005, 3037, 3157,
3535
Dissertations, Academic
2556
Divination--Guatemala
0618
Dodge, John, 1751-1800.
0836
Documents on Microfilm
3209
Doerschuk Site 0600
Dogrib Indians see
Thlingchadinne Indians
Don Juan, 1891-. 0516-
0518, 2817
Dorset Culture 0626
Drama 1175, 1663, 1704,
1989, 2663, 2931, 3307
Draper, Lyman Copeland,
1815-1891. 3122
Draper Site, Ontario 1051
Dresden Codex 0593
Drug Abuse 1290.5, 3462
Drum 3262
DuBay, John Baptiste,
1802-1887., 1793
Duck Valley Indian Res-

ervation (Idaho and
Nevada) 2021
Dull Knife 2319
Dumont, Jean Paul, 1940-.
0885
Dundley, Joseph, 1647-
1720. 2090
Duston, Hannah Emerson,
b.1657 2087
Dutton Site, CO 2970
Dwellings (see also Cliff
Dwellings) 0782, 0874,
0973, 1068, 1342, 1353,
2151, 2260, 2317, 2637,
2692, 2990, 3418
Dwellings--Mexico 1011,
1012, 2152
Dzibilchaltun Site 0106

Ealy, Taylor F. (Taylor
Filmore) b.1848 2171
East St. Louis Stone
Quarry Site, IL 2156
Earthworks (Archaeology)
2204
Eastburn, Robert, 1710-
1778. 0907
Eastern Indians, Wars
with, 1722-1726. 2442
Eastern States 1182,
1288, 1603, 1853
Eastern Woodlands see
Woodland Indians
Eastman, Charles Alex-
ander, Santee Sioux,
1858-1939. 2142, 3458
Eastport Site, MI 0267
Ecology 2072, 2254, 3286
Economic Anthropology
2274
Economic History--Mexico
0381, 0705
Economic History--Latin
America 0381, 0433,
0635
Economic History--North
America 0336, 0457,
1530, 1617, 1667, 1773,
2159, 2273, 2294, 2361,
2569, 2593, 2660, 3010,
3043, 3215, 3223, 3347,

3365, 3411
Ecuador 2519, 2735.5,
2739, 3421, 3422
Carchi (Province)
1109
Quito Region 2735.5
Education 0037, 0084,
0677, 0892.5, 0992,
1082.5, 1163, 1231,
1290.5, 1737, 1928,
2238.5, 2319, 2320.5,
2547, 2645, 2701, 2854,
2962, 2984, 3191, 3206,
3207, 3210, 3479, 3499
Education--Curriculum
1157.5, 1283.5, 2217.5,
2709, 2831.7
Education, Bilingual
2319.5
Education, Higher 0307,
0405, 0923, 2320, 2387,
2448, 3222, 3538
Educational Administra-
tion see School Manage-
ment and Organization
Effigy Mound 1549
Egli Site 1426
Eiseley, Loren, 1907-
1977. 0575
Elementary School
Teachers 0769
Eliot, John, 1604-1690.
0937, 1107, 2196, 2735
Elk Island Site, Manitoba
3512
Employment 1025, 1575
Encyclopedias and Dic-
tionaries (see also
Glossaries; Language
and Languages) 0807-
0809, 1869, 2249, 3161
Energy see Power Re-
sources
England--Biography 1238
English Literature--
Translation from Indian
Languages 0082
English Poetry--Trans-
lations from Indian
Languages 3090
Environment 1196, 1465,

lations into English
0451
Mayhew, Thomas 2735
Mayo Indians 0703
Mazahua Indians 2062
Meadowcroft Rockshelter,
  PA 0024-0026, 0259,
  0487
Medals 2551
Medical Anthropology 2581
Medical Care 1157.2,
  1795, 3191, 3338
Medicine--Latin America
  2381, 2382, 2756
Medicine--Mexico 2381,
  2756
Medicine--North America
  0209, 0578, 0698, 0786,
  1034, 1086, 1203, 1734,
  1795, 1803, 1893, 2183,
  2210, 2381, 2382, 2405,
  2803, 3080, 3084, 3282,
  3433, 3517
Medicine, Botanic 0698
Medicine Bundles 1034
Medicine Hat Site, Al-
  berta 2607
Medicine Lodge, KS 3523
Medicine Men (see also
  Shamanism) 1540, 2392
Medicine Wheels (Stone
  Circles) 0922
Meek, Joseph Lafayette,
  1810-1875. 3270
Megalithic Monuments 3152
Meigs, Return Jonathan,
  1740-1823. 2019
Mendelhall Privy Site,
  Wilmington, DE 0846
Mendieta, Geronimo de,
  d. 1604. 2463
Menominee Indians 1692,
  2278, 2331, 2389, 2450,
  2886, 2958, 3261
Mental Healing 1341
Mental Health 1731
Merchants 0127
Merivale, Herman, d. 1874.
  2031
Merrimack Valley (NH and
  MA) 1744

Meas Verde National Park
  0237, 0527, 2135
Metal Working (see also
  Goldwork; Silversmith-
  ing) 0346, 0360
Methodist Church 1082.5
Methvin, John Jasper,
  1846-. 1082.5
Meth Rebellion 1067,
  1526, 2212
Mexican Americans 2378.5
Mexico (see also Yucatan)
  0666, 0993, 1720, 1726,
  1810, 2076, 2259, 2308,
  2355, 2952, 2976
  Alta Vista, Zacatecan
    1719, 2471
  Belize 0319, 1183,
  Caracol (Chichen
    Itza) 1089
    1664, 2109, 3114
  Chiapas 0248, 0376,
    0520, 1403, 1543,
    1807, 1860, 1954,
    1957, 2397, 2737,
    3025, 3026
  Chichen Itza 0320,
    1089, 1494, 2137,
    2655
  Chihuahu (State) 1913
  Cholula 2359
  Coapa 1860
  Coatzacoalcos Region
    0601
  Corazones 1397
  Huasteca 2749
  Jonotla (Puebla) 2598
  Loma San Gabriel 0398
  Monte Alban (State)
    0298, 0299, 0301
  Oaxaca 1068, 1069,
    1544, 2308
  Oaxaca Valley 0298,
    0300, 0594, 0606,
    0936, 1545, 3138
  Papaloapan Basin 2976
  Potam 2954
  Quintana Roo 1352,
    1353
  San Andres, Cholula
    2359

Grassy Narrows, Navaho,
Onondaga, Pine Ridge,
Pyramid Lake, Rosebud,
San Carlos, Seneca,
Tonawanda, Tongue, Warm
Springs. 0007, 0512,
0734, 1306, 1617, 1827,
2030, 2273, 2321, 2638,
3189, 3214, 3215, 3482
Rhode Island 1055, 3165
Ridge, Major, ca.1771-
1839 3433.5
Riebeth, Carolyn Reyn-
olds, 1898-. 2638
Riel, Louis, d.1885 1067,
1529, 2212
Rio Grande--Water Rights
0881
Rio Ramos Site 0398
Ritchie, William
Augustus, 1903- 0712
Rites and Ceremonies (see
also Marriage Customs
and Rites; individual
tribes)
Rites and Ceremonies--
Latin America 0537
Rites and Ceremonies--
Mexico 0225, 1081, 2008
Rites and Ceremonies--
North America 0004,
0065, 0100, 0216, 0277,
0291, 0341, 0727, 0936,
1095, 1171, 1177, 1265,
1442, 1510.5, 1799.5,
1958, 2279, 2367, 2502,
2867, 2869, 2989, 3004,
3076, 3300, 3309, 3471,
3472, 3480
Riverhaven Site, Erie
Co., NY 1779
Rivers Site, Addison Co.,
VT 0397
Roads (see also names of
individual roads) 0654,
2344, 2505
Roanok Island, NC 0894
Robertson, Samuel C.
(Samuel Churchill) d.
1893 1563
Rock Paintings 1244,

1245, 1909, 1976, 2776,
2882
Rogersm John, Chippewa
Chief 2689
Rosebud Indian Reserva-
tion, SD 1268
Ross, John, Cherokee
Chief, 1790-1866. 2233,
2234, 2605, 2704
Round Lake, Canada 2688
Round Top Site, Broome
Co., NY 1802
Rowlandson, Mary 2713,
2714
Royal Proclamation of
1763 3129
Running 2255
Rupert, Henry, 1855-
Washo Shaman 1331
Ryders Pond Site, Kings
Co., NY 1942

SCAPULA (Information Re-
trieval System) 3052
Sac Indians see Sauk
Indians
Sacagawea, 1786-1884 0583
St. Francis River, Canada
0741
St. Lawrence Area 2220,
2514
St. Lawrence Island 1529
Salish Indians 0093,
0505.5, 0714, 1285,
1297, 2122, 2226, 3057,
3093, 3425
Salmon Site, NM 0019,
0316
Salt 0103
San Antonio Frutal Site
0418
San Blas Site 2235
San Carlos Indian Reser-
vation, AZ 0595
San Juan Island, WA 1760,
2893
San Juan River Basin 2504
San Lorenzo Tenochtitlan
Site 0601, 0606
San Salvador 0632
Sand Creek, Battle of,

LIST OF TRIBES
CITED IN SUBJECT INDEX

with area locations:
L = Latin America; M = Mexico
N = North America excluding Mexico

Abnaki (N)
Acoma (N)
Aleuts (N)
Algonquian (N)
Apache (N)
Arapaho (N)
Araucanian (S)
Arawak (L)
Arecuna (L)
Arikara (N)
Ashluslay (L)
Athapaskan (N)
Atsina (N)
Atsugewi (N)
Aztecs (M)

Bannock (N)
Barasana (L)
Basketmaker
(M, N)
Bella Coola (N)
Beothuk (N)
Bororo (L)
Brotherton (N)
Brule (N)

Caddo (N)
Caddoan (N)
Cadioeo (L)
Caingua (L)
Cakchikel (L)
Calusa (N)
Campa (L)
Canelo (L)
Carib (L)

Catawba (N)
Cayuga (N)
Chalchihuitl
(M)
Chane (L)
Cherokee (N)
Cheyenne (N)
Chiapenac (M)
Chichimecs (M)
Chinook (N)
Chippewa (N)
Chiriguano (L)
Choctaw (N)
Chol (M)
Choroti (L)
Chumashan (N)
Clackamas (N)
Comanche (N)
Cree (N)
Creek (N)
Crow (N)
Cuna (L)

Dakota (N)
Delaware (N)

Fox (N)

Gosiute (N)
Guahibo (L)
Guarani (L)
Guayaqui (L)

Haida (N)
Hidatsa (N)

Hopi (N)
Houma (N)
Hualapai (N)
Huicho (M, N)
Huron (N)

Inca (L)
Ingalik (N)
Inuit (N)
Iowa (N)
Iroquois (N)
Ivuyivik Eskimo
(N)
Ixil (L)

Jemez (N)
Jicarilla (N)
Jivarian (L)
Jivaro (L)

Kainah (N)
Karok (N)
Kaskaskia (N)
Kawchottine (N)
Kickapoo (M, N)
Kiowa (N)
Kiowa Apache
(N)
Klamath (N)
Korak (N)
Koyukon (N)
Kuri Kuru (L)
Kwakiutl (N)

Lacandon (L, M)

653

Lakota (N)
Lenape (N)
Luiseno (N)
Lumbee (N)

Mahican (N)
Maidu (N)
Makah (N)
Mandan (N)
Mashpee (N)
Massachuset (N)
Mataco (L)
Matinnecock (N)
Maya (L, M)
Mayo (M)
Mazahua (M)
Menominee (N)
Miami (N)
Miccosukees (N)
Micmac (N)
Mimbres (M)
Miskito (L)
Misttassini (N)
Mixtec (M)
Modoc (N)
Mohave (N)
Mohawk (N)
Mohegan (N)
Montagnais (N)
Montauk (N)
Moravian (N)
Motilon (L)
Moxo (L)
Munsee (N)

Nanticoke (N)
Nascapee (N)
Naskapi (N)
Natchez (N)
Navaho (N)
Nez Perce (N)
Niantic (N)
Nomlaki (N)
Nootka (N)

Oglala (N)
Ohio (N)
Ohlone (N)
Ojibwa (N)
Olmecs (M)
Omaha (N)

Ona (L)
Oneida (N)
Oneota (N)
Onondaga (N)
Oto (N)
Otomi (L, M)

Pai (N)
Paiute (N)
Panare (L)
Papago (M, N)
Passamaquoddy (N)
Pawnee (N)
Pennacook (N)
Penobscot (N)
Pequot (N)
Pima (N)
Pomo (N)
Ponca (N)
Potawatomi (N)
Pueblo (N)

Quechua (L)
Quiches (L)
Quileute (N)

Salish (N)
Santee (N)
Sarsi (N)
Sauk (N)
Secoya (L)
Seneca (N)
Seri (M)
Shastan (N)
Shawnee (N)
Shinnecock (N)
Shoshone (N)
Siksika (N)
Sinons (L)
Sioux (N)
Sipibo (L)
Skagit (N)
Slavey (N)
Sokoki (N)
Spokane (N)
Squawmish (N)
Susquehanna (N)
Susquehannock (N)
Suya (L)

Tanai (N)
Tanomano (L)
Tapajos (L)
Tarahumare (M)
Tarascan (M)
Tarasco (M)
Tenero (L)
Têtes de Boule (N)
Teton (N)
Tewa (N)
Thlingchadinne (N)
Timiskaming (N)
Timucuain (N)
Tinne (N)
Tlingit (N)
Toba (L)
Tolowa (N)
Tsattine (N)
Tsimshian (N)
Tucano (L)
Tunica (N)
Tuscaroras (N)
Tzeltal (M)
Tzotzil (M)
Tzutuhil (L)

Ute (N)

Wampanoag (N)
Washo (N)
Winnebago (N)

Yahgan (L)
Yakima (N)
Yana (N)
Yaqui (N)
Yavapai (N)
Yokuts (N)
Yuchi (N)
Yukian (N)
Yuma (N)
Yurok (N)

Zuñi (N)